SINCE *1900*

THE MACMILLAN COMPANY
NEW YORK · BOSTON · CHICAGO · DALLAS
ATLANTA · SAN FRANCISCO

MACMILLAN AND CO., LIMITED
LONDON · BOMBAY · CALCUTTA · MADRAS
MELBOURNE

THE MACMILLAN COMPANY
OF CANADA, LIMITED
TORONTO

SINCE 1900

A History of the United States in Our Times

OSCAR THEODORE BARCK, JR.
Professor of History, Syracuse University

NELSON MANFRED BLAKE
Associate Professor of History, Syracuse University

NEW YORK · 1947

THE MACMILLAN COMPANY

Preface

THE PITFALLS IN WRITING CONTEMPORARY HISTORY ARE OBVIOUS, BUT the values of its study outweigh them. Never before has intelligent understanding of the role of the United States in world affairs been so much needed; never before has it been so imperative that the American government and the American economy be wisely guided. We are under no illusion that we know all the answers to urgent present day problems, but we are convinced that no one will ever find the answers without a study of the historical development of the issues—particularly since the turn of the century. This consideration has guided our choice of materials and greatest attention has been devoted to the problems that are of current importance. We are well aware of the significance of recent social and cultural trends and we have tried to give them ample treatment. But we have reserved a major portion of our space for the two lines of development which seem to us most impressive—the steady expansion of the functions of government to deal with the complex problems of a new age and the increasing involvement of the United States in global politics.

As far as is humanly possible, we have tried to keep this account free from partisan bias. Desirable in any case, this policy has been a practical necessity with us since we belong to different political parties and hold opposing convictions on many subjects; we have tried to state the facts and leave final judgments to the reader. This does not mean that we have shunned all responsibility for interpretation. On the contrary, we have tried to prepare the ground for fruitful discussion and thought by suggesting the most pertinent arguments for and against the more controversial propositions advanced during the period.

We are indebted to numerous colleagues and professional associates for encouragement and help in this enterprise. We wish to express particular gratitude to artists and newspapers all over the country for generous permission to reproduce cartoons. The opportunity to use these has greatly pleased us, since we are convinced that studying such material is one of the very best methods of projecting oneself back in time and seeing issues as they appeared to intelligent contemporary observers. To our loyal wives we want to pay sincere tribute both for their good sportsmanship in putting up with many inconveniences while we have been at work and for the long hours which they themselves contributed to helping us with proofreading and preparing the index. We of course must accept full responsibility for all errors of fact and judgment.

OSCAR THEODORE BARCK, JR.

NELSON MANFRED BLAKE

Syracuse University

August 21, 1947

Contents

1   THE GOOD OLD DAYS   1

The United States in 1900—Economic Conditions—Religion and Reform—Intellectual Growth—Literature and the Arts

2   THE PROGRESSIVE MOVEMENT   25

Antecedents—Municipal Reformers—Progressivism in the States—
Reform Movement in National Politics—Roosevelt Challenges the
Trusts—Election of 1904—Rooseveltian Reforms

3   THE BATTLE OF THE PROGRESSIVES   53

Election of 1908—Taft and Reform—Republican Insurgency—Rise
and Election of Wilson

4   THE AMERICAN EMPIRE   78

Rise of Imperialistic Thought—War with Spain—Problems of the Dependencies—American Interests in the Far East—Relations with Japan
and China

5   SEARCH FOR SECURITY AND PEACE   103

Acquisition of the Panama Canal—Caribbean Diplomacy—Arbitration
Treaties—Alaskan Boundary Settlement—The United States and the
European Powers

6   THE NEW FREEDOM   123

Wilsonian Reforms—Wilson and the Dependencies—The New Diplomacy—Protecting the Caribbean Lifeline—Problem of Mexico—
Reform Interrupted

7   DIFFICULT NEUTRALITY   149

Decision for Neutrality—Sabotage—Economic Effects of the War—
Anglo-American Controversies—The Threat of War—The *Sussex*
Pledge

8   FROM PEACE TO WAR   180

The Preparedness Struggle—Wilson Seeks Concessions from the
British—Campaign of 1916—The Break with Germany—Why
America Fought

vii

9 WAR FOR DEMOCRACY   207

Raising an Army—Economic Mobilization—Witch Hunting—Advertising America—The War Fronts

10 THE MAKING OF THE PEACE   234

Evolution of War Aims—Armistice Negotiations—Wilson Goes to
Europe—Planning the League—Completing the Treaty

11 WILSON REPUDIATED   254

The Senate and the Treaty—Postwar Reforms—Demobilization—
Labor Unrest—Red Scare

12 THE HARDING REGIME   280

Election of 1920—The Tariff and the Budget—Death of Harding—
The Harding Scandals—America for Americans—The Veterans and
the Bonus

13 KEEPING COOL WITH COOLIDGE   307

The Triumph of Calvin Coolidge—Government and Business—Debt
and Tax Reduction—Battle over Muscle Shoals—The Farm Problem

14 FOREIGN AFFAIRS, 1921–1929   335

The World Court—The Washington Conference—War Debts—The
Paris Pact—The United States and Latin America—Colonial Unrest

15 REACTIONARIES AND REBELS   360

Welfare Capitalism—Suppressing Radicalism—The Ku Klux Klan—
Fundamentalists *v.* Modernists—Youth and the Family—Literature
and the Arts—Popular Heroes

16 PROSPERITY   393

Economic Trends, 1914–1929—The Boom Industries—The Sick and
Subsidized Industries—Business Becomes Bigger—Foreign Trade and
Investments—The Balance Sheet of the Twenties

17 HOOVER AND THE DEPRESSION   422

Election of 1928—The Great Bull Market—The Depression and its
Causes—The Federal Farm Board—The Hawley-Smoot Tariff—Fighting the Depression

18 HOOVER'S QUEST FOR WORLD STABILITY   449

The London Naval Conference—The Moratorium—The New Pan-
Americanism—Movement toward Philippine Independence—Far-
Eastern Troubles

19 THE NEW DEAL BEGINS   476

Election of 1932—The Lame Ducks—The Hundred Days—The Progress of Recovery—Second New Deal—Spending and the Budget

20 BUSINESS AND THE NEW DEAL   500

Monetary Policy—NRA: Experiment in Industrial Self-Government —New Deal Tax Policies—Regulation and Reform—The Tennessee Valley Authority—Public Housing

21 AGRICULTURE AND LABOR, 1933–1939   532

Agricultural Adjustment Administration—Farm Security Administration—The NLRB—Social Security—Birth of the CIO—Wage and Hour Legislation

22 THE NEW DEAL MILITANT   559

Election of 1936—The Supreme Court and the New Deal—Executive Reorganization—The Recession—Attempted Purge—The Hatch Acts —Recess on Reform

23 FOREIGN POLICY, 1933–1937   586

London Economic Conference—The European Nations Default— Hull Reciprocal Trade Program—Recognition of Soviet Union—The Good Neighbor—Failure of Disarmament—Neutrality Legislation— The *Panay* Incident

24 AID TO THE DEMOCRACIES   615

Appeasement at Munich—Impact of the European War on the United States—The Fall of France—Destroyer-Base Deal—The Campaign of 1940—Burke-Wadsworth Act—Lend-Lease

25 PRELUDE TO PEARL HARBOR   643

Improving Hemisphere Defense—The Atlantic Charter—The Shooting War—Mounting Japanese Aggression—Failure of the Peace Talks —Pearl Harbor

26 PREPARING FOR TOTAL WAR   670

Raising an Army—Mobilizing the Home Front—War Finance— Censorship and Information—Problems of the Home Front

27 THE GLOBAL WAR   698

The Rival Forces—Invasion and Conquest of North Africa—Sicily and Italy—The Battle in the Pacific—D-Day—Piercing the Siegfried Line—The Surrender of Germany—Victory over Japan

28 TRIBULATIONS OF TRUMAN   731

Election of 1944—Death of Roosevelt—Demobilization—Reconversion and Price Control—Labor Problems—Republican Victory in 1946— Truman and Congress

29 PROBLEMS OF PEACE AND WORLD ORGANIZATION   765

Better Hemisphere Accord—Broadening Allied Accord—The United Nations—Occupation Problems: Germany and Japan—Relations with Russia—Truman Doctrine—The Marshall Plan

CONTENTS

30 SOCIAL TRENDS DURING PEACE AND WAR   798

Rise of the Negro—Cross-Currents in the South—Women and the Family—Revival of Religion—The Challenge of Science—Education, Literature, and the Arts—Facing the Future

SUGGESTIONS FOR FURTHER READING   825

INDEX   849

SINCE 1900

1

The Good Old Days

THE CLOSING YEARS OF THE NINETEENTH CENTURY AND THE OPENING ones of the twentieth were vastly significant in American history. In 1898 the United States abruptly announced its advancement to the rank of a first-class world power by waging war on Spain, liquidating that country's imperial possessions in the Caribbean Sea, and compelling her to cede the Philippine Islands, 8000 miles across the Pacific from San Francisco. Three years later an assassin's bullet cut short the life of President William McKinley and ended an era in American domestic politics as well. The genial McKinley, like all his predecessors, Republican and Democratic, for thirty years, had been a conservative who believed that the nation's economic life should be subject to as little interference as possible at the hands of government. Theodore Roosevelt, his colorful successor, was sympathetic to new demands which were sweeping the country—demands that government should be more responsive to the popular will and that the state should intervene in economic affairs where necessary to protect the public interest.

Thus were clearly foreshadowed the three themes which were to run through the history of the United States during the next half century. A people largely indifferent to international politics were to be pushed by events into a position of dominating power in world affairs. They were to be compelled to defend democracy not only as a way of government and of life, but to reexamine their own institutions to see whether they squared with the democratic ideal. And finally the American system of capitalism was to be subjected to acid testing. A new generation was to raise the insistent cry that to produce wealth was not enough; a just economic system, it was to be asserted, must provide security as well. Politics were to orient themselves around the rival claims of the parties to foster the economic well-being of the people.

What kind of a nation was the United States, as it stood on the eve of a most significant period of its history? What was America like in the era between the Spanish-American War and World War I—years which millions of Americans now dimly recall as "the good old days"?

WHO WERE THE AMERICANS?

In 1900 the United States was sovereign over a vast empire covering 3,738,000 square miles. Under its jurisdiction lived 84,750,000 persons; 76,000,000 resided within its continental boundaries, the remainder in the outlying territories. The rapidity of American growth had astounded the world. Only 110 years before the United States had possessed but 900,000 square miles of territory and not quite 4,000,000 inhabitants. Between 1790 and 1900 the population under American rule had multiplied by twenty-one.

Except for a small number of Indians (237,000), the residents of the United States in 1900 were an immigrant people. No less than 66,810,000 were descended from white Europeans; of the remainder, 8,834,000 were of African Negro stock, while a mere 114,000 were of Oriental origin.

For three hundred years this stream of immigration had been flowing to America, but it was not until the middle of the nineteenth century that it reached huge proportions. For thirty years after 1850 foreigners entered the country at the rate of about 250,000 a year; then from 1880 to 1900 the annual average jumped to approximately 400,000. But the peak was not yet reached. Between 1901 and 1914 13,000,000 immigrants were admitted, an average of 900,000 a year. The census of 1910 showed that one third of the population was of immediate foreign stock—either foreign-born or of foreign parentage. To some Americans it became a serious question whether immigration had not grown to a volume greater than the country's capacity to assimilate the newcomers in satisfactory fashion.

Particular concern was felt over the changing composition of the alien stock. In 1880, 80 per cent of the foreign-born had come from Germany, Ireland, England, and Canada; but by 1910 this familiar old immigrant element formed only 44 per cent of the foreign-born. Each year was bringing more and more of the so-called new immigration, originating largely in Italy, Austria-Hungary, and Russian Poland. Outnumbering the old immigration for the first time in 1896, the new immigration continued to increase until, in the arrivals of 1907, the ratio of new to old was four to one. Gloomy critics asserted that these Slavic, Latin, and Jewish peoples of eastern and southern Europe were

Italian Immigrants Arriving in the United States. (Brown Bros.)

of a racial stock inferior to that of the northern Europeans who had been predominant in the older generation. Such assumptions were both unscientific and dangerous. But a more valid indictment of the recent newcomers could be made; many of them manifested no intention of becoming naturalized and making America their permanent home. Indeed, nearly one half of the thirteen million immigrants admitted between 1901 and 1914 returned to the old country after a few years. To the American wage earner, it seemed unfair that he should be called upon to compete with this type in the labor market. The American Federation of Labor became one of the principal champions of immigration restriction.

Even more did workers, particularly on the West Coast, object to competition from Orientals. The Chinese were excluded in 1882, but the Japanese did not arouse much alarm until after 1900. In 1880 there were but a bare 2000 Japanese in the United States; by 1900 their number had increased to 24,000, and by 1910 to 72,000. An Asiatic Exclusion League, formed in 1905, gained the support of organized labor and many farmers in its demand for the barring of all oriental immigration. The issue proved to be a delicate and dangerous one, since it involved the relations of the United States and the other new great power of the twentieth century, Japan.

As characteristic of America as the entrance of foreigners into the country was the movement of native stock from section to section. Many were the families which could trace a great-grandfather to New England, a grandfather to the prairie states, and a father to the Far West. In 1890 the frontier line had disappeared from the census map, but the frontier impulse still continued. Farmers still sought free homesteads, while the sick and old sought sunnier skies. Between 1890 and 1910 the population of Arizona, New Mexico, and Oregon doubled, that of Washington and North Dakota tripled, while that of Oklahoma multiplied by six times. In 1890 Los Angeles had 50,000 inhabitants; in 1910 it had 319,000. Three states had been admitted into the Union during the nineties; three more—Oklahoma (1907), New Mexico (1912), and Arizona (1912)—were added after 1900, thereby completing the roster of the forty-eight states.

Americans enjoyed seeing the nation grow, but many were disturbed by the tendency of the cities to enlarge at the expense of the rural districts. Whereas communities having over 2500 inhabitants increased their population by almost twelve million between 1900 and 1910, rural population grew by only four million. This disparity was due not only to the fact that the immigrants thronged to the cities, but to the tendency of the children of the rural population to seek employment in the towns.

The nation was being transformed from a predominantly rural country to an urban one. In 1860, 83 per cent of the people had lived in places of less than 2500 inhabitants; by 1900 the percentage had declined to 60, by 1910 to 54, and by 1920 to 49. But the degree of urbanization was by no means the same throughout the nation. Whereas Rhode Island, Massachusetts, and New York had in 1910 respectively 97, 93, and 79 per cent of their population living under urban conditions, North Dakota, Mississippi, and Arkansas were still more than 87 per cent rural. American politics inevitably reflected the conflict between the points of view to which these far different environments gave rise.

AGRICULTURE AND INDUSTRY

Despite the lure of the city, rural America was enjoying between 1898 and 1914 what was to seem in retrospect its Golden Age. For the majority of the farmers, the hard days of the first pioneers were over. They now lived in comfortable homes near established villages which had stores, churches, and schools. The railroad, rural free delivery, and the telephone had taken much of the isolation and loneliness from rural life. In happy contrast to the eighties and nineties, crops were usually good and prices were gradually rising. What was of equal importance, the prices of the products which the farmer had to sell maintained a fair relationship with the cost of the commodities he had to buy.

There were, however, dark shadows in the picture. In New England, agriculture had been in the doldrums for several decades, and between 1900 and 1910 the number of acres of land under cultivation declined by over 10 per cent. In the South, the lot of the small farmer and the sharecropper was a hard one, while in the West the agricultural situation was profoundly influenced by a new factor. Although homesteading still continued in large volume, the supply of good free land was rapidly diminishing. Many of the farms now being opened up could be cultivated only through new techniques of dry farming or dependence on government-sponsored irrigation projects. It was apparent that in the future agriculture would have to rely increasingly on intensive, scientific methods.

It was in the field of industry that American life was being most rapidly transformed. Between 1860 and 1914 the value of products manufactured in American factories rose from less than $2,000,000,000 annually to more than $24,000,000,000. During the fifteen years preceding 1914, industrial production more than doubled. The change in the relative position of the United States among the industrial nations of the world was striking. From fourth place in 1860, she had risen to first by 1894, and by 1914 she was producing as much as her three nearest competitors—Great Britain, France, and Germany—combined.

As significant as the expanding volume of manufactures was the increasing size of the industrial units. To be sure, there continued to be many small businesses; indeed as late as 1914, 88 per cent of the manufacturing establishments of the country were factories or shops producing less than $100,000 worth of annual output. The remaining 12 per cent, however, employed three quarters of the workers and turned out four fifths of the nation's manufactures. In many of the major industrial fields some single corporation was dominant. Such giants as the United States Steel Corporation, the Standard Oil Company, the American Sugar Refining Company, and the American Tobacco Company were in a position to enjoy extensive influence over prices and production in their respective domains.

The word "trust" had come into common usage to describe an industrial combination which sought to avoid competition by absorbing, controlling, or forcing out of business its competitors or by acting together with them to fix prices or to regulate output. In 1904 there were 318 companies in the United States which might be classified as trusts. Absolute monopoly was difficult to achieve and seldom sought after 1900. The essential usually attempted was the stabilization of the industry and the maintenance of prices. Trusts controlled two fifths of all the capital invested in manufacturing in the country. Twenty-six of these industrial giants were powerful enough to control 80 per cent or more of the total production in their respective fields; fifty-seven controlled 60 per cent or more, and seventy-eight 50 per cent or more. In legal form, most of the trusts could be classified as either outright consolidations or holding companies. In the former, individual competing companies were merged or amalgamated into a single giant corporation and lost their separate identities; in the latter, the constituent companies preserved their separate names and organizations, but were integrated in management by a parent corporation which owned a controlling interest in the stock of each of them.

The trust movement was in its most aggressive phase between 1897 and 1903. Over one hundred great combinations, each capitalized at $10,000,000 or more, were organized during this period. The largest of them all was the United States Steel Corporation, established in 1901 —the first billion-dollar corporation.

The big corporations dominated American economic life, but who dominated the big corporations? Not, as a usual thing, the experienced steelmaker or the expert in railroad transportation. The era was one of finance capitalism. Money was the lifeblood of the large combinations, and it was the bankers who had access to the vast funds of accumulated wealth in the nation. The great corporations could not sell their securities without the services of the investments bankers who took part of their compensation in blocks of stock and demanded a leading voice in management to protect their own interests and those of their clients. Although the United States Steel Corporation, for example, had some hundred thousand stockholders by 1911, the final control of the enterprise rested in the private banking firm of J. P. Morgan and Company.

The year 1913, in which the elder J. P. Morgan died and his son of the same name became head of the famous house, affords an appropriate moment for a glance at the Morgan kingdom. The firm was linked in informal alliance with two other great New York City institutions, the

First National Bank, headed by George F. Baker, and the National City Bank, dominated by James Stillman. These three banks had combined resources of over $600,000,000 and control of seven other New York banks as well as of the great Equitable Life Assurance Company. Direction over the investment of funds totaling some $2,000,000,000 thus lay within the power of three individuals. What this power meant in the control of the great corporations is suggested by the calculation that the Morgan-Baker-Stillman group was represented by 341 directors in 112 corporations having aggregate resources exceeding $22,000,000,-

A Dream of Empire. The desire of the trusts to dominate the world. (By Opper in the *New York Journal*.)

J. P. Morgan, Master of Capital, Who Died in 1913. (Brown Bros.)

ooo. This so-called money trust included banks, insurance companies, transportation systems, and public-utility corporations, as well as large manufacturing establishments.

Sometimes, as in the case of the Rockefellers, the road to financial power seemed to move through other channels, but the end was the same. Wealth secured by the Standard Oil group through the production and sale of oil was used to secure control of great banks. Then the familiar pattern of banker domination worked out to make the Standard Oil backers prominent figures in great industries, railroads, and public utilities in all parts of the nation.

The consolidation of American business life into bigger and bigger corporations, which tended in turn to come under the control of the bankers, was considered good or bad according to the point of view. The large corporations were usually able to produce more efficiently; the enormous productivity of American industry, which was making the United States wealthy and powerful among the nations, was to a large extent a result of big business; the standardization of products and the lowering of their price raised the standard of living for the whole population; banker control was often a conservative, rationalizing influence. Despite all this, however, most Americans were uneasy in the realization that so much power rested in so few hands. Farmers, workers, consumers, small businessmen all shared this fear and looked to the government to do something about the trusts. What this something should be became one of the perennial issues of American politics.

TRANSPORTATION AND COMMUNICATION

The vast area and thriving industry of the United States demanded an intricate system of communications and transportation. The United States Post Office, dating back to colonial days, expanded its functions in 1913 to include parcel post. Supplementing the mails, the country was served by the world's greatest telegraph and telephone systems, while a new medium of communications, wireless telegraphy, had by 1910 proved its value in exchanging messages with ships at sea.

By 1913 the United States had 250,000 miles of railways, constituting 37 per cent of the world's total mileage. Railroad building had been carried on at a feverish pace for eight decades. It was, however, destined to stop with startling abruptness. Between 1900 and 1910, 50,000 miles of new track were laid; during the next ten years only 3000 miles were added; since 1920, almost 20,000 miles of railway have gone out of operation.

The railroads were feeling the competition of interurban streetcar lines. Such lines were built with characteristic American prodigality until a high point of 17,000 miles was reached in 1917. At the time of World War I it was possible to make a vacation trip from almost any sizeable New England town to the seashore resorts without patronizing steam railroads at all, simply by submitting to the inconvenience of innumerable changes from one interurban trolley line to another.

In the end, however, gasoline, rather than either steam or electricity, was destined to provide the cheapest power for moving Americans from place to place quickly. Between 1910 and 1920 the annual production of automobiles in the United States leaped from 187,000 to 2,225,000.

Here was a revolution which was to affect almost every phase of American economic and social life.

The United States was bound together not only by railroads and highways, but by inland waterways. River and canal traffic was much less important than in earlier years, but shipping on the Great Lakes was expanding. And around the ocean circumference of the country there was an active coasting trade, which was to profit enormously by the opening of the Panama Canal in 1914.

The foreign trade of the United States was increasing rapidly. American exports almost tripled between 1890 and 1914, while imports more than doubled. In 1890 farm products composed 75 per cent of the exports and manufactured goods only 18 per cent; by 1914 the proportion of the latter commodities had risen to 47 per cent. The best customer was Great Britain, who took 25 per cent of American exports while providing 16 per cent of the imports. Canada and Germany were tied for second place, each purchasing 16 per cent of the exports. The United States had not yet been very successful in developing markets in either South America or Asia; only about 5 per cent of American exports went to each of those continents, while 63 per cent went to Europe. The total amount of American products sold abroad for the year ending June 30, 1914, was $2,365,000,000; the total imports were $1,906,000,000.

THE LOT OF THE WORKER

In 1910, 7,000,000 Americans worked for wages in factories; 2,638,000 served the transportation system; 1,750,000 were employed in the building trades, and 1,000,000 in mining, while 2,750,000 were unskilled laborers. Although these workers enjoyed conditions sufficiently attractive to draw millions of immigrants from Europe and even to tap the rural population of the United States itself, their share in American prosperity was in reality a modest one. In 1900 the wages for all factory, railroad, and mining workers averaged less than $13 for a fifty-nine-hour week. Working conditions in some respects improved. By 1914 the average work week in the factories had been reduced to fifty-five hours, and the weekly wage raised to $16. The cost of living, however, rose faster than wages; $16 in 1914 bought less than $13 in 1900.

Ambitious to better their lot, 2,750,000 workers were members of labor unions by 1914. Almost two million of this total belonged to unions included within the American Federation of Labor. The one-time immigrant cigar maker, Samuel Gompers, who had organized the Federation in its first form in 1881, continued as president except for

Samuel Gompers. (Acme.)

a brief period in the nineties until his death in 1924, and his philosophy dominated all but a segment of the American labor movement. Gompers was uncompromising in his assertion of labor's right to organize—and, when necessary, to strike—in order to secure higher wages, shorter hours, and better working conditions. By other standards, however, his leadership was conservative. Gompers advocated organization along the lines of skilled crafts, a procedure which proved to be ill-suited for many of the mass-production industries. Unlike European labor leaders, he was completely hostile to socialism. He opposed, moreover, the formation of an independent labor party, preferring that the Federation should limit its political activities to endorsing or refusing to endorse the candidates of the established parties. In seeking legislation, Gompers was also cautious because he feared making labor's position too dependent upon government.

The leadership of Gompers was not accepted in all quarters. The railroad employees, for example, maintained the independence of their own prosperous and powerful Brotherhoods. Another and far different organization was the Industrial Workers of the World. Started in 1905, the I.W.W. loudly proclaimed its radical objective—to unite in one body all skilled and unskilled workers for the purpose of overthrowing capitalism and establishing a socialist state. Although the I.W.W. had its greatest success among the underpaid workers of the logging camps and grain fields of the West, it invaded the East as well and became involved in bitter strikes in Lawrence, Massachusetts, Paterson, New Jersey, and Akron, Ohio. But while the I.W.W. often captured the headlines, its membership probably never exceeded 60,000.

Even unionism in the conservative mold cast by Gompers was opposed by most American employers. Between 1901 and 1910 the union movement suffered one of its most serious setbacks. The iron- and steelworkers' union determined to organize all the plants of the newly established United States Steel Corporation; the corporation directors, on the other hand, voted to oppose any such development. The union was defeated in two great strikes and by 1910 the corporation had freed itself from any need of dealing with organized labor. Such a conspicuous victory for the company encouraged the management of other heavy industries to pursue an antiunion policy. In 1915 a Federal commission of investigation reported: "Almost without exception the employees of the large corporations are unorganized as a result of the active and aggressive 'nonunion' policy of the corporation management. Furthermore, the labor policy of the large corporations almost inevitably determines the labor policy of the entire industry."

Equally determined opponents of unionism were to be found among small employers. The National Association of Manufacturers began an aggressive war on unionism in 1903, while on the local level many employer associations were formed for the support of antiunion activities. Employers could usually count on the support of general middle-class opinion. Labor organizers were denounced as troublemakers, and "vigilantes" were frequently called upon to run them out of town or to break up meetings which they tried to address. Often the authorities of local government not only acquiesced, but cooperated, in such violations of the civil rights of the union representatives.

Furthermore, the unions had many unhappy experiences in the courts. The issuance of injunctions in labor disputes rapidly increased. Federal judges were particularly generous in granting such orders, basing their action on the contention that picketing, boycotting, and other union activities were conspiracies in restraint of trade under the Sherman Antitrust Act. The courts even ruled that individual members of labor unions might be held liable for the acts of the union itself and might suffer the attachment of their bank accounts or of their homes in such litigation.

In only a few fields was unionism accepted as an established institution. The most notable victory was in the clothing industry, where the International Ladies' Garment Workers and the Amalgamated Clothing Workers of America secured privileges most unusual for the day. Not only were regular channels for the consideration of grievances and the arbitration of disputes set up, but agencies were created for employer-worker cooperation in promoting efficiency and healthful working conditions in the industry.

An employer's antiunion policy did not, however, necessarily indicate a desire to subject labor to ruthless exploitation. This was dramatically illustrated on January 5, 1914, when Henry Ford announced that he had established a minimum wage of $5.00 per eight-hour day for his 13,000 employees. Ford's motives in proposing to pay twice what he needed to for labor were not understood at the time, and were perhaps not even clear in his own mind. But eventually a definite theory was worked out to justify the payment of high wages. Industries like the automobile business depended on a large market. How better could such a market be created than through lifting the income of American workers above the subsistence level? Ford's example was subsequently followed by many other employers, and the payment of good wages was combined with honest efforts to improve working conditions in the factories. This became known as "welfare capitalism." It was a trend still in its infancy in 1914, but it served to strengthen the conviction of many middle-class Americans that workers would be better off if they ignored the siren song of the labor-union organizer and placed their faith in the good intentions of management. The wide acceptance of this belief of course hampered the work of union organizers and strengthened the position of antiunion employers, whether or not they were practitioners of welfare capitalism.

RELIGION AND REFORM

Whether they worked in an office, at a bench, or in the fields, millions of Americans were to be found in church on Sunday morning. Church membership expanded at a rate faster than population; between 1900 and 1914 it grew from 36,000,000 to nearly 52,000,000. Particularly rapid was the growth of the Roman Catholic Church. The 13,667,000 members which it listed in 1914 represented an increase of almost 62 per cent since 1900. This remarkable record was linked with the great immigration of those years. Newcomers from Italy, Austria-Hungary, and Russian Poland swelled the Catholic population of the large industrial centers of New England, the Middle Atlantic states, Illinois, Wisconsin, and Michigan.

Despite these gains, Protestants still outnumbered the Catholics almost three to one. The Protestant camp, however, was divided along a multitude of sectarian lines; there were no fewer than seventeen branches of Methodism alone. Nevertheless, there was a growing tendency for these denominational differences to diminish in importance. In many small towns a single church took the place of a number of struggling competing denominations. In the large communities, where the denominations preserved their separate identities, there were ministerial associations and other agencies for better coordinating the activities of the several churches. Crowning the whole Protestant structure, the Federal Council of the Churches of Christ in America was organized in 1908 through the cooperation of thirty-three evangelical bodies.

Interdenominational cooperation was also facilitated by the growth of a more liberal theology which placed much less emphasis on fine points of doctrine. Young ministers trained in the large Northern theological seminaries were likely to be "modernists," critical of the older beliefs. Although Protestant congregations were often more orthodox than their pastors, the sermons of the young liberals usually escaped criticism—provided they were not too long. Protestantism in the urban areas of the nation was being quietly guided toward a milder and more tolerant creed.

In the rural districts, on the other hand, the "hell and damnation" school of preaching still held the field. When the local pastor's efforts seemed to falter, some traveling evangelist would visit the town to call sinners to repentance in highly emotional revival meetings. Most prominent among the evangelists by 1914 was the Reverend William A. ("Billy") Sunday. An ex-baseball player, Sunday preached in a way so sensational and energetic that he attracted tremendous crowds. He

Billy Sunday. (Brown Bros.)

invaded the cities and inspired thousands of converts to throng to the front of the specially constructed tabernacles in which his meetings were held—to "hit the sawdust trail," in the slang phraseology of the evangelist himself.

Despite the apparent vigor of the churches, urban manners and morals were changing in a way that shocked those who retained something of the old Puritan spirit. An older generation of evangelical church members, brought up to frown upon dancing and card playing, were distressed to find their children insisting that these were innocent amusements. Still more upsetting was the changing place of Sunday in American life. Newspapers, baseball games, moving pictures, and "joy riding" all intruded upon the quiet observance of the Sabbath. Militant Protestants denounced the innovations and called for the enforcement of the local blue laws. After a visit by Billy Sunday to Scranton, Pennsylvania, Bible-classmen there rented the baseball field and stood guard each Sunday to see that the grounds were not used.

But the losing fight to preserve the old-fashioned Sabbath did not consume all the energies of the churches. By 1914 the movement known as "Social Christianity" had already made impressive progress. City parishes began to develop a program that would keep the church open seven days a week, providing wholesome recreation for the young and ministering to the needs of the poor. There was a quickening of the religious conscience in response to some of the important social problems of the day. In 1908 a general conference of the Methodist Episcopal Church adopted a resolution stating that the organization of labor into unions was not only the right of the workers, but was "of great benefit to society at large." Several other denominations established associations or committees to study labor problems, and the Federal Council of Churches urged the abolition of child labor, the reduction of the work day, the establishment of old-age insurance, and the "most equitable division of the products of industry that can ultimately be devised." Like modernist theology, however, this type of liberalism was more likely to stir enthusiasm in the pulpit than in the pew. The effort of the churches to advance the cause of social justice never took on the aspect of a crusade.

Not that the crusading spirit was dead. On the contrary, few causes have ever enlisted more wholehearted support from church members than did the campaign against alcoholic beverages. So tragic were the broken homes and broken lives caused by intemperance that millions of well-intentioned people determined to drive the liquor business out of American life. All the churches, Catholic and Protestant alike, had their temperance societies. The extreme goal of legislative prohibition, however, was adopted only by the evangelical Protestants. The Methodist Episcopal Church gained particular prominence in the movement. "We must realize," a trade periodical of the liquor industry warned in 1914, "that the entire Methodist Church is a solidified, active, aggressive and obedient unit in this war on our trade." The Methodist Board of Temperance, Prohibition, and Public Morals established its headquarters in Washington and lobbied for state and Federal antiliquor laws.

Even more powerful was the American Anti-Saloon League, organized in 1893. By 1914 the league was employing hundreds of agents and speakers, and spending hundreds of thousands of dollars annually in a many-pronged offensive against "Demon Rum." The league kept a careful record of the votes of all legislators and was singularly successful in rewarding its friends and punishing its enemies.

The third of the active "dry" organizations, the Women's Christian Temperance Union, had been functioning since 1874. Its greatest victory before 1914 had been the enactment of laws in all states requiring that instruction in the evil of intemperance be given in the public schools. Like the Anti-Saloon League, the W.C.T.U. was nonsectarian, but it drew its chief support from Protestant church members.

The prohibition movement enjoyed particular success in the South, where many were eager to keep liquor from the Negroes, and in the Midwest, where the Methodists and Baptists had their greatest strength. By the end of 1914 the sale of intoxicants had been declared illegal in nine states, while five others had voted to put prohibition into effect within the next two years. In many states where the dry forces had not yet gained state-wide prohibition, there were local-option laws permitting towns or counties to outlaw the trade. By one device or another, the saloon had been driven from most of rural America. In the cities, however, the enemy was still firmly entrenched.

It was obviously difficult to make local prohibition effective when liquor could be ordered by mail from neighboring communities. The Anti-Saloon League consequently concentrated its activities on securing Federal legislation. In March, 1913, the Webb-Kenyon Act, passed over the veto of President Taft, made illegal the shipment of intoxicating liquors into any state, territory, or district where they were intended to be used in violation of local law. In December of the same year the prohibition forces induced Senator Morris Sheppard of Texas and Representative Richmond P. Hobson of Alabama to present to Congress a resolution providing for national prohibition by Constitutional amendment. The proposal did not emerge from committee during that session of the legislature, but it did serve to mark out an objective toward which all the militant foes of liquor could thenceforth drive.

INTELLECTUAL GROWTH

Although the churches were still potent influences in shaping American society, they had lost much of their domination over intellectual life. Much of the prestige which in earlier generations had been attached to the theologians now belonged to the scientists. The astounding advancement of knowledge which had characterized the nineteenth century continued on into the twentieth.

Although this progress was international in character, the United States contributed its full share of great minds. Among American scientists who enjoyed a world-wide reputation were A. A. Michelson, who measured the speed of light with unequaled accuracy, Franz Boas, who demolished many of the myths connected with the concept of race, Thomas Hunt Morgan, who developed the gene theory of heredity, and Jacques Loeb, who sought through researches at the Rockefeller Institute to determine the exact nature of physiological processes. Experimental biology, according to a German expert in the field, was "preeminently an American science."

Much of this scientific research was along lines which seemed remote from the daily life of the average citizen. He could scarcely comprehend the profound implications of Einstein's theory of relativity or of Loeb's parthenogenesis in the egg of a sea urchin. The work of the chemists, however, often touched ordinary life more closely. When the man in the street learned that coal tar was being transformed into coloring matter for cake frosting, and wood pulp into sausage casings and rayon underwear, he was willing to concede that synthetic chemistry was working miracles.

It was when science joined hands with medicine that the most obvious contributions to human welfare were made possible. Mosquitoes, flies, lice, and ticks, it was discovered, were not only pests but carriers of disease. Medical scientists learned that hookworm was one of the great enemies of the South, an enemy that did not kill his victim, but sapped his energies, leaving him tired, indolent, and despondent. A widespread campaign, aided by Rockefeller money, was waged to eradicate this disease and thus contribute to the rehabilitation of a whole section of the nation. Preventative medicine was meanwhile making smallpox, typhoid fever, and diphtheria very rare, instead of very common, diseases.

No speedy magic was discovered to dispel the terrors of tuberculosis. But the work of Edward L. Trudeau at Saranac Lake, New York, demonstrated that nature would cure many cases if patients were treated at sanitariums where rest, good food, and proper amounts of sunlight were provided. Early diagnosis of the ailment was found to be of prime importance. Through the activities of public health authorities and of the National Tuberculosis Association, founded in 1904, the annual death rate from tuberculosis of the lungs was reduced from 181.8 per hundred thousand population in 1900 to 128.2 in 1914.

EDUCATIONAL ADVANCEMENT

To many reflective thinkers, the methods which science employed were even more significant than the results achieved. Rejecting all preconceptions, scientists based their hypotheses on the results of observation and experiment. Might not philosophers do the same? John Dewey, the most influential American philosopher of the period, repudiated belief in absolutes. Truth, he asserted, was the successfulness of ideas which we frame as instruments for the achievement of our purposes. Dewey's views were put to work particularly in the field of education. Since reality was not fixed or complete, authoritarian methods of teaching fell into disrepute, and stress was placed on the importance of learning through experimentation and practice. Social efficiency and not mere knowledge, it was asserted, should be the aim of education.

Other Americans than John Dewey had an interest in education. People at large had abiding faith that the solution of almost every national problem lay in improved schooling made available to more and more young people. The statistics of educational expansion were impressive. Between 1898 and 1914 enrollment in elementary schools grew from sixteen million to more than twenty, while that in high schools and colleges more than doubled. Much of this increase was in the South, which was just recovering from the grievous blows suffered by its institutions of learning during the Civil War and Reconstruction periods. As the number of students who went to high school and college increased, there were significant changes in the courses which were offered. Latin and Greek received less emphasis, while vocational training along many different lines was now available.

Colleges and universities became much less dependent on the churches for support than they had been a generation before. New patrons were found among men who had gained wealth in banking or industry. The Rockefellers generously endowed the University of Chicago; Edward Stephen Harkness bestowed princely gifts on Yale; George F. Baker gave $6,000,000 to found the Harvard Graduate School of Business Administration.

Although such gifts were of inestimable value to the cause of higher education, they were not without their dangers. Some university presidents and deans, it was suspected, placed more importance on keeping the money rolling in from wealthy benefactors than in defending academic freedom. In 1915 a Federal commission asserted that there was developing "a degree of control over the teachings of professors

in our colleges and universities which constitutes a serious menace."
While this may have been an overstatement, it was true that in several
well-known incidents college instructors had lost their jobs, not because they were poor teachers, but because they were suspected of
being "unorthodox" in their economic or political views. Concern
over this situation was one of the things which led in 1914 to the organization of the American Association of University Professors.

The desire to learn often continued past the years of formal schooling. Many American women found an opportunity to widen their intellectual horizons through lectures and study classes sponsored by
women's clubs. Large and small communities alike received annual
concentrated doses of both entertainment and education when traveling
Chautauqua companies set up their big canvas tents in town. There
such notables as Theodore Roosevelt and William Jennings Bryan
might be seen and heard.

THE AMERICAN PRESS

The most powerful influence working upon the adult mind was the
periodical press. In the fourteen largest cities alone daily newspapers
had reached a circulation of over forty million by 1914, while the
circulation per issue of all periodicals—daily, weekly, monthly, and
quarterly—went over the two hundred million mark.

Americans might take pride in many of the achievements of their
journalists. The newspapers were larger, contained more news, and
were more readable than most English or European papers. They introduced to the public such talented humorists as "Mr. Dooley" (Finley
Peter Dunne), George Ade, Don Marquis, and Franklin P. Adams.
Courageous crusades were frequently made for good causes. The *New
York World*, for example, forced an investigation into the mismanage-
ment of New York life insurance companies, exposed police corruption
in New York City, and aroused the public conscience on the issue of
campaign contributions by the large corporations. Through the weekly
and monthly magazines many evils in the political and business world
were pointed out.

There was, unfortunately, another side to the picture. American
liberals were disturbed by the heavy dependence of the periodical press
upon advertising. In 1911 Will Irwin revealed in a series of magazine
articles that newspapers often shaped their editorial policy and either
played up or suppressed news stories according to the wishes of their
advertisers. The desire to expand their circulation led many publishers
to give an unwarranted amount of space and emphasis to stories of

scandal and crime. Paradoxically, the same Joseph Pulitzer who made the *New York World* an outstanding champion of reform, contributed much to the development of "yellow journalism." He was speedily outdone, however, by William Randolph Hearst. By 1914 Hearst was the owner of papers in New York, Chicago, Boston, Atlanta, San Francisco, and Los Angeles. Wherever they appeared, they were easily identified by their cheap sensationalism, their pseudo radicalism, and their irresponsible jingoism.

The newspapers expanded their circulation not only by featuring murders and divorces, but by introducing so-called features—comic strips, recipes and menus, puzzles, bedtime stories, and advice to the lovelorn. Many of these features were syndicated. This development, combined with the growth of newspaper chains and the increasing dependence of all papers on the great news services like the Associated Press and the United Press, imposed a monotonous similarity upon most American papers. The day of colorful editors like James Gordon Bennett, Horace Greeley, Henry J. Raymond, and Charles A. Dana, and of famous reporters like Richard Harding Davis was passing; the newspapers were becoming impersonal products of machinelike journalism.

LITERATURE

The same demand for easy, rather than profound, reading material carried over from the world of newspapers into the realm of books. Historical novels had a tremendous vogue around the turn of the century; by 1914 the trend was toward sentimental stories like those of Kate Douglas Wiggin and Gene Stratton Porter, entertaining studies of American character like those of Booth Tarkington, red-blooded tales of the North like those of Rex Beach, and earnest narratives conveying a rather obvious moral like those of Harold Bell Wright. Probably the best of the popular writers was Winston Churchill. His historical novels, *Richard Carvel* and *The Crisis* had enjoyed great success in 1899 and 1901, and his popularity was still great in 1913 and 1914 when his fictional appeal for Social Christianity, *The Inside of the Cup*, led the list of best sellers.

The minority of readers who were repelled by the shallow romanticism of the popular novelists applauded the growth of realism. The pioneers of the new school, William Dean Howells and Henry James, were firmly established by 1900. The former's most important work was already done; the latter wrote three of his greatest novels, *The Wings of the Dove*, *The Ambassadors*, and *The Golden Bowl*, early in the twentieth century. Of the younger school, Edith Wharton and Willa

Cather were outstanding. Most of Mrs. Wharton's novels were penetrating studies of New York society, but her masterpiece, *Ethan Frome* (1911), was a powerful tragedy laid in a rural New England setting. Miss Cather attracted the attention of the discerning in 1913 with *O Pioneers*, a finely written story of Bohemian and Scandinavian immigrants in Nebraska. Two promising careers were cut short in 1900 and 1902 when Stephen Crane and Frank Norris died after writing a few works of real power. Jack London lived longer, but his early promise was not fulfilled; he could not resist the temptation to gain wealth by giving the public the romantic stuff it craved. The author who most stubbornly resisted the popular taste for an unvaried diet of sweetness and light was Theodore Dreiser. His first novel, *Sister Carrie* (1911), dealt with prostitution in so frank a fashion that Dreiser had difficulty getting it published. Later novels, *The Financier* (1912) and *The Titan* (1914), told the story of a ruthless American businessman. *The Titan* was so brutally direct that Dreiser's publishers became frightened again and attempted to suppress the book.

American poetry suffered from the same shallowness as American fiction. The popular poets were such genial versifiers as James Whitcomb Riley. Largely unrecognized by the general public, however, a young and singularly gifted generation of poets was learning its craft just prior to World War I. The oldest of the new school was Edwin Arlington Robinson, who was powerfully helped by the patronage of President Theodore Roosevelt. Less fortunate was Robert Frost. His early work was rejected by American editors and publishers. Not until *A Boy's Will* (1913) and *North of Boston* (1914) were published and acclaimed in England did Frost find honor in his own country. Both Robinson and Frost wrote poems that were remarkable for their insight into life and for their beauty of diction, but their work showed no radical departure from earlier verse forms. The champion of free verse and every other form of poetical experimentation was Amy Lowell, whose *Sword Blades and Poppy Seeds* appeared in 1914. These three poets were all New Englanders, but the Midwest was to share in the revival. Vachel Lindsay, Carl Sandburg, and Edgar Lee Masters, all from Illinois, were just beginning to attract attention by 1914.

THE FINE ARTS

American achievement in the fine arts was still small. Painters were hardly recognized as useful members of society and indeed they often preferred to live abroad. This was the case of John Singer Sargent, who studied art in Paris and for most of his life practiced his craft in

England. Some of the most notable of Sargent's work, nevertheless, was done in the land of his birth. He accepted lucrative commissions to paint the lords of Wall Street and their wives and daughters. Boston was vastly proud of the ornate murals with which Sargent decorated her Public Library and her Museum of Fine Arts. While the name of the fabulous Sargent had become a household word, many scarcely less talented and much more authentically American artists were appreciated only by a discerning few. There were, for example, Winslow Homer, who conveyed to canvas the rugged beauty of the Maine coast, Albert Ryder, who was to art what Poe was to literature—a creator of dark, mysterious fantasies, and Thomas Eakins, who not only painted many notable portraits but discovered significant new themes in Negro life and in the world of sport. Or there were John Sloan and George Bellows, who recorded colorful scenes of New York City—its bars, prize fights, and slums.

Although the lot of the serious artist was not an easy one, there were fortunate individuals who won both fame and fortune through their dexterity with pencil and brush. The magazine illustrations of Charles Dana Gibson, James Montgomery Flagg, and Howard Chandler Christy enjoyed a tremendous vogue. The "Gibson girl" was indeed an influence to be reckoned with. She was the lovely, smartly dressed young lady every American girl imagined herself in her dreams.

Sculpture interested the general public more than did painting. After all, a people proud of its history could not fail to think it appropriate that the figures of its famous statesmen and generals should be carved in stone for the adornment of its parks and public buildings. Fortunately, a generation of talented American sculptors was available for the task. The most prominent of these was Augustus Saint-Gaudens, but memorable work was also done by George Gray Barnard, Daniel Chester French, and Lorado Taft.

By 1914 American architecture showed signs of an important revival. To men of imagination, steel and concrete offered the material and big business the patronage for a bold departure from conventional building models. The "skyscraper" was the most dramatic, if not the only, expression of this "functional architecture." Louis Sullivan was the pioneer of the new school; Frank Lloyd Wright, Daniel Burnham, Cass Gilbert, Gilbert F. Chase, and Raymond Hood were some of its most successful exponents. Already the New York skyline was something justifying a trip to New Jersey—or even to Brooklyn—to see. The pride of the city was the Woolworth Building, fifty-seven stories high, designed by Cass Gilbert and completed in 1912.

The state of American music was peculiar. Millions of little Americans were industriously practicing Schumann's *Happy Farmer* on the parlor piano; thousands of Caruso records were being purchased for the new phonographs; the Metropolitan Opera Company of New York was the world's finest company; the symphony orchestras of Boston, Philadelphia, Chicago, and New York were among the world's greatest. These facts suggested that the United States was a nation of music lovers. But piano playing was mostly a polite accomplishment with which young ladies were expected to impress their young gentlemen callers; the phonograph was a novelty; the opera and symphonies brought real pleasure to a select few. Before World War I Americans seldom became great musicians, more seldom still prominent composers. The opera companies and the large orchestras were almost exclusively supported by women. The menfolk looked upon occasional evenings spent at the opera house or the concert hall as a form of torture which they had to endure as a concession to their wives' desire to dress and go to some fashionable place.

But Americans did thoroughly enjoy music in a lighter vein. Operettas and musical comedies had long runs and millions of Americans hummed their ·hit tunes. The public taste for this type of music was well served. In all the world there was no more skilled creator of captivating melodies than Victor Herbert.

Americans also loved to dance, and the new type of dance music which was to conquer the world was just evolving in 1914. Irving Berlin's *Alexander's Ragtime Band* was published in 1911; W. C. Handy's *Memphis Blues* and *St. Louis Blues* appeared around 1912. The birthplace of jazz seems to have been New Orleans; thence it spread to the big excursion boats which played the Mississippi River ports. Jazz captured Chicago, and then moved east to New York. The first prominent jazz orchestra, the Dixieland Band, was organized in New Orleans around 1905, moved from city to city, and finally took both New York and London by storm in the years following 1916.

These then were the "good old days." Viewed in close perspective, they do not seem a golden age. The United States was prosperous, but its prosperity did not extend to all groups. The nation was religious, but its church members did not invariably practice righteousness. The country was full of schoolhouses, newspapers, and books, but popular taste in literature, art, and music was shallow. The days between 1900 and 1914 linger in affectionate memory, not because they were perfect, but because they were untroubled by the most acute of present anxieties.

2

The Progressive Movement

IN 1901 AMERICA PASSED FROM THE AGE OF MARK HANNA INTO THE AGE of Theodore Roosevelt. During the presidency of the amiable William McKinley, Hanna had played the role of national Republican boss and had kept the Federal government safely quarantined from the contagion of crusading reform. After McKinley's death, however, the power of the millionaire industrialist declined. Under the new Chief Executive, young and sensitive to changing trends of opinion, the tone of government soon changed. Radical reformer Roosevelt was not —at least while he occupied the White House—but he deeply mistrusted that close alliance between business and government which Hanna had embodied. Aggressively, but seldom rashly, he began an attack upon the more flagrant abuses of the old system. Roosevelt and the progressive movement became synonymous to millions of Americans, although actually progressivism was something older and bigger than the President.

POPULISM

For three decades before Theodore Roosevelt assumed his high post there had been rising discontent with certain aspects of American political and economic life. One of the first groups after the Civil War to voice dissatisfaction with existing conditions was the debt-burdened farmers of the West and South, who raised an impressive protest against "big business" and its control over Federal and state government. The Patrons of Husbandry, better known as the "Grange," organized in 1867 for purposes of economic betterment and social improvement, became during the seventies a crusading order, insisting on the passage of state laws to regulate the railroads and other corporations. The Grangers built their own plow and harvester factories and established other co-

25

operative activities in an attempt to emancipate the farmers from the exorbitant prices charged by greedy industrialists. In the states of the Middle West they turned to politics with considerable success. The legislatures which they controlled passed the so-called Granger laws which regulated the railroads. In the field of national politics agrarian discontent of the seventies and early eighties gave birth to the Greenback party, aimed at easing the burden of debt through currency inflation.

The conservatives, however, were well entrenched. The railroads combatted the Granger laws both in the legislatures and in the courts. Many of the regulatory measures were either repealed or rendered ineffective. The farmers' cooperatives were ruined by patent suits and cutthroat competition. By 1885 both the Granger and Greenback movements had spent their strength.

But the economic difficulties of the farmers had not been ended; indeed, they became more acute than ever. In the late eighties, therefore, the so-called Farmers' Alliances were formed to renew the battle; their members were pledged to combat "the encroachments of concentrated capital and the tyranny of monopoly; . . . to oppose, in our respective political parties, the election of any candidate to office . . . who is not thoroughly in sympathy with the farmers' interests."

After some local success, especially in 1890, the farmers sought the support of the industrial workers in launching out on the seas of national politics. In 1892 the People's party, better known as the "Populist," was born. Its platform was a challenging document. "Corruption," said the preamble, "dominates the ballot-box, the Legislatures, the Congress, and touches even the ermine of the bench. . . . The newspapers are largely subsidized or muzzled, public opinion silenced, business prostrated, homes covered with mortgages, labor impoverished, and the land concentrating in the hands of the capitalists. . . . The fruits of the toil of millions are boldly stolen to build up colossal fortunes for a few, unprecedented in the history of mankind; and the possessors of these, in turn, despise the Republic and endanger liberty. From the same prolific womb of governmental injustice we breed the two great classes—tramps and millionaires." To fight these evils, the Populists demanded the issuance of more money (both paper and silver), a graduated income tax, government ownership of railroads and telegraph, conservation of the national domain, restriction of immigration, election of Senators by direct vote of the people, adoption of the initiative and referendum, and the inauguration of the secret ballot by the states. The presidential candidate of the Populists in 1892, James Weaver, polled more than a million popular votes, a definite sign of the discontent that was rampant. The total vote would undoubtedly have been larger had the industrial workers given wholehearted support to the movement.

In 1896 agrarian radicals captured the Democratic party. William Jennings Bryan made a spirited campaign for the presidency on a platform that incorporated many of the Populist demands of 1892, although it subordinated all other planks to that demanding unlimited coinage of silver. Despite Bryan's sweeping victories in the West and South, the conservatives managed to carry the election for McKinley. After this exciting contest, the revolt of the farmers subsided during the period of prosperity which began in 1897. But although free silver was dead as a political issue, a vestige of Populism survived. The farmers had been imbued with fear of corporate wealth and monopoly, and this fear of big business was destined to be one of the principal ingredients in the progressive movement after 1900.

SOCIALISM

The citadels of American capitalism were meantime being vigorously assaulted from another direction. For decades a few Americans had been familiar with the teachings of Karl Marx. A segment of the American labor movement associated itself with the short-lived First International, and local socialist groups were organized in various parts of the country. In 1877 the latter were merged into a national organization, the Socialist Labor party. Before 1890 this was more an educational society, aimed at spreading Marxist views throughout the United States, than a political party. Then from 1890 to 1914 the movement was dominated by a brilliant immigrant from the Dutch West Indies, Daniel DeLeon. Opposing all half-way measures, DeLeon demanded a proletarian revolution aimed at the "unconditional surrender of capitalism." To most Americans he seemed far too radical. His militancy and hostility to the established labor union movement repelled all but his own small coterie.

In 1888, however, the socialist case was put into a form that appealed to a vastly larger American audience than could ever be attracted to the pure gospel of Karl Marx. Edward Bellamy's Looking Backward was a fascinating novel in which the injustices of contemporary society were contrasted with an Utopian America of the year 2000 where all industry was merged into one great trust or national syndicate. Everyone had a job; no one was permitted to live off the labor of others. This book had a striking success; nearly a million copies were sold within ten years. Nationalist or Bellamy clubs were instituted to promote the author's ideas; a weekly newspaper, the *New Nation,* appeared for a time to spread his views. Bellamy's fame was of short duration, yet he contributed much to making socialism seem respectable. Since he repudiated the doctrine of class struggle and proletarian dictatorship, he appealed to many middle-class idealists who shied away from the more ruthless aspects of Marxism.

Socialism's most valuable convert was Eugene V. Debs. Originally a labor leader, he was sent to prison for his part in the Pullman strike of 1894. There he spent much of his time reading Bellamy, Marx, and other socialist authors. As a result of this study, he became one of the organizers of the new Socialist party which emerged as a rival of the Social Laborites. The sincerity and eloquence of Debs won him the support of many thousands. As presidential candidate of his party, his popular vote steadily increased from 95,000 in 1900 to 900,000 in 1912.

By other standards also the Socialists seemed after 1900 to make themselves a force to be reckoned with in American life. Victor Berger, who had helped found the party, was sent to Congress as a representative from Wisconsin; a Socialist mayor, Emil Seidel, was elected in Milwaukee. Hundreds of Socialist periodicals were published and there was a large Socialist faction within the American Federation of Labor.

Although the ultimate goal of the Socialists was the establishment of a cooperative commonwealth, they presented a series of immediate demands which were in reality only an advanced brand of Populism. In addition to public ownership of railroads, public utilities, and mines, they sought government relief for the unemployed, a shorter work week, abolition of child labor, social security legislation, income and inheritance taxes, equal suffrage, initiative and referendum, proportional representation, and abolition of the Supreme Court's right to pass on the constitutionality of legislation.

While never more than a minority of Americans called themselves Socialists, the followers of Debs, like the Populists, helped to educate the American public to the idea that government should intervene in American economic life for the sake of social justice.

CRITICISMS OF AMERICAN SOCIETY

Numerous other criticisms were directed at the American way of life. In 1879 there was published Henry George's *Progress and Poverty,* a book which showed evidence of much original thought. The paradox of degrading poverty as the seemingly inseparable companion of progress was explained as arising out of the private ownership of land—

the natural resource to which all men ought to have equal right as they had to air and sunlight. George advocated as a remedy, not confiscation, but the single tax. This tax would take from the landlord for the benefit of society the economic rent of land, that is, the social value which is created by no labor of its owner, but which arises through the growth of cities, proximity to markets, or the discovery of mineral resources. The collection of the single tax, George taught, would obviate the need for tariffs or taxes on the products of human labor. It would destroy monopoly, speculation, inflation, and depressions. Even readers who regarded George's remedy as oversimple found his graphic descriptions of the inequalities of American life profoundly moving. He did secure converts who formed single-tax societies to spread the gospel to others. George combined politics with theory, and his defeat for the mayorship of New York City hastened the decline of the single-tax movement.

Henry George's indictment was followed in 1894 by a bill of particulars through the publication of *Wealth Against Commonwealth* by William Demarest Lloyd. This was a careful study of the way in which a great monopoly, the Standard Oil Company, had been created. It was a shocking revelation of ruthless competition, railroad discrimination, and legislative bribery. Using his training as a journalist, Lloyd served as a pathfinder for all subsequent investigators who delved into trust activities.

The type of patient fact-finding which Lloyd developed was utilized particularly after 1900 by a talented group of writers generally known as the "muckrakers." This label was intended to convey a rebuke when it was applied to the school by Theodore Roosevelt in 1906, and some of the more irresponsible of the authors, who placed sensationalism ahead of fact, may have deserved such condemnation. Many of the muckrakers, however, were careful in their research. They painted a dark picture of American political and economic life only because they had discovered the unpleasant truth. Ida M. Tarbell's *History of the Standard Oil Company* was based upon five years of concentrated study, and Lincoln Steffens spent years of painstaking—and dangerous—effort in investigating political corruption in a score of American cities and states while writing *Shame of the Cities* and *Enemies of the Republic*.

Such research cost thousands of dollars. At first it was largely paid for by one man, S. S. McClure, with the motive of securing timely articles for *McClure's Magazine*. The venture was so successful from the point of view of circulation increase that McClure employed other writers as well to hunt for skeletons in the American closet. Ray Stannard Baker investigated both the labor unions and the railroads; Burton J. Hendrick, the life-insurance business; and George Kibbe Turner, prostitution in Chicago. McClure himself explored the crime situation and revealed that between 1881 and 1895 murder in the United States had increased six times as rapidly as the population, and was thirty times as frequent per million of population as in the European countries.

Other magazines soon followed *McClure's* lead. *Everybody's Magazine* published articles by Charles Edward Russell on the Beef Trust, as well as the lurid series "Frenzied Finance" in which Thomas W. Lawson revealed how stock-market operators like himself gambled with the savings of others. Samuel Hopkins Adams described the patent medicine racket through the medium of *Collier's*, while Hearst's *Cosmopolitan* entered the field with "The Treason of the Senate" by David Graham Phillips. It was the sensationalism of this last series which led directly to President Roosevelt's stinging denunciation of muckraking at a Gridiron Club banquet in April, 1906.

Muckraking died a lingering death after 1906. True, magazine articles of the now familiar type continued to appear, but their quality was in general sadly inferior to the careful work of Lloyd, Steffens, Baker, and Miss Tarbell. One important exception, however, should be noted. *The History of the Great American Fortunes* (1910), by Gustavus Myers, was a three-volume work based on years of careful, competent research. The same author also wrote severely critical studies of Tammany Hall and the Supreme Court.

Readers who preferred their muckraking in fictional form could ponder over the so-called problem or sociological novels of the period. The popular Winston Churchill was an accurate weather vane registering the fact that the literary wind was blowing from a new quarter. He turned from historical romance in 1906 to produce *Coniston*, a study of New Hampshire politics, and followed this in 1908 with *Mr. Crewe's Career*, based on a similar theme. Churchill painted a black picture, although he held out the hope that politics needed only the intervention of good men to purify them. A much less optimistic view of American society was given by *The Jungle*, Upton Sinclair's shocking study of the meat-packing industry, and by *The Octopus* and *The Pit*, two powerful novels by Frank Norris, which depicted the ruthlessness of the great railroads and of the speculators in wheat.

The new critical evaluation of the American political and economic system found its way into academic circles as well. Scholars like Richard T. Ely and Thorstein Veblen transformed the study of economics from a mere rationalization of the existing order into a challenging examination of its predatory character. Political scientists and historians like J. Allen Smith and Charles A. Beard subjected the Constitution itself to critical examination and came to the conclusion that that famous document came into being not so much as the result of divine inspiration as from the ingenuity of human beings seeking to protect property interests against an excess of democracy.

MUNICIPAL REFORMERS

When James Bryce wrote his famous study, *The American Commonwealth* (1888), he expressed the opinion that the most conspicuous American failure had been in the field of municipal government. The muckraking writings of Lincoln Steffens indicated that conditions had not materially improved by 1902. It was obvious that if men of action wanted to attempt the purification of politics in the United States, they could find abundant opportunity at the local level. In scores of cities reform administrations were brought into power during the first decade of the twentieth century, an indication that the light had been seen.

Samuel M. Jones, a successful factory owner, was elected mayor of Toledo, Ohio, in 1897 through the efforts of the local Republican boss and certain business interests. The new mayor soon discovered that he was supposed to grant a favorable franchise to a street-railway company in gratitude. He rebelled against becoming a party to such graft, thereby provoking a bitter fight with the Republican machine. As a result, he was denied the Republican nomination for reelection; but he ran as an independent, won, and continued in office until his death in 1904. Jones had gained the nickname of "Golden-Rule" because of his attempts to apply that Christian principle in his business dealings; he carried the same spirit into his administration of the city government. He took night sticks away from the policemen, introduced free kindergartens into the public schools, and established public playgrounds for the children. Jones fought unsuccessfully for public ownership of the utilities of the city. Good evidence of the fear he instilled in the hearts of his opponents is the fact that the stock of the Toledo street-railway company jumped twenty-four points the morning after his death.

The Toledo reform movement did not die with "Golden-Rule" Jones. The following year his disciple and former secretary, Brand Whitlock, became mayor. During his four terms, Whitlock continued to battle against machine politics. His most notable achievement was the securing of a new city charter which provided for initiative, referendum, recall, and direct nominations.

Events followed a similar course in Cleveland. Tom L. Johnson had had a typically American business career during the eighties and nineties when he amassed a fortune through the steel industry and the manipulation of street railroads. A monopolist himself, Johnson enlisted in the crusade against monopoly after reading the works of Henry George. In 1901 he was elected mayor of Cleveland where he gave the people an administration so energetic and efficient that Lincoln Steffens described him as "the best mayor of the best-governed city in America." Johnson brought the street railways under municipal control, forced a reduction of their fares to three cents, and attacked tax assessment abuses. After eight years in office, Johnson was defeated, but in 1911 a new reform mayor, Newton D. Baker, was elected to continue the struggle for Johnson's ideals.

Jones and Johnson were the most picturesque of the municipal reformers, but they had many imitators. Attempts were made to clean out such Augean stables as St. Louis, Minneapolis, Jersey City, San Francisco, Denver, and even New York. Many brave victories were won, but unfortunately few of them proved to be permanent. All too often the grafters took to storm cellars while public indignation waxed strong, only to emerge again, almost as evil, when the voters returned to complacency.

Many reformers believed that the solution to the problem lay in new forms of city government. Galveston, Texas, devised one such innovation following the disastrous tidal wave and hurricane of 1900 which took the lives of one sixth of the population and destroyed one third of the city's property. To meet the emergency extraordinary powers were placed in the hands of a commission of five. The experiment was so successful that a new city charter was presently drafted to make the commission form of government permanent. Interest in the Galveston venture led to the inauguration of similar plans in other cities. The scheme worked out in Des Moines, Iowa, combined the superior efficiency of commission government with certain democratic checks in a blend that served as a model for many other communities. Another widely copied plan was that devised by Dayton, Ohio, in which a commission acted like a board of directors for the city, while the actual municipal administration was entrusted to a city manager, a nonpolitical executive hired to run the government along lines of business efficiency. In one form or another, commission government had been introduced into 210 American communities by 1912, with varying degrees of success.

PROGRESSIVISM IN THE STATES

These years witnessed a demand for a multitude of particular reforms, but all of them may be reduced to two general principles. The
progressives—and the word is here used to include not merely the members of a new political party in 1912, but to cover liberals of all parties
who were seeking to advance social justice through political action—
wanted to purify politics and to eliminate the worst abuses in American business life. The cleansing of politics required the destruction of
"invisible government," or government dominated by the bosses; this
overthrow, the progressives believed, could be achieved by devising
means whereby all the voters could participate in all the processes of
government. The elimination of economic abuses entailed government
regulation of business; the doctrine of laissez faire must bow to the
doctrine that government should be used as a positive agency in promoting human welfare.

In attempting to achieve these fundamental principles, the progressives
found a particularly fruitful field for activity within the forty-eight
states. The great political bosses maintained themselves through their
control of state governments; they could best be forced to abdicate by
the revolt of men of good will within their own feudal preserves. In
these years, moreover, it seemed that the bulk of the necessary regulation of business might be secured through state legislation enacted under
the so-called police power, that is, the power that enables a state legislature to pass laws for the protection of the public health, morals,
safety, or general welfare.

The campaign against the bosses is best exemplified in the career
of Robert M. LaFollette of Wisconsin. Entering politics as an ambitious
young lawyer, he first became a district attorney and then a representative to Congress. In the latter role he discovered that he was supposed
to take orders from Senator Philetus Sawyer, a wealthy lumber man
who, supported by big business, controlled the Republican party in
Wisconsin. LaFollette not only asserted his independence of the machine, but threw his energy into a fight against Sawyer. The rebel's conduct kept him out of office for nine years, but during that period he
worked doggedly to build up an anti-Sawyer bloc within the Republican party of the state. To defeat the old machine it was necessary to
create a new one, committed to the interests of the people as against
those of the great corporations. LaFollette's triumph finally came in 1900
when he was elected governor by the largest majority in Wisconsin

Robert M. LaFollette. (Brown Bros.)

history. He was reelected in both 1902 and 1904; from 1906 until his death in 1925 he represented his state in the United States Senate.

The program which LaFollette carried into effect in his home state was given wide publicity as the "Wisconsin idea." To curb the power of the bosses, he secured a law which took the naming of the candidates of the political parties out of the control of caucuses and conventions and gave it to the voters in direct primary elections. The privileged position of the railroads and other corporations was attacked in legislation which required the corporations to pay a larger share of the taxes, enlarged the power of the state railroad commission, and prohibited the acceptance of railroad passes by public officials. Other laws subjected inheritances to a progressive tax, provided for workmen's compensation in case of industrial accidents, and aimed at the conservation of the forests and water power of Wisconsin.

No less important than Wisconsin as a laboratory for trying out new ideas in government was the state of Oregon. In 1891 the Australian or secret ballot was adopted; in 1899 a new registration law was passed; in 1902 the initiative and the referendum was introduced; in 1904, 1908, and 1910 respectively a direct primary law, a corrupt practices act, and a measure providing for the recall were placed on the statute books. The successful fight for all these reforms was led by William S. U'Ren, a quiet man who avoided public position and campaigned for reform through the agency of voters' organizations. Like Brand Whitlock, Tom Johnson, and Robert LaFollette, U'Ren had been powerfully influenced as a young man by reading Henry George's *Progress and Poverty.*

In almost every state the party Goliaths found themselves challenged by youthful Davids. Among the men who gained recognition as anti-machine governors were Joseph W. Folk of Missouri, Albert B. Cummins of Iowa, Hiram W. Johnson of California, Theodore Roosevelt and Charles Evans Hughes of New York, and Woodrow Wilson of New Jersey. Franklin D. Roosevelt was much younger than these men and his part in the progressive movement was a minor one; but it is worthy of note that he first attracted attention in 1910, when, as a New York state senator, he led a fight of independent Democrats in the legislature against the party bosses.

Everywhere the progressives placed great importance on the establishment of new devices of democratic government. The direct primary in some form was eventually introduced into all of the states; twenty-one states adopted initiative and referendum procedures; eleven states made provision for recall of state officials. Women's suffrage became a part of the progressive program; by 1914 the male monopoly of the voting booth had been broken in eleven states—all west of the Mississippi. The direct election of United States Senators was a universal progressive demand. Since, as a Constitutional amendment, it required a two-thirds vote of the very chamber it sought to reform, it was not finally achieved until 1913. Prior to that time, however, twenty-nine states devised ingenious machinery which in effect took the power of election out of the hands of the state legislators and put it into the hands of the people.

This was a period of significant progress in social legislation. Despite conservative opposition and the hurdles frequently erected by the courts, workmen's compensation acts were passed in forty-two states between 1900 and 1920. During the first thirty years of the century all except five states enacted laws limiting the number of hours that women could work; practically all of the states prohibited or restricted the employment of children, although many of the laws were inadequate. Laws limiting the work day for men were less frequent, but several states restricted the hours of labor in certain occupations, such as mining. About one third of the states enacted measures embodying minimum-wage standards for women and children. Conditions that long had been taken for granted suddenly aroused the public conscience and brought remedial legislation. Thus in the three years between 1911 and 1913, twenty states passed mothers' assistance acts, providing pensions for widows with dependent children. The first state to set up an old-age pension system was Arizona in 1914, but the state supreme court found the act unconstitutional.

THE REFORM MOVEMENT IN NATIONAL POLITICS

For three decades before 1900 all branches of the national government had been in conservative hands. Cleveland, the only Democratic president of the period, was as resolutely opposed to all forms of radicalism as were his Republican contemporaries, Hayes, Arthur, Harrison, and McKinley. The composition of the Senate had been strongly influenced by the undemocratic method of its election; many of its seats were held by wealthy businessmen, enjoying their reward for having contributed generously to party campaign chests; other seats were occupied by the great state bosses themselves, men like Roscoe Conkling, Thomas C. Platt, and David B. Hill of New York, or Matthew Quay and Boies Penrose of Pennsylvania. In the House of Representatives, the dictatorial rule of Speakers like "Czar" Reed speedily schooled Congressmen in the virtues of party regularity and the perils of insurgency. As for the third branch of the government, the Supreme Court was never more bitterly condemned in its history than during the middle nineties when it upheld the injunction under which Eugene V. Debs was sent to prison for his part in the Pullman strike, when it refused to break up the Sugar Trust as a combination in re-

straint of trade, and when it declared that a Federal income tax was unconstitutional. This series of decisions damned the court as a guardian
of special privilege in the eyes of angry farmers and laborers.

To be sure, public opinion forced a few breaches in the conservative
dike. The Pendleton Act of 1883, authorizing the establishment of a
merit system in the Federal civil service, was dependent upon presidential action for its implementation and still left much patronage under
control of political leaders; it represented, however, a defeat for the
bosses. The clamor of the debt-stricken West resulted in silver coinage
measures permitting some increase in the volume of money, although
much less than was demanded. Most important of all, in 1887 and 1890
respectively, Congress yielded to popular demand by passing the Interstate Commerce Act and the Sherman Antitrust Act—two pioneer steps
in the Federal regulation of business. The first of these declared illegal
some of the most common abuses of the railroads—a good part of which
the roads themselves were glad to see curbed—and created the Interstate Commerce Commission (ICC); the second in terms impressive
but vague declared that ".every contract, combination in the form of
trust or otherwise, or conspiracy, in restraint of trade or commerce
among the several states, or with foreign nations, is . . . illegal."

Both of these acts proved cruel disappointments to the hopes of the
reformers. The powers of the ICC were so circumscribed that shippers
found themselves without adequate remedy against the unfair rates
and the discrimination still practiced by the railroads, while the Sherman Act became almost a dead letter through the unwillingness of the
Attorneys General to initiate suits and the narrow interpretation given
the law by the courts. In United States v. E. C. Knight Co., et al., a
case arising out of the formation of a trust controlling some 95 per
cent of the country's sugar production, the Supreme Court ruled that
manufacturing was distinct from commerce and that a monopoly in
manufacturing was not a conspiracy in restraint of trade within the
meaning of the Sherman Act. Later decisions of the nineties, while upholding the act, did so in terms which encouraged lawyers to believe
that industrial holding companies would not be disturbed.

ELECTION OF 1900

Such was the situation in 1900 when Mark Hanna easily arranged the
renomination and reelection of President McKinley. The latter was at
the height of his popularity due to the speedy victory achieved in the
Spanish-American War and the growing prosperity which the country had enjoyed since 1897. These were the issues stressed in the Re-

publican platform along with the maintenance of the gold standard, the high protective tariff, and American control over Hawaii and the Philippines.

The only excitement at the Republican convention was over the naming of the vice-presidential candidate. Matthew Quay of Pennsylvania and other local bosses resented Hanna's dictatorial leadership and sought to assert their independence by rejecting Hanna's choice for second place on the ticket. Party to this plot was Senator Thomas C. Platt, the powerful New York state boss. He advocated giving the nomination to Theodore Roosevelt, not because he loved Roosevelt, but because he longed to remove him from the governorship of New York, a post which Platt wanted to see occupied by some less impulsive politician. When news of this plan "to kick him upstairs" first came to the governor's ears, he objected strenuously. But the rank and file of the Republican party, particularly in the West, took up the idea of Roosevelt for vice-president with enthusiasm. The reluctant candidate, flattered by this impressive acclaim, in the end accepted the nomination. The shrewd Hanna regarded this development with many misgivings.

Roosevelt's rise to national political stature at the age of forty-one had been dramatic. He belonged to a prominent old New York family and had received his schooling at Harvard. He was trained for the legal profession, but ill health and the lure of politics turned him away from that vocation. Seeking to build up his physical strength, he lived several years on a Western ranch. The experience influenced him profoundly; here he completed the formulation of his philosophy of "the strenuous life," here he made friendships and developed a great enthusiasm for the traditions and virtues of the frontier. Meantime, during a period of residence in the East which had been interspersed with his life in the West, he had entered New York state politics and served three terms in the Assembly where he had shown an interest in reform legislation not altogether pleasing to older politicians. In 1886 he ran for mayor of New York City, but was badly defeated by his Democratic opponent, Abram Hewitt. His energies were given a new outlet, however, when he was appointed to the Federal Civil Service Commission by President Harrison. He supplemented his administrative work with speeches and articles on civil service matters, thereby strengthening the position of the commission. Following this service, Roosevelt became police commissioner of New York City, where he displayed independence, vigor, and a flair for provoking violent controversy.

Roosevelt campaigned actively for McKinley in 1896 and was rewarded with the post of Assistant Secretary of the Navy. There he played a leading part in building up the strength of this service and preparing it for effective participation in the war with Spain—a conflict which Roosevelt welcomed with enthusiasm. Not content with a desk post during the war, the young politician resigned his position and secured a commission as lieutenant colonel of the First Volunteer Cavalry—the famous Rough Riders, composed in large part of recruits from Roosevelt's beloved West. The new colonel saw action in Cuba, particularly in the battle of San Juan Hill, where a disproportionate share of the glory fell upon his willing shoulders. He returned to the United States a hero, and Boss Platt, taking advantage of his popularity, secured his election in 1898 to the governorship.

Platt soon repented of his action. He and the new governor did not openly quarrel; the latter was too well aware of the requirements for practical political achievement for this. But Roosevelt refused to give the boss anything approaching a free hand; he insisted on reasonably honest appointments and he advocated certain reforms which Platt disliked. From the boss's point of view the governor was irresponsible and impulsive. This was the situation which impelled Platt to seek a way out by steering Roosevelt into the vice-presidency—usually a dead-end street in American politics.

The Democrats, with their 1896 schism healed, once more endorsed William Jennings Bryan of the liberal Western wing. The platform insisted that the primary issue was imperialism which the party vigorously opposed with the statement: "We assert that no nation can long endure half republic and half empire and we warn the American people that imperialism abroad will lead quickly and inevitably to despotism at home." Consequently, the Philippines must be granted independence as quickly as possible. The decorations of the convention hall echoed these sentiments with such statements as "Lincoln abolished slavery; McKinley restored it." Public approval of the Gold Standard Act prevented Bryan from making free silver the paramount issue, although he once more came out boldly for bimetallism. Other planks opposed the protective tariff as a breeder of trusts, favored enlarged powers for the Interstate Commerce Commission, advocated a canal through Nicaragua, supported direct election of United States Senators and more aid for the workingman, and attacked what was called government by injunction.

The campaign was featured by Bryan's swing around the circle during which he made as many speeches as he had in 1896. McKinley again conducted a front porch appeal to the voters, but his young running mate proved a match for the Democratic presidential candidate with a vigorous tour of the country. Some Republicans refused to come out for McKinley, chiefly because of his failure to support progressive measures, yet their defection was not sufficient to disrupt the well-built organization which Hanna had constructed.

The result was an overwhelming victory for McKinley who secured 292 electoral votes to the 155 received by Bryan. The conservative candidate's majority over his radical Democratic rival was more decisive than four years before when the count had been 271 to 176. Hanna and his big-business friends had reason to hope that the threat of popular revolt against their dominance had been thoroughly smashed. But there were two weaknesses in the conservative position. One was that the country's demand for reform was much more widespread and insistent than the election figures of 1900, reflecting national pride in the military victories of 1898 and joy over the return of prosperity, seemed to indicate. For example, although McKinley's popular vote reached 7,200,000, Bryan received nearly 6,400,000 ballots, and Debs, the Socialist candidate, nearly 100,000. The second was that only one life now lay between the presidency and Theodore Roosevelt, who already perceived the new direction from which the political winds of the twentieth century were likely to blow.

ROOSEVELT CHALLENGES THE TRUSTS

McKinley served only six months of his second term. On September 6, 1901, when the President was attending a Pan-American Exposition at Buffalo, New York, he was shot by Leon Czolgosz, a demented Polish fanatic. After an eight-day fight for life, McKinley succumbed to the wound.

Theodore Roosevelt thus achieved the presidency at forty-two, the youngest man to assume that position. He immediately asked McKinley's cabinet to continue in office [1] and announced his intention of

---

[1] There were eventually many changes. The cabinet officers under Roosevelt were: Secretary of State, John Hay of Ohio followed by Elihu Root of New York in 1905 and Robert Bacon of New York in 1909; Secretary of the Treasury, Lyman J. Gage of Illinois followed by Leslie M. Shaw of Iowa in 1902 and George B. Cortelyou of New York in 1907; Secretary of War, Elihu Root followed by William H. Taft of Ohio in 1904 and Luke E. Wright of Tennessee in 1908; Secretary of the Navy, John D. Long of Massachusetts followed by William H. Moody of Massachusetts in 1902, Paul Morton of Illinois in 1904, Charles J. Bonaparte of Maryland in 1905, Victor H. Metcalf of California in 1906, and Truman H. Newberry of Michigan in 1908; Attorney-General, Philander C. Knox of Pennsylvania followed by William H. Moody in 1904 and Charles J. Bonaparte in 1906; Postmaster-General, Charles E. Smith of Pennsylvania followed by Henry C. Payne of Wisconsin in 1902, Robert J. Wynne of Pennsylvania in 1904, George B. Cortelyou of New York in 1905 and George von L. Meyer of Massachusetts

carrying on his predecessor's policies. But Roosevelt was temperamentally incapable of treading cautiously in another man's footprints. Nor was he a man content to sit idly by while big business and the political bosses ran the country. Love of power and love of applause impelled him toward independence, while a highly developed instinct for predicting popular trends made it possible for him to take up the leadership of new causes.

One of the first signs that the Roosevelt regime was shifting from the policies of the McKinley era came on February 18, 1902, when the conservatives were shocked to learn that the administration had decided to prosecute the newly organized Northern Securities Company as a combination in restraint of trade. Immediately prices on the stock market fell sharply and J. P. Morgan hurried to Washington in an unsuccessful attempt to induce the President to halt the proceedings.

In attacking the Northern Securities Company, Roosevelt was challenging the interests of the great Morgan himself, as well as those of two of the country's most powerful railroad magnates, James J. Hill and Edward H. Harriman. This $400,000,000 holding company was the device through which these three titans had made peace after a famous financial battle of 1901. At that time Hill and Morgan, who dominated the Great Northern and Northern Pacific Railroads, had aroused the anger of Harriman, who controlled a third of the large transcontinental lines, the Union Pacific, by buying the Chicago, Burlington, and Quincy, on which all three of the systems were dependent for connections with Chicago. Harriman fought back by purchasing enormous blocks of Northern Pacific stock. Morgan's domination over this company rested upon an insecure minority interest and he became involved in a wide buying campaign to prevent control from passing into the hands of his ambitious rival. The struggle was so violent that the price of Northern Pacific stock was run up from 110 to 1000 and a panic was precipitated in the stock market where shorts were fighting desperately to fulfill their contracts. So confused did the situation become that only through litigation in the courts would it have been possible to determine which party had won. Characteristically, the contestants abruptly decided to join hands rather than to continue their costly contest. The Northern Securities Company was thereupon organized by the three principals as a holding corporation to unify the manage-

in 1907; Secretary of Agriculture, James Wilson of Iowa; Secretary of the Interior, Ethan A. Hitchcock of Missouri followed by James R. Garfield of Ohio in 1907; Secretary of Commerce and Labor (post created in 1903), George B. Cortelyou followed by Victor H. Metcalf in 1904 and Oscar S. Straus of New York in 1906.

ment of the Great Northern, the Northern Pacific, and the Chicago, Burlington, and Quincy.

The government now charged that the new combination would have an illegal monopoly over transportation in the whole Northwest. Proceeding cautiously because of the conservative attitude of the courts, Attorney General Philander Knox spent two years collecting evidence against the company. Finally in 1904 the Supreme Court, in a five-to-four decision, upheld the government's contention and ordered the dissolution of the Northern Securities Company. Roosevelt's victory in the courts did not restore competition among the Hill, Harriman, and Morgan lines. By a "community of interest," or unwritten agreement, they achieved most of the purposes which they would have gained through the Northern Securities Company. But the case, nevertheless, was of great importance. It brought back to life the moribund Sherman Act and it demonstrated to a doubting citizenry that even the rich and powerful were answerable to the laws. Moreover, it served with other factors to discourage for a time the creation of new trusts.

The contest gave President Roosevelt a new and popular title; he was now dubbed the "trust buster." Subsequently he sought to justify his laurels by ordering action against numerous other combinations, including the Standard Oil Company, the American Tobacco Company, and the Meat Trust. But the significance of these activities has sometimes been overrated. Fewer antitrust suits were instituted under the long Roosevelt presidency than during the four years of his successor, William Howard Taft. The Rough Rider, moreover, emphasized that not all trusts were bad; there were good ones which were the result of natural causes in the business world and thus should be left alone so long as they operated within the law. Roosevelt's words often hurt more than did his deeds; to be branded as "malefactors of great wealth" by the President of the United States was a new and disquieting experience for the leaders of big business. These verbal attacks made the public more conscious of the evils of monopolies and increased the demand for addititonal regulatory legislation. And, because of community of interest, Roosevelt found it easier to regulate trusts than to actually "bust" them.

Perhaps the President's most constructive step in dealing with the new economic problems was to secure from Congress in February, 1903, authorization for the establishment of a Department of Commerce and Labor with a cabinet post for its head. Within this new Department a Bureau of Corporations was organized to gather facts and figures concerning the great industries of the nation—information that provided evidence for the antitrust suits. In the same month Federal prosecution of trusts was aided by the passage of the Expediting Act, under which government suits against illegal combinations were given precedence on the court calendars, thereby ending the delays which had characterized the period of the nineties.

ROOSEVELT AND LABOR

During the fall of 1902 Roosevelt had to deal with a serious strike in the Pennsylvania anthracite coal fields. The mines were largely owned by the large coal-carrying railroads. The miners worked long hours for pay that lagged behind the rising cost of living; they had to patronize company stores where they paid tribute in the form of high prices to their employers; living quarters in the mining "patches" left much to be desired. Resentful of these conditions, the miners joined the United Mine Workers, then under the leadership of an energetic young worker, John Mitchell. In 1900 they won a 10 per cent wage increase, due largely to pressure exerted upon the operators by Republican party leaders who disliked labor troubles in an election year. The raise was considered inadequate by 1902 when the miners struck again, this time seeking a 20 per cent wage increase, an eight-hour day, improved working conditions, and union recognition. The operators, headed by George F. Baer, president of the Reading Railroad, were determined

The Fatted Steer: "I just wonder what he is going to do?" (By Rehse in the *St. Paul Pioneer Press.*)

not only to resist these demands but to break the union. Baer's opinion of collective bargaining was immortalized in a widely quoted letter in which he asserted that the interests of the workers would be taken care of not by "labor agitators" but by "the Christian men to whom God in His infinite wisdom has given the control of the property interests of the country."

The strike involving 140,000 men began on May 12. By mid-September no progress had been made toward a settlement, the price of anthracite had risen from $5 a ton to over $30, and worried householders started to fear a coalless winter. It seemed imperative even to conservative politicians that the President do something about the situation, although neither law nor precedent offered any satisfactory basis for executive action. At Roosevelt's behest, Mark Hanna conducted secret negotiations with Mitchell and J. P. Morgan, who had extensive interests at stake and was worried lest the continuation of the strike bring more regulatory legislation for big business. But "Divine Right" Baer refused all proposals of compromise.

Finally the President summoned representatives of both sides to meet with him at a White House conference on October 3. Mitchell there offered to submit the miners' demands to an impartial commission to be appointed by Roosevelt, but Baer and his colleagues not only refused this suggestion but rebuked the President for his unwillingness to use Federal authority to break the strike as Cleveland had ended the Pullman strike of 1894.

In the days following the White House conference Roosevelt made no secret of his disapproval of the conduct of the operators. He allowed it to be known that he was contemplating calling out the army to take possession of the mines and operate them. If this were a bluff, the mine owners did not care to call it. After negotiations conducted by Secretary of War Elihu Root with J. P. Morgan, the operators finally consented to submit the controversy to arbitration. They insisted, however, that the President's commission should include no representative of organized labor. The miners protested against this reservation and a new deadlock was threatened. But Roosevelt adroitly overcame the difficulty by appointing E. E. Clark, the head of the railway conductors' union, describing him as an "eminent sociologist" rather than as a representative of labor.

The commission, headed by Judge George Gray, spent four months questioning more than five hundred witnesses before it handed down its decision on March 21, 1903. Only a part of the miners' demands was granted. They were given a 10 per cent raise, a nine-hour day, and

the right to submit future grievances to a board of conciliation, representing both owners and miners,[1] but were refused union recognition
and other concessions. Their victory was at best a modest one. Yet
Roosevelt's departure from earlier precedents was important. For the
first time the Federal government intervened in a labor controversy
not to uphold the employers against their rebellious workmen, but
in a way calculated to protect the interests of the general public and
bring about a peaceful solution without prejudice to either party. The
President's action was sharply criticized in conservative circles.

Roosevelt's sympathy with the miners did not indicate an unqualified
approval of labor unionism. On the contrary, he publicly opposed the
closed shop and denounced the radicalism of more aggressive labor
leaders. He frequently expressed the opinion that his duty was that of
steering a middle course, thus saving the country from socialism by
punishing the excesses of predatory wealth on the one hand and of
lawless agitators on the other.

THE ELECTION OF 1904

As President, Roosevelt continued the policy which he had followed
as governor of New York in alternately defying and appeasing the Republican bosses and the wealthy business interests. He did many things
of which the Old Guard disapproved and yet he shrank from any break
with Mark Hanna and his friends final enough to injure his chances
for reelection or the success of his legislative program. Despite his
caution there was some talk among the Old Guard late in 1903 that
the Republican nomination should be given to some less impulsive politician. The one most mentioned was Hanna himself, although the
Ohioan refused to avow his candidacy. The conservatives would not
take Hanna's refusal seriously, but on February 15, 1904, the powerful
boss died and the President's control over the party machinery then
became complete. The Old Guard no longer had anyone who could
seriously challenge the popular Teddy, as Roosevelt was now affectionately called by the masses.

Consequently, when the convention met at Chicago, Roosevelt was
nominated without opposition. The naming of Charles W. Fairbanks,
Senator from Indiana, as his running mate was a sop to the conservative
wing. The platform was largely confined to recounting the achievements of the administration, with emphasis upon trust busting and the

[1] Were the conciliation board unable to reach a decision, the final settlement would
be made by the Federal circuit judge of the district. Under this arbitration agreement,
there was comparative peace in the anthracite coal fields until after World War I.

acquisition of canal rights, rather than on specific pledges for the future.

Bryan's defeats made his renomination in 1904 unlikely. Many Democrats were tired of his constant harping on the dead issue of free silver and they wanted a more conservative and practical candidate. There was considerable talk of drafting Cleveland again and it was said that big business, normally Republican, would support him as an antidote to Roosevelt. The ex-President, however, refused to allow his potential candidacy to develop; instead, he threw his backing in favor of Judge Gray, who had headed the coal arbitration commission. The Bryan element favored William Randolph Hearst, but the convention delegates, meeting at St. Louis, nominated Judge Alton B. Parker of New York, a representative of the conservative Cleveland wing of the party. Although Parker was rather colorless, the Democrats felt that he might be able to defeat Roosevelt in New York State, a requisite for victory. The platform was also negative and was featured by the failure to endorse a silver plank, the result of Parker's refusal to run unless the gold standard were "firmly and irrevocably established."

A dull campaign followed, enlivened only near the end by Parker's charge that George Cortelyou, who was both Secretary of Commerce and Labor and Republican National Chairman, had used information gained from the Bureau of Corporations to extort money from monopolistic corporations for the benefit of the Republican campaign fund and had promised immunity from antitrust prosecutions as a reward. Roosevelt did not deny that his party had accepted the usual donations from corporations, but indignantly asserted that the charges of blackmail were "monstrous"; he was, he said, "unhampered by any pledge, promise or understanding of any kind, save my promise, made openly to the American people, that so far as in my power lies I shall see to it that every man has a square deal, no less and no more."

Roosevelt won a sweeping victory on election day, November 8. Parker did not carry a single state outside of the Solid South, and even lost Missouri which had been in the Democratic column consistently since the Civil War. The Roosevelt popular vote was 7,628,834 to Parker's 5,084,491, while the electoral count was 336 to 140. Never before had a presidential candidate received so large a vote in the electoral college, nor so great a popular majority.

ROOSEVELTIAN REFORMS

Conscious now of the full extent of his popularity, Roosevelt moved further toward progressivism than he had during his first term. Early in

Theodore Roosevelt. (Brown Bros.)

1906 the Pure Foods and Drugs Act and the Meat Inspection Act were passed. The former prohibited the manufacture, sale, or transportation of adulterated, misbranded, or harmful foods, drugs, or liquors, and required that medicines containing dangerous drugs should carry a label stating the character of the contents. The latter authorized Federal inspectors to examine meat shipped in interstate commerce and to see that sanitary conditions were maintained in slaughtering houses. This moderate extension of the principle of Federal regulation into new fields followed the shocking exposures of Upton Sinclair's book, *The Jungle*, and the spirited preachments of Dr. Harvey W. Wiley, chief chemist of the Department of Agriculture, who had been advocating such legislation for years.

Meantime, the issue of further railroad legislation became acute. Loud complaints of exorbitant rates and discrimination were still heard on every hand, and the powers granted to the Interstate Commerce Commission in the Act of 1887 had proved inadequate to meet the problem. In 1903 the Elkins Act was passed to deal with the practice of rebating which the railroads themselves had come to regard as a nuisance. Departure from the published rates was made the sole test of discrimination and shippers who accepted rebates were made subject to fines as well as railroads which gave them.

But the problem of high rates still remained. The President tried to secure remedial legislation under the Townsend-Esch Bill in 1904; the Congress, however, made more independent by the election year, refused to pass the measure. Consequently, after his reelection, Roosevelt devoted a considerable part of his annual message of December, 1904, to a demand for the enlargement of the power of the Interstate Commerce Commission. In answer, the Hepburn Bill, conforming to the executive wishes, was passed by the House of Representatives, but a Senate committee killed it. It was overwhelmingly approved again by the new House in February, 1906. In the Senate, however, a conservative faction led by Elkins of West Virginia and Aldrich of Rhode Island worked hard to emasculate the measure, and Roosevelt for a time allied himself with Democrats and independent Western Republicans in a bitter struggle with these saboteurs of his program. In the end, the President was compelled to compromise and the bill was passed in a form somewhat disappointing to the progressives. The Hepburn Act expanded the Interstate Commerce Commission from five to seven members and extended its authority to cover express companies, sleeping-car companies, pipe lines, and railroad terminals. The most important new power bestowed upon the commission was that of nullifying rates found, upon complaint of shippers, to be unreasonable and, in such cases, to state the maximum rate which would be reasonable. The orders of the commission were to be binding upon the carriers unless set aside by the courts, with the burden of initiating such litigation being transferred from the commission to the carriers. Progressive Westerners criticized the extensive powers still reserved for the courts to delay and reverse the orders of the commission and they regarded the Hepburn Act as seriously deficient in not authorizing the commission to appraise the value of the railroad properties—a step which Senator LaFollette argued was an essential preliminary to determining whether rates were bringing more than a fair return to the carriers. Whatever may have been its shortcomings, the measure saved the Interstate Commerce Commission from oblivion and gave it its first really important powers. Shippers were prompt to take advantage of the Hepburn Act; more complaints were registered with the commission in the two years after the passage of the measure than in the nearly two decades before. A number of rates were reduced, sometimes through commission action, sometimes through voluntary decision of the carriers. Yet these reductions did not result in bankruptcy for the railroads, as had been widely predicted by the conservatives during the fight over the Hepburn Bill.

Another act of 1906 made the railroads engaged in interstate commerce liable for the injuries sustained by their employees. Although this measure was invalidated by the Supreme Court, a similar act passed in 1908 was upheld.

CONSERVATION

Theodore Roosevelt's most enduring work was done in the field of conservation. For decades the national domain had been passing out of the hands of the Federal government into those of private owners. With careless generosity, not only agricultural land, but forest regions, mineral deposits, oil fields, and water-power sites had been given over to ruthless exploitation without thought for the future needs of the country. Roosevelt's great love for the outdoors and for the West ideally equipped him for the task of laying down a new policy. Taking advantage of legislation that had been on the books since 1891 but which had been applied on only a small scale by his cautious predecessors, Roosevelt withdrew from public sale 150,000,000 acres of forest land. There were no such laws covering mineral deposits and water-power sites, but the President went blithely ahead anyway, withdrawing additional millions of acres by executive order. Reclamation was also given emphasis. As early as 1902 the Newlands Act was passed, appropriating Federal funds for the construction of irrigation projects in the arid lands of the Southwest; the funds realized from the sale of land thus rendered arable were to be devoted to further reclamation.

Roosevelt had a great flair for publicity; by numerous clever devices he succeeded in making the American public conservation-conscious. In December, 1907, his annual message to Congress contained a striking survey of the whole problem of conservation and the development of the nation's resources. The next year a great conservation conference was held at Washington, with governors, legislators, scientific experts, and prominent citizens from all parts of the country in attendance. A declaration of principles was drawn up which urged the extension of the forest fire fighting service, protection for sources of navigable waterways, control over timber cutting on both public and private lands, and government retention of subsoil rights, especially coal, oil, and natural gas. Roosevelt's most enthusiastic lieutenant in these activities was Gifford Pinchot, head of the Federal Forestry Service. Pinchot was appointed chairman of a National Conservation Commission, which coordinated the work of the various agencies involved in the program and made an exhaustive inventory of the national resources. This commission was not authorized by Congress, nor was it the first such executive agency appointed by Roosevelt. The legislature, now tired of the President's extension of authority, passed a measure which refused appropriations for the continuation of any commission for which the Congress had not specifically provided. The Conservation Commission therefore soon found itself without funds and had to give up its work temporarily. Another outgrowth of the national conservation meeting was the extension of the movement within the states; by 1909 forty-one state conservation commissions had been established. Also approximately fifty agencies representing private societies and organizations were set up to sponsor the movement. And just before Roosevelt left office, an international conference, representing several of the countries of North America, agreed to cooperate in preserving the natural resources of the continent.

THE PANIC OF 1907

In 1907 the country suffered a brief interruption in the unrivaled prosperity which it had been enjoying for ten years. Several railroads went into receivers' hands, thirteen New York City banks failed, and elsewhere serious unemployment and wage cuts were to be found. It was largely a bankers' panic brought about through speculation and rash management, but conservatives did not miss the opportunity to lay their troubles upon the shoulders of the President; they asserted that the depression had been caused by the business community's lack of confidence in the policies of the administration. This responsibility Roosevelt denied, but certain concessions to Wall Street were, nevertheless, made.

One morning during the worst phase of the panic Roosevelt was called away from his breakfast table to meet two envoys from J. P. Morgan. They confided to the President that a large New York financial institution would fail unless a quantity of shares in the Tennessee Coal and Iron Company were taken off its hands. The United States Steel Corporation stood ready to make the purchase, but its management desired to know whether this action would be viewed by the government as a violation of the Sherman Antitrust Act. The President replied that he did not feel it his duty "to interpose any objections." Thus did the "trust buster" give his tacit blessing to a transaction whereby the country's largest corporation acquired control of one of its most important competitors at a bargain price.

Roosevelt tried to prevent future bankers' panics through signing the Aldrich-Vreeland Act of 1908. This provided that the Treasury Department might lend emergency currency to the amount of several hundreds of millions of dollars to banks hard hit by monetary inflexibility. Furthermore, a National Monetary Commission, headed by Senator Aldrich, was established to find some solution for the nation's banking and currency problems. This was the forerunner of the Federal Reserve System, initiated in 1913.

In the field of civil service reform, Roosevelt showed the same interest as when he had been a commissioner under Benjamin Harrison. He developed new methods for improving the efficiency of the merit system and for promoting men of proved worth. The number of positions filled through competitive examinations was materially increased; the most notable additions being the diplomatic corps, the consular service, and more of the lesser postmasterships. As a wise politician, however, Roosevelt did not press the advantage too far and thus he did not incur the opposition of the bosses. The color line was not drawn when making appointments, although it must be admitted that the President was not always tactful when naming Negroes to Federal posts. He was quick to track down rumors of malfeasance in office and once corruption or dishonesty was proved, he was just as quick to remove the erring officials. Through his efforts, conditions were improved in the Post Office Department and in the methods of selling public lands. In the main, he was very successful in obtaining competent men for administrative positions, men who were loyal to him and zealous in the promotion of the progressive movement.

As indicated in the Tennessee Coal and Iron incident, there were frequent inconsistencies in Roosevelt's conduct. He often disappointed the more advanced liberals of the country. He refused to be drawn into any really serious quarrel with the "standpatters" of his party, men like Speaker "Uncle Joe" Cannon of the House and Senator Aldrich. He shunned the cause of tariff revision which was, in the opinion of many progressives, the most promising way of attacking the monopolistic practices of big business, although there was, in truth, no widespread popular demand for such reform. Obviously Roosevelt was no radical. He was by his own description an intelligent conservative, seeking to preserve free enterprise by curbing the most flagrant abuses in the system, abuses which were likely to lead to really revolutionary discontent. He had numerous defects of character—vanity, bellicosity, impulsiveness. But his faults were easily forgiven by the great American public which loved him for his youthful energy, his zest for adventure, his gift for vivid phrasemaking, and his staunch patriotism.

3

The Battle of the Progressives

THE PROGRESSIVE MOVEMENT, HERALDED BEFORE 1900 BY PROPHETS IN advance of their time and by rumblings of protest among the farmers and laborers, became during the presidency of Theodore Roosevelt a popular religion. After the Rough Rider left the White House, the new gospel continued to have magnetic appeal, but Roosevelt's successor, the unfortunate Taft, try though he might, could not retain the allegiance of all the faithful. The movement rose to a climax in 1912 with three parties clamoring for the approval of the voters, each claiming to be more devoted to the cause of true reform than its rivals.

THE CROWN PRINCE

William Howard Taft became President in 1908 through the efforts of Roosevelt. Such was the latter's popularity and power that he could have easily secured a third term for himself, but he had publicly renounced any intention of seeking such an honor immediately after his electoral triumph of 1904. He gave the matter of choosing a successor serious consideration. After weighing the great merits of Elihu Root, who had been Secretary of State since 1905, Roosevelt decided that Root was too conservative to appeal to the voters in their increasingly progressive mood. Instead, he threw his support to Taft, who had succeeded Root as Secretary of War. Fat and genial, Taft was judged to have good potentialities as a vote winner, while Roosevelt respected his administrative ability and his loyalty to the reform policies of the administration.

At the Republican national convention in Chicago, Taft was nominated on the first ballot, with James S. Sherman of New York as his running mate. The platform was a moderately progressive document. It called for a strengthening of the Interstate Commerce and Sherman

William Howard Taft, *third from left*. (Brown Bros.)

Antitrust Acts, for conservation and good roads, for a postal savings system, and even for a revision of the tariff. Not accepted, however, were more radical planks advocated by LaFollette and his friends, which would have pledged the party to legislation requiring the publicity of campaign expenditures, the valuation of railroad properties, and the direct election of Senators.

The Democrats returned to the leadership of Bryan, nominating him on the first ballot at their Denver convention. John W. Kern of Indiana was nominated for the vice-presidency. The platform condemned the Republican party as the organization of "privileges and private monopoly." It demanded laws prohibiting corporations from contributing to campaign funds, new antitrust legislation, and laws limiting the issuance of injunctions in labor disputes.

THE LABOR ISSUE

The election of 1908 was notable for the more prominent part taken by organized labor. Samuel Gompers had always placed the achievement of collective bargaining above the enactment of legislation, but by 1908 a situation had arisen which could only be met by political action. The utilization of Federal court injunctions to break strikes had become increasingly common since Attorney General Olney's well-publicized success in dealing with the Pullman strike of 1894. Indeed, the interference of the courts with labor union activities took extreme forms after 1900.

In 1902 the hatters' union, attempting to support a strike by the employees of D. E. Loewe and Company of Danbury, Connecticut, declared a nation-wide boycott against the Loewe Company's products. The next year the company filed suit in the Federal district court for triple damages of $240,000 against the officers and members of the United Hatters of North America, asserting that the boycott had been a conspiracy in restraint of trade under the Sherman Act. Although the case was not finally disposed of until 1917, the union lost the principal bastions of its defense in February, 1908, when the Supreme Court ruled in the so-called Danbury Hatters' case (Loewe v. Lawlor) that such a boycott constituted an interference with interstate commerce under the Sherman Act. The implications of the decision were most alarming to organized labor. Not only might a union be rendered liable for civil damages for its strike and boycott activities, but individual union members might be held responsible for the actions of union officers and might suffer the attachment of their homes and savings.[1]

Another evidence of the vulnerability of labor-union activity to attack through the courts came in the Bucks Stove case. A controversy between the foundrymen's union and the Bucks Stove and Range Company resulted in the inclusion of the company's name among the eighty or more listed in the *American Federationist* on the so-called unfair list—or list of concerns deemed unfair to labor and from whom members of the AFL should not buy. The company thereupon appealed to the courts and in December, 1907, the Supreme Court of the District of Columbia issued an injunction ordering the American Federation of Labor and its affiliated bodies from further prosecuting their boycott. Like the Danbury Hatters' case, subsequent litigation kept the issue before the courts for years. In 1909 jail sentences were imposed upon Samuel Gompers and two other officers of the AFL for contempt of court in violating the injunction. Gompers was saved from serving his sentence through a technicality, but the whole issue of the use of the injunction in labor controversies and of labor's status under the Sherman Act was brought once again into the center of the stage.

Gompers and other labor leaders traveled first to Chicago and then to Denver in an endeavor to secure planks in the Republican and

[1] The case was finally settled for $234,000 in 1917; the greater part of this amount was raised by organized labor.

Democratic platforms of 1908 promising the enactment of legislation limiting the issuance of injunctions in labor disputes and requiring trial by jury in contempt cases where the alleged contempt did not occur in the presence of the court. The Republican response to these demands was not satisfactory; indeed, the platform upheld "the authority and integrity of the courts" and insisted that "their powers to enforce their process and to protect life, liberty, and property . . . be preserved inviolate." On the other hand, the Democrats received the Gompers delegation cordially and incorporated most of its demands in the party platform.

The American Federation of Labor followed its traditional nonpartisan political policy to the extent of refraining from a formal endorsement of the Democratic party, but the inadequacy of the Republican platform and Taft's personal shortcomings were emphasized. Therefore labor's rank and file could hardly mistake which candidate was favored by the Federation leaders. The issue was given more prominence by the fact that Taft was alleged to have been an "injunction judge" during his earlier years on the bench.

AN UNFORTUNATE BEGINNING

Gompers's support of Bryan, however, was a poor counterweight to Roosevelt's support of Taft. Thus, when the votes were counted in November, the crown prince's victory was discovered to be scarcely less sweeping than that of his sponsor four years before. The electoral count was 321 to 162; the popular vote, 7,700,000 to 6,500,000, while the Republicans continued in secure control of both Houses of Congress.

Under the circumstances Roosevelt, and the rest of the country as well, assumed that the personnel and policies of the new administration would be almost identical with those of the old. But from the beginning, Taft, urged on by his family, showed an inclination to go his own way. Only two of his cabinet officers, Secretary of the Navy Meyer and Secretary of Agriculture Wilson, had been serving under Roosevelt. The outgoing President was unhappy about the situation since he had understood that it was Taft's intention to retain at least five of the Roosevelt cabinet. The ex-President particularly resented Taft's rejection of Secretary of the Interior James R. Garfield, a great champion of conservation, and of Attorney General Luke Wright, to whom Roosevelt had offered this post in 1908 with the assurance that he would be wanted in the official family of the incoming President. Conspicuous among the new faces under Taft were those of Philander

Knox of Pennsylvania, the new Secretary of State—who had served for a time as Roosevelt's Attorney General—and George B. Wickersham of New York, Attorney General,[1] both prominent corporation lawyers and therefore regarded with suspicion by the progressives.

The Republican party had pledged itself to a revision of the tariff and Taft quickly called the new Congress into special session to redeem this promise. The House Ways and Means Committee under the chairmanship of Sereno Payne of New York prepared a bill making numerous departures from the rates of the Dingley Tariff, which had been on the books since 1897. In general the new rates were lower than the old and in this form the Payne Bill passed the House of Representatives. In the Senate, however, the measure had to run the gauntlet of the Finance Committee headed by the powerful Senator Aldrich. Amendments to a total of 847 were made, generally in the direction of higher rates. Debate on the floor of the Senate was unusually acrimonious.

[1] Other cabinet members were: F. MacVeagh of Illinois, Secretary of the Treasury; J. M. Dickinson of Tennessee, Secretary of War; F. H. Hitchcock of Massachusetts, Postmaster General; R. A. Ballinger of Washington, Secretary of the Interior; and C. Nagel of Missouri, Secretary of Commerce and Labor.

The Temptation of William. Speaker Cannon and Senator Aldrich attempting to persuade President Taft to support high protection. (By Rehse in the *St. Paul Pioneer Press.*)

Western Republicans led by LaFollette denounced what they regarded as a betrayal of the campaign pledge, while the Aldrich faction countered with the assertion that only "a revision" of the tariff had been promised and that the legislators had a free hand to change it either upward or downward. Ten insurgents carried their revolt to the point of voting with the Democrats against the measure, but they could not prevent its passage. Since the House and Senate had passed the bill in different forms, a conference committee was necessary. Here a few reductions were made in the Senate schedules, but the Payne-Aldrich Tariff as finally passed and signed by the President on August 5, 1909, was a bitter disappointment to progressives. Since every tariff measure covers thousands of items, it is difficult to compare one act with another; of the revision of 1909 it can only be said that despite reductions in some schedules and raises in a few others, no significant change had been made in the system of high protection maintained since the Civil War. The indignation of the insurgents was only intensified when Taft attempted to defend the act in a speech at Winona, Minnesota. "I would say without hesitation," the President told his audience, "that this is the best tariff bill that the Republican party has ever passed, and therefore the best tariff bill that has been passed at all . . ."

THE BALLINGER AFFAIR

While controversy over the tariff was still raging, the administration fell under violent attack for its alleged sabotage of Rooseveltian conservation policies. The new Secretary of the Interior, Richard A. Ballinger, was, like the President, a cautious lawyer. He believed that the Roosevelt administration in its enthusiasm for conservation had sometimes exceeded its legal authority. With Taft's support Ballinger proposed to proceed in the future with much more scrupulous regard for juristic niceties. To the ardent Gifford Pinchot, still head of the Forestry Service, such circumspection immediately aroused the suspicion that the new Secretary was in league with large corporate interests greedy to gain control of the nation's mineral reserves and water-power sites. A month after Taft's inaugural Pinchot was protesting vigorously against the action of Ballinger in opening again to private entry extensive water-power sites which Roosevelt had set aside during his last days in office. On this occasion Taft took Pinchot's side and ordered the lands in question to be restored to the forestry reserve, but the friction between the Secretary of the Interior and the Chief Forester continued and deepened.

Ballinger's integrity was also doubted by one of his own subordinates, Louis R. Glavis, the twenty-five-year-old chief of the Field Division. Ballinger insisted upon approving the claims of one Clarence Cunningham and others to extensive coal and timber lands in Alaska. Glavis had been investigating these claims and had become obsessed with the suspicion that they were fraudulent and that the whole affair was a conspiracy designed to enable a Morgan-Guggenheim syndicate—the embodiment of sinister big business—to gain control of a valuable portion of the public domain. Rebuffed in his protests to Ballinger, Glavis confided his suspicions to Pinchot who took the unusual step of sending the young man directly to the President. Unmindful of the explosive possibilities of the affair, Taft dealt with it in a hasty and superficial manner. Accepting the assurances of the accused Ballinger himself that Glavis's charges were unfounded, the President wrote a public letter to the Secretary, exonerating him and requesting him to dismiss Glavis.

Conservation—already a holy cause to millions of Americans—now had a martyr. The insurgent bloc in Congress took up the case of Glavis with enthusiasm, while sensational attacks upon the Interior Department

With Both Feet. The insurgents and Democrats attacking the Payne-Aldrich Tariff. (By Rehse in the *St. Paul Pioneer Press.*)

were published in the great muckraking magazines: *Hampton's, Mc-Clure's,* and *Collier's.* Much was made of the fact that before his appointment to office Ballinger had upon one occasion acted as private counsel for the Cunningham group. Pinchot, taking up the issue with characteristic zeal, finally took the serious step of writing an indignant letter to the insurgent Senator Dolliver of Iowa, which was read on the floor of the Senate. Suffering the same fate as Glavis, the Chief Forester was dismissed for insubordination. This was a much more important action. Glavis's name had been known to only a few; Pinchot's was a household word where it had become synonymous with the whole cause of conservation. Furthermore, Pinchot, as everyone knew, was the intimate friend of Theodore Roosevelt.

This was not the end of the embarrassing ramifications of the Ballinger affair. A Congressional committee held extended hearings during 1910, hearings in which the Glavis-Pinchot charges were pressed by the brilliant liberal lawyer, Louis D. Brandeis. Although the investigating committee's standpat majority supported the conduct of Taft and Ballinger, the administration's victory was a hollow one since a minority report sharply criticized the President and advised the censure and removal of the Secretary. Moreover, some new facts about the case, brought to light under the sharp questioning of Brandeis, provided ammunition for additional newspaper attacks upon the administration. In March, 1911, Ballinger decided that his health would not permit him to continue in office and he was replaced by a conservationist of the more zealous school, Walter Fisher of Chicago. Under the new Secretary the controversial Cunningham claims were withdrawn by the government.

In the judgment of most recent historians, Secretary Ballinger was the victim of considerable injustice in the attacks which finally drove him from office. Apparently he was a real, though legalistic, friend of the conservation cause and innocent of any corrupt dealings in connection with the Cunningham claims. His principal accusers, Glavis and Pinchot, were honest and sincere, but mistaken. Whatever the merits of the controversy, however, the effect of the whole affair at the time was most damaging to the Taft administration. Both the Ballinger incident and the Payne-Aldrich Tariff contributed to Republican humiliations at the polls in 1910. For the first time in eighteen years the voters sent a Democratic majority to the House of Representatives, while the Republican majority in the Senate was reduced from twenty-eight to ten.

TAFT AND REFORM

Despite dissension within Republican ranks and reviving Democratic strength, the Taft administration achieved not a little for the cause of reform. Even the unfortunate Ballinger had to his credit several new conservation laws enacted by Congress upon his advice. The President was given authority to withdraw from entry other lands in addition to forest reserves; the public lands were reclassified according to a scientific survey of their resources, and the title of surface holdings was separated from the coal, oil, natural gas, asphalt, or phosphates below surface, rights to which were to be leased rather than sold. In 1911 the Appalachian Forest Reserve Act was passed, appropriating $8,000,000 over a period of four years for the purchase of lands controlling the sources of important streams in the White Mountains and the southern part of the Appalachian chain.

In the Justice Department Attorney General Wickersham, though accounted a conservative, demonstrated great zeal in the enforcement of the Sherman Act, initiating nearly eighty suits against the trusts. His most notable victories came in 1911 when the Supreme Court ordered the dissolution of the American Tobacco Company and the Standard Oil Company of New Jersey in the forms which those combinations had then attained. Gratifying though these decisions were to those who feared the trusts, jubilation could not be complete. These corporate monsters, chopped into pieces, showed a discouraging vitality in their dismembered parts; indeed they often continued to act like single organisms. Moreover, the Standard Oil decision revealed an inclination upon the part of Chief Justice White and a majority of his colleagues to narrow the scope of the Sherman Act by judicial interpretation. Because of the law's broad and general terms, said the Chief Justice, it seemed clear that their application "necessarily called for the exercise of judgment"; "the standard of reason" should be resorted to in determining whether or not the statute had been violated in any given case. In a dissenting opinion by Justice Harlan, the so-called rule of reason was condemned as an usurpation of power upon the part of the Court; in effect, argued Harlan, the Court was amending the statute. Many legislators became convinced that new antitrust legislation was imperative. The Senate Committee on Interstate Commerce reported that, although it respected the intelligence and integrity of the Supreme Court, it found in itself "unwillingness to repose in that court, or any other court, the vast and undefined power which it must exercise in the administration of the statute under the rule which it has promulgated." Taft, however, defended the principle laid down by the Court.

New railroad legislation was passed in 1910. Under the procedures of the Hepburn Act railroad rates fixed by the carriers were collected by them unless and until some shipper complained that they were unreasonable and the commission, after investigation, ordered them to be changed; meantime, shippers had to continue paying the high charges. By the new Mann-Elkins Act the commission was empowered to suspend newly announced rates for a period not exceeding ten months and decide during that time whether the rates were reasonable. Furthermore, the commission might act upon its own initiative without waiting for some shipper to complain. Other provisions of the new measure extended the jurisdiction of the commission over means of communication as well as transportation and revived the old prohibition against charging more for a short haul than for a long haul over the same route. A Commerce Court was instituted to expedite appeals from the orders of the commission, but the court proved unpopular and was abolished by Congress in 1913. LaFollette failed in 1910, as he had before in 1906, to have the commission authorized to appraise the property of the railroads as a basis for determining rates, but this principle was finally incorporated in the Physical Valuations Act of 1913.

With President Taft's approval Congress passed the Sixteenth (1909) and Seventeenth (1912) Amendments to the Federal Constitution. The former granted to Congress the power to lay and collect taxes on income from whatever source derived; the latter provided for the direct election of United States Senators. Both of these proposals had long been on the program of American progressives. In 1913 both amendments secured ratification from the required number of states and were proclaimed in effect. The Payne-Aldrich Tariff Act had, in a sense, anticipated the Sixteenth Amendment by applying a 1 per cent tax on corporation earnings over $5000, a form of trust control.

Another demand of the progressives was met by a law of 1910 requiring the publication of the names of persons who contributed to campaign funds in Federal elections, the amounts contributed, and a detailed account of the expenditures of the candidates and the purposes for which the expenditures were incurred. In 1910 Congress established postal savings banks, which proved of great benefit to small investors who were suspicious of large private banks. Two years later the parcel-post system was begun, a blow at the monopolistic express companies. Taft gave his approval to both of these measures despite charges by the banks and express companies that they were socialistic.

A special commission was appointed to promote increased efficiency and economy in the national government, and the Department of Commerce and Labor was divided with each new head subsequently received into the cabinet. In an effort to publicize the child labor problem, as well as other related issues, a Federal Children's Bureau was established. The merit system was extended to include the lesser postmasterships and Alaska was granted a greater degree of self-government through being given a territorial status.

But these good deeds were not enough to make Taft a hero to the progressives. Two things in particular brought political disaster to the President. In the first place, Taft was not Roosevelt; he lacked the explosive energy and colorful personality of his famous predecessor and he failed to publicize his own good works. More important still, the reform movement had turned toward new objectives. The Taft administration was progressive according to the standards of 1900 or 1905; it was not when judged by those of 1910, the standards of Senators LaFollette and Albert J. Beveridge of Indiana, or of Governor Hiram Johnson of California.

Illustrative of the limits beyond which Taft's progressivism would not go was the Arizona constitution issue. In 1911, both Arizona and New Mexico, having drawn up constitutions imbued with the liberal spirit then pervading the West, applied for statehood. A joint measure, the New Mexico-Arizona Enabling Resolution, was approved by Congress, but President Taft vetoed it on August 22, 1911, because the Arizona document provided for the recall of judges. He regarded that clause as "so pernicious in its effect, so destructive of independence in the judiciary, so likely to subject the rights of the individual to the possible tyranny of a popular majority" that he could not give his assent. Not until Arizona removed the objectionable provision was its admission—along with that of New Mexico—granted in 1912. Then, once in the Union, the Arizona citizens proceeded to add the questioned clause and there was nothing Taft could do about it. To the progressives, this presidential opposition to the recall of judges placed Taft definitely in the conservative, standpat category, and more so because in 1911 and 1912 Roosevelt was giving his support to at least the recall of judicial decisions.

THE STRUGGLE OVER RECIPROCITY

In one of the most important battles of his administration Taft found the progressives fighting against a measure which he expected them to approve. This was the reciprocity agreement between the United States and Canada, signed January 21, 1911, by which more than one hundred items were to be placed on the free list and the tariff was to be reduced on more than four hundred others. In the President's opinion this arrangement promised many advantages. Its effect would be to modify the unpopular Payne-Aldrich Tariff—which should commend it to Democrats and insurgent Republicans; on the other hand, it would make for closer ties between the United States and its neighbor to the north and widen the market for American manufactures—considerations likely to appeal to regular Republicans.

But LaFollette and his Congressional followers charged that the reciprocity arrangement would be of benefit only to Eastern industrialists, while Western interests would be injured by the importation of Canadian cattle, hides, and grain. A strange alliance of insurgents and ultraconservatives opposed the treaty, while Republicans loyal to the President and Democrats united to support it.

Due to the well-known difficulties of securing a two-thirds Senate majority for the approval of formal treaties, it had to be stipulated that the tariff changes should be made by independent but parallel legislation in the two countries. In the United States the House of Representatives passed the necessary bill in February, 1911, but the Senate failed to take action before it adjourned on March 4. The President refused to be thwarted and called the newly elected Congress into special session in April. Once again the House, now controlled by the Democrats, approved the measure, but in the Senate a bitter fight developed. The National Grange and other farm organizations lobbied against reciprocity, while Taft sought to enlist public support for it. In vigorous speeches in New York and Chicago he charged that the opposition was inspired by a "contemptible union" of the lumber and paper interests and "those who claim vociferously to represent the whole farming industry of the United States." On June 21, 1911, the Senate finally passed the bill by a vote of fifty-three to twenty-seven. For the moment it was a great triumph for Taft, although one which would have been impossible without the support of the Democrats; of the President's own party members, twelve insurgents and twelve regulars had voted against the measure.

But the ill fate which pursued so many of Taft's ventures overtook this one as well. For almost half a century Canadian statesmen had sought a reciprocity treaty with the United States in order to enjoy again the benefits which had followed an earlier agreement between the two countries in effect from 1854 to 1866. Now that such an agreement had been actually worked out and accepted by the American

Congress, however, the whole project was wrecked through its involvement in Canadian domestic politics. The treaty had been the work of the veteran Liberal Prime Minister, Sir Wilfrid Laurier; it was opposed by Sir Robert Borden and the Conservatives. The latter asserted that reciprocity would injure the British mother country, that it would result in American exploitation of Canadian resources, and, above all, that it would pave the way for the eventual annexation of the Dominion by the United States. The Conservatives pointed out that the Hearst papers had been agitating for such an annexation for many years and that Speaker Champ Clark hoped "to see the day when the American flag will float over every square foot of the British North American possessions," which he believed could be accomplished by gradual economic means. Even President Taft had spoken of the "light and imperceptible" ties that bound Canada to the mother country. The issue forced a dissolution of the Canadian Parliament and in the resulting general election the Liberals and the cause of reciprocity went down together in humiliating defeat. To make matters worse for Taft, in the United States the Western progressives charged the President with full responsibility for the failure—although they themselves had not favored the project.

REPUBLICAN INSURGENCY

The political dexterity of Theodore Roosevelt had prevented any serious schism within the Republican ranks while he remained in the White House. Each succeeding month of the Taft administration, however, widened the gulf between the party conservatives and the extreme progressives. In the Senate serious insurgency dated from the fight over the Payne-Aldrich Tariff, while in the House the incident most clearly foreshadowing a party split was the fight of 1910 over the powers of Speaker Joseph G. ("Uncle Joe") Cannon. Following precedents laid down by Speaker "Czar" Reed in the early nineties, Cannon had ruled the House with an iron hand since he first gained the Speaker's post in 1901. He appointed the Republican majority on all committees and named their chairmen, being thus enabled to reward the faithful and discipline the rebellious. Moreover, he himself served as chairman of the powerful Rules Committee which determined procedure and made whatever special orders might be necessary. To call up a bill a Representative had to negotiate humbly with the Speaker in his private chambers. Otherwise measures never emerged from committee, nor did their sponsors secure permission to address the House. In March, 1910, Representative George W. Norris, a Republican from Nebraska, launched a sudden attack upon the Speaker's autocratic powers. He moved that the Committee on Rules be henceforth elected by the House and that the Speaker be excluded from membership upon it. Although caught momentarily off guard, Cannon fought desperately to retain his full powers and he had the support of all the standpatters. But after an excited debate which continued without interruption for almost thirty hours, the Speaker was beaten. About forty insurgent Republicans voted with the Democrats for Norris's motion. Cannon thereupon dramatically offered to vacate the Speakership, but the insurgents, including Norris himself, voted to retain the old veteran, personally a likeable character. The following year the Democrats, placed in a majority by the election of 1910, voted still further restrictions upon the Speaker's powers. All committees were henceforth to be chosen by the Ways and Means Committee which, in its turn, was made up of members designated by the caucuses of the majority and minority parties.

As Republicans approached the parting of the ways, the President elected to stand with the conservatives. In his private correspondence he alluded to men like LaFollette and Norris as "yellow dogs," and he discriminated against the whole insurgent group in distributing the patronage. Despite Taft's attempt to read them out of the party, however, all the progressives except Senator Beveridge triumphantly survived the election of 1910, while many of the conservatives were repudiated by the voters.

THE PROGRESSIVES ORGANIZE

On January 21, 1911, the National Progressive Republican League was organized by a group which made clear its intention of opposing Taft for renomination in 1912. Senator Jonathan Bourne of Oregon was elected president of the League, but it secured most of its energy from the tireless Senator LaFollette. The evangelical spirit of the movement was sounded by Louis D. Brandeis, one of its founders, who declared: "We are confronted in the twentieth century, as we were in the nineteenth century, with an irreconcilable conflict. Our democracy cannot endure half free and half slave. . . ."

Throughout 1911 a LaFollette-for-President boom appeared to be making great progress. In April a conference of Congressional insurgents passed a resolution inviting the Wisconsin Senator to become a candidate for the Republican nomination. At a progressive convention held in October at Chicago, informally chosen representatives from many states gathered and endorsed LaFollette's candidacy. Lincoln Steffens of muckraking fame was active in this movement, as were

Gifford Pinchot, his brother, Amos, and James R. Garfield, Roosevelt's Secretary of the Interior. A group of liberal millionaires, including Medill McCormick of Chicago, Joseph Fels of Philadelphia, and Rudolph Spreckels of San Francisco, gave financial support, while Senator LaFollette poured out his energy in touring the country and making innumerable speeches.

ROOSEVELT RETURNS TO POLITICS

How would Theodore Roosevelt stand in the coming contest? No question in American politics aroused such interest as this.

Immediately after Roosevelt left the White House in 1909, he departed for big-game hunting in Africa. Following this, he toured Europe where he was treated as visiting royalty by emperors, kings, politicians, and educators. But the most gratifying tribute of all was the enthusiastic welcome he received from his own people when he returned to America on June 16, 1910. While he was still abroad, standpatters and insurgents had bombarded him with indignant accounts of their opponents' conduct and, with the popular hero home again, these efforts were redoubled. Both the supporters of Taft and those of LaFollette made pilgrimages to Oyster Bay, Roosevelt's Long Island home, to enlist his backing in the intraparty conflict.

Splitting. The break between Republican regulars and insurgents. (From the *Brooklyn Eagle*.)

Although no longer feeling the cordial friendship which had once marked his relations with Taft, Roosevelt for many months refrained from any public criticism of his successor. Without taking sides between the two factions of the party, he participated in the campaign of 1910— with unhappy results. Induced by his friends to accept nomination as chairman of the New York Republican state convention, he found his election opposed by conservatives and only secured the post after a close vote of the delegates. His friend, the progressive Henry L. Stimson, won the nomination for governor, but was defeated in November by the Democrat, John A. Dix.

The ex-President's western speaking tour in behalf of his party was equally ill-starred. His references to Taft were so noncommittal as to offend both standpatters and insurgents, while conservative opinion was deeply shocked by his speech on the "New Nationalism," delivered at Osawatomie, Kansas, on August 31, 1910. Here Roosevelt said that property, which man's labor had made, must be "the servant and not the master of the commonwealth." The people "must effectively control the mighty forces which they have themselves called into being." The New Nationalism put national need before sectional or personal advantage, regarded the executive power as the steward of the public welfare, and demanded of the judiciary that it "be interested primarily in human welfare rather than in property." To make these things possible, he advocated a number of "square deal" reforms including greater regulation of corporations, a revision of the tariff, income and inheritance taxes, broadened conservation, compensation legislation for workers, regulation of child labor, and the direct primary. He had already championed the cause of the initiative, referendum, and recall.

Despite these ultraprogressive expressions, Roosevelt declined to join the National Progressive Republican League after its organization in 1911. Throughout most of the year he remained silent in the face of pleas from his liberal friends that he become a candidate for the Republican presidential nomination. LaFollette still stood unchallenged as the hope of those who wanted to deny renomination to President Taft.

All this time Roosevelt's growing irritation with Taft was revealed only in his private conversations with his friends. Not until November 16, 1911, did the general public read words from the ex-President's pen severely critical of his successor. On that date *The Outlook*, of which Roosevelt was now one of the editors, carried the Rough Rider's caustic comments on the recently announced antitrust suit brought by the Taft administration against the United States Steel Corporation. He took violent exception to the government's contention that he had been misled during his presidency when he gave approval to the Steel Corporation's purchase of control in the Tennessee Coal and Iron Company.[1] Moreover, he criticized the whole direction which the Taft antitrust campaign was taking. Nothing was to be gained, he said, "by breaking up a huge industrial organization *which has not offended otherwise than by its size.*" Unless they were guilty of wrongdoing, the large corporations should be handled by regulation, not by "destructive litigation" in the courts.

This public blast at the administration revived the hopes of Roosevelt's admirers that he would try for the nomination. By January, 1912, it was clear that the progressive rank and file, as well as most of its leadership, would swing over from LaFollette to Roosevelt if the latter said the word. The Wisconsin Senator's fortunes were already sinking fast when they were finally destroyed by a tragic incident. On February 2, 1912, LaFollette spoke at a banquet given by the Publishers Association in Philadelphia. Overtired from his numerous activities and worried because of the illness of one of his daughters, the insurgent leader shoved aside his prepared manuscript and indulged in a two-hour tirade against the big newspaper interests represented by his listeners. His disgusted audience walked out on him and the rambling, repetitive speech came to an end at last with the orator slumping to his seat and allowing his head to sink to the table. LaFollette's loss of self-control was only temporary, but the incident provided an opportunity for progressives who wanted to shift their support to Roosevelt to assert that they had no choice in the matter because of LaFollette's condition.

The truth was that Roosevelt had already decided to seek the nomination for himself. During January he dispatched his devoted follower, Frank Knox of Michigan (later to be Secretary of the Navy under another Roosevelt) to secure the signatures of seven progressive governors to a letter—composed by the Rough Rider himself—begging him to make the race against Taft.[2] On February 24, 1912, Roosevelt's reply to the appeal of the seven governors was made public: "I will accept the nomination for President if it is tendered to me, and I will adhere to this decision until the convention has expressed its preference." This was the formal announcement of his candidacy, but his campaign to secure it had actually begun three days before. In his so-called Charter of Democracy speech at Columbus, Ohio, he had come out for the ini-

---

[1] See above, p. 50.
[2] The governors were Walter R. Stubbs of Kansas, Chase S. Osborn of Michigan, Herbert S. Hadley of Missouri, Chester H. Aldrich of Nebraska, Robert P. Bass of New Hampshire, W. E. Glasscock of West Virginia, and J. M. Carey of Wyoming.

tiative, the referendum, and the recall of judicial decisions. The same day he had replied to the question of a reporter with the vivid phrase: "My hat is in the ring, the fight is on and I am stripped to the buff."

TAFT VERSUS ROOSEVELT

The quarrel between the ex-President and the man whom he had put into the White House now became a bitter one. Speaking of extreme progressives, Taft condemned them as "neurotics"—a word which Roosevelt indignantly assumed was aimed at him. In April the President denounced his predecessor in an angry two-hour speech at Boston, while Roosevelt replied twenty-four hours later in a meeting at Worcester, Massachusetts; Taft, his opponent declared, had been "disloyal to every canon of decency and fair play"; he would never have become President had not Roosevelt kept his promise in spite of infinite pressure to break it. "It is a bad trait," the Colonel cried, "to bite the hand that feeds you."

Throughout the spring there was a feverish campaign to secure delegates for the national convention. Within the Republican rank and file Roosevelt's popularity was still great. In thirteen states where presidential primaries were held, he secured 281 delegates as against 71 for Taft and 36 for LaFollette. In the remaining states, however, the delegates were chosen by older, less democratic means. There the Old Guard was able to muster most of the delegations for Taft.[1] Preconvention polls indicated that Taft had about 550 delegates, enough to nominate him, while Roosevelt had approximately 100 less. Twelve days before the convention, the Republican National Committee convened to decide 252 cases in which there was a dispute as to who were the properly chosen delegates from a particular state; some of the challenged delegations were for Roosevelt, some for Taft. The progressives hoped to win enough of the cases—many of them trumped up for this purpose—to overturn the Taft majority. But the National Committee was dominated by the conservatives and decided against the Rooseveltians in almost every contest.

The progressives refused to surrender. Two days before the convention opened Roosevelt went to Chicago, the convention city, where he received a fervent welcome from his admirers. That night he addressed a crowded mass meeting at the auditorium. His closing words were so moving that they were quoted throughout the country:

---

[1] The results in the states having primaries do not prove that Roosevelt would have carried the other states if he had had a democratic chance. The states having primaries were usually the most advanced progressive territory anyway.

We fight in honorable fashion for the good of mankind; fearless of the future, unheeding of our individual fates, with unflinching hearts and undimmed eyes; we stand at Armegeddon, and we battle for the Lord.

On June 18 the convention began its sessions and was immediately thrown into an uproar by two issues. The progressives challenged the right of seventy-two Taft delegates to their seats and moved to substitute seventy-two Rooseveltians. This motion was declared out of order and the contested delegates were allowed to occupy their places while the convention voted for permanent chairman; their votes helped to elect the conservative Elihu Root by a vote of 558 to 501 over the progressive Francis E. McGovern, governor of Wisconsin. This was an all-important victory for the Old Guard because it kept them in control of the machinery of the convention. When the Rooseveltians then renewed their attempt to unseat the Taft delegates, Root, following good legal precedents, allowed the latter to vote on their own cases despite angry cries of "theft," "fraud," and "steam-roller" hurled at him from the floor and the galleries. Most of the Roosevelt backers, on orders from the candidate himself, refused to recognize the legitimacy of the convention and declined to vote either in the adoption of the platform or the balloting for candidates. Consequently, Taft was nominated on the first ballot and James S. Sherman was again selected as his running mate.[1]

The Republican platform recognized the popular demand for reform by advocating maximum-hour laws for women and children, workmen's compensation acts, reforms in legal procedure, a simpler process than impeachment for the removal of judges, additions to the antitrust laws, revision of the currency system, publicity of campaign contributions, and parcel post.

On June 22, the night following the nomination of Taft, the defeated faction held an informal meeting. Roosevelt addressed the assembly in moving terms and announced plans for the organization of a new party, the Progressive. The delegates were directed to return to their homes, ascertain the sentiments of their communities, and reconvene on August 5 in a representative convention to adopt a platform and name candidates.

THE RISE OF WILSON

With a Republican split assured, Democratic hopes soared and the nation watched with eager interest the proceedings of their national

[1] Sherman died before election day so Nicholas Murray Butler, president of Columbia University, was substituted.

convention which opened at Baltimore on June 25. The leading contenders for the nomination were Champ Clark of Missouri, the popular
Speaker of the House of Representatives, Governor Judson Harmon of
Ohio, Representative Oscar W. Underwood of Alabama, and Governor Woodrow Wilson of New Jersey. The first three of these were
politicians who had been in the public eye for many years. Wilson, on
the contrary, had been chosen for his first public office only two years
before.

The New Jersey governor, who was destined to snatch the coveted
nomination from the clutches of his more experienced rivals, had been
born in Staunton, Virginia, in 1856. His ancestors were of Scotch-Irish
stock and his father was a Presbyterian clergyman—facts that go far
toward explaining the austere sense of duty, the frequent stubbornness,
and the deep religious conviction which were to be so characteristic of
Wilson as President. After graduating from Princeton and studying
law, Wilson set up in practice in Atlanta, Georgia. But he disliked his
first-chosen profession and turned to teaching. After securing his doc-
torate at Johns Hopkins and teaching at several other institutions, he
returned to Princeton, his alma mater, as professor of government and
history. He was successful as an author, his ablest book, *Congressional
Government*, going through twenty-four editions between 1885 and
1913. A competent scholar and prolific writer, Wilson's real genius,
however, was in his command of the spoken word. He was a lecturer
and public speaker of captivating grace and power.

In 1902 Wilson was chosen president of Princeton and henceforth
enjoyed a wider audience for his talents. His career as an university
administrator, however, was anything but placid. Faculty politics,
usually spirited enough in any institution, took a particularly bitter form
at Princeton where Wilson and Graduate Dean Andrew F. West fought
a seven years' war over the administration and expansion of the graduate
school. Another controversy arose when Wilson attempted to democra-
tize undergraduate social life by the elimination of exclusive eating
clubs. The president's activities alienated many of the rich patrons of
the university and created a powerful opposition faction among the
trustees. By 1910 Wilson's position had become so difficult that he required little urging to accept the Democratic nomination for governor
of New Jersey, thus launching out on a new career.

The idea of running Wilson for the governorship was sold to the
Democratic state bosses by Colonel George Harvey, the publisher of
the *North American Review* and *Harper's Weekly*. As early as 1906
Harvey had publicly expressed his conviction that the gifted head

of Princeton might make an excellent President of the United States. What attracted the New York publisher was not Wilson's liberalism but his apparent conservatism. Up to this point in his career Wilson had given little indication of sympathy with the aims of the progressives; he had condemned the regulatory legislation of the Roosevelt administration and opposed Bryan's leadership of the Democratic party as dangerously radical. All this, thought Harvey, was excellent; through Wilson he hoped that conservative Easterners of the Cleveland-Parker stamp would regain control of the Democratic organization. Harvey, it should be noted, was the friend of and spokesman for some of the most powerful figures in Wall Street.

The election of Wilson to the governorship of New Jersey was the necessary preliminary to Harvey's further plans, and to this end he secured the cooperation of ex-Senator "Jim" Smith and "Jim" Nugent, New Jersey's Democratic bosses. The machine men had some hesitation in working to secure the nomination for a candidate whose background was so unorthodox from the politician's point of view, but the New Jersey Democrats greatly needed an electoral victory and the advantage of putting such an eminently respectable name at the head of the ticket was obvious. There was some hesitation on Wilson's side as well, but at length he gave his assent. The bosses engineered the nomination; Wilson accepted in a dramatic speech in which he asserted that the nomination had come to him unsolicited and that, if he were elected, he would enter upon his duties "with absolutely no pledges of any kind." In November, 1910, Wilson was one of twenty-six Democratic governors elected in the great uprising against the Republicans.

Because of the circumstances of his nomination, Wilson was looked upon with grave suspicion by New Jersey progressives, both Democratic and Republican. He soon displayed, however, a sturdy independence which won them to his side. Although the voters of the state had indicated in a preferential primary that they wanted James Martine for United States Senator, Boss "Jim" Smith attempted to secure the post for himself. When Smith refused to retire from the contest, the new governor put the issue directly to the people in a series of speeches, and the legislature elected Wilson's man. The bosses were aghast at the ingratitude of the man whom they had elevated to the governorship, but Wilson's spectacular defiance of the machine brought him national attention. Under the scholar-politician's aggressive leadership, the New Jersey legislature passed a drastic election reform law, a public-utility regulation act, and an employers' liability bill. The state's corporation laws, so hospitable to big business that New Jersey had become known as the "mother of trusts," were now radically amended. Wilson aroused further interest by an effective speaking tour of the West during the summer of 1911, during which he advocated the initiative, referendum, and recall—all favorite demands of the progressives.

Swinging steadily toward liberalism, Wilson found Colonel Harvey's continued support embarrassing because Harvey's Wall Street connections were well known. In December, 1911, the governor practically asked Harvey to stop advocating his nomination, thereby making a bitter personal enemy who was destined later to play a leading part in defeating Wilson's cherished project for a league of nations. Harvey's place within Wilson's inner board of strategy was taken by another honorary colonel, Edward M. House of Texas. Colonel House was a quiet man of refinement and wealth who loved to play the political game from behind the scenes. He had become very powerful in Texas politics and was now eager to enter the national field. Unlike Harvey, House's sympathies were with the progressives. Indeed, he published anonymously in 1912 an utopian novel, *Philip Dru, Administrator*, which told the story of the sweeping reforms made in the United States by a benevolent dictator. Meeting for the first time in November, 1911, Colonel House and Wilson became close friends, and Wilson relied heavily on this shrewd Texan for political advice during the next months. House encouraged the governor to cut loose from Harvey and to court the Western faction of the party in general and Bryan in particular. Fortunately for Wilson and House, Bryan was a good Christian and disposed to forgive the governor for having expressed the wish in 1907 that the Great Commoner might be knocked "once for all, into a cocked hat."

Although having no chance to secure another nomination for himself after his three defeats, Bryan proved to be the most powerful figure at the Baltimore convention. To be sure, his attempt to secure the chairmanship in the place of the conservative Judge Parker, the choice of the national committee, was voted down in a close contest; but he did succeed in having a bold platform adopted that called for immediate downward revision of the tariff, strengthening of the antitrust laws, presidential preference primaries, prohibition of corporation contributions to campaign chests, a single term for the President, and the revision of the banking and currency laws. His most dramatic maneuver came on the third day of the convention when he unexpectedly offered a resolution which read in part: "As proof of our fidelity to the people, we hereby declare ourselves opposed to the nomination of any candidate for President who is the representative of or under obligation to J. Pierpont Morgan, Thomas F. Ryan, August Belmont, or any other member of the privilege-hunting and favor-seeking class. . . . We demand the withdrawal from the convention of any delegate or delegates constituting or representing the above-named interests." It was a direct challenge to the Tammany delegation and to Ryan and Belmont, both Wall Street millionaires, who were present as delegates. The resolution threw the meeting into an uproar, and Bryan consented to delete its most offensive parts. In amended form, however, it was overwhelmingly adopted.

Forty-six ballots for the presidential nomination were taken before the necessary two-thirds majority could be obtained by any candidate. Champ Clark was in the lead throughout the early balloting and had an actual majority on the second day of voting when Tammany boss Charles Murphy suddenly shifted the backing of the New York delegation to him at the expense of Harmon. But Clark's chances were ruined when Bryan announced that Murphy's action indicated that the Speaker was accepting the help of predatory big business. Bryan then threw his influential backing to Wilson and this switch in the end proved decisive in securing the nomination for the crusading governor. Thomas R. Marshall, governor of Indiana, was chosen as the party's candidate for vice-president.

THE BOLT COMPLETE

The first national convention of the National Progressive party opened in Chicago on August 5. The meeting was unique for its atmosphere of religious enthusiasm. "John Brown's Body" and "Onward Christian Soldiers" were sung by the inspired delegates, and ex-Senator Beveridge of Indiana delivered a passionately eloquent keynote address. In the same spirit was Roosevelt's speech the next day accepting the presidential nomination of the new party. Hiram Johnson was given the second place on the ticket. A platform was adopted calling for the whole calendar of reform: direct primaries, direct election of Senators, initiative, referendum, and recall, a speedier method of amending the Constitution, women's suffrage, the limitation of campaign expenditures, the prohibition of child labor, a "living wage," the eight-hour day, a Department of Labor, conservation of national resources, the strong national regulation of interstate corporations, and the establishment of a Federal industrial commission comparable to the Interstate Commerce Commission.

THE ELECTION OF WILSON

Republicans throughout the country had to choose between loyalty to the historic party and alignment with the secessionists. Naturally the bulk of the machine politicians as well as the businessmen supported Taft, while idealists and reformers rallied happily to the so-called Bull Moose standard. Many individuals, however, took an unpredictable course. Such outstanding insurgents as LaFollette and Borah refused to support the third-party movement, while among Roosevelt's most active supporters were Boss "Bill" Flinn of Pittsburgh, millionaire publisher Frank A. Munsey, and George W. Perkins, former partner of J. P. Morgan, who became chairman of the Progressive National Committee.

The campaign was really one of personalities. All three candidates claimed to be friendly to the cause of reform; all three party platforms were liberal documents. Particularly hard it must have been for the puzzled voter to discern wherein the New Nationalism proclaimed by Colonel Roosevelt differed from the New Freedom promised by Governor Wilson. On one issue alone did the two take sharply opposed positions. Roosevelt had always distinguished between good and bad trusts; he now emphasized that what was needed was not new legislation and prosecutions designed to break large corporations into small, but Federal regulation of the trusts to preserve their good points and eradicate their evil. Wilson took the contrary position; excessive size in corporations was in itself a bad thing because it gave them too much power, both economic and political; the antitrust laws should be strengthened and clarified. Both Roosevelt and Wilson were deeply influenced by the thinking of other men on this problem. The former adopted the arguments of Herbert Croly, whose influential book, *The Promise of American Life*, had appeared in 1909; the latter accepted the ideas developed by Louis D. Brandeis in numerous writings, and especially in the volume entitled *Other People's Money*.

Roosevelt's reputation for radicalism in 1912 was largely due to his advocacy of the so-called recall of judicial decisions. The idea was deeply shocking to all conservatives, even though in the Progressive platform the phrase was given very careful definition. It was there made clear that such a recall was to apply only when an act passed under the police power of the state was held by the courts to be unconstitutional under the state constitution. Under these circumstances the people were to have an opportunity to vote on the question whether they desired the act to remain as law despite the decision.

All three candidates engaged in long speaking tours before large audiences. Wilson kept his talks on a high plane, considering only the issues. On the other hand, both Taft and Roosevelt descended to slinging mud at each other in bitter fashion. An almost disastrous incident occurred at Milwaukee on October 14, when a "poor creature," John Chrank, shot the Progressive candidate, supposedly to prevent him from serving a third term. Fortunately the wound was not fatal.

In November the election gave the result which any intelligent observer could have predicted. By an overwhelming electoral majority Woodrow Wilson was chosen President; he had 435 ballots, Roosevelt 88, and Taft 8. Of the popular votes, Wilson had secured 6,300,000 or 42 per cent; Roosevelt, 4,000,000, or 27 per cent; and Taft, 3,500,000, or 23 per cent. The schism had enabled a candidate with a minority of the popular ballots to win. Almost a million Americans showed their distrust of all three candidates by backing Eugene V. Debs, the Socialist. The new Congress also showed the effects of the Republican split; the House would consist of 290 Democrats to 145 Republicans and Progressives; the Senate, 51 Democrats to 45 of the opposition.

4

The American Empire

THE CLOSING YEARS OF THE NINETEENTH CENTURY WERE CLIMACTIC ones in American diplomatic history. They marked the end of an era of comparative isolation and the beginning of an epoch during which the United States emerged as a world power. Although the conclusion of the war with Spain is generally accepted as the dividing line between the two periods, actually the shift was gradual; the war merely hastened and accentuated it.

As a result of that war, the United States gained numerous insular possessions and, the appetite whetted, secured others in which it had been previously interested. The administration of some of those newly acquired lands overseas—particularly those in the Far East—raised unusual problems and turned American diplomatic interest again toward that part of the world. In order to settle those problems, the United States became involved with numerous other nations and thus emerged from its shell of isolation.

THE RISE OF IMPERIALISTIC THOUGHT

Since approximately 1890 a series of events had combined to bring an end to that comparative isolation and to make the United States a world-minded nation. In 1890, the American frontier was officially closed. While it is true that there were still millions of acres available for homesteading, American citizens were beginning to look about for new spheres to conquer. Industry, growing mightily since the Civil War, had reached a point where it was producing more goods than the home market could sustain. Consequently, new markets were being sought to buy the surplus. At the same time, these mercantile interests were looking for new sources of raw materials to keep their ever-expanding factories going. This combination of desire for new markets and for new areas for investment could not long be held in check.

78

Manifest Destiny, dormant since the early 1870's as Americans moved into the West, rehabilitated the South, and promoted industry, once more emerged; but it was a new form of destiny, one motivated both by economics and by needs of national defense. The foremost proponent of the revised doctrine was a prominent naval officer and writer, Captain Alfred Thayer Mahan. Captain Mahan firmly believed that the bulwark of American defense was a strong navy, and to be strong, the navy must have additional bases from which to operate. Therefore he brought to life again the theories that had been advocated by William Seward, Secretary of State during the Lincoln-Johnson era: the United States should extend its control over potential bases in both the Caribbean and the Pacific. To Mahan, the original Monroe Doctrine was not so important now. Since the United States could not adequately defend southern South America, he felt that the nation should concentrate primarily upon the West Indies and the countries bordering on the Caribbean and the Gulf of Mexico. He was also a firm believer in an interoceanic canal under complete American control. This canal, strongly protected by Caribbean bases, would furnish the avenue to the Pacific, where the United States must also necessarily have naval outposts.

Captain Mahan was likewise convinced that his country must develop markets in the Far East, and China, the center of that trade, must be kept politically independent. He did not believe in territorial expansion as such, for the United States had enough land as it was; but the acquisition of bases was an essential adjunct for the maintenance of the United States as a world power. By the middle 1890's Mahan was a firm supporter of close cooperation with Great Britain, whose outlook, he believed, was similar to that of the United States.

A vociferous, although inept, apostle of these views was the young Henry Cabot Lodge of Massachusetts. He lacked the broadness of vision which Mahan enjoyed, however, and was much less cautious. In many ways he was like the War Hawks of 1812. He felt that Canada should be annexed, Cuba taken by force from Spain, and the islands of the Pacific snatched from the grasping hands of European expansionist nations. Yet Lodge did not contemplate the means by which those objectives could be obtained—nor the effects. He was an out-and-out jingoist at this particular time and had considerable influence among the younger generation.

Combining the wisdom of Mahan with the rashness of Lodge was Theodore Roosevelt, who first made his presence felt on the national scene while serving as Assistant Secretary of the Navy under President

McKinley. Like Mahan, he was a prime supporter of a bigger and better navy, and the efficiency which the naval forces showed during the war with Spain was due in part to his efforts.

The larger navy which Mahan and Roosevelt were advocating was beginning to materialize. In addition to their pleas, contributing factors to the growth of the naval arm, a necessity for imperialism, were the prosperous condition of the treasury around 1890 (approximately the time when Speaker Reed said that the United States was a billion-dollar country), troubles with Chile which made the nation realize its naval deficiencies, and the difficulties with Great Britain and Germany over Samoa.

In the 1890's, philosophers, sociologists, and religious leaders were teaching and preaching doctrines which tended to support imperialism. The philosophers and sociologists concluded that Anglo-Saxons were particularly endowed with the faculty for spreading their beneficent rule to other parts of the world. And religious leaders, particularly those with missionary instincts, felt that it was the Christian duty of Americans to spread the Gospel in foreign parts.

Newspaper editors in all parts of the country were likewise pressing the demand for Manifest Destiny. Of course the publishers of the Hearst-Pulitzer school were thinking primarily in terms of sensational headlines and consequently of increased circulation, but the majority of the editors looking for new lands to conquer were expressing in their columns the views of their readers. Thus it was evident that the new Manifest Destiny was growing in popularity as the 1890's progressed. The expansionist theory was being supported by naval leaders, by politicians, by educational and religious leaders, by investors, and by industrialists.

True, there were vigorous opponents of imperialism. President Grover Cleveland in his second term (1893–1897) indicated his opposition by withdrawing the Hawaiian annexation treaty from Senatorial ratification. Many New Englanders were strong in their denunciations of expansion. Severe critics of growing big business could see in imperialism only another medium for promoting greater profits for the capitalists. Isolationists regarded external holdings as un-American.

If the advocates of expansion were to have their way, they needed something which would unite their varied, scattered forces. The incident which served to coalesce those forces, to win new converts, to cause the United States to embark definitely upon an imperialistic course, and to make it, as a result, a world power was the Spanish-American War.

THE WAR WITH SPAIN

The "splendid little war," as John Hay called it, had both deep and surface roots. For a century Americans had been interested in Cuba, while Spaniards had feared that the United States might seize that rich and strategic island. The situation had brought numerous diplomatic crises, particularly during the fifties and the seventies. But the more immediate causes for the war grew out of the Cuban revolt which broke out in 1895. Spanish measures of repression were harsh, and the atrocity stories which horrified America had an unfortunate basis in fact, although they were frequently exaggerated in the propaganda of Cuban juntas and the columns of the "yellow" press. American investments amounting to $50,000,000 and trade worth $100,000,000 were imperiled by the insurrection; American health was threatened by the plague conditions in Cuban "reconcentration camps." Public opinion in the United States demanded that the Spanish government cease hostilities and grant the Cubans their own government. President McKinley tried to withstand the pressure of the so-called war party and achieve these ends without war, but in the end this proved impossible. Revelation of the Spanish ambassador's criticism of the President and the tragic explosion that destroyed the *Maine* aroused American feelings to a demand for war which neither McKinley nor Congress could withstand.

On April 11, 1898, McKinley asked Congress for authority to intervene; on April 19 Congress responded with the passage of four resolutions which amounted to a declaration of war. The fourth of these, the so-called Teller Amendment, however, was a concession to the anti-imperialists since it disclaimed any intention on the part of the United States to annex Cuba; the ultimate objective of American policy was declared to be "to leave the government and control of the Island to its people."

Judged by twentieth-century standards the Spanish War was not a great military struggle. The American army was woefully unprepared as far as leadership, manpower, and equipment were concerned. President McKinley quickly had to issue calls for volunteers to participate in what was considered at first to be a major struggle. Few in the United States realized the numerous problems that had to be faced. The navy, steadily increasing in size and efficiency since about 1890, was in much better shape than the army and, thanks to the foresight of Secretary of the Navy Long and his assistant, Theodore Roosevelt, the various fleets were at strategic points when hostilities started. Fortunately for the

United States, Spain was worse off, despite an apparent supremacy on paper.

The fighting began on May 1, when Admiral George Dewey, who had been ordered to the Far East shortly after the blowing up of the *Maine*, successfully attacked the Spanish fleet in Manila Bay. What was considered the major campaign did not open until about June 1, when the Atlantic fleet under Admiral Schley and Admiral Sampson succeeded in bottling up the Spanish navy at Santiago, Cuba. Not until three weeks later did the American army invade that island. After several misfortunes, Santiago was captured and the Spanish fleet was destroyed while attempting to escape. By the middle of July the Americans were in practical control of the whole of Cuba. General Miles had an even easier time dominating the near-by Puerto Rico. While the fighting around Manila continued, the disastrous blows of the Americans, added to political and economic troubles in the homeland, compelled Spain to ask for armistice terms on July 26.

This speedy victory made Americans forget that their country was still largely unprepared. Instead, they felt a new sense of power; had not a European power been brought to its knees in less than three months? Now it was the destiny—perhaps even the duty—of the United States to assume its rightful place in affairs of the world and to make its wishes and interests felt everywhere.

THE TREATY OF PARIS

This feeling of world-mindedness and new-found power was expressed at the peace conference, held in Paris from October to December, 1898. Although the United States had entered the war supposedly only to obtain freedom for Cuba, she emerged from the conference with Puerto Rico, Guam, and the Philippines, together with a guardianship over Cuba until its inhabitants were ready to govern themselves.

The treaty ran into difficulties in the Senate where the anti-imperialists rallied under the leadership of George Hoar of Massachusetts to delay ratification. They argued that it was un-American to have imperial holdings; they refused to admit that the nation could be half free and half subjugated; they asserted that all democratic governments secured their consent from the governed; they raised the bogey of foreign entanglements. The administration forces, basing their support of the treaty upon the varied imperialistic arguments, finally won the day, aided in no small part by William Jennings Bryan. Bryan, a professed anti-imperialist, nevertheless desired peace first of all. Moreover, Bryan realized that if his followers did not support the treaty, the Philippines would remain under Spanish control. The only hope for the freedom of the islands was by ratifying the document. He therefore persuaded some of the treaty opponents to change their minds, saying that the issue of imperialism could be settled by the people themselves in the election of 1900. Even then the treaty was just squeezed through by a vote of fifty-seven to twenty-seven on February 6, 1899. A majority of the supporters—forty—were Republicans; a majority of the opponents—twenty—were Democrats.

Before the century was over, imperialism and the theories of Mahan were given added impetus when, in 1898, the United States annexed Hawaii by joint resolution of Congress, and secured the island of Tutuila in the Samoan group, with its excellent coaling station and naval base of Pago-Pago, as a result of a tripartite arrangement with Great Britain and Germany in 1899.

Thus, as the twentieth century opened, the United States had given up its previous isolation. Through its recent victory, it had secured insular territories in the Caribbean and the Pacific. Additional bases in the Pacific had been acquired by peaceful diplomatic action. The European powers were showing an unaccustomed respect for America. The nation was now definitely a world power, and with that position came new responsibilities and new interests. Dealing with those responsibilities and interests furnished the major task of American diplomacy in the opening years of the new century.

KEEPING THE PLEDGE WITH CUBA

The Teller Amendment of April, 1898, mentioned above, had stated: "That the United States hereby disclaims any disposition or intention to exercise sovereignty, jurisdiction, or control" over Cuba "except for the pacification thereof, and asserts its determination, when that is accomplished, to leave the government and control of the Island to its people." With the conclusion of the war with Spain, however, the United States was not fully ready to put this pledge into effect. Fear of a counterrevolution by the Spanish residents, the appalling illiteracy, the lack of training in self-government, and the fear that were the United States to withdraw at once some other power, perhaps Germany, might step in delayed fulfillment of the promise.

Therefore an American military regime was immediately established, with General Leonard Wood eventually serving as governor general. Wood's administration was characterized by important work in these fields: (1) improving the transportation facilities of Cuba, with special attention to the construction of a road throughout the length of the island; (2) making Cuba more healthful, aided by the Army Medical Corps under Major Walter Reed who was able to discover that a certain type of mosquito was responsible for the spread of the disastrous yellow fever; and (3) the development of an educational system to cut down the illiteracy and train the inhabitants to govern themselves.

By the middle of 1900 Governor Wood, after conferring with the Cuban leaders, felt that the islanders were ready for self-government. A constituent assembly, selected by a limited franchise, convened in November. By February, 1901, this group, guided by Wood, had drawn up a constitution which provided for three branches of government and separation of powers, but made no mention of Cuba's relationship with the United States. The War Department refused to give its approval to the document as it stood, so Secretary of War Root and General Wood collaborated in drawing up the so-called Platt Amendment which was made a rider to the Army Appropriation Act of March, 1901. Of the seven articles of this amendment, the most important were: (1) the "Government of Cuba shall never enter into any treaty or other compact with any foreign power . . . which will impair . . . the independence of Cuba, nor in any manner authorize . . . any foreign power . . . to obtain by colonization or for military or naval purposes . . . control over any portion of said island"; (2) Cuba shall not "assume or contract any public debt to pay the interest upon which . . . the ordinary revenues . . . shall be inadequate"; (3) Cuba agrees "that the United States may exercise the right to intervene for the preservation of Cuban independence, the maintenance of a government adequate for the protection of life, property, and individual liberty"; (4) Cuba will continue the sanitation program; and (5) Cuba will lease or sell coaling stations and naval bases to the United States to aid in the Cuban defense.

The Cubans did not like the Platt Amendment as they believed that it infringed on their sovereignty; but they realized that the cherished self-government would not be attained unless they added the amendment to their constitution. Therefore, with many misgivings, they made the necessary addition and, to strengthen the right of American intervention, the amendment was made the basis for a treaty between the two nations in 1903.

As soon as the Cuban constitution was approved by the American Congress, preparations were made for the first election. Presidential victory was gained by Tomas Estrada Palma, whose long exile in the United States had acquainted him with democratic procedures. Following Palma's inauguration in May, 1902, American troops were withdrawn and the island left to its destiny. The ending of the military occupation of Cuba was a great surprise to other nations, who had not believed that such a valuable prize would be given up. There were some objections in the United States, particularly among those who had investments in Cuba and the advocates of Manifest Destiny. However, a promise had been made and reiterated, so the honor of the United States was at stake. Furthermore, had the United States continued to remain in Cuba, there assuredly would have been considerable trouble with the inhabitants, and in withdrawing the United States had sufficient ties through the Platt Amendment to insure against Cuba falling prey to some hostile nation.

During Palma's first administration Cuba progressed along all lines. Her economic advance was aided by the United States. President Roosevelt realized that Cuba needed a ready market for her chief crop, sugar, and the natural one was the United States. The Dingley Tariff rates, however, were so high that they tended to exclude that commodity. Consequently, he demanded that Congress amend those rates to allow

Cuba, the Beginner. Uncle Sam getting Cuba ready for self-government. (By Bart in the *Minneapolis Journal*.)

the sugar to enter at less than the usual duty. The protectionists in the legislature, backed by the Louisiana sugar growers, refused to make the necessary changes until the President sent a strong message demanding action. Then, in December, 1903, the Congress accepted a measure allowing reductions of from 20 to 40 per cent on imports from Cuba and at the same time ending sugar reciprocity agreements with other countries. Cuba was greatly aided by this act and she showed her gratitude by becoming one of the leading purchasers of American goods.

When Palma was reelected in 1905, the Cuban opposition, charging him with dictatorial tendencies, threatened to start a civil war. Secretary of War Taft sent troops to the island in 1906 and reestablished military government. American advocates of annexation became active again, and even Roosevelt wrote to a friend: ". . . I am so angry with that infernal little Cuban republic that I would like to wipe its people off the face of the earth . . ."

During this period of intervention, the governorship was chiefly in the hands of Charles Magoon of Nebraska, who had had experience as an executive in the Canal Zone. His work consisted mainly in developing commerce, industry, and agriculture, in promoting road building and other public works, in enacting new election laws, and in establishing a more effective educational program. Nevertheless his administration was unpopular in Cuba and he was charged with extravagance, with establishing a bureaucracy, with making too extensive a use of the pardoning power, and even with corruption. A subsequent American investigation of these charges, however, showed that they were groundless.

When the Cubans were again thought ready to govern themselves, an election was held resulting in victory for the Liberal, José Gomez, and, in January, 1909, the American administrative and military intervention was ended. Once more the United States had lived up to its promise that it would not keep Cuba, and American public opinion, seeing order restored in the island, overwhelmed the annexationist minority. Yet this second period of military rule indicated that the United States would brook no disorder within the small neighbor's territory.

THE PUERTO RICAN EXPERIMENT

Puerto Rico, with its 3435 square miles of territory and population of nearly a million, approximately 60 per cent of whom were whites, was part of the booty gained in the war with Spain. The islanders were largely illiterate, with no training whatsoever in the field of self-government. Under the treaty terms it was provided that "the civil rights and political status of the native inhabitants . . . shall be determined by Congress." No promises had been made concerning the future, but the general sentiment throughout the United States was that the Puerto Ricans should be treated fairly.

Immediately after annexation the island, which was in a bad way economically—and made worse by a severe hurricane in the summer of 1899, was placed under military rule. The several military governors, as in the case of Cuba, did excellent work economically, educationally, and medically.

Then in April, 1900, permanent civil government was established under the Foraker Act. There was a governor and an executive council of eleven, named by the President with the consent of the Senate. At least five councillors were to be Puerto Ricans. Six executive departments were created, each of which was headed by a council member, usually an American. The insular legislature was made up of the council, which served as the upper house, and the House of Delegates, elected by the qualified voters. The court system was based on the United States model. The inhabitants were designated as "citizens of Puerto Rico," entitled to the protection of the United States but not to all the privileges of American citizenship. This form of government bore a striking resemblance to that which the Americans themselves had once "enjoyed" under British rule.

The system thus established, which represented the views of the dominant Republican party in the United States, remained in force without essential change until 1917, despite the fact that the political arrangements did not work altogether smoothly. The Puerto Ricans were dissatisfied because they seemed to be placed in a position of inferiority through the denial of American citizenship, and they were especially distressed because the control of the executive departments was kept from the hands of the assembly. The result was friction and a series of petty quarrels between the governor and his council on the one hand and the House of Delegates on the other which are reminiscent of the eighteenth-century conflict between British colonial executives and the American colonists. Just as in those cases, the popular branch of the legislature tried to close the purse strings. The Congress of the United States foiled such tactics, however, with a law of 1909 which stated that in case the House of Delegates failed at any time to vote the necessary appropriations, the amount approved for the preceding year would be collected. Although better administrators were sent out and the government now worked more smoothly, it cannot be said that the Puerto Ricans were any more enthusiastic over American control.

In spite of the political bickerings, there is no doubt that under American rule Puerto Rican economic conditions—though still far from prosperous—developed beyond anything the island had previously known. It is true that the advantages did not affect all lines of production equally and that the important coffee industry even declined somewhat, but the total exports and imports were considerably larger than in the past. In addition, Puerto Rico secured improved means of transportation, modern sanitation which thwarted the dread hookworm, and better schools which decreased the widespread illiteracy. The United States assuredly was showing its good intentions, but the primary problem of civilized government under normal conditions is to secure the consent of the governed, and in that regard she was deficient.

PHILIPPINE DIFFICULTIES

The most novel immediate question raised by the war with Spain was that of control of the Philippines, consisting of seven thousand islands of varying size and inhabited by seven million persons, many of them uncivilized. Many dialects were spoken in the islands and a variety of religions practiced. The great majority of the American people regarded the rule of the islands as a trust and desired to educate the Filipinos to self-government in the American sense as soon as possible, although it seemed to leading Republicans that a long course of education would be necessary before the natives could be trusted to conduct a modern administration. It was, of course, inevitable that the Filipinos, after their experience with Spain, would not appreciate the American point of view and that unhappy consequences would result.

After the surrender of Spain, American control did not extend beyond the environs of Manila and, when it became evident that the United States did not intend to recognize the Philippine Republic under Emilio Aguinaldo, that leader and his supporters resorted to arms. Two days before the treaty of peace was ratified, the Filipino insurgents attacked the American troops at Manila. As their forces were numerous and fairly well equipped, the situation seemed serious.

In regular warfare, however, the Filipinos proved unable to offer very effective resistance to the Americans who were soon heavily reenforced, with the volunteers for the Spanish War being replaced as quickly as possible by regulars. In a few months the insurgent government was broken up and all its chief officers captured except Aguinaldo, who succeeded in eluding his pursuers. In this struggle the American forces showed remarkable efficiency and zeal, but the campaigning was most difficult because of the delays occasioned by the rainy season, the character of the country, and the trouble in controlling large districts with small garrisons.

The spirit of the insurgents was not broken. Realizing at length the strength and weakness of the Americans, they decided in November, 1899, to disband their organized forces and resort to guerrilla warfare exclusively. This decision increased the problems of the Americans, and the fighting was now carried on with increased ferocity. Public opinion at home became disturbed by persistent reports of outrages committed by American troops against Filipino captives, and this sentiment finally forced a Senatorial investigation. The testimony clearly showed that the methods of American soldiers had in many cases been ruthless. Yet in extenuation it appeared that the situation was very trying and that the officers as a rule had tried to prevent the atrocities. Such incidents are unfortunately the almost inevitable result of guerrilla warfare.

Meantime the military operations were actively pushed and, in February, 1901, Aguinaldo himself was tracked down and captured by General Frederick Funston as the result of a daring ruse. Contrary to expectation, Aguinaldo's capture had little effect on the insurgents, but the end was only a matter of time; the last resistance ceased in April, 1902.

The earliest American rule in the archipelago was necessarily military, with first General Otis and then General MacArthur [1] serving as military governor. Even before the ratification of the peace treaty, however, President McKinley named a commission of five to study conditions in the islands and to report on the best means of control. In January, 1899, this First Philippine Commission, headed by President Schurman of Cornell University, began its careful investigation and subsequently presented an elaborate report. The commission concluded that the natives were as yet incapable of self-government; the report included a very useful account of the conditions and resources of the Philippines, about which Americans knew little.

Acting on the commission's recommendation, McKinley therefore named a second commission made up of Chairman William Howard Taft and four other members in March, 1900. Unlike the first board, this was to be a permanent administrative body and was especially charged with the delicate task of organizing a system of government beginning with the municipalities and then extending to the provinces.

[1] The father of General Douglas MacArthur of World War II fame.

When the commissioners believed that a civil, as distinct from a military, central government could be established, they were to submit the necessary recommendations. The Second Philippine Commission was to be the supreme legislative authority in the islands, subject to the President through the Secretary of War, but the military governor was to be retained as chief executive. All these important steps were taken by President McKinley by virtue of his military power as commander-in-chief.

It was naturally felt that some more permanent legal basis was desirable for such an important action, and this was provided by Congress in March, 1901, through the Spooner Amendment to the Military Appropriation Act. This conferred upon the President complete military, civil, and judicial power over the Philippines until Congress should provide otherwise. The measure, although good for immediate practical purposes, constituted a rather remarkable step for a Congress acting under the American system of government, for it made President McKinley virtually dictator of the archipelago.

Taking advantage of his new power, McKinley wisely made certain alterations in the government of the islands. Taft was appointed civil governor and the authority of General MacArthur was limited to the districts in which the insurrection had not been crushed. A little later three native members were added to the commission, and the administration was divided into four executive departments, each in charge of one of the American commissioners.

The task assigned was carried out with excellent judgment. Governor Taft showed much ability and laid the foundation for the reputation which later helped to make him President. A system of municipal government was first established, largely elective but based on a carefully limited suffrage and retaining something of the old Spanish forms and names. These municipalities were subject to rigid supervision. The commission next proceeded to institute provincial government in those areas where conditions made it possible. The governors of these provinces were elected by the councils of the several municipalities, but the other officers were appointed by the commission. Effective control of provincial affairs was lodged in a board of three, consisting of the governor, the treasurer, and the supervisor of public works. Under this system there was very little independent self-government in local matters, yet it was hoped that the arrangement of limited franchise and careful supervision, especially over the public purse, would constitute a training school through which the natives would be prepared for larger self-control. About thirty-five provinces were organized by Governor Taft during the first year of his administration. The commission had, however, to make special provisions for the Moro Province, inhabited by warlike Mohammedans, where elective government was manifestly impossible.

Upon the whole these arrangements worked well and, by an important act of July 1, 1902, Congress confirmed what the President and the commission had done, although requiring that in the future the civil governor and other executive officers named by the President were to be approved by the Senate. The measure also provided for further progress. A census of the islands was to be taken, and two years thereafter elections were to be held for a general assembly. When this body convened, it was ordained that the legislative power in the islands was to rest in a bicameral congress—the elective assembly as the lower chamber and the commission as the upper. The act further declared the natives to be citizens of the Philippines and extended to them nearly all of the provisions of the American Constitution. Life, liberty, and property were guaranteed, but not trial by jury.

Although the work was carried out rather slowly, the plans for the elections were finally completed. More than 100,000 Filipinos voted and, in the fall of 1907, eight years after the institution of American rule, the Philippine Assembly met. Nothing revolutionary happened, although the Nationalist party, which stood for speedy independence, gained a majority over the Progressives, who favored evolution under American rule. The Nationalists, while expressing their desire for freedom, wisely refrained from following an aggressive or violent course, and the existence of the assembly did not greatly complicate the situation.

The duty of creating the best possible system of government for these new wards was, however, only one of the numerous tasks which the possession of this vast and populous archipelago entailed. Particularly important were the settlement of the question of the Friars' land and the introduction of a new system of education.

The Friars' land problem was vital because the dominant position which had been held under the Spanish regime by the three prominent religious orders—the Dominicans, the Augustinians, and Recollectos—had much to do with the discontent of the natives. The Friars held about 400,000 acres of the best land in the islands and had established a system under which the Filipinos could cultivate it only by renting it on shares for long periods. The revolt against Spain in 1896 had been largely the outgrowth of Filipino hostility to this condition, as well as the alleged immorality among the members of the religious orders. During the revolt the Friars had been largely dispossessed, but they still continued their claims, while the native holders naturally regarded the captured soil as their own. The best way out, according to the commission, was to purchase the disputed acreage—which it was authorized to do under the Act of 1902—but the Orders demanded too high a price. Lengthy negotiations were needed, including a trip by Taft to the Vatican, before the price was lowered to $7,239,000, a sum which was admitted to be more than the actual value of the land; but the commission regarded this concession to the diplomatic skill of the Holy See as a proper one to secure satisfaction to all concerned. Further problems, however, remained, for the idea was to sell the land on fair terms to the tenants, while the feeling was prevalent among the Filipinos that they were already entitled to the property. As time passed, the titles were granted to the natives upon very liberal terms.

Perhaps no aspect of American control deserves more praise than the active and successful effort to develop an educational system. The next organized invasion after that of the army was one of American teachers, who promoted a school plan vastly superior to that of the Spaniards. Because of the difference in tribal speech and the absence of a written literature, English was made the basis of instruction. Normal schools were quickly established for the training of native teachers, and a university on the model of American state universities was founded at Manila. Under the Spanish regime, manual toil of all kinds had been regarded as something to be avoided, but, in the face of the most deep-seated prejudice, the American schools made commendable progress in their efforts to popularize technical and agricultural education.

Nevertheless, the results should not be exaggerated. The difficulties to be faced were still great. An Oriental people change slowly, and some of the measures devised to force upon the Filipinos a premature enthusiasm for "American liberty" had exactly the opposite effect. Moreover, the refusal of Congress to grant adequate financial aid to the Filipino schools retarded the work and limited in a disappointing way the numbers reached.

THE INSULAR CASES

Meantime, the outcome of the Spanish War had brought the United States face to face with some of the most complicated questions of political theory and constitutional law that Americans have ever had to meet. While the United States had often acquired territory before, with the exception of Alaska it had been land contiguous to the United States and was manifestly destined to be admitted some day to the Union. The case of Alaska naturally caused little trouble since most of it had remained so long unoccupied, but it seemed absurd to many Americans that distant islands, inhabited by races so dissimilar to themselves as those of the Philippines, should ever become states. Yet, on the other hand, the idea of the Stars and Stripes waving over permanently subject peoples was abhorrent to many of the best and wisest, like Senator Hoar, Carl Schurz, and other leading anti-imperialists.

And, after the deed was done, the complications did not cease. Many well-informed men held that the new lands had at once become parts of the United States, and their inhabitants were citizens just like those of the older American territories. It seemed indeed absurd that Moros and headhunters should have all the privileges of the Bill of Rights and the Fourteenth Amendment, yet there were not a few thinking Americans who contended that under the American form of government nothing else was possible. The Constitution spoke nowhere of subjects, but only of citizens.

The other view was, of course, that the Constitution did not extend automatically to the new lands because they were "dependencies," subject to the rule of Congress and that the Constitution would not apply to them until it was extended by act of the "sovereign legislature." This view appeared to be good common sense, but it was not easy to find basis for it in the Constitution. Especially was it hard to think of Congress bound by the limitations of the Constitution within the continental United States, but doing anything it pleased regarding life, liberty, and property outside of those geographical limits.

Nevertheless a searching of the precedents proved decidedly favorable to those who held the second view. In the case of Louisiana and also of Florida it had undoubtedly been the idea of the government and of leading contemporary statesmen that the provisions of the Constitution did not apply until formally extended by Congress, and American legal practice in dealing with these territories had been based on this theory. In the cases of the Gadsden Purchase, Alaska, and Harrison's treaty for the annexation of Hawaii, it had been specifically stated that the inhabitants should be admitted to full citizenship in the United States. Although these examples were possibly not conclusive in the matter of legal principle, they nevertheless stood out very strongly against the idea of automatic extension. It was the attitude of McKinley's administration that the rights and privileges of the Constitution did not extend to the peoples of Puerto Rico and the Philippines, and it based its policy toward them on this theory.

The vital questions involved came in due time before the Supreme Court. These cases are generally referred to as the insular decisions and were decided mainly in 1901. The first case, DeLima v. Bidwell, turned on whether duties on goods from Puerto Rico could be collected under the Dingley Tariff Act. The court held, but only by a vote of five to four, that Puerto Rico was not a foreign country and therefore the duties could not be collected.[1] This, however, did not reach the real heart of the matter. Although it was settled that the Dingley Act did not apply automatically, it was not decided whether Congress had the right to place special duties on merchandise imported from the islands.

This further question at once arose. When the Foraker Act was passed, the President and perhaps the majority of the American people wished Puerto Rican products to come in free. The sugar interests, however, were opposed and were able to force a provision into the measure which placed a 15 per cent duty on imports from Puerto Rico until 1902. The validity of this requirement was now tested in Downes v. Bidwell, decided in May, 1901. The crux of the matter lay in this question: did the provision of the Constitution that all duties must be uniform throughout the United States apply to Puerto Rico? In the Downes v. Bidwell case the Supreme Court decided that the Foraker Act was valid, and thus that the Constitution does not automatically follow the flag. Again it was a five-to-four division, and in the minority were Chief Justice Fuller and Justice Harlan, who enjoyed a particularly high legal reputation. Moreover, the majority did not agree in their reasoning, although concurring in upholding the validity of the act.

It is difficult to contemplate the decision with equanimity. Yet it must be admitted that even if it involved bad political science and questionable law, it applied well to the existing situation. If the United States had to rule over Filipinos and Puerto Ricans, it would be highly inconvenient to grant them all the rights of American citizens. But even decisions of the Supreme Court could not govern irrevocably the thinking of the American people. In the minds of many opposition still remained to permanent domination over peoples regarded as inferior, nor could the implied pledge to prepare the Filipinos for eventual independence be forgotten.

Generally speaking, the issue was drawn between the major political parties. The Republicans, highly susceptible to the influence of big business and rather inclined to view with complacency the peculiar virtues of American progress, regarded independence for the Philippines as impracticable until the remote future. The Democrats, on the other hand, more or less committed against imperialism by William Jennings

[1] Directly after, the same doctrine was held in the case of the Fourteen Diamond Rings regarding goods from the Philippines.

Bryan, favored early freedom for the national wards. To anyone un-acquainted with the sudden changes of American politics, this reversal since Civil War days of views on the general subject of race capacity might seem indeed surprising.

AMERICAN INTERESTS IN THE FAR EAST

The occupation of the Philippines and, to a lesser extent, of Hawaii, Guam, and Samoa, revived American interest in the Far East, an interest that had been largely dormant since before the Civil War when Secretary of State Daniel Webster and his immediate successors had worked for equality of privileges and commercial facilities for all nations doing business with China.

Following the Civil War that interest had lagged and, even as late as March, 1898, a British proposal for joint action in the Far East to protect the open door was sidetracked in United States official quarters. Then came the war with Spain and the resultant annexation of Far Eastern territory. Very speedily did the American attitude change. Part of the reason was economic: American exporters in quest of new markets and importers in search of new sources of supply wanted their full share of Far Eastern commerce. Part of it was strategic: that region must be kept at peace so that the new insular holdings could be defended more easily and at less cost.

The major trouble spot was China, whose weakness had been clearly demonstrated by her overwhelming defeat in the Sino-Japanese War of 1894–1895. Japan and the major powers of Europe had been quick to seize advantage by securing spheres of influence in Chinese territory. France obtained a ninety-nine-year lease to Kwangchow-wan; Britain gained Wei-hai-wei and Kowloon; Russia took over Port Arthur; Germany secured Kiaochow; Japan was showing interest in Fukhien and Korea; and Italy was striving to keep pace with the rest. It was no coincidence that these spheres centered around important ports. The United States had not participated in those spoils, but she was interested in what might happen. Suppose each trespassing power closed its ports to the commerce of all but its own ships? Certainly, then, American trade would suffer increasingly. Furthermore, the closed-port theory might lead to antagonisms, war might follow among the contestants, and the American hold on the Philippines might be lost. At the least, the United States would have to increase her military and naval establishments in that part of the world.

Consequently, the McKinley administration was finally willing to heed the urgings of Lord Charles Beresford, a British admiral and publicist, Alfred Hippisley, an Englishman employed in the Chinese customs service, and W. W. Rockhill, an American who had spent years in the Far East. Secretary of State John Hay, following the example of John Quincy Adams, took over the leadership for the United States in promoting a policy of British origin.[1] On September 6, 1899, he sent similar notes to Great Britain, Germany, and Russia, and two months later to France, Italy, and Japan. The gist of these messages was that no country should interfere "with any treaty port or vested interest within any so-called 'spheres of interest' or leased territory it may have in China"; within each sphere the Chinese government should collect all duties provided for in its tariff treaties; and each power concerned was asked not only to approve these statements but to try to persuade the others to agree also.

The replies from most of the powers were equivocal, with support of the so-called Open-Door doctrine made contingent upon ratification by the others. The Russian answer, indeed, was practically a rejection. Secretary Hay was displeased with the result, but he determined upon a bold stroke. On March 20, 1900, he publicly announced that all the nations concerned had given their support in "final and definitive" terms to his proposal. None of the powers dared challenge his statement lest the others consider it as grasping. Thus for the time being at least, the United States diminished the danger of a commercial war in the Far East and secured for its citizens economic advantages which otherwise would have been lacking.

Secretary Hay was not finished however. In June, 1900, a faction of Chinese nationalists, popularly known as the "Boxers," began a fanatical attempt to drive out the invaders of their precious land. Several hundred of the "foreign devils" were killed, and the British legation at Peking, where many found refuge, was for weeks besieged by the Boxer forces. An international army of twenty thousand, of whom twenty-five hundred were American troops from the Philippines, had to be dispatched to effect a rescue. By the middle of August the siege was raised and the Boxer rebels dispersed.

Again the United States had to go to China's aid. On July 3, 1900, Hay added to the Open-Door principle the additional policy of attempting to preserve the territorial integrity and independence of China. The other powers did not formally accept Hay's principles, but the dismemberment of the empire was prevented by working one country's territorial greed against that of another. Furthermore, the possible

---

[1] There was this difference. The British in 1899 wanted the United States to do this; such had not been Canning's wish in 1823.

bankruptcy of China through payment of a proposed billion-dollar indemnity was avoided when the United States prevailed upon the other nations to cut their demands by two-thirds. China showed her gratitude by concluding a commercial treaty which was particularly favorable to her benefactor. The good relations were further accentuated when the United States returned (in 1908 and in 1924) approximately three-quarters of her $24,440,778 share of the Boxer indemnity. In turn, China used this money for scholarships in the United States granted to out-standing Chinese students.

The Open-Door policy was not entirely altruistic. American traders and investors desired more of the Chinese commerce than they had been getting. Also, as has been pointed out, the United States was possibly more interested in general peace in the Far East than in the specific safeguarding of China's territorial integrity. It is extremely doubtful whether the United States would have fought to force inter-national recognition of the Open Door, but at least the sponsorship of it thwarted, for the time being at least, the aims of other powers to secure control of China's trade. Furthermore, the very fact that those powers yielded to Hay's diplomacy indicated that they recognized that the United States had become a world power too.

Hay was not always consistent in his policies. At the close of 1900— the very year in which he made his public statements about preserving Chinese territorial entity—the Secretary secretly tried to secure a naval base for the United States in Southern China. The deal was frustrated through the opposition of the Japanese government, which chided Hay for his forgetfulness.

RELATIONS WITH JAPAN

After 1900 English and American proponents of the Open Door watched with growing concern while Russia extended more and more complete domination over Manchuria and even made gestures toward Korea. The British government, with the approval of most Americans, countered Russian imperialism by entering upon an alliance with Japan in 1902. This diplomatic development encouraged the Nipponese to attack Port Arthur suddenly in 1904, thus precipitating the Russo-Japanese War. Toward this contest the United States government maintained an official neutrality, but there was little attempt to disguise the strongly pro-Japanese character of its sympathies. Indeed, accord-ing to Roosevelt's own story—which has been questioned—he went so far as to warn France and Germany that the United States might go to the assistance of Japan were either of them to enter on the side of

Russia. Whatever the truth of this tale, it is certain that Roosevelt responded eagerly when the Japanese government intimated to him in ultrasecrecy that it would welcome his good offices in bringing the war to an early conclusion, whereby the fruits of initial Japanese victories would be ensured. Fortunately for the President, Russia—convulsed by internal revolution—was also secretly eager for peace. Roosevelt was therefore upon certain ground when he issued his public invitation to the belligerents for a peace conference to be held in the United States. The resultant Treaty of Portsmouth of 1905 pleased the President since it was moderate enough to maintain a balance of power and since he subsequently received the Nobel Peace Prize for his part in bringing it about.

The surprising military strength displayed by Japan impressed upon the Roosevelt administration the desirability of an understanding to safeguard American interests in the Philippines. Accordingly, President Roosevelt authorized Secretary of War Taft, upon completing a special mission to Manila, to proceed to Tokyo to sound out Japanese plans. Toward the close of July, 1905, Taft and Prime Minister Katsura concluded the so-called Agreed Memorandum. Under this arrangement the United States was to allow Japan a free hand in Korea in return for a promise that she had no designs upon the Philippines. Before the year was over, Secretary Root indicated his full support of this memorandum by telling the Japanese ambassador that in the future the United States would deal with Korean problems only through Japan.

This Agreed Memorandum was kept secret from the American people for many years. Certainly it was not in accord with the announced policy of the Open Door. Later, Root tried to defend this secret diplomacy by saying that the only way to have stopped the Japanese trespass in Korea was through war. He inferred that Congress would not have made a declaration and, if it had, the people would not have stood for it. Therefore, "all we might have done was to make threats which we could not carry out."

Although the Agreed Memorandum normally would be considered an indication of full cordiality between the two nations, actually beneath the surface there were definite signs of ill-feeling. Japanese jingoists, unacquainted with the initiative taken by their own government, believed that American diplomatic intervention in their war with Russia had deprived them of territory and large financial indemnity. On the other hand, Americans along the Pacific coast, headed by labor interests, were worried over increased Japanese immigration, particularly of unskilled workers with a low standard of living. While a Congressional bill for complete exclusion of the Japanese failed because of Roosevelt's opposition, the San Francisco local authorities enacted in October, 1906, an ordinance preventing Orientals from attending the regular city schools. Immediately Japan objected on the ground that a treaty with the United States gave her nationals the same rights as those enjoyed by the most favored nation.

President Roosevelt supported this contention, but the Constitution gave him no authority to act in a local matter. The President, however, used other means to end this "wicked absurdity." He called the Republican leaders of California to a White House conference in which he persuaded them to use their influence to have the obnoxious statute repealed. And in this stand he was backed by most of the press of the nation, which feared war, so great was the Japanese resentment. The San Francisco authorities, influenced by the higher-ups and the absence of public backing, amended the school law so that Japanese children "of proper age and preparation" could attend the regular schools.

Then, in an effort to stop further local or state actions of a similar nature, Roosevelt concluded the "Gentlemen's Agreement" of 1907. Under this protocol, Japan promised to stop her citizens' immigration to the United States at the source, thereby helping her to save face.

"Get Out O' There, Ye Foolish Boy." Uncle Sam trying to prevent California from antagonizing Japan. (From the *Cleveland Plain Dealer*.)

Although she adhered to the agreement satisfactorily, legislation discriminatory against Japanese aliens continued to be passed in California.

Roosevelt did not wish Japan to believe that his intervention in the school law case meant that he was fearful of Japanese strength. Indeed, he wrote to one of his friends in July, 1907, ". . . I am none the less anxious that they should realize that I am not afraid of them and that the United States will no more submit to bullying than it will to bully." Consequently, he decided to send the American battle fleet of sixteen battleships with numerous torpedo craft and auxiliaries around the world, with a stop at Japan. This would show that the United States, now with the world's second largest navy, was prepared in case Japanese jingoists were strong enough to have their country declare war. When the announcement was made in the summer of 1907 there were immediate protests. The press in the East asserted that it was a foolhardy move which would leave the Atlantic shores unprotected and place the fleet in an open position for a possible Japanese attack. Congress, led by the Senate Naval Appropriations Committee, refused to furnish the money necessary for the venture. The President, however, answered this with the statement that there were enough funds available to get the fleet to the Pacific where it would stay until Congress changed its mind. And thus Roosevelt had his way.

When the fleet reached Japan, the officers and crew were enthusiastically greeted. Perhaps this enthusiasm was engendered by what a Hearst newspaper called "the size of the fleet." At any event, the trip around the world did help the cause of peace and, at the same time, it indicated the growing power and world-mindedness of the United States.

While the fleet was on the high seas, Secretary Root affected a promising agreement with Japanese Ambassador Takahira in November, 1908. Its terms provided for mutual support for the Pacific *status quo*, noninterference with each other's possessions, mutual backing of the independence and territorial integrity of China, and general reiteration of the Open-Door principle. Unfortunately this was not a treaty, but simply an executive arrangement; yet under it Japan gave her most adequate endorsement of the Hay theory up to that time.

But the Root-Takahira pact did not soothe the feelings of many Americans, for the fear was still prevalent in the United States that Japan was the outstanding enemy. Why should not the United States strike now before Japan became too strong? This attitude was accentuated during the Taft administration when a Japanese syndicate sought to gain control of Magdalena Bay in Lower California in 1911. Immediately the cry was raised that the syndicate was really a Japanese governmental agency which wanted the Bay as a future naval base from which to attack the United States. So great was the furore that the syndicate dropped its plans. But to make sure that it did not happen again, Senator Henry Cabot Lodge introduced into the Upper House the so-called Lodge Corollary to the Monroe Doctrine, which was approved by the overwhelming vote of fifty-one to four in August, 1912. This resolution declared "That when any harbor or any other place in the American continents is so situated that the occupation thereof for naval or military purposes might threaten . . . the safety of the United States, the Government of the United States could not see without grave concern the actual or potential possession of such harbor or other place by any Government, not American. . . ." While this corollary was not endorsed by President Taft, the American people considered it a twentieth-century version of the hallowed Monroe Doctrine. This attitude did not improve relations between the two countries.

DOLLAR DIPLOMACY IN CHINA

The Open Door was supposedly in jeopardy again during Taft's presidency. In 1910 occurred the Chinese revolution which overthrew the Manchu Dynasty and made China nominally a republic. The immediate result was to submerge the Chinese in problems of reorganization, particularly economic. Taft, along with Secretary Knox, became worried over the proposal of French, German, and British bankers to enter the picture by constructing the Hukuang Railroad through Southern and Central China. Taft felt that the building of this line might destroy the Open Door. Consequently, the State Department prevailed upon J. P. Morgan to establish an American syndicate to participate in the railway development. About the only effect of this action was to make the European powers suspicious of American designs, and even the Morgan interests were not enthusiastic about entering the project.

Also Taft was fearful of the Russo-Japanese railroad interests in Manchuria, the extension of which the President believed was endangering the territorial integrity of China. Therefore he proposed to the several European powers and to Japan that their bankers combine with those from the United States to loan China sufficient money to buy the railroads in question. The other powers were not in sympathy with the proposal, and the American bankers had to be practically forced to participate. The State Department, however, finally worked out a six-power arrangement for lending $125,000,000 to China; but before the loan could go through, Woodrow Wilson became President. In March, 1913, he publicly announced through the press that such a loan would weaken China's sovereignty and might lead to future interventions. If the American bankers wanted to go ahead, they would do so at their own risk; they could expect no backing from his administration. Thus did Taft's efforts at so-called dollar diplomacy in China fail. His honesty of intention could not be doubted, but his methods only served to promote closer Russo-Japanese accord and to weaken the *status quo* arrangements which Theodore Roosevelt had made with Japan.

In administering its new empire, the United States showed considerable ability and restraint. There was little effort made to subjugate the inhabitants in the style of earlier European imperialism. While there were complaints from those inhabitants, actually they were far better off in every way than they had been.

But in delving into Far Eastern problems the United States was storing up numerous diplomatic headaches. Unwilling to back up its policies with force, the government had to rely largely upon diplomatic maneuvering which consisted of playing one nation against another. This worked as long as the several powers involved feared one another. As the century progressed, however, the American position, founded principally upon what might be called bluff, became untenable. The United States was compelled either to retire in humiliation or fight.

5

Search for Security and Peace

THE SPHERE OF AMERICAN DIPLOMACY IN THE FIRST DECADE OF THE
twentieth century was not limited to solving problems of colonial administration or to trying to maintain the Open Door in China and peace
in the Far East. There were other matters as well which had to be given
full attention. In order to maintain its newly won position as a world
power, the United States felt the need of constructing an interoceanic
canal, of seeing that the approaches to that waterway were protected,
and of developing a closer spirit of accord in the Western Hemisphere.
Likewise, the United States assumed the responsibility of promoting
world peace. She continued to be a prime supporter of the doctrine of
arbitration for settling international disputes.

THE ACQUISITION OF THE PANAMA CANAL

The Spanish-American War finally made the United States realize
the necessity of having an interoceanic canal. The sixty-eight-day voyage of the *Oregon* around the Horn and the acquisition of Guam and
the Philippines, plus the annexation of Hawaii and Tutuila in separate
negotiations, brought forth in forceful fashion the need of a waterway
between the Atlantic and Pacific oceans; otherwise the new possessions
in the Pacific could not be adequately protected. True, this was not the
first time that the subject of such a canal had been broached. Spaniards
of the early sixteenth century had considered such an avenue; Thomas
Jefferson had proposed a connecting link; mid-nineteenth century supporters of Manifest Destiny, already eying California, had backed such
a project as a means of speeding transportation to the hoped-for West
Coast. Indeed, in 1846 Minister Bidlack had concluded a treaty with
New Granada, the predecessor of Colombia, granting a right of way
across the Isthmus of Panama· but a railroad, rather than a canal, was

constructed along the right of way. Even while the Bidlack Treaty was being debated in the Senate, jealousies developed between the United States and Great Britain over the Central American region. These were settled, however, in the Clayton-Bulwer Treaty of 1850, in which the signatories agreed that neither would seek to fortify or exercise exclusive control over any canal built through Central America.

During the Civil War there was a revival of interest in a canal, for it might afford the means by which the Confederate raiders could be destroyed more quickly. With the conclusion of hostilities between the North and the South, however, the country reverted to matters domestic. The canal problem came up again when the French, proud of their Suez achievement, established an international company which secured from Colombia construction rights across the isthmus. This action led President Hayes in 1880 to declare that any canal connecting the Atlantic with the Pacific must be under American control because it would form "a part of the coastline of the United States." The failure of the French-sponsored company, amidst a widespread scandal, removed the fears of foreign control, but nevertheless under both Presidents Garfield and Arthur efforts were made to have Great Britain modify the Clayton-Bulwer Treaty so that the United States could build and control a waterway. Britain, however, refused to yield her position, and President Cleveland, on assuming office, agreed that she was right. Then the international company was reorganized as the New Panama Canal Company, but its financial resources were not sufficiently large to make much progress. In the early 1890's, several American companies were formed with the purpose of either completing the work of the French company or starting anew, possibly in Nicaragua, but they soon realized that such a project was too great for private concerns to cope with.

At the conclusion of the war with Spain, an interoceanic canal was still a dream, yet the American people were demanding that it be made a reality. In 1899, Secretary of State John Hay, following the earlier advice of Richard Olney, Cleveland's Secretary of State, began negotiations with Great Britain for the modification of the Clayton-Bulwer Treaty. On February 5, 1900, Britain showed her friendship by agreeing to the so-called First Hay-Pauncefote Treaty. Under this arrangement, the United States might build and manage a canal through Central America, but Britain still held that the canal must be neutralized and unfortified under approximately the same rules as those governing the Suez Canal. The United States Senate refused to ratify this document as it stood. Instead, the Upper House made a number of changes,

the most important of which denied the international character of the
canal and provided for American defense of the proposed waterway.
Britain would not accept these amendments, so Hay had to start all
over again. On November 18, 1901, a compromise was reached in the
Second Hay-Pauncefote Treaty: the Clayton-Bulwer arrangement was
definitely superseded, the United States could build and manage a canal
which, although theoretically neutralized, would be under the protection of the United States, and the clause barring fortifications was removed. The only restricting article of importance insisted that the
canal be open to the nations of the world on terms of equality. This
time the Senate offered no opposition to ratification. Somewhat later,
Britain conceded the right of the United States to fortify the canal
since there was nothing in the treaty to forbid such action. These
British concessions indicated the growing accord between the two nations. Another sign of friendly feeling was the gradual reduction of the
British fleet and garrisons in Caribbean waters; thus Britain was admitting American supremacy in that area.

Meantime, President McKinley, in anticipation of the success of
Secretary Hay, had appointed a commission headed by Admiral Walker
in the spring of 1899 to investigate the feasibility of the two major canal
routes, Panama and Nicaragua. The Walker Commission finally made
its report two days before the Hay-Pauncefote Treaty was concluded,
and it favored the Nicaraguan site. The chief reason for this decision
was that the stockholders of the New Panama Company were demanding $109,000,000 for their rights across the isthmus. Were this amount
paid by the United States, the total cost for a Panama canal would be
greater than that through Nicaragua.[1]

The chief executive, now Theodore Roosevelt, was most anxious to
begin the construction of the canal, a project in which he had long
been interested. While he probably preferred the Panama route, he
refused to pay the outrageous sum which the New Panama Company
was asking. Consequently, in December, 1901, he gave his outward
blessing to the Hepburn Bill for a canal through Nicaragua, which
passed the House of Representatives early in January, 1902, by the one-
sided vote of 308 to 2. Meantime, the Panama Company stockholders,
realizing that the Hepburn Bill would pass unless something were done
and knowing that their own rights would be worthless were a canal
built through Nicaragua, forced out their officers who had made the

[1] The Walker Commission reported that construction costs alone would be: for
Panama, $144,000,000; for Nicaragua, $190,000,000. The addition of $109,000,000 to the
Panama construction cost would therefore make the total Panama amount $60,000,000
more than the Nicaraguan.

$109,000,000 demand. The stockholders then offered to sell their priv-
ileges for $40,000,000. According to the Walker Commission, this was
a reasonable sum. Therefore the Spooner Amendment was added to the
Hepburn Bill in the Senate, substituting the Panama route if the United
States could get the company's rights for the $40,000,000 figure and
secure satisfactory permission from Colombia. Thanks to administration pressure and volcanic eruptions near the site of the proposed
Nicaraguan route, the amended Hepburn Bill passed both Houses by
overwhelming majorities and was signed by President Roosevelt on
June 28, 1902.

The remaining obstacle, Colombian permission, was the most difficult.
After long negotiations, Secretary Hay finally concluded the Hay-
Herran Treaty in January, 1903. Under the terms of this convention,
the United States was to lease a 6-mile-wide strip across the Panama
isthmus with full construction rights in return for a cash payment of
$10,000,000, and an annual rental of $250,000. The United States Senate
ratified this arrangement on March 17, despite the protests of some
members that the treaty did not give the United States sovereign
authority over the canal zone. After nearly two months of debate,
however, the Colombian Senate unanimously rejected the treaty in
August. The reasons were numerous: Colombia believed that the Hay-
Herran pact might destroy her sovereignty over Panama; public opinion
in many sections of Latin America was against the construction of a
canal; and Colombian politicians desired larger payment, either from the
United States or, what is more probable, from the New Panama Company. Regardless of the reason, Colombia, a sovereign state, had a perfect right to reject the treaty.

To President Roosevelt, however, the Colombian action was that of a
grasping, "antisocial" nation, willing to retard world progress. He
referred to those responsible as "the foolish and homicidal corruption-
ists at Bogotá." The President's insistence that the Panama project must
go through reached the ears of Panamanian leaders, who were extremely
dissatisfied with Colombian rule and who saw in the rejection of the
treaty the loss of revenue for their province. These leaders quickly
found support in the person of Philippe Bunau-Varilla, a stockholder in
and former engineer of the New Panama Company, who stood to lose
financially if the canal were not built through Panama. Another con-
spirator was William N. Cromwell, an American lawyer who was looking after the legal interests of the company and who was seeking to
form another company to buy out the French rights. Cromwell let it
be known to the Panamanian leaders that the United States would

probably look with favor upon a revolution in Panama. This view was strengthened by the arrival in Panama waters of the USS *Nashville*, and the knowledge that other warships were on their way. The commander of the *Nashville* had orders to "prevent the landing of any armed force with hostile intent, either Government or insurgent, at any point within fifty miles of Panama," thereby upholding the New Granada Treaty of 1846 under which the United States had promised to keep open the right of way across the isthmus.

Greatly encouraged by the turn of events, the Panamanians successfully revolted against Colombia on November 3, 1903. Many Colombian troops joined the rebels, the *Nashville* landed sailors and marines who prevented Colombia from sending reinforcements, and within twenty-four hours the revolutionists were in complete control after a practically bloodless *coup d'état*. On November 4 the Republic of Panama was declared, followed two days later by United States recognition. At the same time, Bunau-Varilla was named by the new government as special envoy to the United States. By February, 1904, the Hay-Bunau-Varilla Treaty had been drawn up and ratified. Under its terms, the United States guaranteed the independence of Panama, secured a perpetual lease to a 10-mile-wide canal zone, and agreed to pay Panama the same amounts that were offered to Colombia in the rejected Hay-Herran Treaty.

Colombia was naturally incensed by the incident and charged that the United States had fomented the revolution. But while undoubtedly Roosevelt and the State Department knew what was being planned and

The Man Behind the Egg. The intrigue promoting the Panama Revolution. (By Drake in *The New York Times*.)

did indirectly encourage the uprising through statements that the canal must be built through Panama, there is no concrete proof that the United States gave any direct assistance to or plotted with the rebels in any way. True, Roosevelt said in both 1908 and 1911, "I took the Canal Zone and let Congress debate," but it was a usual Roosevelt characteristic to make himself later the hero of any important action that occurred during his administration. The month before the revolt, he had written that while privately he would be "delighted if Panama were an independent state," he would do nothing publicly to encourage a revolt. And in his annual message to Congress of January, 1904, he justified the actions of the United States on the grounds of the treaty with New Granada, American national interests, and the need of the world for the canal. This justification, however, did not ring true to the ears of citizens of Colombia and some of the other Latin-American nations.

With the diplomatic problems surmounted, those of construction next had to be faced. Differences of opinion concerning the type of canal, Congressional red tape, disputes over control and methods, and the search for an efficient labor supply held up the work during the initial years. Finally, in 1907, President Roosevelt, anxious to see "the dirt begin to fly," placed the construction in the hands of army engineers commanded by Lieutenant Colonel George W. Goethals. Colonel William Gorgas of the Army Medical Corps supervised in competent fashion the improvement of sanitary and health conditions in the Canal Zone. The work then began in earnest and, despite many natural obstacles, featured by numerous landslides, the Panama Canal was opened to traffic on August 15, 1914. The cost, $375,000,000, was higher than had been anticipated but, considering the advantages of the waterway to the United States and to the world, it was more than worth the price. And Roosevelt regarded obtaining the route and its actual construction as his greatest achievement.

In anticipation of the opening of the canal, Congress passed the Panama Canal Act in August, 1912. This measure established the toll rates to be charged the users of the canal. It exempted, however, American ships engaged in the coastwise trade from any payment. Britain immediately protested that this exemption was contrary to that clause of the Hay-Pauncefote Treaty which stated that the canal should be open to the nations of the world on an equality. Not until March, 1914, was President Wilson able to persuade the legislature that treaty obligation went ahead of national self-interest and that the exemption should be removed.

CARIBBEAN DIPLOMACY

Interest in the Panama Canal had an important effect upon American diplomacy. The policy which resulted was aggressive, perhaps even militant, and is referred to as the Caribbean or big-stick diplomacy. It was based on the assumption that, were the United States to construct a canal, she must protect it. No possibly dangerous foreign power could be allowed to obtain a foothold near the approaches to such a canal; no little hemisphere republic could be permitted to reach the verge of bankruptcy or of disorderliness which might result in foreign intervention. The Monroe Doctrine must be brought up to date to meet the situation.

Theodore Roosevelt was not the first to employ big-stick diplomacy. During the 1890's American nationalists became fearful lest, under the guise of a dispute over a boundary between British Guiana and Venezuela, the British might extend their control over territory in a strategically important Caribbean area. Cleveland's Secretary of State, Richard Olney, demanded that this controversy be submitted to arbitration, and flatly stated: "Today the United States is practically sovereign on this continent, and its fiat is law upon the subjects to which it confines its interposition." The British at first denied that the United States had any right to intervene but, after Cleveland backed up his Secretary with a stern special message to Congress in which he said that all the power of the United States would be used to prevent British encroachment on Venezuelan territory, Great Britain began to retreat. Not that Britain feared the United States—her navy, for instance, was five times greater than the American—yet as Minister Bayard wrote, "The United States is the last nation on earth with whom the British people or their rulers desire to quarrel." The English were worried about the European situation and their country's traditional isolation was now looking much less splendid.

Britain consequently submitted to the American demand, with a few face-saving safeguards, and the arbitral tribunal of 1899 awarded her most of the disputed territory. But through her acquiescence in the new and broadly extended interpretation which Olney had given to the Monroe Doctrine, Britain was paying the price of American friendship by accepting the supremacy of the United States in the Western Hemisphere. One of the chief evidences of this acceptance was the British ratification of the Hay-Pauncefote Treaty in 1902.

Even while the negotiations for a canal were proceeding, Venezuela again became a trouble center, this time over debts owed to the citizens of at least ten countries. British and German creditors, tired of being refused payment of either interest or principal, appealed to their respective governments in 1901 to intervene in their behalf. Germany took the lead among the creditors by offering to submit the debt problem to the Hague Court for arbitration, but Venezuelan dictator Cipriano Castro, who was in part responsible for the extravagance which had caused the debt, refused the proposition. Consequently, Great Britain, with more at stake financially than the other creditors, suggested forcible collection, a move which President Roosevelt did not oppose. He accepted British and German assurances that such action would not result in the annexation of territory and therefore the Monroe Doctrine would not be at stake; furthermore, he felt that Venezuela was in the wrong in not agreeing to arbitration. Indeed, he wrote in 1901 that if a Latin-American country misbehaved, "let the European country spank it."

Encouraged by Roosevelt's policy of noninterference, Great Britain and Germany, followed eventually by Italy, began a blockade of Venezuela in December, 1902. Although there was no declaration of war, the ships of the little Venezuelan navy were captured and two were sunk. Castro now abruptly changed his tune and through the United States requested arbitration. The creditor states agreed in principle, but insisted on maintaining the blockade until all the details could be arranged and an agreement to arbitrate was finally signed in February, 1903. The blockade, thus continued for over two months, was extremely irritating to American public opinion, especially when it resulted in incidents like the bombardment of a Venezuelan coastal town. Significantly the Germans rather than the British were the targets of most of this indignation. Even Roosevelt became restive and suspicious, urging the German ambassador to have the arbitration settlement arranged and the blockade ended as soon as possible. Although professing faith that the German Kaiser would keep his pledge and refrain from any attempt to secure South American territory, the President kept the American navy mobilized at Puerto Rico as an additional insurance that the Monroe Doctrine would be respected. In later years Roosevelt asserted that he compelled the Kaiser to accept arbitration by an ultimatum in which he threatened to send the fleet to Venezuela, but the contemporary evidence to support this story is not convincing. Be that as it may, the importance of the whole affair was that the European powers did not institute the blockade until they learned it would not be opposed by the United States, and their decision to accept arbitration was hastened by the knowledge that the blockade was resented by American public opinion. The so-called second Venezuela affair, like the first, resulted in an impressive recognition of the strength of the United States in the Western Hemisphere.

President Roosevelt was made wary by this affair. With the diplomatic negotiations for the canal concluded, he did not want similar incidents to develop in other backward Latin-American countries which might enable creditor nations to intervene and perhaps obtain a foothold dangerous to the security of the canal. The United States, he believed, must use its police power to prevent chronic wrongdoing within the republics bordering on the approaches to the isthmus. This need was brought to the fore in 1903 when the Dominican Republic, following years of dictatorship and civil war, found herself unable to meet financial obligations owed to several European countries, notably France and Italy, and to the American-controlled San Domingo Improvement Company. After numerous efforts at settlement by arbitral means, the United States signed a protocol which stipulated that if the republic did not pay what it owed, the American government would have to take over the administration of Dominican customs receipts. The Dominican authorities failed to heed the warning, no payments on the debt were made, and both France and Italy considered the possibility of intervention. Consequently, in October, 1904, a financial agent of the United States was placed in charge of the customs houses under a temporary arrangement.

President Roosevelt justified his action in his annual message to Congress in December, 1904, and again a year later. Telling passages in these two messages were:

If a nation shows that it knows how to act with reasonable efficiency and decency in social and political matters, if it keeps order and pays its obligations, it need fear no interference from the United States. Chronic wrongdoing . . . in the Western Hemisphere . . . may force the United States, however reluctantly, in flagrant cases of wrongdoing or impotence, to the exercise of an international police power. . . . We must make it evident that we do not intend to permit the Monroe Doctrine to be used by any nation on this Continent as a shield to protect it from the consequences of its own misdeeds against foreign nations. . . .

This was the so-called Roosevelt or Big-Stick Corollary of the Monroe Doctrine and was the logical extension of the Olney interpretation of the previous decade. Its promulgation was another evidence that the United States realized that it had become a world power; considering the catering of the European powers to that Doctrine in the second Venezuela affair, perhaps it was only natural that the United States should expect that the big-stick theory would also be recognized.

Under this doctrine of American police power in the hemisphere and to make the temporary arrangement with the Dominican Republic more satisfactory and permanent, Secretary Hay sought a treaty which would give the United States the right to collect Dominican duties and to pay the creditors. In February, 1905, President Morales approved the suggestion that 45 per cent of the customs be used for Dominican government expenses and that the rest take care of the debt. Furthermore, the United States was to be empowered "to restore the credit, preserve the order, increase the efficiency of the civil administration, and advance the material progress and welfare of the Dominican Republic." This agreement was not approved by the United States Senate, largely because of the belief that the executive branch was overstepping its authority. President Roosevelt, however, believed that it was the duty of the United States to establish a financial protectorate. He asserted that "those who profit by the Monroe Doctrine must accept certain responsibilities along with the rights it confers." Consequently, he put the protocol into effect by executive order.

Under this agreement, the United States did excellent work in the Dominican Republic. The Dominican government received more income from its 45 per cent share of the customs than it had previously from the full receipts, and at the same time its debt was scaled down materially. In 1907 the American Senate, seeing this progress and having temporarily put aside partisan bickerings, ratified a treaty which provided that the Dominican debt, now fixed at $17,000,000, should be paid with the aid of a $20,000,000 loan advanced by American bankers. That debt could not be increased and an American receiver of customs was appointed to collect all receipts. This financial protocol lasted until 1924.

During the remainder of Roosevelt's administration and throughout the greater part of Taft's four years in office, the Dominican Republic was peaceful politically. The republic's trade developed rapidly and her program of public works was beneficial for the inhabitants. No effort was made by the United States to exploit the Dominicans in any way. Yet by 1911 the political leaders, tired of political peace, began to chafe under orderly government. An era of rebellions began, which subsequently led to the establishment of American military and political control.

This intervention in the Dominican Republic under Theodore Roosevelt was the forerunner of what came to be called dollar diplomacy which reached its zenith under Taft. Briefly stated, dollar diplomacy means this: a chaotic and nearly bankrupt country, facing possible intervention by a European nation potentially unfriendly toward the United States, had to be saved from such a fate by the United States, using the Roosevelt corollary as justification. The United States would set up a financial protectorate and prevail upon private bankers to lend money to the backward state, and the bankers in turn would demand that their loans be protected. The United States therefore would establish a political protectorate as well, usually with the aid of American marines—which would lead finally to a military protectorate as well. Elections would then be supervised and would result in the selection of a president favorably disposed toward the United States and the American banker creditors. Owing his position to American favor, this president would then grant concessions to American investors who would subsequently reap the profits. This dollar diplomacy in so far as it affected Latin America was promoted under the guise of safeguarding the Panama Canal. As Taft's Secretary of State Knox said: "Thus the malady of revolutions and financial collapse is most acute precisely in the region where it is most dangerous to us. It is here we seek to apply a remedy." But at another time Knox tried to place this diplomacy on a higher plane: "If the American dollar can aid suffering humanity and lift the burden of financial difficulty from states with which we live on terms of intimate intercourse and earnest friendship, and replace insecurity and devastation by stability and peaceful self-development, all I can say is that it would be hard to find better employment." President Taft was not always so altruistic, however, as he definitely considered dollar diplomacy in terms of advantage for American investors. In one of his speeches he said: "This Administration, through the Department of State and the foreign service, is lending all proper support to legitimate and beneficial enterprises in foreign countries, the degree of such support being measured by the national advantages to be expected . . ."

Such a remedy as Knox and Taft advocated was deemed necessary for Honduras in 1909. That Central American republic could not pay the interest on its bonds, most of which were held by British investors. Fearing the possibility of British intervention, Knox finally persuaded American bankers to take over the Honduran debt in 1911. There was no financial protectorate established, as had been the case in the Dominican Republic. Similar trouble coupled with political chaos in Nicaragua led to the placing of that state's customs houses under an American collector, a move that was aided in no small measure by the presence of an American warship and marines. The Taft administration then refused to recognize the new Nicaraguan president until he secured American loans sufficient to pay off his country's foreign debt. The people of Nicaragua did not like the high-handed actions of the United States and it was only through threats of force that the financial protectorate was established. Haiti, one of the insular republics, was beginning to show signs of economic troubles also. Consequently in 1910, the State Department prevailed upon four American banks to buy up a large number of the bonds of Haiti's National Bank. This opened the way for further intervention under Wilson.

Dollar diplomacy in connection with Latin America was definitely economic imperialism. While Taft used the excuse that only through American interventions and investments could the backward republics be made stable, peaceful, and civilized, one of the primary motives was to give American bankers and investors a profit. And it cannot be said that dollar diplomacy improved Pan-American relations.

PAN-AMERICANISM

The attempt to bring the republics of the hemisphere more closely together diplomatically, economically, and culturally—or Pan-Americanism—had originated in recent times under James G. Blaine, who served as Secretary of State under Garfield and Benjamin Harrison. The first modern Pan-American meeting, held in Washington in 1889–1890, discussed arbitration agreements, a customs union, uniform weights, measures, copyright and patent laws, and a trade dollar, but did not accomplish much. The novelty of the plan, the suspicions of American motives, and mutual jealousies all combined to prevent the Washington conference from attaining its objectives. However that meeting did smooth the way for future sessions and did establish the forerunner of the Pan American Union, a clearing house for varied information of value to the republics.

The first conference of the new century, held at Mexico City in 1901–1902, did not open auspiciously. The United States had just finished its war with Spain, a war which, to the Latin-American mind, had turned from an altruistic battle to free Cuba into an imperialistic contest. It was feared that that imperialism had not been satisfied, and the next American objective might be the smaller states of the Western Hemisphere. The United States delegates tried to quiet these apprehensions by proposing that all international disputes be submitted to arbitration. Unfortunately, this suggestion did not receive unanimous backing, although a goodly minority of the republics supported the proposition. A majority, however, did back the theory that financial problems, which could not be settled by normal diplomatic procedure, be submitted to arbitration through the media suggested at the Hague Conference of 1899.

Nor did the next session, meeting at Rio de Janeiro in 1906, begin on a note friendly toward the United States. The forcing of the Platt Amendment upon Cuba, the Panama Revolution, intervention in the Dominican Republic, and the promulgation of the Roosevelt Corollary made several of the other republics wary of American intentions. Furthermore, Argentina, rival of the United States for hemisphere leadership, had her own solution for the controversial debt problem. This Drago Doctrine stated that armed force must not be used to collect financial obligations, a theory in a sense opposed to the Roosevelt corollary. Disagreement over the issue might have broken up the meeting had it not been for the conciliatory attitude of Elihu Root, chairman of the United States delegation. Root agreed to have the matter of debt collection submitted to the Second Hague Conference, scheduled to meet the following year. He was also able to keep diplomatic discussions at Rio at a minimum and to concentrate on the promotion of economic and cultural accord.

Following this meeting, Root visited seven other Latin-American countries in an effort to promote better relations within the hemisphere through greater sympathy and understanding. He was well received in each of the republics as he stressed the need of cooperation for peace and security. Indeed, Elihu Root might well be called the originator of the policy of the Good Neighbor. President Roosevelt, commenting on Root's trip, wrote: "We in this country do not realize how wonderful it was and how much good he has done." It was also Root who prevailed upon Andrew Carnegie to contribute a large sum of money toward the construction of the building in which the Pan American Union is housed.

The Buenos Aires conference of 1910 saw greater harmony among the now twenty-one republics than heretofore. All the members signed a pact to arbitrate any financial differences that arose among them. The Pan American Union was reorganized in a way that proved satisfactory to most of the previous objectors. Such matters as uniform patents, copyrights, and trademarks, the improvement of communications, health, and sanitation, and the interchange of students and professors occupied the major attention of the delegates.

The United States also used its good services in trying to effect accord among the Central American republics, which were constantly battling with each other. After a war between Guatemala on one side and El Salvador and Honduras on the other in 1906, President Roosevelt, aided by President Díaz of Mexico, sought a solution. But opposition from Dictator Díaz of Nicaragua, who believed the United States was trying to dominate Central America, prevented a satisfactory settlement and the strife broadened. Consequently, in 1907, Roosevelt and the Mexican Díaz again called a conference of the republics which was held in Washington. This meeting resulted in the ending of Central American hostilities, in the establishment of a Central American International Bureau to promote unity, and in the organization of the Central American Court of Justice which was to serve as a tribunal to arbitrate future quarrels among the members. The International Bureau did excellent work along the lines of the Pan American Union; unfortunately, however, the tribunal was not a success—and the United States was largely responsible for its failure.

ARBITRATION EFFORTS

The growing interest of the United States in world affairs and, more particularly, in the pacific settlement of controversies, was well indicated under both Roosevelt and Taft. The first sign of this attitude had been shown at the first Hague Conference, which had been called by the Czar of Russia in November, 1899. The United States was one of the twenty-six nations represented, with Ambassador to Germany Andrew D. White as head of the American delegation. A "Convention for the Peaceful Adjustment of International Differences" was drawn up, under which disputes between nations might be settled by mediation, by international tribunals of inquiry, or by the Permanent Court of Arbitration (which was not a court in the real sense, but a panel of jurists from which arbiters could be chosen for any specific controversy) for which the Hague conferees provided. White played a prominent part in overcoming Germany's opposition. In ratifying the work of the Hague meeting, however, the United States Senate insisted that incidents arising under the Monroe Doctrine were outside the scope of the permanent court.

The first case which came before the Hague Court concerned the so-called Pious Fund. In the seventeenth century the Catholic Church had established a trust fund to convert the Indians of California to Christianity. When the fund's administrators, the Jesuits, were expelled from the Spanish Indies, the King of Spain assumed the dispensing of this fund until the Wars of Independence. Then the new Mexican government took charge. In 1848, the United States gained California and the Catholic bishops sought control of the money. Mexico, however, refused to turn it over, so the bishops subsequently brought the case before a mixed commission which decided in their favor. Mexico then paid some of the interest, but stopped after a few years. In the 1890's the United States government, at the behest of the archbishop of San Francisco and the bishop of Monterey, took up the case and Mexico promised to abide by the decision of the anticipated Permanent Court. In 1902 the judgment was handed down in favor of the clerics, a judgment to which Mexico conformed. Thus the combined efforts of the two neighboring nations showed that arbitration could work under the Hague plan.

THE ALASKA BOUNDARY SETTLEMENT

That another long-standing difference could be settled by peaceful means was shown in the controversy over the boundary between southern Alaska and Canada. The Klondike gold rush at the end of the century made Canadians ambitious to secure control of the Lynn Canal and the port of Skagway. The United States insisted, however, on an interpretation of earlier treaties which would maintain exclusive American domination of this stretch of coast.

Since 1899 Secretary Hay had tried to effect a settlement, but without success. The British government, at the insistence of Canada, asserted that the issue should be submitted to an arbitration in which some foreign umpire would have the deciding voice, but the American government maintained the position that the Canadian claims had so little basis that American rights should not be thus jeopardized. Instead, Hay suggested that the question should be decided by a commission of three American and three British members. No decision could then be reached unless one of the commissioners voted against the contentions of his government. When in 1903 Britain finally consented to this proposition, President Roosevelt turned not to impartial jurists for his appointments to the commission, but to politicians: Secretary of War Root, Senator Lodge, and ex-Senator George Turner of Washington, on whom he could depend to hold out for the claims of the United States. The British government named Lord Alverstone, the Lord Chief Justice of England, and two prominent Canadians. Given this tribunal, the United States could scarcely lose its case, but Roosevelt took aggressive steps to assure a clean-cut victory. By every possible channel he sought to impress upon the British government how unfortunate the consequences might be if Lord Alverstone did not cast his vote against the Canadian contentions. In the end the British jurist did vote with the Americans for a decision that ruled out most of the Canadian claims. Despite Canadian protests, the issue was ultimately settled on this basis.

THE HAY ARBITRATION TREATIES

After taking so prominent a part in the establishment of the Permanent Court at the Hague, the Roosevelt administration not merely showed the way in referring special cases to it, but tried hard to secure arrangements with other nations by which the parties agreed to submit all cases coming within what international jurists then regarded as the scope of arbitration to this tribunal. The First Hague Conference as part of its work had prepared a model treaty through which the contracting parties would promise to refer all such problems to the Permanent Court.

Secretary Hay negotiated fourteen treaties on this model, chiefly with Great Britain, France, and Germany, by December, 1904. They all excepted from arbitration questions affecting the vital interests, independence, or honor of the contracting parties. As these exceptions were precisely the things which caused war, the negotiation of such instruments did not go very far. And as far as Great Britain was concerned, the United States had already arbitrated to great mutual advantage matters which might fairly be called vital. Nevertheless, the action of Hay helped at least to advertise the idea of arbitration.

When these treaties were submitted to the Senate for ratification, there was trouble. The Senate feared that its power over all treaties as laid down in the Constitution was being threatened. Some Senators also professed doubt lest questions arising out of the repudiation of debts by some of the states would be subjected to arbitration. The Upper House therefore amended the treaties in such a way as to alter the "special agreements" under which the various questions were in each case to be arbitrated into special treaties subject individually to the advice and consent of the Senate. Angered by this tenacity, Roosevelt withdrew the treaties from further consideration. He said at the time:

I think that this amendment makes the treaties shams, and my present impression is that we had better abandon the whole business rather than give the impression of trickiness and insincerity which would be produced by solemnly promulgating a sham.

THE SECOND HAGUE CONFERENCE

The Second Hague Conference of 1907, also called by the Czar, was signalized from the American point of view by the fact that the nations of Latin America were invited to attend at the insistence of Elihu Root. The United States delegation was headed by Joseph Choate and General Horace Porter. As far as limitation of armaments and securing a real world court were concerned, this meeting accomplished little more than had the first. The American representatives exerted their efforts largely toward obtaining definite guarantees of the rights of neutrals and of neutral commerce during war. But such difference of opinion arose that the best that could be done was to have the matter referred to a supplementary naval conference which was scheduled to meet at London in 1908.

That naval gathering produced in 1909 the famous Declaration of London, which was practically a maritime code defining absolute and conditional contraband, blockades, and the right of search. It also laid down clear rules for the conduct of belligerents and neutrals during wartime. Great Britain, however, refused to ratify this declaration. Thus, at the outbreak of World War I, the Declaration could be regarded as international law only by a tremendous stretch of imagination.

The Second Hague Conference likewise took up a problem of special interest to the United States and its Latin-American neighbors—the Drago Doctrine. The delegates refused to accept that doctrine as it stood, but instead amended it to read that armed force should not be used to collect debts unless the debtor country refused to arbitrate.

Shortly after the 1907 meeting adjourned, Secretary of State Root

The Angel of Peace: "Help Help!" Can the Big Stick work at the Second Hague Conference? (From the *New York World*.)

began to negotiate arbitration treaties similar to those engineered by Hay. During the remainder of Roosevelt's second term he was able to complete twenty-five of them with all the leading powers except Germany. Amended so as to guarantee the rights of the Senate in each individual case, these treaties were duly ratified.

THE TAFT-KNOX TREATIES

Taft and his Secretary of State, Philander Knox, were ready to go further than to adopt documents rendering lip service to arbitration but actually excepting everything which might cause war. As Taft said in October, 1911:

We now have treaties of arbitration . . . in which we agree to submit all questions that do not affect our national honor and do not affect our vital interest. Well, that seems to me to be an agreement to arbitrate everything that is highly unimportant. . . . If arbitration is worth anything it is an instrumentality for avoiding war. But, it is asked, would you arbitrate a question of national honor? I am not afraid of that question. Of course I would.

Following this theory, Knox negotiated two remarkable treaties with France and Great Britain, popularly known as the "Taft-Knox Treaties," which went the whole way in providing for the submission to arbitration of all justiciable disputes whatsoever. Again there was much criticism from the more nationalistic elements. Ex-President Roosevelt became an outspoken opponent of agreements which might involve "national honor." And the Senate proceeded to emasculate the documents by exempting from arbitration questions involving immigration, state debts, and the Monroe Doctrine. Thoroughly disgusted, Taft thereupon withdrew the treaties from further consideration.

However disappointing was the progress toward general arbitration, the peaceful settlement of specific controversies through arbitration continued. In 1909 the United States and Great Britain agreed to submit to the Hague Court the troublesome question of the rights of American fishermen in Newfoundland waters—a question which had been vexing the diplomats since 1782. The Court's decision in 1910 provided a workable compromise which safeguarded the rights of both the Americans and the Newfoundlanders.

THE ALGECIRAS CONFERENCE

In 1905 President Roosevelt became deeply involved in a tangled web of European diplomacy. By a dramatic visit to Tangier, Morocco, in 1905 the German Kaiser raised the protest of his government at the steps which France was taking to extend a protectorate over the North

African country. Germany brusquely demanded that the Morocco
question be submitted to an international conference. France, strongly
supported by Great Britain, refused and there was grave danger of a
European war over the issue. The Kaiser, who had been courting Roosevelt ever since he became President, urged the American chief executive
to support Germany in her conference demand. Roosevelt at first refused to take the problem seriously and ridiculed the "pipe dreams" of
the German emperor. But when he became convinced that the danger of
war was actually great, he sought to mediate between the angry governments. Fortunately Roosevelt was on terms of closest intimacy with
both the French ambassador at Washington, Jules Jusserand, and the
German envoy, Baron Speck von Sternburg, and through them he finally
suggested an acceptable formula under which the conference could be
held.

Early in 1906 the diplomatic representatives of the powers interested
in the Morocco question met at Algeciras, Spain. Roosevelt sent an
American delegation, headed by Henry White, the ambassador to Italy.
American participation was justified on the grounds that the United
States had treaty rights in Morocco and some slight trade to protect, as
well as on the more defensible principle that America had an important
interest in the preservation of world peace.

White at Algeciras and Roosevelt in Washington worked hard to
bring about a settlement. Although the President strove to maintain
his role as friendly mediator between the European rivals, he had from
the beginning believed that France was in the right. Consequently, on

Is Miss Morocco Worth It? (From the *Minneapolis Journal*.)

crucial issues, the American weight was thrown to the side of France and England. The General Act of Algeciras finally accepted by the powers saved the face of Germany by paying lip service to the independence of Morocco and to the principle of the open door for trade, but actually left France free to increase her influence over the disputed country. A typically Rooseveltian flourish marked the conclusion of the conference. The President sent word to the reluctant Kaiser that if he would accept the settlement, Roosevelt would pay public tribute to the German monarch's contribution to peace. The Kaiser agreed, and within the next few days the President received a delegation of German war veterans at the White House. To them he gave William credit for the Moroccan settlement.

Roosevelt's action during this crisis was subjected to some criticism as a departure from the traditional American policy of noninvolvement in European affairs. The President, however, was intelligent enough to see how dangerous to all Western civilization a general European war would be. He worked earnestly during these years to dispel the mutual fears and suspicions that were threatening world peace.

6

The New Freedom

M ANY AMERICANS HAD BEEN SO ABSORBED BY THE TAFT-ROOSEVELT feud in 1912 that they had paid scant attention to the candidate who had won the election. It was a common assumption that a man of Wilson's background must be an effete intellectual, certain to be dominated by the practical politicians of his party. Such a judgment, however, showed little knowledge of Wilson's actual record as college professor, university president, and governor of New Jersey. The new President, reserved and scholarly though he seemed, possessed an inflexible will and a fighting heart. He was, moreover, a student of American government, who had drawn from his research the conclusion that the President of the United States should be both the leader of his party and of the nation.

THE NEW ADMINISTRATION

Influenced by Colonel House, who was somewhat fearful that his friend in an excess of idealism might ignore orthodox Democrats and fill his cabinet with independents, Wilson selected an official family which rewarded the various sections of the country and the different factions within the party in a traditional way. Steeling himself to what the situation demanded, he bestowed the Secretaryship of State upon the man he had often criticized in the past, William Jennings Bryan. Sophisticated Easterners loved to ridicule the new head of the State Department, to laugh at his dinners where parched foreign diplomats found nothing stronger than grape juice in their glasses, and to be vastly amused when he took time off from his official duties to lecture in Chautauqua tents. But Wilson quickly learned to respect Bryan's sincerity, to value his sturdy common sense, and to accept gratefully his advice on political matters—a subject on which the Secretary certainly spoke from experience, whatever the deficiencies in his diplomatic education. Another Bryanite appointed to the cabinet was Secretary of the Navy Josephus Daniels, newspaper editor from North Carolina. Wilson wanted to make Louis Brandeis either his Attorney General or his Secretary of Commerce, but the financial community was so hostile to the rumored appointment that he had to give up the idea. Instead, James C. McReynolds of Tennessee was made Attorney General and Congressman W. C. Redfield of New York Secretary of Commerce. As his Secretary of the Treasury, Wilson chose William Gibbs McAdoo of New York, a prominent Wilson delegate at the Baltimore convention, whose most notable achievement hitherto had been in promoting the construction of the railroad tunnels under the Hudson River from New York to New Jersey. The prominence of Texas in Wilson's prenomination campaign was recognized in the appointment of a veteran Congressman from that state, Albert S. Burleson, as Postmaster General, and David F. Houston as Secretary of Agriculture. For the Secretaryship of the Interior, Wilson selected Franklin K. Lane of California, who had made a notable record as a member of the Interstate Commerce Commission. The first man to head the Department of Labor, newly separated from the Commerce Department, was Congressman William B. Wilson of Pennsylvania, a member of the miners' union. Lindley M. Garrison of New Jersey became Secretary of War.

Although the new President was firmly committed to a program of progressive reform, he avoided any declaration of war against old-line Democrats whose votes he would need. By courting Champ Clark and Representative Oscar W. Underwood, he sought to smooth over the wounds left by the Baltimore convention. Moreover, he learned to acquiesce while Postmaster General Burleson dispensed patronage with a practiced hand to Representatives and Senators and Bryan found posts within his Department and elsewhere for "deserving Democrats."

But if much of the old in political practice survived under Wilson, much that was strikingly new was introduced. His inaugural address was both eloquent and bold. After itemizing the need for tariff and currency reform, for further regulation of the trusts, and for measures benefiting labor and agriculture, he concluded with these stirring words:

This is not a day of triumph; it is a day of dedication. Here muster, not the forces of party, but the forces of humanity. Men's hearts wait upon us; men's lives hang in the balance; men's hopes call upon us to say what we will do. Who shall live up to the great trust? Who dares fail to try? I summon all honest men, all patriotic, all forward-looking men, to my side. God helping me, I will not fail them, if they will but counsel and sustain me!

Scarcely a month after taking office, Wilson gave a striking demonstration of the role which he believed the chief executive should play. He appeared at the Capitol in person, where, facing the two Houses of Congress and packed galleries, he appealed for tariff revision. He was thereby boldly breaking a precedent established by Thomas Jefferson and followed religiously by succeeding executives for more than a century. This was only the first of such appearances. Again and again through the next eight years Wilson went before Congress to ask for legislation or to outline his policies. Few Presidents have ever led their parties with such a firm grip as did this one-time college professor.

TARIFF REFORM

The first dividend from the Democratic victory was the Underwood Tariff, passed by a special session of Congress in 1913 after six months of debate. During the last two years of the Taft administration a Democratic-Insurgent coalition had passed several bills which would have materially altered the Payne-Aldrich schedules had they not been vetoed by President Taft. After Wilson's election in November, 1912, the House Ways and Means Committee under Chairman Underwood began framing a general tariff measure, and the preliminary work was well advanced by the time the special session opened in April, 1913. The new bill was designed to reduce the cost of living by placing wheat, corn, sugar, meat, eggs, and milk on the free list, along with raw wool, flax, and shoes. Duty-free also were iron ore, pig iron, steel rails, rough lumber, paper, and wood pulp. On hundreds of other items the protective principle was maintained, but levies were reduced in accordance with President Wilson's theory that "the object of the tariff duties henceforth laid must be effective competition, the whetting of American wits by contest with the wits of the rest of the world." On luxuries, such as precious stones, furs, perfumes, and fashionable garments, the old rates were left unchanged. Taken as a whole, it was by no means a radical abandonment of protection, but it did offer the first genuine downward tariff revision since the Civil War. The Tariff Board provided for in 1909 was under attack as political and the Democrats abolished it, but in 1916 the need for a fact-finding board was again recognized and a bipartisan commission under Professor Taussig of Harvard was appointed.

One of the most important features of the new bill was its provision for a graduated income tax, made possible by the Sixteenth Amendment, ratified in February, 1913. The rates proposed were moderate. Incomes of less than $3000 for unmarried persons and of less than

$4000 for those married were exempt; incomes in excess of these figures were subject to a normal tax of 1 per cent and graduated surtaxes reaching a level of 6 per cent on incomes in excess of $500,000.

Under the skillful leadership of Representative Underwood the bill passed the House on May 8 without significant change. In the Senate, however, a hard fight developed. There the Democratic margin of control was small and many Senators were tempted to seek amendments which would safeguard the protection enjoyed by their own constituents. So active were the lobbyists that the President took the unusual step of appealing to the public against their activities. In a statement given out to the press he said:

It is of serious interest to the country that the people at large should have no lobby and be voiceless in these matters, while great bodies of astute men seek to create an artificial opinion and to overcome the interests of the public for their private profit. . . . Only public opinion can check and destroy it. . . .

In the end, wavering Democrats were kept in line and the measure was passed in substantially its original form. It was a tremendous victory for the new President—one secured on an issue which Roosevelt had avoided and Taft had taken up to his own hurt.

Economists watched with interest to see how American economic life would be affected by the new measure. They were destined, however, to be provided with no adequate data. Within ten months after the Underwood schedules went into effect international trade was completely disrupted by the outbreak of World War I. Conditions continued to be highly abnormal as late as 1921 when the Republicans returned to power and promptly rewrote the tariff laws according to their own doctrines.

The income tax, although at first disappointing as a revenue producer, revealed some interesting data on the concentration of wealth in the country. Of 120 individuals paying taxes in 1916 on incomes of a million dollars or over, 100 lived in three states: 74 in New York, 16 in Illinois, and 10 in Pennsylvania.

THE FEDERAL RESERVE SYSTEM

Wilson was a hard taskmaster. While the tariff debates were still in progress, Congress was given a new assignment—the complicated and difficult task of banking and currency reform. Serious faults in the banking structure of the country had been discernible for many years. Bank reserves were not mobilized in a manner to meet depositors' runs on fundamentally sound institutions. Small town banks followed the practice of depositing their reserve funds principally in the banks of larger cities; these in turn deposited in the great metropolitan banks. Since the funds of these banks were available for speculative loans, the banking structure of the entire country was likely to be jeopardized by trouble in the securities market. The system furthermore tended to drain funds from rural districts where credit was badly needed and concentrate them in the cities where they encouraged speculation. Credit was inelastic. Banks unable to borrow themselves were often compelled to refuse to make new loans to their clients or to renew old ones, even when perfectly good security was offered. Currency was also inelastic. Instead of expanding and contracting as business increased or diminished, national bank notes were fixed in amount by the number of government bonds available for purchase by the banks.

Following the bankers' panic of 1907, a National Monetary Commission, under the chairmanship of Senator Aldrich, had studied the problem for four years. The Commission's analysis of the situation had been of the utmost value, but its suggested remedy, a strong central banking association controlled by private bankers, was politically impossible. Aldrich was regarded by the progressives as ultraconservative and a spokesman for special interests; the great bankers, moreover, were in particular disrepute because of revelations concerning the

The Citizen and the Income Tax. (By May in the *Detroit Times*.)

"money trust" which had been made in 1912 by a special Congressional committee headed by Representative Arsene Pujo of Louisiana.[1]

An inner circle of Democratic leaders began an intensive study of the banking problem soon after the 1912 election. Colonel House, a former banker himself, conducted private discussions with the leading financiers of the country, while the task of actually drafting a bill was taken up by Representative Carter Glass of Virginia, the chairman of the House Banking and Currency Committee, assisted by Paul Warburg, a big banker, and Professor H. Parker Willis of George Washington University. Although the bill which Glass first drafted was criticized by the bankers as unsatisfactory to their interests, it aroused the excited hostility of Secretary Bryan as a surrender to the "money trust." A countermeasure representing Bryan's demand for strict government control was drawn up by Senator Robert L. Owen of Oklahoma, chairman of the Senate Banking and Currency Committee, with the assistance of the progressive lawyer, Samuel Untermyer of New York. President Wilson's first impulse was to side with the Glass version, but Brandeis, to whom he turned for advice, strongly supported Bryan and Owen on some of their main contentions. In the end, the President accepted two important principles that the Westerners had been contending for: that the central governing board of the new system should be made up exclusively of government appointees and that the new currency to be issued should be an obligation of the United States government rather than of the banks.

Out of all these discussions a compromise measure was at length prepared. The Glass-Owen or Federal Reserve Bill provided most of the facilities of a central banking system, but at the same time brought banking under a form of government control. Despite misgiving on the part of both Western radicals and Wall Streeters, the bill, with its essential principles intact, became law in December, 1913.

Instead of a single central bank, the new legislation provided for the establishment of twelve regional banks to serve so-called Federal reserve districts. The stock of these Federal reserve banks was to be entirely owned by the member banks, that is, all the national banks of the country and such state banks and trust companies as cared to join.

The Federal reserve banks were primarily bankers' banks. They received deposits from the member banks and these had to be large enough to cover the reserves which the law required to be maintained

[1] See above, pp. 6–8, for a discussion of the "money trust" based upon the findings of the Pujo Committee. Much of the interesting data compiled by the committee was brought to light through the questioning by its aggressive counsel, Samuel Untermyer of New York.

against the deposits in the member banks. The banking reserves of the country were thus concentrated in a few large reservoirs, where they could not be used for speculative purposes.

Member banks might borrow from the Federal reserve banks through the rediscounting of commercial paper. This meant that the member banks could use high-grade notes, drafts, and bills of exchange on which they had advanced money to their own customers as the basis for securing loans for themselves. Through this process the banking funds of the country became mobile; they moved quickly to the places of greatest business activity.

One of the most important functions of the new Federal reserve banks was to put into circulation a new kind of currency, the Federal reserve notes. As Bryan had insisted, the new notes were made a direct obligation of the United States government, redeemable in gold and acceptable for all public dues. In issuing them, the government received and held as security commercial paper which the Federal reserve banks had taken in through their rediscounting activities. Although the law required a 40 per cent gold reserve to be maintained, the new currency possessed to a large degree the elasticity so lacking in the old national

"Old Hickory" Jackson to "New Hickory" Wilson: "Shake!" (By May in the *Detroit Times*.)

bank notes. When business flourished, commercial paper increased in volume. This paper, through the process of discounting, flowed into the Federal reserve banks and was available to serve as collateral for the issuance of Federal reserve notes. When business activity lagged, this process was reversed and the volume of notes in circulation was reduced.

The Federal reserve banks also received the deposits of the Federal government and acted as the government's financial agents. This permitted the eventual abandoment of the unsatisfactory system of keeping Federal funds in independent treasuries.[1]

Despite strong opposition from the bankers, an independent agency, the Federal Reserve Board, was created to supervise the new system. The board consisted of the Secretary of the Treasury, the Comptroller of the Currency, and five other members appointed by the President with the consent of the Senate and serving for ten years each. Each Federal reserve bank was to have a board of nine directors, six of whom were elected by the member banks and three appointed by the Federal Reserve Board. That board was given extensive powers to examine the books of the Federal reserve banks, to remove their officers, and even to order them to suspend operations. Probably the most important function of the board, however, was to approve the rediscount rates fixed by the Federal reserve banks. This power provided, to a certain extent, a governor on the economic machinery of the country; a low discount rate encouraged borrowing and business expansion; a high rate discouraged them.

The Federal Reserve Act in operation proved to be on the whole very satisfactory. The shock of World War I to American economic life was cushioned by the new system, while the Federal government could scarcely have financed American participation in the hostilities had not the new organization of banking been substantially completed by 1917.

Even after the reform of 1913, however, there still remained many weaknesses in the American banking situation. The country had many more state banks than national; for the former, membership in the Federal Reserve System was not compulsory, and a majority of them stayed outside. Although 80 per cent of the combined banking resources of the nation were held by institutions belonging to the Federal reserve organization, the small state banks not joining outnumbered the member banks two to one. Proposals that membership be made compulsory for all institutions were opposed on the grounds that such action would violate states' rights. The Federal Reserve Board, moreover,

[1] The independent treasury system was finally terminated by Act of Congress in 1920.

had little control over the banking policies and practices of even the member banks as the banking disasters of the great depression demonstrated.

THE TRUST PROBLEM

On January 20, 1914, President Wilson appeared once again before Congress, this time to ask for new antitrust legislation. Several bills were immediately introduced to conform with the President's suggestions and, after several months of debate two of them were passed, the Federal Trade Commission Act and the Clayton Antitrust Act.

The first of these measures provided for a bipartisan commission of five members, who should be appointed by the President with the approval of the Senate to serve seven years each. The commission was given extensive powers to compile information concerning the organization and conduct of corporations engaged in interstate commerce. Furthermore, it was to investigate the manner in which corporations that had been adjudged guilty of violating the antitrust laws carried out the decrees of the courts. Unfair methods of competition were declared to be unlawful, and the commission was empowered to issue orders requiring any person or corporation believed to be using such unfair methods to "cease and desist" from doing so. The orders of the commission, however, were subject to review in the Federal courts.

The Clayton Antitrust Act, an amendment of the Sherman Act of 1890, prohibited certain corporate practices such as price discrimination, exclusive selling or leasing contracts, and purchase by one corporation of the stock of a competing corporation, whenever the effect of such action might be "to substantially lessen competition or tend to create a monopoly in any line of commerce." Furthermore, no person might be a director or officer of more than one bank, if one of the banks had deposits, capital, surplus, and undivided profits aggregating more than $5,000,000; nor could a person be a director of more than one corporation if the corporations were competitors and if one of them had capital, surplus, and undivided profits of more than a million dollars. The chief difference from the Sherman Act was that the new law was designed to be primarily preventive rather than punitive. The interdicted corporate practices were declared illegal per se without proof of actual monopoly or conspiracy.

Particularly important were the provisions of the Clayton Act dealing with the rights of workers. "The labor of a human being," the measure asserted, "is not a commodity or article of commerce." Neither labor unions nor farmers' organizations were to be considered illegal combinations in restraint of trade under the antitrust laws, provided they were in lawful pursuit of their objectives. The rights of laborers to strike, to picket peaceably, to pay out strike benefits, or to boycott an employer were recognized. No Federal judge was to grant an injunction in any case growing out of a labor controversy unless necessary to prevent irreparable injury to property; trial by jury was to be granted in contempt cases unless the contempt was committed in the presence of the court. Samuel Gompers hailed these provisions as a "Magna Carta" for labor, but time was to prove that the rights secured had definite limitations. Judicial interpretation of the Clayton Act narrowed its scope so that many antilabor injunctions continued to be granted by the Federal courts.

The underlying philosophy of the Federal Trade Commission Act and the Clayton Act is obvious. The liberals of 1914 refused to accept the socialist assumption that the trend toward monopoly was inevitable and that the public could only safeguard its interests through nationalizing the trusts. They believed, on the contrary, that competition was the answer to the country's economic ills. If the corporations could be compelled to compete, and the competition kept open and fair, monopolies would be impossible, small business would survive, and consumers would be protected. No more than had the Sherman Act did the legislation of 1914 actually halt the trend toward business consolidation; but it did lead to a reform of some of the cruder business practices.

The Department of Justice under Wilson brought numerous actions under the antitrust laws, while the new Federal Trade Commission was vigorously active, receiving over two thousand complaints between 1914 and 1921 and issuing 379 "cease and desist" orders against such practices as false advertising, false statements against competitors, bribery, adulteration of goods, and misbranding of fabrics. The commission, together with the Justice Department, secured the dissolution of the International Harvester Company in 1918 and the Corn Products Refining Company the following year. But American participation in World War I encouraged tremendously the growth of big business, while the Supreme Court in the United States Steel Corporation case (1920) refused to order the breakup of the company upon the ground that despite its huge size it was not following monopolistic practices. Furthermore, the antitrust crusade lost much of its fervor after 1917.

THE NEW FREEDOM FOR AGRICULTURE AND LABOR

The Wilson administration witnessed the development of a broad program to improve the lot of the nation's farmers. Increased appropriations were secured from Congress for the support of the Department of Agriculture, which now took on enlarged activities including that of providing a market news service. New Federal legislation provided for the uniform grading of staple crops, for regulating trade in agricultural staples, and for developing a better system of warehousing. The Agricultural Extension Act of 1914 made it possible through Federal and state cooperation to place in each of the 2850 rural counties of the nation two agents to do farm demonstration work. Roadbuilding was stimulated by the Federal Highway Act of 1916 under which the Federal government expended money for rural roads on condition that its appropriations be matched by those of the states.

One of the most urgent of the farmer's needs was for facilities whereby he might secure loans upon more favorable terms. The Federal Reserve Act provided a measure of improvement in the situation, but not until 1916 were the farmer's demands more directly met. The Federal Farm Loan Act established twelve Federal Land Banks in the various sections of the country. These were authorized to loan money to cooperative farm-loan associations made up of farmers who wanted to borrow. The farmer gave a mortgage on his real estate to the association; the association in turn deposited the mortgage with the Land Bank. The initial capital of the Land Banks was to be subscribed by private investors, with the government making up any deficiency. Additional funds were to be raised by the sale of tax-exempt bonds secured by the mortgages held by the Land Banks. Supervision of the system was lodged in a Federal Loan Board, composed of the Secretary of the Treasury and four other members appointed by the President.

Although at first private capital was suspicious of the project and supplied but $200,000 of the $9,000,000 required to set up the system, a steadily larger proportion of private investment developed until by 1930 the government had disposed of almost all the stock it had originally been compelled to subscribe. Local farm-loan associations numbered 4659 in 1930, while the Federal Land Banks held about $1,000,000,000 worth of farm mortgages.

The Wilson administration was hardly less responsive to the demands of labor. The American Federation of Labor leadership had given Wilson its support in 1912, as it had Bryan in 1908. Its most appreciated reward was the amendment of the antitrust laws to protect labor union activity from judicial interference, but other legislation in which labor was deeply interested was also passed. In 1915 the LaFollette Seamen's Act, designed to protect merchant sailors from many injustices, became law. In 1913 a Board of Mediation and Conciliation was established to deal with railroad labor controversies, while in 1916, under circumstances which will be discussed in a later chapter, the Adamson Act, to institute an eight-hour day for railway employees, was pushed through Congress under Wilson's urging. The President supported the movement to secure a Federal child labor law, a project which Senator Beveridge had vainly urged during the Theodore Roosevelt administration. The Keating-Owen Child Labor Act of 1916 excluded from interstate commerce goods produced in factories where child labor was employed, but was held unconstitutional by the Supreme Court (Hammer v. Dagenhart, et al., 1918). An attempt to achieve the same end in 1919 through levying a 10 per cent tax on the net income of factories and mines employing children was likewise held invalid (Bailey v. Drexel Furniture Company, 1922).

On the issue of immigration restriction, however, Wilson and organized labor took opposing stands. The latter advocated legislation to exclude from the country immigrants who could not pass a literacy test, but the President, following the example of Cleveland and Taft, vetoed the bill embodying this principle passed by Congress in 1915. Congress enacted a similar bill in 1917 and, when Wilson again opposed it, his veto was overridden and the literacy test at last became law.

WILSON AND THE DEPENDENCIES

The spirit of the New Freedom was carried into the administration of the outlying possessions. In one of his early messages to Congress Wilson asserted that the United States must move toward granting independence for the Philippines "as steadily as the way can be cleared." In naming the Philippine Commission the President gave a majority of the places to Filipinos, while as governor general he appointed Francis Burton Harrison of New York, who administered the islands in a liberal spirit which aroused the nationalist ambitions of the natives. Wilson and Harrison were severely criticized by Taft, who had been the first governor of the islands, and by other prominent citizens on the ground that the Filipinos should not be encouraged to expect an early grant of independence for which they were not ready.

The administration, however, refused to deviate from its course. In 1916, after a hot debate, Congress passed the Jones or Philippine Organic Act, which stated in its preamble that "it is, as it has always been, the purpose of the people of the United States to withdraw their sovereignty over the Philippine Islands and to recognize their independence as soon as a stable government can be established therein. . . ." [1] To

---

[1] An attempt by some Democratic Senators to amend the measure to provide independence within four years was defeated.

speed that day the act reorganized the government of the archipelago in a manner designed to increase native participation and responsibility. The old Philippine Commission and Assembly were abolished and legislative power was now lodged in a senate and house of representatives, both to be elected by Filipino citizens who could meet certain property or literacy qualifications. Executive power was to be exercised by a governor general appointed by the President of the United States with the consent of the American Senate. Most of the other executive officers were to be appointed by the governor general with the consent of the Filipino senate.

The Jones Act took a long step toward delivering the islands to native rule, despite extensive veto powers over acts of the insular legislature retained by the governor general and the President. In execution the new organic law proved even more liberal than it appeared on paper due to policies followed by Harrison. By executive order, he created a Council of State consisting of the governor general, the presidents of both legislative houses, and the six Filipinos who headed the executive de-

The New Gate. The Senate and the House viewing with delight the effect of the literacy test upon immigration. (From the *Minneapolis Journal*.)

partments. This body, theoretically existing for the purpose of co-ordinating the activities of the executive and legislative branches, actually determined the policies of the government until it was abolished by Harrison's successor, General Leonard Wood.

Somewhat similar to the Jones Act for the Philippines was the Jones or Organic Act for Puerto Rico passed by Congress in 1917. There, too, legislative power was entrusted to a senate and house of representatives, both elective, while executive responsibility continued to be vested in a governor appointed by the President of the United States. In the case of Puerto Rico, however, no commitment was made on the question of the future status of the island; the Puerto Ricans were promised neither independence, nor dominion status, nor statehood. They were, however, granted United States citizenship.

THE NEW DIPLOMACY

President Wilson aspired to bring the same spirit of reform into the conduct of American foreign affairs that he had to domestic problems. Ever an idealist, he hoped to base his foreign policy on enduring principles of justice and morality. He was deeply suspicious of professional diplomats who all too often advocated what was expedient rather than what was right. Wilson was particularly disturbed by the close alliance of the State Department and Wall Street which had grown up during the Taft administration—the era of frankly avowed dollar diplomacy.

Scarcely two weeks after his inauguration Wilson had occasion to make plain his intention of repudiating this alliance. At the invitation of the Taft administration, a group of American bankers had arranged to cooperate with bankers of five other powers in a consortium or international loan to the Chinese government. Representatives of J. P. Morgan and Company sought from Secretary Bryan a statement of the attitude of the new administration toward the project. In a statement to the press on March 19, 1913, Wilson expressed his emphatic disapproval. The conditions of the loan, he said, threatened the administrative independence of China; the United States government might, through connection with the project, become involved in a forcible intervention. Altogether, the plan was "obnoxious to the principles upon which the government of our people rests." The American bankers, unenthusiastic about the proposition anyway, acquiesced in the President's position and withdrew from the consortium.

Economic imperialism in Latin America was even more bluntly condemned. First, in a statement to the press on March 11, 1913, and later

in a speech at Mobile, Alabama, the following October 27, Wilson
lashed out at "special groups and interests." At Mobile the President
said of the relations of Latin-American governments with foreign
capitalists:

They have had harder bargains driven with them in the matter of loans
than any other people in the world. Interest has been exacted of them that
was not exacted of anybody else, because the risk was said to be greater; and
then securities were taken that destroyed the risk—an admirable arrangement for those who were forcing the terms! I rejoice in nothing so much as
in the prospect that they will now be emancipated from these conditions,
and we ought to be the first to take part in assisting that emancipation.

Wilson went on to make an important statement of policy: "I want to
take this occasion to say that the United States will never again seek
one additional foot of territory by conquest."

Such were the standards upon which Wilsonian foreign policy was
based. Like most idealists, however, the President often found the practical application of his principles a matter of most perplexing difficulty.
More than once, indeed, the Wilson administration became involved in
a line of conduct quite incompatible with Wilsonian ideals.

IN BEHALF OF PEACE

Despite the striking differences in background between Wilson and
Bryan, they saw alike on many issues. The Secretary of State was delighted by his chief's repudiation of imperialism, and the President in
turn gave hearty support to a project which Bryan had been sponsoring
for many years. The essence of the latter's plan was that the United
States should enter treaties with as many different nations as possible,
pledging that all questions in dispute between the signatories which
diplomacy should fail to adjust should be submitted to an international
commission. The nations should agree not to resort to any act of force
until after the commission had had an opportunity to investigate and report—a proceeding which must be completed within one year. The
agreements embodying these principles became known as "cooling-off
treaties," since one of the advantages of the plan was believed to be the
unlikelihood of two nations going to war over an issue if they had waited
a year for the report of an international commission. England, France,
and most of the other great powers were included among the thirty nations entering into such treaties with the United States. But Germany
rejected the proposition; other governments, she objected, would request similar treaties with her, and to sign them would deprive her of
the advantages to be derived from her superior military preparedness.

Bryan negotiated with the Senate as successfully as with the foreign diplomats involved and encountered no difficulty in securing senatorial assent to all but one or two of the treaties. Only twenty-two of them went into effect, however, because of ratification difficulties with the signatory states.

Like all of Bryan's activities, the "cooling-off treaties" were subjected to considerable ridicule, and they were, to be sure, frail bulwarks against the whirlwinds of war which were to be unloosed in 1914. As late as 1938, however, nineteen of them were still in force and they have had some influence on the thinking of diplomats struggling to build more effective peace machinery.

A more ambitious proposal was pushed by the administration in 1915 and 1916, after Bryan had been succeeded as Secretary of State by Robert Lansing. This was for a Pan-American pact in which the twenty-one republics should mutually guarantee the independence of the member states under republican forms of government, as well as their territorial integrity. The project, which was the brain child of Colonel House, failed, due largely to the opposition of Chile. Even more than the Bryan treaties, however, the pact idea influenced Wilson in his later work on the Covenant of the League of Nations.

MORE CANAL DIPLOMACY

The great Panama Canal, opened to traffic in 1914 although not finally completed until 1920, continued to involve the United States in a tangle of diplomatic problems. The Colombian government had never ceased to protest the steps by which Theodore Roosevelt "took" the Canal Zone. The Taft administration attempted without success to placate this neighbor, and the problem was still acute when Wilson and Bryan took over. In 1914 a treaty between the United States and Colombia was arranged whereby the United States expressed "sincere regret" for the incident of 1903 and promised to pay Colombia $25,000,000. This attempt to right an old wrong was typically Wilsonian, but it was blocked in the United States Senate where friends of Roosevelt indignantly opposed any such American acknowledgment of guilt. Not until 1921, when Roosevelt was dead and Wilson had left the White House, did a similar treaty, although without the expression of regret, secure ratification—this time under the sponsorship of a Republican administration which possibly was not unmindful of the recent discovery of oil in Colombia.

Another diplomatic problem inherited from the Taft regime was the tolls issue. In 1912, it will be recalled, Congress had enacted legislation fixing the tolls for the canal when it should be opened. This act stipulated that American ships engaged in the coasting trade should be permitted to use the waterway without charge. The British government protested against this arrangement on the grounds that it violated the Hay-Pauncefote Treaty of 1901 which said that the canal should be "free and open to the vessels . . . of all nations . . . on terms of entire equality." Taft and Secretary Knox, excellent lawyers, had held that the words "all nations" meant all nations other than the United States, and that the American government was within its rights in giving preference to its own citizens. All foreign experts in international law, however, believed that the United States had promised not to make such a discrimination. One of many thoughtful Americans believing that the Taft-Knox interpretation was wrong was Elihu Root, who had assisted Hay in the negotiations of 1901. The British took a serious view of the controversy and were particularly aroused by the refusal of the Taft administration to consent to submit the case to arbitration.

Wilson had not given the subject any particular attention until after he moved into the White House, but he gradually became convinced that the United States was in the wrong and that the exemption clause was a definite breach of good faith with Great Britain. Despite the embarrassing fact that the Democratic platform of 1912 had upheld the exemption principle, Wilson made a personal appearance before Congress on March 5, 1914, to request "a voluntary withdrawal from a position everywhere questioned and misunderstood." "I ask this of you," the President concluded, "in support of the foreign policy of the administration. I shall not know how to deal with other matters of even greater delicacy and nearer consequence if you do not grant it to me in ungrudging measure." This somewhat cryptic language probably referred both to Wilson's general aspiration to bring the United States to a position of moral leadership in world affairs and to his more specific need of enlisting Britain's support for his Mexican policy, presently to be discussed. The bill to repeal the exemption clause precipitated a stormy debate—especially in the Senate, but it was finally passed. Wilson's victory on the issue raised the reputation of the United States for fair dealing in the eyes of all foreigners, particularly those of the British.

PROTECTING THE CARIBBEAN LIFE LINE

Despite Wilson's repudiation of imperialism in theory, the exigencies of canal diplomacy drew his administration into more than a little imperialism in fact. Indeed it became involved in more armed interventions in Latin America than were any of its predecessors—interventions in

Mexico, Cuba, Haiti, and the Dominican Republic. It followed policies that tended, like those of the Roosevelt and Taft administrations, to reduce the Caribbean states to the ranks of protectorates of the United States. The American empire was enlarged, moreover, by the addition of the Virgin Islands, purchased from Denmark in 1917 for $25,000,000.[1] The administration's Caribbean policy, seemingly so inconsistent with Wilsonian principles, is largely to be explained by the outbreak of World War I. Both the State and Navy Departments were seriously alarmed lest Germany or some other belligerent seize territory in the Western Hemisphere that might be used as a base for operations against the Panama Canal.

The most serious of the Wilsonian interventions was in Haiti. In that island republic conditions approaching anarchy had developed by 1914. Politics were characterized by civil war, assassination, and mass executions. The situation endangered the lives and property of foreigners and threatened to bring about intervention by some European power. American financial interests were jeopardized, especially the considerable stake of the National City Bank of New York in the National Bank of Haiti. In order to protect the gold reserve of the latter institution, American naval officers landed in December, 1914, and removed $500,000 from the bank's vaults. The money was then deposited in the National City Bank of New York pending a reform of Haitian finances. Meantime, pressure was exerted upon the insular government to accept a financial arrangement with the United States like that of the neighboring Dominican Republic. This pressure brought no result, and affairs arose to a climax on July 27 and 28, 1915. On the first of these days President Vilbrun Guillaume Sam infuriated the opposition party by summarily executing 167 political prisoners; this bloody massacre was followed the next day by a rising of the mob against the Haitian executive. He was hunted down in the French legation and literally torn limb from limb. That afternoon United States marines landed and began an occupation destined to continue nineteen years.

Under the vigilant eye of Admiral W. B. Caperton of the American navy, the Haitian legislature proceeded to elect a president acceptable to the United States. The new government then entered into a treaty with the United States whereby provisions were made not only for an American receivership of Haitian finances, but for the organization of a constabulary trained and officered by Americans and for restrictions

[1] Negotiations for purchase had begun immediately after the Civil War, but had failed for a variety of reasons. Now in 1916, Wilson insisted that a plebiscite be taken before the deal was completed. The inhabitants of the islands voted overwhelmingly in favor of annexation by the United States.

upon Haitian sovereignty more extensive than those embodied in the famous Platt Amendment. In 1918 the island republic, efficiently policed by the new constabulary, voted 69,377 to 335 for the adoption of a new constitution in whose drafting Americans had taken a leading part.[1]

American intervention brought many material reforms to Haiti. A sanitary program to improve health conditions was instituted, roads were built, the currency was stabilized, and the government's financial house put in order. But there was a dark side to the picture. Haitian resistance to foreign control brought drastic action; more than two thousand Haitians were shot by American marines in pacifying the country. American public opinion was shocked by stories of atrocities and forced labor.

Events in the Dominican Republic followed a similar, if less spectacular course. Financial receivership proved insufficient by itself to assure stable political conditions. Civil war resulted in intervention by American marines in 1916, which continued until 1924. Once again the establishment of an American protectorate meant material benefits for the population, but brought uneasy consciences to United States citizens who believed in "government by the consent of the governed." In 1917, the United States once again sent troops into Cuba, where they remained until 1922. They did not, however, establish military rule as in 1906, but merely served as a warning to the Cubans to remain orderly.

Nicaragua had been one of the most active fields of Taft's dollar diplomacy and at the end of his term a treaty embodying striking advantages for the United States had been drafted. By this agreement the latter would secure a renewable ninety-nine-year lease of the Great and Little Corn Islands, the privilege for a like period of establishing a naval base on the Gulf of Fonseca, and a grant in perpetuity of the exclusive right to build an interoceanic canal across Nicaraguan territory. In return, the United States would pay Nicaragua $3,000,000, but the consent of the United States would be necessary to the disbursement of this payment, a stipulation obviously in the interest of American bankers who had loaned money to Nicaragua. The advantages of thus guaranteeing that no foreign government should secure control of

[1] Assistant Secretary of the Navy Franklin D. Roosevelt said in the course of a campaign speech in 1920: "You know, I have had something to do with the running of a couple of little republics. The facts are that I wrote Haiti's constitution myself, and if I do say it I think it is a very good constitution." The Haitians did not think so at the time, however, for they were practically compelled by the military to vote for it. Thus the overwhelming vote for adoption is misleading.

a water route rivaling the Panama Canal were so obvious that Wilson and Bryan decided to support the treaty. They even agreed to a Nicaraguan suggestion that clauses similar to the Platt Amendment should be incorporated. But the Senate revolted at the proposal of establishing so undisguised a protectorate and rejected the treaty. In 1916, however, a new agreement, the Bryan-Chamorro Treaty, incorporating the original terms without the protectorate clauses, was approved by the Senate and carried into effect.

THE ACID TEST: MEXICO

Although the events just related seem to belie the sincerity of the new diplomacy's repudiation of imperialism, Wilson's forbearance in dealing with a difficult situation in neighboring Mexico marks a really sharp departure from the methods of dollar diplomacy.

From 1876 to 1911 Mexico was ruled by Porfirio Díaz, a military dictator who maintained strict order and encouraged foreign investment. To Americans resident in the country or doing business there, Mexico under Díaz seemed in happy contrast to strife-ridden nations elsewhere in Latin America. But the beneficence of the dictator's rule was more apparent to foreigners exploiting Mexico's resources and to the privileged few among the Mexicans themselves who had amassed fabulous wealth than it was to the masses. The peasants, sunk in ignorance, remained in a condition of peonage which was almost slavery, and much of the land was monopolized by wealthy aristocrats who owned enormous estates.

Revolution broke out in 1910, and the following year Díaz fled to Europe where he soon died. His successor as president was Francisco Madero, an idealist and reformer, but a gentle soul hardly equipped to control the explosive forces now unleashed. Civil war swept the country, and foreigners, fearing for their lives and property, remembered longingly happier days under Díaz.

In February, 1913, Madero was the victim of shocking treachery. One of his generals, Victoriano Huerta, rebelled against him, imprisoned him, and proclaimed himself president instead. A few days later Madero was killed, almost in cold blood. Foreign diplomats in Mexico shrugged off the murder as an unfortunate, but understandable, act of Latin violence and recommended that their home governments recognize the new regime—a step which seemed likely to restore the conditions of the Díaz dictatorship. Most of the European powers, including Great Britain, acted upon this advice. Had it not been the last month of Taft's term, the United States government would undoubtedly have followed

Woodrow Wilson. (Brown Bros.)

the same course, but instead the decision was left to the incoming administration.

Wilson believed that the circumstances of Huerta's seizure of power created grave doubt as to whether his government should be recognized. He regarded Huerta as a murderer and suspected that he was much more popular with foreign, especially British, oil interests than he was with the Mexican people. Evidence of this was the continuing civil war in which Venustiano Carranza, governor of the northern state of Coahuila, was showing himself a formidable rival. Despite widespread American criticism that the denial of recognition to a *de facto* government was against American diplomatic precedent dating back to the days of Thomas

Jefferson, Wilson let the months slip by without according recognition to the Huerta regime. Through unofficial channels he sought to have Mexican factions accept a plan providing for an armistice in the civil war, an early, free election to be supported by all groups, a pledge by Huerta that he would not be a candidate in this election, and the agreement of all parties to abide by the election results. Characteristically, Wilson chose for his agent to present these proposals, not a professional diplomat, but ex-Governor John Lind of Minnesota, one of Bryan's friends.

When Huerta refused this invitation to remove himself from Mexican politics, Wilson fell back upon a policy known as "watchful waiting" —that is, of refusing recognition to Huerta but resisting at the same time the loud demand set up by eager American jingoes for United States military intervention to set the Mexican house in order. By refusing recognition, Wilson expected that Huerta could not long remain in power. Defending this policy before Congress on August 27, 1913, Wilson declared: "We can afford to exercise the self-restraint of a really great nation which realizes its own strength and scorns to misuse it. It was our duty to offer our active assistance. It is now our duty to show what true neutrality will do to enable the people of Mexico to set their affairs in order again, and wait for a further opportunity to offer our friendly counsels."

Waiting proved scarcely a popular policy in many quarters, especially since Mexican civil strife resulted in damage to American property and death to more than seventy American citizens between 1913 and 1915. Theodore Roosevelt demanded intervention, and Wilson's policy was vigorously denounced in Congress. Senator Albert Fall of New Mexico, who had close connections with American oil magnates, was one of the President's leading critics.

At the end of 1913 Wilson modified his own policy to the extent of adopting active measures to try to force Huerta out. The British government, grateful for Wilson's leadership in the fight against the Panama tolls exemption clause, agreed to withdraw its support from Huerta. Moreover, in February, 1914, the President lifted the arms embargo, imposed the preceding year, thus greatly assisting the rebels, Carranza and Francisco Villa. Despite these blows, Huerta still clung to power. Indeed his defiance of the "Colossus of the North" was an important factor in winning for him a considerable backing among his own people.

In April, 1914, a crisis developed which seemed almost certain to bring about the full-scale American intervention which Wilson had been trying to avoid. On the ninth of the month, American sailors engaged in loading supplies for an American naval vessel were arrested at Tampico by a Mexican force and paraded through the streets to jail for having allegedly violated martial law. The men were soon after released by the Mexican commanding officer, who apologized for the ignorance of his subordinate in making the arrests. But Admiral Mayo, in command of the American fleet at the scene, was not satisfied with this verbal expression of regret. He demanded that within twenty-four hours the Mexican authorities should submit a formal apology and disavowal of the act, together with an assurance that the officer responsible for the incident would receive severe punishment. As a further measure, the admiral's ultimatum demanded that the Mexicans "publicly hoist the American flag in a prominent position on shore and salute it with twenty-one guns, which salute will be duly returned by this ship." The expression of regret which Mayo demanded was transmitted, but Huerta balked at giving orders for the salute.

Wilson could scarcely refuse to back up his admiral, despite the dubious wisdom of the latter's unauthorized ultimatum. On April 20 the President went before Congress to ask approval for using the armed forces of the United States "in such ways and to such an extent as may be necessary to obtain from General Huerta and his adherents the fullest recognition of the rights and dignity of the United States . . ." After a two-day debate, Wilson was voted this authority: 323 to 29 in the House and 72 to 13 in the Senate.

Full-scale war now seemed likely. "I'd make them salute the flag if we had to blow up the whole place," asserted Senator Chilton of West Virginia, while Senator Borah said: "This is the beginning of the march of the United States to the Panama Canal." Indeed, events beyond Wilson's power to control seemed to be forcing his hand. Even before the authorization to use force had passed Congress, the President was informed that a German merchant ship was about to deliver a cargo of arms to the Huerta faction at Vera Cruz. Fearful lest possession of more munitions should strengthen the Mexican usurper and provide him with equipment to use against the United States, Wilson gave the order for armed action. On April 21, Vera Cruz was bombarded and occupied by American marines after considerable bloodshed.

Since the seizure of Vera Cruz served only to strengthen the defiance of Huerta, further military operations seemed inevitable, when a way out of the situation was offered from an unexpected quarter. On

April 25, the diplomatic representatives of Argentina, Brazil, and Chile, the so-called ABC powers, called at the State Department with an offer to mediate in the Mexican imbroglio. Wilson's immediate acceptance of the proposal brought him enthusiastic praise throughout Latin America. Not only did it show friendly deference by the United States to the opinion of the republics to the South, but it indicated that Wilson's repudiation of aggressive designs toward Latin America was sincere. It was, in the opinion of the Springfield *Republican*, "worth dozens of Pan-American conferences. . . . It establishes a precedent; possibly it opens an era."

The chief contribution of the mediation proposal to the actual Mexican situation was to ease over the crisis caused by the Tampico and Vera Cruz incidents. The plan for a general Mexican settlement worked out at a conference of representatives of the ABC powers, the United States, and Mexico at Niagara Falls, Canada, failed because Carranza refused to accept it. The United States, however, evacuated Vera Cruz without salute and in July Huerta gave up the struggle to hold the Mexican presidency and fled the country. To Wilson's admirers, Huerta's final downfall seemed complete vindication of both the President's policy and his tactics in pursuing it.

Unfortunately, however, the potentialities of the Mexican situation for creating embarrassing complications for the new diplomacy were not yet exhausted. Carranza became president of the Mexican Republic and in October, 1915, Wilson, after consultation with other American states, accorded him recognition. But civil war continued due to the claim of Villa that he, rather than Carranza, was the true champion of the principles of the martyred Madero. Villa showed his resentment of Wilson's recognition of the Carranza regime and his desire to embroil Mexican-American relations by a series of indignities against the "gringoes." In January, 1916, eighteen American citizens were massacred at Santa Ysabel, Mexico. Once again the demand for forceful intervention swept the United States and, when on March 9, 1916, a band of Villa's followers crossed the border and sacked Columbus, New Mexico, killing eighteen Americans, Wilson had to act. General John J. Pershing was ordered to lead a cavalry force into Mexico and capture Villa dead or alive. Carranza gave grudging consent to an agreement under which either American or Mexican government troops might operate across the border to suppress the rebels.

Pershing failed to capture the elusive Villa, and the American operations led to serious friction between the Carranza regime and the United States despite the observance of diplomatic niceties. Finally, in

February, 1917, with the United States near a state of war with Germany, the enterprise was abandoned and Pershing's men were withdrawn. Once again Wilson's critics denounced his failure to adopt a policy of wholesale intervention and thorough housecleaning in Mexico, asserting that the Villa episode had been humiliating to the prestige of the United States. It should be noted, however, that the administration's reaction to the border raids had at least been sufficiently vigorous so that there were no further incidents of this kind.

Although the continuance of the Mexican revolution after 1917 involved still more diplomatic problems, the entry of the United States into World War I shifted American attention away from the maelstrom of Mexican politics. Whether the whole course of American policy was to be praised or condemned depended largely on the partisan sympathies of the critic. Wilson's own evaluation of his policy was embodied in his message to Congress in December, 1916:

We have been put to the acid test in the case of Mexico, and we have stood the test. Whether we have benefitted Mexico by the course we have pursued remains to be seen. Her fortunes are in her own hands. But we have at least proved that we will not take advantage of her in her distress and undertake to impose upon her an order and government of our own choosing . . . that we seek no political suzerainty or selfish control.

REFORM INTERRUPTED

For leadership in domestic reform, Wilson had possessed unusual training. He was a student of government and of the new economic and social problems with which government had to deal. For leadership in foreign affairs, his training was much less adequate. His interests had been to a large degree focused on purely American issues. Yet through one of history's ironies it was destined that Wilson should be compelled to deal not only with vexatious issues in Latin America, but with problems of world politics more momentous than had any President before his time. In August, 1914, Germany invaded Belgium, and Europe became involved in the first general war since the defeat of Napoleon a century before. From that time on, America's relationship to the great conflict absorbed to an ever-increasing degree the attention both of the President and of the nation.

The progressive movement did not end abruptly with the advent of war. Liberal legislation continued to be enacted and, as late as 1920, the Nineteenth Amendment granting women's suffrage was added to the Constitution. But the crusading spirit of the earlier years was gone. After the United States finally entered the war itself, the mood of the country passed into a period of indifference and then of hostility to the progressive point of view. For fifteen years after the conclusion of hostilities this conservative reaction continued. Not until the country was engulfed by the great depression did a great new demand for reform and change make itself heard.

7

Difficult Neutrality

THE OUTBREAK OF WORLD WAR I FOUND THE PEOPLE OF THE UNITED States ill prepared to understand its causes and implications. Americans had been concerned during the preceding years primarily with matters of domestic importance—the tariff, the reform of banking, antitrust legislation, and social justice generally. If they had interests of a diplomatic nature, those interests had to do mainly with affairs of the hemisphere: the construction of the Panama Canal, intervention in the smaller republics, and, more immediately, the Mexican problem. Little attention had been centered on the European scene.

Thus the public had not realized that since about 1870 the European powers had gradually become more antagonistic toward one another and that alliances had been formed which needed but one little incident to arouse the long-engendered animosities to a state of war. One alliance included Germany, Austria, and Italy; the other, France, Russia, and Great Britain. Balance of power, spheres of influence, nationalism, and commercial rivalry were motivating factors in promoting the groundwork for growing unrest between the two rival groups.

The assassination of Austrian Archduke Francis Ferdinand at Sarajevo, the capital of Bosnia, on June 28, 1914, was the incident which brought on the war. It made newspaper headlines in the United States for a day or two, but the average American thought that it was just another of those Balkan troubles, just another flare-up following the Balkan Wars. Few Americans knew who the Archduke was, and fewer bothered to get out their dust-covered atlases to learn where Sarajevo was located. If there were trouble brewing, it would soon blow over. Nor did the State Department seem especially anxious about the whole affair; no reports from the diplomatic corps overseas indicated that anything serious would develop. Secretary Bryan was busy with his "cooling-off" treaties, while President Wilson was centering his attention on the forthcoming mediation meeting at Niagara Falls, where the Mexican trouble might be settled. True, he asserted that he was "deeply shocked at the atrocious murder"; but there is no indication that he gave it further thought or realized its potentialities at that time.

WILSON AND HIS DIPLOMATIC ADVISERS

President Wilson might be called a practical idealist. A student of political science and history, he had a wide knowledge of the workings of both the British and American governments. From his studies, he became firmly convinced that the United States had a mission to perform in the world. It must serve as the model of righteousness, a theory that may have grown as well from his Calvinistic background. If the nation came out boldly for the promotion of international law and adhered to all of its precepts, then other countries would be forced to fall in line with the American position. Force might have to be used to secure for American citizens their international rights, but force should be only the last resort. Diplomacy, plus the firm assertion of right, would accomplish more than arms. A streak of stubbornness, added to a reluctance to accept advice, sometimes prevented the President from accomplishing as much as he might have under other circumstances.

His first Secretary of State was William Jennings Bryan, who was picked, not because of any previous experience in the field of diplomacy, but as a reward for his political strength within the Democratic party which had helped secure Wilson's nomination. Normally, Bryan had considerable common sense in matters of domestic policy, and there were few contemporaries who could compare with him in judging the American political temper. He had an antipathy to war; indeed he might be classed as a pacifist. His beliefs were indicated in his efforts to make his "cooling-off" treaties universal. Sometimes the State Department was weakened by the Secretary's absence from Washington at critical times, engaged in speechmaking for the Chautauqua and other circuits. Although Wilson and Bryan eventually came to the point where they could not agree on fundamental policy, the President had high respect for Bryan's sincerity and uncanny ability to know what the average citizen was thinking.

Bryan's major assistant and eventual successor was Robert Lansing, who entered government service as State Department Counselor on April 1, 1914. Trained in general law, Lansing's marriage to the daughter of a former Secretary of State, John W. Foster, caused a shift to

William Jennings Bryan. (Brown Bros.)

international law and diplomacy. Although not a warmonger, Lansing was more belligerent than his superior, and although he did try to secure full recognition of American rights from all the warring countries, he was more and more inclined to be pro-British.

The United States was not particularly well represented in the belligerent capitals. Walter Hines Page, ambassador to Great Britain, was ill prepared for this diplomatic position. Moreover, so certain was he that Britain was entirely in the right that he did his best not only to prevent his country from weakening England's stand, but to bring the United States into the war on Britain's side. In Berlin, the American ambassador was James Gerard, who had little knowledge of European diplomacy, and he appeared to be more interested in society. From practically the outset of hostilities he was against Germany. While Myron Herrick in Paris was an oldster in the field in comparison with Page and Gerard, there is nothing to show that he understood the implications of the growing European tension any more than did his fellow Americans. Brand Whitlock, representing the United States in Belgium, was better known as the reform mayor of Toledo and as a writer than as a diplomat. With such contacts in European capitals, it is perhaps no wonder that the Wilson administration did not realize that war was impending.

Neither the State Department nor the ambassadors abroad, however, played as prominent roles as might have been expected. As one magazine of the time expressed it: "Every President has to be, in the big matters, his own Secretary of State, and Mr. Wilson will undoubtedly continue to determine for himself the main features of our foreign policy." German Ambassador Bernstorff echoed this sentiment when he asserted that "Wilson decides *everything*" on matters of international policy; and Wilson himself had written: "When foreign affairs play a prominent part in the politics and policy of a nation, its Executive must of necessity be its guide. . . ." Moreover, the President believed that more could be learned about diplomacy "at country houses and dinner tables" than through regular diplomatic channels. Consequently much of the groundwork for Wilsonian diplomacy was done by unofficial agents of the President himself. This method had worked satisfactorily in Mexican relations; why should it not be as effective in dealing with European problems? Thus, Edwin M. House, honored with a political colonelcy by his native state of Texas, secured for himself the task of being the *alter ego* of the President in European diplomacy. Colonel House sometimes made mistakes; yet his intentions were good and he was able to make contacts where regular government agents could not.

As hostilities progressed in Europe, Colonel House believed that the war could be ended by mediation, and he influenced Wilson to his way of thinking. He also concluded early in the struggle that the Allied cause was just, thus seeing eye to eye with Page and Lansing. In the spring of 1914, when war clouds were gathering over Europe, Colonel House persuaded Wilson to send him to that continent. The Texan was primarily interested in establishing a concert of powers, of which the United States would be a member, to ensure a long-range peace. He also planned to divert European attention from local differences toward colonial expansion. Despite the fact that he visited the leaders of the major powers during the hectic days of June and July, he did not seem to realize that a war was in the immediate offing. Indeed, in his correspondence with President Wilson, he made no mention of the archduke's assassination.

THE DECISION FOR NEUTRALITY

The first intimation Americans had that war in Europe might develop came on Sunday, July 26, 1914, when the newspapers carried the information that Austria had severed relations with Serbia because the latter had failed to accede to the terms of Austria's twenty-four-hour ultimatum. Worried by the grave illness of his wife (who died on August 6), President Wilson paid little attention to this report. Not until Tuesday evening, the 28th, when a message from Ambassador Herrick, describing the European situation "as the gravest in history," did the chief executive realize the urgency of the problem, and even then he felt it necessary to contact Page before taking any positive step. During this interval, Austria declared war on Serbia, Germany on Russia, France on Germany, Germany on Belgium, and Britain on Germany. The unforeseen maelstrom had burst in full fury.

No American doubted the wisdom of neutrality at this point. Had not neutrality been the traditional policy of the United States since Washington had issued his famous proclamation of 1793? European troubles should not concern the nation any more in the twentieth century than they had in the closing years of the eighteenth. As a student of history, the President believed that he must retain the American

Play in Your Own Back Yard. Uncle Sam, backed by the ABC powers, attempts to promote neutrality with a 60-mile zone along the Atlantic coast. (From the *San Francisco Chronicle*.)

tradition; furthermore, he had been elected on a platform which stressed domestic reform. His achievement of the New Freedom, already under way, might depend in large part upon the absence of other interests. War was regarded as a threatening diversion, and he did not like it.

Consequently, on August 4, he issued a more or less routine proclamation of neutrality. After announcing that "a state of war unhappily exists," the President asserted that no one in the United States "shall take part, directly or indirectly, in the said wars, but shall maintain a strict and impartial neutrality." He warned American citizens that all the provisions of the Penal Code of the United States, enacted on March 4, 1909, would be rigidly enforced. That code defined the individual acts "forbidden to be done, under severe penalties, within the territory and jurisdiction of the United States." Yet the citizens were promised that there would be no interference "'with the free expression of opinion and sympathy, or with the commercial manufacture or sale of arms or munitions of war." Belligerents, however, were warned against using American waters and territory for hostile purposes.

Still not comprehending the depth of European animosities, Wilson felt that widespread hostilities might be stemmed through America's "influence for peace." On both August 4 and 5 he offered the good services of the United States for mediation, believing that Colonel House had laid a good groundwork for conciliation during his "great adventure" in Europe. Naturally, those services were rejected, although the warring countries did allow American representatives to handle their interests where they had been forced to withdraw their diplomatic corps. The President did not believe that the European contest would seriously implicate the United States; he constantly spoke of World War I at the outset as one "which cannot touch us" or "with which we have nothing to do."

At this time majority American opinion was strongly behind the President's position. Even Theodore Roosevelt, often considered a constant jingo, praised Wilson's stand and wrote that Americans should be thankful they lived in a nation at peace, safe from the horrors of war.

Despite this support, Wilson knew that more than thirty-two million of the nation's ninety-two million inhabitants were of foreign birth or had one or both parents foreign born. Consequently, he believed he should reinforce his policy by making a direct appeal to the people. His message, issued on August 19, read in part:

The effect of the war upon the United States will depend upon what American citizens say and do. Every man who really loves America will act and speak in the true spirit of neutrality, which is the spirit of impartiality and fairness and friendliness to all concerned. . . . The people of the United States are drawn from many nations, and chiefly from the nations now at war. . . . Some will wish one nation, others another, to succeed in the momentous struggle. . . . Such divisions amongst us would be fatal to our peace of mind and might seriously stand in the way of the proper performance of our duty as the one great nation at peace . . . The United States must be neutral in fact as in name during these days that are to try men's souls. We must be neutral in thought as well as in act. . . .

Again Theodore Roosevelt supported Wilson when he wrote: ". . . Nothing but urgent need would warrant breaking our neutrality and taking sides one way or another."

While the majority of Americans probably did honestly strive to be "neutral in fact as well as in name," there was a definite swing in favor of the Allied cause as the war progressed. Although the Germans as a people were not disliked, the ruling caste of the German Empire was not so highly regarded. Those leaders' demands for their rightful place in the sun, their boasts of the supremacy of Germanic civilization or *Kultur*, the strutting of Prussian officers, the Kaiser's "Me und Gott" proclamations did not appeal to the average American. What was worse in American eyes were the Germanic acts of violence. The disregard of Belgium's neutrality was the most heinous of all and was accentuated by Chancellor Bethmann-Hollweg's reference to the nearly century-old neutrality treaty as a mere "scrap of paper." (Furthermore, the atrocity stories about the mistreatment of Belgian civilians, which reached a high point in the Report of the Bryce Committee on Alleged German Atrocities (published in the United States shortly after the *Lusitania* sinking—a most strategic time), were wholly believed by most Americans. While it has since been proved that most of these stories were propagandist fabrications, Americans at the time were so shocked by the invasion of Belgium that they were ready to believe anything. German efforts at counterpropaganda were wholly inadequate and they suffered in translation.)

On the other side of the picture, the kinship of Americans to Britons, based on common language and institutions, was strong. The friendship between the two countries in recent years was bearing full fruit, aided in no small way by the American feeling that Germany had tried to hurt the United States during the same period. The accounts of the progress of World War I came chiefly from Allied sources and were undoubtedly colored to play up Allied victories and heroism. The taxicab-transported French army, the first "hundred thousand" Britons who went to the defense of Belgium, the slogan "They Shall Not Pass" all stirred up American emotions in favor of the Allied cause. The Allies definitely had the advantage in these battle reports: they had cut the cable between Germany and the United States early in the war; except for very brief wireless dispatches, German accounts had to come by mail which followed a circuitous route before reaching its destination; most of the American correspondents were with the Allied armies, not only because of preference, but because of the speedier means of filing their stories.

Monetary considerations closely linked the two great English-speaking countries. American bankers loaned money to Britain and naturally felt that an Allied victory would result in speedier repayment. While munitions makers would have sold their wares to both groups of contestants, British control of the seas made delivery to Germany impossible. Therefore American munitions trade was entirely with the Allies and brought a pro-Ally feeling. The same can be said for trade in general.

The British were not content to rely simply on these factors. Throughout most of the period between the outbreak of war and American entrance, they maintained a well-organized propaganda distribution center, referred to as Wellington House. Under the able leadership of the prominent publisher, Lord Northcliffe, the articles from Wellington House kept pounding at German atrocities, the righteousness of the Allied cause, the danger of a German victory to the whole world, the duty of the United States to enter on the Allied side to aid the triumph of democracy. Sir Gilbert Parker, a Canadian novelist whose writings were well known in the United States, was placed in charge of propagandist activities directed toward America. Through free news service, pamphlets written by prominent Britons, and lecturers, Parker did excellent work.

The German-American author, George Sylvester Viereck, aided by Frederick F. Schrader, tried to offset the work of Wellington House with a newspaper entitled *The Fatherland, Fair Play for Germany and Austria-Hungary.* The effort was amateurish, feeble, and un-American in comparison, and before long Viereck confessed defeat. Subsequently he admitted that he had failed to comprehend the strength of the opposition. Other German attempts, liberally supported from the Embassy, had no greater success.

France was probably better liked by most Americans than was Britain. They still remembered their history sufficiently to know that France had come to the assistance of the United States during the Revolution. Perhaps the time had now come to repay that debt. There was also a feeling of sympathy because France was the victim of vicious invasion. Russia, on the other hand, was little known or liked by the general public.

In the long run, however, the invasion of Belgium, the German submarine warfare with its destruction of American lives, and the belief that the Allied cause was that of democracy and right were the prime factors in the swing from neutrality in thought and action to a definite feeling that the Allies must win, even though such a victory be gained only through American participation. In this feeling, public opinion, especially in the East, ran far ahead of President Wilson.

SABOTAGE

Even if German propagandist efforts had been as competent and as effective as the Allied, those efforts undoubtedly would have been offset by the attempts on the part of agents of the Central Powers to disrupt the industrial life of the United States, especially in the fields of munitions and transportation. This sabotage was asserted to be in retaliation for American shipments to the Allies, but American opinion bitterly resented these destructive attempts and they played no small part in the growth of a pro-Ally feeling.

Directed chiefly from the German Embassy with money supplied largely by the German government, the sabotage leaders were German Ambassador Count Johann von Bernstorff, Austrian Ambassador Constantin Dumba, Captain Franz von Papen, the military attaché to the German Embassy, Captain Karl Boy-Ed, the naval attaché, Dr. Heinrich Albert, commercial attaché, Wolf von Igel, and Franz von Rintelen, who worked more or less independently from his New York City headquarters. Perhaps three thousand agents were under the supervision of the higher-ups.

Secret-service activities took many forms. German agents tried to send their government information about the amount of munitions being produced in the United States. They attempted to prevent the exportation of military supplies or to destroy the ships which carried them. Strikes were fomented in munitions plants. False passports were secured for German reservists so that they might reach the Fatherland in the guise of American citizens. Manifests were forged in an effort to get supplies, like fuel, to German warships and submarines which were attacking Allied merchantmen. Were the Allies to learn the source of those supplies, there might develop antagonism toward the United States. German agents also cooperated with Irish revolutionists in America and, through such organizations as the American Embargo Conference and the German-American National Alliance, tried to prevail upon Congress to pass measures inimical to the Allies.

American newspapers had a field day playing up sabotage cases, actual or fancied. Many of the incidents blamed upon German agents were normal accidents, but, as in the case of Belgian atrocities, the American public was more than ready to accept every large fire, every explosion as another example of sabotage. Consequently, the hostility toward Germany grew. Lansing likened the attitude to the witch-hunting of colonial days.

Yet there is no doubt that saboteurs were responsible for some of these incidents. The millions of dollars which the German and Austrian embassies dispensed could not all have gone in vain. The British seizure of the luggage of the lecturer-journalist James F. J. Archibald when he landed at Falmouth revealed a number of letters indicating the scope of the plans. One of these written by Ambassador Dumba read in part: "It is my impression that we can disorganize and hold up for months, if not entirely prevent, the manufacture of munitions in Bethlehem and the Middle West, which in the opinion of the German Military Attaché, is of importance and amply outweighs the comparatively small expenditure of money involved. . . ." This message, plus Dumba's unfortunate reference to President Wilson and his "self-willed temperament," forced the administration to demand the Austrian's recall on September 22, 1915. Another document seized from Archibald revealed that von Papen had referred to "these idiotic Yankees." The German attaché escaped dismissal on this occasion, but by the end of the year both he and Boy-Ed proved so obnoxious that Wilson insisted upon their leaving the country. And Dr. Albert absent-mindedly left his briefcase on a New York City elevated train. In it there were found documents showing that Germany was trying to foment strikes and to prevent munitions shipments.

The watchfulness of the American secret service, commanded by William J. Flynn, nipped most of the German plots in the bud. At least two attempts to blow up the Welland Canal were frustrated, as were also bomb plots against numerous DuPont plants, the Bethlehem Steel Works at Newcastle, Pennsylvania, and many others. On the other hand, the explosion on the evening of July 30, 1916, at the Black Tom (New Jersey) docks of the Lehigh Valley Railroad brought death to two persons and property damage of $22,000,000. Subsequently, Germany admitted her responsibility and paid for this destruction.

On the whole, whatever the extent of these and other disruptive actions, Germany did not achieve her objective—to cripple American industrial activity. And, indeed, she lost because these efforts turned opinion in the United States against her, and prepared the ground for the entrance of America into the war against her.

ECONOMIC EFFECTS OF THE WAR

As the foremost maritime and industrial neutral, the United States was bound to be affected by the outbreak of World War I, despite Wilson's assertion that the contest would not touch the American people. Even the President realized that American trade would boom. The warring countries must necessarily seek supplies of all kinds from the United States; there would be calls from European neutrals who previously bought from nations now at war; and markets all over the world would look to America to stock their larders.

To carry the supplies for demands which were sure to come, Congress passed on August 18, 1914, the Ship Registry Act which provided that foreign-built ships owned by American corporations could be more easily and speedily admitted to United States registry. Because this was but an emergency measure and was decidedly slow in results, the President sought additional legislation to enable the government to buy, build, and lease ships; private business interests and Congressional opposition delayed final action on this request for two years. On September 2, however, the Bureau of War Risk Insurance was set up with a fund of $5,000,000 to provide insurance for American merchant vessels and their cargoes unable to obtain reasonable terms from private firms.

The expected increase in American exports did not materialize at once. Indeed, there came instead a decided drop, particularly in wheat and cotton. The growers of these staples were especially hard hit because the large exports of 1913 had encouraged them to produce more during the first war year. For example, the wheat production of 1914 was approximately 20 per cent higher than for the previous year. But in August, 1914, none was exported to Germany. In August, 1913, the United States sold abroad 257,172 bales of cotton; in August, 1914, less than 10 per cent of that amount was exported, and the decrease was even greater for September. With the decline in exports, the price of cotton dropped from 12½ cents a pound to 7¼ cents. An effort was made to peg the price at 10 cents; another, to subsidize the growers; and still another, to persuade patriotic citizens to buy bales to preserve the price. The demand for copper and steel likewise fell off, and the textile industry was hurt when German dyes became unavailable. As Seth Low, president of the New York Chamber of Commerce, said in mid-August, 1914: "Europe has placed an embargo on the commerce of the world."

When the first shock of war wore off and the nation realized that events in Europe would help, rather than hurt, American industry, confidence was gradually restored. By the spring of 1915 the threatened panic was definitely averted. The Allies, turning their industrial efforts primarily to the war effort and expending their backlog of prewar commodities, sought more and more supplies from the United States; an increasing number of ships became available to take care of that demand; and in turn American production in many fields was speeded up. Germany could have used the output of American factories as well, but British control of the seas precluded the delivery of purchases. Indeed, only one German ship, the large submarine *Deutschland*, was able to reach the United States and return to Germany after the British blockade was established.

The growth of American exports to Europe is shown in the following table:

	Exports to Europe	Imports from Europe	U. S. Favorable Balance
1913	$1,449,573,000	$864,666,000	$ 584,907,000
1914	1,399,296,000	788,517,000	610,779,000
1915	2,573,408,000	546,362,000	2,027,046,000
1916	3,813,278,000	633,317,000	3,179,961,000
1917	4,061,729,000	551,144,000	3,510,585,000
1918	3,858,698,000	318,121,000	3,540,577,000

The one-sided character of this trade is revealed by these figures:

	Exports to Allied Nations	Exports to Central Powers
1914	$ 824,861,000	$169,290,000
1915	1,991,748,000	11,879,000
1916	3,214,481,000	1,160,000

Thus exports to the Allies nearly quadrupled in that three-year period, whereas in 1916 the Central Powers secured less than 1 per cent of their 1914 imports from the United States.

Naturally the Germans felt bitter about the situation. They asserted that since only the Allies were being helped by American exports, the United States government should lay an embargo, at least on munitions. But, as the Wilson administration pointed out, to impose such an embargo during wartime would be an obviously unneutral act. Under the principles of international law, the fact that the Allies could secure goods from America and Germany could not was simply the fortunes of war. Bryan wrote on January 24, 1915: ". . . There is no power in

the Executive to prevent the sale of ammunition to the belligerents."
And he pointed out at the same time that Ambassador Bernstorff had
admitted that "under the general principles of international law, no exceptions can be taken to neutral states letting war materials go to Germany's enemies."

The biggest export increases were in so-called war necessities. In
1914, $6,250,000 worth of explosives were sold; in 1917, more than
$800,000,000. Iron and steel exports grew from $25,000,000 in 1914
to more than $1,000,000,000 in 1917. The value of wheat sent abroad
mounted from $88,000,000 to nearly $300,000,000 during the same
period. Prices rose almost in the same proportion as export values. For
example, wheat sold for less than $1.00 at the opening of the war;
shortly after the United States entered hostilities, it took nearly $3.00
to buy a bushel. American production of iron ore grew from 40,000,000
tons in 1914 to approximately 75,000,000 tons in 1917; the copper increase in the same period was from 1,150,000,000 tons to 1,885,000,000;
wheat, from 760,000,000 bushels to nearly 900,000,000.

STOCKS AND LOANS

Fear that the $2,700,000,000 European-owned American securities
would be dumped in the United States market caused the New York
Stock Exchange to close down on July 31, 1914. Not until December
12 was the danger deemed sufficiently averted to allow limited trading,
although not until the following April did full regular stock dealings
begin. After the resumption of open sales, prices of stocks, especially of
the so-called war babies, mounted rapidly. What European-owned
securities were sold after that time did not materially affect the American exchange.

But the enormously expanded purchases of American commodities
threatened serious trouble. The Allies could not afford to ship all their
gold to the United States to pay for what they bought, nor did the
United States want to dislocate both its own and the European monetary economy by such a transfer. Thus only about a billion in gold
found its way to America. Approximately $1,500,000,000 worth of
American securities were disposed of by European owners to offset the
unfavorable balance, but not for long could the Allies count on these
limited resources to pay for their purchases in America.

If the trade were to continue, the Allies would have to secure loans
in the United States. When the issue was first raised, however, Secretary of State Bryan wrote to J. P. Morgan on August 14, 1914, in
answer to the banker's query: "There is no reason why loans should

not be made to the governments of neutral nations, but, in the judgment of this government, loans by American bankers to any European
nation which is at war are inconsistent with the true spirit of neutrality." Morgan and other bankers considered this Bryan statement
an administration ban, although there does not seem to be any proof
that Wilson held this view. But, as the war progressed, as the pro-
Ally feeling grew, and as the realization developed that the loans would
be spent in the United States to promote American industry and balance the increasing export trade, the bankers decided that the Bryan
statement was no longer binding. They were perhaps influenced by
the sentiment of the new Secretary Lansing, who wrote to President
Wilson on September 6, 1915, that both he and Secretary of the
Treasury McAdoo believed that "the flotation of large bond issues by
the belligerent governments" was the only solution to the overfavorable
trade balance.

Before the month was over, Morgan, representing a syndicate of more
than sixty New York banks with affiliates numbering approximately
fifteen hundred throughout the nation, subscribed to a $500,000,000
loan for the French and British governments through the Reading Commission. The promise of those governments to repay was the only
collateral—a sure indication that American bankers were convinced of
eventual Allied victory. The bankers also floated four Allied loans
totaling another $500,000,000 during 1916, loans backed by American
utility and industrial securities still owned by the Allies. In addition,
$75,000,000 in Russian bonds were sold in the American market.

By the end of 1916, the Federal Reserve Board became worried
about the effect of these sales. Its warnings caused a suspension of loans
until the following January, when England sold $250,000,000 worth of
gold notes in the United States, and two months later France disposed
of $100,000,000 in similar securities.

On the other hand, Germany was able to sell only between $16,000,-
000 and $20,000,000 worth of short-term bonds in the early days of
the war. Since she could not secure war supplies in return, she used a
goodly part of the proceeds for propaganda and sabotage.

CONTRABAND CONTROVERSIES

Although relations between the United States and Great Britain had
been unusually friendly for nearly two decades, that friendship was
sorely tried early in World War I. The insular Britain insisted from the
outset that she must dominate the seas in order to maintain her life line
and to prevent supplies from reaching the enemy. Therefore she re-

fused to accept the Declaration of London of 1909 which, among other
things, had defined the various types of cargoes in the following way:
absolute contraband, consisting of actual war material destined for the
enemy; conditional contraband, made up of goods that might be used
for purposes of both war and peace, but which were contraband if it
could be proved that they were going to enemy governments or their
military forces; and noncontraband or free goods, including commodities like food, wood, certain ores, and cotton, which were essential for
the life and industry of civilian groups.

When on August 5, 1914, Britain first announced the commodities
which she would consider absolute and conditional contraband, the
United States apparently had no cause for worry because the British
list was practically the same as that drawn up at London. Yet soon

"Scat!" President Wilson trying to protect American commerce from British
interference. (By Carter in *The Sun*, New York.)

Britain declared that there might be "certain modifications and additions . . . indispensable to the efficient conduct of their naval operations"; moreover, no mention was made of a noncontraband list.

President Wilson was disturbed by this and had the State Department send a warning on September 26, 1914, that the vague British position was "highly prejudicial to the neutral rights of commerce" and might stir up "bitter feeling among the American people." After reading this note to Sir Edward Grey, the British Foreign Minister, Ambassador Page said that he did not agree with its tenor, and that he and Grey could easily find some means of getting around it. Furthermore, British Ambassador Cecil Spring-Rice was quick to inform Grey that Wilson's advisers, particularly Colonel House, were not in full accord with the note. Consequently, Grey evidently assumed that Britain could do about as she pleased without danger of American reprisal. Thus Wilson's desire to take a firm stand on neutral rights at the very outset was defeated in part by both his ambassador and his personal advisers.

As the war progressed and England's position became precarious, she receded from her original position of August 5, 1914. In a series of orders in council she gradually added to the absolute contraband list a number of materials previously conditional, notably gasoline, cotton, and rubber. Her argument was that new methods of warfare had been introduced in this struggle and these added commodities were now being used directly by the fighting forces. The most unusual addition was food as a result of the German order that all wheat, flour, and corn within the German borders were to be commandeered. Britain concluded that this was being done to ensure edibles for the German army; *ipso facto*, food must be contraband and so could be seized by British blockaders. The ultimate was reached on April 13, 1916, when Great Britain removed all distinctions between absolute and conditional contraband. Thereafter more than 225 commodities might be seized from neutral ships.

Had the Wilson administration taken a firm stand in the beginning, Britain might not have acted as she did because she could not afford to make an enemy of the United States. So why did the President, with his strong views on neutral rights, temporize until it was too late to force a change in the British position? Some observers believe that he feared to establish an embargo, knowing what one had done to his country a century earlier; others feel that a strong anti-British step would have jeopardized Democratic chances in the Congressional elections of 1914; some assert that he did not wish to interfere with American exporters, who were making money in spite of the seizures; and, finally, it is said that Wilson from the beginning wanted the Allies to win and, as long as American lives were not lost through British infringements, he would only protest, not act. Of course, too, the statements of his pro-Ally advisers usually frustrated the efforts of the President when he did become incensed.

VISIT AND SEARCH

Another potential source of disagreement over the Declaration of London concerned the definition of a blockade. The declaration's version was that a blockade must be effective and impartial, it must be announced in a formal decree, it must not prevent access to neutral ports nor allow capture of ships going to nonblockaded ones. Nor did the declaration recognize the doctrine of continuous voyage—that is, that goods could be seized on the way to neutral ports if it could be proved they were ultimately destined for enemy territory.

On the excuse that Germany had sown mines indiscriminately in the North Sea and along the Irish coast, Britain announced on November 4, 1914, that the whole North Sea area was a military zone. Lest neutral ships be sunk by such mines or by Allied war craft under suspicion of being enemy ships, they should enter that sea only through the Strait of Dover. As it turned out, when they followed the British warning, neutral merchantmen could easily be searched by British authorities.

Obviously British apprehension about the safety of neutral shipping was related to the inability of the British to conduct effective searches on the high seas.[1] For with the advent of the submarine menace she argued that it was unsafe for her warships to conduct a lengthy search at sea. Therefore many a neutral ship was taken to a British port and held there, sometimes for months, partly because of man-power shortage for the search and partly because the contraband goods were sometimes well disguised and hidden, needing X-ray machines to discover them.

No attention was paid to American protests that such delays often resulted in deterioration of cargoes and increase in shipping rates, not to mention the illegality of the proceedings. After the original outbursts of indignation, however, American shippers calmed down because they were well compensated by Britain for the inconveniences they had

[1] The Declaration of London stipulated that a belligerent ship which stopped a neutral merchantman suspected of carrying contraband must make the search at the scene. Were any contraband discovered, it could be removed and the merchantman allowed to continue.

suffered. And to Britain, prevention of the arrival of such contraband in Germany was more important than strict observance of the international maritime code.

The close tie-up between the contraband issue and the blockade was indicated more clearly by the order in council of March 11, 1915, which Britain asserted was an answer to the German decision of the previous month to initiate submarine warfare around the British Isles. This order attempted to throw a complete cordon around Germany through seizing contraband that might conceivably reach her from ships of all flags, regardless of their immediate destination. Great Britain insisted that this was not a blockade in the normal sense, and thus Allied patrol ships could range far from the vicinity of the ports and coasts immediately under ban to stop vessels suspected of carrying goods that might eventually reach Germany. Moreover, the patrol would not necessarily have to be effective. Thus the doctrine of continuous voyage was put into effect. Many cargoes destined for Norwegian, Swedish, Danish, and Dutch ports were seized by the British on the grounds that the inhabitants of those countries were buying more in wartime than they had during peaceful years; the surplus must be going to Germany.

On March 30, the State Department protested that this order was in defiance of the Declaration of London. Before the British replied, however, the sinking of the *Lusitania* largely diverted American attention from the illegality of the "blockade." Not until July 24 did Sir Edward Grey state that he believed that Germany's actions, such as the rape of Belgium, the use of poison gas, and the sinking of ships without warning, were much worse than the American charges against his country. He avowed that the British measures did "conform to the spirit and principles of the essence of the rules of war." And finally he pointed out that the United States had applied the doctrine of continuous voyage during the Civil War and had been upheld by its Supreme Court. Was the present British position any different, he asked? Although more notes were exchanged as late as April, 1916, the British refused to back down on their decision to exclude Germany from as much commercial contact as possible with the rest of the world. In fact, the British position was stated simply: "We have necessity on our side; you have the law—what is left of it—on your side: we'll not seriously quarrel." And serious quarrels were averted, partly by the growing pro-Ally spirit in the United States and partly because whenever there was serious tension, some German action usually occurred which appeared much worse in American eyes.

ADDITIONAL ANGLO-AMERICAN CONTROVERSIES

Another source of American complaint over British actions developed from the British custom of raising the American flag over their ships to escape from German submarines. Secretary Byran made the first protest on Februray 10, 1915, against what he called the "general use" of the flag of the United States by merchant ships of belligerents. He weakened the objection, however, by admitting that "occasional use" as a *ruse de guerre* might be condoned by his country, although such use must not have the official sanction of the British government. And President Wilson "regretted the necessity of sending the note," only giving his approval because he did not wish to strengthen "the hands of Germany in their extraordinary threat to destroy commerce."

Grey's reply of February 20 asserted that it had long been common usage to fly neutral flags to escape enemy action. He pointed out that Union ships had done so during the Civil War. Was now the United States so unfair as to deny similar privileges to Great Britain? Thus, with a practical refusal to abandon the practice, Grey concluded the argument.

British and French censoring of American mail brought additional protests. During the first sixteen months of the war, the Allies were content with simply examining all letters going through their territory, regardless of origin and destination. At the end of 1915, however, the scope was broadened to include mail on ships which merely stopped at their ports. Both Allies found excuses whenever the United States objected. Then in May, 1916, when America admitted the belligerent right to seize merchandise in letters, it practically conceded the Allied privilege to examine first-class mail.

American opinion was aroused by this censorship because it was asserted that Britain secured valuable trade information for its firms and delayed the completion of American bids and contracts. Moreover, the Allied answers to State Department protests were considered insulting. The administration would not go so far as the public wished with its objections. True, in the fall of 1916, Lansing did prepare a note which categorically demanded a change in Allied conduct, but Wilson would not allow it to be sent. Thus, in the absence of forceful official demand on America's part, Britain and France continued with their widespread censorship. They were able thereby to confiscate large quantities of contraband which would have helped Germany.

The British practice of arming their merchantmen for defense against submarine attacks in turn gave the Germans an excuse for not giving warning before trying to sink such ships. As far as the United States was concerned, it brought up the delicate matter of the status of passengers on those ships. Even the pro-Ally Lansing was forced to admit on January 7, 1916, that "merchant vessels . . . carrying an armament . . . should . . . not possess the immunities attaching to private commercial vessels of belligerent nationality. . . ." Furthermore, there was the problem of whether armed merchantmen of a belligerent could rightly enter an American port. But all the administration efforts to make England see the position of the United States were as unavailing as had been the attempts in other fields.

For several weeks in 1916 England lost much ground in American public opinion through her mishandling of events in Ireland. Radical nationalists in Ireland sought to take advantage of England's involvement in war to secure full independence; some even urged a military alliance with Germany as a means of attaining this goal. Since the aspirations of the radicals obviously depended on a German victory, their supporters among Irish-Americans tried to prevent the United States from going to England's assistance. They cooperated with German-American groups in mass meetings of protest against the policies of the Wilson administration, which they considered to be pro-British. Moreover, a small group of Irish-American leaders made contact with Ambassador Bernstorff in an attempt to secure backing for the proposed Irish revolt. The German reply was encouraging and for the first few months of 1916 John Devoy of New York and other leaders of Clanna-Gael, the radical nationalist society, were in close touch with the German embassy. But a succession of disasters befell the Irish volunteers who made their bid for independence during Easter week, 1916. The British eventually quelled the uprising, 15 of the Irish leaders were executed, 145 were sentenced to long terms of imprisonment, and 1841 were sent to England for internment.

The severity of the British retribution shocked many Americans. In the eyes of all Irish-Americans, the executed Irish leaders were martyrs in a holy cause. The staunchly pro-Ally *New York Times* pronounced the executions to be "incredibly stupid." Senator Borah of Idaho condemned them on the floor of the Upper House, and the Senate approved a resolution expressing hope that the British government would extend clemency to Irish political prisoners. The journalist, David Lawrence, wrote: "The truth is, Great Britain in a few days has alienated many of her sympathizers—almost as many as Germany alienated when the *Lusitania* was sunk." Consequently, pro-Ally elements for the time being found it difficult to use their most effective argument—the contrast between the brutality of the Huns and the humane principles of the British and French.

Up until the time when Germany began her unrestricted submarine warfare, the United States had more grievances against Great Britain. But the growth of a pro-Ally feeling and the fact that no American lives were lost as a result of British infractions of international law prevented a break in relations between the two Anglo-Saxon nations.

THE EARLY SUBMARINE THREAT ⌣

(American relations with Germany were largely concerned with the latter's submarine warfare, which threatened the safety of American lives on the high seas. The German proposal to isolate the British Isles through the medium of the submarine was first made in the fall of 1914 in order to stop the increasing flow of American munitions to Britain. Yet there were objections voiced by some of the German leaders: there were probably not enough submarines to establish an effective blockade, and vigorous American protests over their use would undoubtedly be forthcoming.)

By January, 1915, however, the British navy was establishing a tighter ring around Germany. This fact, plus the feeling that the United States was not protesting enough about England's actions toward neutrals, caused a change in German policy. Thus several British merchant ships were torpedoed without warning before the month was over.

This fateful start was followed on February 4, 1915, by an official German announcement that after the 18th "the waters surrounding Great Britain and Ireland including the whole English Channel are hereby declared to be comprised within the seat of war. . . . All enemy merchant ships found in these waters . . . will be destroyed although it may not always be possible to save crews and passengers. . . ." Because British ships were wont to fly neutral flags, vessels of nonbelligerents would expose themselves to danger if they entered this zone.

In anticipation of American protest, Ambassador Bernstorff hastened to inform the State Department that Germany was forced to retaliate because the British had flouted "all the principles of international law" and neutrals had "generally acquiesced," to the detriment of Germany. In carrying out her plan, Germany would try "to avoid violence to neutral ships in so far as they are recognizable." Mistakes, he admitted, might be made.

To Wilson and his advisers, especially Robert Lansing, the German proposal to sink ships without proper care for the safety of passengers and crews presented a delicate problem. As an ardent advocate of neutral rights, President Wilson felt he must do all in his power to prevent this from happening. Were he to nip the plan in the bud—before Germany had a submarine fleet sufficiently large to accomplish its objective —he might be performing an outstanding service for humanity. Yet at the same time, he must not allow Britain to continue to fly the American flag from her ships; to do so would give Germany greater reason to continue the sinkings of merchant ships. Therefore, upon the suggestion of Secretary Bryan, it was agreed that notes of protest be sent on February 10 to both offending parties. The one to Britain vigorously objected to the "general use" of the American flag by English merchantmen; but its severity was softened, as has been mentioned, when the British learned that Wilson regretted his action because he did not believe that the two types of misdeeds were in the same category.

The note to Germany did not conceal in any way Wilson's position. The President considered that the sinking of any merchant ship, even one owned by a belligerent, without preliminary visit and search, was "unprecedented in naval warfare." Were Germany to sink an American ship, though it be by mistake, the United States must regard the act as an "indefensible violation of neutral rights" for which the perpetrator would be held to "strict accountability."

When the German officials received this message, their opinions were divided. Chancellor Bethmann-Hollweg and Foreign Secretary Gottlieb von Jagow believed it wise to placate the United States; the navy men, on the other hand, thought that a month and a half of submarine warfare would put an end to the British blockade. Since no agreement could be reached, the ultimate decision was left to the Kaiser who, through navy pressure, took the position that the submarine war against enemy merchant ships must go on, but that it was never the intention of Germany "to destroy neutral lives and neutral property . . . as the American Government appear to have erroneously understood." Submarine captains were ordered to abstain "from violence to American merchant ships when they are recognizable as such."

On learning of this German position, Wilson tried to effect an agreement between Britain and Germany to forestall submarine warfare. All American food sent to Germany would be distributed only to civilians through American agents; and England would agree not to interfere with the shipments. Germany should give up her proposed submarine sinkings, and both sides should cease indiscriminate mine laying and the flying of neutral flags. Neither party would accept the Wilsonian compromise. On March 1, Germany said she would agree to the proposition only if raw materials were added to her import lists; two weeks later, Great Britain roughly rejected it entirely, and countered with a blockade of her own. A less yielding ambassador than Page might perhaps have accomplished better results.

AMERICAN LIVES ARE LOST

Although many an Allied ship was torpedoed after this compromise failed, the first incident to arouse the American public was the sinking of the British *Falaba*, carrying both passengers and munitions, on March 28, 1915, with the loss of one American life. Warning had been given by the submarine captain, who also allowed twenty-three minutes for the passengers to get off. The fatal torpedo was fired before all aboard the *Falaba* were safe because of the presence of other British ships in the vicinity.

Wilson, Bryan, and Lansing could not agree on the substance of the protest that should be sent to Germany. While Lansing was in favor of severing relations and Wilson believed that the German act was "an unquestionable violation of the just rules of international law," Bryan was inclined to feel that Americans who traveled on belligerent ships did so at their own risk. He wanted the President to prevent Americans from continuing such travel. Wilson, however, refused to turn from his theory that citizens of neutral countries had a right to travel on the seas, even though aboard a merchant ship of a belligerent. Considerable correspondence and numerous conferences were held among the three, without reaching any solution; it was apparent, however, that the President was leaning more and more toward the Lansing point of view.

During these discussions, the United States learned that the *Cushing*, an American steamer clearly displaying the American flag, had been attacked by a German plane, but with no resulting loss of life, and three days later, the *Gulflight*, owned by the Gulf Refining Company, was torpedoed. The tanker reached port, but two of the crew were drowned and the captain died of shock. There may have been an excuse for the *Gulflight* incident, because the tanker was with several British trawlers, from which she was seeking information about securing a French pilot to guide her to Rouen. The submarine captain may have believed that she was part of a convoy, particularly since she broke out the American flag at the last moment. The submarine, fearing attack, had fired the torpedo while submerged, to escape possible ramming by one of the trawlers.

Germany was prompt to admit her errors. She "very much regretted" the "unfortunate, unintentional" incidents and promised "full recompense." And on May 6, Chancellor Bethmann-Hollweg informed the German Admiralty that he would not "assume responsibility for a further aggravation of our relations with the neutral powers by a continuation of the U-boat war in the manner thus far conducted . . . Further attacks by our U-boats upon neutral ships [must] be avoided under all circumstances." After some protests from the Admiralty that such a course would defeat the purpose of Germany's blockade, it grudgingly gave in; no more American ships were torpedoed prior to February, 1917.

THE "LUSITANIA" TRAGEDY

While this discussion was going on, the *Lusitania* was sunk off the coast of Ireland on May 7, 1915, with the loss of 1198 lives, of which 124 were American. Immediately there developed in the United States, already stirred by the previous incidents, a demand for war. The press made much of the deaths of helpless women and children. Theodore Roosevelt called the sinking an act of piracy. While it has since been shown that the sinking was not planned, the fact that warnings had been printed by the German embassy in American newspapers against neutral citizens sailing on any belligerent ships, and telegrams similar in nature had been sent to those who had booked passage on the *Lusitania*, convinced many Americans at the time that it had been a deliberately plotted crime.

Yet the President would not heed the pleas of the war element. On May 13, he received word from Ambassador Page to the effect that British respect for the United States would end were war not declared against Germany. The presidential reply was voiced in a Philadelphia speech the following evening. A telling excerpt was:

. . . The example of America must be the example not merely of peace because it will not fight, but of peace because peace is the healing and elevating influence of the world and strife is not. There is such a thing as a man being too proud to fight . . . a nation being so right that it does not need to convince others by force that it is right.

Thus Wilson was not going to commit the country to war because of the *Lusitania*. He was sure that his position on neutral rights was so just that victory for those rights could be won by reasoning rather than through use of force. Many Americans condemned Wilson's stand. Again Theodore Roosevelt was his most severe critic. To the ex-President, Wilson was a "Byzantine logothete," surrounded by "flubdubs, mollycoddles, and flapdoodle pacifists." But these and other attacks failed to move the President from his reasoning.]

On May 13, the first *Lusitania* note was sent, signed with the greatest reluctance by Secretary Bryan. It began with a statement that Germany had been previously warned against such incidents, and then it emphasized that a submarine could not adhere to the following points of international law: the right of visit and search, the right to take prizes, the ability to take care of passengers and crews, and the need to give adequate warning before opening fire. Therefore Germany must prevent "the recurrence of anything so obviously subversive to the principles of warfare. . . ." Secretary Bryan offset to some degree the demands of the note by informing Austrian Ambassador Dumba that there was no widespread demand for war in the United States, but that the note was sent to satisfy American public opinion, which insisted on a protest.

The German reply was noncommittal, although it did say that the *Lusitania* was armed and carried munitions; therefore the sinking was perfectly justified. The drafting of the second note of the United States occasioned considerable discussion among Wilson's advisers. In it the President categorically denied that the ship was armed and carried explosives.[1] He refused to concede that Germany might violate "the rights of humanity" in retaliation for England's nonobservance of property rights; the two violations had nothing in common. Nor did Germany's excuse that the submarine, a new weapon, was not covered by the Declaration of London hold water.

Secretary Bryan refused to approve this draft, asserting that the United States could not remain neutral if it failed to protest England's failure to abide by international law while severely proclaiming its rights against Germany. When the rest of the cabinet supported the President, Bryan resigned his position on June 8. His successor, Robert Lansing, as has been pointed out, was quite definitely pro-Ally and certainly less of a pacifist. With Bryan's opposition removed, the second note, in practically its original form, was sent on to Germany. Again the German reply failed to meet the American points, much to the dissatisfaction and disappointment of many citizens, like Theodore Roosevelt,

---

[1] There has been great controversy whether the *Lusitania* was armed; the most thorough investigator asserts definitely that it was not. There is no doubt it carried several thousand cases of rifle cartridges, but they were not "explosives" in the terminology of international law. The fact is, however, that the submarine captain did not know whether it was armed, nor did he make any effort to find out. And he did break the rules of war by not giving warning. Therefore the question of the ship being armed is merely academic.

who were of the opinion that there should be less writing and more fighting.[1]

THE "ARABIC" PROMISE

Notes were still being sent back and forth across the Atlantic in the fruitless endeavor to dispose of the *Lusitania* problem when news reached the United States of the sinking of the British *Arabic* on August 19, 1915, with the death of two American citizens. So belligerent was American opinion that Ambassador Bernstorff, on his own responsibility, hastened to give the State Department what has been called the *Arabic* pledge: "Liners will not be sunk by our submarines without warning and without safety of the lives of noncombatants, provided that the liners do not try to escape or offer resistance." Bernstorff probably felt justified in making this pledge because, on June 5, submarine captains had been ordered not to attack the larger passenger ships, even though they belonged to the enemy. He was subsequently reprimanded for his promise, but he had succeeded in temporarily quieting American opposition. Nevertheless, the American State Department renewed its protests of the violation of the "rights of humanity"; so on October 15, 1915, Chancellor Bethmann-Hollweg expressed regret for the *Arabic* sinking, promised that an indemnity would be paid, and assured the United States that such stringent orders had been given to submarine captains "that a recurrence of incidents similar to the *Arabic* case is considered out of the question."

President Wilson regarded the *Arabic* pledge as a victory for his notewriting method of diplomacy. The war spirit quickly died down; even the belligerent Theodore Roosevelt accepted the result as "most gratifying." And Wilson could write toward the close of September: "The country is undoubtedly back of me in the whole matter. . . ." He did wonder, however, how long a policy of patience toward Germany would be a virtue for the United States. Germany still had not admitted that Wilson was right in his assertion that search must precede an attack upon a merchant vessel which did not try to resist, and that such an attack must not cause death or injury to citizens of neutral countries. Moreover, the American contention had been pressed to the point where the United States could hardly avoid drastic steps if the German sinkings were resumed.

---

[1] In February, 1916, Germany did agree to pay indemnity for the American losses in the *Lusitania* sinking, thereby admitting her liability. But since this offer was not accompanied by a statement that the act was illegal, Wilson refused to accept its adequacy. Therefore the affair was still unsettled when the United States entered the war.

THE HOUSE–GREY MEMORANDUM

Meantime, while the controversies with both groups of belligerents were mounting, President Wilson was still hopeful that peace offers would be accepted. Encouraged by certain statements in letters from Sir Edward Grey in the early fall of 1915, the President and Colonel House concluded that the latter should go to the Allied capitals to ascertain whether the leaders were ready for a peace based upon justice. Were they to show willingness, then President Wilson would send out invitations to a peace meeting. If Germany accepted the olive branch and, at the subsequent conference, an adequate accord were reached, the hostilities would be ended and the Wilsonian aim would be a success. In order to be a complete triumph, however, the peace arrangements must necessarily include provision for disarmament and a league of nations. On the other hand, were Germany to refuse to attend such a conference, Wilson and House thought that it might be desirable for the United States to enter the war on the Allied side and thus speed the defeat of Germany and the return of world peace.

House sailed forth on another "great adventure" in December, 1915. For the next two and a half months he conferred with the heads of government of Britain, France, and Germany. His Berlin reception was none too cordial, and his writings indicate that he was convinced that neither the Kaiser nor his subordinates were favorable to a peace that would satisfy either the opposition or Wilson. In the French capital, he found the government quite noncommittal, largely because of the belief that Germany would never submit to the Allied wishes. In London, however, there was a hearty reception, just as House had expected. After lengthy conferences, Grey and House came to an agreement on February 22, 1916, which the Briton committed to writing as the famous House-Grey Memorandum. The heart of the document was this:

Colonel House told me [Grey] that President Wilson was ready, on hearing from France and England that the moment was opportune, to propose that a Conference should be summoned to put an end to the war. Should the Allies accept this proposal, and should Germany refuse it, the United States would probably enter the war against Germany.

Colonel House expressed the opinion that, if such a Conference met, it would secure peace on terms not unfavorable to the Allies; and, if it failed to secure peace, the United States would leave the Conference as a belligerent on the side of the Allies, if Germany was unreasonable. . . .

When House returned to America, Wilson gave his approval to the memorandum with one significant amendment; he inserted the word "probably" before Grey's statement that in case Germany were un-reasonable at the proposed conference, the United States would leave the meeting as a belligerent. Wilson hoped that the Allies would now support him in a move to secure peace. But not even the assurance that the United States might enter the war to force upon Germany terms acceptable to the Allies was tangible enough to induce the British gov-ernment to act upon the proposal. The abortive negotiations, which were kept secret, only resulted in making it more difficult for the Wil-son administration to secure concessions from the British and French on such issues as those of the blockade and the arming of merchant ships.

THE GORE-MCLEMORE RESOLUTIONS

Although Congress did not know about the House negotiations, there were some members of the legislature who believed that the President's shift toward preparedness and his more vigorous position in regard to Germany meant that Wilson was planning to bring the nation into war. Moreover, there was a disposition among members of his own party to challenge Wilson's leadership in anticipation of the 1916 elec-tion; were they to force the President to show his hand concerning his policy toward the European conflict, his Democratic opponents might be able to make a strong case against him with the voters.

While numerous resolutions concerning control of munitions makers, embargoes on armaments exports, and the like were introduced in Con-gress by those seeking to embarrass the administration, the real fight was staged over the so-called Gore-McLemore Resolutions. On the premise that the loss of American lives on belligerent ships might bring the na-tion into war, this opposition asserted that American citizens must be barred from such travel. On January 5, 1916, Democratic Senator Thomas P. Gore of Oklahoma proposed that passports be denied to citizens who contemplated sailing on ships of belligerent nations; sev-eral days later, he added the principle that American noncontraband must be fully protected from any interference on the high seas. While these propositions were being discussed by the Upper House, Repre-sentative Jeff McLemore of Texas was working on a similar proposal which would forbid Americans from traveling on armed ships flying the flag of a nation at war.

The President vigorously opposed these Gore-McLemore Resolu-tions because he believed that they would restrict the neutral rights for which he had been struggling since the beginning. Moreover, he realized that he must scotch these opponents in order to maintain his leadership. On the other hand, many Congressmen, especially Democrats, were just as insistent that the resolutions be passed. By mid-February it seemed as though the President might be defeated. Secretary Lansing was "very much alarmed," and Speaker Champ Clark felt that if they came to a vote, the House would support the resolutions by at least a two-to-one vote.

Wilson still had a strong string for his bow. He conducted a series of conferences with the party leaders [1] at which he made the defeat of the resolutions a matter of party loyalty. The President also wrote a number of letters to key men in the legislature in which he stressed the same thought. One of the most important messages was to Senator William J. Stone of Missouri, chairman of the Senate Foreign Relations Committee, dated February 24, in which Wilson stated his position. This letter read in part:

. . . You are right in assuming that I shall do everything in my power to keep the United States out of war. I think the country will feel no uneasiness about my course in that respect. . . . But in any event our duty is clear. No nation, no group of nations, has the right while war is in progress to alter or disregard the principles which all nations have agreed upon in mitigation of the horrors and sufferings of war; and if the clear rights of American citizens should ever unhappily be abridged or denied by any such action, we should, it seems to me, have in honor no choice as to what our own course should be. . . . We covet peace, and shall preserve it at any cost but the loss of honor. . . .

Despite the redoubled efforts of his opponents, the President achieved victory when the Senate turned down the Gore-McLemore proposals by a vote of 68 to 14, and the House by 276 to 142. The disappointed Gore then tried to force the administration's hand by resolving that when American lives were lost as a result of submarine action without warning, war should be declared. But the President, still in control of the legislature, succeeded in having this proposal tabled.

THE "SUSSEX" PLEDGE

(Scarcely had this opposition at home been stilled than news of another incident reached America. The unarmed French *Sussex*, plying across the English Channel, was torpedoed without warning on March 24, 1916. Although the ship managed to limp into port, a number of lives were lost and many other passengers, including several Americans,

[1] One of these conferences may have been the much-publicized "Sunrise Conference" with Democratic leaders which was supposed to have been held some time between February 22 and early April; the most likely time was February 25. There is so much disagreement about this meeting and what is said to have taken place at it that the authors have not seen fit to include it in the main text.

were injured. Secretary Lansing was quick to write a memorandum advocating an immediate rupture of diplomatic relations with Germany since this method of submarine warfare could no longer be tolerated.) ⏝Wilson refused to allow this memorandum, which was directly against the German stand, to be sent to the warring nations until a month after the attack on the *Sussex*. He believed that to do so would mean war with Germany; he still thought that the American position could be maintained through negotiation. Colonel House, on the other hand, considered that the time had come to sever relations with the German government. By so doing, Wilson could secure the undivided support of the American people and the praise of the Allies. Thus, were a peace conference to be held, the President would play a more important role in it.

Wilson finally yielded sufficiently to have Bernstorff warned that a break would come unless Germany mended her ways. And at the same time (April 6, 1916) he informed Lord Grey: "Since it seems probable that this country must break with Germany . . . and since, if this country should once become a belligerent, the war would be prolonged, I beg to suggest that . . . you might wish now to consult with your allies . . ." along the lines of the House-Grey Memorandum. This was the nearest approach to the prediction that the United States might be involved in war that the President had thus far made; yet he was still a believer in a negotiated peace.

⏝While Wilson was considering the contents of a note on the *Sussex* case, Germany gave her version of the affair on April 12. She said that the submarine commander had insisted he had not attacked a merchant ship, but a war vessel. Wilson, however, declared that this was a "direct untruth." And since Germany was not contrite, the first *Sussex* note was sent on April 18. After calling submarine attacks the "most terrible examples of . . . inhumanity," it said "unless the Imperial Government should now immediately declare and effect an abandonment of its present methods of submarine warfare against passenger and freight-carrying vessels, the Government of the United States can have no other choice but to sever diplomatic relations with the German Government altogether." The United States would do this "with the greatest reluctance," yet such a step might be necessary "in behalf of humanity and the rights of neutral nations."

⏝When informed of the contents of this note, many Americans in the East believed that war was in the immediate offing—and welcomed it. In the West, however, the feeling prevailed that it should be averted. The great majority of Congressional members of both Houses likewise believed that the attack upon the *Sussex* did not warrant hostilities. Germany thought that war might soon come, and Bernstorff was given instructions to render German ships in American ports useless to the United States. And Britain, in an effort to speed the entry of the United States into the conflict, gave a cautious apology for her actions against which America had protested.

Germany, however, did not desire war with the United States at this time. On May 4 she replied that her government was "prepared to do its utmost to confine the operations of war for the rest of its duration to the fighting forces of the belligerents." There would be no more sinkings of merchantmen without warning or without an effort to save lives, unless such ships offered resistance or tried to escape. To put this pledge into operation, however, the United States must insist that Great Britain conclude the restrictions upon neutrals. Otherwise Germany "would then be facing a new situation in which it must reserve itself complete liberty of decision."

Through Lansing's influence, President Wilson on May 6 refused to express satisfaction over Germany's apparent change of heart or to say that he would take up again with Britain her infringements of neutral rights. Instead, he concentrated on the fact that the rights of Americans must be respected by Germany regardless of what other countries did. "Responsibility in such matters," he concluded, "is single, not joint; absolute, not relative."

Since Germany made no reply, Wilson assumed that the *Sussex* pledge would be kept, temporarily at least, without the proviso. The war spirit among Easterners again faded as no more American lives or property were lost through submarine action until the following year. The Mexican problem, domestic affairs, and the election of 1916 took the spotlight as the belief grew that Wilson had averted war.

8

From Peace to War

DESPITE THE FACT THAT THE RELATIONS WITH THE GERMAN EMPIRE perceptibly improved during the remainder of 1916 because the *Sussex* pledge removed the submarine controversy from its dangerous phase, there is no doubt that the United States had been on the brink of war with the Central Powers in the early part of that year. To numerous Americans the danger was not wholly averted, and they continued to clamor for adequate preparedness in case of another flare-up which would lead the nation into war. In spite of additional causes for strained relations with the Allies, the pro-Ally feeling continued to develop in the United States and even President Wilson, successfully reelected, was influenced by this trend. Moreover, as 1916 came to a close, Germany realized that her only hope for victory lay in unrestricted submarine warfare. The result was that the *Sussex* pledge was eventually broken, neutral rights were denied, American lives and property were threatened, and the United States finally concluded that war with Germany was necessary.

THE PREPAREDNESS STRUGGLE

Although Wilson had originally held to the thesis that the European war would not touch the United States, the feeling grew that, were hostilities to continue, the nation would inevitably be drawn into the struggle. Consequently, the question arose as to the best means of avoiding that possibility. In seeking answers, no unity of opinion was to be found in the early years of the war. Some Americans believed that the question could best be answered by refusing to supply the belligerents with war materials, thereby preventing antagonism from developing against the United States. Others considered that the preventive could be found through actively working for mediation be-

tween the contestants to bring an early peace. Still another group felt
that the United States could be kept out of the conflict by paying no
attention to belligerent infractions of American rights and to insults;
the country should turn the other cheek. And another element asserted
that preparedness was the best method of avoiding war; the realization
that American might was growing would cause other powers to think
twice before antagonizing the United States. These numerous points
of view were vigorously debated during the early days of the European
conflict; each group believed it had the best solution for keeping the
country out of war.

There were numerous organizations devoting their energies against
war when World War I broke out. Perhaps the best known were the
Carnegie Endowment for International Peace and the World Peace
Foundation. The latter had been established in 1910 by the prominent
publisher, Edward Ginn. Both movements were engaged in disseminating books and pamphlets to impress the public with the folly of

Watch Your Step. The advocates of preparedness show the danger of lack of
preparedness. (By Marcus in *The New York Times*.)

war. The number of peace societies grew with the advent of war. In addition to the American Society for the Judicial Settlement of International Disputes, the American School Peace League, and the Church Peace Union, there were the Women's Peace Party, with Jane Addams and Carrie Chapman Catt as sponsors, the Anti-Militarist League, which obtained its backing chiefly from the colleges, and the National Peace Council.

The majority of these so-called peace organizations were fully loyal and patriotic; their members were honest in the opinion that peace was the proper objective of the United States. Not all were against preparedness, but preparedness must be developed with the view to keeping the country out of war. That might be a difficult task, however, because enlargements of the army and navy might promote a martial spirit among American citizens; or belligerents, seeing America arming, might attack before preparedness was complete. Therefore, said these proponents of peace, the best course would be to keep preparedness at a minimum and concentrate upon mediation between the belligerent groups.

In another category was the American Embargo Conference, which had the support of those with pro-German sympathies and which attempted to influence Congress through letters and telegrams to ban shipments of American munitions and supplies to the belligerents. Germany would be helped were the United States to remain neutral. And German propaganda was used to influence Americans to join any peace organization in the hope that the result would be to lessen the chances that the United States might join the Allied cause.

Considerable publicity attended the effort of Henry Ford to promote conciliation between the European contestants. He believed his mediation would be readily accepted because, as he expressed it, "The fighting nations are sick of war." Influenced in part by the great loss of life among the troops and in part by persons like Jane Addams and Madame Rosika Schwimmer, Ford chartered the Scandinavian liner, *Oscar II*, and set out for Europe in December, 1915, to "get the boys out of the trenches before Christmas." The sixty delegates who went along were a heterogeneous group, and the accompanying newspapermen had a field day in poking fun at the "Peace Ship." Although Ford's motives could not be questioned, the movement, needless to say, did not accomplish its purpose; indeed, it served only to hurt the peace cause as the American public took the whole matter as a huge joke. Later projects had to endure ridicule because of the laughter which the Ford plan had originally engendered.

The outstanding pacifist was William Jennings Bryan, particularly after his resignation as Secretary of State in June, 1915. In speeches and in the columns of his paper, *The Commoner*, he preached the folly of both war and preparedness. He continued to try to prevent Americans from traveling on the high seas, especially aboard belligerent ships. He hurt his case, however, by becoming more bitter with the passage of time—and thus less convincing. Moreover, unwittingly he played more and more into the hands of the pro-German elements, and therefore the feeling grew in some quarters that he was not entirely loyal to the United States.

The first prominent advocate of preparedness as an antiwar measure was Henry Cabot Lodge's son-in-law, Congressman Augustus P. Gardner of Massachusetts. On October 15, 1914, Gardner requested Congress to form a National Security Commission to inquire into conditions of the army and navy and to report on how close they were to war strength. He backed his proposal with the assertion that the United States was totally unprepared to defend itself and warned Congress that the belligerents might some day attack America. The legislature, perhaps persuaded by administration opposition to the suggestion, refused to approve the Gardner project. The Congressman, however, kept alive the plan by appealing to Americans throughout the country and by establishing preparedness organizations.

Two of the earliest such agencies were the National Security League and the American Legion, Incorporated. The former had as its chief objective to "insure for the nation an adequate system of national defense." General Leonard Wood and Theodore Roosevelt were prime leaders in the organization which, centering in New York, had branches throughout the country. The American Legion, likewise inspired by Wood and Roosevelt, worked for the establishment of a military training program and for the enrollment of a variety of specialists like engineers, automobile drivers, and telegraph operators. Through these means, several hundred thousand trained volunteers would be available in case the nation were attacked. Were war not to materialize, these volunteers might be used for police work, particularly to prevent sabotage.

Backed by many prominent Americans, Wood started his plan for voluntary military training for businessmen at Plattsburg, New York, in the summer of 1915. At the outset, this was but a small-scale project where approximately 1200 men secured the rudiments of military knowledge. The following year, however, the movement was expanded; at least four camps were attended by some 12,000 men. In general, the administration opposed this work and, it must be admitted, the Plattsburg plan touched only a small number of Americans.

Meantime, Theodore Roosevelt, tired of what he called the milk-and-water policy of President Wilson, was becoming the outstanding critic of the administration and the most vigorous advocate of preparedness. In January, 1915, he explained the need for adequate defense in *America and the World War*, and followed this in 1916 with *Fear God and Take Your Own Part*, in which he decried the folly of turning the other cheek. This thesis was also upheld by Hudson Maxim in *Defenseless America* (1915) and by Frederick L. Huidekoper, who had been working for a larger army and navy for almost a decade, in his *The Military Unpreparedness of the United States*. Huidekoper pointed out that in past wars in which the United States had been involved, many soldiers had needlessly been slaughtered because they lacked military training. After war started was too late to begin preparing; in addition to greater loss of life, there was larger monetary expense, not to mention the danger to the nation.

Although Wilson undoubtedly favored the Allied cause from the beginning, he did not make public his views. Instead, he tried his best to maintain an official neutrality; never, he insisted, should the United States be drawn into the European conflict. The President believed at first that the preparedness movement might endanger America's role as potential peacemaker. Thus Wilson opposed the efforts of the army and navy leaders in their support of the National Security League, believing that they wanted an increase in strength as a prelude to American entrance into the war. In a speech before Congress on December 8, 1914, Wilson said: "We shall not alter our attitude . . . because some amongst us are nervous and excited. Such a change would merely mean that we had lost our self-possession." He continued to place reliance upon a "citizenry trained and accustomed to arms" rather than upon a large standing army. The navy should be a medium for defense, not for attack. Without executive approval of preparedness, nothing could be done, and military appropriations were kept at the low prewar level.

As the war progressed, however, the President began to change his position. He saw American rights being denied on the high seas; perhaps the preparedness advocates were correct in their belief that a mighty arm would do the most good in upholding international law. By May, 1915, Wilson started talking openly about the need of a larger navy; two months later he initiated plans for improved national defense; and near the close of the year, he came out strongly for preparedness when he addressed a Democratic rally in New York City.

A more forceful and definite plan was placed before Congress on December 7. The President said he would soon request the legislature for larger appropriations for both the army and navy, and hoped Congress would grant speedy approval. He also expected to ask for increased governmental control over the merchant marine. These requests were to come because "the war has extended its threatening and sinister scope until it has swept within its flames some portion of every corner of the globe." He insisted, however, that he was not seeking war. "We regard war merely as a means of asserting the rights of a people against aggression. . . . But we do believe in a body of free citizens ready and sufficient to take care of themselves. . . . At least so much by way of preparation for defense seems to me to be absolutely imperative now."

THE FIRST PREPAREDNESS MEASURES

Opinion for preparedness was now rapidly gaining ground, despite the original support given the Gore-McLemore Resolutions and the activities of the antiwar associations. In the late winter and spring of 1916, the President was committed to the theory that an increased army and navy were necessary to maintain American rights. Congress was once more under control; would the people support Wilson's new thesis? To make the test, Wilson made a series of speeches in key cities, especially of the Middle West, during January and February; important sentences from some of these addresses were: "We must be ready . . . upon the shortest possible notice . . ."; "This country should prepare herself, not for war . . . but for adequate national defense"; "The force by which the authority and right of the United States are to be maintained and asserted" should be secured, as well as "a great navy second to none in the world." Even in the supposed antiwar Middle West his audiences received these opinions enthusiastically. This confirmed Wilson's decision to ask preparedness legislation from Congress without further delay.

On March 4, 1916, Senator G. E. Chamberlain of Oregon, chairman of the Military Affairs Committee, introduced a bill for a general increase in the armed forces, and two days later Representative James Hay of Virginia proposed a similar measure in the Lower House. The passage of such legislation was aided by the raids of Villa, the Mexican revolutionary leader, upon American towns; delay, however, was occasioned by Congressional disagreement over details. Finally, on June 6, the Hay or National Defense Act was signed by the President. It provided for a gradual increase of the regular army from the existing 90,000 men to a minimum of 175,000 and a maximum of 220,000; the Federalization of the National Guard, which was to be built up to 400,000 men; the establishment of officers' reserve corps; and compulsory military training for youths over the age of sixteen in high schools and colleges.

American support for the Hay Act was indicated by the numerous preparedness-day parades throughout the land. That there was some opposition, however, was shown at San Francisco where, on July 22, Thomas Mooney and Warren Billings were accused of throwing a bomb among the paraders. Their subsequent trial and imprisonment became a *cause célèbre*.

The navy, which Wilson desired to be second to none, was not forgotten. On August 29, 1916, the President placed his signature on the Naval Construction Act; between $500,000,000 and $600,000,000 were to be spent over a three-year period for the building of at least five battle cruisers and numerous lesser craft. Also, after debate of nearly two years, Congress established the United States Shipping Board on September 7. This government agency was empowered to lease, buy, build, and operate merchant ships through an Emergency Fleet Corporation. Fifty million dollars were appropriated as the original operating fund.

Sometimes considered primarily as a phase of the New Freedom, the Adamson Act may be included as well as a preparedness measure. Because of the demand of the four railway brotherhoods for an eight-hour day and time and a half for overtime in March, 1916, and the subsequent refusal of the railroad operators either to agree or arbitrate, the unions scheduled a strike to begin on Labor Day, 1916. The government tried its best to offer mediation through the United States Board of Mediation and Conciliation, which had been established under the Newlands Act of 1913, but little attention was paid to this agency.

The proposed strike threatened to tie up the transportation facilities of the nation. Were this to happen, the flow of war material to the Atlantic coast would be stopped and the general preparedness program delayed. Wishing to avert a calamity, President Wilson tried to prevail upon the railroad owners to relent, at least to the extent of granting the eight-hour day, which had "the sanction of the judgment of society in its favor." When this proposal also failed, the President went before Congress on August 29 and explained the gravity of the situation. The legislature quickly responded with the Adamson Act of September 2, which gave the workers the working day they sought, although overtime pay was to be prorated. A fact-finding commission was established to consider a general overhauling of the powers of the Interstate Commerce Commission and of the Newlands Act. This measure satisfied the brotherhoods and the strike was called off. The President was widely criticized in employer circles for surrendering to the threats of labor, but he felt justified in his action to keep preparedness rolling.

WILSON SEEKS CONCESSIONS FROM THE BRITISH

Meantime, Wilson continued his efforts to secure recognition of neutral rights and to bring the war to an earlier conclusion through note-writing and mediation proposals. In a letter of May 16, 1916, to Colonel House, he outlined the policy which he believed should be followed in view of the *Sussex* pledge which Germany had just given. The removal of the submarine issue focused attention on the "altogether indefensible course" Great Britain was pursuing with regard to neutral trade and her "quite intolerable interception" of mail being carried by neutral ships. Recently there had been added "the great shock" American opinion had received from the course of the British government toward the Irish rebels. According to Wilson, he was faced with this alternative: "The United States must either make a decided move for peace (upon some basis that promises to be permanent) or, if she postpones that, must insist to the limit upon her rights of trade . . . with the same plain speaking and firmness that she has used against Germany."

What Wilson hoped was that the British government would accept the idea of a peace conference convened according to the plan of the House-Grey Memorandum of the previous February. Sir Edward Grey insisted, however, that the project was premature. A negotiated peace on the basis of the existing military situation would be to the exclusive advantage of Germany. Furthermore, such a peace would strengthen the prestige of German militarism and render ineffective and insecure any convention for maintaining future world order.

Despite the coolness of the British response, President Wilson discussed the possibilities of peace in one of the most important of his speeches—that of May 27, 1916—before a convention in Washington of the League to Enforce Peace. With the causes and objects of war, Wilson declared, the United States was not concerned. Nevertheless, Americans were "participants, whether we would or not, in the life of the world", with obligations and interests in all that "affects mankind." Americans believed these fundamental things: first, that every people had a right to choose the sovereignty under which they should live; second, that the small states of the world had a right to enjoy the same respect for their sovereignty and for their territorial integrity that great nations insisted upon; and, third, that the world had a right to be free from every disruptive disturbance that had its origin in aggression and disregard of the rights of peoples and nations. In the most important sentence in the speech, Wilson asserted that the United States was "willing to become a partner in any feasible association of nations formed in order to realize these objects and make them secure against violation." If the warring nations would consent, he would be glad to initiate a peace movement on the basis of such a settlement with regard to their own immediate interests as the belligerents might agree upon. This movement must be accompanied by the formation of "an universal association of the nations to maintain the inviolate security of the highway of the seas for the common and unhindered use of all nations of the world, and to prevent any war begun either contrary to treaty covenants or without warning and full submission of the causes to the opinion of the world—a virtual guarantee of territorial integrity and political independence."

Thus for the first time Wilson publicly associated himself with the idea of a league of nations. In private correspondence, however, he had written as early as 1914 that after the war there would have to be an organization of the nations, all bound together for the protection of the integrity of each.

Wilson's advocacy of a league to enforce peace and his offer to mediate in the war were unwelcome to all the belligerent governments. Germany wanted peace, but she wanted it on her own terms; Ambassador Bernstorff was instructed to block any attempt on the part of the American President to mediate. The Allies, particularly the British, were indignant because Wilson had said that the United States was not concerned with the causes and objects of the war. After temporizing throughout the spring and summer, Sir Edward Grey bluntly notified Colonel House in August that England would not contemplate peace until the Allies considered the moment had come to make it.

(Unable to make progress in his efforts to secure an early end to the war, Wilson sought to obtain from Britain and France promises to respect more scrupulously America's rights as a neutral. But here, too, he was doomed to disappointment. Far from relaxing the blockade of Germany, the British government was determined to strengthen it since it was the most effective weapon which England could use against its dangerously powerful antagonist. Nor would the British and French abandon the practice of intercepting and censoring American mail bound for European countries, both belligerent and neutral.)

A particularly irritating issue arose in July, 1916, when the British government made public a "black list" which included the names of many American firms. This meant that British nationals were forbidden to do business with concerns suspected of trading with Germany. The penalty imposed upon such American companies was a serious one since the world's shipping, banking, cable communications, and insurance were largely under British control. The publication of this particular list only brought to public attention a practice which the British had been quietly following for many months. Apparently some firms were black-listed only because they had officials with German-sounding names.

American opinion was thoroughly aroused. Wilson wrote to Colonel House one of the angriest letters of his career, saying:

I am, I must admit, about at the end of my patience with Great Britain and the Allies. This black list business is the last straw. I have told Spring-Rice so. . . . I am seriously considering asking Congress to authorize me to prohibit loans and restrict exportations to the Allies.

Although Wilson did not take this step, Congress placed a powerful weapon in his hands by authorizing him to prohibit the importation into the United States of the goods of any country which, contrary to international law, forbade the importation into its own or any other country of American goods. The President, however, decided against using this power. The United States was dependent on so many British-controlled raw materials that such an action might prove a boomerang.

Yet American reaction was sufficiently violent to cause the English to make a few concessions. The cases of some of the affected corporations were reconsidered and some names removed from the list. On the basic principles involved, however, the British government was unyielding.

Wilson has been severely criticized for not following up his sharp protests against both the black list and other Allied violations of American rights with some effective form of pressure, such as an embargo. In considering this matter, it must be remembered that the United States had experimented with such measures a century previously during the Napoleonic Wars. Wilson, an historian as well as a political scientist, was thoroughly familiar with these precedents and very reluctant to see history repeat itself; on the earlier occasion, embargo and nonintercourse had seriously damaged American commerce and created desperately hard times for the American farmer without securing the recognition of American rights. The President in particular wanted to avoid the sort of situation represented by the War of 1812, when the United States had become involved in a great world conflict on what was probably the wrong side. Although often irritated by British policy, Wilson was careful not to allow any Anglo-American quarrel to reach the point where there was any likelihood of the United States drifting into war on the side of autocracy and militarism.

THE CAMPAIGN OF 1916

Wilson's election in 1912 had been possible only because of the quarrel within the Republican ranks and the consequent formation of the Progressive party. The Progressives, however, proved to have little vitality except as they drew upon that of the dynamic Theodore Roosevelt—and Roosevelt's interest in quixotic politics rapidly subsided. Much though the ex-President hated the Republican Old Guard, he detested Wilson more. The Congressional elections of 1914 had shown clearly that the Progressive party was dying; some of its supporters had gone over to the Democratic party and others had returned to the Republican fold. Although that election had resulted in strengthening the Democratic control of the Senate with fifty-six seats instead of the former fifty-one, the administration majority in the House had been sharply reduced; the Democratic members had declined from 290 to 231.

During the next two years the disintegration of the Progressives continued. Roosevelt was still the party's idol, but he wanted no part in any new three-way contest such as that which had led to Wilson's victory in 1912. What he hoped instead was that the regular Republicans might be induced to nominate him in 1916 and that he might triumphantly return to the White House as the candidate of both the Republican and Progressive parties. But the Old Guard felt too bitterly about the quarrel of 1912 to permit this. They wanted the Progressive vote, but not the Progressive hero. Another factor that strengthened the determination of the Republican leaders not to allow the nomination of Roosevelt was that no man in America was more hated by the German-Americans, whose votes the leaders hoped would beat Wilson.

What the Republicans needed was a candidate who had not bolted in 1912, but whose record, nevertheless, was sufficiently liberal to attract the Progressives. They also needed a candidate who had not been so outspoken on the war as to alienate the German vote; yet at the same time they could not afford to name a man open to the charge of being pro-German. This was a hard bill to fill and one which automatically ruled out such prominent statesmen as ex-President Taft, Elihu Root, or Henry Cabot Lodge. The field, in fact, soon reduced itself to one man—Justice Charles Evans Hughes of the Supreme Court. Hughes had first secured prominence in 1905 by his fearless investigation of insurance company scandals in New York; from 1907 to 1910 he had been a successful governor of that state. These things in his record appealed to liberal voters. On the other hand, conservative Republicans noted with approval that Hughes had been appointed to the Supreme Court bench by President Taft in 1910, that he had been a sound judge, that his judicial position had prevented his taking any stand in the party quarrel of 1912. Both conservative Republicans and German-Americans noted with distinct approval one final fact about Hughes— it was common knowledge that Roosevelt did not like him.

Early in June, 1916, the Republicans and the Progressives held their separate conventions in Chicago. The younger party marked time to see whether the Republicans would not in the end accept Roosevelt after all. But the voting soon demonstrated Hughes's strength and he secured the nomination on the third ballot. Charles W. Fairbanks of Indiana, who had been Vice-President from 1905 to 1909, was named as running mate. The platform was brief; it denounced the Democratic administration for failure to protect the rights of American citizens, especially in Mexico, stressed the need for preparedness, and attacked both the Underwood Tariff and the merchant marine program.

The Progressives then nominated Roosevelt for President and John M. Parker of Louisiana for Vice-President. Their program repeated the slogans of 1912 and attacked Wilson's foreign policy, while demanding military and naval preparedness. But the party which the Rough Rider had created in 1912 was killed by its own parent. A letter from Roosevelt, declining the Progressive nomination and announcing his intention of supporting Hughes, was made public too late for the convention to name another candidate. The Progressive National Committee, by a divided vote, gave its endorsement to Hughes and then adjourned, never to meet again. Most of the Progressives returned to the Republican fold; a minority became Democrats.

The Democratic convention assembled later in June at St. Louis. It quickly proved a triumph for the President. Not only was he renominated by a vote of 1092 to 1, with Thomas Marshall of Indiana again as his running mate, but the platform was largely his handiwork. It pointed with pride to the legislation passed by two Democratic Congresses and acclaimed the administration's patient Mexican policy. It praised American neutrality in the European war, but said that it was the duty of the United States to join with other countries of the world in an association of nations.

The plank which Wilson considered most important and on which he wanted to fight the campaign was a ringing assertion of Americanism linked with a denunciation of "hyphenism"—the divided loyalty of some German-Americans and other groups of recent foreign stock. On June 14 (Flag Day), the very day on which the St. Louis convention was holding its opening session, the President and his cabinet members were marching in a great preparedness parade in Washington. Wilson's address later in the day warned: "There is disloyalty active in the United States, and it must be absolutely crushed."

Events in St. Louis proved the greater popularity of a different slogan. In the keynote speech of Martin H. Glynn of New York, he defined the avoidance of war as being the paramount issue of the campaign. Glynn cited numerous examples in the past history of the country when dangerous controversies had arisen between the United States and some other nation; in each case he hammered home the point: "But we didn't go to war." The delegates were wild in their enthusiastic approval and it was obvious that Wilson's strongest political asset was his success in keeping the United States insulated from the world conflagration. A sentence in the platform capitalized on this: "In particular we commend to the American people the splendid diplomatic victories of our great President, who has preserved the vital interests of our Government and its citizens, and kept us out of war." As a summary of the President's past policy, the slogan "He kept us out of war" was true enough; had the President wanted to get the country into war, he could easily have brought about such a step at almost any time during the year between the sinking of the *Lusitania* and the receipt of the *Sussex* pledge. Yet it was, nevertheless, a dangerous slogan when regarded as a guarantee for the future. Wilson told one of his advisers: "I can't keep the country out of war. . . . Any little German lieutenant can put us into war at any time by some calculated outrage."

The campaign which followed was more notable for colorful incidents than for the quality of the debate on the issues. Several of these incidents involved the hyphenate problem. Radical Irish- and German-Americans, determined to make their influence felt during the campaign, claimed credit for inflicting a defeat upon the President in his adopted state. In a September primary, the Democratic voters of New Jersey renominated Senator Martine despite Wilson's opposition. Jeremiah O'Leary, head of the rabid Anglophobe organization known as the "American Truth Society," dispatched an exuberant telegram to the President, saying: "Senator Martine won because the voters of New Jersey do not want any truckling to the British Empire nor do they approve of dictatorship over Congress. Your foreign policies, your failure to secure compliance with all American rights, your leniency with the British Empire, your approval of war loans, the ammunition traffic, are issues in this campaign." Wilson's reply was immediate and crushing:

Your telegram received. I would feel deeply mortified to have you or anybody like you vote for me. Since you have access to many disloyal Americans and I have not, I will ask you to convey this message to them.

This O'Leary incident captured headlines all over the country, and the Democratic National Committee sought to capitalize further upon it by charging late in the campaign that Hughes had made a deal with a group of German-Americans and Irish-Americans which included the wicked O'Leary. Hughes's reply was an admission that he had permitted such a group to interview him, but a denial that he had promised them anything or that he had known who O'Leary was when he met him. *The New York Times*, supporting Wilson, chortled: "A few days ago who would have suspected in the bustling Jeremiah O'Leary the successor, as a candidate slayer, of the grave and reverend Burchard."

Hughes's campaign was full of embarrassments. His speeches, while vigorously critical of the President, were vague as to any alternative policy. His cautiousness in dealing with the submarine issue was in sharp contrast with the fiery speeches of Roosevelt, who denounced in ringing terms German policy and Wilson's weakness in dealing with it. He likened the President to Pontius Pilate, and then apologized to Pilate. Roosevelt's language was of such a character as to dismay the Irish and German groups which were working for Hughes. Ambassador Bernstorff, in fact, decided that Germany had more to lose than to gain in a Republican victory and so informed German-Americans who looked to him for advice.

The costliest blunder of the Republican campaign was committed in California. In this important state Hughes unwisely complied with the wishes of the conservative bosses and shunned Governor Hiram Johnson, who had been the Progressive vice-presidential candidate in 1912 and was now running for the United States Senate. Therefore Johnson made no effort to have his own followers support Hughes. When the ballots were counted in November, it was revealed that Johnson had carried the state by almost 300,000 votes, while Hughes was losing it by 4000.

California's electoral votes proved to be decisive in an extremely close election. The first editions of the newspapers on the morning after the balloting announced that Hughes had won, for he had carried all of the large eastern states—New York, Pennsylvania, Massachusetts, and New Jersey—upon which victory had hitherto always hinged. In the Midwest, moreover, he had won the strategic states of Illinois, Indiana, and Michigan. To win all these and yet lose the election seemed impossible, but Hughes did it. To Wilson went the Solid South, plus Maryland, New Hampshire, and Ohio; the balance of power proved to be in the states west of the Mississippi, all of which the President carried except Oregon, Iowa, South Dakota, and Minnesota. After several days of uncertainty, the final electoral vote was revealed as: Wilson, 277, Hughes, 254. The popular vote gave Wilson 9,129,600, Hughes, 8,538,-200, and Benson (Socialist), 585,000.

The defeat of Hughes in such a close contest obviously depended on other factors than his snub of Johnson. Had he carried states like Ohio or Kansas, he could have afforded to lose California. The general weakness of his campaign was that it depended on appealing both to the elements that wanted a more genuine neutrality than that of the Wilson administration, and to those who wanted a more energetically pro-Ally course of action. On domestic issues also Hughes was unconvincing. Wilson, on the other hand, derived effective political support from organized labor, which liked the Adamson Act, and from farmers, who were grateful for the Farm Loan Bank Act, also passed in 1916. Women now voted in most of the western states, and they were particularly responsive to the slogan: "He kept us out of war."

The effect of the O'Leary incident is not clear. Many votes were won to Wilson by his vigorous condemnation of hyphenism, but many others were lost. Thousands of Irish resented what they considered a slur upon their loyalty and refused to vote for Wilson. The President failed to carry any one of the six states—New York, Pennsylvania, New Jersey, Massachusetts, Connecticut, and Illinois—in which the largest number of Irish votes were concentrated.

The Democrats maintained their control of the Senate where they secured fifty-three seats. In the House, however, 216 Republicans were elected to 210 Democrats. Enough of the nine independents, who held the balance of power, allied with the Democrats, however, to permit the latter to reelect Champ Clark as Speaker when the new Congress met for the first time in April, 1917.

THE APPEAL FOR PEACE

Late in the campaign Wilson clearly revealed how difficult it was to keep the United States at peace. In a speech he said: ". . . this is the last war . . . that involves the world that the United States can keep out of. I say that because I believe that the business of neutrality is over. . . . I mean this, that war now has such a scale that the position of neutrals sooner or later becomes intolerable." So far as the war now raging was concerned, Wilson realized that the longer it continued, the more difficult American neutrality would become.

United States diplomatic representatives in Germany kept the President informed of a sharp contest within the German government, a contest on whose outcome America's chances to remain at peace depended. The most important admirals, von Holztendorff and von Capelle, were pressing for the resumption of ruthless submarine warfare. On the other hand, Ambassador Bernstorff was sending solemn warnings that this would bring the United States into the war and, for the moment, the Kaiser, Chancellor Bethmann-Hollweg, and Foreign Secretary von Jagow were holding out against the extremists. But how long could or would they continue to do so?

The German government was anxious for peace. Indeed, during the summer of 1916 Chancellor Bethmann-Hollweg had authorized Bernstorff to inform the United States that Germany was prepared to have President Wilson issue an appeal for a peace conference. Instead of delivering this information directly to President Wilson or the State Department, Bernstorff first conferred with Colonel House. The colonel's answer was that the United States and the President would do nothing until after the election was over. Nevertheless, this German move strengthened Wilson's ambition to act as peacemaker.

Although Wilson had no intention of allowing himself to be used as a tool of German diplomacy, for reasons of his own he considered it imperative, as soon as the election was out of the way, to make an earnest move for peace. Unless he did so, and did so quickly, he privately informed Colonel House, the United States would "inevitably drift into war with Germany upon the submarine issue."

Throughout most of November Wilson struggled with the drafting of a note to the belligerent powers requesting that they state the terms upon which they would consider peace, preferably in an international conference. Secretary Lansing and Colonel House had little sympathy with this project; they felt that the time was not ripe for such a move and that it would be resented by the Allies. Lansing, indeed, believed that Germany was not observing the *Sussex* pledge and that therefore the United States should break diplomatic relations with her.

Overriding the objections of his advisers, however, the President continued to formulate his appeal. On December 12, an event occurred which threatened to dull the prospects of his peace move—prospects which were none too bright to begin with. The German government unexpectedly made its own peace offer. No terms were suggested, and the spirit of the maneuver was typified by a speech which the Kaiser made to his troops in Alsace. In the conviction, he said, that the Germans were "the absolute conquerers," he had proposed negotiations. In such a context it is little wonder that the very word "peace" seemed an insult to Allied ears.

Wilson's position was most unpleasant. To proceed with his peace moves now would inevitably bring the charge from the Allied camp that he was acting in collusion with the Germans. Yet to give up the idea was to accept without struggle a situation that was likely to make it impossible for him to keep the country out of war. From the American representatives in Germany came the information that, if the German peace offer should fail, the Chancellor would be subjected to greater pressure than ever for a renewal of ruthless submarine activities.

Finally, the President's desire for peace won out and, on December 18, 1916, he sent identical notes to each of the belligerent governments. The document was phrased in language as carefully neutral as possible, calling attention "to the fact that the objects which the statesmen of the belligerents on both sides have in mind in this war are virtually the same, as stated in general terms to their own people and to the world." Wilson did not propose peace; he did not offer mediation. He only asked from each warring nation a statement of the specific terms upon which the contest might be concluded, as well as what guarantees each country would require for its future security. Then, he said, all might learn, neutrals as well as belligerents, "how near the haven of peace may be for which all mankind longs with an intense and increasing longing."

The Allied reaction was not enthusiastic. Russia refused to make any statement about its future. France regarded the proposition as a "gross trap" really engineered by Germany. Lloyd George refused to admit Wilson's statement that Allied war aims were "virtually the same" as those of the Central powers—and King George V is said to have wept when he read that phrase. The venerable Lord Bryce well summarized the English attitude when he wrote to an American friend: "We are quite sure that the German Government would not accept any terms we could offer nor could we accept any they would offer. They claim to negotiate as conquerors, we mean to defeat them. We think nothing short of their defeat will ensure peace for the future." The British, however, were somewhat cheered by a careless statement of Lansing to newspapermen in which he said: "The sending of this note will indicate the possibility of our being forced into the war." Despite the Secretary's subsequent assurance, given out to the press at Wilson's insistence, that the government was not contemplating any change in its policy of neutrality, British condemnation of the peace move became less bitter.

The German government, on the other hand, was alarmed by the original Lansing statement and returned to its earlier policy of opposing Wilsonian mediation. It refused to state specific peace terms, except to Allied delegates sent to some neutral city. Bernstorff was informed, moreover, that that neutral city would have to be in Europe, where the negotiations could be free from "American indiscreetness and intermeddling."

The Allied reply, sent on January 10, 1917, stated that Germany and Austria-Hungary were responsible for the war and that the peace settlement must protect Europe from another outbreak of such "brutal covetousness." A series of specific demands followed: Belgium, Serbia, and Montenegro must be restored and indemnified by Germany; France, Russia, and Rumania must be evacuated and indemnified; past conquests from Allied nations returned; Italian, Slav, Rumanian, and Czechoslovak minorities liberated; peoples subject to Turkey freed; Poland given autonomy under the Czar; and a league of nations established. These terms could, of course, be achieved only through complete Allied victory. Their publication was intended to end all talk of a negotiated peace.

Faced with this situation—with Germany refusing to state any peace terms at all and with the Allies giving terms so far-reaching as to make immediate peace impossible—Wilson reacted in a way completely characteristic of his own conception of democratic leadership. He determined to make a direct appeal to the peoples of the warring nations over the heads of their governments. Such was the purpose of the carefully prepared address which the President delivered to the Senate on January 22, 1917. He took it for granted, he said, that mere terms of peace between the belligerents would not satisfy the belligerents themselves. What was necessary was to create a force to guarantee the permanency of the settlement, so powerful a force that no nation or combination of nations could withstand it. No such league for peace that did not include the United States would suffice to keep the future safe against war; yet there was only one sort of settlement that the people of America could join in guaranteeing. It must be "a peace without victory. . . . Victory would mean peace forced upon the loser, a victor's peace imposed upon the vanquished. . . . Only a peace between equals can last. Only a peace the very principle of which is equality and common participation in a common benefit." Besides this, the settlement in order to be durable must be based on the principles of government by the consent of the governed, freedom of the seas, and disarmament. In other words, "in every discussion of the peace that must end this war it is taken for granted that peace must be followed by some definite concert of power which will make it virtually impossible that any such catastrophe should ever overwhelm us again."

By many critics this is considered the greatest of Wilson's public papers—a message of prophetic power which, had it been heeded, might have saved the peoples of all countries from untold suffering. But, despite the heartfelt approval of much American opinion and that of liberals even in the belligerent countries, the speech was denounced in many quarters. Several leading Republican Senators attacked bitterly the idea of American participation in a league of nations which would employ force to maintain peace. The phrase "peace without victory" greatly offended the Allies; that of government by the consent of the governed seemed dangerous to the Central Powers.

The desperate odds against Wilson's success in his campaign for a negotiated peace were becoming daily more obvious, but the President did not give up. On the contrary, he renewed pressure upon the German government to state the terms on which they would be willing to bring the war to an end.

END OF THE "SUSSEX" PLEDGE

The President was aware throughout this period that strong elements within German official circles were pressing for resumption of ruthless submarine warfare. It was this knowledge that had made him so energetic in his appeals for peace. What the President did not know, however, was that the struggle over policy in Germany was over. The militarists had won. The most powerful generals, Hindenburg and Ludendorff, had come to the support of the admirals, and on January 9, 1917, the Kaiser had issued the fateful command:

I order that the unrestricted submarine warfare be launched with the greatest vigor on the 1st of February. You will immediately take all the necessary steps, taking care, however, that this intention shall not prematurely come to the knowledge of the enemy and the neutral Powers.

Bernstorff's dispatches had left little doubt that this step could be taken without bringing the United States into the war, but the German officials decided that this would have to be risked. Admiral von Capelle expressed the opinion that from the military standpoint the assistance which the Allies would secure from the entrance of the United States into the war would "amount to nothing." The military authorities had convinced themselves that ruthless submarine warfare would so injure British economic life and so terrify the English people that the war would end in a complete German victory within a few months. The German authorities may also have been influenced by the American election of 1916, resulting in Wilson's success on a pledge of "He kept us out of war." This undoubtedly was interpreted in Germany as a mandate from the American people to continue to remain out of the war during the second term as well. Thus the change in German policy would not bring American retaliation.

On the afternoon of January 31, 1917, Ambassador Bernstorff delivered to Secretary Lansing a brusque note: after February 1, Germany would forcibly prevent all navigation, that of neutrals included, in a zone around Great Britain, France, Italy, and in the eastern Mediterranean. All ships within that zone would be sunk on sight. One American steamer, not carrying contraband, might sail to and from Falmouth, England, each week, provided three "vertical stripes, one meter wide," alternately red and white, were painted on the hull and superstructure; furthermore that ship must fly a red-and-white checkered flag from both stern and masthead, it must be lighted at night, and follow a course mapped out by the German authorities. To indignant Americans reading the note in their newspapers, this patronizing weekly concession to a single ship, striped like a barber pole, seemed the ultimate in insult.

In a desperate effort to induce Wilson to postpone a diplomatic break, Ambassador Bernstorff on this same day confided to Colonel House the specific German peace terms for which the President had been asking. But Wilson was no longer interested. For the Germans to expect him to continue his efforts for peace at the very moment when they were tearing up the Sussex pledge was a mockery.

During the next forty-eight hours the President pondered over his next move. Then, on the afternoon of February 3, he appeared before Congress and in a somber address announced that all diplomatic relations between the United States and the German Empire had been severed. But, he added, "I refuse to believe that it is the intention of the German authorities to do in fact what they have warned us they will feel at liberty to do. . . . Only actual overt acts on their part can make me believe it even now." Should such acts occur, he concluded, he would come before Congress again to ask for authority to use any means that might be necessary "for the protection of our seamen and our people." Four days later, by a vote of seventy-eight to five, the Senate passed a resolution endorsing the President's action.

ARMED NEUTRALITY

Although the only two American ships to be sunk by German submarines in February were given warning so that no American lives were lost, American shipping was badly demoralized. Many vessels remained in port, and an insistent demand went up that the government should protect the ships by providing them with navy guns and gunners. Wilson struggled against this step, which would obviously bring the country closer to war. Indeed the cabinet was almost in revolt over the issue.

By the end of the month, however, Wilson's advisers had practically won him over to acceptance of the idea. Just at this critical moment the President learned of a piece of German intrigue which more than any other single thing destroyed all his trust in German good faith.

In the middle of January, 1917, German Foreign Secretary Zimmermann had dispatched to the German minister in Mexico a coded message, informing him of the decision to resume unrestricted submarine warfare on February 1. In case war between Germany and the United States resulted, the minister was instructed to propose an alliance with Mexico on the following basis: the two countries should make peace and war together; Germany would give general financial support; and it was to be understood that Mexico would use the war against the United States "to reconquer the lost territory in New Mexico, Texas, and Arizona." It was furthermore suggested "that the President of Mexico on his own initiative should communicate with Japan suggesting adherence at once to this plan; at the same time offer to mediate between Germany and Japan."

British naval intelligence officers had intercepted this message when it left Germany; the British government, however, had shrewdly refrained from handing it over to American officials until German-American relations had approached a breaking point. On February 25, the Zimmermann note was in Wilson's hands; on the next day he appeared before Congress to ask approval for the arming of American merchant ships.

To understand the indignation with which the President regarded this German invitation for Mexico and Japan to join in an attack upon the United States, it must be remembered that the document bore a date showing that it had been prepared at the very time when the German officials were urging Wilson to continue his efforts for peace. All this was bad enough; but a few days later the President learned of further circumstances that seemed to aggravate the outrage. In order to send and receive confidential messages concerning the proposed peace negotiations, Ambassador Bernstorff had been granted the unusual privilege of exchanging cipher messages with Berlin through the American State Department; it was through an abuse of this hospitality that the German government had sent the Zimmermann note to Bernstorff for retransmission to Mexico. British intelligence officers, for their part in this amazing episode, had unblushingly intercepted the message en route between the American Embassy in Berlin and the American State Department.

Aware of the tremendous effect that publication of the Zimmermann note would have on public opinion, Wilson at first hesitated to give it out to the press. But he soon decided to do so, and the news of the incident was published throughout the country on March 1. Great excitement was aroused, and the rising war spirit of the nation was obvious to all observers. There were some, however, who asserted that the Zimmermann note was a British forgery, calculated to force the United States into war on the side of Great Britain. This charge was invalidated when Secretary Zimmermann admitted his authorship.

Despite Wilson's personal appeal and the warlike mood of most of the country, the bill for arming merchant ships did not become law. True, the measure passed the House by a vote of 403 to 14, but in the Senate a group of eleven legislators, headed by Senators LaFollette of Wisconsin and George Norris of Nebraska, succeeded through a spectacular filibuster in preventing the measure from coming to a vote before the adjournment of Congress on March 4. The President bitterly condemned these obstructionist Senators in a statement to the press: "A little group of willful men, representing no opinion but their own, have rendered the great Government of the United States helpless and contemptible." Consequently, much against his original wish but realizing now the need for speedy action, Wilson himself, on March 12, gave the order for the arming of merchant ships. He used as his authority a statute which had originally been passed during the administration of John Adams in 1797.

Most American opinion, however, was clamoring for still more drastic measures. The events of the past six weeks had already aroused great indignation; now news of the sinking of several American ships, the *Algonquin,* the *Vigilancia,* the *City of Memphis,* and the *Healdton,* mostly without warning, and the resultant loss of American lives, brought the country to a fighting pitch.

Just at that moment, the dramatic news came out of Russia that popular demonstrations had forced the abdication of the Czar and the establishment of a constitutional government. America emphatically approved; the United States was the first government in the world to recognize the new regime. The event seemed to clarify the issues of the war; now the Allied cause appeared to be truly that of democracy struggling against absolutism. No one felt this more keenly than did Wilson. "If our entering the war," he said, "would hasten and fix the movements in Russia and Germany, it would be a marked gain to the world and would tend to give additional justification to the whole struggle."

With those two developments, the actual sinking of more American ships, and the news of the Russian Revolution, Wilson at last made up his mind that his country must enter the war. But to make doubly sure that he was right, he called a special cabinet meeting on March 20 and, without informing the members of his own position on the subject, he asked them their opinion as to what course the United States should follow under the circumstances. With but little discussion, the Cabinet quickly supported a declaration of war against Germany. On the following day, March 21, the country heard the news it had been expecting; the new Congress was being called into special session to receive a Presidential message on "grave questions of national policy."

Since this message could mean but one thing, war, it was an impressive assembly which President Wilson faced in the House chamber on the evening of April 2. Directly in front of the Speaker's desk sat the Justices of the Supreme Court. On one side were the cabinet officials and, immediately behind them, the diplomatic corps, sitting for the first time on the floor of the House. Other distinguished visitors crowded the galleries. After the Representatives had taken their places, the Senators filed in, most of them wearing or carrying little American flags.

Wilson's address was worthy of the occasion. First, he reviewed the history of the submarine controversy, stressing, not the loss of property involved, but "the wanton and wholesale destruction of the lives of non-combatants, men, women, and children, engaged in pursuits which have always, even in the darkest periods of modern history, been deemed innocent and legitimate." Property could be paid for, the lives of peaceful and innocent people could not be. German submarine activities were "a warfare against mankind." Therefore he asked that Congress declare the recent course of the Imperial German

Government to be in fact nothing less than war against the government and people of the United States and that it formally accept the status of belligerent. Then followed an eloquent statement of America's war objectives. With the German people, Wilson asserted, the United States had no quarrel; it was not upon their impulse that their government acted in entering the war. The United States would fight for the ultimate peace of the world and for the liberation of its peoples, the Germans included. "The world must," he said, "be made safe for democracy." After admitting that it was a fearful thing to lead a great peaceful people into war, he concluded with these stirring words:

But the right is more precious than peace, and we shall fight for the things which we have always carried nearest our hearts,—for democracy, for the right of those who submit to authority to have a voice in their own Governments, for the rights and liberties of small nations, for a universal dominion of right by such a concert of free peoples as shall bring peace and safety to all nations and make the world itself at last free. To such a task we can dedicate our lives and our fortunes, everything that we are and everything that we have, with the pride of those who know that the day has come when America is privileged to spend her blood and her might for the principles that gave her birth and happiness and the peace which she has treasured. God helping her, she can do no other.

The President's address was frequently interrupted by wild applause; there was no question but that Congress and the country would follow his leadership. The opponents of war were beaten and they knew it. On April 4 there was a spirited, but brief, debate in the Senate on a resolution declaring that a state of war existed between the United States and Germany. Senator LaFollette, supported by Norris and Stone (of Missouri), fought against the measure, yet it was passed late that evening by a vote of eighty-two to six. All the next day the House debated, and the final ballot was not taken until three o'clock on the morning of the sixth. The Representatives approved the war declaration by a vote of 373 to 50; Miss Jeannette Rankin, the only woman in Congress, voted with the minority. That afternoon of April 6, 1917, President Wilson signed the declaration, and the United States was at war with Germany.

WHY AMERICA FOUGHT

In later years much was said and written about why the United States went to war in 1917. One school of thought held that Americans had been tricked by British propaganda; another, that bankers and munitions makers had insisted upon the country's active participation to save the money which they had loaned to the Allies and to make bigger profits; a third, that Wilson had from the beginning wanted to lead the nation into the war and that he had deliberately adopted policies designed to bring about this result.

British propaganda there was, and in abundance, but the Germans were scarcely less active. Why did the majority of Americans believe the British and not their opponents? Fundamentally, it was because the Allies had the stronger case. Although many of the atrocity stories were exaggerated or untrue, the deeds which most hopelessly damned the Germans in the eyes of most Americans were things which could not be denied, things like the violation of Belgian neutrality and the sinking of the *Lusitania*. These actions seemed to show that Germany was utterly ruthless in seeking to fulfill her ambitions. Moreover, educated and influential Americans, particularly if they lived in the East, tended to see the issues of war in exactly the same light as did the same kind of people in England. The best spokesmen for the Allied cause were respected citizens like Theodore Roosevelt, Elihu Root, Leonard Wood, Henry Cabot Lodge, and ex-President Charles W. Eliot of Harvard, men whom it would be absurd to think of as the paid propagandists of Great Britain.

It is undeniable that American financial involvement in the war had become very great by 1917. And American industry had boomed on war orders, while British control of the seas resulted in American munitions going almost exclusively to the Allies. Furthermore, when the Allies ran out of money, they secured loans through American bankers. Undoubtedly these economic factors did help to stimulate strong pro-Ally sentiment among industrialists and financiers. But the sentiment of those individuals would not have been much different had such trade and loans been prohibited. The charge that Wilson himself was influenced by the bankers to ask Congress for a declaration of war is absurd. Not only does it receive no support from the documents, but it entirely misrepresents the character of a man who placed much more value in ideals and principles than he did in dollars, and who was particularly suspicious of suggestions that could be traced to Wall Street.

Nor does the theory that Wilson plotted from the beginning to get the country into the war hold together. To be sure, he was pro-Ally and anti-German, but he was less so than almost any other public man who had a similar background—less so, for example, than Page, House, Lansing, and most of the members of his cabinet. He accepted the idea that the United States might in the end have to enter the war and, if it did so, he certainly intended that it should be on the Allied side. But he much preferred that the United States should keep out and use its great influence to bring about a just and durable peace. Instead of becoming more pro-Ally, Wilson had, by January, 1917, become "really neutral," an admission that came from Ambassador Bernstorff himself. The conclusion is inescapable that it was the submarine issue that was decisive. Had not the German government decided to return to unrestricted submarine warfare, the United States might easily have remained neutral; but with the German announcement of the return, there was nothing honorable left for Wilson to do except ask for war, particularly after the stand he had taken in the *Sussex* affair. Only through war, Wilson believed, could the United States maintain the long-cherished doctrine of freedom of the seas.

WIN THE WAR ON THE OTHER SIDE OR WE SHALL HAVE TO FIGHT IT ON THIS SIDE OF THE ATLANTIC

An Ounce of Prevention Is Worth a Pound of Cure. (By Stinson in the *Dayton Daily News*.)

On the other hand, a more effective criticism of Wilson is that, although he really desired to keep the United States out of war, he followed policies which defeated his purpose. This was the accusation of Senator LaFollette in the debate on the declaration of war. According to the Wisconsin legislator, the Democratic administration made a fatal mistake. It had "assumed and acted upon the policy that it could enforce to the very letter of the law the principles of international law against one belligerent and relax them to the other." That thing, LaFollette continued, no nation could do without losing the rights that went with "strict and absolute neutrality."

The question which must be answered in the final analysis is this: Was World War I a struggle of such a character that the United States could afford the kind of "strict and absolute neutrality" which LaFollette was thinking about? Such neutrality might have resulted in a crushing defeat of Britain and France and so resounding a victory for the Central Powers that the German military caste would have been encouraged to seek further triumphs. Would such an outcome to the war have been desirable from the standpoint of American interests? Looking back from our present vantage point, the answer seems obvious. Complete German dominance of Europe, followed as it must inevitably have been by mastery of the Atlantic Ocean, would have created such a new situation in world politics as to affect most seriously the security of the United States. Since this was so, "strict and absolute neutrality" was as unrealistic in the years following 1914 as it was in the years following 1939. Wilson may be criticized for not having stressed the issue more in his war messages. Probably he himself did not see it clearly. It was characteristic of him that he thought and talked more in terms of legal rights and moral principles than in those of national interest.

Once having accepted the idea of war, Wilson laid great stress on the ends he hoped to gain: the furtherance of democracy, insurance of the rights and liberties of small nations, and the establishment of a league of nations. He assumed that he spoke for the entire nation in stating these war aims, and in the exaltation of the moment it seemed that he did. As time went on, however, it became apparent that many Americans, while accepting the necessity of war against Germany, rejected the Wilsonian conception of the ultimate war objectives.

9

War for Democracy

THE UNITED STATES WAS AT WAR, BUT WHAT DID WAR UNDER SUCH CIR-
cumstances mean? How did one nation fight another 3000 miles away?
Americans both in civilian life and official position were not sure.

The navy was thrown into the struggle at once. Since the German
submarine campaign had brought the country into the world conflict,
it was natural that American warships should join with the British and
the French in a great combined effort to clear the Atlantic of the undersea raiders. Indeed, even before the actual declaration of war, Rear
Admiral William S. Sims had been quietly sent to England, and by
April he was ready to help plan joint operations of the British and
American navies. Sims was soon promoted to the rank of vice-admiral
and given command of all naval ships of the United States in European
waters. In May the first of these—a flotilla of destroyers—reached
Queenstown, Ireland, and gradually thereafter a large part of the navy
was transferred to trans-Atlantic bases. Special help in destroying submarines was desperately needed by the English, who were losing several hundred thousand tons of shipping each month.

The Allies were not slow in making other needs known. Within
three weeks of the declaration of war, British and French war missions
arrived in the United States. Eager to find outlets for their patriotic
zeal, Americans gave the envoys an enthusiastic greeting. Foreign Secretary A. J. Balfour, the head of the British delegation, received the unusual honor of being invited to address the House of Representatives.
The heartiest welcome, however, was reserved for Marshal Joffre, who
was popularly credited with having saved France at the first battle of
the Marne. The famous war hero was lionized to such a degree that most
Americans failed to realize that the actual head of the French mission
was not Joffre, but René Viviani, a former premier.

First of all, it was money that the missions were seeking. The British had served as bankers for the Allied cause for almost three years; now they were hard pressed for further assets that could be converted to the purchase of food and munitions. Even before the missions arrived in Washington, that need had been anticipated in the Emergency Loan Act, passed by Congress without a dissenting vote and signed by the President on April 24. This measure authorized adding $5,000,000,000 to the national debt in the form of bonds bearing 3½ per cent interest. Three billion of this the Treasury was empowered to loan at the same interest rate to nations "engaged in war with the enemies of the United States." The first advances to Britain and France under this authorization were made on April 25. Many more loans were to follow, and other states at war with Germany hastened to send their own war missions to secure a share in the distribution. During the next eighteen months, more than $7,000,000,000 was loaned by the American government to the governments of Great Britain, France, Italy, Russia, Jugoslavia, and Cuba. Most of the money was spent in the United States for the products of American factories and farms.

Naval support, money, and goods—these things obviously the United States could contribute to the campaign against the Central Powers, but this, most observers in April, 1917, believed, was about all the nation could do. That the United States could create a large army, train it, equip it, and transport it over 3000 miles of submarine-infested water to the western front seemed fantastic not only to the Germans, but to the British, the French, and most Americans as well.

Notwithstanding the apparent impossibility of large-scale military support, Marshal Joffre appealed to the American authorities to send at least a small force to France at once. Although Americans did not realize it at the time, the French were dangerously weary of the war. Their burdens seemed too heavy to be borne much longer. It was hoped that the sight of fresh American troops, no matter how few, marching through Paris would stiffen sagging French morale. As early as May 8 Wilson and Secretary of War Baker decided to respond to Joffre's appeal. Major General John J. Pershing, who had but a few months before been pursuing Villa through northern Mexico, was designated to command the American Expeditionary Force. On June 26, 1917, the first American regiments began to disembark at St. Nazaire, France.

Pershing's initial command contained about 14,500 men, enough to parade and receive the plaudits of the French, but a mere handful as armies were counted in 1917. After examining the military situation, the American general came to the immediate conclusion that the Allies

General Pershing and Secretary of War Baker. (Brown Bros.)

were too much weakened by three years of war to launch a winning offensive. Only American intervention on a large scale, Pershing believed, could break the stalemate and crush the enemy. On July 6 he informed the War Department that plans "should contemplate sending over one million men" by the next May, with additional millions to follow. In short, the impossible would have to be accomplished.

RAISING AN ARMY

Although the project of sending a million soldiers to France was a new and breath-taking one, the idea that the existence of a state of war would require a greatly enlarged army for national defense was not. When war was declared, the General Staff advocated immediate conscription, and President Wilson and Secretary Baker accepted the principle at once. They believed that in a democracy the obligation for military service should be universal. Furthermore, they had ample warning of the difficulties involved in recruiting as a result of the recent experience of the British, who had depended on volunteering during the first years of the war. The greatest weakness of the system had proved to be, not that it failed to bring large numbers of men into the armed forces, but that all too often it brought the wrong men, or the right men at the wrong time. There was wastage of man power as men gave up vital production jobs to answer the call of king and country, or as fine potential-officer material left school to serve as privates and contribute an appallingly large proportion of the early casualties of the war. "The idea of a selective draft," wrote Wilson to a doubting Congressman, "is that those should be chosen for service in the Army who can be most readily spared from the prosecution of the other activities which the country must engage in and to which it must devote a great deal of its best energy and capacity."

The Selective Service Bill, which was introduced into Congress in April, originated in the office of General Enoch H. Crowder, the Judge Advocate General of the Army. It was written largely by Captain Hugh S. Johnson, who had recently been with Pershing in Mexico and who was destined sixteen years later to be one of the most colorful figures in the early days of the New Deal. The most striking characteristic of Johnson's scheme was that the draft should be administered, not by the army nor by Washington bureaucrats, but by public-spirited civilians serving in their own local communities.

Despite the democratic machinery proposed, the Selective Service Bill was not passed without a struggle. Speaker Champ Clark expressed the blunt judgment that "in the estimation of Missourians there is precious little difference between a conscript and a convict." The Democratic chairman of the House Military Affairs Committee, Dent of Alabama, opposed the measure; therefore the leadership in the fight to secure its passage had to be entrusted to Julius Kahn of California, a Republican and a naturalized American born in Germany. One of the points of controversy was over the age limits for registrants. The War

Department preferred to have men from nineteen to twenty-five; Congress, however, rebelled at the thought of drafting youths too young to vote. Eventually the limits for the first registration were placed at twenty-one to thirty.

The most bitter issue of the debate was an amendment proposed by admirers of Theodore Roosevelt, which would have made it mandatory for the President to accept volunteer units in the army under their own officers. This project reflected the patriotic ambition of the ex-President to raise a division of volunteers and lead them into battle on the western front, just as the Rough Riders had been recruited in 1898. Roosevelt had begun accepting tentative enlistments to such a unit as soon as war had been declared; on April 10, he had called on Wilson at the White House to urge that his volunteers be accepted. The idea was typically Rooseveltian—colorful and exciting—and it aroused the enthusiastic support of many Americans. But the army was thoroughly opposed. Modern war was declared to be a business for professionals; to commission a civilian to command an expeditionary force would be a disastrous precedent; the use of political generals in the Civil War had cost the lives of many soldiers. Wilson and Baker accepted the adverse decision of the professional soldiers and used the strength of the administration to prevent the amendment of the Selective Service Bill in such a way that Roosevelt's division would have to be sent to the battle front. Instead, the President was left at liberty to accept volunteer units, or to reject them.

The bill was finally passed and signed by Wilson on May 18. Without delay the President settled the issue raised by the Roosevelt volunteers by issuing a blunt statement that this was "not the time for compliment or for any action not calculated to contribute to the immediate success of the war." The rebuff to the popular ex-President inevitably aroused controversy. Wilson's action was attributed by many to petty jealousy and partisanship. Similar accusations were brought against both the President and Secretary Baker when it became obvious that General Leonard Wood was to be kept in the United States, rather than given active command in France. But here again the civilian heads of the army were basing their policy upon professional advice. Pershing was chosen for the European command because he had had more recent experience and because he was younger and in better health. Once selected, Pershing was given a free hand in choosing his subordinates, and he was opposed to using Wood in any capacity.

The President designated June 5 as registration day, and the event was awaited with some anxiety. Memories of draft riots during the Civil War haunted certain gloomy souls; Senator Reed of Missouri predicted that the attempt to enforce conscription would cause the streets of American cities to run with blood. But nothing of the kind occurred. On the appointed day more than nine and a half million young men appeared before 4557 local selective service boards and filled out their registration blanks. The registrants of each board received serial numbers in the order of filing. On July 20, Secretary of War Baker took his place before a large bowl containing 10,319 capsules—the largest number registered with any single board. While cameras clicked, he drew out the first capsule and read the number on the slip it contained. The news was flashed throughout the country that men holding serial number 258 would be the first called for classification before each local draft board. The drawing continued until each registrant had been assigned a call number. Eventually all were grouped into five classes, based upon their availability for armed service, their obligations toward dependents, and the degree of importance attached to their civilian occupation. A total of 3,706,544 registrants were placed in Class I—subject to military duty. As men became twenty-one years of age, they were enrolled in later registrations. Since the needs of the services seemed likely to outrun the resources of the twenty-one to thirty age group, all men between the ages of eighteen and forty-five not previously registered were required to enroll on September 12, 1918. All told, 24,-234,021 men registered under Selective Service during World War I. Thousands of men did not wait for the draft, but enlisted in the Regular Army, the National Guard, the Navy, or the Marine Corps. This continued until August 9, 1918, when the government discontinued volunteering for all the services. On April 2, 1917, just before

c. 1917 by John T. McCutcheon.

Selective Conscription Will Pan Out Well. (From the *Chicago Tribune*.)

Wilson's war message to Congress, the total number of men in the armed forces was 378,619; on Armistice Day, 1918, the number had grown to 4,791,172.

TRAINING THE ARMED FORCES

Finding the men, however, was comparatively easy. Transforming millions of civilians into soldiers was immeasurably more difficult. First of all, the men had to be housed. In June, 1917, construction was begun on sixteen camps to receive the draftees and volunteers. Each camp had to be a complete city, equipped to quarter and feed 48,000 men. Impatient critics sniffed at the wooden barracks, recreation centers, and modern plumbing. Soldiers pampered with these luxuries, they asserted, would be soft for the conditions of the battlefields. But the experience of other wars had taught that unhealthy training centers were likely to kill more soldiers than would enemy bullets.

The building of the camps was a miracle of speedy construction. Even so, they were far from completed on September 5, 1917, when the first men of the new National Army were mobilized. Not all of the 687,000 men called up in the first draft were in cantonments by Christmas.

General Pershing had notified the War Department that he wanted all instruction for the new soldiers to "contemplate the assumption of a vigorous offensive." The problem of finding a sufficient number of instructors to teach the methods of warfare which had been worked out on European battlefields was difficult. In part it was solved by the employment of numerous British and French officers, loaned to the American Army for this purpose.

One of the most serious needs was for officers. Fortunately, General Wood had foreseen this and at Plattsburg, New York, and elsewhere the process of giving officer training to intelligent civilians had been started well before the country's involvement in war. The War Department set up special officer training camps where university students and other young men, competitively selected, were given intensive three-month courses, after which those found competent were commissioned as second lieutenants.

ECONOMIC MOBILIZATION

Under authority of the Army Appropriation Act of August 29, 1916, there had been created a Council of National Defense, comprising six cabinet officers—the Secretaries of War, Navy, Interior, Agriculture, Commerce, and Labor. This council had advisory powers only, but it was charged, among other things, with the "coordination of industries and resources for the national security and welfare," and with the "creation of relations which will render possible in time of need the immediate concentration and utilization of the resources of the Nation." To furnish essential information for this council, the President was directed to appoint an Advisory Commission of seven specially qualified persons to serve without compensation. The men picked for this work were: Daniel Willard of the Baltimore and Ohio Railroad, who advised on transportation problems; President Hollis Godfrey of Drexel Institute, engineering and education; Howard Coffin, a leading automotive engineer, manufacturing and munitions; Dr. Franklin H. Martin, medicine and surgery; Bernard Baruch, a successful Wall Street operator, raw materials; Julius Rosenwald of Sears, Roebuck, supplies; and Samuel Gompers, president of the American Federation of Labor, labor relations.

Although for some months the activities of these commissioners consisted largely of conferences and discussions, by March, 1917, a considerable organization had developed, consisting of committees of experts drawn from varied lines of industry. But in handling the problems involved in guiding the transition of the national economy from a peace to a war basis, the National Defense Council and its dollar-a-year advisers were laboring under serious handicaps. They lacked authority, their advice was often ignored, and the various agencies of the government worked at cross-purposes. Moreover, there was criticism that in counseling the government while maintaining a place on the pay rolls of private corporations, the men attached to the Advisory Commission were serving two masters, whose interests did not always coincide. Gradually more and more work was assumed by new powerful and independent administrative bodies, staffed by men who had cut their ties with private business. These agencies in turn came to be largely dominated by individual administrators with vast power.

One such independent agency was already in existence when war was declared. This was the United States Shipping Board, established under an act of September 7, 1916, and actually organized in January, 1917, under the chairmanship of William Denman of California. The Board was empowered to buy, lease, or build ships and operate them through the Emergency Fleet Corporation. The increasing emphasis placed on expansion of the merchant marine may be measured by the growth of the government-supplied capital which was poured into the enterprise. Originally fixed at $50,000,000, it had been enlarged to $1,934,000,000 by October, 1917.

Ships were bought, seized, and built. As soon as war was declared, 105 enemy-owned vessels interned in American ports were turned over to the Shipping Board. Their former crews, anticipating this action, had attempted to render these ships useless by damaging vital machinery. Ingenuity and hard work, however, made possible the repair of the vessels, and they were put into service within a few months. The Emergency Fleet Corporation also commandeered some four hundred ships in the process of construction in American shipyards, mostly for British and Norwegian owners.

The necessity of embarking on the building of new ships in great volume led to a bitter controversy between Chairman Denman, who believed that wooden ships could be built quickly and cheaply, and Major General George W. Goethals of Panama Canal construction fame and now manager of the Emergency Fleet Corporation, who asserted that steel ships should be the chief item in the program. Eventually the President had to accept the resignation of both men and appoint Edward N. Hurley, a Chicago businessman, to head both board and corporation. Not only were both steel and wooden ships now built, but even concrete vessels. Many new shipyards were opened, the largest being that at Hog Island, near Philadelphia, and many ingenious methods of speeding up construction were devised. Ship design was standardized, many parts were prefabricated in various factories, and the work of the shipyards simplified to the point where it was primarily one of assembly. By the fall of 1918, forty-four steel ships and ninety-six wooden ones were coming off the ways each month. Despite these striking achievements, not many of the new ships actually went into service before the armistice. The most effective work of the Shipping Board was that of coordinating the use of existing vessels in an efficient manner.

A second powerful agency of economic mobilization was the Food Administration. As early as April 11, 1917, the Council of National Defense recognized the importance of the food problem and created a committee on food supply and prices with Herbert C. Hoover as chairman. Hoover was a man in whom the public took a great interest. Successful as a mining engineer in the United States, China, and Australia, he was representing extensive business interests in London at the outbreak of war. Heading a committee organized to aid American tourists placed in serious difficulties by the onset of hostilities, Hoover handled the job so effectively that he was placed in charge of the newly created Belgian Relief Commission. Within a few weeks he became a world figure because of his success in helping the Belgians without arousing the opposition of either the Allies or the Germans. When the United States abandoned neutrality, Hoover had to terminate his work in Belgium and return to the United States. His recent experience made him the ideal man to head the American food administration.

Hoover at once objected to the purely advisory character of his committee; he demanded full 'powers and a free hand. On May 20, 1917, he was named Food Commissioner and made independent of the Council of National Defense, but not yet did he have sufficient legal authority to take the drastic steps which he believed necessary. In June, Congress began to consider the Lever Bill which proposed the establishment of government control over the production and distribution of both food and fuel. The powers which were to be granted over a whole vast area of American economic life had no precedent in the history of the United States. Farmers were much opposed to such a "dictatorship" and asserted that the administration was pushing the proposal because of its subservience to organized labor.

After extensive debate, the Lever Act was passed on August 10, 1917. In its final form, it gave the President authority to erect controls over foods, feeds, fuels, and fertilizers, and the machinery and equipment for producing them. It fixed a minimum price of $2.00 a bushel for the 1918 wheat crop and empowered the President to set in advance the minimum price for succeeding years. The antiliquor forces won a striking victory by forcing into the measure a section prohibiting the use of food to manufacture "distilled spirits for beverage purposes" and authorizing the President to forbid such use for "malt or vinous liquors."

Hoover was now appointed Food Administrator, and the volunteer organization he had already built up was given legal basis. Much of the agency's activitiy was educational. Housewives were not subjected to formal rationing, but they were enjoined to use up leftovers, to substitute dark bread for white, and to observe wheatless Mondays and Wednesdays, meatless Tuesdays, and porkless Thursdays and Saturdays. The menfolk were exhorted to plant victory gardens even if it meant sacrificing the front lawn. Yet Hoover did not hesitate to use coercive powers when necessary. The activities of millers were conducted under a strict licensing system. Hoarding and profiteering were severely dealt with. Farmers were encouraged to produce through the establishment of a fixed price for wheat of $2.20—twenty cents above the minimum guaranteed by the Lever Act. To stabilize the market, a government-owned Grain Corporation was established, and this precedent led later to the creation of a Sugar Equalization Board. Increased production and conservation made possible the exportation to the Allied nations of three times the amount of foodstuffs shipped to the same countries before 1914.

Another war agency deriving its authority from the Lever Act was the Fuel Administration, headed by Harry A. Garfield, son of a former President of the United States and himself president of Williams College. The price of coal was fixed sufficiently high to stimulate production and the public was implored to use fuel sparingly. The importance of gasoline to modern war was reflected in a ban, enforced by public opinion alone, upon all but essential driving on Sundays.

Despite Garfield's efforts, transportation tie-ups resulted in a serious fuel crisis in January, 1918. Thirty-seven ships loaded with munitions were held up in New York harbor for lack of coal. Before the public had become aware of the seriousness of the situation, the startling news came out of Washington that for five days starting January 18 all factories east of the Mississippi, except plants making munitions or other essential supplies, were to be closed and that thereafter "heatless Mondays" were to be observed for the next nine weeks. Garfield's order was denounced as both arbitrary and unnecessary, but the President upheld the action of his Administrator.

And, By Ginger, He Can Play 'em All! But it keeps Uncle Sam busy these days. (By Donahey in the *Cleveland Plain Dealer*.)

The fuel emergency was an outgrowth of a transportation crisis which had come to a showdown the month before. One of the voluntary bodies organized by the Council of National Defense had been a Railroads War Board, made up of prominent rail executives. Although the Board's power was only advisory, much had been done to coordinate the operations of the independent lines, and a system of freight priorities had been worked out to expedite the movement of vital supplies. Serious problems, however, had arisen. Tremendous quantities of freight moved to the Atlantic coast for shipment to Europe with the result that cars, which could not be unloaded fast enough, jammed the yards of Eastern terminals, while the rest of the country was starved for "empties." The onset of winter accentuated all these difficulties. Therefore, on December 28, 1917, the President, acting under authority of the Army Appropriation Act of 1916, took over the management of all the rail lines of the country. William Gibbs McAdoo, Secretary of the Treasury and Wilson's son-in-law, was made Director General of the Railroads and he proceeded to develop an organization under which the lines were operated as a single consolidated system.

Less known to the general public than the well-advertised activities of Hurley, Hoover, Garfield, and McAdoo, was the work of the War Trade Board, headed by Vance McCormick. A number of laws culminating with the Trading-with-the-Enemy Act of October 6, 1917, conferred power on McCormick's agency to control all American exports and imports. Through a system of licenses and the black-listing of firms in neutral countries, the British blockade of Germany was powerfully implemented and each month the economic strangulation of the enemy came closer to fulfillment.

BERNARD BARUCH: ECONOMIC DICTATOR

Meantime the need of arming and equipping a vast military machine had made the government the most important customer of American industry. But the difficulty was that the government contracted for the products of the nation's factories not as a single unit, but through numerous separate agencies which competed vigorously against each other. The confusion was increased by the separate purchasing activities of the Allies and by the shortages which inevitably appeared as one industry bid against another for essential raw materials. The Council of National Defense struggled with various expedients to bring order out of chaos, and finally on July 28, 1917, the War Industries Board was created with Frank A. Scott, a Cleveland manufacturer, as its first chairman. The most important functions which the new board began to exercise were those of setting up a system of priorities and of fixing prices for numerous essential raw materials.

Like all the creations of the Council of National Defense, the War Industries Board, as originally organized, had merely advisory powers. Neither government purchasing agencies on one side nor businessmen on the other were under any legal obligation to follow its orders. The need for giving the board an independent status similar to that of the Shipping Board, the Food Administration, and the other war agencies became increasingly apparent and in 1918 it was reorganized. Bernard M. Baruch was named chairman and given vast powers, while the board was removed from the jurisdiction of the Council of National Defense and made an independent administrative agency directly responsible to the President.

In the end, the vast organization built up by Baruch acted as a clearing house to which all the government purchasing bureaus and those of the Allies submitted their requirements. The board then planned how these were to be met and which needs were to be given precedence over others. The search for new sources of critical raw materials led Baruch's lieutenants to survey not only the resources of the United States, but those of the entire world. The construction of new industrial plants was made possible, and existing ones were guided in their conversion from civilian to war production. The country had passed for the time being under a planned economy, and Baruch, affable and diplomatic though he was, wielded the vast powers of an economic dictator.

There were many disappointments in war production. To create a vast aircraft industry out of nothing proved much more difficult than anticipated by easygoing optimists. By Armistice Day about eleven hundred planes and approximately thirty-two thousand "Liberty" motors had been manufactured, but American aviators in combat had only about two hundred of them. Not until three months before the Armistice were Browning machine guns available in quantities sufficient to equip the American troops at the front, while the war was over before American-made heavy artillery appeared in France. In many lines, as in shipping, American production was just beginning to achieve large volume when hostilities ceased. This led to pointed criticisms of the administration in both Congress and the press. But to the Germans, the wonder was not that the Yankees produced so little, but that they produced so much. When the Kaiser's generals undertook in later years to explain why the Fatherland lost the war, they gave full credit to American industry, and they uttered the name "Baruch" with regretful awe. Strangely enough, it had remained for the United States—antimilitary in tradition though it was—to develop the organization of "total war."

LABOR AND THE WAR

One of the country's greatest assets during 1917 and 1918 was the patriotism and loyalty of Samuel Gompers. Not only did the president of the American Federation of Labor use his influence to combat radical socialists, who sought to convince the workers that the war was merely for capitalist aggrandizement, but he endeavored to prevent strikes and to allay the natural uneasiness with which union men saw women and nonunion labor recruits streaming into jobs in war plants. The general public, observing Gompers fraternize with the great industrialists of the Council of National Defense, was as much amazed as though the vision of the wolf dwelling with the lamb had suddenly become reality.

On the issue of wages, however, labor's patience had definite limits. With the cost of living going rapidly up and the country's wage scales none too generous to begin with, there were demands for pay increases on every side. In taking over the management of the railroads, the government found itself confronted with a particularly serious situation. Despite increases during 1916 and 1917, 80 per cent of all the railroad employees received only $100 a month or less. The government proceeded to make substantial raises. In the words of Director McAdoo these were not only adjustments to meet the rising cost of living, but were intended "to find a just and equitable basis which would outlive the war and which would give a living wage and decent working conditions to every railroad employee." The war had made the government the country's greatest employer, with thousands of workers receiving pay in government-owned shipyards and war plants. Moreover, many private construction companies and factories were working on war contracts on a cost-plus basis. On every hand, the payment of higher wages seemed infinitely preferable to serious labor controversy.

Disputes and strikes, however, still threatened production in many quarters. On April 8, 1918, a National War Labor Board was appointed with ex-President Taft and Frank P. Walsh, a prominent labor lawyer, as joint chairmen. The board was to hold hearings and make recommendations when all other methods of settling labor controversies had failed. During the next year the board heard more than a thousand cases. In the few instances where the parties showed an inclination to ignore its rulings, the President used or threatened coercion. Thus the

War Department commandeered the Smith and Wesson plant at Springfield, Massachusetts, after noncompliance by its management, while workers in Bridgeport, Connecticut, who resisted orders of the Taft-Walsh Board, were threatened with cancellation of their draft deferments.

Other important new agencies were the War Labor Policies Board with Felix Frankfurter as chairman, which worked out uniform labor standards for those employed by the government, and the United States Employment Service, which found jobs for 3,700,000 men and women.

WHERE THE MONEY CAME FROM

Waging modern war involved the expenditure of money in amounts which seemed fabulous to Americans accustomed to peacetime national budgets of less than $750,000,000 annually. Between July 1, 1917, and June 30, 1920, the outlays of the United States government averaged $12,500,000,000 each year.

A few prominent citizens believed that the war could be financed on a "pay-as-you-go" basis. The American Committee on War Finance, headed by Amos Pinchot, advocated such a policy, and Senator LaFollette urged it in the Senate—largely because it would penalize American war manufacturers whom he suspected of having forced the country into hostilities. Most Americans, however, believed that taxes sufficiently heavy to pay the war bills as they came in would paralyze national economic life. Secretary of the Treasury McAdoo eventually recommended that one third of the costs be met by taxation and the remainder by loans. Most businessmen thought that this was too much; they would have preferred the ratio of taxes to loans to be about one to five, the ratio of Federal financing during the Civil War.

After six months of deliberation, the Revenue Act of 1917 was passed in October. Excise taxes were levied on nearly everything in sight; in addition to such familiar tax victims as tobacco and alcoholic beverages, the list now included transportation, communications, insurance, automobiles, pianos, phonographs, amusements, jewelry, patent medicines, and even chewing gum. The principal controversy had been over fixing the rates at which incomes and war profits should be taxed. The income tax was a recent addition to the regular tax structure and no one knew just how much the recipients of large incomes could or should be obliged to pay. After allowing $1000 exemption for unmarried persons and $2000 for heads of families, the final schedule provided for graduated taxes which rose from 2 per cent on the lowest taxable incomes to 67 per cent on all income in excess of $2,000,000. Corporations were taxed at the rate of 6 per cent of their net income, while profits in excess of what was considered normal both on the basis of invested capital and prewar earnings were taxed at rates graduated from 20 to 60 per cent.

Never before had the United States government attempted to lay such heavy taxes directly on individuals and corporations. Yet the war machine demanded still more. The Revenue Act of 1918 raised income tax rates to 6 per cent on the lowest brackets and 77 per cent on incomes in the highest level, now defined as those in excess of $1,000,000. The corporation income tax rate was doubled, while excess profits were subjected to an 80 per cent levy in the highest bracket.

Meantime the government was borrowing money from its own citizens in amounts hitherto deemed impossible by practical financiers. When McAdoo was planning the first Liberty Bond drive, J. P. Morgan advised him to fix $1,000,000,000 as the goal. The optimistic Treasury head decided to seek $2,000,000,000 instead. When the books were closed on this first loan, this quota was oversubscribed by more than $1,000,000,000. Succeeding loans were equally successful and, in the end, the four Liberty Loans and the Victory Loan, which was sold just after the Armistice, brought into the Treasury $21,448,120,330. School children and other persons of small means contributed another $800,-000,000 through the purchase of thrift stamps and war-savings certificates.

The Liberty Bond campaigns were skillfully organized through committees in every city, town, and village. Moving-picture programs were interrupted so that the patriotic appeal could be made from the stage by "four-minute" speakers, while in cities like New York, stage and screen celebrities contributed their services to sell the bonds. So successfully was the message hammered home that more than twenty-one million individuals purchased bonds during the fourth loan drive.

The United States spent almost $22,000,000,000 in direct war expenditures and loaned another $10,000,000,000 to its cobelligerents. Just about one third of the total outlay was raised by taxes and two thirds by loans; war financing, in short, followed closely the recommendations of Secretary McAdoo.

WITCH-HUNTING

As soon as war was declared, many Americans became acutely spy-conscious. They imagined that they saw mysterious lights at night, or asserted that German agents were plotting to poison Red Cross bandages or to wipe out entire communities by planting germs in the public drinking water. Such hysterical ideas were not entirely unnatural since there had been some evidence of German sabotage activities during the days of neutrality. German-Americans were suspected of disloyalty and were the victims of numerous local persecutions. Sometimes serious incidents occurred, as when Robert Prager, a German-American Socialist, was lynched by a mob in Collinsville, Illinois.

Congress enacted new laws empowering the government to deal drastically with treasonable activities. The Espionage Act of June 15, 1917, provided penalties running to $10,000 fine and twenty years' imprisonment for those who should willfully cause or attempt to cause insubordination in the armed services or obstruct recruiting. Also subject to punishment were persons who willfully made false reports and statements with intent to interfere with the operation or success of the military and naval forces. The Postmaster General was authorized to bar from the mails any letter, pamphlet, book, or newspaper which violated any provision of the act or which advocated treason, insurrection, or forcible resistance to any law of the United States. Attempts to use the mail for these purposes were punishable with fines up to $5000 and five years' imprisonment.

Drastic though the Espionage Act was, especially as vigorously administered by Attorney General Gregory and Postmaster General Burleson, still more powers were granted in the Trading-with-the-Enemy Act of October 6, 1917. In addition to its sections dealing with the control of foreign trade, the law authorized the appointment of an Alien Property Custodian to take over and administer the property of enemy aliens resident in the United States and that of corporations controlled by enemy nationals. Furthermore, it empowered the President to set up a censorship over all channels of communication between the United States and other countries, and widened the Post Office Department's powers to exclude material from the mails in a manner which amounted to an effective censorship of the foreign-language press. On April 20, 1918, the Sabotage Act was passed, making it a Federal offense to injure or destroy war material or utilities or transportation, whether public or private.

Still the advocates of ruthless suppression of all subversive activities were not satisfied. On May 16, 1918, the so-called Sedition Act became law. This amended the Espionage Act of the previous year to provide penalties for saying or doing anything to obstruct the sale of Liberty Bonds, for uttering, writing, or printing "any disloyal, scurrilous, or abusive language" about the form of government of the United States, or the Constitution, or the armed forces, or the flag, or language intended to bring these institutions into contempt or disrepute, or for advocating the curtailment of war production. The powers of the Postmaster General were further extended to exclude any written matter of this description from the mails. This Sedition Act was far more drastic than the Espionage Act because the government had now only to prove that an accused person had used disloyal language; it was no longer necessary to prove that some harmful consequence to the war effort had followed or was likely to follow.

The Department of Justice proceeded to take vigorous action under these laws. 1532 persons were arrested for disloyal utterances, 65 for threats against the President, and 10 for sabotage. But actual plots were few. Now that the unwanted war had come, all but a few German-Americans proved to be thoroughly loyal and eager to show their patriotism. Such pro-Germanism as survived was not often expressed where unsympathetic neighbors were likely to hear.

The principal victims of the espionage laws proved to be Socialists and other radicals who opposed the war on ideological grounds, rather than because of sympathy for the enemy. Mrs. Rose Pastor Stokes was sentenced to ten years' imprisonment for asserting, "I am for the people and the government is for the profiteers." A higher court later set aside the conviction, but Eugene V. Debs was not so fortunate. Before he was finally pardoned by President Harding on Christmas Day, 1921, the veteran head of American Socialism served thirty-two months of a ten-year sentence imposed upon him for a speech delivered to a Socialist convention at Canton, Ohio, on June 16, 1918, in which he referred to the war as the supreme curse of capitalism. Leaders of the I.W.W. who were accused of using the war situation to bring about the downfall of the existing economic system, were dealt with even more severely. One hundred of them were brought to trial in the Chicago court of Judge Kenesaw Mountain Landis. Although the trial lasted 138 days, the jury needed but four hours to find all the defendants guilty. Judge Landis sentenced the fifteen most prominent leaders to twenty-year terms, thirty-five others to ten years, and the rest to less drastic penalties. The fines imposed aggregated $2,300,000. This was a blow from which the I.W.W. never really recovered.

Freedom of the press suffered even more than freedom of speech. The watchful eyes of Postmaster General Burleson's assistants were everywhere. Papers carrying articles accused of violating the espionage acts were penalized, not only by having the single offending issue barred from the mails, but by being declared unmailable for the future no matter how circumspect their conduct. Such was the fate of German-American newspapers like the Philadelphia *Tagenblatt*, Irish-American papers like the *Gaelic American*, and radical periodicals like the *Masses* and the Milwaukee *Leader*. The record of the Wilson administration in suppressing the expression of unpopular doctrines during wartime was inconsistent with its notable progressive achievements of earlier years. But in judging that record, it must be remembered that the government was acting at the response of insistent public opinion and was widely criticized as being too lenient. "Disloyalty"—a word of dangerously vague meaning—was for the time being considered the most heinous of crimes.

The unpopularity of all things German reached ludicrous extremes. Public demand compelled the statue of Frederick the Great in Washington to be taken down and ignominiously stored away in the basement of a War Department building. Local officials ordered instruction in German to be halted in many public schools; German operas and opera singers were boycotted; the great violinist, Fritz Kreisler, was not allowed to play in a concert at East Orange, New Jersey. To the ultrapatriotic, German measles became "liberty measles," dachshunds "liberty pups," and sauerkraut "liberty cabbage."

ADVERTISING AMERICA

Soon after the United States entered the war, the Army and Navy Departments urged upon President Wilson the necessity of strict censorship of the news to prevent vital information from reaching the enemy. The newspapers, however, violently protested against the establishment of such controls. In his perplexity, Wilson turned with relief to the suggestion of George Creel, a dynamic free-lance journalist and editor, who asserted that what was needed was not censorship in the conventional sense of the word, but an agency which should provide the press with the fullest possible information about the war effort, relying upon voluntary cooperation of the newspapers to refrain from publishing material that might help the enemy.

The President promptly appointed a Committee on Public Information, with the Secretaries of State, War, and the Navy as members and Creel as executive head. Like so many other war agencies which had started as committees or boards, the Committee on Public Information speedily became a one-man affair. Unencumbered by his fellow committeemen and loyally supported by Wilson, Creel built up a vast organization engaged in a great variety of activities.

The first modest function assumed by Creel's staff was to serve as a liaison agency between the various government departments and Washington reporters. The C.P.I.'s offices were open twenty-four hours a day, grinding out mimeographed releases for the newspapers, releases that were soon given a more pretentious form by being published daily in a new periodical, the *Official Journal*.

But Creel soon organized more ambitious projects. His job, as he conceived it, was to sell the war to the American people and Wilson's ideals of a democratic peace to the world. On the domestic front, leading American illustrators, men like Charles Dana Gibson, James Montgomery Flagg, Howard Chandler Christy, and Joseph Pennell, contributed their efforts to preparing a remarkable series of war posters. College professors under the leadership of Guy Stanton Ford, Professor of History at the University of Minnesota, wrote popular pamphlets explaining the nation's war aims. The varied talents of novelists, dramatists, musicians, actors, and motion-picture directors were all employed in arousing the patriotic enthusiasm of the country. Perhaps the most remarkable of Creel's feats at home was the enlistment of 75,000 speakers or "Four-Minute Men." These privates in the C.P.I. army fired 7,555,190 speeches at their fellow-countrymen assembled in moving-picture theaters, lodge meetings, schools, and churches; they even invaded lumber camps and Indian reservations where they found some of their most enthusiastic audiences. The Four-Minute Men sold Liberty Bonds, explained the draft, urged food and fuel conservation, and attacked rumor-mongers.

Creel was a devoted disciple of Wilson. He believed that the great war speeches in which the President gave expression to his abiding faith in democracy, his hatred of militarism, and his hope for future peace and a better world should be given the widest possible audience. Through C.P.I. agencies abroad, the speeches were translated and published in almost every country. A volume of Wilson's messages became a best seller in China, and the text of one address was used as a schoolbook in Madrid.

But the audiences which Creel most of all wanted to reach were the German army and the German home front. Therefore C.P.I. pamphlets printed in German were showered down from airplanes and shot over no man's land from guns. Some of the propaganda bombs consisted of facts, figures, and pictures designed to impress the enemy with the size of the American war effort and the hopelessness of further resistance; others were translations of Wilson's speeches offering a just peace if the Germans would rebel against their war lords. The effectiveness of these tactics was evidenced by the frantic attempts of the German government to stop its subjects from reading the C.P.I. literature.

Creel made mistakes. He believed that truth was his best weapon; yet under the pressure of war psychology, he and his lieutenants sometimes distorted the facts. He sold Wilsonian idealism so completely to the common people of the world that they were bitterly disillusioned when the peace settlement fell short of perfection. He was worse than tactless in his dealings with Congress where he made dangerous enemies not only for himself but for Wilson. Despite these shortcomings, Creel's accomplishments were remarkable. He was a pioneer in the field of political warfare and, as truly as Pershing and Baruch, he was one of the architects of German defeat.

THE WAR FRONTS

The German High Command had resorted to unlimited submarine warfare in the twin beliefs that this weapon would bring speedy victory and that, even though the United States might enter the war, it would be unable to exert any effective military pressure. During the spring and summer of 1917 both German premises seemed all too sound. The submarine campaign was dangerously effective, while America's unreadiness for real fighting was evident to friend and foe alike.

Unless the seas could be rendered tolerably safe for Allied shipping, Germany's defeat was apparently impossible. When Admiral Sims took over his European command, a convoy system had not yet been instituted. The British did not have destroyers enough for the task, and they doubted, moreover, that merchant ships could be kept in formation and moving at the same speed. Even the antisubmarine patrols then in use needed many more ships than were available. In answer to frantic messages from Sims, the Navy Department hurried into Atlantic service every vessel that could be used against U-boats. The building of new destroyers and subchasers was given priority over every other type of naval construction.

The battle against underwater raiders became a grim contest in which new methods and new tactics were constantly being tried. Improved means of detection and more powerful depth charges helped in this struggle. Despite the difficulties involved, more and more shipping moved in convoys protected by destroyers and other small naval craft. The most ingenious stratagem attempted was that of bottling up the submarines in the North Sea by laying a string of mines all the way from Scotland to Norway. This gigantic task had not been completed when the war was ended by the Armistice, but already it had proved effective. One out of every ten German submarines attempting to cross the barrier was destroyed, and many more were so badly damaged that they had to return to port. The morale of the German crews was seriously shaken.

The success of the antisubmarine campaign was to be measured not alone by the steadily declining toll of Allied shipping losses after April, 1917, but also by the safety in which American soldiers were ferried across the Atlantic. It was the proud boast of the navy that not a single doughboy lost his life in the passage.

Pershing had asked for a million men by the end of May, 1918, but it seemed impossible that he would get them. Up to March 1, 1918, only 291,000 had been sent across. The delay was caused in part by the necessity for building camps and training the recruits and draftees in America; but an equally serious problem was that of finding the shipping space to carry the men to France. American facilities were entirely inadequate for the task, and the British found it difficult to help, since submarine losses had put such a strain on their own merchant marine. They could spare ships for transporting American soldiers only by diverting them from carrying vital supplies to England itself. This they were at first most reluctant to do.

This British hesitancy in loaning ships to ferry American troops was closely linked with an issue of the utmost delicacy which was being violently contested behind the scenes. That issue was nothing less than the disposition which should be made of the troops once they reached France. From the beginning, General Pershing had insisted that there must be a separate American army, fighting on its own sector of the front under its own commanders. The British and French authorities viewed this proposition with dismay. They feared that the war might end in a German victory while Pershing hoarded his men until he had enough for an effective army. Moreover, with the quality of the American troops untested and with the American high command so inexperienced in handling large-scale operations, it seemed actually dangerous to entrust any very sizable section of the front to Pershing. Instead, the British and French wanted the American units to be used as replacements in the Allied armies already in the field. Lloyd George and Clemenceau appealed over Pershing's head to Wilson, but the President stood by his commander in the field. So long as this difference of opinion continued, the British hated to gamble their precious shipping on the American Expeditionary Force.

Pershing was not unwilling to loan units to the Allies for limited periods of time or to meet special emergencies. On the contrary, he recognized that this would provide valuable training for the men. In this way, battalions of the American First Division participated in combat with the French army in Lorraine as early as October 21, 1917. This was part of the training which preceded the actual establishment of an American sector on January 19, 1918, when the First Division, under Major General Robert L. Bullard, took over a quiet section of the front near Toul in eastern France.

The Germans made a desperate effort to win the war during 1918. Several factors were in their favor. In November, 1917, the Kerensky government in Russia had been overthrown by the Bolsheviks. The following March the new government submitted to the harsh terms imposed by Germany in the Treaty of Brest-Litovsk. Not only was Russia now out of the war, but Germany had secured access to the agricultural wealth of the Ukraine. Moreover, the bulk of the Kaiser's armies were shifted to the western front to add weight to the great offensive with which the high command hoped to pound Britain and France into surrender. For four months the Allied line was subjected to a succession of terrific hammer blows that again and again secured temporary break-throughs and threatened complete disaster. The peril of the situation was increased by the fact that the British and French were without adequate reserves and that the two armies were still operating under separate commands, with each hesitant to spare units needed to hold its own front in order to rescue some sector held by the other army.

The Germans launched the first of their great blows on March 21. The plan was to attack along the Somme where the British and French lines joined, to break the line at that point and pin the British back against the English Channel. The offensive was so powerful that the Germans drove more than 30 miles in six days—greater gains than either side had been able to make on the western front since 1914. A wide gap was temporarily torn in the Allied line, but desperate countermeasures by the British and difficulties encountered by the Germans combined to permit a new stabilization of the front.

The masterful Ludendorff, commanding the German juggernaut, threw a second great offensive into motion on April 9. Having tried out the right flank of the British, he now attacked the left in Flanders. Again the Germans made a deep penetration, but failed to keep the offensive rolling.

These near disasters served to drive home two lessons. First, the separate Allied armies needed to come under unified command. Second, American reinforcements were imperative. After a series of conferences in March and April, General Ferdinand Foch was designated Com-

mander-in-Chief of the Allied Armies. Pershing at once offered him all
resources which the Americans had overseas, agreeing that the establishment of a separate American army should be delayed until the military situation improved.

Herculean efforts were now made to move American troops across
the Atlantic, with the British diverting as much of their shipping to
this service as possible. Approximately 85,000 soldiers were carried to
France in March, 120,000 in April, and then for the next six months an
average of 263,000 a month. The first million men arrived by July 1,
despite all difficulties, and, by Armistice Day, a million more had come.
The incoming American troops had only a few months before been
civilians and they required more training behind the lines before they
were ready for active combat. But as spring gave way to summer along
the European front, more and more Americans moved to the fighting
zones.

Neither friend nor foe had had as yet much opportunity to measure
the quality of the American forces. The first real test came when the
First Division, serving in a French sector, received the assignment of
attacking Cantigny, a village of strategic importance near the tip of the
Somme salient which the Germans had driven into the Allied lines during their March offensive. Not only did the Americans take Cantigny
on May 28, but they held it against seven German counterattacks during the next two days.

On the day before the American capture of Cantigny, however, the
third and most dangerous of the German blows of 1918 had been
struck against the left flank of the French army in a sector to the west
of Rheims. Covering their movements with complete secrecy and starting the offensive with a great gas attack, the Germans took the rough
hills known as the "Chemin des Dames" and broke straight across the
Aisne River in the first day's assault. During the next three days the
French suffered heavy casualties and were thrown back to Château-
Thierry on the Marne River, only 50 miles from Paris. Once again
American troops—this time the Second Division and units from the
Third and Twenty-eighth—were thrown into battle under French
high command. The French and Americans succeeded in stopping the
German drive. Then, after a week's desperate fighting, attacking Amer-
ican forces took Belleau Wood, a vital position whose capture helped
stabilize the line again.

The Germans still maintained the initiative and were able to launch
two more offensives. The first of these, thrown against the Allied lines
to the west of the Marne salient in June, was halted after a gain of 6

miles. The second, begun on July 14 in the Champagne sector around Rheims, aimed at splitting the French front and rolling down the Marne Valley to Paris. "If my offensive at Rheims succeeds, we have won the war," said Ludendorff. But it was stopped, with American troops once more fighting at the side of the French.

FOCH STRIKES BACK

This was the final turning point of the war. The Germans had thrown all their resources into these five mighty blows; thereafter the preponderance of strength lay with the Allies as more and more American divisions became ready for action.

As soon as it was obvious that the Germans had been stopped at Rheims, Foch directed his first great counterblow—an attack against the Germans' Marne salient. American troops were now so well re-

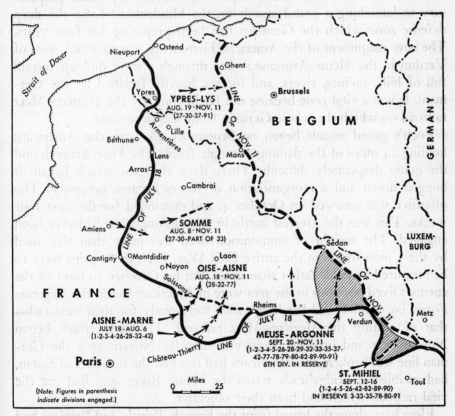

American Participation in the Allied Offensives of 1918. Based on map in *The War with Germany, A Statistical Summary*, Washington, 1919. (By permission of the Central Statistical Office, Office of the Chief of Staff.)

garded that they were used as the spearhead of the drive on July 18. By August 4, the Germans had been driven from the entire salient.

Now at long last Pershing secured command of an army of his own, the First American Army, put together out of divisions which for the past crucial months had been fighting wherever they were needed to strengthen the French and British lines. Pershing assumed command of the new army on August 10, and a month later the new army was ready for its first important assignment, the elimination of the St. Mihiel salient which the Germans had held in the region east of Verdun since 1914. Thirty-six hours after Pershing opened his attack on September 12, the salient was wiped out.

General Pershing hoped for permission to keep his offensive rolling on toward the great fortress of Metz, a vital nerve center in the German communications system. But Foch had other plans. His earlier limited offensives had aimed at improving the Allied position preparatory to launching a grand assault on the Hindenburg Line, the deep defense zone which the Germans had been preparing for four years. The new assignment of the American First Army was to attack west of Verdun in the Meuse-Argonne sector through a most difficult terrain full of hills, ravines, rivers, and forests, heavily fortified by the Germans. It was a vital zone because not far beyond lay the Mézières-Metz railroad on which the whole German front was dependent.

Foch's grand assault began on September 26, with the Americans holding 24 miles of the flaming 200-mile front. The First Army found the going desperately difficult. Three days after the attack began, it bogged down and a reorganization of forces became necessary. The offensive was renewed on October 4, and continued for the next four weeks. This was the greatest battle in which Americans had ever been engaged. The weight of ammunition fired was more than that used by the Union forces in the entire Civil War. Each day's gains were to be measured in yards rather than miles. But by October 30 most of the enemy's fixed positions in the area were in American hands, the Argonne Forest lay behind, and Pershing's men were ready for their next task— that of cutting the Mézières-Metz railroad. This new attack began November 1 and brought decisive results. By November 7 the German line was broken, the Americans had reached the outskirts of Sedan, had established bridgeheads across the Meuse River, and had cut the vital railroad which had been their objective.

Elsewhere along the broad front the French, British, and Belgians had been equally successful. The Hindenburg Line was everywhere broken, and the Germans had been pushed back toward their own borders.

Disasters even more catastrophic had befallen the Central Powers in the Balkan and Italian theaters. On September 29 Bulgaria accepted Allied armistice terms, Turkey followed suit October 30, and Austria-Hungary finally surrendered on November 3.

Acknowledging that the war was lost, the German High Command had urged as early as October 1 that the Kaiser's government should seek an armistice. Preliminary negotiations had begun on October 3 and had been hastened along by the crumbling of the western front and the spread of revolution throughout Germany. On November 7, German delegates passed through the lines to receive Foch's terms. On November 11, in a dramatic meeting in the Forest of Compiègne, the armistice was signed and, at 11 A.M. that day, the military phase of World War I came to an end.

This military victory was not achieved without cost. The total American casualties were 321,100, of whom 39,000 were killed in action, 14,000 died of wounds, 62,700 died of disease, 201,000 were wounded, and 4400 were taken prisoner. Seven per cent of all those mobilized were on the casualty list. Compared to the 73 per cent casualties suffered by the French and the 36 per cent by the British Empire, American losses were extremely light. It should be remembered, however, that American troops were in the front lines only a few months. The actual battles in which the Yanks engaged were among the most bitterly fought and most bloody in American history.

10

The Making of the Peace

WHEN ON OCTOBER 3, 1918, PRINCE MAX OF BADEN, NEWLY APPOINTED German Chancellor, sought to bring hostilities to a halt, he addressed his request for an armistice, not to Premier Clemenceau of France nor to Prime Minister Lloyd George of England, but to Woodrow Wilson. Moreover, the Chancellor's note stated: "The German Government accepts, as a basis for the peace negotiations, the program laid down by the President of the United States in his message to Congress of January 8, 1918, and in his subsequent pronouncements, particularly in his address of September 27, 1918." How had Wilson and Wilson's ideas come to occupy so central a place on the stage of world affairs?

EVOLUTION OF PEACE AIMS

As soon as the war began, shocked Americans began to consider the means by which such events might be prevented in the future. On June 17, 1915, the League to Enforce Peace was organized at a great meeting in Independence Hall, Philadelphia. Under the leadership of ex-President William Howard Taft and A. Lawrence Lowell, president of Harvard University, the new association advocated the establishment of an international court of justice to which all "justiciable" questions, which might arise between nations in the future, should be submitted and the employment of the joint forces of a league of nations against any state which rejected these procedures. The League to Enforce Peace had considerable success, local chapters were founded throughout the country, and hundreds of speakers urged its program.

Even before the formation of the new association, President Wilson had been thinking along the same general lines and, as time went on, he made it abundantly clear that he considered the establishment of some kind of a league of nations as the essential foundation to the building of any permanent peace after the war. Sir Edward Grey's corre-

234

spondence with Colonel House indicated that the British government also favored the organization of such a league. Indeed, British public opinion appeared to demand it.

By January, 1917, Wilson had formulated other principles which would have to undergird a durable postwar settlement. In his "Peace without Victory" speech he asserted that it must be a peace between equals and one which recognized the ideal of government by the consent of the governed, freedom of the seas, and disarmament. His war message three months later declared that the United States was entering the contest to make the world safe for democracy.

By the end of 1917, however, there arose an insistent public demand for a much more specific statement of war aims than Wilson or any other Allied statesman had yet made. The demand was partially the result of the publication by the newly established Bolshevik government in Russia of the text of secret treaties found in the Czarist archives. These treaties pointed to an old-fashioned division of spoils in case of an Allied victory. Repudiating these pacts, the Bolsheviks gave wide publicity to the ideals upon which they believed peace should be based: no annexations nor indemnities, and self-determination for subject nationalities. The effect of these developments was to raise searching questions. To what end were the peoples of all the belligerent nations being called upon to make such terrible sacrifices? Was it simply to serve the territorial ambitions of the rival powers? Or was there some happier alternative—some hope that, when the guns were stilled, a better world would emerge?

Wilson's answer to these questions was embodied in the most famous of all his state papers, the speech to Congress on January 8, 1918, in which the "Fourteen Points" were set forth. As the basis for an enduring peace, Wilson advocated:

1. "Open covenants of peace, openly arrived at. . . ."
2. "Absolute freedom of navigation upon the seas . . . alike in peace and in war," except as the seas may be closed by international action for the enforcement of international covenants.
3. "The removal, as far as possible, of all economic barriers and the establishment of an equality of trade conditions. . . ."
4. Reduction of armaments "to the lowest point consistent with domestic safety."
5. Impartial adjustment of all colonial claims in which "the interests of the populations concerned must have equal weight with the equitable claims of the government whose title is to be determined."
6. Evacuation of all Russian territory and an unhampered opportunity for Russia to determine her own political development and national policy.

7. Evacuation and restoration of Belgium without any attempt to limit her sovereignty.

8. All French territory to be freed and the invaded portions restored, "and the wrong done to France by Prussia in 1871 in the matter of Alsace-Lorraine . . . should be righted. . . ."

9. Readjustment of the frontiers of Italy "along clearly recognizable lines of nationality."

10. Freest opportunity of autonomous development for the peoples of Austria-Hungary, but without destroying the country.

11. Rumania, Serbia, and Montenegro to be evacuated and restored, Serbia accorded free and secure access to the sea, and the relations of the several Balkan states to one another determined "along historically established lines of allegiance and nationality. . . ."

12. An independent Polish state including "the territory inhabited by indisputably Polish populations, which should be assured a free and secure access to the sea. . . ."

13. Secure sovereignty for the Turkish portions of the Ottoman Empire, but other nationalities then under Turkish rule should be assured security of life and an opportunity for autonomous development, and "the Dardanelles should be permanently opened as a free passage to the ships and commerce of all nations under international guarantees."

14. "A general association of nations must be formed under specific covenants for the purpose of affording mutual guarantees of political independence and territorial integrity to great and small states alike."

This speech made a tremendous impression—not because it contained many novel or unfamiliar ideas, but for the contrary reason that it stated in memorable phrases the thoughts which were running in the minds of people in many countries. Only three days before, Prime Minister Lloyd George had stated British objectives in very similar terms.

Wilson returned to a discussion of the objects of the war and the bases of a just peace in several other speeches during 1918. On February 11 he appeared again before Congress to comment on German and Austrian war aims that had recently been set forth in the enemy capitals. To the Fourteen Points he now added "Four Principles." The second and fourth of these were particularly appealing; the former asserted "that peoples and provinces are not to be bartered about from sovereignty to sovereignty as if they were mere chattels and pawns in a game . . ."; the latter stated "that all well-defined national aspirations shall be accorded the utmost satisfaction that can be accorded them without introducing new or perpetuating old elements of discord and antagonism. . . ." In a Fourth-of-July address at Mount Vernon, the President spoke of the "Four Ends" for which the United States and the Allies were fighting. The first of these called for "the destruction of every arbitrary power anywhere that can separately, secretly, and of its single choice disturb the peace of the world. . . ." All four objects, Wilson declared, could be summed up in a single sentence: "What we seek is the reign of law, based upon the consent of the governed and sustained by the organized opinion of mankind."

The last of the great war speeches was that of September 27, 1918, when President Wilson spoke at the Metropolitan Opera House in New York City on the occasion of the opening of the Fourth Liberty Loan. To the Fourteen Points and its corollaries were now added "Five Particulars." Those meriting special mention were the first, saying: "The impartial justice meted out must involve no discrimination between those to whom we wish to be just and those to whom we do not wish to be just . . ."; and the third, stating: "there can be no leagues or alliances or special covenants and understandings within the general and common family of the League of Nations."

ARMISTICE NEGOTIATIONS

When in the fall of 1918 the German officials acknowledged to themselves that they had lost the war, they turned to the Fourteen Points as a drowning man might clutch at a piece of floating timber. By appealing to Wilsonian idealism, they desperately hoped that they might secure lenient treatment for the Central Powers. Accordingly, it was to the American President that Prince Max addressed his request of October 3 for an armistice. Wilson, however, proved to be not so naïvely eager for immediate peace as the Germans thought that he would be. While Foch hammered back the German lines, the President exchanged notes with the enemy government, demanding categorical acceptance of the principles which he had laid down in his war speeches, a promise to evacuate all Allied territory, a cessation of submarine attacks upon passenger liners, and an assurance that the arbitrary power of the Kaiser and of the German generals had been placed under constitutional checks. Only after his adroit diplomacy had secured these things did the President consent on October 23 to transmit the German armistice request to the Allies.

Now the problem was transferred to the European capitals. The military commanders had to decide whether it was expedient to halt hostilities, and, if so, on what terms. The British General Haig thought that mild armistice terms should be offered so as to ensure their acceptance; Pershing preferred that there should be no armistice at all; Foch, whose decision was final, favored an armistice with terms so drastic that there would be no possibility of Germany's renewing the war. Meanwhile, the heads of the Allied governments were debating whether or not they would accept the Fourteen Points as the basis of peace. They were at first reluctant to do so, and Colonel House had to warn them of the possibility that refusal might result in the United States dropping out of the war. Finally, after studying an interpretation of the famous document prepared by Frank I. Cobb and Walter Lippmann, two able journalists who were acting as advisers to Colonel House, the Allied statesmen accepted the Wilsonian principles with one reservation and one elucidation. The second of the Fourteen Points, relating to freedom of the seas, they asserted, was "open to various interpretations, some of which they could not accept. They must, therefore, reserve to themselves complete freedom on this subject when they enter the peace conference." This reservation obviously reflected the ideas of the British; those of the French were represented in the stipulation that the restoration of invaded territory to which Wilson had referred must include compensation by Germany "for all damage done to the civilian population of the Allies and their property by the aggression of Germany by land, by sea, and from the air."

On November 5, President Wilson informed the German government of the Allied reply; if the Germans wanted to proceed, they could learn the actual armistice terms by sending representatives through the lines to meet General Foch. The Germans did so at once; their envoys received Foch's terms on the eighth, appealed to Berlin for further instructions, and finally signed the armistice agreement in the Forest of Compiègne on November 11. This agreement provided for a cessation of hostilities, German evacuation of all non-German territory, Allied occupation of both banks of the Rhine, and German delivery to the Allies of vast quantities of military equipment. Compliance with such terms would make it virtually impossible for the Germans to renew hostilities.

The first Armistice Day was one of delirious rejoicing. Wilson's own happiness was reflected in an exultant statement which he gave out to the newspapers:

The armistice was signed this morning. Everything for which America fought has been accomplished. It will now be our fortunate duty to assist by example, by sober friendly counsel and by material aid in the establishment of a just democracy throughout the world.

It is no wonder the President used such phrases. The triumph of his principles appeared to be as complete as the victory of the Allied arms. Not only had the Fourteen Points been accepted as the basis of peace by friend and foe alike, but German military autocracy seemed utterly vanquished. The peace-hungry German people, convinced that the Kaiser's continued presence on the throne was a barrier to the granting of an armistice, had risen in revolt. On November 9 the government had been turned over to the Socialists, who proclaimed a German republic, and the emperor had fled across the border into Holland. It was another great victory for the American statesman who had called for "the destruction of every arbitrary power."

THE RISE OF REPUBLICAN OPPOSITION

Actually, however, Wilson's position was less impregnable than these diplomatic victories would indicate. Not only in Europe but in America there were powerful elements which did not accept his leadership and were waiting for the first opportunity to make their opposition felt.

The most influential of living Republicans was still Theodore Roosevelt, and Roosevelt's hatred for Wilson had become more and more intense with the passing of the years. Thoroughly loyal and patriotic, Roosevelt supported the war in vigorous public speeches, but at the same time he maintained a constant barrage of criticism against the way in which the Wilson administration had actually organized the war effort. He was particularly contemptuous of the Wilsonian peace program, even though as early as 1910 he himself had expressed in an important address the idea that world peace must be backed up by force. Even after the war had begun, Roosevelt had said that if the idea of an international police power was utopian, then we must choose between "Utopia or Hell." Yet by 1918 his dislike for Wilson had taken him so far that he tried to sabotage Wilson's October negotiations with Germany by calling upon the Senate to repudiate the Fourteen Points. "Let us dictate peace by the hammering guns," he declared, "and not chat about peace to the accompaniment of clicking typewriters. . . ."

Equally hostile was Senator Henry Cabot Lodge of Massachusetts. He and Roosevelt were close friends, and for years in their private correspondence they had heaped scorn upon the professor in the White House. Like Roosevelt, Lodge thought that an association of nations to enforce future world peace was an excellent idea—up to the time when Wilson appropriated the project for himself. In 1915, Lodge had asserted: "The great nations must be so united as to be able to say to any single country, you must not go to war, and they can only say that effectively when the country desiring war knows that the force . . . is irresistible. . . ." A year later he had repeated and elaborated on this conviction in a notable address before the League to Enforce Peace. But following Wilson's fervent plea for a league in his "Peace without Victory" speech of January, 1917, the Massachusetts Senator had reversed himself completely, warning the Senate that such an international organization might enforce Oriental immigration upon the United States or "might plunge us into war at any moment at the bidding of other nations."

The Republican leaders were naturally eager to return to power in the national government. As practical politicians, they believed that the country was normally Republican and that the Democrats had enjoyed their brief hour of glory only because of animosities within the ranks of the dominant party. With the Congressional election of November, 1918, approaching, strenuous efforts were made to patch up the old quarrel. A new and energetic national chairman, Will H. Hays of Indiana, was appointed, while Roosevelt, Taft, and Root appeared together on public platforms as a visible demonstration to their admirers that the battle of 1912 was forgotten. Wilson was accused of desiring a negotiated peace with the Kaiser rather than unconditional surrender, and the third of the Fourteen Points was depicted as a threat to the protective-tariff system. Democratic Congressmen, worried by the aggressiveness of the opposition, beseeched the President for help. Somewhat reluctantly, he responded with an appeal to the voters, given out to the newspapers on October 24. Among other things, he said:

If you have approved of my leadership and wish me to continue to be your unembarrassed spokesman in affairs at home and abroad, I earnestly beg that you will express yourselves unmistakably to that effect by returning a Democratic majority to both the Senate and the House of Representatives. . . . The leaders of the minority in the present Congress have unquestionably been pro-war, but they have been anti-administration. At almost every turn since we entered the war they have sought to take the choice of policy and the conduct of the war out of my hands and put it under the control of the instrumentalities of their own choosing. . . . The return of a Republican majority to either house of the Congress would . . . be interpreted on the other side of the water as a repudiation of my leadership.

Wilson's appeal proved to be a blunder. It offered the Republicans the excuse for casting off the restraint that they might have felt over attacking the President during wartime. Chairman Hays denounced Wilson's words as "ungracious . . . wanton . . . mendacious." The President, it was charged, had cast a slur upon Republican patriotism.

When the votes were counted on November 5, it was learned that the new House of Representatives would have 237 Republicans, 191 Democrats, and 7 Independents, while in the Senate there would be 49 Republicans and 47 Democrats. It was a defeat for the President's party and also for the President himself since, in his own words, Wilson had defined confidence in his leadership as one of the issues of the campaign. The exultant victors asserted that the President had been decisively repudiated by the voters. In reality, it was by no means certain that this was so. The war was obviously nearly over, and many of those who went to the polls expressed with their ballots their impatience with wartime restrictions or their sentiments on local issues rather than their opinion of Wilson. Republican victory under the circumstances was probably inevitable, but it was made more damaging to the President than it needed to have been by the role he had assumed during the campaign.

Perhaps the most fateful result was to make it certain that Henry Cabot Lodge would become chairman of the Senate Foreign Relations Committee in the new Congress. In this powerful position, Lodge would have ample opportunity to place obstacles in the path of the man whom he detested.

WILSON GOES TO EUROPE

Before the month of November was over, the names of the American peace commissioners were announced. Wilson had long before decided to attend the peace conference in person; to go with him he now named Secretary of State Lansing, Colonel House, General Tasker H. Bliss, and Henry White. It was a competent group. Next to the President himself, Lansing and House were obviously the two best informed men in the country on the diplomatic developments of the past several years, while Bliss and White were extremely able. The former was not only a military expert, but a scholar with an excellent grasp of European economic and political problems; the latter had had an unusually distinguished and valuable diplomatic career, having held important posts in London, Paris, and Rome.

The President's opponents, however, criticized his appointments severely. Natural though it might seem that the President should wish to go to Paris himself, he was breaking a precedent. Earlier Presidents had always remained in the White House while they left to other men the actual work of negotiating treaties of peace. Wilson's decision to head his own delegation was attributed to his vanity or to his "Messiah complex." The commission was further criticized as giving inadequate recognition to the Republicans. True, White was a Republican, but not an active partisan. Why had the President ignored such distinguished leaders as Hughes, Taft, and Root? Finally, unfavorable comment stressed the absence of Senators on the delegation. This was resented as a slight to the body which must give its consent to the ratification of any peace treaty. Although much of this criticism was mere partisanship, it does appear that Wilson's failure to take with him to Paris at least one prominent Senator from each party was a serious mistake—a mistake that played directly into the hands of his enemies.

On December 4, 1918, the liner *George Washington* left New York, bound for France with the peace commission and scores of advisers and experts on various problems. Key men from the war administrations were aboard, as well as numerous college professors and other specialists in history, geography, and economics. These experts had been assembled by Colonel House over the course of the past year. Known as "The Inquiry," they had been assembling facts and figures at their headquarters in New York City for many months. Even this evidence of earnest preparation for the serious tasks ahead was ridiculed by unfriendly newspapers, which sneered at "Colonel House's troupe of performing professors."

The *George Washington* docked at Brest on December 13, but not for another month did the peace conference begin its work. During this period of waiting, President Wilson visited Paris, London, and Rome. Everywhere he received a most extraordinary welcome. The enthusiasm of the crowds that lined the streets surpassed anything that men could remember. With pathetic trust, common people in all countries were counting on the American President to achieve an impossible goal—that of securing a perfect peace settlement.

LIONS IN THE PATH

At the very moment when Wilson was enjoying his greatest triumphs, the dangers that confronted him were clearly evident. Behind him in America his opponents were ceaseless in their activity. Even before the President sailed, Theodore Roosevelt had warned in a statement to the press:

Our allies and our enemies and Mr. Wilson himself should all understand that Mr. Wilson has no authority whatever to speak for the American people at this time. His leadership has just been emphatically repudiated by them. . . . Mr. Wilson and his fourteen points and his four supplementary points and his five complementary points and all his utterances every which way have ceased to have any shadow of right to be accepted as expressive of the will of the American people. . . .

This bitter document was one of Roosevelt's last contributions to American public discussion. The ex-President was a desperately sick man, fighting a losing struggle with a tropical ailment that he had contracted during an adventurous trip to the Amazon in 1913. On January 6, 1919, he died.

But Henry Cabot Lodge remained very much alive. On December 21, 1918, he addressed the Senate at length, stating his belief that the Allies should be permitted to make any territorial settlement that they desired without Wilson's interference, and that the League of Nations should not be included as a part of the peace treaties. The Senate, he said, could, and often had, refused to ratify treaties; many other agreements —and these were significant words—had been "virtually amended." Without waiting to see what kind of league of nations would be proposed, Lodge was already laying careful plans to oppose it. He even went to the extreme of suggesting to Henry White that the latter should communicate these ideas to leading Allied statesmen in order to encourage them to oppose the President; but White honorably refrained from acting upon the suggestion.

On the European front, several major obstacles lay in the President's path. Four years of bitter struggle and hardship had created a great public demand for stern punishment of the country which universal Allied opinion held guilty for the war. There had been a 1918 election in England as well as in the United States; Lloyd George had been victorious, but the most popular electoral appeals had been such incendiary slogans as "Hang the Kaiser," "Squeeze the Germans until the pips squeak," and "Make Germany pay for the war." In France, Clemenceau had received an impressive vote of confidence from the Chamber of Deputies under circumstances that indicated popular expectation that he would demand rigorous handling of the hated *Boche*.

Equally dangerous to Wilsonian idealism was the network of secret treaties which had been formulated by the Allied governments before the United States declared war. Italy, as her reward for abandoning neutrality in 1915 and entering the struggle against her former allies, had been promised a strategic frontier in the Alps and along the Adriatic, which would extend her rule not only over "unredeemed" Italians but over thousands of Germans and Slavs as well. Rumania had been promised a large section of Hungary, while Russia, France, and Great Britain had planned a partition of the Turkish Empire. Japan had secured from her hard-pressed Allies their assent to her keeping Germany's Pacific islands north of the equator, as well as German political and economic rights in the Shantung Peninsula on the China coast.

Wilson had long been aware of the existence of most of these documents. Indeed, his appeal for "open covenants of peace, openly arrived at" expressed his disapproval of such bargains. But he refrained from any study of their details. Wilson considered that the entry of the United States into the war, as well as the negotiations leading to the armistice, created a new situation in which the secret treaties should be ignored. Each part of the settlement should be made on the merits of that particular case, without regard to previous agreements. Wilson soon discovered, however, that the Allied statesmen were determined to insist stubbornly on the fulfillment of these old pledges.

The work of peacemaking had to be carried on in an atmosphere of haste and confusion that was hardly conducive to long and patient consideration of any single problem. Treaties of peace had to be made not only with Germany, but with Austria, Hungary, Bulgaria, and Turkey as well. The new states which were making their appearance on the map had to be committed by a separate series of treaties to the decent treatment of their minorities. But these were only the least of the anxieties of the Peace Conference. All Europe appeared to be tottering on the edge of chaos. A score of petty wars had broken out—both civil wars between rival factions in the same state and wars between neighboring nations over disputed boundaries. There were, moreover, unemployment, hunger, and discontent everywhere.

Such unrest seemed doubly dangerous because of the situation in Russia. Might not the wildfire of Communism spread west across the whole continent? This was the greatest of all the fears haunting the peacemakers and impelling them to make important decisions in frantic haste.

In other ways as well, the work of the Peace Conference was hampered by affairs in Russia. That great country was convulsed by civil war, and the Allies were uncomfortably involved. After the Soviet government had made its separate peace with Germany, Allied expeditionary forces had been sent into various parts of Russia to try to prevent military supplies from falling into the hands of the Germans. American troops were involved in these operations, both around Archangel and Murmansk and in eastern Siberia. The armistice of November, 1918, ended the necessity for trying to protect the military supplies, but by this time the Allies had become entangled in virtual alliances with anti-Bolshevik armies resisting the authority of the Soviet government in various sections of the country.

No question confronting the statesmen at Paris was more perplexing than that of trying to shape a Russian policy. The French government favored all-out military action to suppress the Communist regime, but Lloyd George and Wilson urged instead that Bolshevik and anti-Bolshevik leaders be brought together around a conference table to see whether a way to bring the Russian civil war to an end might not be discovered. When this effort failed, President Wilson, with Lloyd George's approval, sent William C. Bullitt, a youthful Philadelphian attached to the peace commission, to Moscow on an unofficial and highly confidential mission. Bullitt brought back to Paris a Bolshevik offer to make an armistice, come to a conference, and acknowledge Russia's debts to the Allies, if the latter would restore diplomatic relations and terminate their intervention in Russian internal affairs. When news of these negotiations leaked out to the French and British press, there was such loud condemnation that the whole matter had to be dropped.

The consequence of these failures was most unfortunate. The Allied policy of supplying and encouraging the anti-Bolsheviks continued—not with sufficient volume or energy to be effective, but just enough to plant in the hearts of Soviet leaders a bitterness and suspicion of the Western democracies which would plague international relations for the next generation. The Wilson administration, reluctant from the beginning to send American troops into Russia, began evacuating them from North Russia in May, 1919, and from Siberia in January, 1920. Not until 1933, however, did the United States accord diplomatic recognition to the Soviet government. The hated regime, which had overthrown capitalism in Russia and accepted a separate peace with Germany, was unrepresented at the Peace Conference. Not only did this make it impossible for the Allied statesmen to draw boundary lines in eastern Europe, but, what was still more important, no place was provided for vast Russia in the new League of Nations, nor was it in any way brought into the concert of powers which would have an interest in preserving the peace settlement.

PLANNING THE LEAGUE

On January 18, 1919, the Peace Conference held its first plenary session. Open meetings such as this one, where the delegates of all the nations which had broken relations with Germany were represented, were held on only a few occasions thereafter, and then merely to ratify decisions reached elsewhere. All the important work of the conference was done by smaller groups. From January to March the most important of these was the Council of Ten, which Wilson and Lansing attended along with the two highest ranking delegates from Great

The Big Four at Paris—Lloyd George, Orlando, Clemenceau, and Wilson. (Brown Bros.)

Britain, France, Italy, and Japan. Even this proved too cumbersome a body, and from March to June, while the most important issues were being threshed out, the Council of Four, Lloyd George, Clemenceau, Wilson, and Orlando (Premier of Italy), dominated the scene. Most of the work of the conference was done behind carefully guarded doors, with only brief and juiceless communiqués being issued to the press. Critics protested that this was hardly the open diplomacy which Wilson had advocated. But, although the President tried to secure more privileges for the journalists, the other leaders prevailed with their contention that full publicity would advertise each occasion of difference between the victors and stiffen the resistance of the vanquished.

Wilson won two important points early in the negotiations. Against the wishes of France and such British Dominions as Australia and South Africa, the American President prevented the victorious powers from carrying through an outright annexation of the German colonies and the Arab territories of the Turkish Empire. Instead, the mandate principle was accepted. This meant that those areas should be held under a form of trusteeship; the mandatory power should administer them under conditions which would protect the rights of the natives and provide for general supervision by the League of Nations. The President's second early achievement was securing immediate consideration for the League of Nations and an acceptance of the principle that the League should be made an integral part of the peace treaty instead of postponing this issue for a later conference.

A League of Nations Commission, with Wilson as chairman, set itself energetically at the task of drafting a constitution for this new international body. Much preliminary work had already been done by British, French, and American experts and, after long and exhausting night sessions, the document was finally whipped into such form that it could be presented to a plenary session of the conference on February 14.

The proposed Covenant provided for an Assembly in which every member state, large or small, would have one vote, and for a Council on which the Big Five—Great Britain, France, Italy, Japan, and the United States—would have permanent seats, with temporary seats allotted to four of the smaller powers. In addition to the Assembly and the Council, which were to meet at stated intervals and might be specially convened to deal with emergencies, there was to be a permanent Secretariat to assemble information for the use of the League and to receive and publish the texts of any treaties entered into by the member states. Many functions were to be undertaken by the League, including the establishment of a Permanent Court of International Justice, the formulation of plans for international disarmament, the supervision of mandates, the safeguarding of world health, and the promotion of fair conditions of labor. But the League's most important responsibility was to preserve peace. Any future war or threat of war was to be considered a matter of concern to the whole League; members of the League agreed to submit any controversy between them likely to lead to war either to arbitration or to inquiry by the Council, and not to resort to war until three months after an award or report had been made; moreover, if all the members of the Council other than those representing parties to the dispute agreed to certain recommendations, members of the League were bound not to go to war against any nation which complied with these recommendations. Should any member of the League resort to war in disregard of these pledges, it was to be punished by economic sanctions; and the Council, as a last resort, might recommend joint military action against the offending power. What President Wilson regarded as "the heart of the Covenant" was Article 10, which read:

The Members of the League undertake to respect and preserve as against external aggression the territorial integrity and existing political independence of all Members of the League. In case of any threat or danger of such aggression the Council shall advise upon the means by which this obligation shall be fulfilled.

The day after this draft of the Covenant was presented to the full conference, Wilson embarked on the *George Washington* for America. Congress was about to adjourn and the President had to be available to sign bills and take care of various affairs which had accumulated during his absence.

At Colonel House's suggestion, Wilson entertained the members of the Senate Foreign Relations Committee at a White House dinner on the evening of February 26. Until nearly midnight the President explained the Covenant to the Senators and answered their questions. The Democratic members of the committee were much impressed; the Republicans were not. It was questionable whose attitude was most ominous: that of Senator Brandegee of Connecticut, who cross-ex-

Getting a Taste of It. Wilson giving Congress the first sample of the League of Nations. (By Donahey in the *Cleveland Plain Dealer*.)

amined Wilson like a district attorney, that of Senator Lodge, who kept silent most of the evening, or that of Senators Borah of Idaho and Fall of New Mexico, who refused to attend at all.

The President's failure to win over the skeptics was made all too clear less than a week later. On March 4, the last day of the session, Senator Lodge requested unanimous consent for consideration of a resolution, asserting that "the constitution of the League of Nations in the form now proposed to the peace conference should not be accepted by the United States" and that the whole proposal should be postponed until after peace was made with Germany. Immediate objection was registered by a Democratic member—just as Lodge had hoped. This gave him his opportunity to read into the *Congressional Record* the names of thirty-nine Republican Senators, or Senators-elect, who would have voted for the resolution had they been given the opportunity. This challenge to the President, henceforth known as the "Round Robin," had been the idea of Senator Brandegee; its support by thirty-nine Senators was of serious import, since only thirty-three votes were required to block the ratification of a treaty.

The President was entirely unwilling to yield to the threat of the Round Robin insofar as that maneuver sought to compel him to separate the League Covenant from the peace treaty. If this were done, he feared that the world's best opportunity to secure a league would be lost and the project would be subjected to indefinite delay. On the evening of this same March 4, Wilson and Taft addressed a huge and enthusiastic audience in the Metropolitan Opera House in New York City. In a fighting speech, the President accepted the gauge of battle flung down by his opponents. When the treaty was completed, he said, not only would the Covenant be in it, but so many threads of the treaty would be tied to the Covenant that the Covenant could not be dissected from the treaty without destroying the whole vital structure. That the treaty itself might be rejected, the President apparently had no fear.

On the other hand, Wilson was not hostile to criticisms of the plan which were really constructive. Following his return to Paris on March 14, a careful study was made of all the suggestions which had been offered by prominent Republicans like Taft, Lowell, Hughes, and Root, and by Democrats like Bryan and Senator Hitchcock of Nebraska. Lodge also had been urged to make specific recommendations, but had refused to do so. Although the President believed that the plan as already drafted adequately safeguarded American rights, he decided to ask for a number of amendments in order to satisfy hesitant Senators. The League of Nations Commission was reconvened, and numerous concessions to the United States were written into the Covenant. The right of a member state to withdraw from the League was recognized, as was also the right to refuse a mandate. Domestic questions such as immigration control and tariffs were specifically exempted from League jurisdiction and provision was made that, for all important questions, the Council and the Assembly would have to agree unanimously upon any course of action. Finally, and most important, it was stated that nothing in the Covenant should be deemed "to affect the validity . . . of regional understandings like the Monroe Doctrine. . . ." The formal recognition of this historic American policy represented a striking diplomatic victory.

Wilson thus fought for and won modifications in the Covenant which had been demanded by American opinion, but in order to do so he found it necessary to moderate his opposition to certain things that the other powers were seeking.

COMPLETING THE TREATY

The period from March 14, when the President returned to Paris, to June 28, when the Treaty of Versailles was finally signed, was one of great and exasperating difficulties. Always frail in health, Wilson aged perceptibly during these weeks of anxiety and overwork. For several days in April he was confined to his bed with an attack of the deadly influenza which had been sweeping both America and Europe.

Clemenceau fought savagely for drastic treaty provisions which he believed vital to French security: French annexation of the coal-rich Saar Basin, detachment of the strategic Rhineland from Germany and its establishment as an independent buffer state, French military occupation of bridgeheads across the Rhine for thirty years, and a crushing reparations burden for the defeated foe. Wilson opposed this program as not only being inconsistent with the Fourteen Points, but as providing the seeds of future war. Except on the reparations issue, Lloyd George supported the President. Compromises were finally arranged. In the Saar only the coal mines went to France; the administration of the area was entrusted to the League of Nations for fifteen years, after which there was to be a plebiscite to determine the final disposition of that territory. The Rhineland remained a part of Germany, but was to be permanently demilitarized. Allied troops were to occupy territory along the Rhine for fifteen years. In order to secure Clemenceau's consent to these decisions, security treaties were signed under which Great Britain and the United States pledged themselves to come to the support of France in case she were the victim of unprovoked aggression.[1]

On the reparations issue Wilson was opposed by both Lloyd George and Clemenceau. The American delegation contended that a definite sum should be fixed in the treaty, that it should be based upon a reasonable estimate of Germany's ability to pay, that the period of payments should not extend longer than thirty years, and that Germany's responsibility should be limited to paying for the restoration of devastated areas. Although the President successfully withstood pressure to have Germany's obligations stretched to cover the whole cost of the war, he had to give in to the British contention that Allied pensions bills should be added to civilian damages assessed against the enemy. In the end, the Treaty of Versailles compelled Germany to sign a blank check —a promise to accept a bill which would be compiled and presented to her by a Reparations Commission in 1921. Thirty-three billion dollars, the sum eventually demanded, proved to be far more than Germany could or would pay.

Two issues which provoked particular anxiety were the Italian demand for Fiume and the Japanese determination to take over Germany's political and economic rights in the Shantung peninsula. Wilson believed that to permit Italy to annex Fiume would be a gross injustice to the new state of Jugoslavia, whose economic position would be highly insecure without the use of this important Adriatic port. He attempted to appeal over the heads of Orlando and the other Italian delegates directly to the Italian people, but the gesture failed. Orlando absented himself from the conference for several weeks, returning to Rome where he was given impressive evidence of popular backing in his struggle with Wilson. The Fiume question had to be left unsettled in the Paris treaties.[2] On the Shantung question, the President's sympathies were all with the Chinese spokesmen, who argued that the German leasehold at Kiaochow and the railroad and mining properties owned by Germans in the peninsula should revert to China. Japan, however, had a very strong position. She was in actual possession, having ousted the Germans by military force when she entered the war in 1914; she had compelled the Chinese government to confirm her rights in 1915 and 1918; she had secured the assent of Great Britain and France to

[1] The treaties never went into effect since they were to remain inoperative unless both Great Britain and the United States ratified them. The American treaty was never reported out of the Senate Foreign Relations Committee.

[2] In 1924 Jugoslavia finally acquiesced in Italian annexation of Fiume in return for certain Italian concessions giving Jugoslavia port facilities and an outlet to the sea.

these arrangements by secret treaty in 1917. Fearful lest Japan might quit the conference and refuse to join the League, Wilson gave in. The treaty assigned Germany's economic rights and holdings in Shantung to Japan, although in a separate unsigned declaration the Japanese promised that they would eventually withdraw their troops and restore sovereignty over Shantung to China, keeping only the economic concessions. The Chinese representatives registered their indignant protest over this settlement by refusing to sign the treaty.

At last, after many stormy sessions, the victorious powers agreed on the terms which were presented to the representatives of the new German Republic on May 7. No oral discussion was permitted, but the Germans were allowed to file written protests and counterproposals. At the urging of Lloyd George, a few concessions were made, although Wilson agreed on the whole with Clemenceau that the Germans should be required to accept the treaty as written without further change or delay. The final crisis came in June, when the German cabinet resigned rather than give approval to the document. Foch was then ordered to march into the heart of Germany unless the Allied terms were accepted within a specified time. The Germans bowed to the ultimatum and on June 28 the treaty was signed at a dramatic ceremony in the Hall of Mirrors at Versailles.

The Treaty of Versailles has been severely criticized both by those who think it was too soft and by those who consider it was too harsh. The former regret that Wilson interfered in any way with Clemenceau's program for the complete crippling of the enemy; the latter denounce the President for not having compelled the other leaders at Paris to accept his ideas in every detail. To the first line of criticism it may be answered that a document which provided for the almost complete disarmament of the defeated enemy as well as for the absolute demilitarization of the zone on which his defense from attack on the West depended should have given ample security to France and the rest of Europe. That it did not was due far less to deficiencies in the treaty itself than to divisions of opinion and weakness of will, which permitted Hitlerite Germany to flout its provisions with impunity.

The more valid indictment of the Treaty of Versailles is that it involved a breach of contract with Germany, which had accepted the 1918 armistice after an explicit stipulation that the Fourteen Points and the other Wilsonian principles should serve as the basis of the peace settlement. As finally drafted, the treaty sinned against the spirit if not the letter of the Fourteen Points. Although most of the points can be said to have been given embodiment in some part of the document, the terms imposed upon the vanquished were in the aggregate severe: loss of her entire colonial empire, loss of sizable areas of her territory and population within Europe, loss of important economic resources, limitations on her sovereignty, acknowledgment of war guilt, and a crushing reparations obligation. Two unfortunate results followed from this severity: German opinion was easily aroused by demagogues to regard the whole settlement as so intolerable as to require repudiation at whatever cost; on the other hand, a guilt-complex came to obsess English and American liberals who became so acutely conscious of the shortcomings of the treaty that they failed to see how dangerous it was not to insist upon the fulfillment of its terms. But, if the treaty was too harsh, this at least can be said: it would have been harsher still had not Wilson gone to Paris to fight for his principles. That the great idealist had to compromise on many points was unfortunate, but not to be avoided under conditions as they existed in 1919.

The Treaty of Versailles has, unhappily, been more closely examined for its sins than its virtues. Yet it did not lack for the latter. More nearly than on any preceding map of Europe, boundary lines now followed the principles of nationality. Moreover, the Covenant of the League of Nations offered a more promising opportunity for international cooperation than the world had ever known before. Indeed, the President, whose eyes were not blind to the treaty's faults, consoled himself with the thought that whatever was unjust in the settlement might eventually be adjusted through procedures provided in the Covenant. That the League did not in practice function this way was not his fault.

Shortly after the signing of the treaty, the weary President embarked on the *George Washington* for home, leaving Colonel House to deal with the great volume of business that still remained unsettled at the conference. Months of bitter controversy with the Senate lay ahead.

11

Wilson Repudiated

Pᴿᴱˢᴵᴰᴱᴺᵀ WILSON RETURNED FROM PARIS TO A COUNTRY THAT WAS IN a vastly different mood than that of 1917 and 1918. The strongest impulse of the American people was to put the war into the background and to seek a return to patterns of living that the war had disturbed. In the resulting retreat from idealism, Wilson's hope for participation of the United States in a new world order was shattered, while control over domestic policies passed into the hands of men who were hostile to his leadership.

DELAY ON THE TREATY

The President's confidence that the changes in the Covenant which he had secured during his second stay at Paris would disarm his opponents proved to be entirely unwarranted. Lodge announced to the country that the League in its second form was worse than in its first, and he went ahead with his plans to attack the whole Wilsonian settlement.

The Republican leader was a master strategist. His first achievement was to secure the organization of the newly elected Senate in a way certain to create difficulties for the President. Through a well-planned filibuster the Republicans had held up the passage of necessary appropriation bills before the old legislature adjourned on March 4, 1919. This action made it necessary for Wilson to call the new Congress into special session in May. Thus the opposition was given ample opportunity to form its battle lines before the President returned to America with the completed treaty. Not only was Lodge made chairman of the powerful Senate Foreign Relations Committee, but the latter was packed with anti-League Republicans.

On July 10, the day after his return, the President appeared before the Senate to submit the treaty and to make a personal appeal for its ratification. His position still seemed strong. Even his most bitter opponents were of the opinion that if the treaty came to an immediate vote it would probably be approved without change. Therefore their strategy had to be one of delay. The Foreign Relations Committee began a leisurely consideration of the document which held it up for the next two months. Lodge killed two weeks by reading the entire treaty line by line, sometimes to an empty committee room. Six weeks more were devoted to public hearings during which self-appointed spokesmen of Ireland, China, India, Egypt, Italy, Persia, and the Ukraine, together with many others who claimed to be experts on specific problems, were allowed to register their protests against various details in the settlement.

The committee then called upon the President to place all his records of the Paris negotiations at its disposal. This Wilson refused to do—a refusal which gave credence to the charge that he was concealing something. Instead he invited the committee to confer with him at the White House on August 19. There, after reading a prepared statement in which he tried to answer the various arguments that had been offered against the treaty, he permitted himself to be questioned for three and a half hours during which he was asked about every controversial issue. Article 10 of the League Covenant, already under bitter attack, was carefully considered. Of this undertaking "to respect and preserve as against external aggression of the territorial integrity and existing political independence of all Members of the League," Wilson pointed out that the Council of the League could only "advise upon" the means by which the obligation should be carried out in any particular case. Unless the United States were already involved in the controversy, no advice at all could be given without the assent of the American representative. Moreover, the vote of the Council was only advice, which each government would be free to reject if it pleased. Article 10 created "a moral, not a legal obligation." It left Congress absolutely free to put its own interpretation upon the commitment in all cases that called for action. Notwithstanding this fact, Article 10 seemed to Wilson "to constitute the very backbone of the whole Covenant. Without it the League would be hardly more than an influential debating society."

Concerning reservations to the treaty, he could see no objection to the Senate passing resolutions interpreting the sense in which the United States accepted the obligations of the Covenant, provided they were not made part of the formal ratification itself. He did, however, strongly oppose reservations which would have to be accepted by other signatories. Not only would they indefinitely delay final ratification, but they would cause other governments to follow the American example so "that the meaning and operative force of the treaty would presently be clouded from one end of its clauses to the other."

But the President made no converts. As in the February conference, the Democrats went away convinced that Wilson had met every reasonable objection, while Lodge and his followers persisted in their contention that the treaty should be ratified only with important reservations, if at all.

PUBLIC OPINION AND THE LEAGUE

Both supporters and opponents of the League counted upon the creation of a vast tide of popular sentiment that would overwhelm the opposing faction. At first the pro-League forces seemed to have the better of it. Out of 1377 newspaper editors polled by the *Literary Digest* in April, 1919, 718 unconditionally favored the League, 181 opposed, and 478 favored it conditionally. Thirty-two state legislatures passed resolutions favoring the entrance of the United States into some form of international organization, thirty-three governors were similarly on record, while pro-League sentiment was also very strong among editors and Protestant clergymen. The League to Enforce Peace was at the height of its power and influence; it staged meetings throughout the country in which the ratification of the treaty without reservations was urged. A prominent figure in the movement's activities was William Howard Taft, who sharply denounced the partisan maneuvers of his fellow Republicans.

But the anti-Leaguers were also extremely active. A self-constituted general staff held frequent meetings—usually in the Washington home of Senator Brandegee, occasionally in that of Mrs. Alice Roosevelt Longworth, T. R.'s energetic daughter. Prominent in the so-called cabal were Senator Borah of Idaho, Senator Johnson of California, Senator Knox of Pennsylvania, Senator McCormick of Illinois, and Colonel Harvey, publisher of the influential *Harvey's Weekly* and bitter enemy of the President since their break in 1911. Two multimillionaires of Pennsylvania, Henry Clay Frick and Andrew W. Mellon, provided the group with ample funds. The Hearst press was already engaged in violent denunciation of the League; its efforts were now supplemented by the publication of a great mass of literature warning against the perils of foreign entanglements. A League for the Preservation of American Independence was formed and meetings were organized to protest against "the evil thing with a holy name."

Opponents of the League found willing allies among the American Irish. The latter would probably have regarded the League as a sinister Anglo-American alliance under any circumstances, but a series of events in 1919 intensified their hostility. Irish-Americans from all sections of the country gathered in a large convention at Philadelphia in February, where they adopted a resolution proposed by the venerable Cardinal Gibbons calling upon the Peace Conference "to recognize the right of the people of Ireland to select for themselves without interference from any other people the form of government under which in the future they shall live." A distinguished Irish-American commission headed by Frank P. Walsh, former co-chairman with Taft of the War Labor Board, appeared in Paris to demand that Eamon de Valera be permitted to present to the conference the cause of the Irish Republic of which he claimed to be president. Wilson was not unsympathetic to the cause of Irish nationalism and he tried to arrange a meeting between the Irish-American delegation and Lloyd George, but his efforts were frustrated by the repercussions which followed that delegation's trip to Ireland. The trip demonstrated that the Irish-Americans and the Irish in Ireland were thinking in far different terms from the ideas of the British Prime Minister. While the English were still devising Home Rule plans, the Irish had set up the framework of an independent government. Englishmen learned to their great amazement and indignation that Walsh and his colleagues were touring Ireland conveying the greetings of America to this new republic. When they returned to Paris, they found that Lloyd George had ostentatiously withdrawn his promise to meet them. What was worse, Wilson took the attitude that the indiscretion of Walsh made it impossible for him to take any further action on behalf of the Irish-Americans without giving offense to the British. The delegation sailed for home, convinced that Wilson and the Peace Conference had failed to consider the rights of small nations—the principle which had been so loudly proclaimed throughout the war.

The anti-League Senators found their first audiences among the Irish-Americans. The League was portrayed as a menace both to Irish and to American independence, and the Friends of Irish Freedom spent hundreds of thousands of dollars in a widespread advertising campaign against ratification of the treaty. Irish opinion, which would have been a powerful factor at any time, was mobilized during these months as never before or since. Immediately after the failure of Ireland to secure a hearing at Paris, Eamon de Valera had come secretly to the United States. When his presence was at length made public, he at once became the symbol for the whole nationalist movement. In city after city,

Irish-Americans gave him a regal welcome. De Valera was less bitterly anti-League than most leaders in the United States, but inevitably the mass meetings which greeted him became violent expressions of anti-League and anti-Wilson feeling.

American opponents of the League made shrewd use of the state of Irish-American opinion. When they thundered against the iniquity of Article 10, they used Ireland as an example of a situation in which the United States might become involved. In vain the supporters of the League argued that American obligations could not be so interpreted as to force the United States to aid in the coercion of a people fighting for their independence. The misleading contention that the British Empire had been given six votes in the Assembly to the one allotted to the United States also impressed the Irish, who did not stop to ask whether Britain's influence over the vote of South Africa or of Canada would in fact be as great as that of the United States over the votes of the Republic of Panama or of a dozen other small neighboring states.

Alarmed by the success of his opponents in delaying action and beclouding the issues, Wilson set out in September on a speaking trip to carry his cause directly to the people. He visited the states of the Midwest, of the Pacific coast, and of the Rocky Mountains. During the space of twenty-two days, he traveled more than 8000 miles and delivered thirty-seven speeches averaging an hour in length. For a frail man of sixty-three, already overtaxed by the labors of many preceding months, this was too much. After his speech at Pueblo, Colorado, on September 25, Wilson suffered a serious breakdown. All thought of further activity had to be abandoned and the President's special train speeded back to Washington. The day after his return he was stricken with partial paralysis and was ·never again a well man. During the crucial final rounds of the battle over the treaty, Wilson was desperately sick, confined to his bedroom where he received little news from the outside world except through his wife and his doctor. Observers disagreed as to whether the heroic effort that had cost the President his health had strengthened his cause. He had been greeted by large and enthusiastic crowds, many of his speeches had been remarkably eloquent, thousands of listeners had been impressed by his impassioned earnestness. But he had gained no additional support in the one place where he most needed it—in the Senate, and the fickle public listened just as enthusiastically to the speeches of Borah, Johnson, and McCormick who had pressed hard on the President's heels during the tour.

THE DEFEAT OF THE TREATY

The Senate Foreign Relations Committee finally made its recommendations on September 10, 1919. The majority report, concurred in by nine of the ten Republican members (McCumber of North Dakota refused to accept it), advocated no less than forty-five amendments to the treaty and four reservations. Six of the seven Democrats signed a minority report calling for ratification without change. The stage was now set for a long debate on the floor of the Senate. Every conceivable argument was raised against the document. The Shantung settlement was bitterly denounced, the charge that the British would dominate the League through their six votes was repeated again and again, and Article 10 was depicted as a most dangerous entanglement.

Behind all the heated oratory, the situation was this. All but about seven of the Democratic Senators were willing to vote for the treaty without change; it is difficult to say, however, whether they really favored the League or wished to support their party head. The Republicans, on the other hand, were divided into three factions of about equal size. Fourteen were the so-called irreconcilables, determined to vote against the treaty so long as it incorporated the League in any form; a second group were strong reservationists, at heart probably anti-League, but believing with Lodge that it was better tactics to emasculate the treaty with amendments than to attempt to secure its outright rejection; the rest were mild reservationists, sufficiently pro-League to side with the Democrats in voting down the direct amendments which Lodge first tried to put through.

In the end Lodge performed an adroit feat of political generalship. He united the three factions of his party to the support of fourteen so-called Lodge reservations, which passed the Senate in November. The mild reservations supported them because they hoped that a way would thus be paved for the ratification of the treaty; the irreconcilables gave Lodge their votes because they were ready to help any maneuver that would weaken the League. The most important of the reservations was one practically nullifying Article 10 of the Covenant; it stated that the United States assumed no obligation under the article unless Congress decided to act in a particular case. Other reservations claimed for the United States complete freedom to declare any issue a domestic question excluded from the jurisdiction of the League and the sole right to interpret the Monroe Doctrine, withheld assent from the Shantung settlement, and asserted that the United States would not be bound by any decision of the League in which member states of the British Commonwealth cast in the aggregate more than one vote. Several other reservations were equally damaging to the idea of the League and equally likely to be objected to by other signatories to the treaty. Lodge undoubtedly knew that, if the treaty were accepted by the Senate in this mutilated form. Wilson would not attempt to secure its ratification by the other powers. In fact, Lodge had taken a leading part in killing arbitration treaties in 1905 and 1911 by just this device.

Wilson's position on the issue raised by Lodge was made clear in a letter to Senator Hitchcock of Nebraska, the Democratic leader. The President expressed the hope that the friends and supporters of the treaty would vote against the Lodge resolution of ratification since it provided not for ratification, but "rather for nullification of the treaty."

On November 19, when the important roll call was finally taken, only thirty-nine Senators voted to approve the treaty with the Lodge reservations, while fifty-five opposed it. The nays were cast by forty-two Democrats, most of them guided by the advice from the White House, and thirteen Republican irreconcilables, who were opposed to a League whatever the safeguards. The sentiment of the Senate on ratification without reservations was then tested, but only thirty-eight Senators, all but one of them Democrats, would support the treaty in unadulterated form, while fifty-five opposed it, the reservationists joining forces with the irreconcilables.

It seemed fantastic that, although there were only seventeen Senators who were completely opposed to the treaty, ratification could not be secured. Moderates from both parties sought to discover an escape from the impasse through a bipartisan conference which held numerous sessions in January, 1920. The Democrats offered to accept several reservations, including one to Article 10 which had been drafted by Taft. The conference made such apparent progress that the irreconcilables became alarmed and threatened to bolt the party if Lodge gave ground. In the end, the Massachusetts Senator refused all terms except complete Democratic acquiescence in the Lodge reservations, and therefore the attempt at compromise failed.

On March 19 the Senate took the final vote on the treaty. The fourteen Lodge reservations had been strengthened rather than weakened and a fifteenth reservation of Democratic parentage had been adopted —a reservation stating that in the judgment of the United States Senate the Irish people were entitled to a government of their own choice. The treaty with its fifteen reservations came within seven of the two-thirds vote necessary to secure its ratification; now forty-nine Senators voted for it and thirty-five against it. Half of the Democrats who voted against the treaty with reservations the previous November now voted for it, convinced that ratification in this form was better than no ratification at all. But the other half voted against it, following the advice of Wilson incorporated in another letter from the White House. Once again it was their votes, added to those of the irreconcilables, which killed the treaty.

An interesting—though not particularly profitable—speculation is whether the result would have been different if Wilson had retained his health. Perhaps pro-League public opinion would have been more effectively rallied. Perhaps the President would have been more conscious of the realities of the situation. In the latter case, he might have seen the need for Republican votes and, by timely compromise, won the support of the more reasonable reservationists. Such an outcome of the struggle ought to have been possible if the good offices of Taft and other pro-League Republicans had been employed. But to compromise was impossible for the Wilson of 1920; many critics considered this his fatal weakness, although his admirers have insisted that compromise would have been equivalent to surrender.

Failure to ratify left the United States legally at war with Germany. The Republicans, anxious to end Wilson's wartime powers, attempted to meet this difficulty by passing the so-called Knox Resolution which simply repealed the declaration of war, but Wilson returned it to Congress with a stinging veto. Consequently, the official state of war continued until it was brought to an end in 1921 by the Harding administration with a Congressional resolution and a separate treaty between the United States and Germany.

President Wilson never lost faith that American opinion would eventually rally to the League in such volume as to override the obstructionists. He looked forward to the 1920 election as "a solemn referendum" on the issue. But as will be shown later, the election proved to be meaningless as such a referendum. What the American people really thought of the League in November, 1919, in March, 1920, or in November, 1920, is difficult to determine. Undoubtedly time worked to the advantage of the anti-Leaguers. Over the course of the months, the combined efforts of irreconcilable Senators, the nationalist press, and the Irish succeeded in convincing millions of Americans that the League was a sinister plot against American independence. Millions of others did not lose their faith in the ideal, but they became hopelessly divided in opinion as to how to realize it. Taft first and later other leaders of the League to Enforce Peace shifted their ground, giving up their fight to secure the treaty without change and urging

ratification with the Lodge reservations, even though they considered
some of them "harmful." Others believed that the President was right
and that the Lodge reservations were impossible to accept because they
nullified the treaty. Baffled and confused, more and more Americans
became tired of the whole debate and more than willing to forget both
the war and the League.

WILSON'S ECLIPSE

In domestic as well as in foreign affairs the country was deserting
Wilson's leadership. For months Wilson's attention was diverted from
domestic issues by his absorption in the task of peacemaking and his
fight to secure American acceptance of the Treaty of Versailles. After
this his physical collapse and long illness prevented his giving effective
attention to the important problems of reconstruction facing the nation. The loneliness of the President's position was accentuated by his
estrangement from men who had been his advisers for many years. In
February, 1920, Secretary of State Lansing was asked to resign—for
the ostensible reason that he had convened unauthorized cabinet meetings while Wilson was ill, but actually because of the evidence which
had accumulated for months indicating that the Secretary and the
President did not agree on fundamental policies. This quarrel was inevitable, but Wilson's break with his most intimate adviser, Colonel
House, is less easy to understand. Perhaps it arose out of House's fond-
ness for compromise at a time when Wilson was less and less willing
to listen to suggestions that he should make concessions to his opponents.

Quite apart, however, from Wilson's physical inability to provide
his old-time aggressive leadership, the country was not in a mood to
accept his advice when it was offered. Already disillusionment was widespread. To the returning soldier, there was little glamour to be attached
to his recent experiences; the mud of France, trench warfare, wholesale death and destruction left memories both vivid and unpleasant.
Those who had stayed at home were disgusted by the greedy scramble
for the spoils of war which had marked the Paris Peace Conference.
They were irritated by the continuance of wartime controls and the
unchecked rise of prices. Veterans and civilians alike wanted nothing
so much as to return to old prewar patterns of living, but the road back
was a rocky one.

POSTWAR REFORMS

The reaction against idealism did not prevent certain of the prewar
reform movements from achieving their goals during the months after

the armistice. Indeed, the demand for both prohibition and women's suffrage had been accentuated by the war itself.

The Anti-Saloon League and its allies, already very strong, took immediate advantage of the opportunity offered by the war. The brewery business was denounced as unpatriotic because it was dominated by German-Americans, while great stress was laid upon the danger of the liquor trade to the morals of the soldiers and upon the iniquity of diverting scarce grain into the manufacture of intoxicants. The Lever Act of 1917 included clauses prohibiting the use of grain for the manufacture of distilled liquors and making it permissive for the President to extend the ban to beer, ale, and wine. Acting under this authority, Wilson ordered the breweries to close in October, 1918. Ten days after the armistice a law—curiously known as the "War Prohibition Act"—was passed, making it unlawful to sell intoxicating beverages after June 30, 1919, until the President should proclaim the end of the war and demobilization period.

This date was, in fact, destined to be the last day on which intoxicating beverages were legally sold in the United States for more than fourteen years. Before "war prohibition" was over, prohibition by Constitutional amendment had been declared in effect. On December 28, 1917, Congress had passed and sent to the states the Eighteenth Amendment by which "the manufacture, sale, or transportation of intoxicating liquors within, the importation thereof into, or the exportation thereof from the United States and all territory subject to the jurisdiction thereof for beverage purposes" was to be prohibited. Congress and the several states were to have concurrent power to enforce the amendment by appropriate legislation. Ratification was secured with surprising speed and ease. By January 16, 1919, thirty-six states, the necessary three quarters, had approved the amendment, which was proclaimed in force one year later. Eventually all the states except Connecticut and Rhode Island joined in the ratification.

The actual definition of intoxicating beverages as well as drastic penalties for their manufacture or sale was provided by the Volstead Act, passed by Congress over Wilson's veto in October, 1919. The specification that all liquors containing more than 0.5 per cent alcohol were banned was criticized by many who denied that light wines and beer were in fact intoxicating, but the Supreme Court upheld the law (Hawke v. Smith, 1920, and Rhode Island v. Palmer, 1920). The enforcement of legislation which a large section of the public considered a violation of personal liberty proved to be one of the most troublesome problems of the 1920's.

Meantime, the nation's participation in a crusade to make the world safe for democracy and the magnificent support given by women to the war effort had undermined male resistance to the demand for women's suffrage. In June, 1919, Congress accepted the Nineteenth Amendment, which specified that the right of citizens to vote should not be denied by the United States or any state "on account of sex." Ratification met some opposition in the South where Alabama, Maryland, and Virginia rejected the amendment. The fact, however, that 1920 was an election year worked to the advantage of the suffrage advocates. Republicans vied with Democrats in striving for the political credit of having given the women the vote, and in August, 1920, the consent of the thirty-sixth state was secured. The amendment was declared in effect in time for the ladies to cast their ballots for Harding or Cox. In operation the Nineteenth Amendment did not bring the immediate purification of politics which the more ardent suffragettes had promised, but neither did it produce the dreadful consequences predicted by the misogynists.

DEMOBILIZATION

The task of demobilizing more than four million men in the armed services was accomplished quickly. By the middle of April, 1919, four thousand men a day were being discharged, and nearly half of those in training camps in the United States had been dismissed. Even before Wilson returned with the completed treaty of peace a million and a half members of the A.E.F. were back on American shores. This was almost as spectacular an achievement as getting them overseas because only American ships were used on the return voyage. Thanks, however, to the speedy conversion of cargo ships into transports and the service of various types of naval vessels, the homecoming of the troops was speeded up. With the exception of less than twenty thousand men

Can She Live Up to Expectations? (By McCutcheon in the *Chicago Tribune*.)

under General Henry T. Allen, serving as an American Army of Occupation in the Rhineland, all of the expeditionary forces were once more in the United States by January, 1920.

It is questionable whether so rapid a demobilization was wise. Soldiers were given $60 discharge pay and a ticket home according to military units and without any consideration of employment opportunities in the sections of the country affected. Often the veteran faced many weeks without work because of local conditions. The problem was accentuated by the abrupt and planless termination of war contracts, which threatened many industrial units with bankruptcy. Thousands of war workers, moreover, were seeking new jobs along with the returned veterans. All this resulted in a serious situation during the early months of 1919. Labor Department sources estimated that there were a million unemployed on January 30, 1919, and that number increased at the rate of a hundred thousand a week for more than two months thereafter.

The Federal government did little to help during the crisis. In Wilson's message to Congress of December 2, 1918, he expressed the opinion that the American people knew their own business, were quick and resourceful in making adjustments, and self-reliant in action. He advocated, therefore, that there be a minimum of governmental direction over the processes of reconstruction. The President's principal adviser on economic matters, Bernard Baruch, concurred in this judgment, and by January 1, 1919, the powerful War Industries Board had closed shop. Even the limited program which the President did recommend was largely jettisoned by the Republican-dominated Congress. The United States Employment Service, which had placed more than four and a half million workers in jobs over the course of sixteen months, was compelled to scrap 80 per cent of its machinery in March, 1919, just when it was most needed for the reconversion period. The service was killed by the refusal of Congress to make sufficient appropriations to support it due both to the general impulse to cut down the huge expenditures of the government and the unpopularity of this particular agency with employers who accused it of being staffed with doctrinaire social workers, oversympathetic with the cause of labor unionism. The Congressional drive for economy led also to the rejection of proposals for the expansion of public works and for grants to rehabilitate the physical property of the railroads in bad condition because of overuse during the war.

Similar motives operated along with the opposition of the National Grange to defeat the so-called Lane Plan, a scheme sponsored by the Secretary of the Interior for Federal and state cooperation in a bold reclamation project to provide both employment and farms for returned veterans. One of the few measures actually passed by Congress was the Vocational Rehabilitation Act of June, 1918, which set up a Federal Board for Vocational Education to train disabled veterans for jobs. Several thousand men were placed in colleges and schools throughout the country, but the program, nevertheless, proved a great disappointment because it never benefited more than a small percentage of the 230,000 Americans disabled during the war.

Many states and municipalities took a broader view of their responsibilities during the reconstruction period. States like New York, Oregon, and Indiana made generous appropriations for state employment services to serve both the veterans and displaced civilian workers. Employment bureaus were also maintained by welfare agencies all over the nation. The task of coordinating these activities for the benefit of the discharged servicemen was entrusted to Colonel Arthur Woods, formerly police commissioner of New York City and at this time Assistant to Secretary of War Baker. In the end over one million men were placed in jobs through these channels. Massachusetts, Minnesota, and fifteen other states passed bonus acts for the benefit of the veterans; New York and Oregon voted grants to assist veterans in securing an education; California and New York provided for an expanded program of public works; several western states passed legislation promising cooperation with the Lane Plan for settling veterans on reclaimed lands and, when Congress failed to act, California went ahead with a land settlement program of its own.

The greatest help, however, in carrying the country safely through the period of demobilization came from an unexpected quarter. By the summer of 1919 the post-armistice depression was giving way to an extraordinary postwar prosperity. The war had ruined for the time being the German export trade and seriously injured the British. For several months American exports soared to dizzy heights. They totaled slightly less than $8,000,000,000 for 1919 and considerably more than that for 1920—over three times their 1913 level. The domestic market was similarly active. There was an orgy of spending as wartime savings were poured out for commodities that had been difficult to buy during the period of hostilities. Particularly prosperous was the automobile business. The boom, however, was an unhealthy one. All Europe was impoverished by the war, and the export business was cut in half as sharply as it had risen. With wartime controls relaxed, domestic prices jumped to such an unreasonable level as to dry up demand, while warehouses bulged with the huge inventories carried by overoptimistic businessmen. During 1921 the country suffered a serious economic depression. But the short-lived prosperity of the fall of 1919 and the following winter did at least ease the problems created by the rapid demobilization of the armed forces.

GETTING THE GOVERNMENT OUT OF BUSINESS

During the war advanced liberals had watched with approval while the Federal government not only built and operated millions of tons of shipping, but took over the management of the railroad, telegraph, telephone, cable, and radio systems of the country. Some at least of these economic activities, they hoped, would remain permanently nationalized or at least subjected to much more rigorous public control than before the war. Conservatives, on the other hand, had acquiesced in government operation of these enterprises with great misgiving and, as soon as the armistice was signed, they demanded that business be turned back to private control as speedily as possible. In the case of electrical communications they had a complete victory. At midnight, July 31, 1919, these properties were returned by act of Congress to their owners without any condition attached other than that the rates established by the Postmaster General should be continued for four months unless changed by authority of the government.

The railroads, however, constituted a somewhat different problem. Although high wartime costs resulted in the Railroad Administration suffering a loss of $1,000,000,000 during the twenty-six months of its existence, government operation had by certain other standards been an interesting and not unsuccessful experiment. Particularly impressive had been the greatly improved efficiency made possible by operating the railroads as a single system without wasteful duplication of facilities. Progressives demanded either the continuance of government operation or the return of the roads under conditions which would consolidate the wartime gains. McAdoo, who headed the Railroad Administration until January, 1919, and Walter D. Hines, his successor, both recommended that Federal control should be continued for five years while the whole railroad problem was subjected to intensive investigation. The Railroad Brotherhoods vigorously supported a plan, drafted by Glenn E. Plumb, their legal representative, under which the government would purchase the roads and operate them through a tripartite board representative of the government, management, and employees. One half of the net earnings would be set aside for the payment of the bonds issued to finance the government purchase; the other half would be paid to the employees and executives as dividends on wages.

Congress, however, turned its face against both government ownership and operation. On March 1, 1920, the lines were turned back to
private management under the terms of the Esch-Cummins or Transportation Act of 1920. This important law not only provided for government support to the railroads during the difficult transition period,
but laid down as well significant principles governing the future regulation of transportation. For a period of six months after the return of
the lines, the government guaranteed to the carriers a net return equal to
the rentals which they had been receiving from the Railroad Administration; rates, fares, wages, and salaries were all to be frozen at existing
levels during the guarantee period unless changes were authorized by
the government. As a further help to the carriers, a revolving fund of
$300,000,000 was set up from which the railroads might secure loans,
upon approval of the Interstate Commerce Commission, for a period of
two years after the resumption of private control.

The commission was enlarged to include eleven members instead of
nine and was given important additional powers. Its consent was now
made necessary to the issuance of new railroad securities and the construction or abandonment of track. It could fix minimum as well as
maximum rates and it could set aside rates fixed by state authorities if
these were found to be prejudicial to interstate commerce. For the purpose of rate-fixing the commission was authorized to divide the country into districts, in each of which rates were to be fixed at such a
level that the carriers of the district would earn an aggregate net income equal to a fair return upon the aggregate value of their properties.
Since, however, under the same rates strong railroads might earn unreasonable profits while weaker lines were suffering losses, a controversial "recapture clause" was written into the act. Any carrier earning
more than 6 per cent on the value of its property was required to place
one half the surplus in its own reserve fund and to pay over the other
half to the commission which would place it in a general contingent
fund. This fund would be used by the commission either to make loans
to the weaker companies for capital expenditures or to purchase equipment which would be leased to them.

The most striking change of policy in the railroad legislation of 1920
was that under which cooperation and consolidation of the carriers was
favored. Not only was the Interstate Commerce Commission empowered
to relax the long-short haul clause under certain circumstances and to
permit forms of pooling formerly prohibited, but it was directed to
prepare a plan under which the railroad properties of the country
would be consolidated into a limited number of systems. Thus it was

frankly recognized that enforced competition as the panacea for all railroad abuses had failed and that the public interest would best be served by encouraging the strong carriers to take over the weak under strict government regulation.

Finally, the Transportation Act provided new machinery for handling labor problems. There had been considerable Congressional support for compulsory arbitration and the outlawing of railroad strikes; indeed, the Senate had passed the Esch Bill in a form incorporating these principles. The House rejected this extreme procedure, however, and the act as passed provided instead for the establishment of both railroad boards of labor adjustment and a national Railroad Labor Board. The former, to be set up by agreement between the carriers and their employees, were to hear grievances over rules and working conditions. Wage disputes and any grievances not settled by the adjustment boards were to be referred to the Railroad Labor Board, a body composed of nine members appointed by the President; three of these were to be chosen from a list nominated by the employers, three from a list drawn up by the employees, and three appointed without restriction to represent the public. The board was given wide powers to compel testimony, but its findings were not binding upon either party. A discussion of the problems which confronted the board during its short life and which killed it in 1926 is included in a later chapter.

In many ways the shipping problem was even more complex than the railroad situation. In the former case it was not a matter of the government returning to private management enterprises that had all along been privately owned; rather it was one of deciding what should be done with some two thousand ships which had been built or purchased since 1916 with government money. During the export boom of 1919 the problem was not acute since some three hundred operating companies willingly kept existing routes in operation and developed new ones on a cost-plus basis under the supervision of the Merchant Fleet Corporation and the Shipping Board. But the collapse of international trade in 1920 brought unpleasant results. There was no longer enough business to provide attractive commissions to the operating companies and their number fell from three hundred to forty. Oftentimes the government-owned ships were simply abandoned in foreign ports. The losses to the government from its shipping operations reached $16,000,000 monthly by 1921.

Once again the formula favored by Congressional conservatives was a speedy return to private enterprise. The Merchant Marine Act of 1920 directed the Shipping Board to transfer the government-owned ships quickly and on easy terms to private ownership. Except under special circumstances, the ships might be sold only to corporations in which a majority of the stock was held by American citizens; indeed, if the ships were to be used in the coasting trade, the companies had to be at least 75 per cent American controlled. The Merchant Fleet Corporation was to operate the ships which could not be sold; it was to establish new shipping routes and maintain them until private capital could be induced to take them over; it was given a revolving fund of $25,000,000 and empowered to make loans to companies willing to operate the new routes.

The shipping problem was too complex to be solved by any single wave of the wand. The methods by which the Shipping Board carried out its mandate under the act of 1920 provided material for controversy for many years. The nub of the problem was this: high costs made it unprofitable for American shipping to compete with foreign lines; yet an American merchant marine was vital to national defense. The only possible answers were government operation at a loss or private ownership and operation with subsidies. It required many years for American opinion to accept the inevitability of choosing between these alternatives.

LABOR UNREST

During the war labor relations had been abnormal. The American Federation of Labor leaders had attempted with fair success to prevent strikes. At the same time, however, workers had demanded substantial increases in wages and the Federal war administrations had favored their demands in order to keep industrial peace and maintain production. From the standpoint of most employers, labor had become entirely too assertive and it seemed imperative to resist firmly the trend toward increased power for labor-union leaders once the war was over. The unions, on the other hand, were determined not only to preserve their wartime gains, but to secure new concessions. They pointed out that the cost of living after the armistice was constantly rising and that many of the workers, even after pay raises, were worse off than they had been before the war. With both management and labor in an uncompromising mood, all the elements for serious industrial warfare were present. During 1919 more than four million American workers were at one time or another out on strike, and the number of such disputes reached 3630.

In many of these contests labor was victorious. Such was the result of walkouts of the New York clothing workers, the New York harbor

workers, the New England textile employees, the New England telegraph operators, and the New York actors. But these victories—mostly
won early in 1919—hardened public opinion against labor, and the
strikes of the later months of that year were much less successful.

Particularly damaging to the cause of unionism was the alarm felt all
over the country when Seattle, Washington, was the scene of a general
strike in February. There trouble started in the shipyards and became
serious when sixty thousand workers in all trades struck on February 6
in support of the demands of the shipworkers. Strict order was maintained by the strikers and an attempt was made to carry on essential
services. But even though the strike failed and was called off after
five days, the spectacle of the economic life of a great city being thus
tied up was widely cited as evidence of the danger of Bolshevism in the
country—an interpretation of the event given wide publicity through
the speeches of Seattle's Mayor Ole Hansen. This feeling that labor was
getting out of hand and was threatening revolution received additional
impetus from the occurrence of a more serious general strike in May
across the border in Winnipeg, Canada.

Against this background the story of the three most important labor
controversies of 1919 must be considered.

THE STEEL STRIKE

In the steel industry there was much discontent among the workers
over their conditions. The working day was frequently twelve hours,
and the average for employees in some of the plants was about sixty-
nine hours for a seven-day week. Nor was it unusual for the operators
to call upon the men to labor on twenty-four-hour shifts.

In an effort to remedy the situation, twenty-four unions of the American Federation of Labor established a steelworkers' organizing committee which attempted to unionize the men during the summer of
1919. Prominent in the movement was William Z. Foster, who was
reputed to be anything from a Communist to a syndicalist. When the
organizing committee demanded an eight-hour day, a six-day week,
the ending of the twenty-four-hour shift practice, and collective
bargaining, Judge Elbert H. Gary, chairman of the board of the United
States Steel Corporation and general spokesman for the whole industry,
refused to recognize the right of the group to speak for the men.

Consequently, a strike was scheduled for September 22. President
Wilson's effort to avert the danger failed when the union officials rejected his plea to postpone the walkout. On the appointed day, approximately 280,000 men left their jobs, chiefly in Chicago, Youngs-

town, Ohio, Buffalo, New York, and several plants in Pennsylvania. Gradually more workers joined the walkout until there were at least 300,000 in the strikers' ranks. There was disorder around some of the steel mills and, during the disturbances, at least four persons were killed and more than fifty wounded. At one time Federal troops under General Leonard Wood were moved into Gary, Indiana, where martial law was declared and picketing limited.

Public opinion, formulated in no small part by an antilabor press, turned more and more against the strikers. The feeling was widespread that Foster was promoting un-American agitation and also that the workers had gained enough during the war itself. A back-to-work movement gained momentum by January, 1920, the strikers' committee acknowledged failure, and the strike was declared at an end.

The strike had a curious aftermath. Public opinion, which had been so generally adverse to the workers while the dispute was in progress, showed signs of a reversal after it was over. In large part this was due to the harrowing picture of actual labor conditions in the steel industry contained in the report of a special investigating committee of the Interchurch World Movement. This report, to which were appended the names of an impressive list of Protestant churchmen headed by Bishop Francis J. McConnell of the Methodist Episcopal Church, denied that the strike had been Red-inspired and asserted that it had been the natural result of the labor policies of the United States Steel Corporation—policies that were based not alone on low wages and long hours, but included arbitrary management, bribery, spying on the workers, and stirring up racial animosities to prevent employees from forming a common front. The corporation indignantly denied the truth of this indictment, but under the pressure of public opinion and after proddings by President Harding, the twelve-hour day was eliminated from the steel industry in 1923.

THE BOSTON POLICE STRIKE

Boston policemen after the armistice were in a rebellious mood. Their station houses were crowded, they were compelled to buy their own uniforms, and, worst of all, with the cost of living soaring they continued to be paid according to prewar scales based upon a minimum of $1100. In the summer of 1919 the Boston Social Club, to which the police had belonged for thirteen years, applied for a charter from the American Federation of Labor. Police Commissioner Edwin U. Curtis had forbidden any such affiliation and he proceeded to take stern disciplinary action against the officers of the club. Nineteen men were threatened with suspension from the force, bringing the situation to a crisis. Mayor Andrew J. Peters, a Democrat, and a Citizens' Committee sought to mediate with the following formula: the leaders who were in trouble were to be reinstated, the police were to be permitted to maintain a union but without outside affiliations, and an opportunity should be provided for the men to present their grievances. But the commissioner refused to compromise; instead he carried through the threatened suspensions and, by a vote of 1134 to 2, the men decided to strike.

On September 9 the police left their posts and shortly thereafter ruffians, hoodlums, and lawbreakers of every description began to take advantage of the situation. Stores and homes had to be boarded up to prevent looting. The next day Mayor Peters called out that part of the state guard resident in Boston, over which he shared authority with the governor, and this action proved effective in restoring order. On the third day of the strike, Calvin Coolidge, the Republican governor of Massachusetts, intervened and took the situation into his own hands. He called out the rest of the state guard and appealed to the Secretary of War for a promise of Federal troops in case any attempt was made to stage a general strike.

The policemen realized that they were defeated and were ready to

When the Policeman Strikes. (Kirby in the *New York World*.)

return to work. But here they found themselves opposed by Curtis who refused to take back any of the strikers and proposed to enlist an entirely new force to take their places. Samuel Gompers attempted to intercede, but Coolidge, standing firmly behind his commissioner, rebuked the AFL head with a stinging public telegram. "There is no right," Coolidge asserted, "to strike against the public safety by any-body, anywhere, any time."

It reveals much concerning the prevailing mood of the country that Coolidge's rebuke to Gompers and his stern disciplining of the Boston policemen made him a national hero and a possibility for the Republican presidential nomination in 1920. Even President Wilson added his congratulations to those showered down upon the Yankee champion of law and order.

ENTER JOHN L. LEWIS

John L. Lewis, destined to be a prominent figure in labor circles for the next three decades, became president of the United Mine Workers in 1919. His first task was to lead the workers in the bituminous coal fields in their struggle to achieve a program of far-reaching demands which included a national contract, a 60 per cent wage increase, and a thirty-hour minimum work week. The pay demand was large because the bituminous miners, unlike the anthracite workers, had had no wage increase since September, 1917, even though the cost of living had risen sharply.

When the operators rejected these terms, a strike was called for November 1, 1919. Lewis was solidly supported by the miners, but the Federal government permitted the dispute to continue only a little over a week before intervening. On November 9, Attorney General Palmer secured from a district court judge in Indiana a sweeping injunction based on the Lever Act, the law still on the books under which the government had been given its extraordinary wartime powers over food and fuel. The officers of the United Mine Workers were ordered to cease all activities tending to encourage and maintain the strike in the bituminous coal industry. To the reporters Lewis commented: "We cannot fight the government," and an order declaring the strike officially at an end was duly issued.

Despite Lewis's gesture of compliance, the miners did not actually go back to work until a month later when the union accepted President Wilson's proposal that the issues in controversy be submitted to arbitration. After extended hearings the arbitral body awarded the miners a 27 per cent wage increase, but no shortening of hours.

THE RED SCARE

The strike epidemic in itself would have been enough to convince many conservative Americans that dangerous radicalism was abroad in the land. This feeling was many times intensified by events in Europe. The Bolsheviks had seized control of Russia in November, 1917, and made a separate peace with Germany the following March. Despite counterrevolutionary attempts and foreign interventions the hated Reds had not only clung to power in Russia, but had boldly raised the banner of world revolution. For a time during 1919 universal proletarian revolt seemed a possibility both to hopeful radicals and trembling conservatives. The German Communists held the city of Berlin for a few days; the Hungarian Communists ruled their country for five months; unrest boiled high in Italy and elsewhere in Europe; there were ominous rumblings in India and the British Empire.

There was an intoxicating quality in the news which led a few extremists in the United States to the point of dangerous action. Late in April, 1919, a bomb was found in the mail of Mayor Ole Hansen of Seattle, a conspicuous Red-baiter. A day later the colored maid of Senator Thomas R. Hardwick of Georgia, an advocate of immigration restriction, had her hands blown off when she opened a mysterious package addressed to her employer. Timely investigation in the New York City Post Office disclosed sixteen packages containing bombs addressed to prominent persons in public life. Some twenty other deadly bundles were discovered passing through the mails elsewhere. Among the prominent citizens marked for death were Attorney General Palmer, Postmaster General Burleson, Supreme Court Justice Holmes, Federal Judge Landis, J. P. Morgan, and John D. Rockefeller. A month later several bomb explosions occurred in widely scattered parts of the country, one of them wrecking the Washington home of Attorney General Palmer. The most sensational of these outrages took place on September 16, 1920, when a terrific blast in noonday crowded Wall Street caused the death of thirty-eight persons, injury to hundreds of others, property damage to the extent of $2,000,000, and untold harm to the nerves of the masters of capital.

These and other similar incidents were more an index of the unusual strain of the times than of the real strength or intensity of the revolutionary movement in the United States. Actually radical ranks were divided and confused by the turn of events. A right-wing minority of the Socialists led by John Spargo had withdrawn from the party when it went on record in 1917 as condemning American participation in the war. This loss had not been serious, but in 1919 a more important crisis developed. Left-wing Socialists sought to capture the party machinery and affiliate with the Communist Third International and, when this attempt failed, the extremists split off into two new groups: the Communist party and the slightly less radical Communist Labor party. On orders from Moscow the two were united in the spring of 1920 as the United Communist party. Meantime, the Socialist Labor group continued to regard itself as the true Marxian party, the Industrial Workers of the World continued on its separate way, and the Anarchists would have nothing to do with any of the others. The total number of all these radical groups has been estimated at less than 0.2 per cent of the American population. There could be little menace from that small number.

To middle-class Americans, however, a Red was a Red. They were ignorant or indifferent to the fact that the Socialists had purged Communists from their own ranks or that Anarchists were anti-Bolshevik in sentiment. All radicals were branded as un-American because of their hostility to the war and because of the preponderance of recent immigrant stock in their ranks. In Weirton, West Virginia, 118 foreigners, members of the I.W.W. and involved in the steel strike, were compelled by the police to kiss the flag. In New York City a mob of ex-soldiers and civilians wrecked the office of the *New York Call*, a leading Socialist newspaper. Most serious of all was the clash at Centralia, Washington, on Armistice Day, 1919. Three parading members of the American Legion were killed by gunfire from I.W.W. headquarters and one other lost his life during the ensuing turmoil. The affair was surrounded by great controversy. The Legionnaires asserted that the attack was unprovoked; the I.W.W. members claimed to have been defending their hall against an attempt to wreck it as it had been wrecked the year before. Guilty or innocent, the I.W.W. was severely punished. Of twelve men accused of complicity in the shooting, one was taken from his cell by a mob and lynched, while the others were given prison sentences ranging from twenty-five to forty years. But this was not all. Throughout the Northwest I.W.W. halls were demolished by irate citizens; over one thousand of the detested group were arrested and it was difficult to find lawyers who were willing to undertake their defense.

Prosecution of individuals for merely belonging to the I.W.W. or any other radical organization was made possible by the enactment of criminal syndicalist laws in thirty-two states making it illegal to belong to organizations advocating the overthrow of the government by force. Twenty-eight states made it a punishable offense to display the Red flag as a political emblem.

Although ultrapatriots were unsuccessful in their attempt to secure a new Federal sedition act which would be even more severe than the wartime legislation, the Federal government did enforce existing laws drastically against the radicals. President Wilson could not forgive the Socialists for their opposition to the war and refused to pardon Debs and others who had been sent to prison for their activities. Not until Christmas Day, 1933, were the Federal prisons finally cleared of the last of the fifteen hundred of those originally convicted.

A particularly effective antiradical weapon was a law passed by Congress in October, 1918, authorizing the Secretary of Labor to arrest and deport any alien who advocated revolution himself or belonged to any organization which advocated the overthrow of government by force, assassination of public officials, no human government, or the unlawful destruction of property. In 1920 the Secretary's authority was extended to permit the deportation of aliens who had been convicted under the wartime espionage laws. The first wholesale deportation occurred in December, 1919, when the *Buford,* popularly referred to as the Red or Soviet Ark, left for Russia with 249 alien radicals aboard.

Meantime, Attorney General Palmer was preparing a drastic blow. For many weeks during 1919 Department of Justice operatives gathered data on the Communists and Anarchists. Spies were employed to gain access to the secret meetings of these radicals and secure the names of the leaders. In the absence of Secretary of Labor Wilson, who was ill, a subordinate in the Labor Department obligingly supplied Palmer with three thousand deportation warrants, which were served on January 2, 1920, in carefully prepared, simultaneous raids upon radical meeting places in all parts of the country. Everyone found on the premises was arrested, whether or not the agents actually had a warrant for the particular individual, whether or not he was a member of the Communist party, or whether he was an alien or a citizen. Other radicals were apprehended in their homes. Even persons attempting to visit the jailed suspects were themselves arrested on suspicion of affiliation with the proscribed groups. Some four thousand persons all told were rounded up. Their treatment after arrest was often harsh and the deportation hearings were conducted without counsel or other judicial safeguards. Only 556 of those arrested were in the end deported; some of the others were turned over to state authorities for punishment under the criminal syndicalist laws, but the majority were eventually released for want of evidence. Palmer's high-handed procedure was enthusiastically applauded by the great mass of the public who hated and feared the alien radicals; a few thoughtful citizens, however, were seriously disturbed by the un-American conduct of the government itself. Charles Evans Hughes spoke gravely of "violations of personal rights which savor of the worst practices of tyranny."

While the country was still greatly excited over the arrest of the alien radicals, the New York Assembly attempted to outdo the Attorney General in its assertion of 100 per cent Americanism. Five regularly elected assemblymen, representing districts in New York City, were expelled simply because they were members of the Socialist party. Hughes led the New York Bar Association in a vigorous, but ineffective, protest against this action. The former Supreme Court justice and presidential candidate wrote: "This is not, in my judgment, American government. . . . I count it a most serious mistake to proceed, not against individuals charged with violation of the law, but against masses of our citizens combined for political action, by denying them the only resource of peaceful government; that is, action by the ballot box and through duly elected representatives in legislative bodies." The Assembly attempted to follow up its action by passing several drastic anti-radical laws proposed by the so-called Lusk Committee, but the measures were vetoed by Governor Alfred E. Smith.

The Federal Congress also refused to be contaminated by the presence of Socialists. Victor Berger, second only to Debs in prominence in the party, had been an outspoken opponent of American participation in the war. His activities had led to a trial under the Espionage Act in December, 1918. He was convicted and sentenced by Judge Landis to twenty years in prison, but this conviction was later set aside by the Supreme Court because of the judge's prejudicial conduct. In the spring of 1919 Berger appeared in the House of Representatives to which he had been duly elected by the voters of his district the preceding November. But his right to sit in the House was promptly challenged. The case was referred to a special committee which reported against him, and on November 11, 1919, the seat was declared vacant. The next month the voters of Berger's district named him again in a special election, even though Democrats and Republicans had united on a single candidate to oppose him. His case went back to the House and once again that body voted to exclude him, despite the plea of Representative James R. Mann of Illinois, the Republican floor manager, who said:

I do not share the views of Mr. Berger, but I am willing to meet his views in an argument before the people rather than to say we shall deny him the opportunity to be heard when selected by the people in the legal form and invite them, in effect, to resort to violence.

Not until Berger was elected for a third time in 1922 did the House allow him to occupy a seat.

Thus in an atmosphere of narrow nationalism and intolerance, the Wilson administration, which in better days had been dedicated to much different ideals, drew to a close.

12

The Harding Regime

THE ELECTION OF 1920 WAS HELD WHILE THE UNITED STATES WAS STILL in the throes of reaction against everything that was deemed un-American, while the voters were demanding a return to full peacetime conditions, and while the feeling was still growing that the League of Nations was not the cure-all for world ills which Doctor Wilson had prescribed. Under the circumstances, the national canvass was not settled on the merits of the respective platforms propounded by the several political parties. Instead, the voters were motivated by the desire to return as quickly as possible to the "good old days" of the prewar era—or to "normalcy" as the Republican presidential candidate so popularly called it. And to regain "normal" conditions, almost everything Wilsonian, and especially everything connected with diplomacy, must be repudiated. The political trend in favor of the Republicans, which had started with the Congressional elections of 1918, was now running at full tide. The worth of the candidates was of less import than the wish for a change.

THE REPUBLICAN CONVENTION

The Republican delegates gathered in Chicago on June 8, 1920, on a note of optimism. The Progressive-Conservative split had been largely healed; the death of Theodore Roosevelt in January, 1919, had robbed the Progressives of their outstanding vote getter; mutual animosities within the various party factions were largely forgotten in the desire to bring defeat at last to Wilsonian Democracy. Indeed, Keynoter Lodge set the convention stage when he said: "Mr. Wilson and his dynasty, his heirs and assigns, or anybody that is his, anybody who with bent knee has served his purpose, must be driven from all control of the government and all influence in it."

Since the Republican presidential nominee would probably win in the November election, there was a spirited contest for delegates to the convention. Indeed so numerous were the Republican seekers of that nomination that as early as February, 1920, Harry M. Daugherty, a small-town Ohio lawyer who hoped to emulate his fellow Ohioan, Mark Hanna, by becoming a President-maker, had wishfully predicted a deadlock. Then, "at the proper time . . . some fifteen men, bleary eyed with loss of sleep and perspiring profusely with the excessive heat, will sit down at a big table. I will be with them and will present the name of Senator Harding to them, and before we get through they will put him over." As it turned out, Daugherty was substantially correct in his prediction, but in "putting over" Harding, he was aided by numerous circumstances.

Were Theodore Roosevelt alive, he probably would have had the nomination easily, possibly by acclamation; but his death threw the Republican nomination race wide open. The man who was originally expected to win was General Leonard Wood; many Republicans believed that he had inherited the Roosevelt mantle, and the fact that the Wilson administration refused him permission to go overseas in World War I made him an excellent choice to turn the Wilson regime out of office. Detrimental to his selection was his military background and the fact that he had been one of the first advocates of military preparedness; among an electorate desirous of a speedy return to prewar conditions, Wood was not an admirable selection. Second in line was Governor Frank Lowden of Illinois, a self-made man who had an excellent record in Congress and in the governorship; detrimental was his connection by marriage with the Pullman millions. Hiram Johnson had the backing of the Western Progressive group and his strong fight against the League made him a good candidate among the irreconcilable, isolationist elements. Governor Coolidge, Herbert Hoover, President Butler of Columbia University, and Senator Warren G. Harding of Ohio were among the other possibilities.

One of the foremost factors leading to the deadlock came during the contest between Wood and Lowden for convention delegates. The more or less self-appointed manager of the Wood campaign was Colonel William C. Procter, a prominent soap manufacturer. Procter set out to raise $1,000,000 from a number of his wealthy friends, each of whom was to contribute $20,000. Nothing loath, the Lowden supporters likewise started a huge fund. Hiram Johnson, whose own war chest was far from full, became incensed over the lavish sums expended in favor of his rivals and, through his fellow irreconcilable, Senator Borah, an investigation of campaign expenditures was begun in the Upper House by the so-called Kenyon Committee. The report of this committee, made public just before the convention, revealed that the Wood forces had spent $1,773,303, while the Lowden-for-President group had expended $414,000. From that time on, the chances of General Wood for the nomination dwindled rapidly, while the Lowden hopes, although not so badly damaged, were materially impaired.

Contributing also to the Wood failure was the fact that the general would not bow down to the "interests"—both big business, especially oil, and Senatorial. Yet on the first ballot he led, with Lowden a close second, and the other candidates strung out, Harding occupying sixth place. On the next three ballots there was considerable vote lending and jockeying of forces without any decision being reached. When it was conceivable that Wood might obtain the necessary majority, the Lowden group would go all out against him, and in similar fashion the Wood adherents cut Lowden's presidential hopes. The party's elder statesmen, especially Senators Lodge, Brandegee, Reed Smoot of Utah, and Charles Curtis of Kansas, along with Colonel George Harvey— who was now on the Republican side, did not wish the potential deadlock to continue over the week end; were it to do so, both the delegates and the voters at large would realize the disunity within the Republican ranks. Therefore, at four o'clock Friday afternoon, Chairman Lodge, through a successful parliamentary maneuver, secured adjournment until Saturday morning.

During the interim, the leaders were in almost constant conference in the Blackstone Hotel. They also conversed by telephone with Senator Boies Penrose, the powerful boss of Pennsylvania, who was ill at his home. They all agreed that the choice must be a man who had opposed the League as Wilson fashioned it, but who had backed the Lodge reservations; he must also be a strict organization man who had not joined the revolt in 1912 but who had not antagonized the Progressives; he must not be like the cold, reserved Wilson; and most of all he must be one who would follow the orders of the party leaders. After looking over the field, they decided that Harding best filled the bill. Around two o'clock on Saturday morning the word began to circulate that Harding was the choice of the inner circle.

While there were more ballots taken on Saturday, the result was not long in doubt. The Harding votes increased with each successive canvass until finally on the tenth he received the coveted nomination. For the vice-presidency, Governor Calvin Coolidge was named on the first ballot. A *New York Times* editorial of Sunday, June 13, expressed the opinion of many Americans about the Harding nomination. The editorial read in part:

The Chicago convention presents a candidate whose nomination will be received with astonishment and dismay by the party whose suffrage he invites. Warren G. Harding is a very respectable Ohio politician of the second class. . . . Senator Harding's record at Washington has been faint and colorless. He was an undistinguished and indistinguishable unit in the ruck of Republican Senators who obediently followed Mr. Lodge. . . . Governor Coolidge for Vice President really shines by comparison with the head of the ticket.

Yet Harding was the type the party leaders wanted. It mattered not that some wit quipped that the ticket should be "stood on its head."

The platform was no more distinguished than was the presidential candidate. On the important League issue, it carefully avoided a definite position. After asserting that the party stood "for agreement among the nations to preserve the peace of the world," which could "be done without the compromise of national independence," the platform denounced Wilson's Covenant because it would not bring peace and because it contained "stipulations not only intolerable for an independent people but certain to produce the injustice, hostility, and controversy among nations which it proposed to prevent." The platform writers undoubtedly hoped to retain the allegiance of the irreconcilable element through the denunciation of the Covenant and of the Taft-Root group through the promise to work for the preservation of peace. The platform endorsed the return of the railroads and the merchant marine to private ownership, increased immigration restriction, and greater protection for American manufactures. The development of Federal power under Wilson was attacked, as was also his policy toward Mexico. The army and navy, the Republicans asserted, would not be reduced to their former weak position under a Republican administration, while effective aid for the farmer, increased Federal assistance in the educational field, and a sound, economical administration would be assured.

THE DEMOCRATIC CANDIDATE AND PLATFORM

There is evidence to show that Wilson hoped to run for a third term in order to carry into operation his League of Nations, but his illness and the turn of public opinion made this impossible. Indeed, by the summer of 1920 he was opposed by several factions within his own party. Thus the quest for the nomination rested chiefly among Attorney General A. Mitchell Palmer of Red-baiting fame, William Gibbs McAdoo, and Governor James Cox of Ohio. Probably McAdoo was the ablest of these three, but the fact that he was President Wilson's son-in-law reacted against him in the long run. For thirty-nine ballots at the San Francisco convention the issue was in doubt. On the fortieth the shift toward Cox began, and he was finally victorious on the forty-fourth. As his running mate, Assistant Secretary of the Navy Franklin D. Roosevelt was nominated, partly to capitalize on the magic Roosevelt name.

The Democratic stand on the League was unequivocal: "We advocate the immediate ratification of the treaty without reservations which would impair its essential integrity." The domestic features of the New Freedom, with specific emphasis upon "adherence to the fundamental progressive principles of social, economic, and industrial justice," were endorsed, along with economy and reduction of taxation. Women's suffrage, additional Federal educational aid, statehood for Puerto Rico, and independence for the Philippines were other prominent planks. An effort was made to obtain the Irish vote in a plank extending sympathy to Ireland.

The Socialist party had been hard hit by the war. Splits within the ranks were numerous, and public opinion largely assumed that the Socialists had been un-American during the contest. Nevertheless, Eugene V. Debs was nominated again, although he was serving a term in Atlanta Prison for his antidraft activities. The Farmer-Labor party also entered the contest with a platform urging government ownership of natural resources, railroads, and mines, repudiation of the Versailles Treaty, restoration of diplomatic and economic relations with Russia, and a series of social-economic reforms that were reminiscent of Theodore Roosevelt's New Nationalism. With Parley P. Christensen of Utah as the standard bearer, the Farmer-Laborites hoped to gain the support of liberals, members of labor unions, and farmers.

NO SOLEMN REFERENDUM

The Republican leaders, fearful of what Candidate Harding might say, kept him in his Marion, Ohio, home for a front-porch campaign. The Democrats, following Wilson's advice, tried to make the election a "solemn referendum" on the League. Cox's swing around the circle, however, during which he came out boldly for Wilson's international policies, made little impression on the electorate.

Harding's position vacillated. He condemned the Wilsonian League with sufficient vigor to keep the support of the Johnson-Borah faction in the party, while ambiguous references to the desirability of a real "association of nations" encouraged internationally-minded Republicans to remain loyal to the party. To prevent pro-League Republicans from throwing their votes to Cox, thirty-one of the party's most respected leaders, including Root, Hughes, Hoover, and Stimson, issued a statement denying that the issue was "between a league and no league," and implying that a vote for Harding was a vote for the League with reservations. Thus the issue continued to be confused, and voters who wanted the League voted for Harding as well as those who did not. But it made little difference because the League was a dead issue in so far as most of the voters were concerned. Nor was the electorate swayed by efforts in some quarters to play up rumors about Harding's supposed Negro blood. More successful were Republican appeals to the Irish and German voters to repudiate Wilson's foreign policy.

The electorate wanted a change, and the belief was that the change would come sooner and be more effective under Republican rule. Thus Harding was swept into overwhelming victory. He secured more than 16,000,000 popular votes to Cox's 9,000,000; the 61 per cent of the total which the Republican candidate obtained was one of the most impressive

How Long Can He Resist? Candidate Harding tied to his front porch. (By Kirby in the *New York World*.)

majorities in American history.[1] The electoral totals gave Harding 404 to 127 for Cox. The Republican sweep was complete in the new Congress as well. In the Upper House, they had a majority of 22; in the Lower, of 167. But the victory was not one of party; it was brought about by "resentments" and the desire to repudiate Wilson.

HARDING AND HIS HELPERS

The new President was by no means fitted for his position, as he himself readily admitted. Born and brought up in a rural Ohio community, he had finally settled down in Marion, married an ambitious, fairly wealthy widow who urged him on to greater things, and became owner-editor of the local *Star*. Eventually he entered state politics, where at first he was affiliated with the Foraker or Standard Oil faction. He served in the state legislature and as lieutenant governor, but was defeated for the governorship in 1910. During the 1912 split, he remained a thorough conservative; indeed, he made the nominating speech for Taft at the Chicago convention. In partial reward and aided by a factional quarrel in Ohio, he was elected to the United States Senate in 1914. During his term in the Upper House he voted as he was told—and thus opposed the League as drafted, but favored it with the Lodge reservations.

Harding presented a good appearance and was an excellent orator of the old school. His speeches were more remarkable for their verbosity than for their content. Thus he was a good keynoter for the convention of 1916. He was not a deep thinker and he knew little about national domestic problems and less about international affairs. He was genial and easygoing to the point of weakness. The new President thought everyone was his friend, and friends were to be rewarded and trusted—but some of them let him down. That was one of the fatalities of the new regime.

For his Secretary of State Harding wanted his fellow Senator, Albert Fall of New Mexico; the suggestion aroused such a storm of protest that he was dissuaded from making the appointment. Therefore the post went to Charles Evans Hughes, who did a remarkably fine job. Another good appointment was that of Herbert Hoover as Secretary of Commerce. The Treasury headship was given to Andrew D. Mellon, a Pittsburgh millionaire affiliated with the aluminum interests. He proved a good choice as far as running the finances smoothly and economically

---

[1] The Republican vote was double that of 1916, while the Democratic total was approximately the same as in the previous election. Debs secured 900,000 votes, and Christensen, 26,000.

were concerned, but his ideas on taxation were vigorously attacked by liberals. The desire to give plums to his friends, however, caused Harding to appoint what proved to be some of the worst elements within the party. To his backer, Harry Daugherty, went the Attorney Generalship, while Fall was made Secretary of the Interior.[1]

THE RETURN TO TARIFF PROTECTION

One of the first steps taken to return to normalcy was to provide for raising the tariff schedules above the levels of the existing Underwood Act. In addition to the wish to overthrow everything connected with the Wilson regime and to return to Republican protectionist principles, more tangible factors were at work. As part of the postwar reaction there was developing a stronger feeling of nationalism, and with it a desire for greater self-sufficiency. And how could that self-sufficiency be better promoted than through a higher tariff? Then, too, a new American chemical industry had resulted from the war, while other industries, especially metallurgical enterprises, had grown rapidly. Were they now to be sacrificed on the altar of free competition? There was the feeling that they would not survive were German-made competing products allowed to enter the American market with little or no duty.

The farmers joined in the demand for higher import duties. True, the farmers had made money during the wartime boom, but they used their additional income to buy more land or more equipment. With the cessation of hostilities, however, the bottom dropped out of the agricultural market, and the farmers found themselves left with a huge surplus which they could not sell at prices adequate to meet their overhead. Those who had borrowed from the banks or who had mortgaged their property were threatened with bankruptcy or foreclosure. Their dissatisfaction was quickly reflected in Congress, where their representatives had established the so-called Farm Bloc by the spring of 1921. Under the leadership of Republican Senators William S. Kenyon of Iowa and Arthur Capper of Kansas, Representatives and Senators of both parties from agricultural communities combined to demand aid for their constituents. So great was the voting strength of the bloc that unless some remedial legislation were passed, it might disrupt the agenda of the party in power.

Even before President Wilson returned from Versailles the movement

---

[1] Will Hays of Indiana, chairman of the National Committee, received the usual Postmaster Generalship. James J. Davis of Pennsylvania, Secretary of Labor; John W. Weeks of Massachusetts, Secretary of War; Edwin Denby of Michigan, Secretary of the Navy; and Henry Wallace of Iowa, Secretary of Agriculture, were the other cabinet members.

to raise the Underwood rates had begun. The President sought to thwart this trend by sending a special message to Congress in which he asserted that there was no need "in the immediate future" for "any general revision of our system of import duties." He pointed out that Europe was, and would be for years to come, in the process of rehabilitation and without the means for developing quickly along industrial lines. Therefore, he concluded, "no serious danger of foreign competition now threatens American industries."

This message, however, did not quiet the demands of the various groups advocating protection. Consequently, in his annual statement to Congress in December, 1919, Wilson again attempted to stem the movement. The war, he asserted, had made the United States a creditor nation, and the favorable balance which it now enjoyed with Europe could be paid for in the following ways: by sending gold to the United States, which he believed was undesirable as it would adversely affect the economies on both sides of the Atlantic; by extending further credit to European purchasers, which was not wise as United States government loans were sufficiently large already; and by exchange of goods. The last was the most beneficial to all parties concerned. Therefore, Wilson sensibly concluded, "If we want to sell, we must be prepared to buy."

The American groups, especially the farmers, who were hard hit by the depression of 1920, were not content to listen to the presidential economic moralizing. They wanted action to alleviate their troubles, and the action must take the form of upward tariff revision. In this stand they were aided by the growing dissatisfaction with Wilsonianism, by the Republican majority in Congress, by the decisive election results of November, 1920, and by the rapidly forming Farm Bloc. In anticipation of the incoming Harding regime, the House Ways and Means Committee, under the chairmanship of Joseph W. Fordney of Michigan, began hearings in January, 1921. Anxious to rush through a temporary measure to quiet the farmers, a bill was introduced in February to increase the rates on agricultural imports. After quickly passing both Houses, it fell before Wilson's veto on March 3. Telling parts of the veto-message were:

It is obvious that . . . the imports can have little or no effect on the prices of the domestic products. . . . What the farmer now needs is not only a better system of domestic marketing and credit, but especially larger foreign markets for his surplus products. . . . Clearly measures of this sort will not conduce to an expansion of the foreign market. . . . I imagine there is little doubt that while this measure is temporary, it is intended as a foun-

Governor Fuller of Massachusetts, President Harding, and Senator Lodge. (Acme.)

dation for action of a similar nature of a very general and permanent character. If ever there was a time when America had anything to fear from foreign competition, that time has passed. . . .

The advent of Harding, however, brought a definite change in administration policy. In a special message to Congress on April 12, 1921, the new executive placed a new tariff law on the emergency list. "I believe," Harding said, "in protection of American industry, and it is our purpose to prosper America first." Consequently, the Wilson-vetoed measure was revived, again rushed through the legislature, and signed by the President on May 27, 1921, as the so-called Emergency Tariff. Under it the duties on corn, wheat, meat, wool, and sugar were raised to about the Payne-Aldrich levels. The Farm Bloc was highly pleased with this victory for which it was in so large part responsible. The farmer constituents were under the impression that protection would increase the prices of foodstuffs to their wartime level.

The tariff law of 1921 was only a temporary measure, to last until a broader and more definitive act was worked out. The House Committee on Ways and Means, still presided over by Representative Fordney and continuing to have a Republican, protectionist majority, now went to work in earnest. The Fordney Bill emerged from the committee on June 29, 1921. Considering the committee composition, the temper of the country, and the fact that the Farm Bloc, having won its point in the emergency measure, could not very well oppose higher rates to help other groups, it was only natural that the rates were considerably higher than in the Underwood Tariff. Just about three weeks later the House approved the bill with scarcely any change.

The Senate Finance Committee, headed by Porter McCumber of North Dakota, was even more protectionist. It worked until April, 1922, on the Fordney Bill, adding more articles to the dutiable list and raising the rates on the already taxable commodities. In the Senate debates, which lasted for four months, two thousand amendments were made which forced the rates higher still. Strong lobbies were at work to help special interests. This was especially true of the dye industry, which had the backing of the advocates of greater military protection because many of the ingredients needed for that industry were also required in the manufacture of explosives.

In conference, the House usually relented in favor of the Senate changes, and the measure, now called the Fordney-McCumber Bill, was finally approved on September 19, 1922, to give the United States its highest import rates in American peacetime history. The duties on wheat, rye, corn, beef, lamb, sugar, and wool were higher than under the Payne-Aldrich levies. Chinaware, jewelry, cutlery, dyes, chemicals, toys, laces, and cotton goods were given substantial increases. The Congress hoped by changes to have the cost of production abroad plus duty equal the cost of production in the United States. Production costs were constantly varying, however, so in order to maintain the precarious balance, the act stipulated that the Tariff Commission should constantly study those foreign and domestic costs. When any inequalities arose, the commission would so advise the President, who might raise or lower the existing rates as much as 50 per cent to achieve stability.

The protection afforded by the Fordney-McCumber Tariff did not bring all of the expected results. The farmers were no better off and looked around for other cures. American exports did not materially increase because European countries, particularly France, raised their own tariff barriers in retaliation. The net result was to start tariff wars, which adversely affected international trade, and to develop greater nationalism. As the decade progressed, more and more American manufacturers, seeking broader markets for their products, established branches in foreign countries and thereby escaped the higher import levies. In the United States the temporary conclusion of foreign competition encouraged again the concentration of industrial control in fewer hands. European debtor nations, unable to sell in the American market, found it more and more difficult to pay their wartime obligations.

The Tariff Commission became a center of criticism. The industrial interests felt that the commission's reports to the President were neither fair nor sound. The Democrats, particularly after 1926, charged that the members were motivated by political partisanship. As far as trying to maintain the production-cost balance was concerned, Harding and Coolidge together raised the duties on specific commodities thirty-two times and lowered them but five.

Yet there was no organized demand for a general revision of the Fordney-McCumber Tariff during the rest of the twenties; indeed, in the campaign of 1928 both major parties urged the continuation of protection. Important factors in this absence of demand were: the prosperity which the United States enjoyed until 1929 and the fear a tariff change might disturb it; the industrialization of the South, originally the opponent of protection; and the attitude of the farmers who, although still unhappy, did not blame protection for their troubles. As far as income was concerned, the Fordney-McCumber Tariff was bringing in more than $500,000,000 annually, a jump of $200,000,000 over the Payne-Aldrich receipts.

THE BUDGET ACT

In the quest for more efficient and economical administration, there had been urged for many years a better budget system for the Federal government. The existing practice, under which the various executive departments, quite unrelated to one another and without cooperation, tried to secure for themselves as much of the annual appropriations as possible, was wasteful, extravagant, and haphazard.

Not until the Treaty of Versailles had been concluded, however, did President Wilson give ear to the reformers. Then the need to deal with the postwar problems of debt and tax reduction led him to ask Congress, in his annual message of December 2, 1919, to provide for the more efficient planning of Federal expenditures. His particular suggestion was that the responsibility for drawing up the budget should be placed in the hands of the executive branch, which would secure estimates from the different departments of government for the ensuing fiscal year. The only changes which Congress should make in the executive budget would be through a special appropriations committee of each House.

In the fall of 1920 the legislature passed a measure which conformed in general to Wilson's wishes, but Wilson vetoed it because it contained a clause which he believed placed an unwarranted, unconstitutional check upon the executive. Although the House quickly removed the objectionable part, the Senate had not acted before that session ended. Nevertheless, Wilson continued to press the demand. In December, 1920, he once more made a plea for the passage of his original plan, saying: "I cannot overemphasize the necessity of economy in government appropriations and expenditures."

Shortly after his inauguration, Harding took up the issue in the Wilsonian form, making his request in his message to the specially convened Congress in April, 1921. The result was the passage of the Budget and Accounting Act two months later. This measure provided that each department, bureau, and agency of government should submit to the President its fiscal needs. He would then consider the feasibility of each and present the amended total budget to Congress on the opening day of every regular session, along with a financial report of the nation. That report would include an estimate of income and expenditures for the coming fiscal year and the financial picture of the preceding year. Only through a special committee of each House could departments appeal for a change. To assist the President in his work, a new Budget Bureau was to be established, and a Director of the Budget was to be appointed for fifteen years.

The executive budget system did work out much better than had the old method. It was more in line with the English plan of attempting to work out some relationship between receipts and expenditures. True, there were still many weaknesses, for Congress frequently did change materially some of the items in the executive proposals. Charles G. Dawes of Illinois, who had gained fame as purchasing agent of the Expeditionary Forces in World War I, was the first Director of the Budget, a position which he filled both colorfully and efficiently. When Dawes became Vice-President in 1925, his place was taken by the equally firm and able General H. M. Lord.

The Harding administration also faced numerous other problems of the postwar era. Immigration restriction, the politically dangerous bonus issue, the equally troublesome farm problem, the matter of tax reduction, and its attendant complication of lowering the debt were all given initial consideration. Completion of the formula for each, however, was not achieved during Harding's term, which was suddenly and unexpectedly shortened by death.

The voters were not entirely satisfied by the delays in settling the several important affairs nor by the failure of the country to return to prosperity as speedily as had been anticipated. Thus in the Congressional elections of 1922 the Republican majority in the Senate was cut from 22 to 6, and in the House from 167 to 15. It is doubtful, however, whether even a stronger President could have accomplished much more during the period of reaction.

THE DEATH OF HARDING

The Presidency was a hardship for Warren Harding. Used as he was to a life of comparative ease and freedom, he did not readily take to his burdensome task. In his own way he did try to fulfill the obligation of his office. But the more time he spent in dealing with the affairs of the nation, the more hours he devoted to golf, poker, and other diversions. The combination of harder work and more strenuous play was bad enough for a constitution that had been allowed to run down, despite its outwardly robust appearance; the situation became worse when Harding eventually realized that his supposed friends, upon whom he counted so much when he appointed them to public office, were betraying his trust in them. By early 1923 rumors were beginning to circulate that all was not well in certain quarters of the administration. Harding did not know how long it would be before the storm would break, to be followed by a flood of recrimination. His nature was such that he blamed himself for what his appointees did.

As an outlet for his mental and physical troubles, he decided upon a speechmaking tour of the country, which might serve as well the purpose of bolstering his position with the people. The trip began on June 20, 1923. Enthusiastic audiences in St. Louis, Kansas City, Denver, Salt Lake City, and other western communities greeted his speeches on farm problems, taxation, railroad reorganization, the World Court, and prohibition. He drove a binder in Kansas, visited miners in Montana, saw the glories of Zion National Park, and participated in rodeos and pageants. Little time was allowed for relaxation; he was constantly in the public limelight. All this took additional toll of a mind and body already at the danger point. By the time of embarkation for Alaska, the President showed definite signs of strain, which were augmented by additional news of the deceit of his friends. The sea voyage did not give him the expected respite and, after his return to Seattle on July 27, his advisers urged him to cancel the remainder of his itinerary. This

Harding refused to do. That evening, however, after a strenuous speech under a broiling sun, his physician, Dr. Charles Sawyer, had to be summoned. The President was suffering from what was diagnosed as ptomaine poisoning, the result of eating none-too-fresh crabs.

Harding was hurried to San Francisco where consultants were called in. His condition failed to improve as pneumonia set in, followed by a stroke of apoplexy which brought death on August 2. The nation's grief was sincere. The funeral cortège from San Francisco to Washington, and then to Marion, was watched by mourning millions. Hundreds of eulogies were delivered for the man who was a martyr to the burdens of the presidency. Not until some time after his burial did the expected storm break, and only then did the public at large realize that the scandals of his administration were the worst in American history. It was then, too, that all sorts of rumors cropped up about his "mysterious" death; among them was the story that his wife poisoned him. The fact that no crabs were on the menu accentuated these tales. In all probability the strain of office, the weakened constitution, and the absence of will to live combined to bring Harding's death.

PRESIDENT CALVIN COOLIDGE

Vice-President Calvin Coolidge had the oath of presidential office administered to him by his father early on the morning of August 3, 1923, in the family home at Plymouth, Vermont, where he had been vacationing. With his accession to this high office there began a period of remarkable national material prosperity which contributed to make him popular. He was well prepared for his new position. A graduate of Amherst College, trained for the law, he had made politics practically his vocation. Coolidge capably filled a number of local posts, served in the Massachusetts state legislature, and finally as governor. His stand in the Boston police strike made him a national figure and brought him the vice-presidential nomination in 1920.

There was nothing spectacular about Coolidge. He lacked the energy of Roosevelt, the idealism of Wilson, and the glad-handedness of Harding. But he made up for those deficiencies by having the confidence of the people, to whom he appeared as an average American—the type who could steer the nation along its normal road in competent fashion.

The new President was primarily a party man of the conservative school. Laissez faire was his doctrine, and he relied for advice, not upon the Republican liberals, but upon the businessmen and lawyers. Economy in government was the general theme of his nearly six years in office, and he vetoed many a bill because of the proposed expenditures involved. Little social legislation was enacted during his administration and there was little effort to enforce the existing regulatory measures against big business. This seemed to fit the mood of the country for there was no widespread public demand for the continuation of the Square Deal or the New Freedom. The vast majority of Americans were concerned with matters materialistic rather than idealistic, and Coolidge was the man who would assist them. The ship of state was never to be in danger while he was on the bridge, but the skipper never was to venture into uncharted seas.

THE HARDING SCANDALS

The first problems which President Coolidge faced as titular party head arose out of scandals connected with the administration of his predecessor. As has been said, Harding had definite inklings that all was not well in the spring of 1923, but the facts of corruption were for the most part not brought to light until after his death. Whether Coolidge, who had attended frequent cabinet meetings during his vice-presidency and was in close contact with the men responsible for some of the misdeeds, knew what was taking place it is impossible to judge. After he became President, however, he kept Harding's official family until Congressional pressure and the force of public opinion compelled the resignation or removal of those involved in scandal, and he hesitated to push the cases against them until the evidence was so strong that to have failed to approve the investigation would have weakened his chances for the 1924 Republican presidential nomination. The only charitable thing that can be said in support of Coolidge's laxity is that he may have believed that the charges against Fall, Daugherty, and others were primarily political, brought by the opposition to weaken his party.

The most spectacular of the Harding scandals involved the naval oil reserves. Back in 1912, President Taft had ordered set aside for the use of the navy some 70,000 acres of oil lands in the Elk Hills region of California, and three years later Wilson had added the nearly 10,000 acres at Teapot Dome, Wyoming. Both of these acts were part of the general conservation program; the oil in those reserves was to be maintained until some future time when the navy might find difficulty in securing it from other sources.

When the operations in privately owned neighboring fields endangered the naval reserves during the latter part of the Wilson regime, Congress passed the General Leasing Act of 1920. This empowered the Secretary of the Navy, at his discretion, to "use, store, exchange or sell the oil . . . from lands in the Naval Reserves, for the benefit of the

United States." Secretary Daniels then did lease a small percentage, but he kept the vast majority under naval control.

Shortly after Harding's inauguration, Secretary of the Interior Fall prevailed upon him to issue a secret executive order transferring the reserves to the Interior Department, and the amenable Denby concurred without question. Fall's excuse was the continued draining of the reserves; if he could lease them to private companies, the government would be able to profit from the rentals. He also subsequently intimated that the move would benefit national preparedness—in what way he did not specify.

It was in 1922 that Fall leased the reserves to two powerful oil operators: Teapot Dome to Harry F. Sinclair in April, and Elk Hills to Edward L. Doheny in April and December. Again these were secret transactions, but rumors of Fall's actions eventually began to circulate. Senator LaFollette, to whom any government deal with big business smacked of corruption, thereupon forced through the Upper House a resolution calling for an investigation, which was placed in the capable hands of Thomas J. Walsh of Montana.

Walsh required a year and a half of preparation before he was ready to start the open hearings on October 9, 1923. The testimony was long and complicated. Navy Secretary Denby was shown to be free from any corrupt act, but the furore aroused over his complacency and lack of responsibility caused him to resign in March, 1924, to relieve the President of further embarrassment.[1]

At first Fall made a good impression before the Senate committee; his answers seemed straightforward and convincing. Additional testimony from other witnesses, however, disclosed that he had recently spent some $170,000 on his New Mexico ranch. Walsh then pressed him as to the source of his sudden wealth. Only after many weeks of questioning did the awful truth come out. Fall had received "loans" of $100,000 from Doheny and of nearly $250,000 from Sinclair—who also contributed lavishly to the Republican campaign chest. Fall's resignation did not save him from prosecution, along with Doheny and Sinclair, on criminal charges of conspiracy against the United States. Since the Department of Justice was under fire at the time, special government prosecutors, Owen J. Roberts of Pennsylvania and former Democratic Senator Atlee Pomerene of Ohio, were named in February, 1924, to press the cases. Coolidge, who now strongly backed these special counsels,

---

[1] The Senate had demanded that Coolidge dismiss him. This he refused to do, partly because of his belief that Denby was not guilty of any malfeasance, partly because the Senate had no right to issue the demand.

then made his only public statement about this particular scandal; he said that the guilty ones would be punished and the interests of the government fully protected.

Indictments for conspiracy and bribery were brought against Fall, Doheny, and Sinclair in June, 1924. Delays of various kinds held up the trials for years. All were found not guilty of conspiracy to defraud, but finally in October, 1929, Fall was convicted of accepting a bribe and sentenced to one year in jail—which he did not begin until 1931—and a fine of $100,000. Doheny and Sinclair were both acquitted on the bribery charges. The latter, however, who had been a most unwilling witness throughout the affair, was found guilty of contempt of the Senate—for refusing to answer questions—and also of contempt of court—for having his jurors shadowed; he was fined $1000 and sentenced to a total of nine months in jail. In June, 1924, the government instituted proceedings to cancel the leases. Appeals delayed the final

Will It Prove More Than a Tempest in a Teapot? (From the *San Francisco Chronicle*.)

decision of the Supreme Court until December 28, 1927, when the tribunal stated that the leases, having been secured through fraud and corruption, were no longer valid.

The tendency has been to place emphasis upon the lurid incidents in the oil scandals. But equally significant was the revelation that men in high government posts apparently were willing to sabotage the conservation and defense programs of the nation. The appointment of Fall should never have been made, for he was known to be an opponent of conservation; and Denby was nothing more than a "yes" man who knew nothing about the needs of the navy. It likewise throws a strange light on the workings of American justice that the public official who took the bribes was punished, while Doheny and Sinclair, who did the bribing and stood to profit to the tune of at least $100,000,000 from the leases, should have escaped so easily.

Numerous other betrayals of the public faith were revealed. Custodian of Alien Property Thomas W. Miller, a member of the so-called Ohio gang which trailed Harding to Washington for spoils of office, was found guilty of having secured $50,000 through disposal of patents and other property in his care; he was fined $5000 and sentenced to eighteen months in prison. Jess Smith, Harry Daugherty's right-hand man, committed suicide when he became involved in the transaction. The Department of Justice was likewise under suspicion of collaboration with certain corrupt big business interests. Indeed, Daugherty was accused of conspiracy to defraud the government. For some months Coolidge resisted pressure to remove him from the Attorney Generalship, but when he refused to answer the questions of a Congressional committee on the grounds that he might incriminate himself, the President felt compelled to demand his resignation in late March, 1924. Only jury disagreement kept Daugherty out of prison. His department was involved in the withdrawal of liquor from government warehouses for the benefit of other members of the "gang"; in this way the prohibition experiment was partially sabotaged. Colonel Charles R. Forbes, Director of the Veterans' Bureau, was found guilty of diverting at least $250,-000,000 from his agency into the pockets of himself and his friends through corrupt contract and building abuses; thereby was the rehabilitation program severely injured.

As has been said, Harding was dead before any of these disclosures came to the public knowledge. The Republican party might have been critically affected had he been President when the trials were taking place. While it is true that Coolidge did not do much to bring the perpetrators to account, he did enough to satisfy the voters, who showed in 1924 that they blamed the individuals involved, rather than the party with which they were connected. The easy complaisance with which the general public shrugged off not only the evidence of governmental corruption but the threatened sabotage of the whole conservation, veterans' aid, and preparedness programs is impressive evidence of the extent of the postwar retreat from idealism. The country seemed to have lost its capacity for indignation on such issues. And, to make matters worse, individuals connected with the prosecutions were hounded unmercifully and subjected to trials on fraudulent charges; fortunately, they all survived the attempts to besmirch them.

AMERICA FOR AMERICANS

Coolidge also inherited from his predecessor the growing movement to restrict immigration to the United States. The close of World War I threatened to end the temporary decline in immigration and by 1920 the fear of unbridled admissions from southern and eastern Europe was once more mounting. The opposition to such immigration was increased by the Red scare and the wave of supposedly Communist-influenced strikes in 1919. American labor worried lest the growing unemployment in the United States be accentuated and continued with the arrival of Europeans with a lower standard of living. The old cry that Russians, Poles, Eastern Jews, Italians, and Greeks did not become Americanized as quickly or thoroughly as those of the old immigration was raised again.

Many Americans felt that the literacy test of 1917 was not enough, and indeed by 1920 several amendments to existing acts had already been passed. The most important, largely the result of opposition to un-American "isms," provided for the exclusion or expulsion from the United States of "aliens who are members of the anarchistic and similar classes."

Then came consular reports from various immigration embarkation centers in Europe that millions of inhabitants were anxiously awaiting transportation to the land of the free. Realizing that the existing legislation would not be sufficient to bar the expected influx, the House of Representatives passed a bill in December, 1920, ending practically all entrance into the United States. The Senate, however, substituted a plan for admission on the basis of 3 per cent of the number of natives of each of the European countries in the United States at the time of the 1910 census. On February 22, 1921, the House accepted the Senate version, but President Wilson refused to give his approval to it.

Harding did not feel the same way as Wilson about restriction. Consequently, in his message to the special session of Congress in April, 1921, he asked that the February measure be revived. The legislature quickly complied with the executive wish and on May 19, 1921, the Emergency Quota Act was on the statute books. It was called an emergency measure because of the realization that a permanent act would require more time to draw up—and some stopgap had to be put into effect during the interim. The 1921 act stipulated "that the number of aliens of any nationality who may be admitted under the immigration laws to the United States in any fiscal year shall be limited to 3 per centum of the number of foreign-born persons of such national-ity resident in the United States as determined by the United States census of 1910." Not more than 20 per cent of the annual total were to be allowed to enter in any one month, and the measure was "in addition to and not in substitution for" the previous immigration statutes.

The effects of the Emergency Quota Act were felt almost immedi-ately. For the year ending June 30, 1921, 805,228 immigrants were ad-mitted; for the following year, the first in which the act was in effect, the number dropped to 309,556. While this decrease was one of the purposes of the legislation, it was not wholly satisfactory. Of the 198,082 quota established for nationalities coming under the heading of the old immigration, but 46.4 per cent availed themselves of the op-portunity to come to the United States; on the other hand, 95.3 per cent of the 158,200 new immigrant quota did enter. Something must be done, the restrictionists argued, to limit further the arrival of those from eastern and southern Europe.

There were other troubles as well which affected the issue. As President Harding stated in September, 1921, "I haven't any doubt in the world but the enforcement of the immigration laws is working many a hardship." He was referring primarily to the monthly quota. Those who arrived near the end of the month, after the quota had been filled, were sometimes forced to return to their native land. Families were thereby separated. American steamship companies, competing for pas-sengers, raced each other to get into an American port before the dead-line was up. No effort was made at the port of embarkation to limit the number who sailed; the primary investigation of entrance qualification was made at Ellis Island or some other American immigration station. Congress was constantly being called upon to allow persons to enter in excess of the quota. In general, during the first year the law was in operation, the legislature was very liberal in complying; thereafter there was a tightening of the monthly allotment.

The permanent measure was not ready until 1924, by which time

Coolidge was President. His attitude toward restriction had already been indicated in his message to Congress on December 6, 1923: "New arrivals should be limited to our capacity to absorb them into the ranks of good citizenship. America must be kept American. For this purpose, it is necessary to continue a policy of restricted immigration. . . ." Influenced by the constant agitation of labor, the Johnson Immigration Act was overwhelmingly approved by Congress and signed by the President on May 26, 1924.

Under the new law the quota basis was changed from the census of 1910 to that of 1890—when the new immigration had been small, and the annual quota per cent was lowered from 3 to 2. The monthly quota of 20 per cent was eliminated, and the primary selection of immigrants was made at the ports of embarkation rather than in the immigration stations in the United States. The number of exempted classifications was reduced, and those who could not become naturalized citizens were not to be allowed to enter.[1] The provisions of the quota plan, however, were not to apply to the countries of the Western Hemisphere.

Practically all of the criticisms of the Emergency Quota Act were removed in this 1924 law. Families were no longer divided, fewer persons were turned back after their arrival in the United States, and the rush to get in before monthly quotas were exhausted was ended. Indeed, the annual immigration quotas for 1925 and 1926 were not even reached.[2]

One clause in the act, however, elicited strong protests—that denying admission to those who could not become naturalized. President Coolidge and the State Department opposed this provision and Japanese Ambassador Hanihara wrote a memorandum speaking of the "grave consequences" which might follow this termination of the Gentlemen's Agreement to which Japan had adhered faithfully. But the Hanihara note only stiffened the determination of the exclusionists to have their way despite the fact that, if the Japanese were included under the quota system, not more than 146 could be admitted in any given year. Senator Kenneth McKellar of Tennessee probably expressed the opinion of the majority of Congressmen when he stated: "Whenever we permit a quota of 146, we have established a principle by which in the future Japanese can come in here as the subjects of other nations come in. To that I am

[1] From the very beginning of the republic, naturalization laws applied only to "white" persons. The Supreme Court in the Ozawa case (1922) stated that Japanese were not "whites" within the meaning of the naturalization laws and so could not acquire citizenship by naturalization.

[2] The quotas were 164,667 for each year. In 1925 only 145,971 were admitted; in 1926, 157,423.

opposed . . . because we can never assimilate that race with ours." All attempts to change or postpone this Japanese exclusion clause were fruitless. Thus suspicions of the yellow race bore fruit. Although legislators asserted that the clause was not meant to endanger the friendly relations between the two nations, the day the act went into effect was one of mourning in Japan, punctuated by anti-American demonstrations.

The blow to the new immigration is indicated by the fact that but 14.88 per cent of the total quota was allotted to those in that category, while 84.11 per cent was assigned to the old immigrants.

The immigration legislation did not stop there. The Johnson Act further provided that after July 1, 1927, a new schedule would go into effect. Under it, "the annual quota . . . for each fiscal year . . . shall be a number which bears the same ratio to 150,000 as the number of inhabitants in continental United States in 1920 having that national origin . . . bears to the number of inhabitants in continental United States in 1920, but the minimum quota of any nationality shall be 100." The State, Commerce, and Labor Departments worked hard to determine these so-called national-origins quotas, but the mixtures in the American melting pot made the task a difficult one. Not until 1930 did these quotas, many of them quite arbitrary, go into effect under the National Origins Act of 1929. By that time the depression discouraged immigrants from seeking entrance; yet to make sure that the unemployment situation was not worsened, President Hoover issued an executive order in 1931 lowering the total quota from 150,000 to 48,500. At the same time a ban was erected against those entering from Mexico, normally exempted from the quota, who were merely trying to find jobs—the so-called floaters.

Cogent arguments have been advanced for and against the restrictive immigration legislation of the twenties. Without debating the relative merits, it is sufficient to say that the laws were in line with majority opinion in the United States and with the general postwar reaction. From the economic standpoint, the laws tended to cut off the arrival of unskilled workers and to increase the percentage of entering farmers. Consequently, the measures virtually ended the immigration factor in the struggle for a living wage.

THE VETERANS AND THE BONUS

Even before the armistice was signed, Colonel Theodore Roosevelt, Jr., son of the ex-President, had dreamed of a vast veterans' organization to be formed not from the A.E.F. alone, but from all men who had worn uniform during the great conflict. On February 16, 1919, Roosevelt entertained twenty officers at a dinner party in Paris where he enlisted their support for his plan. One month later an organization meeting attended by a thousand soldiers was held in the same city. There the name "American Legion" was adopted. Later organization gatherings were staged in St. Louis in May and in Minneapolis several months later. On September 16, 1919, the American Legion was chartered by act of Congress. The new organization was a powerful champion of the ideal of patriotism, a vigilant guardian of the cause of national defense, a promoter of many worthy charities, and a sponsor of an active social and recreational program for its members. But to the general public the Legion became best known as a tremendously effective pressure group seeking legislation to benefit the servicemen.

Through the efforts of the Legion's lobbyists, the so-called Fordney Bill passed the House of Representatives in May, 1920, by a vote of 289 to 92. The measure proposed to provide the veteran with "adjusted compensation" in his choice of one of four ways: land settlement, aid in the purchase of city or country homes, vocational training, or bonds on a basis of $1.50 for each day of military service. The bill was buried in the Senate Finance Committee, but the issue of the bonus, as the proposal was soon popularly tagged, became one of the most controversial political issues of the twenties.

Shortly after Harding became President it came up again. To Congressmen the issue was a delicate one. Most of them wanted to cut down expenses and taxes, but to vote against the bonus would mean antagonizing thousands of their constituents who had served in the armed forces. Were the soldiers' demands turned down completely, a veterans' bloc might be formed, to prove possibly disastrous to both major parties. Furthermore, despite the importance of the economy program, the argument of the veterans seemed sound; they had served in the armed forces for approximately $1.00 a day. Those who had remained in civilian life had benefited financially from the great wage increases of the wartime boom. Were not the veterans entitled therefore to some "adjusted compensation" for the time they had spent in the service of their country?

President Harding was able to delay the movement for a time, but in 1922 the veterans' demands could no longer be denied. In March, Representative Fordney reintroduced his 1920 measure, together with a plan of paying the adjusted compensation through the issuance of paid-up twenty-year endowment policies or certificates. The value of these policies would be determined at the rate of $1.00 a day for military service in the United States and $1.25 for service overseas. A veteran might borrow up to one half of the face value of his policy; he could then use this amount to purchase land or a home. On March 23, the Fordney Bill was approved by the House by the one-sided vote of 333 to 70, and the galleries, packed with members of the Legion and other veterans, cheered as each affirmative vote was cast. The Senate was slower to act, and the general feeling in the Upper House was that the tariff should be completed first. The power of the veterans was such, however, that the Fordney Bill was given precedence; on August 30, the Senate gave its approval, 47 to 22.

The President refused to sign the measure, and in his veto message of September 19—which has been called Harding's most impressive state paper—he pointed out that Congress had made no provision for paying for the bonus. He admitted that he was in accord "with the avowed purpose of the bill to give expression of a nation's gratitude to those who served in its defense"; yet the cost, estimated at $3,000,-000,000—one sixth of the public debt—should not be added to the already heavy financial burdens of the total population to help less than five million persons. To do so "would undermine the confidence on which our public credit is builded and establish the precedent of distributing public funds whenever the proposal and the numbers affected make it seem politically appealing to do so."

The House quickly overrode Harding's veto, 258 to 54; the Senate sustained it, although only by four votes—44 to 28. This defeat of the Fordney Bill only served as a temporary check upon the demands of the veterans; thereafter they redoubled their efforts.[1] The problem was therefore dumped in the lap of President Coolidge. On March 18, 1924, the World War Adjusted Compensation Bill, better known as the Soldiers' Bonus Bill, was introduced into the House of Representatives and quickly approved by a vote of 355 to 54. The Senate accepted the principle, but not the form of this proposal with a similarly overwhelming ballot, 67 to 17, on April 23. In the ensuing conference early in May, a compromise was reached: twenty-year paid-up endowment policies were to be given to veterans on the $1.00 a day for home and $1.25 a day for overseas service basis; those who were entitled to $50

---

[1] Not all veterans favored the bonus. Indeed, in 1922 an Ex-Service Men's Anti-Bonus League was established. This organization asserted that the veterans had received all they had been promised, as well as the unexpected $60 discharge pay. Were a bonus paid, the veteran would be "pauperized in body and spirit."

or less were to be paid in cash; the certificates, which averaged $1500 and which bore interest of 4 per cent, were expected to total $3,500,-000,000; veterans could borrow up to 22½ per cent of their face value.

On May 15 Coolidge, following the precedent of Harding, vetoed the bill. Again economy was used as a reason, along with the failure of the bill to provide the wherewithal to finance it. The President likewise opposed it as class legislation and insisted that the payment of adjusted compensation would not end future pension demands. Congress was quick to repass the bill over this veto, the House by a vote of 331 to 87, the Senate by 61 to 27. The legislature was not under Coolidge's thumb and 1924 was an election year. Few members cared to endanger their chances of reelection by voting against the measure.

The bonus or adjusted compensation was not the only form of assistance given the veterans of World War I. On August 9, 1921, Congress provided for the establishment of the Veterans' Bureau, which consolidated the work of three hitherto separate agencies: the Federal Board for Vocational Training, the Bureau of War Risk Insurance, and the Soldiers' Health Service. Colonel Charles R. Forbes of Washington was named as first administrator of this new bureau. Eventually more than forty hospitals and a dozen soldiers' homes were supervised by the Veterans' Bureau, which had numerous regional branches to facilitate its work. Unfortunately, the agency gained a bad name early in its career because of the misdeeds of Forbes; a change in administration, however, brought improvement under which the bureau performed excellent service for those who sought its benefits.

Then in 1924 another amendment was added to the War Risk Insurance Act of 1917. Any neuropsychiatric ills or tubercular infections which struck veterans before January 1, 1925, were now presumed to be the result of war service and such men were entitled to full compensation. Hospitalization and compensation rights were also extended for other illnesses that might have originated during the war. Monthly compensation for disabled veterans was increased to $80, plus $10 for each child. In addition, approximately eight thousand pension acts were passed between 1923 and 1929 to take care of special individual cases. The vocational work and scholarships in schools and colleges continued to be carried on.

By 1931 the number of veterans receiving compensation was nearly 300,000; approximately 100,000 widows were being helped; 230,000 men were on disability allowance; and more than 500,000 had received hospital treatment. The cost of taking physical care of these veterans and their dependents, the borrowings on the certificates, and the administration of the vocational program raised the price of World War 1 considerably. By 1931 the amount paid out through the Veterans' Bureau was $14,000,000,000. While this sum was for a worthy cause, it helped to complicate Republican plans for economy and lowering the public debt—plans which Coolidge and Mellon devoted themselves to fulfilling, particularly after the election of 1924.

13

Keeping Cool with Coolidge

THE CAMPAIGN OF 1924 AND THE YEARS THAT FOLLOWED WERE IN-
dicative of the state of the American mind. The fact that both major
parties nominated candidates who were considered conservative showed
how far they had departed from the liberalism of 1912. Furthermore,
the reforms of the New Freedom were pushed far into the background.
True, there was discontent in various sections of the land, but the cries
of the dissatisfied elements were drowned by the waves of support given
to the reaction in favor of a return to laissez faire. The worship of material success, which had begun to come to the fore with the accession
of Calvin Coolidge in the summer of 1923, was destined to grow in scope
during the next six years.

THE TRIUMPH OF CALVIN COOLIDGE

The Republican party entered the campaign of 1924 with some misgivings. There had been signs of discontent with the regime in the
Congressional elections of 1922 when the party's majority in the national
legislature had been materially cut. Coolidge's support in Congress was
shaky, as the overriding of his bonus veto and the rejection of some
of his legislative proposals demonstrated. Finally and most serious, continued revelations of the scandals under Harding had besmirched the
party with an oily brush.

The nation, however, did not blame Coolidge for the weaknesses of
his predecessor. He seemed to have given the nation the Midas touch—
and growing prosperity covered a multitude of the party's sins of
omission. Full purses made many a voter indifferent toward the ideals
of social justice which had appeared so important a decade before.

When the Republican Convention met in Cleveland early in June,
the nomination was already signed, sealed, and all but delivered to
Calvin Coolidge. This was not simply because the President had the

307

confidence of the nation, but because Coolidge had planned it that way. Shortly after he assumed office, he started the machinery moving. By Thanksgiving, 1923, he had secured the support of most of the conservative Republican wheelhorses. Not content, he then turned to the business interests and, with the competent assistance of William M. Butler, a textile industrialist of Massachusetts who was also an able politician, he received their backing. Consequently, Coolidge was named on the first ballot, receiving 1065 of the 1109 votes cast. Robert La-Follette and Hiram Johnson divided the small remainder. There were, however, a few incidents to mar the President's triumph: some of the LaFollette backers from Wisconsin and North Dakota refused to support a motion to make the nomination one by acclamation and the demonstration given after the nomination seemed singularly lacking in enthusiasm and spontaneity.

The position as running mate was offered to Frank Lowden, largely as a sign of revolt against the dictatorship of Butler. Much to the chagrin of the convention, however, Lowden refused to run. After several substitutes had been considered, among them Senator Borah and Herbert Hoover, the nomination went, apparently by default, to Charles G. Dawes, Director of the Budget.

The Republican platform emphasized the "record unsurpassed" in economy and debt reduction, and asserted that the Fordney-McCumber Tariff was in part responsible for the excellent national recovery. Public utilities must be regulated, but government ownership was out of the question. The Railroad Labor Board, a relic of the Wilson regime, was denounced, along with compulsory arbitration of labor disputes. The eight-hour day was supported, as well as a constitutional amendment to end child labor. Conservation of natural resources, promotion of the merchant marine and aviation, immigration restriction, help for disabled veterans, and an army and navy strong enough for national defense were likewise advocated. In the diplomatic field, the platform praised the work of the Washington Conference as a move toward world peace and urged joining the World Court. The only mention of the scandals came when all corruption was denounced. The platform, like the candidate, was unexciting, but comfortably safe.

THE DEMOCRATIC MARATHON

The Democratic party was by no means united when its convention opened in Madison Square Garden, New York City, on June 24, and the cleavages which developed during the long gathering accentuated still more the diverse elements within the organization. The death of Woodrow Wilson on the preceding February 3 left no one strong enough to handle the situation—and it is doubtful whether even Wilson could have. The Southern delegates, fearing Negro and labor problems, were vigorously opposed to the revival of anything that savored of the New Freedom; the East was Catholic and bitterly opposed to the Ku Klux Klan, which had considerable backing among fundamentalist Southern and Western Protestants. The South, with its growing industrialization, was losing interest in the principle of tariff for revenue only, and with that defection one of the few remaining Democratic issues died. The delegates from the urban districts desired to attack prohibition, but those from the rural sections were "drys."

The two leading candidates were William Gibbs McAdoo and Governor Alfred E. Smith of New York. The former had the backing of the West and the South; he appeared to be the knight who might lead the charge against the big business interests of the East. Detrimental were his relationship to Wilson and his legal activities in behalf of Doheny and the oil group. Smith was looked upon by Eastern liberals as the man best fitted to carry on the quest for social justice; his record as governor was excellent in the field of progressive legislation. But he was a Catholic and a "wet," and thus was anathema to the Klansmen in general and the South in particular.

How Could McAdoo Hope to Win? (By Darling in the *New York Tribune*.)

Each man had enough backing to prevent the other from securing the nomination; neither would yield to the other. Ballot after ballot was taken without a decision being reached. The delegates' nerves were on edge, the galleries, vociferously for Al Smith, got out of hand, and the heat was terrific. The schism grew as the deadlock continued. Not until more than ninety ballots had been taken was there a sign of a break, and then the movement in favor of a compromise candidate, John W. Davis, a wealthy corporation lawyer and diplomat, started. On the one-hundred-third ballot the tired, worn-out, divided delegates selected him. Although able and distinguished, Davis could scarcely be advertised as a great liberal who would appeal to the anti-Coolidge vote. The nomination of Charles W. Bryan, brother of William Jennings, did not strengthen the ticket.

The making of the platform also showed the divisions within the ranks. A plank calling for American entry into the League of Nations was defeated by more than two to one; denunciation of the Klan as un-American failed by the close vote of 546 to 541—and that closeness served to widen the breach; the differences over prohibition were indicated when the only step taken was to criticize the Republicans for their failure to enforce the amendment. The 1922 tariff law was denounced as an aid to monopolies and a detriment to trade. Income taxes, the platform asserted, should be continued, but not the nuisance taxes. The Transportation Act of 1920 must be revised, and the merchant marine must once more come under government control. The farm aid and labor planks were little different from those in the Republican platform, but Republican corruption was roundly condemned. War was frowned upon as "a relic of barbarism"; disarmament was a possible solution. All in all, this document was no more constructive than that of the opposition.

LAFOLLETTE BIDS AGAIN

Senator LaFollette had long been disappointed in the trend away from liberalism. In an effort to stem this reaction, he formed the Conference for Progressive Political Action in 1922, reminiscent of his National Progressive Republican League of a decade before. He hoped through this new organization to capture the Republican party and secure the 1924 nomination for himself.

When Coolidge nevertheless won the party designation, LaFollette charged that it was the result of intrigues on the part of Butler and Coolidge's cabinet advisers. Even before the delegates departed from Cleveland, he laid plans for what he called the second Cleveland convention, scheduled to meet on July 4, at which he would consolidate the various progressive forces and revive the movement for reform and social justice.

This convention quickly named LaFollette for the presidency by acclamation, and subsequently Democratic Senator Burton K. Wheeler of Montana, who had played a prominent part in bringing to light some of the Harding scandals, was nominated as his running mate. This Progressive ticket was endorsed by the Socialist party—a most unusual step as LaFollette was not a member of that party, the Farmer-Labor party, and the American Federation of Labor. The Communists tried to lend their support also, but LaFollette refused it.

The brief fourteen-point platform was the handiwork of LaFollette. The power of the Federal government, it asserted, must be used to crush, not foster, monopolies. Public ownership of water power must be established, as well as control over all natural resources. Rapidly progressive taxes must be assessed upon large incomes and inheritances. An immediate farm-relief program should be enacted, together with a reform of the Federal Reserve System. Direct election of Federal judges and Congressional power to override judicial decisions were sponsored. The child labor amendment should be quickly ratified, and injunctions denied in labor disputes. The foreign policies of the Harding-Coolidge regime were denounced as mercenary, primarily in the "interests of financial imperialists, oil monopolists and international bankers." There should be a general revision of the Treaty of Versailles to bring it more in line with the armistice. Disarmament should be speedy, war outlawed, and a referendum taken before the United States could become involved in hostilities.

COOLIDGE VICTORIOUS

The campaign did not arouse public enthusiasm. Davis made a swing around the circle during which he played up the national scandals and promised that such things would not be found in his administration; yet he did not try to link Coolidge with the Harding corruption. "I make no charges against the honesty and integrity of the present occupant of the White House. I think no man truthfully can," was one of Davis's statements. He tried also to debate the issues, but the listeners were not interested and the Republicans did not challenge his arguments. They were more concerned with defeating LaFollette and said that a vote for him was a vote for revolution and overthrow of the government. Coolidge, hard hit by the death of his son in July, did not seem to show much interest in the election until the early fall. His speeches were few and stressed the economic phases; "This is a business country; it wants a business government" was one of his pertinent statements. LaFollette concentrated his appeal on voters of the Middle and Far West.

The Republican slogan, "Keep Cool with Coolidge," satisfied the listless electorate. The candidate's liberal opposition was divided, as were the Democrats. The general question seemed to be, "Why swap horses in the middle of prosperity?" and no adequate reason could be found by the voters. The November returns gave Coolidge 15,726,016 votes, Davis 8,386,503, and LaFollette 4,822,856; Coolidge had two and a half million more than the combined opposition. The electoral college showed Coolidge with 382 votes, Davis with 136—all from the South, and LaFollette with 13 from his native Wisconsin. The good showing of LaFollette in twelve states of the West, in which he ran ahead of Davis, indicated that old-fashioned progressivism was not entirely dead, but it was not sufficiently strong to support a third party. Coolidge's triumph, though impressive, was largely a negative one; only about half of the qualified electorate bothered to cast their votes.

The Republicans also maintained their control of the new Congress. The new Senate would consist of 50 Republicans, 40 Democrats, and 6 LaFollette men; the House would be made up of 232 Republicans, 183 Democrats, and 20 in the LaFollette bloc.

The inaugural of March 4, 1925, was a simple one, definitely in line with President Coolidge's desire to avoid ostentatious show. Yet more people heard his speech than had listened to any previous inaugural for it was broadcast by radio. And that speech, considered the ablest of Coolidge's career, set the keynote for the next four years. "I favor the policy of economy," he said, "not because I wish to save money, but because I wish to save people." Then he continued:

Economy is idealism in its most practical form. . . . The wise and correct course to follow in taxation and all other economic legislation is not to destroy those who have already secured success but to create conditions under which everyone will have a better chance to be successful. . . . We are not without our problems, but our most important problem is not to secure new advantages but to maintain those which we already possess.

His was to be an administration in which the government did its best to encourage private enterprise and to keep government control at a minimum. There was to be little social legislation, and that in the economic field was calculated to help those "who have already secured success."

President Coolidge and His Cabinet. *Seated, left to right:* Secretary of War Weeks, Secretary of State Hughes, President Coolidge, Secretary of the Treasury Mellon, Attorney General Stone, Secretary of the Navy Wilbur; *standing,* Secretary of Agriculture Wallace, Secretary of Commerce Hoover, and Secretary of the Interior Work. *Not shown:* Postmaster General New and Secretary of Labor Davis. (Acme.)

CONGRESS BALKS

President Coolidge had many difficulties with the legislature, despite its Republican majority. He was the nominal leader of his party, but his following was to be found primarily among the rank and file, rather than among the Congressional members. The Progressive legislators usually combined with the Democrats to attack administration measures, sometimes with success. Furthermore, there was a tendency for Congress to believe that the executive branch was infringing on its prerogatives, and in turn Coolidge resented the Congressional efforts to dominate his office. Yet the President did not try to dictate to the legislature as Theodore Roosevelt and Woodrow Wilson had done; he was content, after a few flare-ups, to maintain the separation of powers. His difficulties with the legislature made Coolidge cautious about his appointments. His tendency was to nominate men whom the Senate would be apt to approve. Consequently, they usually proved to be conservatives, not disposed to challenge big business. This type Coolidge also seemed to have confidence in, as did the nation at large, although many of them were sharply criticized by Progressives and Democrats.

There were a number of changes in the official family after Coolidge first took office. Only Herbert Hoover, Andrew Mellon, and James Davis held their original posts in the cabinet throughout the remainder of the Coolidge regime.[1] Secretary of State Hughes retired in March, 1925, to be replaced by Frank B. Kellogg of Minnesota, who had been serving as Ambassador to Great Britain. Although Kellogg was a hardworking lawyer and was considered competent for the post, he lacked the ability and farsightedness of Hughes. Henry Wallace died in November, 1924, and his position as Secretary of Agriculture was eventually given to William M. Jardine, president of Kansas State Agricultural College. Jardine was an expert on the farm problem and was interested in agricultural cooperative experiments. In the ensuing differences between the President and Congress over farm relief, Jardine took the part of Coolidge.[2]

One of Coolidge's first conflicts with Congress came just before the inaugural of 1925. He had just appointed Harlan Stone, his Attorney General, to the Supreme Court. As Stone's successor the President nominated Charles B. Warren of Michigan, a man high in Republican political circles. In February, 1925, the Senate Judiciary Committee approved this nomination, but a storm of protest developed when Warren's name came before the whole Senate. Democrats and Progressives, led by Senator George Norris of Nebraska, asserted that Warren's Michigan Sugar Trust had broken the antitrust laws and that the nominee had defended his company's actions. When Coolidge saw he would have a fight on his hands, he requested postponement of the final vote; at the same time, however, he denounced the charges of the opposition as false.

On the opening of the new session of Congress, Coolidge again submitted Warren's name. Again the opposition developed. When the vote was taken on March 10, Vice-President Dawes was absent, and without his guiding influence the appointment was turned down forty-one to thirty-nine. Coolidge was furious; contrary to the advice of his party leaders,

---

[1] Hoover, however, did resign shortly before his nomination for the presidency in 1928.
[2] Other cabinet changes were: Curtis Wilbur of California succeeded Denby as Secretary of the Navy; Harlan F. Stone of New York replaced Daugherty as Attorney General; Will Hays was followed by Hubert Work of Colorado, and then by Harry New of Indiana as Postmaster General; and Work took the Secretaryship of the Interior after Fall's resignation.

he resubmitted the nomination a week later, only to be turned down once again by the more decisive vote of forty-six to thirty-nine. The President then considered giving Warren a recess appointment, which would not need Senate approval, but Warren refused to accept it. Consequently, Coolidge had to find a substitute—John Garibaldi Sargent of Vermont, with whom the Senate found no fault and who performed the functions of the Attorney General's office in competent fashion. Thereafter, as has been intimated, Coolidge tried to make sure beforehand whether his appointees were acceptable. True, he did not like this procedure, but he lacked the forceful leadership of some of his predecessors and thus realized he must act in this fashion. Although some lesser appointments were turned down by the Senate, President Coolidge was generally supported in his nominations by the Upper House from this time on.

FACTIONAL DIFFERENCES

The Republican regulars showed considerable contempt for the legislators who had bolted to support LaFollette in the 1924 campaign. The Progressives, headed by Smith Brookhart of Iowa, lost their key positions on committees, had no chance for chairmanships, or were demoted to the bottom of committee lists. This attack was continued when the Republicans in the Senate refused to grant Brookhart his newly won seat and substituted a Democrat. This practical purge of the Republican insurgents helps to account in part for the factional strife which Coolidge encountered during the first half of his second administration. Those insurgents in effect held the balance of power in Congress and, to gain support for the measures they sponsored, they frequently allied with the Democrats to form an effective opposition to administration bills.

The elections of 1926 showed a definite swing toward the left, especially in the Middle West. Brookhart, seeking vindication, defeated the administration-backed Albert Cummins in the Iowa Senatorial primaries and then went on to defeat his Democratic opponent in the November ballot. Gerald Nye of North Dakota also secured reelection over a Presidential favorite. Robert LaFollette, Jr., took the seat of his famous father who had died in June, 1925. In the East, the reaction was likewise shown when a Democrat, David Walsh of Massachusetts, defeated William Butler for the United States Senate, despite the fact that Coolidge asked for Butler's reelection and even went with his family to Massachusetts with the announced intention of casting ballots for the Republican candidate.

While the Republicans managed to retain a majority of forty members in the House of Representatives of the Seventieth Congress, their hold over the Senate was extremely precarious. At the opening session, the line-up indicated that there would be forty-eight Republicans, forty-seven Democrats, and one Farmer-Laborite. Therefore, in order to maintain the small majority, the Republican regulars had to restore the purged insurgents to their committee posts and to promise legislative concessions to that faction.

The matter was further complicated by the fact that two recently elected Republican Senators—William S. Vare of Pennsylvania and Frank L. Smith of Illinois—were denied their seats. Their chief opponent was Senator Norris,[1] who won his point when an investigating committee of the Upper House eventually denied both Vare and Smith their victories because they had spent too much money in securing their elections. It was shown that Vare spent at least $800,000, and Smith practically as much—which probably came from the Insull group. Norris's triumph was short-lived as the governor of Pennsylvania named the reactionary Joseph Grundy to the vacant position.

GOVERNMENT AND BUSINESS

Meantime, the Coolidge administration was showing an increasing tendency to give business a free hand. One of the early indications of this laissez-faire attitude was in the appointments to governmental departments and agencies which had been entrusted with the regulation of big-business activities. The Interstate Commerce Commission had its composition changed from one which favored curbing of practices which were deemed inconsistent with the antitrust laws to one under which laissez faire flourished. The most notable addition to this commission was Thomas F. Woodlock of New York, who had long made his money from railroad stocks. The liberals, led again by Senator Norris, failed to thwart his appointment; they believed that henceforth the railroads would dominate the commission.

In similar fashion the appointment of William E. Humphrey of Washington to the Federal Trade Commission gave the advocates of big business a majority, and that majority proceeded to change the policy of the commission from that of regulating big business to that of giving advice. Moreover, the Tariff Commission underwent an

[1] Norris had persuaded his liberal friends in Pennsylvania to vote for Vare's Democratic opponent, William Wilson. Despite this liberal support and the fact that he carried about every county outside of Philadelphia, Wilson was beaten by Vare's Philadelphia machine.

overhauling, with the new appointees proving to be sympathetic to the wishes of manufacturing groups.

Under the circumstances, businessmen had little reason to complain of governmental interference with their activities during the Harding-Coolidge period. On the contrary, the Department of Commerce under Secretary Hoover sought to make itself helpful to industry in as many ways as possible. Hoover gave the trade association movement his enthusiastic support; in the stabilization of production through voluntary cooperation he saw hope for the survival of small business. The Commerce Department published a handbook designed to promote the movement and sponsored many industrial conferences. A great deal of statistical information was collected and printed by the Department itself, even though the exchange of such data was one of the chief devices through which trade associations hoped to induce their members to restrict production and maintain prices.

What one branch of the government was actively promoting, other branches looked upon for a time with suspicion. The Federal Trade Commission condemned certain trade-association practices, and Attorney General Daugherty prosecuted the concerns which were using the Hardwood Manufacturers' Association for price-fixing activities. In this case the Supreme Court ruled that the gathering of information and statistics among members of such an association was a violation of the Sherman Antitrust Act. "This is not the conduct of competitors," said the Court, "but is . . . clearly that of men united in an agreement to act together . . . to restrict production and increase prices." (American Column and Lumber Company v. U. S., 1921.) The Court took a similar stand two years later in the Linseed Oil case.

For the moment these decisions discouraged the trade association movement, but presently the situation changed. The Court tended to follow the election returns, and in a series of five to four decisions it greatly weakened the antitrust laws. In 1925, for example, the Supreme Court decided in the Maple Flooring Manufacturers' Association and the Cement Manufacturers' Protective Association cases that exchange of statistical information not involving any agreement as to production or prices was legal.

The Justice Department became more lenient, although the several attorneys general in the 1921–1929 era did bring a total of 138 antitrust cases to the courts. Public indifference, plus the attitude of the judiciary, resulted in few convictions after 1925, and the opinion was frequently expressed that the Sherman and Clayton acts were outmoded and should be repealed. Indeed, the Department adopted the practice of advising the organizers of trade associations in advance on the legality of their activities.

There was also a definite change in the policy of the Federal Trade Commission after the appointment of Humphrey in 1925. "So far as I can prevent it," announced this new chairman, "the Federal Trade Commission is not going to be used as a publicity bureau to spread socialistic propaganda." And almost at once he began revising the rules. The first change was that the commission would not "entertain proceedings of alleged unfair practices where the alleged violation of law is purely private controversy redressable in the courts except where said practices substantially tend to suppress competition as affecting the public." Next, the commission decided not to publicize any of its investigations until the cases were settled. These changes were vigorously fought by the commission's minority members and by the liberals generally. Senators Borah and Norris asserted that the commission might as well be dissolved, so completely was it dominated by big-business interests. And it is true that the commission, instead of openly aiding in the prosecution of concerns under the antitrust laws, actively participated in the drafting of codes of ethics or trade-association practice agreements under which members of an industry promised not to use unfair methods of competition such as bribery, misbranding, misrepresentation of products, refunds, discounts, freight allowances, and the like. Sometimes clauses forbidding price cutting more directly were added secretly by the producers; in any case the general tendency of these associations was toward restrictions on production and price fixing. So far indeed was this true that even while the Republicans were still in power the government somewhat modified its policy toward such activities. In 1930, the Department of Justice brought suit against eight of the associations, while the next year Assistant Attorney General John Lord O'Brian reported that an investigation of fifty trade associations revealed that the majority of them were violating the Sherman Act.

By that time, however, the trade-association movement had grown too strong to be wiped out easily. The encouragement of the several agencies of government—the Supreme Court, the Department of Commerce, the Department of Justice, and the Federal Trade Commission —and their preference for modifying questionable business practices through quiet admonition and conferences rather than through the use of more aggressive methods had built up a huge network of business associations. The government practice of cooperating with business rather than bulldozing it was widely praised by industrialists large and small. This was a sign of the materialistic twenties, which was reflected in the statement by one of the leading industrial periodicals: "In these tremendous days of competition between industries . . . the man who tries to fight alone is foolish."

DEBT AND TAX REDUCTION

The struggles between the conservatives and liberals during the twenties were best exemplified in the issues concerning tax reduction, the disposition of Muscle Shoals, and the farm problem.

The peak of gross United States debt was reached on August 31, 1919, with the then staggering total of $26,596,701,648. President Wilson and his successors regarded the reduction of this amount as one of the principal duties of the Federal government. At the same time, however, the several administrations deemed it essential to decrease another burden which rested heavily upon the general public—taxes, which had mounted steadily in size and in number during the war period. There was considerable difference of opinion over the latter problem, which became a political as well as an economic issue during the twenties. The conservatives desired the burden to be lifted most quickly from the wealthy, who could thereby use the amounts hitherto earmarked for taxes to develop national industry and therefore national income. The liberals, on the other hand, believed that the excess-profits, estate and inheritance, and income taxes should be continued at the high rates, with the primary alleviation given those in the lower brackets. President Coolidge and Secretary Mellon were subjected to bitter attacks for not sharing this view.

Despite this controversy, the Federal government not only lowered taxes materially, but by June 30, 1930, had reduced its debt to $16,185,-308,299. This decrease of approximately one third of the national debt in a decade led his conservative admirers to describe Andrew Mellon as the greatest Secretary of the Treasury since Alexander Hamilton.

President Wilson first took up the matter of tax revision in his annual message to Congress on December 2, 1918, when he said: "As much of the burdens of taxation must be lifted from business as sound methods of financing the government will permit, and those who conduct the great essential industries of the country must be told as exactly as possible what obligations to the government they will be expected to meet in the years immediately ahead of them." And early in 1919 Wilson told the legislature that the ordinary taxpayer should be relieved as quickly as possible, not only through simplifying schedules and reducing the rates, but through the speedy elimination of nuisance taxes. In order to take care of government financial need, however, "I take it for granted that its mainstays will henceforth be the income tax, the excess-profits tax, and the estate tax."

The Revenue Act of 1919 did afford some relief for the small taxpayer. Although the exemptions of $1000 for single and $2000 for married persons were maintained, the normal tax rate was lowered from 6 to 4 per cent on the first $4000 of taxable income, and from 12 to 8 per cent on the remainder. The surtax rates remained the same as under the Revenue Act of 1918. Corporation taxes were lowered from 12 to 10 per cent, but the estate and excess-profits levies were unchanged.

With the advent of President Harding, conservative influences predominated. In a series of recommendations to Congress from April through August, 1921, Secretary Mellon urged the repeal of the excess-profits taxes, a boosting of the corporation taxes in partial compensation for the loss of revenue from the excess-profits levies, the ending of most of the nuisance taxes, and a reduction of combined normal and surtaxes to 40 per cent for the fiscal year 1921 and to 33 per cent in after years. Harding indicated his support of his Secretary's proposals in the message to Congress of April 12, 1921. Among other things he said: "The most substantial relief from the tax burden must come for the present from the readjustment of internal taxes and the revision and repeal of taxes which have become unproductive and are so artificial and burdensome as to defeat their purpose. A prompt and thoroughgoing revision of the internal tax laws . . . is . . . a requisite to the revival of business activity in this country. . . . We are committed to the repeal of the excess-profits tax. . . ." And in proposing that repeal Harding showed a major departure from the Wilson suggestions.

Congress, however, did not follow Harding's wishes in the Revenue Act of 1921. The normal income tax and surtax, as well as the corporation tax, continued as before, although the income-tax exemption for married persons was increased to $2500. The excess-profits levy, instead of being abolished, was raised slightly to between 30 and 40 per cent of income in excess of 20 per cent of the capital invested. Some of the nuisance taxes were ended, but a sales levy of 5 per cent on automobiles and 3 per cent on trucks was substituted. Thus this measure was not materially different from its wartime predecessors. The administration's efforts to force a downward revision, especially of the excess-profits taxes, had been foiled largely through the opposition of the Farm Bloc and the Democrats.

For the fiscal year 1922 the most notable changes were a lowering of the surtaxes [1] and an increase of the corporation tax to 12½ per cent. The government revenue from internal revenue fell off in 1922, the result of the lowering of tax rates and the decline in national income due to the depression. Nevertheless, efficient fiscal management resulted in a surplus; consequently, Secretary Mellon urged again a revision of the whole tax program. His most specific request in 1923 was for the elimination of the still high surtaxes. He argued that the wealthy would not invest their money in industry when the government was taking so large a percentage of their profits. Without investments by the rich, new fields of economic enterprise could not be developed. Instead, the rich were investing more and more in tax-exempt securities or in foreign fields to avoid payment of income obligations. The Secretary of the Treasury pointed out that those who had incomes of more than $300,000 in 1916 paid taxes of approximately $1,000,000,000; in 1922, however, government income from the same source was scarcely one third as much.

President Coolidge came to the support of Mellon in his message to Congress of December, 1923. The new executive recommended that the forthcoming Revenue Act of 1924 contain suitable reductions in normal taxes as well as surtaxes with the greatest relief given to those in the lower brackets, but that the excess-profits and estate taxes be eliminated. The President likewise suggested that Congress abolish by Constitutional amendment the issuance of tax-exempt securities. The arguments he gave were similar to those voiced by the Secretary of the Treasury.

The legislature refused to go along with the suggestions of the administration as once again the Farm Bloc and the Democrats combined to oppose the wishes of Coolidge and Mellon. It is true that income taxes on the lower brackets were decreased to 2 per cent on the first $4000, the surtaxes were lowered, and a 25 per cent rebate was allowed on earned income.[2] On the other hand, however, the maximum estate tax was raised from 25 to 40 per cent. Provision was also made for the publication of the name of every person making a tax return, together with the amount of the tax paid. The backers of this section believed that such publicity would make tax evasion more difficult.

[1] The surtaxes had been 1 per cent on incomes of $5000, 2 per cent on those between $6000 and $8000, and gradually rising to 65 per cent on those above a million; in 1922 they were 1 per cent on incomes between $6000 and $10,000, and graduating up to 50 per cent on incomes above a million.

[2] Earned income was defined as that received in compensation for personal efforts like wages and salaries. Unearned income was considered financial return from bond interest and stock dividends. Income under $5000 was regarded as earned, above $10,000 as unearned.

President Coolidge did not like the measure, but he nevertheless signed it on June 2, 1924, because of the government's need of a revenue law for the ensuing fiscal year. His written protest was long and critical. He asserted that the act "does not represent a sound permanent tax policy, and in its passage has been subject to unfortunate influence which ought not to control fiscal questions." Coolidge believed that this Revenue Act represented "tax reduction, not tax reform," and both reduction and reform should be promoted "upon an economic and not a political basis." He denounced the legislature for failing to end tax-exempt securities, while keeping high surtaxes. "This does not mean," the President wrote, "wealth in existence is taxed; it is not. It escapes. It does mean, however, initiative and new enterprise are throttled." He asserted that a combination of high surtaxes, high estate taxes, and a newly established gift tax amount "to a practical confiscation of capital." As to publicity of tax returns, Coolidge believed that it would prove a boomerang. Those who wished to evade payment would henceforth attempt to conceal their assets more cleverly and at the same time that clause was "unwarranted interference with the right of a citizen to privacy."

Coolidge and Mellon were determined that the next revenue measure should be in line with their views and, taking advantage of the new prestige enjoyed by the administration after the election of 1924 and of the good feeling generated by prosperity, they won their point in the Revenue Act of February, 1926, which was approved by an overwhelming vote of both Houses. The normal rates were lowered to 1½ per cent on the first $4000, the surtaxes were radically reduced—the maximum being only 20 per cent on income above $100,000, the estate tax was practically halved, and still more excise or nuisance levies were repealed, as was also the clause requiring publicity of tax returns. There was some discussion in the legislature about raising the exemptions in the lower brackets. Despite Democratic charges that the majority wanted only to relieve the wealthy, the administration won out in keeping the existing income-tax exemptions on the Mellon theory that as many citizens as possible should contribute something to the running of the government.

Although the administration anticipated a drop in revenue as a result of the cuts under this revenue legislation, such a drop did not materialize. Surpluses continued to pile up as the government became the beneficiary of payments on the war debts, back taxes, and the like. The opposition took advantage of the surplus to denounce the administration for intentionally failing to diminish taxes as much as possible so

that the public debt could be paid off more quickly. Mellon was able
to prove, however, that his estimates of tax receipts had been substantially correct and to show that it had been the unexpected payments
which had formed a large share of the surplus. Thus the opposition
failed to make political capital of the problem, and, furthermore, the
majority of the taxpayers were enjoying the boom time of prosperity
and thus did not feel their tax burden appreciably.

In view of the surplus, however, there was a renewed demand for
another reduction in taxes in 1928 to which both major parties were
responsive since it was an election year. There was a difference of
opinion over the amount of revenue that was needed. The administration felt that a decrease of $225,000,000 was all that the Treasury could
stand, while the Democrats urged twice that sum. As had been the case
since 1925, the Coolidge-Mellon theory had its way in the Revenue
Act of 1928. About the only changes from the measure of 1925 were
in the corporation tax which was cut to 12 per cent and in the automobile sales tax which was abolished. The combined decrease was
approximately $190,000,000.

The Daily Grind at Washington. Coolidge constantly practicing economy. (By
Darling in the *New York Tribune*.)

The Coolidge-Mellon tax policy of reducing the tax burdens of the wealthy may have encouraged the era of great prosperity, but it was challenged from many sides. There were those who believed that the basic principle of the graduated income tax—taxation according to ability to pay—was being violated. They questioned, furthermore, whether the wealthy were in fact employing their savings in sound investment; the wild speculation in the stock market suggested that they were not.

Despite these criticisms of the tax policy of the Republican administrations of the twenties, from the purely business standpoint the government was run efficiently. During the years from 1921 to 1929 there was never a deficit. The following table indicates various phases of government economy:

	Receipts from Income and Excess-Profits Taxes	Total Government Receipts (in millions of dollars)	Total Government Expenditures
1921	$3228	$5625	$5538
1922	2087	4109	3795
1923	1691	4007	3697
1924	1842	4012	3506
1925	1762	3780	3529
1926	1974	3963	3585
1927	2220	4129	3493
1928	2175	4042	3643
1929	2331	4033	3848

THE BATTLE OVER MUSCLE SHOALS

As part of the preparedness program, the National Defense Act of June, 1916, had empowered the President to construct and operate power facilities for the manufacture of explosives and fertilizers. Nothing was done until February, 1918, when Wilson ordered the 35-mile Muscle Shoals section of the Tennessee River in Alabama to be used for those purposes. The so-called Wilson Dam was almost completed before the end of Wilson's second term and plants were constructed for the production of atmospheric nitrogen.

Such was the situation when Harding became chief executive. As another step toward normalcy, Harding was determined that the government must retire from the hydroelectric power business. Consequently, work on the Wilson Dam was stopped and Secretary of War Weeks, hoping to dispose of the nitrate plants and the uncompleted dams on which the government had already spent more than $100,-000,000, asked for bids from private industry. One of the first to reply was Henry Ford, who in July, 1921, offered to take a hundred-year lease of Muscle Shoals at a rental of 4 per cent of the construction costs, to buy the nitrate plants which he promised to have constantly available for the manufacture of explosives, and to provide 40,000 tons of nitrogen annually for fertilizer if the government would complete the dams already started.

This proposal was well received by the administration, especially by Secretary Hoover, by the Republican and Democratic leaders in Congress, and by the farm groups—who looked forward to the promise of cheap fertilizer. Senator Norris, however, was vigorously opposed to granting the lease to Ford, and he began a long fight, against tremendous odds, to defeat the offer. Norris believed that Ford was using the cloak of fertilizer manufacturing to cover his desire to secure hydroelectric power for his own purposes. Were that done, undoubtedly the aims of the Federal Power Act of 1920 would be defeated. The Nebraska Senator proposed a substitute. The government should complete the Muscle Shoals dams and plants and then operate them for the manufacture of power, explosives, and fertilizers for the primary use of the army and navy. A special government corporation should be set up to supervise Muscle Shoals and to sell any surplus power to either public or private corporations. Norris did not make this suggestion on the spur of the moment. He had been studying the power problem for years and had reached the conclusion that public-run plants could produce electricity more cheaply than could private concerns. He had figures to show that the government-operated hydroelectric company of the Province of Ontario furnished electricity to local consumers at about one seventh the rates charged in Washington, D. C., by privately owned utility companies.

While the struggle over the two plans was going on, the new executive, President Coolidge, urged in his message to Congress of December, 1923, that the Muscle Shoals property and equipment be sold to the highest bidder, who could then operate the power and fertilizer facilities under private control. It seemed as though this laissez-faire doctrine might win, as in March, 1924, the House approved the lease to Ford by a vote of 227 to 143. But by that time the issue was complicated still more when several private-utility companies, headed by the Alabama Power Company, formed the Associated Power Companies of the South and offered to rent Muscle Shoals for $3,000,000 a year, to produce 50,000,000 tons of fertilizer yearly, to spend $1,000,-000 on a research project which might lead to lower cost of fertilizer to the farmer, and to be regulated in the production of electricity by the Federal Power Act.

Norris, however, was able to persuade his fellow Senators not to act upon either the Ford or Associated Power proposals and succeeded in shelving Coolidge's plan—which was repeated in every annual message. Indeed, before 1924 was over, Ford withdrew his offer in the face of certain defeat. He said: "We have lost our interest in Muscle Shoals. Productive business cannot wait on politics." Nevertheless, President Coolidge and the conservatives in Congress were also able to frustrate Norris's advocacy of government operation throughout the second term. In 1928 the two Houses of Congress did accept a resolution embodying the Norris proposition, but Coolidge killed it with a pocket veto.

This Muscle Shoals controversy was the most notable example of the fight between conservatives and liberals waged during the twenties. By 1928 the contest had developed to a stalemate, with neither Coolidge nor Norris able to have his way. The issue did not die, however; it was to be very much alive during the Hoover regime and to result in eventual victory for Norris under the New Deal.

The failure of the various proposals concerning the future of Muscle Shoals did not prevent other ventures in related fields. The continued spring floods in the Mississippi Valley, culminating in the disastrous one of 1927 which resulted in nearly $400,000,000 worth of property damage and in the loss of homes for 700,000 persons, made the Coolidge administration realize that more definite steps must be taken toward flood control. Consequently, a special commission, consisting of the Secretaries of Commerce, Treasury, War, Navy, and Agriculture, was appointed to supervise the alleviation of suffering and to propose new methods of flood control. The commission's chairman, Herbert Hoover, personally visited the devastated areas and, with Red Cross aid, provided relief and prevented potential epidemics from developing.

The Congress, sensitive to the widespread demand that something be done to prevent future occurrences, finally passed the Jones-Reid Act of May, 1928, under which more than $300,000,000 was appropriated for the erection of levees, drainage basins, and spillways along the dangerous parts of the river. Coolidge urged that the states concerned should bear one fifth of the costs, but the Congress, believing that they had spent and suffered enough, placed the whole financial burden upon the Federal government.

Combining flood control, hydroelectric-power development, and irrigation was the movement to regulate the waters of the Colorado River. In the summer of 1921, Congress authorized seven states [1] to try to effect

---

[1] Colorado, Arizona, New Mexico, Utah, Nevada, California, and Wyoming.

an agreement as to how the waters of that river might be apportioned. Although a tentative arrangement was approved by those states in the late fall of 1922, Congress did not sanction it until six years later. There were numerous reasons for the delay: Arizona and California quarreled over their respective water allotments; engineers differed over method; there was controversy over means of operation; and a struggle developed over the "twilight zone" of Federal-state authority.

Finally, however, these problems were disposed of and, just before Christmas, 1928, Congress passed the Boulder Dam Project Act. This provided for the construction of a 750-foot dam near Las Vegas, Nevada, capable of storing at least 20,000,000 acre-feet of water, for the building of a canal to carry water to the arid Imperial Valley of California, and the erection of hydroelectric-power plants. The cost of the undertaking, estimated at $165,000,000, would eventually be taken care of through the sale of electric power and water privileges to the neighboring states during the next half century. In such sales, local government agencies were to be granted preference over private concerns. The passage of this act marked the beginning of the Federal government's active participation in the production of hydroelectric power, a participation which was to grow during the next decade. It also indicated a partial breakdown of the laissez-faire attitude which had been so characteristic of the Coolidge regime.

THE FARM PROBLEM

In many ways American farming showed remarkable progress in the twenties. New methods permitted the cultivation of vast areas in the semiarid belt of the Great Plains where much land was brought under the plow during World War I and another great area during the twenties. Agriculture was being transformed by another mechanical revolution. Gasoline-powered equipment was taking the place of the horse-drawn machinery of prewar days; the number of tractors in use increased from 230,000 in 1920 to 920,000 in 1930. With new combines which cut, bound, threshed, and sacked wheat as they were pulled through the fields, one man could harvest 40 acres in a day and do work which would have formerly required the labor of fifty men. In planting, similar, if less dramatic, economies were introduced through the use of disk plows and power drills. Nor was wheat the only crop thus mechanized. The corn belt witnessed the increasing use of such machines as the three-row planter, the four-row cultivator, the picker-husker, and the husker-shredder, while through the use of sleds in the cotton fields one man could harvest as much as fifteen hand workers.

The seed which the farmer sowed was much improved. Hybrid corn, for example, grew more quickly than older varieties, yielded heavier crops, and was resistant to many of the diseases which had earlier plagued the farmer. Similarly improved strains of wheat, sugar, and cotton seed were developed, as well as better fertilizers and both materials and methods for insect control.

Parallel progress was made by the livestock raisers. Partly as a result of scientific breeding, but more because of better care and nutrition, hogs produced more pork and lard, steers more beef, and cows more milk. Important work was also done in the control of animal diseases.

But as agriculture became more scientific, it likewise became more expensive. Full advantage of the new methods could be taken only by farmers cultivating many acres, who could afford to make a large capital investment. Corporations appeared upon the agricultural scene. Largest of these was the Campbell Farming Corporation, which owned a domain of 100,000 acres in Montana on which it was producing 500,000 bushels of wheat a year. Similar if smaller enterprises were to be found engaged in the cotton-growing or fruit-raising business. In 1928 there were nine thousand corporation-owned farms in the country.

This corporate organization of agriculture, however, was unusual. Most farms continued to be owned by individuals, but they were becoming larger. By 1930 the average size of farms in the corn belt was already 239 acres, and experts were advocating 640 acres as the minimum desirable size for a family enterprise, while for maximum efficiency they were saying that a farmer would require 1000 or even 2500 acres. The small farmer, usually tilling the less desirable land, found it increasingly difficult to make a living. Many of these small farmers lost their holdings through mortgage foreclosures or sold or abandoned them and became tenant farmers, agricultural laborers, or factory workers in the cities. More and more chose the third of these alternatives. During the seven years after 1921 the nation's agricultural population declined by some three million.

The mechanization of agriculture, however, more than made up for the decline in the number of farmers. Acreage under cultivation had greatly increased during the war under the stimulation of large export markets and government-guaranteed prices. During the twenties not only did this expanded acreage not decline, but it actually increased somewhat due to the rapid growth of agriculture in the Great Plains already referred to. Production of all the great staples remained at high levels.

Yet, while the supply of American farm products remained large, demand for them declined soon after the war was over. Between December, 1919, and December, 1920, wheat dropped from $2.15 a bushel to $1.44, corn from $1.25 to $0.68, and cotton from $0.36 a pound to $0.14. Nor did foreign market prospects improve during the ensuing years. The age was one of economic nationalism; by tariffs and bounties the various countries were striving to promote their own agriculture and to cut down dependence on imports. In this shrinking market, moreover, American foodstuffs were competing with those grown in Canada, Australia, and Argentina.

The domestic demand for agricultural products failed to expand as in earlier generations. Immigration restriction and a declining birth rate meant fewer new Americans to be fed and clothed. Changes in diet and style likewise influenced the market. As a larger proportion of the population followed sedentary callings, less bread and meat were eaten. To be sure, a vitamin-conscious generation consumed more vegetables and fruits, but the contraction of one type of agriculture and the expansion of another was not an easy transition. The cotton grower as well as the textile manufacturer was injured as women began to wear less clothing and rejected cotton in favor of silk and rayon. Finally, the displacement of perhaps eight million horses by automobiles, trucks, and tractors profoundly affected the agricultural situation. Some 35,000,000 acres had been required to grow feed for these animals and most of this acreage was now planted with crops suitable for human consumption.

Denying the urgency of the problem, some critics pointed out that farm prices during the twenties were 25 to 50 per cent higher than they had been in the prewar period and that agricultural exports maintained a substantially higher level than before 1915. Spokesmen for the farmers, however, emphasized a number of important points. In the first place, the prices which the farmer had to pay for manufactured goods were much higher in proportion to 1914 prices than those for which he sold his crops. His real income, therefore, was less than before the war. Moreover, a substantial proportion of the nation's farmers had bought land at the inflated values of the war years. The collapse of prices in 1921 not only gave these farmers a very small return upon the capital which they had thus invested, but when, as was usually the case, they had borrowed the money to purchase the land, low prices made it extremely difficult for them to make their interest and principal payments. Indeed, the growth of mortgage indebtedness on American farms from 3.8 billion dollars in 1912 to 9.2 billion in 1930 was one of the most serious aspects of the situation. The high costs of agriculture were reflected not only in the increased prices of the things the farmer had to purchase and his higher interest burdens, but in higher taxes, higher wages for farm labor, higher freight rates, and higher distribution costs.

The spokesmen for the farmers insisted that prices must be raised to save American agriculture from disaster. But the problem was a difficult one. Tariff protection was ineffective because of the annual surplus which had to be sold in the world market. To raise prices, either the surplus would have to be reduced or exports would have to be subsidized in some manner. The various legislative projects whereby the farmers sought to secure these ends occupied much of Congress's attention during the Coolidge administration.

LEGISLATING FOR THE FARMER

The Emergency Tariff of 1921 did not stop the fall in agricultural commodity prices, and even before this was demonstrated the Packers and Stockyards Act was passed through the efforts of the Farm Bloc on August 15, 1921. This statute attempted to help the raisers of livestock by declaring it unlawful for packers to monopolize the market, to control prices, to establish territorial pools, or to otherwise engage in unfair practices. The Secretary of Agriculture was made supervisor of this legislation, and to him all packers and stockyard operators were compelled to furnish their fee schedules. Were he to consider any charges or practices as unfair, he was empowered to issue "cease and desist" orders in somewhat the same fashion as the Federal Trade Commission. Less than two weeks later Congress enacted the Grain Futures Act, which gave the Secretary of Agriculture similar control over the dealers in wheat and other grains. At the same time, the Agricultural Credits Act broadened the powers of the War Finance Corporation to allow greater loans to agriculture so that farm surpluses could be more effectively taken care of. During the life of this measure (until 1924), nearly $300,000,000 was loaned to farm associations.

Still not satisfied, the Farm Bloc forced through the Capper-Volstead Cooperative Act on February 28, 1922, after ten months of debate. This act reinforced the Clayton Act by once more exempting agricultural organizations from the provisions of the Sherman Antitrust Act. Furthermore, farm associations were allowed to process and market their staples in interstate commerce under the watchful eye of the Secretary of Agriculture.

None of this legislation provided the expected relief, nor did the Fordney-McCumber Tariff, so on March 4, 1923, the Farm Bloc tried again with the Federal Intermediate Credit Act. Under this measure, the Federal Farm Loan Board established twelve new banks—known as the "Federal Intermediate Credit Banks"—separate and distinct from the Land Banks even though they were located in the same towns and had the same officials. The government contributed the $5,000,000 capital for each institution, and each bank had the right to rediscount agricultural paper and to loan money to farm cooperatives for as little as six months and as long as three years. The collateral for these loans was the agricultural products which the cooperatives had in their warehouses. In addition, the farmers' associations were allowed to establish their own credit corporations which could also loan money, while the maximum loans permitted to be made by the Farm Loan and Federal Reserve Banks were increased. By the end of the decade, farmers had borrowed more than $3,000,000,000 from these various sources.

Other concessions to agriculture came when the Fordney-McCumber rate on imported wheat was raised to 42 cents a bushel in 1924, and on butter to 12 cents a pound in 1926. Yet the farmers were coming to the conclusion that a tariff increase would not help a product that was available for export. The price of such a commodity was established primarily by the demand in the world market, which was less than the American farmer wished to secure. A different type of farm relief was advocated by George Peek and Hugh S. Johnson—who were to become more famous under the New Deal—president and attorney respectively of the Moline Plow Company of Illinois. Briefly, the Peek-Johnson plan, first advocated in 1922, proposed that the exportable surplus of an American staple like wheat should be purchased by some government agency at a fair domestic price and then sold abroad at the world market price. The losses incurred in such a plan to peg domestic prices above their world level could be covered by a special tax or equalization fee levied upon the producers of the staple.

This proposal formed the basis for the several measures sponsored in Congress by Senator Charles McNary of Oregon and Representative Gilbert Haugen of Iowa. The McNary-Haugen Bills encountered stormy strife in the legislature in the beginning, and the original plan was amended numerous times between 1924 and 1928.[1] Each new amendment brought additional support. Originally the plan had the backing primarily of the Middle West. Gradually the Southern repre-

[1] The first bill was introduced in January, 1924, and, after months of debate, was defeated in the House on June 3 by a vote of 223 to 153. The second version was voted down in May, 1926, 167 to 112. The third effort passed the House 214 to 178 and the Senate 51 to 43, but was vetoed by President Coolidge. The fourth attempt likewise passed—the House vote was 204 to 121, the Senate, 58 to 23—but again encountered a presidential veto which could not be overridden.

sentatives joined the other members of the Farm Bloc as cotton and tobacco were added to the staples whose price was to be protected, and more votes were gained among the Congressional members from the Far West. Moreover, an increasing number of liberals and men prominent in government circles like Vice-President Dawes, Secretary of Agriculture Wallace, and Frank Lowden added their names to the growing list of McNary-Haugen adherents.

Despite the increased backing for the plan, President Coolidge consistently refused to give his approval, and was supported by his second Secretary of Agriculture, William Jardine, and the Eastern conservatives generally. In addition to the economic problems involved, the situation had political ramifications. Here was an issue that crossed party lines and threatened to develop sectional differences as well. There was the threat of another Populist revolt which tended to affect the conservative wing of the Republican party. It was a phase of the contest between the advocates of laissez faire and the proponents of governmental control and regulation.

One of the first indications that the President was against the McNary-Haugen proposition came in his speech before the American Farm Bureau Federation at Chicago in March, 1924. Coolidge decried the bill as a price-fixing measure which was not needed because the Fordney-McCumber Tariff was already helping agriculture approach normalcy.

His veto message of February 25, 1927, however, was an even more caustic denunciation. Coolidge did not mince words as he asserted that the scheme benefited the growers of only a few staples like wheat, cotton, tobacco, and corn, but did not help agriculture in general. Furthermore, he continued, it provided for price fixing by the government —which was not in accord with his laissez-faire theories. It was unconstitutional [1] because it enabled the Farm Board to levy a tax—the equilization fee and that power was reserved to Congress under the Constitution. The President also believed that the plan would result in further overproduction of the staples involved and would lead to dumping of foreign crops in the American market to take advantage of the artificial prices. Finally, he declared that the Farm Board personnel throughout the country might develop into "an enormous bureaucracy . . . offering infinite opportunities to fraud and incapacity." In concluding his veto message, the President admitted that the lot of the farmer was an unhappy one. He said:

[1] His veto message was accompanied by an opinion of Attorney General Sargent supporting this contention.

The evidence is all too convincing that agriculture has not had its fair share of the national income since the war. Farmers and business men directly dependent upon agriculture . . . are entitled to and will receive every consideration at the hands of the government. To saddle agriculture with unjust, unworkable schemes of government control is to invite disaster worse than any that has yet befallen our farmers. A real farm relief measure must be just and impartial. . . . I have frequently urged such legislation. I wish again to renew my recommendation that some such plan be adopted.

The McNary-Haugen advocates paid little attention to this last presidential statement. Instead they tried to get more support for still another version, which more thoroughly incorporated the suggestions made by Peek and Johnson back in 1922. This measure, passed by both Houses in May, 1928, contained the major parts of each of its defeated predecessors. It provided for the establishment of a Federal Farm Board which would have a $400,000,000 revolving loan fund available for agricultural cooperatives in the marketing of staples. If losses were to be suffered when the surplus was sold in the world market, then an equalization fee would be collected. To explain briefly and as simply as possible how the measure was expected to work, it can be assumed— in a purely hypothetical case with figures reduced for ease in comprehension—that the wheat produced in a given year was 100,000,000 bushels. Of that amount the American market could take care of 75,-000,000 bushels. Under the Fordney-McCumber amendment of 1924 the import tax on wheat was $0.42 a bushel. Even though the world wheat price might be only $1.00, the American farmer, taking advantage of this protection, would desire to sell as near the $1.42 level as possible —say for $1.40. Therefore the Farm Board would lend the wheat cooperatives enough to buy the 25,000,000-bushel exportable surplus at the protected price ($1.40)—and the total farm income from wheat would be $140,000,000. However the exportable amount could be sold at only $1.00 a bushel, or at a loss of 40 cents a bushel. This total loss of $10,000,000 (25 million bushels at 40 cents loss) would be made up from an equalization fee, levied upon those farmers who produced the total wheat supply, which would amount to 10 cents a bushel. The farmers would not object to this tax, for the plan would enable them to get a net of $1.30 a bushel for their whole crop, whereas they would receive only $1.00 if they competed in the world market.

Using the same arguments as in his 1927 message, Coolidge vetoed this new version, and the legislature again could not muster the necessary votes to override him. Laissez faire had once more triumphed. President Coolidge still contended that government aid for a particular class was un-American.[1] Moreover, he felt that the farm situation was gradually improving. That improvement would be speeded if the farmer used more scientific methods and resorted to voluntary crop reduction. Were government aid granted, the farmer would lose his initiative. The selfish ones would grow as much as possible to take advantage of the increased prices which the McNary-Haugen Bill proposed to afford. Thus the situation would worsen. Consequently, both Harding and Coolidge urged the farmers to establish more cooperative associations through which they themselves could agree on what policies to follow and work out their own problems in the true laissez-faire manner. Both Presidents were willing to give advice through the government. For example, in 1921 the first in a series of Commissions on Agricultural Inquiry was established, and the following year a National Agricultural Conference was called under government auspices. Three hundred representative farmers, seventy-five farm officials, and sixty-four businessmen engaged in agricultural manufacturing attended this opening conference. The Farm Bureau Federation was given government blessing, while the Department of Agriculture was constantly sending out bulletins offering suggestions on forming more competent cooperatives and giving various types of advice.

Yet at the end of the Coolidge regime the farm problem was by no means solved. Farm income had dropped from 15 per cent of the national total in 1920 to but 9 per cent in 1929. The farmer's purchasing power was steadily diminishing. The political effect of the resulting unrest was indicated by the fact that both major parties were forced to bid for the votes of the farmers by incorporating promises of agricultural aid in their platforms of 1928.

The Coolidge period was one of conservative supremacy. But the liberals had developed a counterprogram on taxation, power, and agriculture. So long as prosperity continued, the country generally was not greatly interested in these issues, but the economic collapse of the next few years was to transform completely the balance of political power.

[1] Actually, of course, government aid for a particular class—manufacturers—had been defended as "American" since the days of Alexander Hamilton.

14

Foreign Affairs, 1921-1929

Wᴴɪʟᴇ ᴇᴄᴏɴᴏᴍɪᴄ ᴍᴀᴛᴇʀɪᴀʟɪsᴍ ᴡᴀs ʜᴏʟᴅɪɴɢ sᴡᴀʏ ᴀᴛ ʜᴏᴍᴇ, ᴛʜᴇ United States was playing a prominent and varied role in the world of diplomacy. Numerous inconsistencies developed, which were to be expected in a country which had never had any well-defined, long-range international policy. The League was definitely rejected and membership in the World Court postponed, yet the United States attempted to find some other road to world peace. Extreme nationalism was shown in the erection of high protective walls against imports and immigrants on the one hand, although, on the other, the United States showed some willingness to make concessions in the matters of debts, reparations, and disarmament. In Latin-American affairs, Uncle Sam appeared both as dollar diplomat and as good neighbor.

THE KNOX RESOLUTION

President Harding's Secretary of State Hughes was immediately faced with the problem of ending the state of war with Germany, Austria, and Hungary, not only as a diplomatic necessity, but as a means of answering the public demand that domestic wartime controls be concluded. There was no possibility of—or interest in—reviving the Treaty of Versailles issue. Indeed, President Harding was undoubtedly voicing the opinion of the American majority when he said on April 12, 1921, that while he desired to prevent war, "We can have no part in a committal to an agency of force in unknown contingencies; we can recognize no super-authority."

Consequently, the Knox Resolution, which Wilson had vetoed successfully the year before, was passed again and signed by Harding on July 2, 1921. The resolution asserted the state of war "to be at an end," and it reserved for the United States "all rights, privileges, indemnities, reparations, or advantages" accruing from its part in the war and the armistice arrangements, as well as those which it would have obtained had it ratified the Treaty of Versailles.

To Hughes this was a one-sided arrangement that might not stand up in a court of international law. Therefore in August, 1921, treaties were drawn up with Germany, Austria, and Hungary which reiterated the rights claimed by the United States without any commitment to the Treaty of Versailles. They were all duly ratified before the year was over. Hughes subsequently asserted in support of this method of getting the country out of the war:

It was in the interest of the Allies, as well as of ourselves, and it was essential to the cause of peace that we should dispose of the matter by separate treaty; and this was accomplished in a manner confirming our own rights and not derogating from those of the Allies.

THE WORLD COURT

So terrorized by the Republican irreconcilables was the administration that at first the State Department declined even to acknowledge receipt of communications from the League of Nations. Gradually, however, this extreme policy gave way to one of quiet cooperation with many of the activities of the new body. Unofficial observers, sent to the League sessions from the very beginning, were frequently called upon for advisory consultation on nonpolitical matters. Then in 1924 the country was officially represented at the Second Opium Conference. Thereafter, the United States participated actively in nearly fifty meetings of a similar nonpolitical nature. Also there were five envoys permanently stationed at Geneva to take care of American interests at League headquarters.

The Harding and Coolidge administrations hoped to take the further step of associating the United States with the Permanent Court of International Justice provided for in Article 14 of the League Covenant. A stimulus for American admission to this so-called World Court was the decision of the League Council that membership would be open to all nations of the world, irregardless of their membership in the League.

The Court represented an idea in which Americans had been interested since at least 1832 when the Massachusetts State Senate advocated the establishment of a tribunal for the peaceful settlement of international disputes. In 1899 John Hay had instructed the American delegates to the Hague Conference to propose the organization of a permanent tribunal. The American government was disappointed in the makeshift substitute which was then adopted and attempted—again unsuccessfully—to secure a real World Court in the Hague Conference of 1907. Elihu Root as Secretary of State had been particularly interested in the project and in 1920 when the protocol establishing the postwar tribunal was drafted, Root took a leading part. Far from being a sinister foreign conspiracy, the Court therefore was peculiarly American in its philosophy and origin. John Bassett Moore, a leading American expert on international law, was one of the eleven judges chosen in the first election to the Court bench. Later, Charles Evans Hughes and Frank B. Kellogg, both former Secretaries of State, as well as Manley D. Hudson, a prominent professor of international law, served terms as World Court judges.

As Secretary of State, Hughes was an ardent supporter of American entrance into the World Court and succeeded in gaining Harding's backing. However Hughes believed that the United States should append certain reservations to the World Court protocol which would further guarantee the American position. On February 17, 1923, four such reservations were announced: (1) American membership must not commit the United States to any Treaty of Versailles or League obligations; (2) the United States must have equality with League

Enter Uncle Sam, with Escort. (By Harding in the *Brooklyn Eagle*.)

members in the selection of judges to the Court; (3) the United States would pay its fair share of Court expenses; and (4) the Court protocol could not be amended without the approval of the United States, which could withdraw from the Court at any time.

A week after Harding received these Hughes reservations, he submitted the Court plan to the Senate for its consideration, saying: "Our deliberate public opinion of today is overwhelmingly in favor of participation"; but Henry Cabot Lodge cared little for public opinion and kept the project shelved in the Foreign Relations Committee, of which he was still chairman. Disappointed, the President renewed his pleas in public speeches in both April and June, but still the committee took no action. Harding's death did not end the matter, for Coolidge took up the issue again in his first annual message to Congress in December, 1923, with an even more urgent request for Senatorial support. And by that time other factors underlined the need for joining. Several of the bilateral arbitration treaties were up for renewal, and the other signatories, notably Great Britain, France, and Japan, were requesting that disputes might be submitted to the World Court for adjudication.

Public opinion came out more strongly for admission as the Senate continued to refuse to act. Prominent citizens of both parties voiced the necessity for speedy consent; the American Bar Association, the Federal Council of Churches, the American Federation of Labor, and the United States Chamber of Commerce went on record in favor of the action. There were opponents, of course, headed by Senators Lodge and Pepper of Pennsylvania, who advanced their own versions of the strings to be attached to American membership in April and May, 1924. So strong was opinion against them, however, that they were withdrawn without consideration shortly after.

Public opinion forced both major parties to advocate joining the Court in their 1924 platforms. Lodge died during the year, but the chairmanship of the Senate Foreign Relations Committee fell to an even more determined obstructionist, Senator Borah. The issue was still postponed despite a resolution advocating membership overwhelmingly adopted by the House of Representatives on March 3, 1925, and the stress which Coolidge gave to the cause in his inaugural address the next day when he said: "We ought not to withhold our own sanction because of any small and inessential difference. . . . The weight of our enormous influence must be cast upon the side of a reign, not of force but of law; and trial, not by battle but by reason."

Not until December, 1925—two years and ten months after Harding's original message on the subject—did the Court issue reach the floor of the Senate. There the so-called battalion of death—Borah, Johnson, Reed, and their followers—put up a bitter fight, but the measure was finally accepted by the one-sided vote of seventy-six to seventeen. Suspicious Senators had, however, added to the original Hughes reservations a fifth, which constituted a veritable omnibus of safeguards for American sovereignty and dealt particularly with the issue of the Court's power to give advisory opinions.

Immediately Secretary Kellogg forwarded the reservations to the Court members and to the League Council. The Council concluded that some of the reservations might "hamper the work of the Council and prejudice the rights of the members of the League," and so asked that the United States meet with the League members to arrange a compromise. This Council opinion made the battalion of death jubilant since it provided support for their charge that the Court was merely a League tool. Moreover, Kellogg refused the proposed meeting because "the reservations are plain and unequivocal." Nevertheless, a conference was held at Geneva for three weeks in December, 1926, and it finally agreed to accept the American reservations as the price of American admission with the exception of that part of the fifth which read: "nor shall it, without the consent of the United States, entertain any request for an advisory opinion touching any dispute or question in which the United States has or claims an interest."

The Senate refused to approve this compromise, and President Coolidge stood by the Upper House, saying in his December, 1926, annual message that he considered the whole matter closed. Perhaps he was motivated by the election results of the previous month; ten out of fifteen Senators seeking reelection who had voted for the World Court were defeated in campaigns which were interpreted in some quarters as referendums on the admission issue. Although actually this was not the case, the League's refusal to approve all the American reservations did increase the isolationist sentiment in the United States. The matter was then dropped until after the election of Herbert Hoover in 1928.

THE WASHINGTON CONFERENCE

Even though the United States refused to associate itself with the League and the Court, it did try other means to promote world peace during the twenties. The first effort was through the Washington Conference of 1921–1922. This conference was the brain child of Senator Borah, who as early as December, 1920, became worried about existing conditions. Japan was already beginning a broad naval construction program calculated to place her on a par with, or possibly superior to,

Great Britain and the United States. Borah feared lest this might lead to a world-wide naval armaments race which would possibly bring on another war—and war would end the American isolation for which he had struggled.

Therefore he successfully added a rider to the Naval Appropriation Bill on December 14, 1920, which authorized the President to call a conference among the United States, Great Britain, and Japan in order to secure a mutual agreement for yearly naval reductions over a five-year period. Not until July, 1921, was this naval bill with its rider enacted into law. By that time the new Secretary of State Hughes realized that naval armament was only one phase of potential trouble. As he subsequently said: "Without better understanding of the Far East, it would have been idle to deal with proposals of limitation of armament." The American State Department was disturbed by the aggressive foreign policy which Japan had followed during the war when she had entrenched herself in the Shantung peninsula, secured additional rights in Manchuria, and generally threatened the principles of the Open Door and the territorial integrity and independence of China. Nor was the United States satisfied—despite the safeguards in the League of Nations Covenant—that Japan would actually refrain from fortifying the former German islands in the Pacific which she had received as mandates. One of these islands in particular, Yap, Hughes hoped to have internationalized because of its importance as a cable station.

The British government desired a conference on Pacific affairs even more than did the American. Its particular problem was whether to renew the Anglo-Japanese alliance. The British were well aware that the alliance was unpopular in America despite British declarations that their country would never join Japan in a war against the United States. Canada and Australia, suspicious of Japan and hoping for closer relations with the United States, were outspoken in their demand that the alliance be discontinued. Indeed their insistence on the issue at an imperial conference in June, 1921, precipitated the problem and led to the British government's suggesting to Washington a conference on Pacific affairs even before Hughes's project could be presented in London.

Thus when President Harding sent out formal invitations to the naval limitations conference, they included the proposal to discuss as well the problems of the Far East and the Pacific. That being the case, the list of the invited was expanded to include France, Italy, the Netherlands, Portugal, Belgium, and China. All accepted the invitation, although Japan did so with much less enthusiasm than did the others.

On November 12, 1921, an impressive group of delegates gathered in Continental Memorial Hall in Washington. Secretary Hughes, Henry Cabot Lodge, Oscar W. Underwood, and Elihu Root made up the United States delegation; Arthur Balfour headed a prominent British group which included envoys from the Dominions; Premier Aristide Briand, René Viviani, and Jules J. Jusserand were the French delegates; Sao-Ke Alfred Sze, Minister to the United States, and Wellington Koo, Minister to Great Britain, were the Chinese representatives; and Baron Tomosaburo Kato, Minister of the Navy, and Masanao Hanihara supported the Japanese interests. The prominence of these envoys indicated the importance which each country concerned attached to this conference.

After an opening address of welcome by President Harding, Chairman Hughes took over the leadership of the conference. His initial speech proved a bombshell. "The time has come," he said, "and this Conference has been called, not for a general resolution or mutual advice, but for action." And the action he then proposed was actual limitation of naval armaments. The building of all capital ships should cease for ten years; this holiday must affect not only the building programs planned, but the ships still on the ways. Moreover, old ships in service above a certain total tonnage must be scrapped.[1] The comparative naval strength of the nations concerned must be maintained, and the capital ship tonnage of the several countries should be approximately 500,000 for Great Britain and the United States, 300,000 for Japan, and 175,000 for France and Italy. Hughes hoped that this ratio would also be observed for lesser naval craft.

This proposition to scrap at least 1,878,073 tons of combat ships came as a decided surprise to the audience. British delegates, with their country's long tradition of naval supremacy, and the Japanese envoys, who had hoped for naval equality with the other two powers, did not at first seem to be in favor of the plan. A British observer, Colonel Repington, is said to have made the statement: "Secretary Hughes sunk in thirty-five minutes more ships than all the admirals of the world have sunk in a cycle of centuries." The galleries of the hall, however, filled with prominent persons from many countries, were more than enthusiastic. Taking advantage of the shock which his speech had occasioned, Hughes quickly secured an adjournment over the week end before there was an opportunity for the delegates to praise or criticize.

[1] The United States should scrap fifteen old ships and stop work on fifteen new ones having a total tonnage of 845,740; Great Britain, nineteen old and four new totaling 583,375; and Japan, ten old and seven new of 448,958 tons.

And before the conferees met again, newspapers in all parts of the world came out in favor of the Hughes proposition.

On November 15 the discussions began in earnest among a group of representatives who, on the whole, were very cooperative. The main exception was the French delegation, which opposed the extension of the quota system to lesser naval craft and refused to consider the proposal for reduction of armies and land fortifications. Otherwise, there was considerable unanimity of opinion on general terms, although there were some differences over detail.

During twelve weeks of discussion, several important decisions were reached. The foremost was the Naval Limitation Treaty, signed February 6, 1922. This agreement, sometimes called the Five-Power Naval Treaty, listed the capital ships built or building of the United States, Great Britain, Japan, France, and Italy which were to be scrapped. For a period of ten years no new capital ships were to be built except as replacements for vessels twenty years old. The total capital ship replacements were not to exceed 525,000 tons for the United States and England, 315,000 tons for Japan, and 175,000 tons for Italy and France. Nor were the replacement vessels to exceed 35,000 tons each or carry guns of more than 16 inches. Aircraft-carrier tonnage was also limited for each of the contracting parties,[1] and none of these carriers was to be larger than 27,000 tons. No lesser naval ships, excepting transports, should exceed 10,000 tons, and merchant vessels should not be prepared for possible armaments.

Britain, Japan, and the United States also agreed to maintain the status quo on fortifications and naval bases in the Pacific, except for the islands lying off their respective mainland holdings bordering on the Pacific and certain of the larger island groups. The primary American exception from this ban on increased fortifications and bases was the Hawaiian Islands. This Naval Treaty was to remain in force until the end of 1936 unless a signatory gave a two-year notice of intention to terminate it.

Another important agreement was the Four-Power Pact, signed by Great Britain, France, Japan, and the United States. This provided for mutual recognition of insular rights in the Pacific. Were any controversy to arise during the ten-year life of the pact which might involve them in war, the signatories promised to hold a joint conference to promote adjustment of the differences. In case the rights of the signatories were threatened by some other power, the contracting parties agreed to

---

[1] Great Britain and the United States, 135,000 tons; Japan, 81,000 tons; Italy and France, 60,000 tons.

communicate with each other in order to agree on proper measures to be taken. Upon ratification of the Four-Power Pact, the Anglo-Japanese alliance was to be terminated. On August 17, 1923, this pact was declared to be in force.

The Nine-Power Treaty, agreed to by the United States, Great Britain, Japan, France, Italy, the Netherlands, Belgium, Portugal, and China, had as its purpose the desire "to stabilize conditions in the Far East, to safeguard the rights and interests of China, and to promote intercourse between China and the other Powers upon the basis of equality of opportunity." Therefore the signatories promised to respect the political independence and territorial integrity of China and to preserve the Open Door, while China agreed not to discriminate against the nationals of any other power using her railroads or otherwise passing through her territory.

Lesser arrangements at Washington provided that: (1) the United States should have free access to the island of Yap, as well as equality with Japan in the matter of cable communications there; (2) Japan gave up her political rights in the Shantung peninsula and withdrew

More Up to Date. The Four-Power Treaty replaces the cloak of isolation. (By Harding in the *Brooklyn Eagle*.)

from Siberia; (3) the Lansing-Ishii agreement was to be abrogated; [1] and (4) a commission was to be appointed to consider the matter of extraterritorial rights in China.

The achievements of the Washington Conference seemed great at the time and won the immediate acclaim of almost all Americans. Actual limitation of armaments by international agreement was a goal often sought but never before achieved. Subsequent events, however, have made a later generation dubious of the wisdom of many of the decisions of the Washington Conference. Japan's navy, though smaller than those of Great Britain and the United States, was large enough to dominate the western Pacific. After Japanese militarists gained control of Japanese destinies during the thirties, it became painfully obvious that the Naval Treaty had rendered Britain and the United States impotent to challenge her. Disarmament proved a feeble foundation for peace without some effective system of collective security which would prevent an aggressor state from taking advantage of the military and naval weakness of other powers.

THE GENEVA CONFERENCE

The failure of the Washington meeting to extend the quota system to destroyers, cruisers, and submarines led to a race among some of the nations in those fields of construction. The United States, primarily interested in domestic matters, did not participate in this race and even failed to keep its capital-ship tonnage up to the allotted ratio.

Yet by early 1927, President Coolidge became worried about the increase in lesser naval armament, as well as about the strained relations which had been developing between his country and Japan since the immigration law of 1924. These were potential causes for war. Would it therefore not be wise to hold another disarmament conference? So on February 10, 1927, he invited the other four signatories of the Washington Treaty to another discussion to be held at Geneva.

The Geneva Conference, whose six-week sessions opened June 20, 1927, proved a disappointing failure. France and Italy refused to attend at all, while the United States, Great Britain, and Japan were unsuccessful in their search for a formula to extend the quota system to the smaller naval craft. Great Britain, with world-wide commitments

---

[1] The Lansing-Ishii agreement of November 2, 1917, was a wartime attempt to find a formula which would reconcile the conflicting China policies of the United States and Japan, then cobelligerents against Germany. This agreement pledged mutual adherence to the principles of the Open Door and the territorial integrity and political independence of China, but recognized that "Japan has special interests in China, particularly in that part to which her possessions are contiguous."

and a network of island bases, asserted her need for a large number of small cruisers, while the United States—poor in overseas possessions— held out for a small number of large cruisers. The conference's diffi- culties were multiplied through the failure of the governments con- cerned to canvass these controversial questions in preliminary discus- sions, through the presence of professional naval officers opposed to the whole principle of limitation, and through the activities of lobbyists like the American William Shearer who were working to sabotage the project in the interests of munitions and armament firms.

The conference's failure had serious results. Anglo-American rela- tions were more strained than they had been for many years, and American isolationism and nationalism were given strong nourishment.

WAR DEBTS

Another matter of controversy was over the payment of war debts. While the war was still in progress, the United States had loaned to seven countries which were fighting Germany a total of $7,077,114,750. After the armistice, $3,273,364,324 more was granted to these nations and thirteen others hard hit by the ravages of war and in need of cash and supplies to speed rehabilitation.

These twenty debtor states started a movement as early as 1919 to have this 10.3 billion-dollar obligation canceled or at least reduced. The debtors asserted that these loans were actually America's contribution to the war effort before the United States participated actively in the military engagements. Furthermore, the borrowers had used the loans primarily to buy supplies in the United States. The profits accruing to American industry from those sales should be considered sufficient re- payment. Then, too, it would be impossible to pay back in gold; most of the bullion had been drained to the United States in the early days of the war. What little was left in Europe was essential for currency stabilization. The only way to repay, therefore, was in goods, but the increasing American tariff barriers precluded that possibility. France had her own reason for desiring cancellation. During the American Revolution she had loaned the young United States what were then considered large sums. This amount had not been fully repaid, and France had not dunned America for it. Was it now not the time for the United States to reciprocate?

The United States refused to heed these arguments. President Wilson succeeded in averting a discussion of inter-Allied debts at the Peace Conference, and both he and his successors refused to concede that there was any relationship between German reparations to the Allies and the Allied obligations to the United States. Since the money had been loaned by the United States government to European governments without any strings attached, the debtors had both a legal and moral obligation to repay in full. Nor did assertions that the American loans constituted her contribution to the war effort hold good for the postwar aid. Moreover, at the Peace Conference the other victors had obtained land and promises of reparations, while the United States had secured nothing tangible.

The debtors considered the American position greedy, and there were numerous references to Uncle Shylock and the pound of flesh he was collecting from unfortunate Europe. Yet it was not until December 6, 1921, that President Harding requested Congressional authority to effect a settlement of the debt principal and interest of 5 per cent which was in default. The legislature answered on February 9, 1922, with a measure providing for the appointment of the World War Foreign Debt Commission which was empowered

to refund or convert, and to extend time of payment of the principal or the interest, or both, of any obligation of any foreign government now held by the United States, or any obligation of any foreign government hereafter received by the United States arising out of the World War.

The minimum interest should be 4½ per cent and the last maturity date was not to be later than June 15, 1947. Final approval of all settlements must rest with Congress.

The commission [1] immediately started holding conferences with envoys of the debtor nations, trying to reach a compromise in each case based on the debtor's capacity to pay. Great Britain was the first to reach an agreement different from that of the original plan and made possible by a special enactment of Congress on February 28, 1923. Britain promised to pay her whole indebtedness of more than $4,000,000,000 in semiannual installments over a period of sixty-two years at interest of 3.3 per cent. During the next three years twelve other borrowers made varied arrangements with different rates of interest. [2] One of the most recalcitrant and stubborn negotiators was France, which did not come

[1] The members were Secretary Andrew Mellon, who served as chairman; Secretary Hughes, Secretary Hoover, Senator Reed Smoot of Utah, Representative Theodore Burton of Ohio, Representative Charles Crisp of Georgia, and Richard Olney, formerly in Cleveland's cabinet.

[2] Of the remaining seven debtor states, Russia, Greece, and Armenia had not had their new governments recognized by the United States and thus no envoys were received by the commission; Cuba and Nicaragua had already repaid most of their obligations; Liberia was about to receive an American loan to take care of her debt; and, at the time, there was an agreement to postpone consideration of the Austrian debt for twenty years.

to terms until the end of April, 1926. She secured the low interest rate of 1.6 per cent. Italy likewise made a good bargain with her 0.4 per cent interest.

Despite the haggling of some debtors, the total principal plus defaulted interest agreed upon—11.6 billion dollars—to be paid over a period of approximately sixty years at average interest of 2.1 per cent meant that the United States was forgiving about half of the original principal plus original interest of 5 per cent.

Opinions were mixed over these debt settlements. Generally in Europe, but most notably in France and Italy, the Uncle Shylock belief became stronger. In the United States, some liberals agreed with this foreign opinion in regarding the settlements as both unwise and ungenerous. More harm than good would result, they believed. Yet the American majority considered the Europeans as practically defaulters. In Congress opposition was voiced against the low interest rates—which were less than American banks were paying. The isolationist trend was strengthened; if war brought repudiation, the best American policy was to stay out of European troubles. Yet the solving, for the time being at least, of the debt question did clear the air and was therefore a step toward better international relations.

THE DAWES AND YOUNG PLANS

Despite the continued American insistence that the European obligations were not contingent upon the payment of German reparations, the United States did assist in drawing up a plan whereby the reparation payments were speeded up. In turn, the United States would benefit because the sooner the reparations problem was taken care of, the sooner the European debtors would reach an agreement with the United States on war debts. Thus on August 16, 1924, Germany and the Allies ratified the so-called Dawes Plan, for which three Americans were largely responsible.[1] In part this plan provided that the following year Germany should pay the Allies $250,000,000 through income from railroads, industry, and loans, with larger amounts in ensuing years. The United States and the Allies would loan Germany $200,000,000 in gold to facilitate the first payments, to speed up industrial recovery, and to back a new currency issue.

The Dawes Plan worked well at first, but as the payments became larger and Germany realized that there was no ultimate date for the completion of her reparations, she urged a new program. Again the

[1] Charles G. Dawes, Henry M. Robinson, a prominent banker, and Owen D. Young, an outstanding industrialist.

United States played a leading role in finding a solution—this time through the Young Plan of December 22, 1928. Germany was to pay $153,000,000 a year for fifty-nine years, plus a varied scale of "conditional payments" determined by her prosperity. In turn, the Allies agreed to evacuate all German territory by 1930 and to end the supervision of her actions. Were the United States to lower the obligations of her own debtors, Germany would be relieved of some of her reparations.

As to claims of the American government and American citizens against Germany, Austria, and Hungary, they were taken care of in a complicated series of agreements, culminating in the War Claims Act of March, 1928. Various commissioners and umpires awarded—with interest—some $233,000,000 to settle those claims.

NONRECOGNITION OF RUSSIA

The one nation with which the United States did not negotiate for a debt settlement was the Soviet Union. Ever since the Bolsheviks gained control in November, 1917, and repudiated all debts contracted by previous regimes, relations with the United States were strained. The immediate cause for the failure of the United States to recognize the Soviet government was its refusal to admit responsibility for an American loan of $178,000,000 to the Kerensky administration, the confiscation of American property in Russia valued at $443,000,000, and the failure to pay either principal or interest on the $75,000,000 worth of bonds of the old regime sold in the United States. But there were other factors as well. There was the feeling in American official circles that the Soviet administration was not popularly chosen and did not represent the will of the Russian people. Furthermore, the United States charged that the Soviet was spreading propaganda in America calculated to overthrow the existing government—and the average American, fearful of communism and violent strikes, supported his government's contention. Wilson's Secretary of State Colby said, "We cannot recognize, hold official relations with, or give friendly reception to the agents of a government which is determined and bound to conspire against our institutions, whose diplomats will be the agitators of dangerous revolt."

This nonrecognition policy, originating under Wilson, continued throughout the twenties despite the fact that European neighbors did accept Russia into the family of nations. True, there was considerable pressure from American liberals to change this attitude, but Secretaries Hughes, Kellogg, and Stimson, backed by majority opinion including organized labor, refused to be swerved.

THE PARIS PACT

Even before the Geneva Conference had indicated that naval limitation was not a sure path to peace, some Americans were urging that the nations of the world band together to legislate against war. This view was also upheld by Aristide Briand, then French Foreign Minister. To publicize his belief, he devoted a goodly part of his address to the American people on April 6, 1927—in commemoration of the entrance of the United States into World War I—to a proposition that the two nations agree to outlaw war between themselves.

Secretary Kellogg was not quick to accept the Briand proposal. Perhaps he was not interested; perhaps he felt that it was too limited in scope to do much for world peace. Yet there were a number of prominent Americans led by President Butler of Columbia University who gave their support. The press played it up, and the public became enthusiastic. The isolationists saw in the Briand suggestion a way of avoiding war without the commitments of the League of Nations. The archisolationist Senator Borah urged making the agreement multilateral. Petition after petition was sent to the administration with signatures reaching into the millions. The Grange went on record in favor of the outlawing of war.

This enormous tide of opinion forced Kellogg to change his hesitant policy, but it was not until the end of December, 1927, that he was willing to consider the Briand suggestion if it were broadened to include other nations. France agreed to extend the invitation and thus at Paris on August 27, 1928, Britain, her Dominions, Germany, Japan, Poland, Belgium, and Czechoslovakia joined with France and the United States in signing the Paris or Kellogg-Briand Pact. Under its terms the signatories "solemnly declare . . . that they condemn recourse to war as an instrument of national policy in their relations with one another." Furthermore, "the settlement or solution of all disputes or conflicts of whatever nature or of whatever origin they may be, which shall arise among them, shall never be sought except by pacific means." No termination date was provided—the obligation was expected to be perpetual.

The ratifying agencies of the fifteen signatories [1] subsequently gave their approval, usually with reservations. The chief American reservations were that the pact did not cover defensive wars and that the United States regarded the safeguarding of the Monroe Doctrine as necessary for its "national security and self-defense." Backed up by

[1] By 1935 only five countries of the world had failed to sign the pact.

overwhelming public opinion, the Senate approved on January 15, 1929, with the one-sided vote of eighty-five to one.

Fortunately public opinion in many nations supported the outlawry of war, for there was no actual machinery for enforcing the Paris Pact. Hoping to make the agreement more binding, Kellogg proceeded to revive the Root arbitration-treaty plan by negotiating bilateral treaties with eighteen other nations before 1931. The substance of each was that the contracting parties should submit all justiciable differences to some international tribunal, preferably the Hague Court. The Senate, still jealous of its prerogatives, continued to insist on the right to determine what matters should be submitted to arbitration. Yet by 1931 the Upper House was ready to allow more cases than had its predecessors under the Root-Knox-Bryan treaties.

THE UNITED STATES AND LATIN AMERICA

At the immediate close of World War I the relations between Latin America and the United States outwardly appeared to be more friendly than ever before. For the time being the United States had assumed first place among the nations exporting to and importing from the Latin American states. The total value of exports and imports had grown from approximately $700,000,000 in 1913 to about $3,000,000,000 at the opening of 1919. United States loans and investments in Latin America more than kept pace with the commercial interchange. Influenced in large part by the actions of the United States, eight other hemisphere republics had declared war on Germany, with five others severing relations. President Wilson's decision to try to make the world safe for democracy and his subsequent Fourteen Points were well received in the rest of the hemisphere and tended to help the other republics lose their fear for the time being of the Colossus of the North.

The League of Nations was likewise regarded as an additional safeguard for Latin America, and seventeen of the states joined it at once. They saw in the new organization an opportunity to participate in world affairs, to settle international differences by peaceful means, and to have their independence and territorial integrity better protected. The one dark spot was Article 21 of the Covenant, which asserted that nothing in the document should be "deemed to affect the validity of international engagements . . . such as the Monroe Doctrine." All efforts of the Latin-American republics to amend that article were unavailing. The most publicized was the proposed amendment by Honduras:

This Doctrine, which the United States of America have maintained since the year 1823, when it was proclaimed by President Monroe, signifies: All the republics of America have a right to independent existence; that no nation may acquire by conquest any part of the territory of any of these nations, nor interfere with its internal government or administration, nor do any other act to impair its autonomy or to wound its national dignity. It is not to hinder Latin American countries from confederating or in any other forms uniting themselves, seeking the best way to realize their destiny.

Most of the states also joined the World Court.

By 1920, however, the old fear of *Yanqui* imperialism was returning. The failure of the United States to join the League seemed to indicate to the other republics that she was not sincere in her wish for international cooperation. Then, to make that fear doubly strong, came the repudiation of Woodrow Wilson by Congress and by the people in the election of 1920. The wartime trade boom gradually diminished with the return of world peace. This decline of business with the United States was in part due to the failure of American exporters to live up to promises of speedy delivery and of high quality goods. So Latin America turned again to European markets or, as a result of wartime specialization in that part of the hemisphere, to the neighboring republics. The Americans felt they should sell to, not buy from, Latin America.

MEXICAN OIL

Throughout the greater part of the twenties there were strained feelings between the United States and Mexico, brought on by the instability of Mexican politics and complications arising out of the extremely liberal Mexican constitution of 1917.

In 1920, Alvaro Obregón became President of Mexico by revolt and subsequent election. Immediately American investors in Mexican oil and land worried lest he make retroactive Article 27 of the constitution which asserted that subsoil rights belonged to the Mexican nation. They demanded that the new executive approve a treaty which would guarantee their property rights. This Obregón would not do because, as he said, foreigners would have more security than would Mexican citizens. Furthermore, Mexico seemed unable to pay her debt, much of it owned abroad, which had been greatly increased by the recent political chaos. Consequently, the United States refused to recognize the new president.

American nonrecognition not only weakened Obregón's position, but made it difficult for Mexico to secure new loans. Therefore in 1922 the Mexican Supreme Court decided that Article 27 could not affect oil leases acquired prior to 1917, a decision given greater weight by a

similar executive decree in the spring of 1923. This decree was soon
followed by provision for a meeting of an American-Mexican joint
commission, held in the early summer. This commission decided that
subsoil rights gained by Americans prior to 1917 would not be interfered with, that Americans owning land in Mexico who lost their
property through expropriation proceedings—also provided for in the
1917 constitution—should be paid a fair price, and that American
monetary claims would be settled through future joint commissions.
These promises were satisfactory to the United States, which recognized
Obregón in August, 1923. Other major powers were quick to follow
America's lead in this respect.

The next year Plutarco Calles was elected to the presidency. At first
it appeared as though the improved relations would continue. But the
new American Ambassador, James Sheffield, perhaps persuaded by the
petroleum interests, informed Secretary Kellogg that Mexico was ignoring American rights. Kellogg presently charged through the press
that Mexico was not taking sufficiently strong or active steps to in-
demnify American citizens for seized property. In addition, the Secretary hinted that the Calles administration was threatened by revolution
and warned:

. . . it is now the policy of this government to use its influence and its
support in behalf of stability and orderly constitutional procedure, but it
should be made clear that this government will continue to support the
government in Mexico only so long as it protects American lives and American rights and complies with its international engagements and obligations.
The government of Mexico is now on trial before the world.

Calles was angered by Kellogg's implied threat, and he apparently decided that if his country had a bad name, it might as well live up to its
poor reputation. Thus in December, 1925, the so-called Petroleum Law
and the Land Law were passed, placing so many conditions on oil
leases and property rights that they made Article 27 in effect retroactive.
Although the smaller American oil companies and landowners complied
with the provisions of this legislation, the more important ones refused
to do so. They appealed instead for United States protection. Secretary Kellogg, backed by President Coolidge, was inclined to support
them. There followed a year of vigorous note writing between the two
governments which did not ease the situation. To many Americans it
appeared as though war might break out, especially when in January,
1927, Kellogg informed the Senate Foreign Relations Committee that he
had proof that Mexico was the center of Bolshevik activities in the
Western Hemisphere.

The Senate, following the lead of the press and public opinion, refused to believe these charges; both President Coolidge and his Secretary were definitely repudiated when the Upper House on January 27, 1927, approved without a dissenting vote a resolution to arbitrate the whole oil problem. The administration realized it had gone too far. In June, Ambassador Sheffield resigned, to be succeeded by Dwight Morrow, who, though a business associate of J. P. Morgan, was considered an able conciliator. This attitude was indicated by his statement that "we shall not fail to adjust outstanding questions with dignity and mutual respect." Morrow's friendly spirit, plus the need of the Calles administration for money, brought a change in Mexican policy. In December, 1927, the Mexican legislature rescinded most of the 1925 and 1926 measures to which American interests objected; in effect, Article 27 was no longer retroactive. Also a Mexican statute prohibiting the purchase of American goods was repealed, while Morrow was able to secure some justice for Americans whose Mexican lands had been seized and to help temporarily in the troublesome religious situation in Mexico. Another step in the improvement of relations was the good-will flight to Mexico City by Charles Lindbergh,[1] soon to be Morrow's son-in-law.

Thus the air was cleared and friendship restored between the two countries. But the problems of debts, oil, and land were not settled; they were to cause more controversy during the next decade.

MEDDLING IN NICARAGUA

American dollar diplomacy in Nicaragua proved to be a constant source of trouble throughout the twenties. Only the presence of American marines could keep political peace there, and at times even they were unable to preserve order. In an effort to end some of the chaos, Nicaragua was persuaded in 1923 to adopt for use in the next year's balloting a new election law which had been drawn up by an American. This reform, plus the fact that Nicaraguan finances were in much better shape, thanks in part to the efficient American collector of customs, brought the promise of Secretary Hughes that the marines would be withdrawn after the inauguration of the new president. The 1924 election, asserted to be the most fair and honest in the history of Nicaragua, brought victory to a "Conservative-Liberal" coalition. In August, 1925, the American troops left the country. Scarcely had they been withdrawn, however, when a revolt took place, forcing President

[1] Mexico reciprocated by sending her leading aviator, Emilio Carranza, to the United States. Unfortunately, he was killed during a storm on his return flight.

Solórzano to resign and Vice-President Sacasa to flee. The rebel leader, Emiliano Chammoro, set himself up as executive, but the United States would not recognize him.

Heartened by the American position, Sacasa, a so-called Liberal, returned and civil war broke out anew. Therefore in June, 1926, American troops, in greater numbers than before, were sent in. After considerable political maneuvering, a cessation of hostilities was obtained in the early fall and a new election was held which resulted in victory for "Conservative" Adolfo Díaz. Shortly after his inauguration, he was recognized by the United States. But Sacasa, still claiming the presidency for himself and supported by Mexico, established his own administration, and the fighting broke out again. More American troops were then landed to protect Díaz, despite protests and criticisms from other Latin-American republics and from liberals within the United States. Much of the tension in United States-Mexican relations of these years grew out of the contrary Nicaraguan policies being pursued by the two governments.

In the spring of 1927, President Coolidge sent Henry L. Stimson, who had been Secretary of War under Taft, to Nicaragua to seek a solution to the imbroglio. Stimson concluded that Díaz should be kept in power throughout the remainder of his term and that the American marines, now nearly 6000 in number, should keep the opposition in check. Sacasa had to bow to the inevitable, although his fellow "Liberal," Augusto Sandino, kept the revolt alive despite the continued presence of the American fighting forces. Then Stimson arranged for another new election law under which the 1928 campaign was held. José Moncada, a "Liberal," won in balloting supervised by American troops. He promised to establish a national guard, trained by an American officer. When this force was competent to police the country, Coolidge agreed to withdraw the marines. Sandino, however, continued to be a source of trouble, even though Moncada disavowed his actions.

This military intervention in Nicaragua did not help the position of the United States in the Western Hemisphere. The Coolidge excuse for it, however, was indicated to Congress on January 10, 1927:

The United States cannot fail to view with deep concern any serious threat to stability and constitutional government in Nicaragua tending toward anarchy and jeopardizing American interests, especially if such state of affairs is contributed to or brought about by outside influence or by any foreign power.[1]

---

[1] President Coolidge was referring to charges that Bolshevists from Mexico were contributing to the Nicaraguan unrest.

GROWING NEIGHBORLINESS

Fortunately for United States-Latin-American relations there were a number of incidents during the twenties which offset the ill-feeling promoted by affairs in Mexico and Nicaragua. Mention has already been made of the satisfactory settlement of the longstanding differences with Colombia through an American payment of $25,000,000 and the granting to Colombia of equal rights with the United States in the use of the Panama Canal. The Senate ratification of this conciliatory act in April, 1921, by the overwhelming vote of sixty-nine to nineteen indicated a definite change of opinion. American oil interests, desirous of obtaining leases in the rich Colombian fields, played a prominent role in this solution, which was followed by a rapid increase of American investments—between 1922 and 1929 more than $260,000,000 in American capital was so invested—in that Latin-American republic, as well as by the signing of a commercial treaty advantageous to both parties.

The treaties concluded at the Washington Conference showed the other republics that the United States was trying to promote world peace. This belief was accentuated when some of the Latin-American states became disillusioned with the League of Nations as a cure-all for international ills and began to resign from that organization.

In 1924 the last of the American marines were withdrawn from the Dominican Republic. The Dominican government promised to continue the numerous political and economic improvements originating during the American protectorate and to allow the American collector of customs to supervise the local finances until the American loans were repaid.[1] And in Cuba, the American General Enoch Crowder drew up new election laws which temporarily ended the chaotic political conditions there without the use of military force.

The longstanding problem of the Tacna-Arica territory, which had alienated Chile and Peru for decades, was presented to the United States for mediation in 1922. Not until three years later was President Coolidge able to suggest a procedure acceptable to both sides. A plebiscite, arranged by an American commission, was to determine which country would get the disputed land. The plan did not work, however, so toward the close of 1926 Secretary Kellogg urged that the territory be given to Bolivia. That suggestion was no more successful; therefore Kellogg prevailed upon Peru and Chile to restore diplomatic relations

[1] In September, 1940, the United States ended its control over Dominican finances when that government signed an agreement that the payments due American bondholders would form the first lien on general government revenues.

and deal directly with each other. Subsequently, in May, 1929, they asked President Hoover to submit his solution for ending the differences. This was accepted and at last the United States met with success in the attempt to act as impartial mediator in a prominent South American dispute.

Two regular Pan-American conferences were held during the twenties. The first, delayed since 1914 by the war, convened at Santiago, Chile, in 1923. Although the United States refused to make the Monroe Doctrine multilateral, she did give her unqualified support to the so-called Gondra Treaty. This provided for the peaceful settlement of all disputes arising among the American republics. Should a conflict develop, a commission of inquiry was to be initiated as quickly as possible. While the findings of this commission were not binding upon the disputants, they might lead to a means of settlement.

The second meeting was at Havana, Cuba, in 1928. A feature was the opening speech by President Coolidge in which he emphasized the importance of hemisphere cooperation for the development of human rights and pledged that the United States would do her part. Coolidge asserted: "All nations here represented stand on an exact footing of equality," but this principle was not carried to its logical conclusion. When the right of one republic to intervene in the affairs of another was questioned, ex-Secretary of State Hughes vigorously opposed discussion of the issue since it involved not only the recent activities of the United States in Mexico and Nicaragua, but the whole trend of its Caribbean policy since 1905. The United States was supported by Brazil, Bolivia, Chile, and Peru, and the explosive proposal was dropped. Another suggestion that the Governing Board of the Pan American Union serve as a hemisphere court of justice was likewise turned down, largely through American opposition. Despite the contrariness of the United States in these matters, Hughes proved to be an able conciliator in other respects. It was primarily through his efforts that the delegates agreed to have a special conference in Washington the following December to consider the possible extension of arbitration in the hemisphere.

This Washington meeting, called the Pan-American Conference on Conciliation and Arbitration, met on schedule. Its work resulted in long steps toward peaceful settlement of disputes among the republics. First of all, the Gondra Treaty was reaffirmed with the amendment that while the commission of inquiry was making its investigation, the disputants would not resort to war. To this was added a General Treaty of Inter-American Arbitration, under which the states agreed to submit to arbitration all disputes of a juridical nature, but not domestic differences or those arising under the Monroe Doctrine. The decisions of the arbitral tribunal were to be final. And the Protocol for Progressive Arbitration attempted to set the future stage for the abandonment of exceptions to arbitration. Shortly after this session was over, Argentina offered her South American Anti-War Pact, which was similar in content to the Paris Pact. All the republics signed this agreement to outlaw war.

While these efforts to ensure hemisphere peace were taking place, President Coolidge requested J. Reuben Clark of the State Department to draw up a document which would define the proper scope of the Monroe Doctrine. Although this so-called Clark Memorandum was not published until 1930, it did much to improve inter-American relations. It asserted: (1) that the Doctrine was still unilateral—that is, that the United States alone would determine when it was being violated; (2) "the Doctrine does not concern itself with purely Inter-American affairs"; (3) "the Doctrine states a case of the United States versus Europe, not of the United States versus Latin America"; (4) "so far as Latin America is concerned, the Doctrine is now, and always has been, not an instrument of violence and oppression, but an unbought, freely bestowed and wholly effective guaranty of their freedom, independence, and territorial integrity against the imperialistic designs of Europe"; and (5) "it is not believed that this [Theodore Roosevelt] corollary is justified by the application of the doctrine of self-preservation." These statements, including the repudiation of the Roosevelt Corollary, were welcome news to the other republics. The fulfillment of the promises contained in the Clark Memorandum could be called the basis for better relations—relations subsequently known as the "Good Neighbor Policy."

COLONIAL UNREST

The people of Puerto Rico had served their guardian well during World War I by participation in military service, buying war bonds, and aiding the Red Cross. Therefore it was a distinct shock to them when they were rewarded with the appointment of the ill-fitted E. Mont Reily as governor by President Harding in 1921. Reily's failure to consider the wishes and needs of the Puerto Ricans, his replacement of competent judges and other local officials by his own untrained friends, and his increases in the budget to raise the salaries of these newcomers brought protest after protest from the inhabitants, together with a demand for his dismissal. The threat of a Congressional investigation resulted in Reily's resignation early in 1923, and he was succeeded by Horace Towner, who had all the qualities of administrative leadership that were lacking in his predecessor. Towner was described as "one of the best governors the island has ever had."

The Puerto Ricans realized that Towner could not remain in office indefinitely and that he might eventually be replaced by a man of the Reily type. Therefore, in 1924, a delegation went to Washington with Towner's full approval to seek a greater degree of autonomy, including the right of the Puerto Ricans to elect their own governor, who should have considerable power to appoint local officials. President Coolidge was in partial sympathy with this request, but he would not approve all of it, saying "Puerto Rico has a greater degree of sovereignty over its internal affairs than does the government of any State or Territory of the United States." And Congress, through failure to agree, did not give its support to the insular requests.

Then in 1928, the Puerto Ricans asked that they receive the position of a "free state," and employed the services of Charles Lindbergh to send the request to Washington. Nothing came of this petition. President Coolidge again asserted that they had a more liberal government than was to be found in the United States proper, something which they did not seem to realize—but he did not try to explain how citizens of one of the states would react to having their governor appointed by the President.

But if the Coolidge administration showed little sympathy for changes in the administrative system, it was not lacking in humanity. When an extremely disastrous hurricane swept over the island in the fall of 1928 to kill hundreds of people, render several hundred thousands homeless, and destroy millions of dollars worth of property, the United States government quickly appropriated $8,000,000 for repairs and for loans to hard-hit farmers. At the same time the American Red Cross sent over workers and spent more than $3,000,000 to alleviate the suffering. The Puerto Ricans were more than grateful, yet this gratitude did not make them forget their desire for greater autonomy.

The Harding-Coolidge regime also turned deaf ears toward the wishes of the Filipinos for independence. Harding appointed General Leonard Wood as governor of the Philippines, and he proceeded to undo most of the liberal work of his predecessor, Governor Harrison. Using the Philippine Organic Act of 1916 as his authority, Wood used his veto power extensively and thwarted the plans of his department heads. The Filipino legislators, who had enjoyed comparative freedom of action under Harrison, did not like this suppression. Therefore, in

October, 1923, they approved a resolution calling for the dismissal of Wood. But Coolidge, through Secretary of War Weeks, gave Wood his unlimited backing in the use of the veto power, saying, "You are entitled to the support of the Administration and shall have it."

Undismayed by this rebuff, the Filipinos then asked that one of their number be appointed as governor of the islands, and at the same time asserted that the arbitrary actions of Governor Wood were making it impossible for Filipinos to work with him in any capacity. These resolutions concluded with the statement "that the immediate and absolute independence of the Philippines, which the whole country demands, is the only complete and satisfactory settlement of the Philippine problem."

Coolidge's answer to these resolutions took the same form as his reply to the Puerto Ricans. Under American rule, he asserted, the Filipinos were much better off than if they wholly governed themselves. They did not have sufficient experience for an independent career and they failed to consider that they would not have the advantages of free trade with the United States. Thus both Coolidge and Wood continued to suppress the independence movement.

On Wood's death early in 1928, Coolidge named Henry L. Stimson to the governorship. Before the year was over, Stimson, with the President's consent, established another Council of State. This agency consisted of Stimson, the respective heads of the Philippine Senate and House, together with the majority leaders, and the chairmen of the executive departments. Its purpose was to serve as an advisory board for the governor when he felt disposed to call it into session. While this council was not so free or powerful as the one for which Harrison had provided, it was the first step in almost a decade toward autonomy—and additional steps were soon to follow.

The diplomacy of the twenties on the whole could not be called vigorous. President Harding left most of the duties in that field to the State Department—fortunately under the capable administration of Charles Evans Hughes. The Washington Conference was more of a paper than an actual victory for peace, and the settlement of the debts and reparations problems was but temporary. Coolidge, during the early years in office, appeared to base his diplomacy on the same laissez-faire principles on which his domestic policies were based. When he did act, he appeared to be favoring American business interests. Toward the close of his administration, however, he took a more liberal, benevolent view of colonial and world affairs, thereby setting the stage for the more internationally-minded Hoover and Roosevelt regimes.

Reactionaries and Rebels

AMERICAN SOCIAL AND CULTURAL LIFE DURING THE TWENTIES DIS-played many contrary tendencies. It was a period of intolerance and narrow nationalism when the Ku Klux Klan and all that it represented flourished. At the other extreme, it was an age of revolt when women bobbed their hair and took up smoking, when flaming youth drank excessively and went mad over jazz, and when the intelligentsia sneered at the conventions of earlier days. But probably to most Americans it was simply a happy, carefree period when times were apparently good and the exploits of Babe Ruth, Jack Dempsey, Red Grange, and Bobby Jones seemed infinitely more interesting than the activities of the politicians.

THE UNIONS LOSE GROUND

Labor shortage and governmental favor had helped labor unions to almost double their membership between 1914 and 1920. In the latter year more than five million workers were affiliated with unions; four fifths of these belonged to groups included within the American Federation of Labor, the remainder to the Railroad Brotherhoods and various other independents. These gains, however, proved impossible to hold. By 1923 total trade-union membership had dropped to about 3,600,000.

The losses of the early twenties were to a certain degree natural. Many workers had joined unions during the period of rapid growth simply because of temporary factors and neglected to pay their dues afterward. The depression of 1921, moreover, hurt the unions greatly. Labor was then abundant, and employers could give preference to non-union men, while the unions lost their popularity when they could not prevent wage cuts and layoffs. Of equal importance was the aggressive campaign waged by many businessmen to curb what they regarded as the excessive power wielded by organized labor. Trade associations, chambers of commerce, and farmers' groups gave support to a well-organized open-shop movement. In January, 1921, representatives from twenty-two manufacturers' associations met in Chicago and adopted the name "American Plan" for their campaign to combat the unions. During the next several months organized labor encountered a number of bad defeats. A strike by merchant sailors against a proposed wage cut in 1921 tied up shipping for almost two months, but failed with disastrous results for the International Seamen's Union, whose membership fell from nearly 100,000 in 1921 to 18,000 in 1923. Similarly most of the progress made during the war toward organizing the meat-packing industry was lost through an unsuccessful strike in 1922. An open-shop drive in San Francisco had conspicuous success in undermining the position which organized labor had secured in the building industry of that city, while a similar movement in Chicago made great temporary progress.

The unions also suffered serious setbacks in the courts. The provisions of the Clayton Act which Samuel Gompers had greeted as "Labor's Magna Carta" were interpreted very narrowly. In the Duplex case of 1921, the Supreme Court ruled that the immunities granted by the act applied only to employees directly involved in a dispute and that it was illegal for fellow unionists to attempt to support those employees by refusing to service the employer's products. In another case of the same year (American Steel Foundries v. Tri-City Trades Council), labor's right to picket was rigorously limited, while in Truax v. Corrigan, also in 1921, the Supreme Court upheld the right of the courts to issue injunctions in labor disputes. Such orders were in fact issued extensively by both Federal and state courts. Particularly hated by the unions were the "yellow-dog" contracts—agreements under which employees were obliged to promise that they would not become members of any labor union during their employment. The courts used the existence of such contracts as grounds for issuing injunctions forbidding organizers to make any attempts, however peaceful, to enlist members for their unions.

For the unions to lose membership during periods of depression was natural; the remarkable thing during the twenties, however, was that they failed to make up their lost ground during the ensuing years of prosperity. Instead, their total membership in 1929 was only 3,450,000, about 150,000 less than in 1923.

Organized labor's most conspicuous failure was in its inability to

penetrate such major industries as iron and steel, food packing, automobiles, rubber products, chemicals, and electrical equipment. This
failure was due on one side to the determined opposition of the employers; on the other, to the union leaders' uncertainty as to what tactics should be pursued. Much of the latter difficulty came through the
fact that these industries were heavily mechanized and employed for
the most part workers without individual skilled crafts; the old-line unions which constituted the major strength of the American Federation
were ill-suited to attempt the task of organizing them. Although the
Federation did have a few industrial unions like the United Mine Workers, the attempt to establish new ones aroused the jealousy of existing
craft unions who feared an infringement upon their jurisdictions. The
Federation witnessed many sharp fights between the progressives who
advocated more aggressive tactics and the conservatives who counseled
caution. Throughout the decade the latter faction, led by Gompers,
Matthew Woll, and William Green,[1] kept control of the national organization.

The cause of the progressives was injured by Communist attempts to
capture existing labor unions by "boring from within." William Z.
Foster of steel-strike fame organized the Trade Union Educational
League to serve this purpose. Gompers was determined to keep Communists out of the Federation and proceeded to take stern measures,
ousting individuals who had sided with Foster from A.F. of L. conventions and revoking the charters of unions which had fallen under
Communist control. So far did the Federation go in its anti-Red campaign that it put itself repeatedly on record as opposing recognition of
the Soviet government by the United States; in 1930 it even asked for
an embargo on imports from Russia because they were "convict made."
Although most of the progressives within the Federation were scarcely
less opposed to the Communists than were Gompers and Green, their
attempts to advance industrial unionism and more aggressive tactics of
organization fell into disrepute when the Communists began to demand the same things.

The United Mine Workers under John L. Lewis had many difficulties
during the decade. In 1922 the operators sought to cut wages and there
were prolonged and bitter strikes in both the hard- and soft-coal fields.
So high did feeling run at Herrin, Illinois, that twenty-five men, most
of them strikebreakers, were killed. Although the miners won satisfactory settlements in 1922, during later years they proved unable to

[1] Gompers died in 1924. William Green succeeded him as president of the Federation.

hold their gains. Despite Lewis's slogan, "No Backward Step," the bituminous miners were compelled to take severe cuts and to suffer much unemployment due to competition with the nonunion fields in West Virginia, Kentucky, and Alabama. Attempts to organize these areas were sternly opposed by hired mine guards and company-controlled local officials. When the miners resorted to violence also, gun battles and bloodshed resulted. Such was the case in Harlan County, Kentucky, where three deputies and a miner were killed in a pitched battle on May 5, 1931; seven of the miners were sentenced to life imprisonment as an aftermath of this affray. The defeats suffered under Lewis led to rebellions against his leadership. Rival unions were formed and the I.W.W. and the Communists took their turn in organizing campaigns, but they had no greater success than had the burly chief of the United Mine Workers.

Serious strife occurred also in the textile field. The workers in the woolen mills of Passaic, New Jersey, rebelled against low wages and poor working conditions in a strike that began January 21, 1927, and did not finally come to an end until March 1, 1928. The trouble was punctuated by numerous clashes between the police and the strikers. Strike leaders were arrested, as well as outsiders like Norman Thomas, the prominent Socialist, when they attempted to protest against the denial of civil liberties which was practiced by the authorities. The vigorous role played by radicals tended to divert attention from the legitimate grievances of the workers, and eventually the Communists, who had led the strikers originally, consented to retire from the struggle. But even after the workers were adopted by an old-line union, the United Textile Workers, they found it impossible to secure any important concessions from their employers.

During 1929 there were bitterly contested strikes in the southern textile towns of Elizabethton, Tennessee, Gastonia, North Carolina, and Marion, North Carolina. The first of these was notable for the mob violence employed against labor organizers; the second, for the drastic tactics used by the local authorities against the strikers and the resulting clash in which the chief of police was killed; the third, for an incident in which the sheriff and his deputies fired upon unarmed pickets, killing three and wounding twenty-one others, two of whom later died. Against the alliance of company, local governmental authorities, and antiunion mobs, all campaigns to organize the southern textile workers broke down, whether led by Communists as at Gastonia, or by the United Textile Workers as at Elizabethton and Marion.

WELFARE CAPITALISM

The weakness of the labor-union movement of the twenties, however, is not to be completely explained either by the shortcomings of the leadership or by the determination of the antiunion forces. Much of labor's docility resulted from the fact that in many areas workers seemed to be bettering their lots materially without organization. Wage cuts there were during the depression of 1921, but usually pay still remained substantially higher than the 1914 levels. The farmers' bad fortune, moreover, was to a certain extent the workers' good. Food prices, though higher than in 1914, were less so than wages; the result was a gratifying increase in purchasing power. According to the calculation of a leading economist, the workers' real earnings averaged 32 per cent higher in 1928 than in 1914.

The better wages of the twenties were sometimes a price grudgingly paid to keep workers reasonably satisfied and indifferent to the union organizers. On the part of many businessmen, however, they reflected a new philosophy which defended high wages not merely as a necessary evil, but as a positively good thing since they attracted the more enterprising and efficient workers to a particular plant and since they helped build up the purchasing power upon which industry depended for a market for automobiles, radios, electric vacuum cleaners, and the like. Similarly, employers were converted to the shorter work week as a contribution to higher labor efficiency and more leisure time for the workers to consume the products of industry.

Welfare capitalism sought also to improve the conditions under which laborers worked. Highly trained personnel departments hired and fired with more discernment than had old-fashioned foremen and superintendents. Piece rates and working rules were more carefully drafted, and provision was sometimes made for vacations with pay. Recreation halls and cafeterias likewise played their part in keeping the employees contented.

A favorite device of employers during the twenties was the company union or works council. The number of corporations supporting such plans increased from 145 in 1919 to 432 in 1926, when the movement reached a peak of popularity. The company union provided a mechanism under which representatives could be elected to confer with the management on behalf of their fellow workers and through which grievances could be voiced. But such unions were kept strictly under the control of the employer and the extent of their activities was rigidly restricted.

In order to prevent the extension of the company-union movement, many of the old-line unions felt the necessity of cooperating closely with management. Under the Baltimore and Ohio plan, for example, the railroad management under President Daniel Willard agreed to have as much work as possible done by union labor in the Baltimore and Ohio shops, while the machinists' union pledged to make the work of the shops as efficient and economical as possible. The plan's success led to its adoption by several other roads. Another outstanding experiment in management-union cooperation was that developed in the men's clothing industry by the Amalgamated Clothing Workers under the leadership of Sidney Hillman. William Green asserted: "We are cooperating with the managements in the elimination of waste because the working man suffers most of all as a result of waste. We are also cooperating with the managements in the elimination of duplication of effort, and we are not opposing the introduction of improved machinery."

Despite such conservative statements of policy, however, employers in industries not already organized continued to recognize only company unions and to base their labor policies upon the tenets of welfare capitalism. Often they sought to ensure the loyalty of the men through stock-purchase plans—a policy that had unfortunate repercussions when stock prices collapsed in 1929.

SUPPRESSING RADICALISM

The anti-Red hysteria of 1919 gradually subsided in most areas as the extremely small number of real radicals in the country became more apparent. But the I.W.W. and the Communists continued to be highly unpopular as was obvious by the public attitude toward labor controversies where either was involved. The criminal syndicalism laws remained on the books and at least in California were actively enforced. In that state there were 504 arrests under the law between 1919 and 1924, and, when juries began to refuse to convict, the state attorney general secured a court injunction under which I.W.W. organizers could be arrested and tried for contempt of court without a jury for merely soliciting new members for the outlawed organization.

Radicals who fell into the toils of the law on any charge were likely to find judge and jury prejudiced against them. Such at least was the conclusion of thousands of Americans who interested themselves in the Sacco-Vanzetti case. Nicola Sacco and Bartolomeo Vanzetti, two anarchists who had been active in strikes during earlier years, were arrested in 1920 on the accusation of having held up and murdered the paymaster

Sacco and Vanzetti (second and third figures walking in front row). (Brown Bros.)

of a shoe factory in South Braintree, Massachusetts. During their trial the next year, the strong distaste of the presiding judge, Webster Thayer, for all anarchists and these two in particular, was displayed by comments which he made outside the courtroom while the trial was in progress. The district attorney was permitted not only to drive home to the jury the radical beliefs of the defendants, but also the fact that they had fled to Mexico in 1917 to evade the draft. After the two men were found guilty and sentenced to death, defense lawyers started a long campaign to secure a new trial on the ground that the first had been unfair. Despite the weakness of the case against the two radicals and the discovery of new evidence pointing to others as the guilty parties, Judge Thayer refused all motions for a new trial and was upheld in his rulings by the highest court in the state. The controversy over the case reached a climax in 1927. Professor Felix Frankfurter of the Harvard Law School had become convinced that the men had not had a fair trial. He incorporated his findings in a book which proved disturbing reading to thousands of citizens, even many who had no sympathy for radicalism. Nevertheless Governor Alvan T. Fuller allowed the executions to be carried out on August 23, 1927, basing his decision upon his own investigation of the case and that made by a governor's committee headed by President A. Lawrence Lowell of Harvard University. Prominent in efforts to save the two had been newspaper men like Heywood Broun, literary figures like Edna St. Vincent Millay and John Dos Passos, and outstanding lawyers like Frank P. Walsh and Arthur Garfield Hayes. News of the executions brought demonstrations thousands of miles away—in England, France, Italy, Russia, and Latin America. Rightly or wrongly, countless people throughout the world were convinced that Sacco and Vanzetti had gone to the electric chair because of their unpopular opinions and not because they had been conclusively proved guilty of murder.

In California two radical unionists, Thomas J. Mooney and Warren K. Billings, escaped death but nevertheless suffered a long imprisonment for a crime of which many Americans also believed them innocent. Accused of participating in a bomb outrage which took the lives of eight persons in a San Francisco Preparedness Day parade in 1916, Mooney was convicted and sentenced to be hanged, while Billings was given a life term. Due to President Wilson's intercession, the governor of California commuted Mooney's sentence to life imprisonment. The two men remained in prison throughout the twenties despite the fact that the conviction had been secured on flimsy evidence and perhaps on perjured testimony. As in the Sacco-Vanzetti case, the circumstance that thousands of liberals were demanding their release only seemed to stiffen the determination of the state authorities to allow the law to take its course. Not until 1939 were the California prisoners granted a pardon.

THE KU KLUX KLAN

On Thanksgiving night, 1915, Colonel William Joseph Simmons and some thirty friends gathered under a fiery cross on top of Stone Mountain near Atlanta, Georgia, and swore allegiance to the Invisible Empire, Knights of the Ku Klux Klan. During the next ten years such weird scenes as this were repeated thousands of times in every part of the country. Simmons's attempt to found a new organization employing the name and paraphernalia of the old Klan of Reconstruction days, which had been defunct for decades, had no great success at first. Up to June, 1920, the Klan had gained only four or five thousand members and was still to be found mostly in the South. The organization was given a new lease of life when Edward Clarke and Mrs. Elizabeth Tyler were put in charge of its promotional activities. The country was divided into domains headed by Grand Goblins, and realms or states each supervised by a King Kleagle. At the bottom of the organizational

Ku Klux Klan in Church. (Acme.)

pyramid were thousands of local Kleagles who rounded up new members and collected their $10 initiation fees. Four dollars of the latter was retained by the local Kleagle, while $1.00 went to the King Kleagle of the realm, $0.50 to the Grand Goblin of the domain, and the remainder to Imperial Wizard and Emperor Simmons, Imperial Kleagle Clarke, and the rest of the Atlanta oligarchy. With this streamlined machinery well lubricated with money, the Klan had a marvelous growth. Its days of greatest prosperity were from 1922 to 1925, during the regime of Simmons's successor, Hiram Wesley Evans, a Texas dentist.

Defenders of the Klan asserted that it was simply a fraternal order devoted to the praiseworthy ideals of patriotism and Christian morality. Many of its members were attracted either by these professed objectives or by the opportunity which the Klan offered for dressing up in mysterious robes and hoods, for participating in melodramatic rituals, or for talking a strange jargon which featured words starting with the letter "K."

Yet the movement, which had gained perhaps four or five million adherents by 1925, had many sinister aspects. It was fed by group hatreds—White hatred of the Negro, Christian hatred of the Jew, and, above all, Protestant hatred of the Catholic. Klan spellbinders convinced many Americans who should have known better that nuns in convents were prisoners against their will, that the Pope was about to transfer his headquarters from Rome to Washington, or that arms and ammunition were being stored in cathedrals preparatory to the Catholics seizing control of the government. The ends to which the Klan was devoted and the methods which it used depended upon the local situation. In some areas its activities were confined to burning crosses at night, holding mysterious konklaves, and parading through the streets; in others it acted as a vigilance committee, sending warning messages to bootleggers, persons accused of immorality, Negroes lacking in humility, or labor-union organizers. Spokesmen for the Klan always denied that it was guilty of violence, but there appears little doubt that local groups using the costume of the Klan were involved in many flogging incidents, tar-and-feather parties, mutilations, and even killings.

Physical violence, however, was less characteristic of the Klan than were other methods. Catholic and Jewish merchants found themselves boycotted. Schoolteachers who failed to present their subjects in the way prescribed by the Klan were spied upon by their own students, badgered by their superiors, and often dismissed by local school committees. Ministers brave enough to condemn the intolerance of the Invisible Empire found their congregations evaporating and themselves forced to resign. More and more the Klan became involved in politics, rewarding its friends and punishing its enemies until it was a power in states as widely scattered as Oregon, Texas, Oklahoma, Louisiana, Maine, and Kansas. Particularly notorious was the situation in Indiana, where David C. Stephenson used the Klan to establish a virtual dictatorship. But Stephenson's fall was as dramatic as his rise. The suicide of a girl whom he had abducted led to his arrest and conviction for murder. With its state leader condemned to prison for life under such circumstances, the Klan's reputation as the guardian of morality and the champion of law and order was shattered. This scandal was followed by revelations of corruption involving the Klan-elected governor of the state and several other prominent members of Stephenson's machine. Good citizens, who had been taken in by the Klan organizers, resigned in haste, while bad sought to cut their connection with a group so much in disgrace.

Elsewhere the decline of the organization was not so rapid, but by 1926 the peak of the movement had everywhere passed. Two years later the Klan was so much in public disfavor that Imperial Wizard Evans tried to rescue it through banning the use of masks and visors. Yet the removal of much of the secrecy connected with the Klan simply marked a further step in its disintegration. The Invisible Empire's greatest success had come through convincing misguided individuals that its activities were somehow in the interests of Americanism; its collapse followed the belated discovery of what should have been evident from the first—that, whatever the professed ideals of the Klan, its actual objectives and its methods were the antithesis of good Americanism.

FUNDAMENTALISTS VERSUS MODERNISTS

Among the dangerous ideas which certain Americans hoped to repress in postwar years were those challenging old standards of religious orthodoxy. The tendency of a younger generation of Protestant clergymen to doubt the Virgin birth of Jesus, the reality of the Devil and Hell, and the literal truth of every word in the Bible aroused the conservatives who believed that the essential foundations of Christianity were being undermined. As early as 1910 an influential pamphlet entitled *The Fundamentals, A Testimony of Truth* had been published and, with the backing of two wealthy laymen, millions of copies were distributed. This encouraged the growth of a faction calling themselves fundamentalists who sought to purge the churches of hated modernism. The fight was taken to the floor of religious conventions where the conservatives tried to have the unorthodoxy of the liberals condemned, to denominational schools where the two factions struggled for control, and even to individual congregations where fundamentalist and modernist cliques took shape.

Most prominent of fundamentalist laymen was William Jennings Bryan, a Presbyterian. The Great Commoner devoted his last years to a crusade against modernism with the same zeal that he had shown in his earlier struggles against the gold standard, imperialism, war, and liquor. Due in large part to Bryan's campaigning, bills to forbid the teaching of evolution in the public schools were introduced in the legislatures of almost half the states. In Tennessee, Mississippi, and Arkansas the proposal actually became law.

The Tennessee antievolution act, signed by the governor on March 13, 1925, led at once to interesting consequences. The American Civil Liberties Union announced that it would back any schoolteacher who would test the law. Enterprising citizens of Dayton acted quickly to secure a promising show for their own home town. A young high-school biology teacher, John Thomas Scopes, readily agreed to cooperate. According to the testimony of one of his pupils, Scopes told his class "that the earth was once a hot molten mass, too hot for plant or animal life to exist upon it; in the sea the earth cooled off; there was a little germ of one-cell organism formed, and this organism kept evolving until it got to be a land animal, and it kept on evolving, and from this was man." For teaching this departure from the story "of the divine creation of man as taught in the Bible," Scopes was arrested and brought to trial in Dayton during July, 1925.

The young defendant was largely forgotten in the battle of legal giants which the case attracted. William Jennings Bryan threw all his energy into the cause of the prosecution, while the defense was in the hands of Clarence Darrow, the most famous criminal lawyer in America, who was ably seconded by Arthur Garfield Hayes and Dudley Field Malone. The courtroom was crowded with reporters and photographers from all parts of the country, as well as telegraph operators, radio broadcasters, and throngs of curious Tennesseeans who promptly took sides and cheered loudly whenever a telling point was scored.

The trial's most dramatic moment came when the defense summoned Bryan to the stand to testify as an expert on the Bible. Under Darrow's sharp questioning, Bryan proclaimed his belief that the whale swallowed Jonah, that Joshua made the sun stand still, and that the world was created in the year 4004 B.C. The Commoner's defense of the literal truth of the Bible was greeted with loud hurrahs and amens from the

The Outcast in the Bryan Zoo. (By McCutcheon in the *Chicago Tribune*.)

Darrow and Bryan at the Scopes Trial in Dayton, Tennessee. Darrow is in the foreground; Bryan left of center behind the microphone. (Brown Bros.)

courtroom audience, although Darrow contended that the examination had exposed "fool ideas that no intelligent Christian on earth believes." The defense attempted to bring to the stand religious-minded scientists who would have testified that the doctrine of evolution was not inconsistent with Christianity, but the presiding judge ruled that the only question at issue was whether Scopes had taught evolution. Since this was admitted, his conviction was a foregone conclusion.

Hearing the case upon appeal, the Supreme Court of Tennessee upheld the constitutionality of the antievolution law, but set aside Scope's hundred-dollar fine on the grounds that the judge had exceeded his authority in imposing it. By this technicality the door was closed to carrying the case to the United States Supreme Court as the defense had hoped. Bryan was not on hand to witness the final disposition of the case. About a week after the end of the Dayton trial he suddenly died—his demise no doubt hastened by overexcitement and overwork.

Fortunately for the churches, a large middle party existed between the fundamentalist and modernist factions. This group, sometimes called institutionalists, was more interested in the church's work than in its doctrines and helped to prevent the quarrel from reaching the point of schism. The controversy gradually quieted down without a clear-cut victory for either side.

Just how strong the churches really were is difficult to say. A poll of newspaper readers taken in 1927 indicated that 91 per cent professed a belief in God and that this belief was more nearly unanimous among college students than among their elders. Open skepticism was rare—rarer than during some earlier periods of national history. Despite this fact, the number of Americans who were casual and indifferent in their religious attitudes seemed to be growing. No longer was it taken for granted that a solid citizen would be found sedately occupying the family pew each Sunday morning. He was indeed as likely to be found on the golf course, in his car speeding over the countryside, or in bed reading the Sunday paper. Nor would college students any longer accept without challenge the institution of compulsory chapel; on campuses everywhere student newspapers were campaigning—usually with success—for making chapel attendance voluntary. Statistically the churches made a good record: the number of church members continued to grow, the churches gained in wealth and enlarged their social program at home and their missionary efforts abroad; the kind of work represented by the Young Men's Christian Association, the Young Women's Christian Association, and the Knights of Columbus was greatly expanded. To many spiritually-minded individuals, nevertheless, it appeared that the majority of their countrymen were more interested in making money and having a good time than they were in seeking the Kingdom of God.

PROHIBITION PROBLEMS

Millions of good people believed that the ratification of the Eighteenth Amendment had miraculously ended the liquor problem; the sale of intoxicants would at once cease and, with that cessation, poverty and crime would largely disappear and America would enter upon a golden era.

But millions of other Americans had an entirely different attitude toward alcoholic beverages. They had been brought up in households where beer or wine was served with the family meal, where birthday or wedding celebrations were incomplete without a few rounds of drinks, and where the problem of how much an individual should imbibe was a question of personal morals. To such people national prohibition was an interference with personal liberty. They felt that the law was entirely unreasonable and that they were justified in continuing to buy liquor wherever it was available. Many who did not drink themselves, moreover, believed that the prohibition laws were on a different basis than statutes which dealt with crimes like burglary or arson. They did not feel under any obligation to report Volstead Act violators to the police or to vote for city officials who would carry out vigorous enforcement measures.

This hostility or indifference to the law—particularly to be found in the great cities—was the nub of the enforcement problem. With millions of thirsty citizens ready to pay high prices for any kind of alcoholic beverage, it was not long before tens of thousands of other citizens decided to run the not very great risk involved in catering to this demand.

An abundant supply of illegal liquor was available from many sources. In the first place, there were 18,700 miles of border—land, sea, lake, and river—across which foreign manufactured beverages could be smuggled. Some of the nation's greatest cities were near by. For example, ships could stand off Long Island outside United States territorial limits while motorboats and fast launches ran their illegal cargoes onto deserted beaches only an hour's drive from New York City. In the second place, wholesale manufacture within the country soon developed. Illicit stills long antedated prohibition; their earlier use had been in evasion of the revenue laws. Now they simply multiplied to meet the new demand. Stills were inexpensive and easily constructed—in fact hundreds of thousands of householders experimented with their own apparatus in the kitchen or the cellar. Finally, a large amount of liquor was available through diversion from legitimate channels. The rapidly growing chemical industry used 28,000,000 gallons of alcohol annually. Although this was supposed to be rendered unfit for human consumption, large quantities passed secretly into the hands of bootleggers. Breweries supplying the near-beer industry had to produce the real product as a first step, and much of this was not actually dealcoholized as the law required. Physicians, furthermore, were issuing eleven million prescriptions annually under which patients might secure alcoholic beverages for medicinal purposes. Many doctors were more than generous in handing these out, while numerous druggists diluted their medicinal stock and sold the balance illegally.

The distribution of this vast supply of illicit liquor was in the hands of thousands of bootleggers who retailed their ware to the doorsteps of customers or who disposed of it wholesale to speakeasies. How openly the latter often operated in the large cities was described in 1923 by Governor Gifford Pinchot of Pennsylvania, a dry. Reporting on a personal tour of investigation in Philadelphia, he said: "In one saloon the law-breaking drinkers surrounded the illegal bar four deep. It was easy to find, for there was as little secrecy about it as there is about the Washington Monument. Crowds walked in and out. A policeman stood at the very door."

Attempting to combat all this was the Prohibition Bureau of the Treasury Department, employing about three thousand agents. The exploits of at least two of these, Izzy Einstein and Moe Smith, became legendary in the New York area. In order to collect evidence against Volstead Act violators, Izzy and Moe disguised themselves as automobile dealers, milkmen, fishermen, horse dealers, streetcar conductors, Palm Sunday churchgoers, football heroes, trombone players, and turkey salesmen. But no amount of such ingenuity could alter the fact that the bureau was too small and too poorly supplied with money to plug up the real sources of the illicit supply. General Lincoln C. Andrews, one of the many administrators who attempted to direct the bureau during its troubled history, testified in 1925 that only about 5 per cent of the liquor smuggled into the country was being stopped and that only about one out of every ten stills in operation was being seized. To add to the difficulties of the service, the extraordinary opportunities for corruption made it necessary to dismiss in disgrace about one out of every twelve agents hired. Prosecutions under the law created forty or fifty thousand cases annually. For such an increase in their business the Federal courts were not ready; the congestion in their dockets could only be cleared by accepting pleas of guilty in return for a light penalty; over 90 per cent of the cases were disposed of by such "bargain-day" procedures.

The states, to be sure, had been granted concurrent power with the Federal government in enforcing the Eighteenth Amendment. All but six of them passed state-enforcement acts, some of them more severe than the Volstead Act itself. But they showed great reluctance to spend money in the war against liquor; their appropriations for prohibition were only one eighth the sum they were spending for the enforcement of their fish-and-game laws. Of course in traditionally dry territory the local police arrested prohibition law violators promptly, but in wet communities they did nothing except under heavy pressure from their superiors—and such pressure was only rarely forthcoming. Wherever local sentiment was strongly antiprohibition, police, judges, and juries all reflected the situation.

Despite the shortcomings of enforcement, the drys claimed that prohibition had brought important benefits. The open saloon had disappeared in most places, and drinking, particularly by the poor, had been materially reduced. The highly respected economist, Professor Irving Fisher of Yale, considered that prohibition had contributed largely to the prosperity of the twenties, and many employers noted a gratifying decline in the absenteeism and inefficiency which had been a problem —particularly on Blue Mondays—in pre-Volstead days. Other businessmen praised prohibition because of the added purchasing power which was created when money, formerly spent for liquor, was available for Fords and radios.

But the wets asserted that the defects of prohibition far outweighed its merits. They emphasized the widespread violation of the law as evidence that the experiment had been a complete failure, and they claimed that only through repeal of the amendment could the mistake that had been made be rectified.

ORGANIZED CRIME

The consolidation of business so characteristic in legitimate lines was duplicated in business carried on in defiance of the law. Gambling and prostitution were already highly organized; bootlegging steadily became so. The profits to be made by monopolizing the illicit liquor trade of a big city were fabulous, and hardened criminals were prepared either to beat up speakeasy proprietors who refused to buy from them or to wreck their property, while with competitors they were ready to employ even more drastic methods. Such men naturally interested themselves in politics, bribing their friends and intimidating their enemies until they secured such power that they often seemed to have secured complete immunity from the law.

The most spectacular criminal career of the twenties was that of Al Capone. Capone was brought from New York City to Chicago in 1920 by Johnny Torrio who needed a lieutenant to handle his competitors in the struggle to get control of the illegal liquor business of Chicago. By 1929 Capone had replaced Torrio as the "Big Shot"; he had at his command several hundred ruthless gunmen armed with submachine guns and sawed-off shotguns; he largely controlled the sale of liquor to Chicago's ten thousand speakeasies; he was in complete political control of the suburb of Cicero; and he had useful ties with many Chicago politicians and judges. How much money he had made and concealed no one knew, but Federal agents estimated the sum at $20,000,000.

Capone's wealth and power had not been achieved without a struggle and the plentiful spilling of blood. Particularly bitter was the gang war fought between Capone's henchmen and those of his ambitious rival, Dion O'Banion. O'Banion himself was shot to death in his own florist shop by gunmen masquerading as customers, but his gangsters continued to contest Capone and made a grand attempt to assassinate him in 1926 when in broad daylight eight touring cars paraded slowly past his headquarters in Cicero, raking the building with machine-gun fire. Unfortunately the attempt failed. In the most gruesome of all the killings, the St. Valentine's Day Massacre of 1929, seven of the O'Banions were lined up against the wall of a garage by strangers disguised as policemen and then mowed down with machine guns. Between 1920 and 1929 there were more than five hundred gang murders in Chicago, and few of those responsible were ever brought to justice. Not until 1931 did Federal officers finally arrest Capone and secure his imprisonment—and then the charge was not murder, extortion, bribery, or violation of the Volstead Act, but merely tax evasion.

Capone and his numerous imitators in New York, Detroit, and other cities gained much of their wealth through the opportunities created by prohibition. They showed ingenuity, however, in expanding into other lines. They operated or demanded tribute from gambling houses, dog tracks, houses of prostitution, dance halls, and roadhouses. The ancient crime of kidnapping was given an unpleasant revival, with wealthy adults often victims. Innumerable were the so-called rackets of the decade. Small businessmen were compelled to pay for "protection"; those who thought that they did not need this commodity were speedily disillusioned when their trucks were wrecked, their shops bombed, or they themselves were beaten up or killed. Unfortunately for the reputation of the legitimate labor-union movement, these rackets were often operated through the connivance of corrupt union leaders who permitted established unions to be used in this way. Sometimes new unions were organized for no other purpose than to levy tribute upon unfortunate workers and employers. Only less common than the racketeering labor union was the racketeering trade association terrorizing small businessmen until they signed up and meekly paid their regular assessments.

The crime wave which caused so much alarm during the twenties was more a change in the character of criminal activities than an absolute increase in their amount. Murder, robbery, assault, and extortion America had always had, and statistics showed no greater increase in the aggregate number of such offenses than might have been expected with the growing population and urbanization of the nation. What was new and alarming was the large degree of organization among criminals and their wholesale use of high-powered automobiles, machine guns, and explosives. Crime had become big business—and to many thoughtful citizens the most serious aspect of the prohibition problem was that by turning the liquor business over to criminals, a vast opportunity to make crime pay had been opened up.

FLAMING YOUTH

Worry over children must be as old as human parenthood, but perhaps the elder generation of the twenties worried over the younger rather more than was usual. They were shocked in the first place at the revolution in women's dress. Corsets were discarded along with numerous other articles of apparel no longer considered essential. The amount of cloth necessary to garb a woman declined from 19¼ yards in 1913 to 7 yards in 1928. During 1919 and 1920 much shorter than ankle-length skirts had appeared, to the great alarm of moralists. Fashion ordered them down again, but women proved reluctant to obey, and by 1925 the designers had surrendered; skirts became shorter and shorter until they reached the knee in 1927. To aggravate the scandal many bold young ladies began to roll their stockings.

Not content with abbreviating their skirts and exposing their knees, the flappers—as the pert young females of the decade were called—abbreviated their tresses as well. Short-haired women in 1918 were assumed to be Bolsheviks, but by 1924 a vogue for bobbed hair was sweeping the nation. Barbers relegated the cuspidor and the *Police Gazette* to the closet and began to tidy up their shops to please their new customers—but in the end most of the business went to hairdressers.

Before the war the dictum had been that no nice women used rouge or lipstick, or, if she did so, she tried to conceal the fact. During the postwar decade, however, the use of these and other cosmetics increased until their manufacture and sale became a billion-dollar business.

The young woman of the twenties not only looked different, she acted differently. Back in Theodore Roosevelt's regime when his daughter Alice had wanted to experiment with tobacco she had sought to escape parental wrath by blowing her smoke rings carefully up the chimneys of the White House fireplaces. Only the most sophisticated of women used cigarettes. But during the postwar decade the taboo against feminine smoking to a large extent broke down. Shocking as this was to the older generation, women's increasing use of alcoholic beverages was even more so. Among the smart set it became the accepted thing for men and women to drink together at domestic cocktail parties, at country club dances, and at speakeasies. Not only did women drink, some of them drank too much.

All this was a final stage in the feminine revolt which had been in progress for many decades. Women had successfully rebelled against their inadequate educational opportunities, against their unfavorable legal status, against their disenfranchisement. Now they were asserting their right to smoke and drink because men did, and to cut their hair, rouge their cheeks, and wear scanty clothing because it symbolized their independence. Not for long, moreover, were the new manners found solely among the young. To an increasing degree elder women occupied and held the territory which the younger shock troops had captured.

Though many parents were seriously troubled over such issues as have been discussed, what kept them awake nights was their children's rebelliousness in other matters. Sons rudely demanded the use of the family car, daughters hotly asserted their intention of driving off with their boy friends without chaperonage. Often the youngsters did not get home until almost morning and indignantly refused to divulge where they had been or what they had been doing. Or what was perhaps worse, they told their parents exactly what they had been doing and then asked belligerently what the parents intended to do about it.

Significantly enough, Samuel Hopkins Adams, one of the muck-rakers of prewar days, found a theme in this rebellion. Under the pseudonym Warner Fabian, he wrote the lurid novel, *Flaming Youth*, which had a huge popular sale and was syndicated in many news-papers. Shocked parents read about wild parties where young people enjoyed the intoxication of both gin and jazz, of mixed midnight swim-ming excursions, and of petting parties on lonely lanes. Similarly up-setting were *The Plastic Age* by Percy Marks and—on a distinctly higher literary level—the novels of F. Scott Fitzgerald. A sensation of another sort was provided by Judge Ben B. Lindsey, who believed that the breakdown in old moral conventions was so serious that the situation should be frankly faced and a system of "companionate marriage" legalized—a sort of trial marriage which could be terminated at any time by mutual consent, provided there were no children.

Undoubtedly the situation was exaggerated by such writers as these. For the most part, the great revolution in morals probably amounted to simply this: girls were easier to kiss than they once had been, and the automobile offered a much better opportunity. But many of the petting parties went farther; just how large a proportion is a matter of dispute. This flouting of older conventions regarding the relations of unmarried young people was to a large extent inevitable and to be explained as still another aspect of the new freedom which women were demanding. The war, however, with its philosophy of seizing the pleasures of the moment in a world of uncertainties, accelerated the movement.

Disputed though the facts might be as to the actual state of sexual morals during the twenties, one thing was crystal clear. The new generation talked about sex with a frankness that would have been unthinkable to the old. The subject was endlessly discussed not only because of its interest, but because of its fashionableness. The teachings of Sigmund Freud had been familiar to American psychologists since the beginning of the century; his ideas were being popularized for the first time, however, during the postwar decade. Exactly what they meant would have been a little hard for most people to explain, but this did not prevent glib usage of such fascinating new expressions as "inferiority complex," "Oedipus complex," "inhibition," and "libido." In general, laymen gathered the impression that scientists had decided that sex was not only exciting, but important, and that it was dangerous to repress sexual impulses. This offered a comforting rationalization to those who thought it smart to defy the old conventions.

THE CHANGING FAMILY

For better or worse, American family life was being transformed from old to newer patterns. The home was less important as an economic, educational, and recreational center. Functions once performed by the family were more and more being taken over by outside agencies, and whether or not the change was good or bad was a matter of dispute.

Married women, particularly those of the middle-income groups, were now relieved of much of the drudgery which had always been their lot. Bread was a highly commercialized product purchased in stores instead of a masterpiece laboriously fashioned in the kitchen, while many other foods hitherto prepared in the home were now secured at bakery shops or delicatessens. Commercial laundries did an increasing share of the nation's washing. Many tasks, to be sure, still remained to the housewife, but the use of electrical appliances permitted them to be performed more quickly and easily.

Husbands and children too had their crowded schedules of activities, and the result was that many homes became scarcely more than a place where the members of the family checked in for a few hours of sleep each night and had their breakfasts—though rarely together.

An increasing number of American marriages were ending in divorce. In 1900 there were 20 divorces for 10,000 married persons; in 1930 there were 36. By the latter year the chances that any particular marriage would eventually break up were about one in six. Divorce was more common in the United States than in any other country for which statistics were available, with the possible exception of the Soviet Union. But the conclusions to be drawn from this fact were disputed. Many regarded it as evidence that unhappiness in marriage was much greater than ever before. Others asserted that there had always been a great many unhappy marriages and that the high divorce rate meant only that more people were taking this way out of the unfortunate situation. Few denied that there was some connection between the increasing number of broken homes and the youth problem.

Another fact about family life which was undeniable but which was given varying interpretations was the declining birth rate. The rate had been 26.6 in 1910 and had fluctuated within narrow limits until 1921 when it was 27.1; thereafter it fell until it was 19.7 in 1931—a decline of one quarter during the decade. Many Americans considered this a healthy rather than an unhealthy development, asserting that a prime cause of poverty would be removed were birth control practiced by the poor as well as by the well-to-do. The American Birth Control League, organized in 1917, carried on an active propaganda during the twenties under the crusading leadership of Margaret Sanger. Her attempt to open a clinic in Brooklyn in 1921 where birth-control information might be given to low-income groups led to arrest, but the New York courts ruled that such information could be given legally by physicians for health reasons. A permanent clinic was opened in New York City in 1923, and later in many other cities, although in some states they were not permitted. Protestant churchmen disagreed on the moral issues involved. The Committee on Marriage and the Home of the Federal Council of Churches recommended in 1930 that "the church should not seek to impose its point of view as to the use of contraceptives upon the public by legislation or any other form of coercion; and especially should not seek to prohibit physicians from imparting such information to those who in the judgment of the medical profession are entitled to receive it." The General Assembly of the Presbyterian Church, however, criticized this statement of policy as dangerous to morals.

The Roman Catholic Church was uncompromising in its condemnation of both divorce and birth control. The papal encyclical, *Casti Connubii*, issued by Pope Pius XI in 1930, asserted that marriage was a "perpetual and indissoluble bond which cannot be dissolved by any civil law"; that companionate and experimental marriages were "hateful abominations . . . which reduce our truly cultured natures to the barbarous standards of savage people"; and that contraceptive devices were "an offense against the law of God and nature."

LITERATURE DURING THE TWENTIES

The postwar reaction from idealism, notable in so many different areas of American life, affected literature. The nation had an unusually talented group of novelists and poets during the twenties, but their gifts were used in large degree to attack contemporary American culture.

The reading public had its first rude jolt in 1920 with the publication of Sinclair Lewis's *Main Street*. The small midwestern town, usually sentimentalized in literature, was here depicted as dreary, narrow, and hypocritical. Inasmuch as the character of American life was still so largely reflective of such small towns, Lewis's attack appeared to be a general disparagement of American civilization. A succession of other brilliant, but caustic, novels from the same author broadened the indictment. *Babbitt* (1922) satirized the self-satisfaction and crude self-advertisement of the American businessman. In the young doctor of *Arrowsmith* (1925), Lewis created a hero whom he could admire, yet he found at the same time much to criticize in the medical profession. *Elmer Gantry* (1927), the novelist's caricature of a go-getter religionist, gave ample proof—if any were needed—that the church could expect no immunity from his idol-smashing.

The great city, no less than the small, was subjected to literary attack. John Dos Passos in *Manhattan Transfer* (1925) depicted life in New York City as hard and meaningless for the individuals thrown together in the vast net of urban society. An earlier Dos Passos novel, *Three Soldiers* (1921), struck the note of disillusionment with the war which was to recur through the decade.

Disillusionment not only with the war but with the general complexity of modern life was reflected in the novels and short stories of Ernest Hemingway. *The Sun Also Rises* (1926), *Men Without Women* (1927), and *A Farewell to Arms* (1929) show complete indifference to idealistic aspirations or to the problems of society. The Hemingway characters find life's fleeting pleasures only in the most elemental experiences, particularly in physical combat and sex. Hemingway was one of the not inconsiderable group of American intellectuals who spent most of the twenties in Europe.

Both the outer shell of sophistication and the inner kernel of unhappiness characteristic of sensitive young people of "the lost generation" was depicted in the novels of F. Scott Fitzgerald. Early works like *This Side of Paradise* (1921) and *The Beautiful and the Damned* (1922) were regarded by the critics as little more than popular fiction, but *The Great Gatsby* (1926) demonstrated that Fitzgerald had one of the finest talents of his generation.

One of the great literary vogues of the period was for the work of James Branch Cabell. His *Jurgen* (1919) received magnificent advertising when it was banned from the mails as obscene. The charge was unfounded in the opinion of many readers, who believed the treatment of sex in this exotic fantasy to be witty and sophisticated, yet hardly likely to undermine the country's morals.

Of the older generation of novelists whose reputation had been well established before the war, Theodore Dreiser enjoyed most favor with those who were looking for ruthless realism. To these, Dreiser's *The American Tragedy* (1925) was the greatest novel of the decade. Other readers, repelled by the crudities of Dreiser's style, took delight in the beautifully written and thoughtful works of Willa Cather, Edith Wharton, and Ellen Glasgow.

The revival of poetry which had been just beginning in 1914 more than fulfilled its early promise. Edwin Arlington Robinson and Robert Frost reflected their New England background in the austere beauty of their writing; they often found their themes in the frustrations and tragedies of life, but they differed from most of the novelists of the period in upholding the dignity of man in the face of suffering. Carl Sandburg and Vachel Lindsay spoke in the more strident cadences of the Midwest. Cruelty and injustice they attacked fiercely, yet they displayed a basic love for America and a faith in its destiny. The same qualities were to be found in Stephen Vincent Benet, whose attempt at an American epic, *John Brown's Body*, aroused great interest in 1929.

Poetry was not immune, however, to the spirit of the times. Indeed, no work of literature more completely reflected the generation's disillusionment and lack of faith than T. S. Elliot's *The Wasteland* (1922). Ezra Pound's contempt for American democracy was so complete that he not only lived the life of an expatriate, but ended up as a glorifier of fascism. Thus was lost to American literature one of the boldest experimenters with new verse forms. More frequent than such a complete repudiation as this was poetry written in a spirit of detached cynicism and sophistication. In such a vein was Edna St. Vincent Millay's *A Few Figs from Thistles* (1920). Other works by this poet displayed higher sensitivity to beauty and a larger sense of social responsibility, but failed to enjoy the popularity of this lighter work.

Writing done for the American stage has rarely won acclaim as an achievement in literature, yet that distinction was realized by Eugene O'Neill. His plays, *Emperor Jones* (1921), *Desire under the Elms* (1924), *The Great God Brown* (1925), and *Strange Interlude* (1929), showed great psychological insight and much ingenuity in the use of dramatic innovations to carry his meaning. Like so many of his contemporaries, however, O'Neill's emphasis was on the least healthy aspects of American life.

A great influence on the literary life of the twenties was exercised by H. L. Mencken, the editor of the *American Mercury*. This vigorous and outspoken critic of the American scene regarded most of his fellow countrymen as "boobs," "morons," and "yokels," and said so month after month to the delight of his sophisticated readers. One of the leading features of Mencken's magazine was "Americana," a department made up of excerpts from the press chronicling the more idiotic deeds and pronouncements of Americans. A moderate sampling of Mencken's criticism often proved a healthy antidote to the reader's complacency, but an excessive dose was likely to leave him with a cynical contempt for democracy.

HIGH- AND LOW-BROW READING

The number of Americans who prided themselves on reading good books increased during the decade, but they showed a certain timidity in choosing their reading matter for themselves. The Book-of-the-Month Club broadened its list of subscribers until by the end of the twenties some hundred thousand Americans were accepting the judgment of its board of experts in making their periodic purchases. The Literary Guild and other organizations distributed books on the same basis. To be selected through this system was to guarantee the success of any book. One of the unfortunate results, however, was that many scarcely less worthy books which had failed to appeal to the experts were doomed to small sales.

On the other hand, many readers chose books frankly for their entertainment value and were indifferent to their rating as literature. The detective stories of Mary Roberts Rinehart, S. S. Van Dine, and others enjoyed a tremendous popularity, as did also sexy romances like *The Sheik* by Mrs. E. M. Hull. There was a good market for biographies, which varied in treatment from the highly scholarly like Albert J. Beveridge's *Life of John Marshall* (1916–1919) and the beautifully written like Carl Sandburg's *Abraham Lincoln: The Prairie Years* (1926) to the popular types which attempted to psychoanalyze their subjects, to "debunk" national heroes, and to glamourize national villains. Astonishingly successful was *The Man Nobody Knows* (1925), in which Bruce Barton, an expert in advertising promotion, portrayed Jesus as a model businessman.

Self-improvement continued to be the aim of many earnest readers. For them a variety of fare was offered during the twenties, ranging from excellent popularizations like Will Durant's *Story of Philosophy* (1926) to the fabulously successful Emily Post's *Etiquette* (1922).

No reading matter, however, was so widely distributed as daily newspapers, whose aggregate circulation in the United States and Canada reached forty millions in 1929. The trend away from personal journalism and toward standardized, large-scale production methods, already pronounced in 1914, was much accelerated during the next fifteen years—due in part to the rising cost of paper. Newspapers became increasingly dependent upon syndicated material, advertising revenue, and mass distribution. Since costs could be reduced by operating several papers under a single ownership, the number of newspaper chains doubled between 1923 and 1927. Within each city, moreover, the tendency was toward the merger of competing journals; five out of seven Chicago morning papers disappeared in fifteen years, while in Detroit the number of morning papers dropped from three to one. There were two thousand fewer publications in 1929 than in 1914.

Sensational stories of crime and scandal still provided a dependable formula for making a paper popular, as was demonstrated by the striking growth of the New York *Daily News*. This first New York tabloid, which began publication in 1919, achieved a circulation of 1,300,000 ten years later. The success of this brash pioneer invited competition; Hearst's *Mirror* and Bernarr MacFadden's *Evening Graphic* entered the New York field, while similar papers multiplied in other cities.

Magazines also increased their sales. The periodicals which catered to the literary-minded or those interested in fundamental social problems had little share in this prosperity. Muckraking articles, so popular a generation earlier, rarely appeared in the magazines of large circulation like the *Saturday Evening Post, Collier's, The American Magazine,* or the *Ladies' Home Journal.* Instead, their pages were devoted to fiction, light but frequently excellent within its limitations, and to articles praising the achievements of American businessmen. The counterpart to the tabloid was the "confession" magazine. Bernarr MacFadden's *True Stories* and its imitators built up an enormous sale through endless variations on such simple formulas as that of the innocent girl corrupted by the bright lights of the big city and involved in amorous adventures, but reformed and safely married by the final paragraph.

EDUCATION AND LEARNING

The goal of most American parents was to provide their children with greater educational opportunities than they themselves had received. The result was a remarkable increase in the number of pupils attending public high schools: in 1900 public secondary-school enrollment had stood at 519,000; in 1910, 915,000; in 1920, 2,199,000; and in 1930, 4,399,000. With the increase of attendance went important modifications of curriculum to meet the needs of the new pupils. Whereas in 1900 over 50 per cent of high-school students studied Latin and over 56 per cent algebra, the percentages were only 22 and 35 respectively in 1928. Furthermore, many subjects which had not been part of the old high-school course of studies were now offered. Most of these were vocational in character like home economics, manual training, bookkeeping, shorthand, typewriting, and agriculture, but others, notably art and music, were cultural by any definition.

The advent of the automobile made it possible to close many of the one-room schoolhouses of the nation. The children from rural families were now transported by bus to well-equipped consolidated schools where each grade could be taught in a separate room by a special teacher. In order to improve and enrich elementary education in the higher grades, many communities organized junior high schools to include the seventh, eighth, and ninth grades, the senior-high-school course being then reduced to three years.

Colleges and universities also grew rapidly. In 1900 college enrollment was 168,000; in 1910, 266,000; in 1920, 517,000; and in 1930, 1,085,799. Some critics believed that this expansion made advisable a division of higher education between the first two and the last two years. Junior colleges, of which there had been only 132 in 1917, numbered 450 in 1930. This tendency was deplored, however, by those educators who believed that the traditional four-year college course had a unity which should not be destroyed. An increasing number of students now devoted more than four years to their higher education. Training in theology, medicine, dentistry, law, engineering, and business administration was based to an increasing degree on a foundation of three or four years general education in a liberal arts college. A growing number of graduate degrees were granted; the annual crop of Ph.D.'s quadrupled during the decade. Most of this increase was due to the demand for more and better trained college instructors, but a growing number of positions in industry were available to men who had graduate training—notably in chemistry.

University faculty members placed increasing emphasis on their responsibility to develop the body of knowledge rather than merely to transmit the cultural heritage. To catalogue the significant achievements of research in all the specialized branches of learning would be impossible, but a few landmarks must be noted because of their importance to general American thought during the decade. The whole field of American history was surveyed from a fresh and stimulating point of view by Charles and Mary Beard in *The Rise of American Civilization* (1927). Of equal significance as an interpretation of the roots of American culture was Vernon L. Parrington's *Main Currents in American Thought* (1927). The reader who wished to learn how people of every income level and background lived in a typical American community was fascinated by *Middletown* (1929), by Robert S. and Helen Lynd. Profoundly influential in its effect upon thinking in such diverse fields as education, morals, criminology, and philosophy was the purely mechanistic explanation of human behavior aggressively presented by John B. Watson in his *Psychology from the Standpoint of a Behaviorist* (1919).

In the field of physical sciences, Americans like Robert A. Millikan and Arthur H. Compton helped to fill in the details of the newer conceptions of the universe which were taking shape during the twenties following the pioneer work of the great German, Albert Einstein. Two important astronomical observatories in California, Mt. Hamilton and Mt. Wilson, provided international science with data of great value in testing the new theories.

Medical research was generously endowed and achieved many goals. Important advances in surgical technique grew out of the work of the doctors during the war. New uses for the X ray were found both in diagnosis and therapy. The importance of vitamins in nutrition was demonstrated, and the consumption of these miraculous health-givers later became a national fad. Public-health measures virtually eliminated typhoid fever, while diphtheria, scarlet fever, and tuberculosis came under steadily greater control. Life expectancy was raised from 49.24 years in 1901 to 59.1 years in 1927—largely through the reduction of the death rate among infants and children. New techniques for treating burns diminished mortality almost miraculously; at the Johns Hopkins Hospital in Baltimore the use of the new gentian violet treatment resulted in cutting the mortality in such cases from 42 to 5 per cent in two years.

THE ARTS

The prosperity of the twenties encouraged construction, and many of the new edifices displayed striking beauty. Some American architects continued to find their inspiration in classical and medieval models. Henry Bacon's Lincoln Memorial in Washington, D. C., for example, demonstrated anew the appeal of the Greek qualities of simplicity, balance, and proportion. Ralph Adams Cram was deeply interested in promoting the use of Gothic style in ecclesiastical architecture, and many of his ideas found their embodiment in the Cathedral of St. John the Divine in New York City. The suitability of the Gothic style for university buildings was emphasized by Cram-designed buildings at Princeton and West Point, as well as by many beautiful structures at Yale.

America's most distinctive contributions to architecture, however, continued to be made by the disciples of Louis D. Sullivan, the great apostle of functional design. The ten years that followed the armistice were the great age of the skyscraper. In 1922 architects from all countries were invited to submit their designs for the *Chicago Tribune* Tower. The competition, which attracted 260 plans from 23 nations, was won by John Mead Howells and Raymond Hood, but the second-prize design submitted by the Finnish architect, Eliel Saarinen, rivaled the winner in the degree of interest it created. New York City, where the technical requirements of the building ordinances had much to do with the development of setback architecture, prided itself on the loftiness and grandeur of the great buildings constructed there during the twenties. The culmination of the movement was the Empire State Building, designed by Shreve, Lamb, and Harmon.

Outside the boundaries of the United States the best known American architect was Frank Lloyd Wright, who boldly discarded older conventions and carried functional design to its logical limits. Wright advocated taking full advantage of new materials and fitting each building both to its use and environment. His "prairie houses" with their emphasis on horizontal lines close to the earth pointed toward a revolution in residential design. Wright's influence was international in scope, but during much of his career he was too bold for the majority of his timid countrymen.

American painters lacked the originality of American architects. They took their cues from European art during this era and found an outlet for their talents with cubism, expressionism, and surrealism. Yet despite the weakness of the Americans for imported fads, a number of capable artists were at work. Among these were John Marin, Max Weber, Georgia O'Keefe, Thomas Benton, and Rockwell Kent.

Musical appreciation seemed to deepen after the war. The radio brought concerts by the country's great orchestras and soloists into millions of homes, and individuals like Walter Damrosch worked tirelessly to educate the people to understand and enjoy good music. American-born singers like Marion Talley, Carmela and Rosa Ponselle, and Lawrence Tibbett sang with the Metropolitan Opera Company, while in 1927 that great organization presented *The King's Henchman*, an opera written by Deems Taylor with libretto by Edna St. Vincent Millay. In the field of light music, Sigmund Romberg, Rudolf Friml, and Jerome Kern proved worthy successors to Victor Herbert.

Jazz during the twenties began to demand attention as an authentic form of musical expression. Orchestras playing in the new rhythms became increasingly pretentious, with Paul Whiteman's taking the lead in presenting jazz in "symphonic" arrangements. A furious debate was provoked between musical fundamentalists, who regarded jazz as merely unpleasant noise, and modernists, who proclaimed it to be as important an American contribution to art as the skyscraper. One of the best assets of the modernist school was George Gershwin, whose extraordinary talent and success in speaking through the new idiom were hard to resist. Gershwin wrote the music for a number of successful musical comedies during the twenties, but he was eager to express himself in more ambitious forms. Therefore he composed such symphonic works as *Rhapsody in Blue, Concerto in F*, and *An American in Paris*. The first enjoyed the widest success, but many discerning critics much preferred the third. That Gershwin was gifted, few denied, although there was no final judgment possible as to whether he was also great.

THERE WERE GIANTS IN THOSE DAYS

Despite the cynicism of the intellectuals, the age was one of hero worship. Rudolph Valentino, the great screen lover, died in 1926, and the crowd attracted to the New York undertaking parlor where he lay in state extended for eleven blocks. "Shipwreck" Kelly achieved transient glory by sitting on top of a Baltimore flagpole for twenty-three days and seven hours. The whole country wept when the efforts to extricate Floyd Collins alive from a Kentucky cave where he had been trapped failed. And when the Lone Eagle, Lindbergh, flew nonstop from New York to Paris the nation went wild.

Perhaps the most typical heroes of the twenties were to be found in the world of sport. Shrewd promotion willingly abetted by news-

Babe Ruth. (Brown Bros.)

paper and radio reporters aroused the American people to a unique enthusiasm for athletics. Their work was made easier by the circumstance that the sports world had an unusually large number of competitors who were not only capable performers, but colorful personalities as well.

In 1919 "Babe" Ruth, playing for the Boston Red Sox, set a new record by hitting twenty-nine home runs in a season. The New York

Yankees sensed the opportunity for making a profitable investment and purchased the young pitcher-outfielder for $125,000. The Babe's employers never regretted their decision, nor did they refuse the slugger's eventual demand for a salary almost as large as that of the President of the United States. The exploits of Ruth, who hit fifty-nine homers in 1921 and sixty in 1927, brought customers to the Yankee Stadium by the thousands and enabled baseball to retain its popularity despite the growing interest in other sports.

College football was followed avidly by the public. So great was the demand to see games that new stadia were built, many of them large enough to accommodate seventy or eighty thousand spectators. Despite the sputtering of faculty members who complained that the game had become professionalized, alumni insisted on highly paid coaches who could produce winning teams, and the coaches in turn demanded athletic scholarships and other inducements to attract promising material. The best players, men like "Red" Grange of Illinois, and the most successful coaches like Knute Rockne of Notre Dame received thousands of lines of publicity.

Sports taste was catholic, however, and thousands of Americans who did not know the difference between a mashie and a putter followed breathlessly the progress of the great golf amateur, Bobby Jones, through various tournaments. Tennis, once thought like golf a high-brow game, became popularized through the dynamic play of Big Bill Tilden, while women's athletic prowess was demonstrated by another fine tennis player, Helen Wills. In most sports, women's performances could not be compared with those of the stronger sex, but when the American Gertrude Ederle swam the English Channel in 1926, her time was better than that of any of the five men who had completed the difficult journey before her. Even horses had their triumphant careers. Man o' War was a sporting sensation in 1919 and 1920. As late as 1945 he was reported to be living "in luxury" on a beautiful farm in Kentucky—which was more than many of his human rivals for acclaim could say twenty-five years after their peak of glory.

No sport of the twenties could secure more publicity for a single contest than heavyweight boxing. The golden days of the prize ring were attained when the master promoter, Tex Rickard, had as his drawing card the superb performer, Jack Dempsey. On July 4, 1919, Dempsey gained the heavyweight title by knocking out the giant Jess Willard at Toledo, Ohio. The new champion, colorful and aggressive, seemed to carry dynamite in his gloves. Attending prize fights became suddenly respectable, and the crowds which saw Dempsey knock out

The "Long Count"—Tunney-Dempsey Fight at Chicago, 1927. (Acme.)

Georges Carpentier in 1921 and Luis Firpo in 1923 were notable not only for their tremendous size but for the extraordinary number of politicians and socialites who were to be found among the spectators. After Dempsey lost his title unexpectedly to Gene Tunney in 1926, the stage was set the next year for what was perhaps the most highly publicized sports spectacle of the decade, the second Tunney-Dempsey fight at Chicago, when the gate receipts totaled $2,650,000. Newspaper reporters had sent daily stories from the training camps of the two great men for weeks; after the fight was over they devoted endless columns to the important question of whether Tunney had not been the beneficiary of a "long count" in retaining his title.

Such were the twenties. American prosperity was built on a shaky foundation which threatened to collapse. The rest of the world struggled with problems too difficult to be solved and which were destined to involve the United States. But oblivious to the storm clouds on the horizon, the average American had a wonderful time during the age of the supercolossal.

16

Prosperity

WHEN IN HIS SPEECH ACCEPTING THE REPUBLICAN PRESIDENTIAL NOMI-
nation in 1928 Herbert Hoover said: "We in America today are nearer
to the final triumph over poverty than ever before in the history of
any land," he was expressing the belief of almost all Americans. The
United States had enjoyed seven years of extraordinary prosperity and
few indeed were the gloomy prophets who ventured to predict danger
ahead.

ECONOMIC TRENDS, 1914–1929

When war broke out in Europe in 1914, the United States was in
what seemed to be the incipient stages of a serious depression. At first
the onset of hostilities simply increased the nation's economic troubles.
But French and English war orders reversed the trend in 1915 and
a great wartime prosperity began which was much intensified by
actual American participation in 1917. The effect of the armistice was
temporarily upsetting and there was serious unemployment for several
months. This gave way, however, to an extraordinary postwar boom
lasting from the late spring of 1919 to the middle of 1920. This bubble
burst suddenly and the last half of 1920 and most of 1921 witnessed a
severe depression. In the latter year some seven million unemployed
were walking the streets. National income fell from $75,000,000,000
in 1920 to $59,000,000,000 in 1921.

This depression, although grave, was short-lived. Recovery set in
during 1922; by 1925 national income had passed its 1920 level and it
continued to rise until it reached more than $84,000,000,000 in 1929. In
a proud catalogue of progress which Candidate Hoover recited in 1928
these items were listed: over 25 per cent increase in the production of
goods since 1921, the construction of more than 3,500,000 new dwel-

lings, the electrification of nearly 9,000,000 homes, the installation of 6,000,000 telephones, the manufacture of 7,000,000 radio sets, the production of 14,000,000 automobiles, the building of parks, playgrounds, and highways. And in human terms Hoover reported:

We have doubled the use of electrical power and with it we have taken sweat from the backs of man. The purchasing power of wages has steadily increased. The hours of labor have decreased. The twelve-hour day has been abolished. Great progress has been made in stabilization of commerce and industry. The job of every man has thus been made more secure. Unemployment in the sense of distress is widely disappearing.

Such was the impressive evidence of prosperity during the twenties. It was small wonder that few Americans were seriously troubled by darker aspects of the picture which Hoover had omitted to mention.

AMERICA TAKES TO THE ROAD

Much of the prosperity of the period arose out of the rapid growth of new industries and, of these, the automobile business was the most astonishing in the degree of its expansion.

The motor car was an European invention. About 1800 experiments in steam-propelled road vehicles had been made both in England and on the continent but without enough success to displace the horse and carriage. The key discovery of the internal-combustion engine powered with gasoline came through the experiments of French and German engineers between 1860 and 1890. By the eighties it had been demonstrated that such engines could successfully propel vehicles along the roads.

Ingenious Americans soon entered the field. The nineties was a period of endless experimentation with all types of vehicles—steam, gasoline, and electric. It required many years for the superior advantages of the gasoline-driven cars to be generally recognized. Indeed, as late as World War I the Stanley Steamer was still considered by many to be the last word in mechanical perfection. Pioneer builders of gasoline vehicles in America were Charles E. Duryea, who built the first such car in the United States, Henry Ford, Ransom E. Olds, Elwood Haynes, and the Apperson brothers. The new contraptions were extremely crude and undependable, but a moderate demand for them developed among people able to indulge themselves with a rather expensive plaything. At first this trade was served by small shops where the horseless carriages were built to order. Production in quantity began in 1898 when the Mitchell-Lewis Motor Car Company of Racine, Wisconsin, manu-

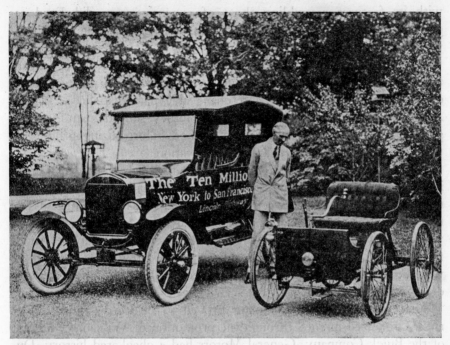

Henry Ford with His First and Ten-Millionth Ford, 1924. (Acme.)

factured five hundred three-wheeled motor vehicles for the European market. Better known companies founded during the next few years were the Locomobile Company of America, the Olds Motor Works, and the Cadillac Company. The Ford Motor Company, destined to revolutionize the industry, was founded in 1903.

Like other manufacturers, Ford at first experimented with a variety of motor types—two, four, and six cylinder. In 1908, however, he began manufacturing the famous four-cylindered Model T. The "tin Lizzies," as the Fords were affectionately called, were ugly to behold, clumsy to drive, and uncomfortable to ride in, yet they provided transportation at a price the average American could afford to pay. In 1908 the Model T was priced at $850, but the figure was reduced again and again until in 1924 a Ford could be bought for $290—if its owner was not too proud to get out and crank it by hand and then race back to the steering gear to adjust the hand throttle and spark before the motor could stall. The Ford joke became a staple commodity in American humor, yet the canny Detroit industrialist accepted without complaint this free advertising and continued to roll out cars and roll in money until he had amassed one of the greatest American fortunes. Not until Chevrolet, produced by General Motors, began to woo away customers with its features resembling those of expensive cars did Ford regretfully forsake the Model T and bring out in 1928 the more conventional Model A.

Ford learned to produce cars cheaply not alone because he concentrated on a single model, but because he pioneered in many techniques of production. Standardized, interchangeable parts had been basic in American industrial success since Eli Whitney started manufacturing guns in 1798, but the assembly-line method of organizing production within a plant was largely a Ford innovation.

Ford's spectacular success encouraged many rivals to enter the field, imitating in so far as their resources permitted his revolutionary techniques of production. Between 1903 and 1926, 181 companies at one time or another manufactured passenger cars. The mortality, however, was exceptionally heavy. By 1926 the number of automobile manufacturers had been reduced to 44; during the next few years many more were destined to quit. By 1930, 90 per cent of the business was being done by six companies.

The General Motors Company proved to be Ford's most serious rival. Organized in 1908 through the promotion of William C. Durant of the Buick Company, General Motors had a checkered history. Durant was brilliant, but reckless, expanding the company rapidly through the purchase of more and more separate concerns engaged in some phase of automotive manufacturing. He lost control of the company in 1910 when it had to be rescued by the bankers, regained command in 1915, and was finally ousted during the depression of 1921. The corporation thereafter was dominated by Morgan and du Pont interests. As late as 1917 Ford was producing nearly four times as many cars annually as General Motors, but during the next decade the gap was closed and the country watched with excitement as Ford's new Model A and General Motors' Chevrolet fought a spirited battle for supremacy in the low-priced field.

The "big two" became a "big three" after the organization of the Chrysler Corporation in 1923 and its purchase of Dodge Brothers five years later. In 1929 Chrysler brought out the Plymouth in a bid for the business being so profitably divided between Ford and Chevrolet. That year Chrysler produced about 450,000 cars as compared with Ford's 1,950,000 and General Motors' 1,900,000, but its share in the business was destined to become larger during the thirties.

Annual production of motor cars in the United States rose from 5000 in 1900 to 181,000 in 1910, 1,900,000 in 1920, and finally reached a peak of almost 4,800,000 in 1929. The number of automobiles registered in the country climbed from 8,226,000 in 1920 to 23,122,000 in 1929. By the latter year there was one car for every six inhabitants. The automobile industry had become the nation's leading business as measured by the value of its annual product; in 1929 that value was nearly $3,500,000,000.

The production of motor cars required vast quantities of steel, plate glass, rubber, leather, aluminum, and copper, while their operation consumed the lion's share of the petroleum products of the nation. In terms of labor the automobile industry not only provided direct employment to some 350,000 factory executives and employees, but gave indirect employment to workers in accessory and tire factories, salesmen, repair men, filling station operators, truck drivers, chauffeurs, and the like until, in the calculation of one authority, some five million persons had jobs in some way dependent upon the automotive business. This was one out of every nine persons gainfully employed in the United States.

The nation's roads were pitifully inadequate to an automobile age, and Federal, state, and local governments found it necessary to spend close to $10,000,000,000 on highway construction during the twenties. So heavy was the traffic that only well-constructed macadam or cement roads would hold up at all. The cost was great, but the major part of it was borne by the motorists. Not only did they have to pay heavy registration and license fees, but between 1919 and 1930 every state in the Union followed the example of Oregon, which pioneered in the levying of a gasoline tax. In 1930 direct and indirect taxes upon those who used the roads accounted for approximately four fifths of the income expended on state highways.

The economic, political, and social implications of the expansion of the automobile industry would be difficult to catalogue completely. Regions like New England, whose agriculture and industry were less prosperous than formerly, found partial compensation through new opportunities of selling their scenery and climate to motorists on vacation. Although Americans traveled more, they depended less on older modes of transportation. The horse and buggy became symbols of the quaint past, and even the electric streetcar and the railroad felt seriously the competition of the cars speeding across the countryside. Particularly was this so when bus companies and commercial trucking concerns began to expand their operations greatly. Many new problems were posed for government. Not only was there highway construction to be organized and financed, but the alarming number of serious accidents involving motorists underlined the necessity for new traffic legislation and strict policing. The automobile made the prohibition and immigration laws more difficult to enforce and helped murderers and bank robbers to make their getaways. For the farmer the new means of transportation brought many benefits; it lessened his isolation and provided an admirable means for him to carry his product to market. Many parents of teen-age boys and girls worried greatly, however, because of the ease with which the younger generation escaped the supervision of the elder through using the new vehicles.

As Americans took to the road, enterprising businessmen made an earnest bid to secure their money. The new state highways were lined with billboards, ornate filling stations, tourist camps, and hot-dog stands. To most citizens this was merely another evidence of the healthy condition of rugged individualism; but sensitive souls complained bitterly that the beauty of the American countryside was being destroyed.

THE AGE OF ELECTRICITY

Another rapidly expanding industry which contributed to the prosperity of the twenties was the electrical business. In 1902 less than 5,000,000,000 kilowatt-hours of electricity had been produced in the United States. This rate of production had more than tripled by 1912 when 17,000,000,000 kilowatt-hours were generated. This, however, was only a small beginning. In 1920 43,000,000,000 and in 1929 97,000,-000,000 kilowatt-hours of electricity flowed through the wires into American homes and factories. Capital investment in the industry was less than $6,000,000,000 in 1910, over $12,000,000,000 in 1920, and more than $23,000,000,000 in 1930.

Who was using this current? Much of it was consumed in domestic lighting. In 1912, only 16 per cent of the population lived in electrically lighted dwellings, but by 1927 this convenience was enjoyed by 63 per cent. And once the home was wired for electricity, the housewife was almost certain to demand some of the electrical appliances which were then available to lighten her domestic chores. According to a calculation of 1926, of sixteen million households equipped with electricity, 80 per cent had electric irons, 37 per cent had vacuum cleaners, and more than 25 per cent washing machines, fans, or toasters. Electric refrigerators, clocks, and stoves likewise became more and more common. Obviously the rapidly increasing use of electricity offered a huge volume of business for manufacturers of household appliances.

But the factory no less than the home was being transformed. In 1914 only about 30 per cent of factory machine equipment had been electrified; by 1929 approximately 70 per cent was run by electrical power.

This permitted a much more efficient organization of production without cumbersome and dangerous systems of belts and pulleys. One of the industrial marvels of the day was the photoelectric eye which counted products, detected flaws, and performed many other functions with uncanny accuracy. Electricity had important special uses in many of the metallurgical and chemical industries.

The rapid growth of the power business presented new problems for government. Advanced liberals insisted that the public stake in the production and distribution of electricity at the cheapest possible rates was so great as to require public ownership. For a time there seemed to be a considerable trend in that direction. In 1902, 815 American municipalities operated their own utility systems; by 1922 the number had increased to 2581. During the balance of the twenties, however, the number declined, largely because power could be more economically generated by large plants serving many cities and industries than by smaller local plants. What was required, in the opinion of advocates of public control, was the generation of hydroelectric power in large volume by state or Federal authorities and its transmission and sale at reasonable rates to municipal distributing systems. Senator George Norris believed that a reasonable amount of public power production would provide a "yardstick" for measuring the rates of the private companies and he hoped to have the Muscle Shoals project developed in this way. Other widely discussed plans called for the production of public power in connection with the building of a proposed St. Lawrence waterway, as well as for combined irrigation-power projects along the Colorado, Columbia, and Missouri Rivers. Private power corporations naturally opposed such government competition with private enterprise, and they had the support of the Coolidge and Hoover administrations. Not until the thirties were the advocates of public power development given much opportunity to try out their theories.

Meantime, the private power industry was being consolidated into larger and larger units. Not only did local distributing companies find that they could purchase power from the larger producing companies more economically than they could generate it themselves, but all operating companies were to an increasing degree brought under the control of holding corporations. The holding companies themselves were often controlled by other holding companies, and this process of pyramiding was carried so far that oftentimes six or more companies were piled on top of one another. By 1929 twelve large systems controlled approximately 76 per cent of the electricity generated in the United States. Finance capitalism was well illustrated in the industry since corporations in which Morgan and National City Bank of New York influence was strong dominated some 37 per cent of the business, while companies within the sphere of influence of the Chase National Bank of New York accounted for about 11 per cent more. A third major group was controlled by Samuel Insull of Chicago. The Insull empire, comprising 10 per cent of the industry, was a fantastic affair. A labyrinth of holding and investment companies had been so built up as to include concerns serving 4741 communities in thirty different states. Insull himself was chairman of the board of directors in sixty-five concerns and president of eleven others.

Although consolidation through holding companies served some economic purpose when judiciously carried out, much of the pyramiding of corporations characteristic of the twenties was against the public interest. The market was flooded with grossly watered securities on which small investors lost millions of dollars during and after the Wall Street crash of 1929. Control of local operating companies, furthermore, was placed in the hands of bankers remote from the scene and often insensitive to the interests of the consumers. Finally, the overcapitalization of the industry and its control by holding companies incorporated in many different states made the problem of rate regulation by state public-utilities commissions extremely difficult.

A cautious beginning toward Federal regulation had been made in 1920 when Congress provided for the establishment of a Federal Power Commission to be comprised of three cabinet members—the Secretaries of War, Interior, and Agriculture. The commission was empowered to issue fifty-year licenses for electric projects on the public lands, reservations, and navigable streams. It could regulate rates on power moved across state lines by the licensed companies and their subsidiaries. The results were not very satisfactory. The cabinet members were too busy with their own departments to give the commission's activities much of their attention, while only a very small proportion of the country's power was being produced under Federal license. Legislation in 1930 provided for the reorganization of the commission; it was now given five full-time members and increased funds, but was granted no additional regulatory authority. Although the demand that the FPC should be given control over the rates of all electricity crossing state lines was not met during the twenties, the liberals did succeed in bringing about an important investigation of the whole utilities problem by the Federal Trade Commission. The most sensational revelation in the hearings before the commission was that utilities companies were spending millions of dollars every year to secure newspaper comment favorable to

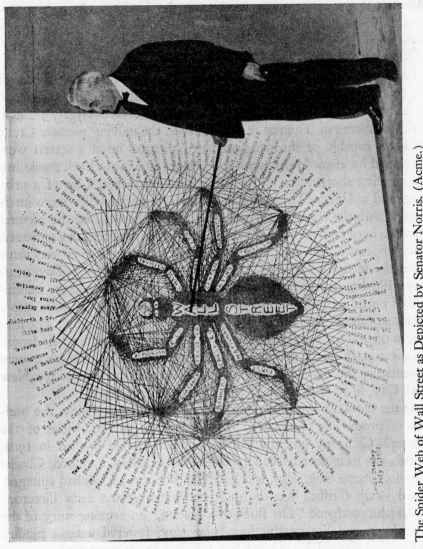

The Spider Web of Wall Street as Depicted by Senator Norris. (Acme.)

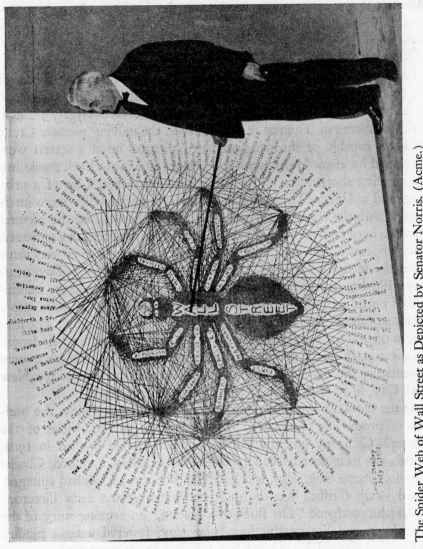

the private control of the electricity business and opposing government ownership. Similar propaganda was being artfully introduced into the educational system at every level from the kindergarten to the university.

MOVIES AND RADIO

Electricity made possible the development of two new forms of entertainment which gained wide popularity and influence, and themselves became big business. The first of these to evolve—largely through the experiments of Thomas A. Edison—was the moving picture. Crude machines capable of throwing animated pictures upon a screen were developed by 1896. In that year an audience in a New York music hall saw the first short movie show—some breaking waves, a bit of a prize fight, and a dancer. Thereafter short subjects occasionally were interspersed with the regular program in vaudeville houses, but the pictures were too hard on the eyes to have much popularity except as a curiosity. They improved, however, and in 1903 the first screen story was made under the intriguing title of "The Great Train Robbery." Two years later a Pittsburgh real-estate operator, one Harry Davis, had the inspiration of putting a movie projector, a piano, and ninety-nine seats into a vacant storeroom and charging 5 cents to see a one-reel show. The idea caught on and by 1907 there were five thousand similar "nickelodeons" in various parts of the country. After 1910 movie theaters became more pretentious; the Strand Theater, which opened on Broadway, New York City, in 1914, was the first of the really large ones.

As the motion picture began to capture the popular fancy, the business of producing films grew. The first large studios, those of the Biograph Company and the Edison Company, were opened in 1906. Within the next decade such favorite stars as Mary Pickford, Charlie Chaplin, Norma Talmadge, and Lillian and Dorothy Gish had emerged. David Wark Griffith was the most celebrated of the early directors. In 1915 he produced "The Birth of a Nation," an exciting story of the Civil War and Reconstruction. The play fostered race prejudice and exalted the old Ku Klux Klan, but despite its shortcomings it enjoyed huge popularity. Cutting loose from stage conventions, Griffith demonstrated the dramatic possibilities of such screen techniques as distant views and close-ups, fade-outs and switchbacks, mob and battle scenes, and exciting flights and pursuits.

The industry had at first been located largely on Long Island, but the superior photographic advantages of California sunlight, as well as certain legal complications, resulted in a wholesale removal to Holly-

Mary Pickford in an Early Movie Studio. (Acme.)

wood. There in 1922 the producers sought to avoid threatened public censorship by organizing the Motion Picture Producers and Distributors of America, Inc. Postmaster General Will H. Hays was induced to resign from Harding's cabinet to head the new project. Under the guidance of the so-called Hays office the industry sought zealously to avoid offending public taste. Overpassionate love scenes, the ridicule of any religious group, the portrayal of crime or sin in which the culprit escaped just retribution were sternly forbidden.

The problem of making the movies talk was a difficult one, but eventually successful systems for synchronizing picture and sound were developed. "The Jazz Singer" starring Al Jolson in 1927 was the first great hit in the new medium. Some two years more elapsed before the wiring of theaters for sound became general.

By the end of the twenties all but the smallest American communities had motion-picture theaters, and between eighty and one hundred million customers each week were paying their money to ride the western ranges with William S. Hart and Tom Mix, to sigh through the romances of Rudolph Valentino, John Gilbert, Greta Garbo, Gloria Swanson, and other popular screen lovers, or to be instructed concerning the magic power of a quality mysteriously known as "It," supposedly possessed in overpowering quantity by Clara Bow. The popularity of these

Station KDKA Broadcasts the Harding-Cox Election Returns, 1920.
(Brown Bros.)

actors and actresses was in fact international. A large export business in films developed and a majority of the pictures shown in almost every country were American-made.

As early as 1903 Reginald Fessenden was demonstrating the possibility of radio telephony in experiments at Washington, D. C. Other pioneers were also at work in the field, and in 1910 Dr. Lee DeForest successfully broadcast Enrico Caruso's voice from the Metropolitan Opera House. Six years later DeForest began experimental broadcasting from High Bridge, New York. Then in August, 1920, the Detroit *Daily News* started the practice of broadcasting news bulletins regularly over its own transmitter for the benefit of amateurs in the Detroit area.

Meantime, in Pittsburgh, Pennsylvania, amateurs had become interested in tuning in the experimental broadcasts made by the transmitters of the Westinghouse Electric and Manufacturing Company. A department store in the city started selling receiving sets and the Westinghouse Company presently decided to provide daily programs for the general public. Radio station KDKA was built and began regular broadcasting on November 2, 1920. The Harding-Cox election returns provided the first program material. The success of this venture induced Westinghouse to erect other stations the next year in Springfield, Massachusetts, Newark, New Jersey, and Chicago. Interest in the new form of entertainment swept the country and, by 1929, ten million sets were in use in the United States.

The problem of who was to pay for the expenses of broadcasting was solved in 1922 when the American Telephone and Telegraph Company's New York station, WEAF, utilized advertising sponsors for its programs; the first "commercial" was one in behalf of the Queensboro Realty Company. The broadcasting business promptly became highly remunerative; by 1927 there were some seven hundred stations in operation. Chaos on the air waves threatened, and the government had to intervene with the establishment of the Federal Radio Commission, which had authority to grant licenses to broadcasting stations and fix their wave length and hours of operation.

The almost inevitable trend of all business toward consolidation was evident in the organization of the Radio Corporation of America in 1919. This company, largely controlled by General Electric and Westinghouse, achieved a commanding position in the sale of radio sets and equipment. In 1926 the National Broadcasting Company, dominated by RCA, was established and soon controlled a chain of broadcasting stations from coast to coast. The rival Columbia Broadcasting System was organized the following year.

MORE BOOM INDUSTRIES

The manufacture of chemicals was scarcely a new industry in the sense that the automobile, movie, and radio businesses were. On the contrary, during the seventeenth century the colonists had begun the production of such commodities as potash and saltpeter. By 1900, moreover, there was extensive manufacture of the so-called heavy chemicals, products like sulphuric acid, soda ash, and caustic soda which were put to important industrial use. Up to 1914, however, the United States was almost completely dependent on imports from Germany for aniline dyes and other prominent synthetic supplies.

The outbreak of war in Europe brought great opportunities. With imports from Germany practically cut off, American textile manufacturers had to turn to American-made dyes, poor though they were at first. A vast amount of important technical information was made available when the Alien Property Custodian seized and assigned to the newly organized Chemical Foundation some four thousand enemy-owned patents for dyes, drugs, and other products. Chemical companies were prospering meanwhile through the huge wartime expenditures for explosives and fertilizers; some 40 per cent of all the explosives used by the Allies were manufactured by E. I. Du Pont de Nemours and Company of Wilmington, Delaware. Wartime contracts permitted vast plant expansion and provided ample funds for research.

The industry, already in a powerful position as it entered the postwar period, was given additional stimulus by the high rates of the Emergency Tariff of 1921 and the Fordney-McCumber Act. By 1929 four of the great American chemical concerns were larger than any of their European rivals. Greatest of all was Du Pont, which in 1930 was making eleven hundred different products in eighty different factories located in thirty different states.

It seemed that the chemical industry had almost limitless possibilities. Plastics had increased in number and utility since the pioneer discovery of celluloid by an American in 1869 until an appropriate product was now available for radio panels, fountain pens, buttons, combs, and hundreds of other uses. Although rayon was not satisfactory at first, it improved in quality and grew rapidly in popularity. New lacquers made of synthetic resins permitted the application of a fine finish to automobiles in two days instead of the twenty-six days formerly required. Other applications of chemistry made possible cheaper fertilizers for the farmer and more durable aluminum pots and pans for the housewife.

Wholesale industrial expansion afforded large profits to the construction business during the twenties, while the prevailing optimism of the period was reflected in the erection of ever-higher skyscrapers. New York City, with its Chrysler Building (77 stories), its Bank of the Manhattan Building (90 stories), and its Empire State Building (102 stories), led the country, but throughout the nation local pride was served by the construction of lofty office buildings. The erection of homes also boomed, particularly since very little housebuilding had been done during the war. Suburban developments were particularly popular as automobiles became more common and city workers accepted this opportunity to acquire homes in quieter, more country-like surroundings. On the other hand, the building of many huge and luxurious apartment houses was evidence that many families preferred to live in the cities and escape the inconvenience of commuting. Like the automobile industry, the construction business was notable for the stimulus it gave to other industries—to the steel, cement, lumber, electrical appliances, plumbing, and heating concerns, for example.

THE SICK INDUSTRIES

Even during the twenties, however, there were a few industries which appeared not to share in the prevailing prosperity. This was notably true of agriculture, which has been discussed in an earlier chapter, but it was true also of bituminous coal mining and cotton textile manufacture.

A combination of factors kept the bituminous coal industry in the doldrums. Fundamentally, the situation was one of overexpansion and overproduction. Furthermore, coal was feeling the competition of newer sources of energy. Whereas 87 per cent of all energy utilized in the United States at the end of the nineteenth century had been derived from coal, the use of petroleum, natural gas, and hydroelectric power had reduced the proportion of coal-produced energy to 45 per cent by the thirties. The price of bituminous coal dropped with disastrous results to the high-cost mines; there was much bankruptcy and unemployment. To make matters worse, many of the older mines which had accepted the union contracts stipulating the payment of reasonably good wages found themselves unable to compete effectively with newer mines, opened in West Virginia, Kentucky, and elsewhere, where an aggressive antiunion policy made it possible to pay low wages.

The cotton textile industry suffered in part from loss of export markets. The growth of textile manufacturing in Japan, India, South America, and China had serious repercussions both in England and the United States. To this blow was added certain changes in feminine apparel. Women wore shorter skirts, less clothing, and preferred silk or rayon to cotton for most of their lingerie and dresses. The total number of spindles actively employed in cotton textile manufacturing in the United States declined by 4,236,000, or about 12 per cent, between 1920 and 1930. Prices fell, mills went bankrupt, and unemployment grew. As in the bituminous coal industry, Northern industrialists found themselves at a very serious disadvantage in competing with newer Southern concerns. The latter had the advantage of proximity to the source of raw material, an abundant labor supply which was willing to work long hours for a low wage, and the use of new machinery, much more efficient than the old equipment of New England factories. Thus the Southern mills were able to expand despite the unfavorable circumstances in which the industry as a whole was placed; the number of spindles in the South was 4,368,000 in 1900, 15,231,000 in 1920, and 18,586,000 in 1930. This development of course multiplied the troubles besetting the industry in New England, where spindles in operation declined by almost one third during the decade.

SUBSIDIZED INDUSTRIES

Businessmen fervently pledged their allegiance to laissez faire, but few interpreted the term to mean that government should abstain from measures directly helping them. The high tariffs of the twenties provided in reality a subsidy paid by the consumer to thousands of industries. Where it seemed necessary, moreover, the Republican administrations of the day did not hesitate to have the government itself pay out money to private business enterprises. This proved to be the case with both the merchant marine and the aviation industries.

The need for a large and healthy merchant marine in case the United States became involved in war was obvious, yet the difficulties in maintaining one proved great. In conformity with the provisions of the Merchant Marine Act of 1920 the Shipping Board sold 1141 government-owned ships to private corporations between 1920 and 1928. Ships that had cost during the war as much as $200 a ton to build were sold for $30, $20, and occasionally as low as $8.00 a ton. Even at these bargain prices, several hundred ships found no purchasers. Almost five hundred of these were allowed to lie idle; the remainder were operated by private companies under contracts so drawn that the companies could not lose but the government could—and did in sums fluctuating between $12,000,000 and $50,000,000 annually. The concerns which had purchased government ships had scarcely better success. They were competing with foreign shipping companies which enjoyed government subsidies, had lower operating costs, and used newer, faster, more efficient vessels. In 1921 almost 43 per cent of American foreign trade was carried in American ships; by 1928 the proportion had dropped to 32 per cent.

Congress tried to rescue the industry with new legislation, the Jones-White Act of 1928. To modernize American shipping, the Shipping Board's loan fund was increased to $250,000,000 from which advances could be made at very low rates of interest to private concerns for the construction of new ships or the rehabilitation of old ones. Furthermore, the government was authorized to enter into long-term contracts with the shipping companies for the carriage of the mails. It was well understood that these contracts would provide a generous if indirect subsidy. By 1933 these payments to shipping concerns for carrying mail reached about $23,000,000 annually, many times what it actually cost to perform the service. Meantime, the government continued to sell its own ships to private companies at a great loss and to loan large sums of money for new construction. Such measures managed to keep the

American merchant marine alive and even to provide it with a few new ships, but the situation was obviously a far from healthy one. Many stockholders and executives connected with the shipping business had grown wealthy on government money, yet the nation had not secured an effective merchant marine.

Aviation was a new industry, but it was far from being a boom enterprise like the automobile business. The famous experiments of Wilbur and Orville Wright at Kitty Hawk, North Carolina, had demonstrated the possibility of flying in a heavier-than-air machine as early as 1903. The first flight of an airplane across the United States, however, did not occur until 1911 when it required nearly seven weeks and was interrupted by numerous forced landings. The World War speeded the development of aviation immeasurably; planes had to be produced in quantity, and thousands of young Americans received training as aviators. In 1918 the first regular air-mail service in the world was instituted between New York and Washington, and the following year an United States Navy seaplane, the NC–4, made the first crossing of the Atlantic by air.

The early postwar years were discouraging ones for the industry. The government was no longer a customer for any substantial number of planes; indeed it was dumping its own surplus aircraft on the market. General William ("Billy") Mitchell preached earnestly the importance of aviation to national defense and even demonstrated that aerial bombing could sink a battleship. His superiors were unimpressed, however, and, when he became disrespectful of them in the heat of his campaign to unify the army and navy air forces, he was first demoted in rank, then court-martialed and forced to retire from the service. Nor was there any extensive market for aircraft among private citizens. Aviation to them was still largely a curiosity; its principal vocational opportunity was to reckless young "barnstormers" who looped the loop and did barrel rolls for the edification of the patrons of country fairs and then sold rides to anyone courageous enough to go up in the air with them.

The Post Office gradually expanded its air-mail service, but up to 1925 the flying was done by its own pilots. In that year the Kelly Act was passed, authorizing the government to make contracts for carrying the mail with private air lines. As a further recognition of the importance of the new business the Air Commerce Act, placed on the statute books in 1926, vested extensive powers over commercial aviation in the Department of Commerce.

The year 1927 was a turning point for the industry. On May 20 of that year Charles A. Lindbergh took off in his plane, "The Spirit of

St. Louis," from the New York airport; thirty-three and a half hours later he landed safely at Le Bourget Field in Paris. The flight, so quietly and competently performed, captured the imagination of the American public and demonstrated the possibilities of aviation as no previous event had done. The "Flying Colonel" became a national hero over night and aviation securities took off on a seemingly nonstop flight themselves; in nineteen months the Wright Aeronautical Company's stock soared from 25 to 245. The air-mindedness of investors was stimulated still further by several other notable flights of these years; in 1926 Commander Richard E. Byrd and Floyd Bennett flew over the North Pole; the next year Byrd organized a trans-Atlantic flight; in 1928 he flew over the South Pole. Meantime, the Atlantic had been crossed also by Clarence Chamberlain and Charles A. Levine and by the famous woman pilot, Amelia Earhart. Two Army Air Corps pilots, Lieutenants Maitland and Hegenberger, flew from San Francisco to Honolulu in June, 1927.

By the end of 1928, there were forty-eight air lines in the United States with a combined length of 20,000 miles which served 355 cities. Licensed aviators numbered eleven thousand.

To an extraordinary degree, however, the industry was dependent upon the patronage of the government. Between 1927 and 1933 over 50 per cent of the output of the aircraft factories was purchased by the army and the navy, and, as late as 1931, 85 per cent of the income of the transport companies came not from carrying passengers or freight, but from the Post Office Department on mail contracts. The rates of payment permitted under the Kelly Act were judged to be inadequate and Congress raised them several times. Finally in 1930 the McNary-Watres Act empowered the Postmaster General to make contracts under which the companies would be paid for providing space for mail irrespective of the weight or volume of the mail actually carried. By 1932 payments on these contracts had risen to nearly $20,000,000 annually, some three times what the Post Office was taking in through the sale of air-mail postage.

The development of aviation was probably important enough to the nation as a whole to justify a policy of subsidies, but the actual administration of the system brought much criticism. Not only were the payments often excessive, but there seemed to be favoritism in their distribution. Hoover's Postmaster General, Walter F. Brown, was accused of having evaded the clauses in the McNary-Watres Act which required competitive bidding, of having allotted the contracts in such a manner that 90 per cent of the government payments were made to three major groups in the industry, and of having brought pressure to bear upon the smaller independent companies to compel them to merge with the larger ones.

THE RAILROADS

The development of air transportation was a potential, rather than an actual, threat to the railroads during the twenties. Their more immediate difficulties lay in the growth of other forms of competition. Fords and Chevrolets were scurrying over the roads on innumerable errands that a decade before would have provided business for the trains. The problem became still more serious as bus lines and trucking companies expanded their activities. Railroad executives complained bitterly that whereas their companies had to expend huge sums of money in maintaining their tracks and roadbeds, these new competitors were enjoying the use of highways built at the taxpayers' expense. To make matters worse from the railroads' point of view, interstate motor transportation was not yet subject to Federal regulation.

The railroads also felt increased competition from waterways. The building of the Panama Canal stimulated interest in similar projects within the nation's borders. In 1918 the new New York State Barge Canal, superseding the historic Erie Canal, was opened to traffic. The Federal government expended large sums of money in projects designed to improve navigation along the Ohio, Missouri, and Mississippi rivers. Once again there was bitterness in the comments of the rail executives; most of these projects, they charged, did not pay for themselves; the railroads were being injured by a form of government-subsidized competition.

The long-range prospects of the railroads looked anything but promising and the carriers were hard hit by the depression of 1921. Yet the evil day was for a little while postponed during the period of Coolidge prosperity. Despite the continued falling off of passenger receipts, freight revenues reflected the satisfactory state of general business activity. Important economies in operation, moreover, were effected. Freight cars were increased in capacity and locomotive design was improved so that longer trains could be pulled. Important experiments were made in the use of Diesel engines, electrification, automatic systems of sorting cars in freight yards, and streamlining. One million and a half railroad employees were operating the country's lines in 1930, whereas two million had been required a decade before.

Increased efficiency, however, was not enough to save the carriers from the devastating effects of the great depression which started in

1929. During the next few years most of the railroads failed to earn their fixed charges, while over 40,000 miles were in the hands of receivers by 1933. Had it not been for lifesaving loans by Hoover's Reconstruction Finance Corporation, bankrupt mileage would have been much greater—greater, in fact, than at any previous period of railroad history.

The Transportation Act of 1920 proved in certain of its provisions hard to administer. The organization of labor adjustment boards proceeded very slowly because of differences between the carriers and their employees. This added to the crushing weight of the problems confronting the National Railroad Labor Board. The board gained the hostility of the unions by recommending wage cuts in 1921 and 1922. When the shopmen walked out in protest against the latter cut as well as against other grievances, their strike was broken with the assistance of an injunction secured by Attorney General Daugherty. The fate of the shopmen, whose union was largely wrecked by their attempt to defy the Railroad Labor Board, contrasted strangely with the treatment accorded the Pennsylvania Railroad, whose refusal to carry out certain of the board's recommendations favorable to the unions went unpunished.

Labor's wholesale opposition to the Labor Board, combined with an attack upon it headed by the Pennsylvania Railroad and several other lines, resulted in the passage of the Railroad Labor Act of 1926. The old board was abolished; in its place was established a permanent Board of Mediation composed of five members chosen by the President. The board's primary duty was to attempt to mediate in railroad labor disputes not settled by direct negotiations or by adjustment boards; if the board's effort at settlement also failed, it was then to urge the parties to submit the dispute to arbitration. The employers and employees could not be compelled to arbitrate, but if they did agree to this form of settlement, the findings of the arbiters were to be binding at law. The arbitration boards were to consist of either three or six members; one or two arbiters were to be named by each of the parties, and they in turn were to choose one or two neutral persons to round out the panel. Should either or both the parties refuse to arbitrate and an interruption in interstate commerce be threatened, the President was empowered to appoint an emergency board to investigate and report to him. The parties were required not to make any change in conditions until thirty days after the emergency board's report. Despite pessimistic predictions by those who remembered the failure of similar legislation passed in 1913, this machinery worked surprisingly well.

The portion of the Transportation Act of 1920 which dealt with the consolidation of the nation's railroads caused difficulties. In the early twenties the Interstate Commerce Commission issued a tentative plan calling for consolidation into nineteen great systems; the railroads protested many details and a revised plan providing for twenty-one systems was published in 1929. Once again the railroads were dissatisfied; they suggested certain regional consolidations based upon their own ideas, but the commission's approval of these was given upon conditions that were unacceptable to the roads. As a result of this deadlock none of the consolidation contemplated in the legislation of 1920 was actually achieved.

For a time the railroads appeared to have found in holding-company organization a device for securing their own kind of consolidation—one which would escape the regulatory powers of the Interstate Commerce Commission. Particularly notorious were the activities of the Van Sweringen brothers of Cleveland, Ohio, who used pyramided holding companies to gain control over railroads having aggregate assets of $2,500,000,000 with an investment of less than $20,000,000. Similarly bold were the operations of the Pennroad Company through which the Pennsylvania Railroad sought to extend its influence into new fields. The ICC was threatened with the undermining of much of its power until the situation was remedied by legislation in 1933.

The "recapture clause" in the Transportation Act also proved hard to administer. The law required that one half of the earnings of the lines in excess of a fair return on their property should be paid into a railroad contingent fund. The commission fixed 6 per cent as a fair return, but commission and carriers disagreed sharply on the valuations of railroad property on which fair return should be figured. The commission laboriously worked out valuations for each railroad, based largely upon what it would have cost to reproduce it in 1914; the railroads contended for a "reproduction cost new" formula which would base valuations upon what reconstruction would cost under the prices of the twenties. In the so-called O'Fallon case (1929), the Supreme Court refused to uphold the commission; the result was to throw the whole issue into great confusion, from which the country was finally delivered by the repeal of the recapture clause in 1933. Since these valuation problems made it also difficult for the commission to base rates upon the formula laid down in the law of 1920, this likewise had to be modified in 1933.

The railroad question continued, obviously, to be one of the major national issues. As time went on, however, the nub of the problem

changed from that of protecting the public against railroad abuses to
that of keeping the roads operating in reasonably solvent fashion.

BUSINESS BECOMES BIGGER

As has been stressed already, the decade of the twenties was an age
of consolidation. Not since the years 1897 to 1903 had political, economic, and social factors blended in an atmosphere so exhilarating to the
promoters of vast enterprises. The movement profited particularly from
the increasing number of Americans eager to invest in stocks, and
willing to buy up in short order almost any new issue of securities
thrown upon the market.

The extent to which business concentration had gone is shown by the
fact that in 1930 the two hundred largest nonfinancial corporations of
the country—forty-five railroads, fifty-eight public utilities, and ninety-
seven industrials—had gross assets of $67,000,000,000. This was almost
one half of all the assets owned by corporations of this character in
the country. By 1930 there were fifteen American companies each of
which had assets of over $1,000,000,000. Mergers resulted in the dis-
appearance of six thousand manufacturing and mining enterprises between 1919 and 1928, while four thousand public utilities and more
than eighteen hundred banks were absorbed by other concerns.

Retail trade had been revolutionized as giant chain stores like the
A & P, Woolworth's, the United Cigar Stores, and Wahlgreen's Drug
Stores spread across the country. In 1929, 27 per cent of American
food sales, 19 per cent of American drugstore sales, and 93 per cent of
variety-store sales were made through the chains.

Although outright mergers were frequent, the most popular device
for consolidating business during the decade was the holding company.
This form of combination had lost its popularity following the adverse decisions of the Supreme Court in the Northern Securities case in
1904 and the Standard Oil case in 1911, but after 1920, when the Court
refused to order the dissolution of the United States Steel Corporation,
corporation lawyers returned to it with great enthusiasm. Not only
were about one quarter of all the nation's industrial concerns brought
under holding-company organization during the next twelve years, but
the method was used with increasing frequency in the railroad and
banking fields.

As corporations became larger, they fell more and more under so-
called management control. So numerous were the stockholders and so
small was the proportion of stock which most of them held that few
ever tried to influence or control the policies of the company; instead

they willingly mailed in their proxies to be voted by a committee of the management. Unwilling to run even a remote risk of a stockholders' revolt, moreover, corporation lawyers specialized in so organizing the companies that the investing public put up the capital through the purchase of bonds, preferred stock, and nonvoting common stock, while control of the enterprise was tightly held by a little group of insiders owning a small issue of voting stock never put on public sale. The growing divorce between corporate ownership and control sometimes made for irresponsibility and bad management.

Despite this trend toward consolidation, however, the single corporation threatening to monopolize a whole field of economic endeavor was less characteristic of the twenties than it had been of the early years of the century. The various Standard Oil companies, for example, controlled only about 43 per cent of the oil business in 1926 as compared with the 80 per cent that had been theirs in 1911, while the United States Steel Corporation's output was approximately 40 per cent of the nation's total instead of the 65 per cent in 1902. But this did not mean a revival of small business. What was developing instead was a situation wherein there were three or four great companies in a field, competing with each other but far outdistancing smaller rivals. This condition, called by the economists oligopoly, was illustrated by the dominance of the automobile field by Ford, General Motors, and Chrysler, in the chemical field by Du Pont, Allied Chemical and Dye, and Union Carbide and Carbon, in motion pictures by Famous Players-Lasky, Metro-Goldwyn-Mayer, Fox, and Universal, and by similar situations in the oil, steel, cigarette, aviation, and electrical industries.

The competition of the giants was a great boon to the advertising business. Enormous sums of money were spent in an attempt to impress upon the buying public the sterling merits of Lucky Strike, Camel, and Chesterfield cigarettes, or the prodigious power of Socony, Good Gulf, or Texaco gasoline. Advertising, however, emphasized the quality of the rival products, rather than their price. Indeed, it was taken for granted that the popular brands of cigarettes would all sell at the same price, as did also the leading brands of gasoline, bread, or milk. Businessmen came to look upon price cutting as unethical. It was assumed, for example, that the figure set by Standard Oil would fix the price charged for gasoline by all the other major companies. Similar price leadership was exercised by the United States Steel Corporation, the International Harvester Company, the National Biscuit Company, and many others.

The desire to stabilize business was reflected also in the organization of trade associations. Such groupings had been in existence since the days of the Civil War, but they increased largely in number and importance during and after World War I. In 1925 there were approximately a thousand of them. Trade association activities took many different forms. Sometimes advertising was done in the interests of the whole industry. For example, when the American Tobacco Company made extensive use of the slogan, "Reach for a Lucky instead of a sweet," the candymakers' association published a series of advertisements emphasizing the healthful food values in their products. Sometimes industrial research was promoted, as at the University of Chicago under the patronage of the Institute of American Meat Packers. Many trade associations undertook to simplify the prevalent business practices in their fields or to standardize products. In such activities they had the full cooperation of Secretary of Commerce Herbert Hoover. The varieties of paving brick were thus reduced from 66 to 4, of sheet steel from 1819 to 261, and of range boilers from 130 to 13.

The temptation was great, however, to direct trade-association activities into less legitimate channels—channels tending toward price fixing, restriction of production, and restraint of competition. Particularly controversial was the so-called open-price movement, which had its original impetus in 1912 from a book entitled *The New Competition*, written by a Chicago lawyer, A. J. Eddy. Upon its title page were these words: "Competition is War and 'War is Hell.'" Eddy's thesis was that cutthroat competition could be avoided and business stabilized if producers would provide each other with complete information about all their transactions—about sales, customers, shipments, production, and prices. By 1921 there were more than one hundred open-price associations engaged in collecting and distributing such information.

FOREIGN TRADE AND INVESTMENTS

About one tenth of the annual production of goods in the United States was sold abroad. As compared with the proportion disposed of in the domestic market these sales were not large, but, to many industries, they represented the difference between prosperity and depression. Hoover, as Secretary of Commerce, was particularly zealous in promoting American export trade. Requests to his department for information about foreign markets rose from 700 to 10,000 a day, and a large corps of commercial attachés and trade experts were sent abroad to advance the interests of the exporters. Other agencies for promoting foreign trade were some fifty export associations which had been granted exemption from the antitrust laws by the Webb-Pomerene Act of 1918, and numerous American banks which were permitted under the Federal Reserve Act to maintain foreign branches.

Thus encouraged, American exports rose from their depression low of 3.8 billion dollars in 1922 to 5.2 billion in 1929. Certain interesting trends were to be noted. Up to 1900 the leading exports had been cotton, wheat, and meat; by 1929 only cotton maintained its leading place —wheat and meat exports being far surpassed by petroleum products, machinery, and automobiles. In 1900, about two thirds of sales abroad had been agricultural products; by 1929 the proportion of these was not more than one third. In 1900, moreover, over three quarters of American exports went to Europe; by 1929 less than one half did so due to increased sales to Canada, Latin America, and Asia.

Imports, no less than exports, were important to the nation's economy. Increasing industrialization led to large purchases of newsprint, vegetable oils, rubber, and various metals like copper, nickel, and tin. As in the case of sales abroad, American purchases from Europe were becoming proportionately less, while those from Canada and Asia were showing notable increases. Republican tariff policies, however, were reflected in the continued excess of exports over imports. In 1929, goods entering the United States were valued at only 4.4 billion dollars, which fell short by $800,000,000 of balancing the country's sales abroad.

Such an annual excess of exports over imports had been usual before World War I. Then it had served a useful function since the United States was a debtor country and required funds to pay dividends and interest to foreign investors who had loaned their money for building American railroads and otherwise furnished capital for the rapid economic development of the country. But the war had radically altered the situation. Many foreigners had had to liquidate their holdings of American securities, while American bankers and the United States government itself had loaned large sums to the belligerents. Even excluding the huge intergovernmental debts, the change in the situation was striking; foreign investments in the United States between 1914 and 1919 had fallen from 6.75 billion dollars to 2.2, while American investments abroad had increased from 3.5 billion to 6.5. The United States, in short, had become a creditor nation.

Ten years after the war conditions were still more radically altered. Foreign investment in the United States had risen again to 6.7 billion— attracted by the dazzling prospects of American industry. But it nowhere nearly kept pace with American investment abroad, which, with the blessing of the American State Department, had risen by 1929 to 15.4 billion dollars. The excess of American exports over imports provided funds for American loans to many foreign governments, as well as for the financing of tin-mine operations in Bolivia, oil projects in Mexico, Venezuela, and Iraq, rubber plantations in the Netherlands East Indies, banana plantations in Central America, and sugar plantations in Cuba. Particularly notable was the large amount of American capital—1.5 billion—invested in manufacturing enterprises in foreign countries, often in foreign branches of American companies. The export of American capital to build foreign factories was so extensive as to threaten the export markets for American manufactured goods.

So long as American capital continued to flow into foreign investments, world economic conditions appeared to be in a state of healthy convalescence. Germany successfully met the reparations payments fixed under the Dawes Plan of 1924, and her creditors in turn made their war-debt payments to the United States. American exports continued in large volume since they were in truth being financed by expanding American investments. But the precarious foundation of this convalescence is obvious. Should American loans abroad cease, disastrous consequences would be inevitable.

THE BALANCE SHEET FOR THE TWENTIES

Seen in perspective, the prosperity of the twenties was by no means entirely fictitious. On the contrary, there was much solid economic achievement. Not only was there a substantial increase in the national gross income, but there were measurable gains both in per capita real income and in the real wages of American laborers. Particularly impressive was the increased efficiency to be found in manufacturing, mining, transportation, and agriculture. Scientific management and improved machinery had made human labor more productive than ever before.

Unfortunately, however, certain other developments of the period proved in the long run so unhealthy as to threaten the whole economic structure. The failure of agricultural prices to maintain an equitable relationship with other prices undermined the security of millions of Americans, while sick industries like bituminous coal mining and cotton textile manufacture involved hardship for many others. Particularly disquieting was the growth of technological unemployment; new machinery seemed to be taking away jobs faster than it created them. It was cold comfort to the man thrown out of work to assure him that his plight was temporary and that ultimately he might expect a new and better job from expanding industry. The transition period was often long and painful, and the rugged individualism of the twenties was entirely opposed to the principle of compulsory unemployment insurance to provide for such cases.

During the Coolidge era men liked to dream that the business cycle had been broken and that the country had entered a period of perpetual prosperity. But the continuance of good times required that distribution keep pace with production, demand with increased supply. Since this was fundamental, the seriousness of a situation in which millions of farmers, miners, and workers failed to secure an ample and stable income is obvious. The price policies of many manufacturers added to the difficulty. The comparative stability of the general price level during the twenties is misleading, suggesting as it does that there was

The Progress of Civilization. Pioneers of the nineteenth and twentieth centuries. (From the *Rochester Democrat and Chronicle*.)

no general inflation. Yet in many lines reductions in cost were effected which failed to be reflected in reductions in price; the result was a species of concealed inflation. Instead of the savings being handed on to the consumers, they were largely diverted to increased profits. Many businessmen preferred to take a large profit on a small volume of business than a small profit on a large volume. But prices higher than they needed to be seriously reduced the purchasing power of the consumers upon which continued prosperity depended. The inflexibility of prices, of course, reflected the restraints upon competition which were so common during the twenties—monopoly, oligopoly, price leadership, and trade-association agreements.

In certain other lines the inflation was not concealed at all. By 1927 the price of most common stock was purely speculative and had lost all contact with the actual earning power of the corporations involved. Yet the great bull market was merely gathering momentum; up and up it went until it reached the fantastic peaks of September, 1929. The housing and real-estate boom of the earlier twenties likewise drove prices to unnatural levels; the most notorious situation was that in the Florida land market where thousands of Northerners were feverishly engaged in buying and selling real estate, much of which they had never seen. Before the hurricane of 1926 and other factors combined to cool the excessive ardor of the speculators, prices had been pushed to grotesque levels.

Speculation in stocks and real estate was particularly dangerous to the continuance of prosperity because it was carried on largely upon credit. The investor preferred to borrow from his broker and buy a large amount of stock on margin rather than purchase a smaller amount outright; the real-estate buyer gave a mortgage for most of the sales price and obligated himself for an indefinite period in the future to make heavy interest payments based upon an inflated valuation of his property. The overextension of credit was, in fact, to be seen on every hand. Hard to resist was the ubiquitous salesman perpetually urging his prospect to "buy now and pay in easy installments." Many a young couple was making payments simultaneously on a bungalow, household furniture, radio, washing machine, vacuum cleaner, and automobile. It was an expensive process because it involved large interest payments; it was precarious since illness, unexpected expenses, or loss of one's job might make it impossible to continue the payments, in which case the unhappy householders might lose both their purchases and the payments which they had already made. But the great banker was often as imprudent as the small householder; many of the securities

—particularly the foreign ones—which he bought for himself and sold to his customers proved to be worthless.

The final weakness in the prosperity of the twenties was its narrow base. In 1929 there were 16,350,000 families in the United States receiving less than $2000 in annual income. This was nearly 60 per cent of all the families in the country, yet they received less than 24 per cent of the national total. A still greater drag on the country's economy was the lowest income group—the 21 per cent of American families who received less than $1000 a year and less than 4 per cent of the national income. Here were the customers who would have to secure purchasing power before the nation would really achieve Hoover's noble goal: "the final triumph over poverty."

17

Hoover and the Depression

IN OCTOBER, 1929, A CALAMITOUS BREAK IN THE NEW YORK STOCK market occurred. This was the dramatic beginning of the greatest depression in world history. Its repercussions were momentous both in domestic and international politics. In England, a Labor government was swept from power; in Germany the political parties upholding the republic were overwhelmed by their anti-republican enemies; in France the situation became so chaotic that no ministry could remain long in authority; in ten of the Latin-American states there were revolutions. And in the United States the great depression blasted the political fortunes of Herbert Hoover despite the fact that few American Presidents have entered the White House with the tremendous prestige that was his in March, 1929.

THE ELECTION OF 1928

On August 2, 1927, the reporters assigned to cover President Coolidge's vacation activities in the Black Hills of South Dakota were provided with an unexpected scoop when the President handed out the terse statement: "I do not choose to run for President in 1928." It was big news because the country was prosperous and contented, Coolidge was at the height of his popularity, and political experts were freely predicting that he would run for a third term and be easily elected. Some of the President's most enthusiastic admirers refused to take his announcement as final and hoped that the movement to renominate him would assume such proportions that he would accept after all. In the absence of any encouragement from the White House, however, the "draft-Coolidge" plan foundered; it lasted only long enough to induce Coolidge's opponents in the Senate—Democrats and Republican progressives—to secure the passage of a resolution on February 10, 1928, stating that any departure from the time-honored custom established by Washington of retiring after two terms in the presidency "would be unwise, unpatriotic and fraught with peril to our free institutions." Coolidge did not give his reasons for not seeking the reelection which would have made him the first man to be President of the United States for more than eight years. His decision may have been based upon respect for the antithird-term tradition, on a knowledge that his health was failing, or upon a canny recognition that prosperity might not last forever.[1]

Coolidge's announcement was the signal for various Republican factions to start promoting the interests of their candidates. Ex-Governor Lowden of Illinois had a faithful following, but his chances for the nomination were injured by his age (sixty-eight) and by the scars left from the Lowden-Wood struggle in the convention of 1920. Vice-President Dawes had demonstrated much executive ability during his career and possessed an unusually colorful personality, but the Senators had never forgiven him for lecturing them on the obsolescence of their rules when he took up the gavel in 1925. Senator Borah of Idaho was a hero to thousands of Republican liberals, yet his name was anathema to most of the conservative Eastern leaders. The aspirations of all these rivals, moreover, were doomed to defeat by the irresistible tide that set in for the nomination of Herbert Hoover. The Secretary of Commerce was unpopular with many of the Republican leaders, but he had tremendous strength among the rank and file of the party. His administration of Belgian war relief had established his reputation as a great humanitarian, his work as wartime Food Administrator had made his name a household word, while his long term as Secretary of Commerce had given him thousands of influential contacts with the business community. Hoover was assured of administration support when he issued a statement in praise of Coolidge's veto of the McNary-Haugen Bill.

At the Republican convention at Kansas City, Hoover was awarded the coveted nomination on the first ballot. The vice-presidential candidate was Senator Charles Curtis of Kansas, who had been serving as majority leader in the Upper House. The platform was a cautious document, promising a continuance of the sound Republican policies which were asserted to be responsible for the nation's prosperity. The troublesome farm problem was recognized in a plank promising governmental assistance in the establishment of a farm marketing system,

[1] Later, in his autobiography, Coolidge asserted that it was the antithird-term tradition that caused his statement.

while prohibition was dealt with in a passage pledging the party to "the observance and vigorous enforcement" of the Eighteenth Amendment. In international affairs the platform advocated the outlawing of war and the further limitation of armaments, but opposed American entry into the League of Nations.

Several candidates, among them Governor Albert J. Ritchie of Maryland and Senator Thomas J. Walsh of Montana, were backed for the Democratic nomination. Their support was weak, however, compared with that accorded Governor Alfred E. Smith of New York. Since his unsuccessful bid for the nomination four years before, Smith had continued to grow in political stature. In 1924 he had been reelected governor despite the fact that Coolidge carried the state by a large majority; in 1926 he had been elected for an unprecedented fourth term. Not only had he proved himself an effective campaigner, but his reform of the New York state government and his advocacy of progressive measures had secured him nation-wide publicity. He was still disliked in the South as a Catholic and a wet, but no bitter-end opposition to him—such as had wrecked the party's chances in the 1924 campaign—was allowed to develop. Instead, the "Happy Warrior," as he had once been described by Franklin D. Roosevelt, received a first-ballot nomination at the Houston convention. An attempt to sugar-coat the pill for the South was made by naming Senator Joseph T. Robinson of Arkansas as his running mate.

The Democratic platform of 1928 was no more inspiring than the Republican. The League of Nations was not mentioned and prohibition was dealt with only in a pledge to make "an honest effort to enforce the Eighteenth Amendment and all other provisions of the Federal Constitution and all laws enacted pursuant thereto." Even on the tariff the Democrats demanded no radical change of policy, promising, on the contrary, duties which would maintain legitimate business and a high standard of wages while permitting effective competition and ensuring against monopoly. Coolidge's farm policy was severely criticized, but the Democratic alternative was left vague.

Fortunately the candidates proved somewhat less evasive than the party platforms. Governor Smith promised to enforce the prohibition laws so long as they were on the books, but he advocated speedy modification of the Volstead Act and eventual repeal of the Eighteenth Amendment. His alternative was a system under which each state would handle its own liquor problem, yet he opposed the return of the saloon and urged the sale of liquor through state stores. Hoover, on the other hand, defended prohibition as "a great social and economic experi-

Alfred E. Smith and Herbert Hoover. (Acme.)

ment, noble in motive and far-reaching in purpose." Smith made his bid for the farmer's vote by accepting the principle of the McNary-Haugen Bill; he advocated also the public operation of the Muscle Shoals project and secured thereby the support of Senator Norris. Hoover outdid Coolidge in his condemnation of such proposals, warning solemnly: "You cannot extend the mastery of the government over the daily working life of a people without at the same time making it the master of the people's souls and thoughts." Despite his stand on prohibition, farm relief, and public power, Smith was no radical. He sought to reassure the country that he would do nothing to interfere with prosperity, and in particular that he would not press for drastic tariff revision. The Smith campaign was essentially conservative, deriving its tone perhaps from the unusual circumstance that a wealthy General Motors executive, John J. Raskob, was serving as Democratic campaign manager.

The election was a heated one, but not because of any widespread interest in the issues. What created excitement was the unorthodox background of the Democratic candidate. A product of Tammany Hall, boasting of his affection for "the sidewalks of New York," he inevitably was viewed with suspicion by millions of small-town Americans. That suspicion was doubled by the knowledge that he was a wet and multiplied many times over by the knowledge that he was a Roman Catholic. Never before had a member of that faith been nominated for the presidency by a major party, and many narrow-minded Protestants—their prejudices heightened by recent Klan propaganda—predicted terrible consequences if Smith were successful. One of the most vicious whispering campaigns was directed against the New York governor.

The Republicans' best argument was the nation's prosperity, for which the party orators naturally took complete credit. And the election returns showed the strength of that argument. Hoover received 444 electoral votes to Smith's 87. The unusual degree of hostility to the Democratic candidate in the South was demonstrated by Hoover's victory in Florida, North Carolina, Tennessee, Texas, and Virginia—states never carried by a Republican since Reconstruction days. Smith suffered further disappointment when he lost his own home state, although he did carry near-by Massachusetts and Rhode Island. Despite the fact that the Democrats won only eight states, Smith's popular vote of 15,016,443 compared very favorably with the nine million votes given to Cox in 1920 and the eight million to Davis in 1924. Hoover's popular vote was 21,392,190; the minor party candidates, Thomas (Socialist) and Foster (Workers or Communist) received only 267,420 and 48,770 respectively. The Progressives made no effort to revive their party during this campaign. As in 1900, the election results were somewhat deceptive. The conservatives seemed completely triumphant, yet the onset of depression was soon to restore progressivism to all its old vigor.

HOOVER: ASSETS AND LIABILITIES

The President who took office on March 4, 1929, had many assets. Before he became a well-known public figure, he had had years of experience in the business world. Trained as an engineer at Stanford University, he had begun in his profession at the bottom, but had speedily acquired a fortune as a mining and railroad expert and promoter. He had spent many years abroad in China, in South Africa, and in England. Both as businessman and government executive, he had developed a passion for facts. He campaigned by quoting statistics; as President, he was continually organizing commissions of experts to study and report on problems. Many of these bodies prepared studies of great interest and importance as, for example, the Committees on Recent Economic Change, on Child Health and Protection, and on Recent Social Trends. Most famous of all was the Commission on Law Enforcement, better known as the "Wickersham Commission," which prepared an exhaustive report on prohibition and related problems. Another outstanding talent of the new President was for organizing cooperative enterprises. As a cabinet officer under Harding and Coolidge, he had been conspicuously successful in helping businessmen to help themselves. In the White House he worked hard to find the solution of important national problems through the same method. Hoover had, moreover, a well-formulated philosophy of government which he upheld with sincerity, if not always with consistency. He objected to government intervention in the business world as not alone injurious to economic life, but to liberty. "Economic freedom," he asserted during the campaign, "cannot be sacrificed if political freedom is to be preserved."

But Hoover had serious liabilities as well. His convictions regarding the proper functions of government were destined to be much more popular during days of prosperity than during days of depression. Moreover, the new President's training, rich in so many respects, was dangerously weak in the field of practical politics. Never before had he held an elective office, never before had he had to deal intimately with a legislative body, jealous of its prerogatives. He was sensitive to criticism, stiff in his personal contacts, cold to newspapermen, and colorless in his public appearances. Most serious of all perhaps, he—like so many products during the golden age of salesmanship—had been overadvertised to the electorate. Depicted as a sort of superman, Hoover's popularity evaporated rapidly when the depression did not disappear at the magician's wand; by 1932 the words "Great Engineer" were usually uttered in a tone of bitterness.

THE NEW ADMINISTRATION

Hoover's inaugural address listed at length the ideals to which he had devoted his leadership. They included:

The preservation of self-government and its full foundations in local government; the perfection of justice whether in economic or in social fields; the maintenance of ordered liberty; the denial of domination by any group or class; the building up and preservation of equality of opportunity; the stimulation of initiative and individuality; absolute integrity in public affairs; the choice of officials for fitness to office; the direction of economic progress toward prosperity and the further lessening of poverty; the freedom of public opinion; the sustaining of education and of the advancement of knowledge; the growth of religious spirit and the tolerance of all faiths; the strengthening of the home; the advancement of peace.

In selecting his cabinet, the new President retained two of his associates in the Coolidge administration, Secretary of the Treasury Mellon and Secretary of Labor Davis. Of the new appointments, the most cherished prize, the Secretaryship of State, went to Henry L. Stimson, who had been Secretary of War under Taft and Governor General of the Philippines under Coolidge. Hoover's good friend President Ray Lyman Wilbur of Stanford University became Secretary of the Interior, while the chairman of the Republican National Committee, Walter F. Brown of Ohio, received the traditional post of Postmaster General.[1]

The retiring Vice-President, Charles G. Dawes, became Ambassador to Great Britain, an important post at any time and in 1929 particularly so on account of Anglo-American disagreement on the issue of naval limitation.

THE GREAT BULL MARKET

During Coolidge's occupancy of the White House stock-market prices had risen almost without interruption. Up to 1927 the advance had been normal since business was expanding and profits were increasing. Thereafter an unnatural and unhealthy trend developed. Business activity leveled off, commodity prices tended to decline, but the prices of common stock soared up and up. On several occasions the market threatened to break, yet in a few days it would steady itself

[1] Other cabinet members were: James W. Good of Iowa, Secretary of War, succeeded during Hoover's first year by Patrick J. Hurley of Oklahoma; William D. Mitchell of Minnesota, Attorney General; Charles Francis Adams of Massachusetts, Secretary of the Navy; Arthur M. Hyde of Missouri, Secretary of Agriculture; Robert P. Lamont of Illinois, Secretary of Commerce, succeeded in 1932 by Roy D. Chapin of Michigan. The Coolidge holdovers eventually resigned: Mellon was succeeded by Ogden L. Mills of New York in 1932, while William N. Doak of Virginia followed Davis as Secretary of Labor in 1930.

and then leap upward again. Hoover's sweeping victory in November, 1928, led to one of the most enthusiastic of these spurts. On September 3, 1929, the bull market reached its final, fantastic peak. Over the course of eighteen months—taking account of split-ups and the issuance of special rights—the stock of United States Steel and Union Carbide had more than doubled in price, that of General Electric, Westinghouse, and Montgomery Ward had tripled, that of Radio Corporation of America had quintupled. Such prices obviously represented speculative, rather than investment, values. American corporations, though enjoying good profits, were not earning the gigantic sums which alone would have justified these transactions. Stock purchasers were gambling recklessly, buying in hope of making a huge profit as the market rose higher and higher.

The situation was as remarkable for the number of people who were involved as for the strange behavior of prices. Back in 1919 when an earlier bull market had been in progress, there had been only six days on which as many as two million shares had been traded on the Exchange. During 1928 and 1929, however, five-million-share days were frequent, and on September 3, 1929, when prices were at their highest, over eight million shares were traded. Before World War I the realm of stocks and bonds was a mysterious area into which the average citizen did not care to venture. The great Liberty Bond drives of war days gave thousands of Americans their first interest in other forms of investment than savings-bank accounts. Further education was provided when large companies like the United States Steel Corporation encouraged stock purchases by their own employees as a form of welfare capitalism. As interest in the stock market grew, Wall Street brokerage houses opened branch offices in all the larger cities, while important banks like the National City Bank of New York had closely affiliated investment branches aggressively scouring the country for new customers. Investment trusts were organized on the plausible principle that purchase of their securities would permit small investors to share in the ownership of diversified lists of holdings chosen by experts. Never before had so many people owned corporation securities. Between 1912 and 1931 the number of stockholders in the Pennsylvania Railroad multiplied three times, in the United States Steel Corporation five, and in the American Telephone and Telegraph Company over thirteen. Much of the political conservatism of the twenties is to be explained by this development.

The most disquieting aspect of the period was the increasing proportion of stocks held on margin—that is, not owned outright, but purchased through a loan from one's broker who held the stock as security. The technique fascinated the uninitiated since through its magic one could apparently buy a great deal of stock with a small investment and then pay for it from the profit realized by its rise. Too late did many small investors discover the catch: if the price of the stock went down they had to put up more and more margin to keep their equity; when they were no longer able to do so, they lost both investment and stock. The banks were involved in these transactions through extensive loans which they made to the brokers for the financing of marginal buying. Such brokers' loans rose from $3,500,000,000 in June, 1927, to over $8,000,000,000 in September, 1929.

The Coolidge administration had watched the bull market with equanimity. Speculators from time to time drew fresh courage from Secretary Mellon's optimistic comments on business conditions, while the usually close-mouthed Coolidge gave the inflationary forces new strength in January, 1928, when he stated publicly that he did not consider brokers' loans too high. The Federal Reserve Board, moreover, took steps during the summer of 1927 to loosen rather than tighten credit. The motive was worthy, since the action was taken at the request of the central banks of England, France, and Germany to assist European business through a threatened crisis. The effect of the lowered interest rates, however, was greatly to increase speculation in Wall Street. So powerful, indeed, was the magnet of the stock boom that Americans began to reduce their investments and loans in Europe in order to buy stocks; worse still, Europeans sent their own funds to America for this purpose. This trend, long continued, presaged disaster for the shaky European economy.

Worried by what was occurring, the Federal Reserve Board tried to stem the trend in 1928 by raising the rediscount rates several times. Yet the bull market continued—fed by more and more brokers' loans. Two days after he took office, President Hoover conferred with the Federal Reserve officials and the conference resulted in an unprecedented action —the board decided to refuse credit to banks which were directly or indirectly financing speculation. Moreover, shortly thereafter Secretary Mellon gave out a curiously veiled warning: "The present situation in the financial markets offers an opportunity for the prudent investors to buy bonds. Bonds are low in price compared to stocks." These actions and warnings halted the bull market only temporarily. Many of the banks, including Federal reserve banks, defied the board's program by offering large credits to the stock market. The government's action resulted in boosting stock-exchange loan rates up to 15 or 20 per cent, but these high rates only encouraged the diversion of money to the call market in preference to less remunerative investments. Even corporations were making such loans from their surplus funds. Throughout the first half of 1929 the Federal Reserve Board maintained its policy of upping the rediscount rates, but the bankers and other lenders of money would not heed the warning.

The American people continued to refuse to believe that disaster lay ahead, and for the most part this was as true of experts as of laymen. Businessmen and college professors talked convincingly of "a new economic era"; the old truism that "what goes up must come down" was amended to read that what goes up will remain on "a permanently high plateau."

THE CRASH

The stock market began to hesitate in September. On the third, prices were at a peak, then they went down but recovered so quickly that on the nineteenth some established new highs. This respite was short-lived. For a month prices fluctuated, but the trend was strongly downward.

Hold On There, Sonny! Ma Columbia fears inflation may cause an explosion. (From the *Rochester Democrat and Chronicle*.)

The decline was not considered alarming and the papers were full of reassuring statements. When Mitchell of the National City Bank arrived in New York from Europe on October 22, he assured the reporters: "I know of nothing fundamentally wrong with the stock market or with the underlying business and credit structure."

On October 23 the situation became suddenly serious when stocks suffered drops averaging eighteen points. The next day panic developed. There were over twelve million transactions on the Stock Exchange and a $240,000,000 bankers' pool, hurriedly organized by the largest financial institutions in the city, had to come to the rescue. Prices were temporarily stabilized, but a few days later they began plunging down again. The blackest day in stock market history was Tuesday, October 29, 1929. An all-time record of 16,410,030 transactions took place; the average prices of fifty leading stocks, as compiled by *The New York Times*, fell nearly forty points. Brokers were deluged with orders to sell from customers who wanted to unload before the market dropped any lower. Many of the sales were involuntary. Traders who had been operating on margin were unable to raise enough money to save their accounts and were sold out. Thousands of Americans saw their life savings thus disappear.

After this terrible day there was no further panic. A stabilizing influence was the welter of comforting statements which came out of Washington and Wall Street. John D. Rockefeller announced: "Believing that fundamental conditions of the country are sound and there is nothing in the business situation to warrant the destruction of values that has taken place on the exchanges during the past week, my son and I have for some days been purchasing sound common stocks." Even with confidence somewhat restored, the process of liquidating the unfortunate marginal traders continued to depress the market and on November 13, prices reached their 1929 lows. In seventy-one days since September 3, American Telephone and Telegraph had fallen from 304 to 197¼, General Electric from 396¼ to 168⅛, Montgomery Ward from 137⅞ to 49¼, and Radio from 101 to 28.

DEPRESSION

So persistent was the belief that America was in a new economic era of perpetual prosperity that even the catastrophe in the stock market failed at first to shake it. On New Year's Day, 1930, Secretary Mellon declared: "I see nothing in the situation which warrants pessimism." And Secretary of Commerce Lamont predicted "for the long run" a continuance of prosperity and progress.

It soon became apparent, however, that the collapse of the stock market was merely the opening crash of thunder for an economic storm of hurricane proportions. Manufacturers found their orders falling off alarmingly, and price cuts failed to revive them. The net income of the 550 largest industrial corporations of the country declined 68 per cent during the next two years. Weak companies were forced out of business, stronger ones operated part time and with sharply reduced personnel. By 1932 industrial production was not more than half what it had been in 1929. The construction business was even harder hit as residential and commercial building together fell to one fifth of their 1929 volume. The railroads, dependent upon a high level of business activity for adequate revenues, were placed in a desperate situation. One third of the nation's mileage passed into receivership. National income dropped from $82,-000,000,000 in 1928 to $40,000,000,000 in 1932.

Wage workers suffered greatly. Until September, 1931, employers generally avoided wage cuts in the belief that their effect would prolong the depression. But even while hourly rates were maintained, the take-home pay of labor was sharply curtailed either because the factories were operating only part time or because what work was available was being spread to provide for as many employees as possible—a practice that was encouraged by the American Federation of Labor. Despite this staggering of employment, more and more workers found themselves laid off. Accurate statistics on unemployment were not obtained and estimates varied widely according to the political leanings of the estimator. Apparently at least ten million Americans were jobless in 1932, however, while in the spring of the following year the number increased to somewhere between thirteen and fifteen million. Moreover, between 1931 and 1933 substantial wage cuts were suffered by those who were fortunate enough to have jobs. The reductions in hourly rates were in most cases less than the reduction in the cost of living, but only a small proportion of the workers enjoyed steady enough employment to be benefited by this.

People in all walks of life found themselves either without income at all or with income sharply reduced. Ministers, teachers, salesmen, salaried executives, and farmers suffered along with industrial workers. Savings painfully accumulated were soon exhausted. People in debt— and there were millions of them—were confronted with specially serious problems. Thousands of farmers and home owners lost their property, and there would have been many more foreclosures had not the real-estate market been so depressed that the creditors postponed taking action. Stock that had been given as collateral for loans was sold when the debts could not be paid, while furniture and automobiles were re-possessed by the finance companies.

If it was a hard time to owe money, it was no great privilege to be a creditor either. Banks were placed in great jeopardy when their debtors defaulted wholesale at a time when stock and real-estate values were so low that the collateral the banks held was often insufficient to cover their outstanding loans. Even during the years of prosperity American banks had failed with alarming frequency, averaging about seven hundred a year. In 1930, however, the number almost doubled when 1326 institutions had to close their doors, while in 1931 the figure rose to 2294 and in 1932 to 1456. It was the smaller state banks, unaffiliated with the Federal Reserve, which failed most frequently, but large city institutions often found themselves in very serious difficulty. Their troubles were multiplied when frightened depositors began to withdraw and hoard their money.

Unfair though it was, the farmers, who had shared very little in the prosperity of the twenties, were particularly hard hit by the depression. Agricultural prices had been considered low in comparison to other prices in 1929, yet by the spring of 1933 the former had fallen 64 per cent from their 1929 level, while the prices of manufactured goods had gone down only 34 per cent. Farmers' cash income dropped from $11,000,000,000 in 1929 to $5,000,000,000 in 1932. The industrialists were able to maintain prices to some extent by reducing production, but the farmers, doing business under ruthlessly competitive conditions, were unable to follow suit. Instead, the warehouses groaned with agricultural surpluses.

CAUSES OF THE DISASTER

The economic collapse, it should be stressed, was world-wide. Some of its roots were to be found in the maladjustment brought about by the war. Millions of lives had been lost and untold property damage caused. A tremendous volume of debt, both internal and intergovernmental, had been created in all the belligerent countries. Europe was crisscrossed by new political frontiers along which economic barriers were speedily erected. Fear for each nation's security led to the maintenance of expensive military establishments. For a few years the seriousness of the fundamental situation was shrouded from view by the fictitious prosperity created by American loans. When the stream of American investment dried up, however, due in part to the superior attractions of the stock market, the European situation deteriorated very rapidly. Stocks fell off in price, unemployment figures grew ominously, and debts were defaulted. America felt the repercussions in many ways, but most directly by a 69 per cent decline in the dollar value of her exports between 1929 and 1932.

Another factor of importance in the world situation was the enormous expansion of production which had occurred during the twenties in the primary industries. For a time international cartels and marketing agreements had succeeded in maintaining prices, but in 1929 and thereafter the market broke disastrously. Coffee fell off one third in price in three months, wool nearly 40 per cent in a year. Other prices declined less rapidly, yet eventually all foodstuffs and raw materials showed the same extreme downward trend. Such great primary producing countries as Canada, Australia, and Brazil were grievously hurt, and their difficulties reacted on the entire world.

America's economic troubles could not all be blamed on outside forces. Factors already discussed—speculation, overextension of credit, inflexible prices, the faulty balance between agriculture and the rest of the economy, the inadequate income of millions of American families —all contributed to the debacle. The country's economic difficulties were increased by abuses in the banking system which permitted dangerous credit inflation during prosperity and endangered the savings of depositors during depression.

During the late thirties much discussion was provoked by the explanation of the depression advanced by Professor Alvin H. Hansen of Harvard University. He stressed the fundamental changes brought about in the American situation by the closing of the frontier, the restriction of immigration, and the declining birth rate. All of these factors tended to reduce the opportunities for private investment. The housing shortage caused by World War I and the new industries of the twenties offered new opportunities for the time being, but their possibilities were largely exhausted by 1929. Nearly all the homes that people could afford had been built, skyscraper office buildings could not find tenants, factories had been expanded to such an extent that their output could not be disposed of in a market where the income did not keep pace with production. Automobiles, radios, refrigerators, and the like had been purchased by most Americans who could afford them—and by some who could not. These were relatively durable goods for which the market in the future would have to be largely a replacement one. Therefore there was little inducement to invest in plants for expanding their production. Savings lay idle in the banks or were gambled in Wall Street because investment outlets were so largely saturated. And as capital expenditures declined, the market for basic goods like steel contracted and the country fell into a declining economic spiral. This "mature economy" theory drew the conclusion that capitalism could only be preserved by government planning and government investment. Although many economists agreed in general with the Hansen thesis, there was considerable debate about what to do about it. Nevertheless it was one of the most powerful influences at work during the later period of the New Deal.

Agri. Market-Act

THE FEDERAL FARM BOARD

In April, 1929, six months before the stock-market crash, Congress met in special session to redeem Republican campaign pledges for farm relief. The administration program called for increased tariff protection and for the establishment of a farm board to promote orderly agricultural marketing. Discussion of the former proposal was protracted and it was not until June, 1930, that the Hawley-Smoot Tariff was passed. The Agricultural Marketing Act, however, was rapidly whipped into shape and received the President's signature on June 15, 1929.

The new law provided for the creation of a Federal Farm Board of nine members to be appointed by the President. A revolving fund of $500,000,000, to be administered by the board, was made available for loans to cooperative marketing associations, owned and controlled by the farmers themselves. In case more drastic measures were necessary, the Farm Board was authorized to establish stabilization corporations to buy and take off the market a sufficient portion of the crop to maintain prices. The Farm Bloc was dubious of the effectiveness of the measure and attempted to amend it by providing for export debentures —a plan whereby the government would pay a subsidy on agricultural exports equivalent to one half the American tariff rate. Hoover so vigorously opposed this that the act was passed in the form which he approved. On the occasion of signing the bill, the President pronounced it "the most important measure ever passed by Congress in aid of a single industry." As chairman of the new Farm Board, he appointed Alexander Legge, president of the International Harvester Company.

The basic idea incorporated in the Agricultural Marketing Act was typical of Hoover. He hoped to help the farmers to help themselves or, in his own words, "with government assistance and an initial advance of capital to enable the agricultural industry to reach a stature of modern business operations by which the farmer will attain his independence and maintain his individuality." The board began its operations in this spirit. Existing cooperative associations were strengthened and enabled to expand; local and state bodies were merged into nation-wide organizations like the Farmers National Grain Corporation, the American Cotton Cooperative Association, the National Livestock Marketing Association, and the National Wool Association. From the revolving fund the cooperatives were permitted to borrow money to build storage facilities, creameries, canning, packing, and processing plants, as well as to finance the marketing of members' crops.

Such activities, however, would benefit farmers more in the future than immediately, and by the end of 1929 the stock-market crash had so upset agricultural prices that the problem of immediate relief was paramount. To an increasing degree, therefore, the Farm Board was diverted from a program of long-range assistance to desperate piecemeal efforts to halt the ruinous fall of prices. Willy-nilly, it had become the first of the great emergency agencies.

In October, 1929, the Farm Board authorized the marketing associations to make loans upon wheat and cotton at fixed prices, and later to purchase some of these commodities. The board felt sufficiently encouraged by this first venture to enlarge its price-pegging policy in 1930. A Grain Stabilization Corporation and a Cotton Stabilization Corporation were established and the two began large-scale operations in the market. During the next three years 370,000,000 bushels of wheat and 1,300,000 bales of cotton were purchased with money advanced by the Farm Board.

During the first two years of these operations the Hoover administration was able to defend the activities of the Farm Board on the ground that, although they had by no means prevented a drastic fall in prices, they had held American prices at a level somewhat higher than those prevailing in the world market. But as time went on the board's activities became progressively less effective. The huge surpluses purchased by the stabilization corporations hung over the market with depressing effect. Moreover, the farmers, trying desperately to maintain their income despite falling prices, continued to produce a large surplus. The Farm Board sought to correct this by asking the farmers for a voluntary reduction of their acreage by 30 per cent. Since each farmer hesitated to reduce his own plantings unless he were sure that all farmers were going to do the same, the plan inevitably failed. More instead of less acreage was planted in 1932.

By the spring of 1932 the necessity of disposing of the Farm Board's surplus holdings was obvious. Large special sales to China, Germany, and Brazil were made, and about one half of the board's stocks was turned over to the Red Cross for distribution to the victims of the depression.

The Farm Board was eventually abolished by executive order of Hoover's Democratic successor in the White House. Losses sustained through loans that could not be recovered and through the disposal of its wheat and cotton holdings brought the total cost of the experiment to about $345,000,000. This was not large compared with other relief expenditures that the government was destined to make, but the Farm Board policy was, nevertheless, a failure since it brought no solution to the fundamental agricultural problem: that of either reducing production or opening up new markets where American staples could be disposed of under conditions which would provide American farmers an adequate income.

THE HAWLEY-SMOOT TARIFF

The other measure of farm relief which the Hoover administration had promised was an increase in the tariff schedules covering agricultural products. The President hoped that the revision would be a limited one and that the rates on industrial goods would be changed only in those exceptional cases where existing duties did not conform with his favorite tariff formula: "the difference in the cost of production at home and abroad." Once the issue was before the House, however, the familiar process of logrolling was soon in evidence. Out of a thousand tariff raises proposed in the so-called Hawley Bill, 75 were on farm products and 925 on manufactured goods. A farm paper warned that if the farmer was not careful he would find himself "paying out $2.00 in increased tariffs on manufactured products, which he must buy, for every $1.00 gain received on farm products." Such warnings were ineffective. Agricultural pressure groups vied with manufacturers' lobbyists in seeking benefits.

Hoover's principal anxiety was to keep the bill free from farm-relief riders and to expand the "flexibility" of the measure through the enlargement of the powers of the Tariff Commission. On both these issues he had difficulty with the Senate. The Farm Bloc succeeded in amending the House bill to include the export debenture plan, while Senator Borah, ever fearful of encroachments by the executive on the legislative branch of the government, headed a Progressive-Democratic-Old Guard-Republican campaign to compel all recommendations of the Tariff Commission to be passed upon by Congress. When a deadlock between the House and the Senate versions of the bill necessitated the appointment of a conference committee, however, the President succeeded in getting the debenture plan out of the bill and the flexible provisions in.

Progressive strength in the Senate had been sufficient to obstruct some of the more excessive demands of the manufacturers' lobbies. Senator Joseph W. Grundy of Pennsylvania, the spokesman of the ultraprotectionists, was in fact disappointed because the measure did not go far enough. But the country's leading economists were of the contrary opinion that the new rates were far too high. Over one thousand of them signed a manifesto appealing to the President to veto the bill. They asserted that the measure would raise prices for the American consumer, would hamper the export of both agricultural and manufactured goods, would be ineffective in helping the producers of staples which had to be sold in the world market, would make it difficult for the interest and principal on American loans abroad to be paid, and would lead to reprisals by foreign governments. Prominent bankers and spokesmen for the export industries also opposed the measure, but it was defended by members of the American Farm Bureau, the National Grange, the American Federation of Labor, and the National Association of Manufacturers. On June 15, 1930, the measure became law with the President's signature.

The Hawley-Smoot Tariff raised the general average of duties from the 33 per cent of the Fordney-McCumber Act to 40 per cent. Rates on farm products were increased from less than 20 per cent to more than 33 per cent. The advantage of this to agriculture, however, was

Careful You Don't Upset Things! A warning against the Hawley-Smoot Tariff. (Reproduced by permission of the *New York World-Telegram*. Copyright, 1929.)

dubious. On the most important staples where an export surplus was produced, the tariff was ineffective in raising prices, while the farmer's cost of living was affected by higher duties on shoes, harnesses, saddles, shovels, spades, lumber, shingles, bricks, and cement. Moreover, the retaliatory measures in foreign countries against which the economists had warned followed speedily. The road of extreme economic nationalism on which the United States had elected to journey was crowded with fellow travelers.

FIGHTING THE DEPRESSION

More than once in American history the Republicans have had the good fortune to witness the beginning of a great upsweep of prosperity coincide with the passage of one of their tariff measures. Such, however, was not the happy experience of the architects of the Hawley-Smoot Act. On the contrary, the business indexes continued their downward spiral relentlessly.

The President had already responded to the crisis with a program typically Hooverian. On November 21, 1929, Henry Ford, Alfred P. Sloane of General Motors, Owen D. Young of General Electric, Walter Gifford of the American Telephone and Telegraph Company, Pierre Du Pont of the great chemical company and other important leaders met the President in a confidential White House conference. He asked for their cooperation in maintaining existing wage rates, in continuing construction, and in spreading available work as widely as possible among employees. The industrialists agreed—contingent upon the President securing from organized labor a pledge not to seek pay increases and to avoid strikes during the crisis. A group of prominent trade-union officials including William Green and John L. Lewis met with Hoover later the same day and gave the required assurances, even going so far as to agree to withdraw certain demands already made. Announcement of this promise of cooperation between industry and labor was given to the press, and two weeks later the President's program was ratified at a White House conference attended by several hundred representatives of the employers and the laborers.

The pledges which had been given were substantially kept by both parties for almost two years. During 1930 an average of only seven out of each hundred firms reporting to the Bureau of Labor Statistics recorded pay cuts as against ninety-two cuts per hundred firms during the depression of 1921. The workers' record was as good. Early in October, 1930, President Hoover, speaking to the American Federation of Labor, congratulated the unions on having held strikes to less than three hundred since their agreement of the preceding September.

Since 1921 Hoover had been an advocate of expanding public works during periods of depression. In November, 1929, he telegraphed governors and mayors all over the country requesting them to increase rather than contract governmental construction, while in his message to Congress the next month he asked for increased Federal appropriations for this purpose. Public-works expenditures by the Federal government rose from their predepression level of around $250,000,000 annually to $412,000,000 in the fiscal year ending June 30, 1930. Thereafter they increased until they reached almost $728,000,000 for the year ending June 30, 1933.

To coordinate the relief activities of private charities and local and state agencies, Hoover established in October, 1930, "The President's Committee for Unemployment Relief" under the chairmanship of Colonel Arthur Woods of New York City. Similar committees of prominent citizens to mobilize relief activities were set up in the various states and local communities.

In September, 1930, the President announced his determination to stop all immigration into the United States on the ground that under existent conditions the newcomers were likely to become public charges. Over the course of the next eight months the influx of foreigners, already sharply cut by the legislation of 1924, was reduced from a monthly rate of about 22,000 to one of 3000. Meantime departures from the country, both voluntary and involuntary, reached 7000 monthly. This latter figure reflected the rigorous deportation policy of the administration. For the four years, 1929–1932, the annual immigration and emigration totals were as follows:

	Immigrants (inward)	Emigrants (outward)
1929	279,678	69,203
1930	241,700	50,661
1931	97,139	61,882
1932	35,576	103,295

This revolution in immigration resulted not solely from the policies of the Hoover administration, but from the disillusionment of foreigners with the United States as a land of unlimited opportunity.

THE DEPRESSION GROWS WORSE

The President and his advisers hoped that these initial steps taken during the first two years of the depression would be successful in tiding over the crisis until recovery could set in. At times victory seemed within grasp; confidence revived and production climbed. Inevitably, however, a relapse would occur. Stocks would plunge down again, factories would lay off more men, farm prices would decline once more. By the fall of 1931 wage cuts were the rule everywhere. The worldwide character of the depression became steadily more apparent, and Hoover struggled during 1931 with the crises caused by the threatened economic collapse of Central Europe and England's departure from the gold standard.

As conditions grew worse, new problems arose. Bank failures and general business uncertainty led to large-scale hoarding both of currency and of gold, while foreigners withdrew funds from the country in alarming volume. This embarrassed the operations of the Federal reserve banks. Although the law required them to maintain only a 40 per cent gold reserve against the Federal reserve notes, the scarcity of eligible commercial paper made it necessary in practice to increase the gold reserve to 75 per cent. This combination of circumstances threatened to force the nation off the gold standard—a possibility which was as terrifying to Herbert Hoover as it had been to Grover Cleveland in the early 1890's.

Elsewhere the contraction of credit brought serious consequences. Home owners and farmers faced foreclosures. Manufacturing concerns and railroads could not borrow. The banks themselves found it difficult to secure additional funds since they could not present eligible collateral to the Federal reserve banks.

Confronted with this situation, the Hoover administration was obliged to expand greatly the range of its activities. At the urging of the President, the banks of the country organized in October, 1931, the National Credit Association with a capital of $500,000,000. Its functions were to rediscount bank assets not eligible in the Federal Reserve System in order to assure the stability of banks against runs and to make loans against the assets of closed banks so that dividends to the depositors might be made. Yet the situation was too serious to be met adequately by this form of self-help. Therefore in January, 1932, Congress accepted the President's recommendation for the creation of the Reconstruction Finance Corporation (RFC). Capital to the amount of $500,-000,000 was advanced by the government, while additional sums up to $1,500,000,000 might be borrowed by the new agency whose function it was to loan money to railroads, banks, insurance companies, and industrial corporations. The first head of this important emergency agency was Charles G. Dawes, the former Vice-President and ambassador to Great Britain. In July, the Emergency Relief and Construction Act gave the RFC greatly extended powers. The amount which it could borrow upon the credit of the United States was doubled and the purposes for which it could advance money were broadened to include the establishment of agricultural-credit banks, loans to states, counties, or cities which were unable to handle their own relief problems, and loans for public or private construction projects which would be self-liquidating.

The Hoover policy of easing the credit situation was further developed through extending the activities of the Federal Land Banks and creating a new system of Federal Home Loan Banks. Since the latter could only loan up to 50 per cent of the appraised value of the mortgagor's property, however, they did little business. To assist the Federal reserve banks and the member banks of the system, the Glass-Steagall Act was passed in February, 1932. This measure permitted the Federal reserve banks to accept a much larger variety of collateral from their borrowers and served the double purpose of freeing vast amounts of gold being held in excess of the legal reserve behind the Federal reserve notes and at the same time making available to the member banks large amounts of credit. The Federal reserve banks now engaged in vast open-market operations, buying more than $1,000,000,000 worth of government bonds during the next few months; this operation was designed to expand credit for the benefit of the whole country. Simultaneously, a vast antihoarding campaign was organized at Hoover's request by Colonel Frank Knox, a prominent Chicago publisher.

PROGRESSIVE AND DEMOCRATIC OPPOSITION

The continuance of the depression despite all that Hoover had done naturally turned public attention more and more to the President's critics. During the first two years of the administration, the conservative Republicans had been in control of the House, but in the Senate their position was not so fortunate. About a dozen of the fifty-six Republicans in the Upper House were progressives; they held the balance of power and, by allying with the thirty-nine Democrats and the sole Farmer-Laborite, they could outvote the administration supporters. The strength of the coalition was demonstrated when Senators Norris and Borah opposed the appointment of Charles Evans Hughes for Chief Justice of the United States in February, 1930, on the ground that his recent legal work had been largely in the employ of the great corporations. Hughes was confirmed, fifty-two to twenty-six, but the size of the opposition vote was a warning of progressive discontent with the conservative trend of recent Supreme Court decisions. Hoover's second appointment to the Court created a much greater controversy. The nominee, John J. Parker of North Carolina, was opposed by organized labor because of decisions which he had handed down as a circuit court judge upholding "yellow-dog" contracts. Negro groups also protested the appointment, and in the end it was rejected, thirty-nine to forty-one. Hoover then substituted Owen J. Roberts of Pennsylvania, who was confirmed by unanimous vote. When another vacancy occurred in 1932, the President obviated the possibility of another bitter fight by naming the liberal and universally respected Benjamin N. Cardozo of New York.

Hoover's difficulties with Congress were greatly increased by the elections of 1930. The Old Guard leaders tried hard to deprive Senator Norris of his seat, even going to the extent of encouraging an obscure grocery clerk also named George W. Norris to enter the Nebraska primary in order to split the votes of the progressive leader and secure the nomination of a conservative. The conspiracy failed, however, when the state courts ruled the grocery-clerk's name off the ballot on a technicality. Norris was renominated and triumphantly reelected. This was only one of the defeats suffered by the administration. The new Senate contained forty-eight Republicans, of whom twelve were progressives, forty-seven Democrats, and one Farmer-Laborite. On the face of the election returns the Republicans appeared to have maintained their control of the House by a very narrow margin, but a number of deaths occurred before the Seventy-Second Congress finally convened in December, 1931. The Democrats found themselves with a majority of four and were able to organize the House, electing John Nance Garner of Texas to the Speakership.

The progressives found the political currents running in their direction for the first time since the Wilson administration. Even during the "lame-duck" session of the old Congress, they showed their strength by pushing through Norris's bill for the government operation of Muscle Shoals. The President, however, subjected the measure to a stinging veto:

This bill would launch the Federal Government upon a policy of ownership and operation of power utilities upon a basis of competition instead of by the proper government function of regulation for the protection of all the people. I hesitate to contemplate the future of our institutions, of our government, and of our country if the preoccupation of its officials is to be no longer the promotion of justice and equal opportunity but is to be devoted to barter in the markets. That is not liberalism, it is degeneration.

The Senate upheld the veto, but the insurgents were unabashed by this setback. A week after the adjournment of Congress in March, 1931, a conference of progressives met in Washington to formulate a program. Prominent in the movement were Senators LaFollette, Norris, and Borah, historian Charles A. Beard, future New Dealers Harold L. Ickes of Chicago, Mayor Frank W. Murphy of Detroit, and labor leader Sidney Hillman. Among the proposals discussed were such anti-Hooverian ideas as large government expenditure for public works, compulsory unemployment insurance, minimum wages, a five-day week, a six-hour day, wider distribution of wealth, social security, child labor laws, and a national economic council.

Neither the Democrats nor the progressives had any opportunity to attempt to secure their objectives until December, 1931, because Hoover refused to heed the demands of his critics that he call the new Congress into special session to deal with the emergency. When the Seventy-Second Congress finally met, conflicts between the legislators and the President were frequent. Hoover regarded the balancing of the budget as an essential step toward recovery. To this principle few of the Congressmen expressed opposition because the theory of deficit spending as a weapon for combatting depressions had as yet few proponents. Nevertheless, it required months of discussion to frame a new revenue bill. The Southern Democrats advocated a manufacturers' sales tax, but the progressive Republican, Representative Fiorello H. LaGuardia of New York, secured enough votes to defeat the proposal. In the end, income-tax rates were raised and nuisance taxes were imposed; the new bill was calculated to increase revenues by $1,000,000,000, but it fell short of what the President requested by some $400,000,000. The President and Congress similarly agreed in principle upon the necessity for economy, but differed on where the axe should be applied. Finally the President secured a reduction in appropriations of only $300,000,000 instead of the $700,000,000 which he had asked.

During this stormy session the President's Congressional opponents raised many issues. One group attempted to challenge the Hawley-Smoot Act with bills which would have made the Tariff Commission answerable to Congress instead of to the Executive, would have directed the President to invite other powers to an international tariff conference, and would have authorized him to negotiate reciprocal trade agreements. Another faction advocated the issuance of more money. The Goldsborough Bill, for example, which passed in the House but failed in the Senate, would have directed the Treasury and Federal Reserve System to expand currency and credit until prices rose to the averages prevailing between 1921 and 1929. A third faction insisted that the Federal government make large appropriations to provide either work or relief for the unemployed. Speaker Garner and Representative Rainey of Illinois were sponsors of a bill which proposed to set in motion a vastly expanded program of public works, while Senators Wagner of New York, LaFollette of Wisconsin, and Costigan of Colorado, along with Representative LaGuardia of New York, were outspoken in their demand for a more adequate program of unemployment relief. All of these measures, however, were successfully blocked by the President.

Nevertheless, not all the work of the progressives was frustrated. They enjoyed an important triumph in securing the passage of the Norris-LaGuardia Anti-Injunction Act in March, 1932. By this law the public policy of the United States was thus stated:

Whereas, under prevailing economic conditions, . . . the individual unorganized worker is commonly helpless to exercise actual liberty of contract and to protect his freedom of labor, and thereby to obtain acceptable terms and conditions of employment, wherefore, though he should be free to decline to associate with his fellows, it is necessary that he should have full freedom of association, self-organization, and designation of representatives of his own choosing, to negotiate the terms and conditions of his employment, and that he shall be free from the interference, restraints, or coercion of employers of labor . . . in the activities for the purpose of collective bargaining or other mutual aid or protection . . .

Yellow-dog contracts, whereby employees agreed not to join a labor union as a condition of employment, were declared to be against this public policy and were not enforceable in any Federal court. Then followed a most specific listing of legitimate union activities which might not be prohibited by any Federal court injunction. Such orders in labor disputes were not entirely banned, but the circumstances under which they could be issued were strictly defined and provision was made for jury trial in any contempt-of-court case arising out of such instances, unless the alleged contempt occurred in the presence of the court. By this important law, organized labor obtained the substance of rights of which the Clayton Act of 1914 had proved to provide only the shadow. With some signs of reluctance Hoover signed this measure.

THE BONUS REVIVED

From the World War I veterans came an appeal for the immediate payment of the bonus. A year before Congress had enacted a measure over Hoover's veto which permitted the veterans to borrow up to 50 per cent on their certificates. In 1932, however, when the depression was even more severe, a demand went up for the payment of the whole amount. A bill to this end, introduced by Representative Wright Patman of Texas, passed the House of Representatives, but, under pressure from the President, was rejected by the Senate in June, 1932. The incident had an unhappy sequel. Starting in May, an increasingly large "Bonus Army" made up of unemployed veterans congregated in Washington to lobby for the Patman Bill. On July 16 Congress adjourned without conceding the veterans' demands, but the Bonus Army lingered on disconsolately in their shanty villages on the outskirts of the capital. Hoover tried to get rid of the unwelcome horde through using government funds to pay their fares home. Some six thousand availed themselves of this help, but five thousand others remained in the city, many of them with their wives and children.

On July 28 they became involved in a fracas with the police in which two veterans were killed and several policemen were injured. Acting immediately upon a request from the District Commissioners, the President called out the army to restore order. Under command of General Douglas A. MacArthur, four troops of cavalry, four of infantry, a machine-gun squadron, and six tanks completely dispersed the Bonus Army and evicted the men from their camps. Whether by accident or design, the shacks in which they had lived were set on fire and burned to the ground. Hoover's defenders stressed the patience which the President had hitherto shown in handling the situation and the fact that no lives were lost in the final eviction; they asserted that a large proportion of the demonstrators were Communists or hoodlums—not veterans at all. Moreover, they said, the shanty village was becoming a menace to the health of Washington. Whatever justification there might have been for the action, however, the incident not only did untold damage to the President's reputation as a great humanitarian, but brought home in shocking fashion to the country the seriousness of the nation's economic situation.

Between President Hoover and his liberal critics there was a clear-cut difference of principle. Hoover believed in using Federal funds and credit to combat the depression, but he thought that the proper place for most of the money to be expended was in strengthening banks, railroads, and other corporations. By so doing, small depositors and investors would be protected, employment would be maintained and expanded, and a process of economic recovery set in motion which would in the end benefit everyone. His philosophy also accepted public works so long as they fulfilled a real need, the distribution of food and clothing to prevent actual physical suffering, and the advance of Federal funds to the states under careful restrictions. But he opposed the direct expenditure of Federal funds to relieve either the unemployed or the farmers, hard-pressed by both ruinously low prices and drought. He held that such direct relief would create a burdensome bureaucracy and destroy the initiative and self-reliance of the recipients.

But Hoover's critics contended that by 1931 and 1932 a condition and not a theory confronted the nation. Panhandlers lined the streets and discouraged men sold apples on the corners. Long breadlines were everywhere to be seen outside private and local relief headquarters. Private charity was near the end of its resources, local governments were threatened with insolvency, the states were without adequate resources. The problem was too big for any lesser agency than the Federal government itself. Moreover, these opponents of the President asserted that money poured into the financial pyramid at the top through the Reconstruction Finance Corporation never seeped down to the bottom. A demand arose for measures that would put purchasing power again into the hands of the millions of individual victims of the depression.

As the election of 1932 approached, it was obvious that not only the harassed President but bankers and businessmen generally had suffered an enormous loss of prestige. A revolution in public opinion had occurred, and those who had been the lords of creation in 1929 were now in disrepute.

18

Hoover's Quest for World Stability

ALTHOUGH PRESIDENT HOOVER FAILED IN MANY RESPECTS IN HIS DO-mestic policies, his international dealings were, on the whole, successful. As has been mentioned, his background and training had been largely international. His work as a mining and railroad expert had carried him to many foreign lands where he became well acquainted with both local and world issues. During World War I his relief management, which was both economic and diplomatic, proved to be conspicuously competent. As Secretary of Commerce during most of the twenties he had become a leading authority in the field of international economics.

During his four years in the presidency, Hoover attempted to use his position and experience to promote world peace. Not only as a Quaker did he oppose war, but he considered armed conflict as a disastrous waste. In the course of the 1928 campaign he set the stage for his administration when he said on August 11, 1928: "Our foreign policy has one primary object, and that is peace. We have no hates; we wish no further possessions; we harbor no military threats." And in his inaugural he promised that the United States would take "a practical part in supporting all useful international undertakings. We not only desire peace with the world, but to see peace maintained throughout the world. We wish to advance the reign of justice and reason toward the extinction of force."

FURTHER REJECTION OF THE LEAGUE AND THE COURT

President Hoover did not believe, however, that the League of Nations was a satisfactory agency for the promotion of the peace that he desired. In his inaugural address he asserted:

Our people have determined that we should make no political engagements such as membership in the League of Nations, which may commit us in advance as a nation to become involved in the settlement of controversies between other countries. They adhere to the belief that the independence of America from such obligations increases its ability and availability for service in all fields of human progress.

Thus Hoover rejected what he considered an entangling alliance and during his term in office there was no public demand developing to cause him to change his policy.

On the other hand, he was willing to have the United States participate directly or indirectly with certain of the League's activities which were not of a political nature. For example, the American adherence to the World Court was strongly urged by Hoover. On March 4, 1929, he said:

American statesmen were among the first to propose, and they have constantly urged upon the world, the establishment of a tribunal for the settlement of controversies of a justiciable nature. The Permanent Court of International Justice in its major purpose is thus peculiarly identified with American ideals and American statesmanship.

Then he concluded with the assertion that he hoped "we may take our proper place in a movement so fundamental to the progress of peace."

This action was to be based upon the so-called Root formula, which had been worked out by a committee, of which Elihu Root was a leading member, sponsored by the League Council in December, 1928. The formula, completed by the fall of 1929, attempted to solve the differences of opinion which had developed between the United States Senate and the League Council back in 1926. First of all the formula provided that all requests for advisory opinions be submitted to the United States. Next, any American objections to these opinions might be discussed with and among the parties concerned. And, finally, the United States might withdraw from Court membership, without endangering its interests, were the other members to refuse to admit that the United States had a "vital" interest.

Both the members of the League and the American State Department found this formula satisfactory. As early as December, 1929, Secretary of State Stimson signed the protocols for the admission of the United States into the World Court with the Root reservations. Not until a year later, however, did Hoover submit the protocols to the Senate for ratification, accompanied by an urgent request for speedy approval. In support of this request, the President wrote:

The provisions of the protocols free us from any entanglement in the diplomacy of other nations. We cannot be summoned before this Court, we can from time to time seek its service by agreement with other nations. These protocols permit our withdrawal from the Court at any time without reproach or ill-will. . . . Through the Kellogg-Briand Pact we have pledged ourselves to the use of pacific means in settlement of all controversies. Our great nation, so devoted to peace and justice, should lend its cooperation to this effort of nations to establish a great agency for pacific settlements.

But like his predecessors, Hoover found it difficult to induce the Senate to approve even so small a step as this toward international co-operation. Although a majority of public opinion and 75 per cent of the press indicated support for the President's plea, another battalion of death was formed in the Upper House, sufficiently large to prevent the issue from coming to a vote during the remainder of Hoover's term. These opponents of internationalism found backing in their obstructionist tactics from the isolationist press, headed by the Hearst papers, which once more headlined charges that the Court was nothing more than an agency of the League with a membership consisting of "international robbers."

THE RENEWAL OF NAVAL DISARMAMENT

Following the comparative failure of the Geneva Conference of 1927, Secretary of the Navy Wilbur secured the introduction of the so-called Butler Cruiser Bill into Congress in November, 1927, providing for the construction of twenty-five light cruisers, nine destroyers, thirty-two submarines, and five aircraft carriers at a cost of $725,000,000. It was stipulated, however, that the building of the cruisers and carriers was subject to the provisions of the Washington Conference and that if another limitation conference were called the President might suspend all or part of this construction program.

While Congress was beginning the debate on this measure, there came the British announcement that they had abandoned two thirds of their proposed naval-building project. To many Americans, especially the advocates of a big navy, this step came too late. The United States should complete the Cruiser Bill provisions within five years and follow a replacement program during the next twenty years. This opinion did not go unchallenged. Senator Borah led the attack upon the bill, asserting that it would lead to "immediate and inevitable war." He was supported by many groups, among them the Quakers, the Federal Council of Churches, and numerous peace societies. This opposition had its way; the Butler Bill was withdrawn in favor of a substitute which cut the program to fifteen cruisers and one carrier at a cost of $274,000,000. The new Navy Cruiser Bill passed the House in March, 1928, but, despite Coolidge's plea for immediate affirmative action, the Senate, through Borah's continued fight, held it up until February, 1929. While this measure did prevent the hurling of a direct challenge against Great Britain, it did threaten a new naval race.

Such was the situation when Hoover assumed the presidency. The new executive worried lest another race begin among the naval nations of the world which might in turn lead to the war he hated. The problem was further complicated by the fact that England and France were having their troubles over parity definitions, while the League was facing the difficult task of trying to arrange a general disarmament conference. True to his inaugural promise, Hoover began negotiations for another meeting of the nations who had signed the Washington Treaty. First he authorized Charles Dawes, now ambassador to England, to confer with the new Labor Prime Minister, Ramsey MacDonald, over the possibility of complete naval parity between the two nations. The talks were quite successful, for most of the difficulties that had appeared at Geneva were ironed out before the end of the summer of 1929. To carry on the rapprochement, MacDonald accepted an invitation to visit President Hoover in early October. Substantial agreement on many issues was reached during their conferences and even before they were over, Great Britain formally invited France, Italy, Japan, and the United States to another disarmament meeting to be held at London. Acceptances from all were quickly received.

The London Naval Conference opened on January 21, 1930. The seven-man American delegation, headed by Secretary Stimson, was ably selected.[1] There were high hopes of success because the preliminary discussions between Great Britain and the United States had developed an understanding that had been lacking at Geneva. Moreover, the admirals and other big navy advocates who had helped to sabotage the efforts in 1927 were conspicuous by their absence.

Despite the favorable auguries, the actual conference did not go smoothly at the start. There was considerable wrangling over unessential details, and France almost broke up the meeting when she sought defensive military agreements with the others before she would consider continuing the naval limitations program.

Gradually, however, the three largest naval powers found a satisfactory solution to the limitation problem, contained in the London Naval Treaty of April 22, 1930. This provided first of all for foregoing the

[1] The other members were Ambassador Dawes, Ambassador Hugh Gibson, Secretary of the Navy Charles Francis Adams, Republican Senator Reed of Pennsylvania, Democratic Senator Robinson of Arkansas, and Dwight Morrow.

construction of the capital ships allowed under the Washington Treaty [1] and for having Great Britain scrap five capital ships, the United States three, and Japan one before the end of 1931. Thus the total capital-ship tonnage would be: for Great Britain, 474,750 (15 ships); the United States, 464,300 (15 ships); and Japan, 272,070 (9 ships). Aircraft-carrier tonnage was also agreed to at approximately the same ratio. Class A cruisers carrying 8-inch guns were limited to 10,000 tons each, with the United States allotted 18, Great Britain 15, and Japan 12. The number of Class B cruisers with 6-inch guns was not allotted, but the total tonnage for each power was limited; the same was true of destroyers and submarines.[2]

An unusual feature was the "escape" or "escalator" clause, which allowed any signatory to build above treaty limits if some other power, not bound by this London agreement, started a construction program which tended to threaten the safety of the signatory. The treaty was to continue in operation until December 31, 1936, with another con-

[1] The United States had been authorized to lay down ten capital ships, Britain ten, and Japan five before 1936.
[2] The tonnage of Class B cruisers was: for the United States, 143,500; for Great Britain, 192,200; and for Japan, 100,450. The advantage for Great Britain was offset by the American superiority in the larger Class A cruisers. For destroyers, the ratio was 10:10:7. For submarines, each of the nations was allowed 52,700 tons, but the maximum size was limited.

Navalism. Japan tilts the scales in her own favor despite the 5-5-3 ratio. (By Bishop in the *St. Louis Star-Times*.)

ference called for 1935 to discuss the feasibility of extending the arrangements beyond that date.

The London Naval Treaty had its weaknesses. France and Italy found fault with the negotiations and with the proposed ratios and refused to enter the agreement. This threatened to upset the whole settlement since either French or Italian construction might cause one of the signatory powers to invoke the escalator clause and embark upon a new building program. American admirals and naval experts, moreover, warned that the limitations agreed upon would prevent the American navy from satisfactorily defending the United States and its outlying possessions.

On the other hand, however, the long desired parity with Great Britain in all naval categories was at last achieved. Moreover, if the signatories lived up to the agreement, the menace of a naval construction race was ended during the life of the London Treaty. Savings of at least $300,000,000 were thereby assured American taxpayers. Yet the United States did not build up to treaty strength and so lost much of its naval superiority over Japan, which took full advantage of her quota.

In the United States, the reception of the London Treaty was, on the whole, good. True, there was some speculation among the citizenry about the cost of bringing the nation up to parity, but that quickly disappeared. The navy personnel, as has been mentioned, did not like the agreement, and they were backed by the jingoist press which asserted that the American envoys had become the dupes of Britain and Japan. Some newspapers even avowed that the United States had become involved in a secret entangling agreement with the other signatories.

When the treaty was submitted to the Senate for ratification early in July, 1930, some of the members of the Upper House demanded that President Hoover turn over to them all of the documents concerning the London meeting. This Hoover refused to do because it was contrary to precedent and might injure future treaty making. Further Senatorial requests for information led him to agree to allow certain key Senators to see all the private papers. Enough of the members were satisfied to approve the treaty on July 21 by a vote of fifty-eight to nine. To make sure, however, that there were no strings attached, the Senate then proceeded to resolve that the nation was not bound by any secret commitment.

President Hoover was not ready to stop with the London Treaty. Thus in 1932 when the World Disarmament Conference, sponsored by the League of Nations, met in Geneva, the American delegates asked for international approval for scrapping all offensive weapons of war. The reception of this proposal was by no means enthusiastic. France led the way in tabling it; she refused to reduce her military arm without adequate proof that she would not be attacked. Hoover was disappointed, of course, but he continued his quest for limitation when the American envoys followed his suggestion by asking that all nations represented at Geneva reduce their armaments approximately 30 per cent. Although there seemed to be widespread support for this proposal, nothing came of it. Even while this disarmament meeting was in session, the peace of the world was threatened by the growing hostilities between Japan and China on the other side of the globe.

THE MORATORIUM

The quest for improved international relations was complicated by a series of events in the economic field which tended to disrupt the settlements that had been made concerning war debts and reparations. By the summer of 1931 France feared that a proposed customs union between Germany and Austria might develop into a political and military alliance. In an attempt to prevent such action, which she believed was aimed at her, France withdrew her credit from a large Austrian bank, already hard hit by the depression. That bank was compelled to close its doors and, with its failure, a number of financially associated German institutions, both banks and insurance companies, tottered on the brink of bankruptcy. In turn, foreign credit, particularly American, was quickly withdrawn from Germany to escape engulfment in the threatened economic collapse. Moreover, American banks holding large amounts in German short-term notes were subjected to worry over the situation.

Fearing an economic catastrophe greater than the stock-market crash of 1929, Hoover acted quickly to avert it. Congress was not in session at the time, but the President secured the consent of twenty-one Senators and eighteen Representatives, all key men and from both parties, to a proposition which he made public on June 20, 1931. This proposed "the postponement during one year of all payments on intergovernmental debts, reparations and relief payments, both principal and interest." [1] On July 6 Hoover was able to report that the European nations concerned had given their approval to the proposal and about two weeks later, at the London Conference on Recovery from the

[1] In December, 1931, Congress approved this moratorium: the Senate vote was 79 to 15, the House, 317 to 100. This act stipulated that the suspended payments should be paid over a ten-year period at 4 per cent interest.

Depression, the international bankers agreed to a similar moratorium on private international obligations.

There is little doubt that this moratorium did ease the international situation. Moreover, for the first time the United States recognized a definite relationship between war debts and reparations. Still there were problems to be considered. German banks were in bad straits as a result of the earlier complication. Fortunately a number of foreign banks, including the Federal Reserve of New York, loaned a total of approximately $100,000,000 in short-term notes to the ailing institutions. While this action saved some of the German banks, it did not prevent the withdrawal of gold from one country after another. Nation after nation was forced to go off the gold standard, culminating in the September, 1931, decision of Great Britain that she too must cease redeeming her currency with that bullion. Thereafter it seemed as though nothing could be done to avert international disaster. Each nation thought primarily of itself. Tariff walls were raised higher in an effort to protect domestic conditions and the local currency media were generally inflated to spur a return to prosperity.

While the moratorium was in effect, the French premier, Pierre Laval, visited President Hoover in late October, 1931. After a series of conversations during which the President soothed Laval's troubled feelings over the failure of the United States to confer specially with France before the moratorium was declared, they both agreed that the question of intergovernmental debts must be considered again before the moratorium was over in order to alleviate the depression and to try to maintain the gold standard. While there were no actual commitments binding their respective countries, Hoover and Laval were ready to do all in their power to make the solution a success. The initiative, they asserted, must be taken by Europe in connection with German reparations.

Germany's creditors took full advantage of the Hoover-Laval proposal and in June, 1932, they met with German representatives at Lausanne, Switzerland. By July 8 they had agreed practically to wipe away more than 90 per cent of the original reparations demands, cutting down their claims to approximately $700,000,000, payable in 5 per cent German bonds. Likewise Germany made provision for the repayment of the loans advanced to her under the Dawes and Young Plans. This Lausanne agreement, however, had a string attached to it. The creditors of Germany said they would not ratify until they had made a satisfactory arrangement for scaling down their own obligations to the United States.

The appeal for war-debt reductions began to reach the United States during the vigorous presidential contest of 1932. The Democrats had already gone on record in their platform against cancellation of those debts. Moreover, neither major party dared to come out in favor of the European proposal because they feared that the American voters, hard hit by the depression, regarded the payment of the war debts as a means of alleviating their own economic distress.[1] Likewise linked with the issue was the matter of reducing armaments and, since the European nations showed no willingness to conform to American wishes on that subject, the Americans were therefore all the more unwilling to follow up the Lausanne proposition with counterreductions.

When Great Britain asked the United States for an opportunity to discuss a reduction of the December 15, 1932, payment, President Hoover and President-elect Roosevelt could not agree as to the method of conference. Thus nothing was done. Consequently, France and four other nations defaulted on their payments, while Great Britain and the remaining debtors did send the full amount of their semiannual obliga-

---

[1] Actually everything pointed to the fact that public opinion favored a benevolent policy toward these debts.

Now If He Just Doesn't Try to Bring His Trunk Along. (Copyright, 1931, by the *Chicago Tribune*.)

tions. They intimated, however, that this might be the last time they could do so unless a new arrangement were made. None was, and thereafter the whole problem was left for the new administration to deal with.

THE NEW PAN-AMERICANISM

The same spirit which President Hoover showed in trying to pacify world troubles was evinced in his Latin-American policy. Shortly after his victory in the 1928 election he visited many of the Latin American countries where he studied the local situations and made contacts which were to prove important later on. Indeed, it was while he was on this trip that he was approached by the leaders of Peru, Bolivia, and Chile on the subject of the Tacna-Arica controversy. Partly through the knowledge he acquired during his visit he was able to find the solution to that long-standing problem. Moreover, this journey aided in bettering the relations between the United States and Latin America; the citizens of the other republics appreciated the fact that such a prominent American came to visit them.

During his term in the White House, Hoover did his best to remove the fears and suspicions which Latin America held toward his country and thereby fostered an improved feeling of cooperation and friendliness in the Western Hemisphere. True, he was aided in this respect by some of the incidents near the close of Coolidge's administration—the naming of Dwight Morrow as minister to Mexico, the drawing up of the Clark Memorandum, and the Washington Conference on Conciliation and Arbitration were the most notable—but they would not have helped the situation long had Hoover not carried on and extended the policy of good neighborliness.

The first official pronouncement of this desire came in Hoover's inaugural address. He said:

I have lately returned from a journey among our sister Republics of the Western Hemisphere. I have received unbounded hospitality and courtesy as their expression of friendliness to our country. We are held by particular bonds of sympathy and common interest with them. . . . We wish only for the maintenance of their independence, the growth of their stability, and their prosperity. . . . Fortunately the New World is largely free from the inheritance of fear and distrust which have so troubled the Old World. We should keep it so.

Yet it was difficult for President Hoover to allay fear and distrust completely because the depression hit some of the Latin republics hard and, to make matters worse, the increase of the American tariff rates under the Hawley-Smoot Act reacted unfavorably upon Latin-American commerce. Half of the republics witnessed the overturn of their governments, largely as a result of troublesome economic times. Several of the Latin-American states had to announce suspension of interest payments on their foreign obligations in October, 1931. President Hoover did not press for payment, however, nor did he threaten military intervention for forcible collection as some of his predecessors had done under similar circumstances. Moreover, the new governments established by those revolutions were almost immediately recognized by the United States as *de facto* ones.

THE WITHDRAWAL FROM HAITI

It was Hoover's attitude toward countries in which the United States had previously intervened and in some of which marines were still stationed which indicated that the spirit of good will and friendship were not passing fancies. For example, in Haiti President Louis Borno, serving his second term, became increasingly unpopular as 1929 progressed because of the popular belief that he was subservient to the wishes of the United States. In December, a strike of students, supported by Haitian politicians, brought the matter to a climax. An attack was made on the American marines near Port-au-Prince, and in the ensuing struggle six Haitians were killed and some thirty wounded.

A few days before this affray, President Hoover had referred to Haiti in his annual message to Congress, suggesting that a commission be sent to the island preparatory to clarifying American policy toward the protectorate. When the news of the outbreak reached him, Hoover sent a special message to the legislature, asking for immediate action. Congress quickly responded by appointing the so-called Forbes Commission in February, 1930, to conduct a thorough investigation of Haiti's problems, to ascertain how the obligations of the United States could be fulfilled, and to suggest when the American troops might be withdrawn.

After a two-months' study the Forbes Commission reported its findings to President Hoover. First of all it praised the work done by American officials in the field of transportation, health, and sanitation. On the other hand, the commissioners concluded that there had been little progress in training the Haitians to govern themselves, the American policy being based "upon the assumption that the occupation would continue indefinitely." Then they went on to recommend that the 1915 treaty rights remain in force until 1936 except where mutual agreement might modify them, that the military high commissioner be replaced by a civilian leader, that the Haitians be trained to take over control of their civil administration and national guard, that a new president be elected by the Haitian legislature, and that the American marines be gradually withdrawn.

With the backing of Congress, President Hoover quickly carried these recommendations into effect. The little-liked Borno was replaced by Provisional President Eugene Roy toward the end of April, 1930, and in October the legislature selected Stenio Vincent as the regular executive. Meantime, High Commissioner General Russell was replaced by Dana G. Munro, a civilian authority on Latin-American affairs. Then, under an agreement of August, 1931, Americans were gradually withdrawn from the various government departments. Differences over financial control, the national guard, and the withdrawal of the marines delayed a settlement until September, 1932, when a treaty was drawn up for the complete American civil and military retirement from Haiti by the end of 1934, although the United States might continue to keep a watchful eye on Haitian finances after that date. Some Haitian opposition to this treaty delayed its acceptance until after Hoover left office. President Roosevelt, however, was able to effect a solution, primarily based on the 1932 treaty, and the last of the marines left Haiti on August 15, 1934.

ENDING MILITARY INTERVENTION IN NICARAGUA

As far as Nicaragua was concerned, it appeared that American relations would be good because shortly before Hoover entered office the Nicaraguan President Moncada had agreed to substitute a national guard for the army, while the United States had promised to withdraw its marines when that guard was ready to police the country. Then in November, 1929, Secretary Stimson asserted that the American garrison of about twelve hundred troops would be withdrawn as quickly as possible. There was some delay because the leaders of both Nicaraguan parties objected. The Secretary then said in January, 1931, that only five hundred troops would remain after the following June, and supplemented that statement in May with the declaration that all marines would leave by the autumn of 1932.

The situation was not to be solved so easily, for early in April, 1931, the rebel leader, Augusto Sandino, openly attacked the Moncada administration. All the efforts of the national guard and the marines could not curb his raids on Nicaraguan communities. At least nine American civilians lost their lives. So serious did the problem become that Secretary Stimson was compelled to inform the Americans resident in the interior of Nicaragua on April 17 that they should retire to the settlements along the coast because of the inability of the marines to protect them. This Stimson statement aroused a storm of debate in the Senate. Some of the members of the Upper House believed it was the proper policy; dollar diplomacy must go. There were others, however, who felt that it was an indication of weakness on the part of the United States. This outburst caused Stimson to clarify his statement. He said that the marines were not trained to fight in the vast jungle area where Sandino had his headquarters, whereas the national guard was. Then he continued with the assertion that the American navy would stand by off the coast, ready to protect "the lives of our nationals wherever they may be found."

Additional complications followed when Sandino's men killed five marines during one of their raids in April, 1932. Again there was Senatorial protest that the lives of American troops were being lost merely to protect a handful of American businessmen. A resolution was introduced, calling for the immediate withdrawal of the marines. And indeed the number had been reduced from almost six thousand to less than one thousand by that time. This Senate proposal might have been carried into effect, however, had not the American government previously committed itself to the supervision of the Nicaraguan election, scheduled for the following fall. Living up to that prior pledge, nearly five hundred marines guarded the polls on election day, November 6, 1932, and prevented the disorders that had been so characteristic in the past. Rear Admiral Clark Woodward of the United States Navy served as head of the election board.

Victory was gained by Liberal Juan Sacasa. Despite the fact that Sandino asserted he would not recognize the new executive, Sacasa took office without incident on January 2, 1933. Shortly after this installation, the last of the American marines boarded the naval vessels off the coast and left the country. Another venture in dollar diplomacy was thereby concluded.

MEXICAN PROBLEMS

Emilio Portes Gil became provisional executive of Mexico in November, 1928. He was not particularly well liked, being considered nothing more than a puppet of the powerful Plutarco Calles. Shortly after, a regular election was scheduled for November, 1929. The political opponents of the administration decided that they would not have a chance in the ensuing campaign so they appealed to the element which had become thoroughly dissatisfied with the anti-church attitude of the government to participate in a revolution. The Catholic group agreed and on March 3, 1929, the day before Hoover took office, the uprising occurred.

President Hoover promptly acted in support of the Gil government. Not only did he proclaim an embargo on all exports of arms and ammunition to the rebellious forces in line with the Arms Embargo Resolution of 1922, but he allowed the Mexican government to buy military supplies in the United States. Moreover, the State Department refused to consider the rebels as belligerents or to receive any of their representatives. Thanks in part to this American attitude, the Mexican administration was able to crush the uprising by the beginning of May, 1929.

Hoover also helped to improve relations between the United States and Mexico by naming the able J. Reuben Clark to succeed Dwight Morrow. Clark continued the policy of friendship which Morrow had instituted. Moreover, the United States immediately recognized Ortiz Rubio, victor in the election of November, 1929. The new executive showed his gratitude by visiting the United States, where he was well received.

Just before Hoover left office another move to strengthen the accord between the two nations was taken. On February 1, 1933, a treaty was signed providing for the settlement of some of the differences which had arisen in connection with control over the Rio Grande in the El Paso region, a movement which, it was hoped, would end the danger from floods.

NONINTERVENTION IN CUBA

The Cuban situation was difficult during the Hoover administration. Cuban President Gerardo Machado had become practically a dictator with the result that popular unrest grew, much aggravated by the falling price of sugar during the depression. Unfortunately, Hoover appointed as envoy Harry Guggenheim, an inexperienced diplomat. The ambassador did his best to keep Machado in office, aiding him in every way, financially and otherwise.

As the Cuban unrest mounted, it became evident in the United States that civil war might break out at any time. Consequently, some Senators urged the United States to intervene toward the close of 1930. Secretary Stimson, however, refused to heed the proposal. He asserted that only actual Cuban chaos warranted such intervention; until that chaos developed, the United States would merely maintain a "close watch" of the situation. In the summer of 1931 an abortive revolt did take place, but the Hoover administration refused to use the Platt

Amendment as an excuse for reestablishing military control. Instead, a completely "hands off" policy was followed, with no effort being made to establish an arms embargo.

To many Cubans the attitude of the Hoover administration was not appreciated. Although pleased that there was no intervention, they felt that the United States was trying to maintain in office the dictatorial Machado, whose regime was becoming more tyrannical. In both countries a demand arose for the abrogation of the Platt Amendment.

For Latin America generally, Hoover followed the policy of recognizing *de facto* presidents without examining the means by which they obtained office. While no regular Pan-American conferences were held, he helped the cause by proclaiming on May 28, 1930, that thereafter April 14 would be celebrated as Pan-American Day. He announced that the American flag would be flown from all government buildings on that date and invited "the schools, civic associations, and the people of the United States generally to observe the day with appropriate ceremonies, thereby giving expression to the spirit of continental solidarity and friendly feeling" which Americans had toward the peoples of the other hemisphere republics.

President Hoover tried hard to alleviate conditions in Puerto Rico. Indeed, he even visited the island and saw at first hand the poverty that was rampant there. On his return to the United States, the President secured from Congress increased appropriations for the improvement of insular conditions. Theodore Roosevelt, Jr., new governor general of the island, also showed great energy and vigor in attempting to end the sickness, the hunger, and the economic hardships which prevailed through the island. The Puerto Ricans appreciated this assistance, with the result that there were few political controversies during the Hoover regime.

THE MOVEMENT TOWARD PHILIPPINE INDEPENDENCE

The question of Philippine independence arose again during Hoover's term. This time, however, the impetus came largely from the United States, with the depression, rather than altruism, playing no small part in developing that impetus. American farmers, their income falling rapidly, did not like to face competition from Filipino cottonseed oil, sugar, dairy products, and cordage, which were allowed to enter duty free. Nor did American workers care to see their jobs taken by cheap Filipino laborers. Moreover, the threat of Japanese aggression in the Far East caused many Americans to believe that the Philippines could not continue to be protected without the expenditure of vast sums which the American taxpayers were not eager to appropriate, and even then it was questionable whether the defense would be adequate.

This combination of anti-imperialists, farmers, and workers was able to exert sufficient pressure upon Congress to pass the Hawes-Cutting Bill on January 12, 1933, despite the objections of another bloc. That bloc consisted of American investors in Filipino resources, the advocates of a bigger navy who saw in the retention of the islands an opportunity to press their cause, and the supporters of imperialism.

The Hawes-Cutting Bill provided for the framing of a constitution by a specially convened Philippine convention, which was to be submitted to the Filipino voters for approval, along with the question of whether independence were desired. It was believed that this initial procedure would take about two years. Were approval given, the Philippines would then begin a ten-year intermediate or probationary period, during which the position of governor general was to be abolished and the American civil control ended except for the supervisory powers exercised by a new American official, the high commissioner. Throughout the probationary period, however, the President of the United States was to be allowed some regulation of Philippine legislation, the Supreme Court could review legal cases, and the foreign problems of the islands would be supervised by the United States. Likewise during those ten years, American military and naval forces would occupy the Philippines. Economically, the right to send commodities to the United States duty free was to be gradually reduced and the competitive commodities placed under a quota system. Moreover, such duty-free exports were to be taxed by the probationary government on a rising scale to help meet the running expenses of government. Immigration to the United States was practically to end.

After the ten years' probation was concluded, complete independence would automatically begin. Then all free trade with the United States would end, unless some commercial arrangement between the two nations effected reciprocity. The United States would be allowed to maintain military establishments and naval bases in the islands and would try to secure an international agreement for the neutralization of the Philippines.

President Hoover wrote a long veto message on January 13, 1933, in which he said he refused to sign the bill because of the economic provisions which he believed would lead to "a degenerating economic and social life, with all its governmental difficulties." He also asserted that during the probationary period American civil control would be weakened "to a point of practical impotence." Nor did he think that the Philippines were prepared to provide the military forces necessary for the preservation of internal order or external defense. The President was supported in his veto by the majority of his cabinet members who considered that if the plan went into effect the United States would be betraying its trust. Secretary Stimson asserted that it would mean a hazardous future for the islands, as well as the disruption of political stability in the Far East and the loss of American prestige in the western Pacific.

The opposing factions were sufficiently strong to pass the Hawes-Cutting Bill over the executive veto. When the plan was presented to the Philippine legislature, however, it was rejected, primarily because of the restrictions on immigration and the failure to continue free trade with the United States. Therefore, although Hoover favored Philippine independence, the failure of Congress to follow his suggestions as to the means delayed the enactment of a mutually satisfactory method until the next administration.

FAR EASTERN TROUBLES

Hoover's quest for international cooperation and peace received a rude jolt in the Orient. Throughout the 1920's revolutionary ferment and civil war in China resulted in numerous incidents that threatened to bring outside intervention reminiscent of the days of the Boxer Rebellion. For example, there were riots in both Shanghai and Canton in 1925 which endangered the property of foreigners. Two years later the British concession in Hankow was attacked by Chinese mobs. Later in 1927 Chinese Nationalist or Kuomintang troops captured Nanking and then proceeded to loot the foreign holdings, with resulting loss of life for numerous foreigners, including Americans. The United States, along with other powers whose nationals had suffered, demanded punishment for the guilty ones, but unsatisfactory replies were received. Some of the nations, notably France, Britain, and Italy, urged economic sanctions against China until complete restitution was given. The United States, however, refused to cooperate and the matter was dropped.

Coolidge and Secretary Kellogg undoubtedly realized that Chinese domestic unrest would not end until a single leader had won out in the civil war and that it would be useless to try to effect any settlement until that time. The administration's general policy was one of trying to cooperate with Chiang Kai-shek, the head of the Nationalist element, in order to hasten the return of peace. For example, in July, 1927, a treaty was made with Chiang under which the United States recognized China's complete control of her tariff. Yet the Coolidge administration was ever ready to protect the lives and property of Americans in China, as indicated by the constant presence of American gunboats in Chinese waters.

By the time of the 1928 election in the United States, Chiang had defeated most of his domestic foes except the Communists and had secured recognition of his government by many of the great powers, including the United States. To show his good faith and his desire for peace, Chiang signed the Kellogg-Briand Pact in August, 1928. Yet these incidents did not settle all of the problems, particularly the controversy between China and Russia over North Manchuria, from which Russia refused to withdraw its dominant influence.

THE SINO-RUSSIAN CONTROVERSY

A series of incidents in the spring and summer of 1929 widened the breach between the two countries. The Chinese, aided by the Manchurians, raided Russian consulates in several Manchurian cities, arrested the consuls and numerous Communists who were charged with breaking a 1924 treaty by spreading anti-Chinese propaganda. This was followed by the seizure of the communications systems of the Chinese Eastern Railway, hitherto under joint management, the substitution of Chinese for Russian officials, and the deportation of Russian employees.

Russia quickly forwarded an ultimatum to Chiang, demanding a prompt conference to solve the problem. She insisted that a solution could not be reached until China revoked her action and restored Russian control over the railway. Chiang's answer was unsatisfactory, so on July 17, 1929, Russia severed diplomatic relations with the Nanking government, and China reciprocated three days later. There was an immediate mobilization of armed forces along the border, with every indication that war would soon break out.

The Kellogg-Briand Pact, which both the Soviet and China had signed, left the responsibility of maintaining peace to each signatory; there was no machinery set up for conciliation and mediation. Secretary of State Stimson, however, insisted that the Pact "necessarily carries with it the implication of consultation" and urged both countries to settle their troubles by peaceful means. The major powers of Europe backed Stimson in this request. Both potential contestants answered that they would not fight except in self-defense. Thus it appeared as though Stimson had won a victory for peace under the Pact.

The ensuing Sino-Soviet conference broke down, however, because of differences over the future of Manchuria, and neither side would accept the mediation of an outside power. Consequently, fighting broke out, the Manchurian provincial forces were defeated, and by Christmas Chiang was compelled to recognize Russian rights in North Manchuria.

Meantime, Stimson was hard at work trying to effect mediation. Germany and Japan refused to join the United States in applying pressure, although Britain, France, and Italy did. The four nations then sent identic notes to the two disputants on December 2, tracing the course of the peaceful efforts since the beginning of the trouble and stressing the importance of abiding by the promises of the Paris Pact. The Stimson note to each added:

The American Government feels that the respect with which China and Russia will hereafter be held in the good opinion of the world will necessarily in great measure depend upon the way in which they carry out these most sacred promises.

The Chinese answer to this multilateral request for peace refused to admit that it had broken the pact and insisted that it was more than ready to submit the differences to mediation. The Russian reply, on the other hand, was anything but satisfactory. The blame for the failure of the negotiations between Russia and China was placed squarely at the doors of China and the United States; China was blamed for not being conciliatory, the United States for meddling after the joint conference was under way. Moreover, said the Russian reply, the issue could not be settled by a third party, particularly when that third party was the United States because

The Soviet Government cannot forbear expressing amazement that the Government of the United States, which by its own will has no official relations with the Soviet, deems it possible to apply to it with advice and counsel.

Thus, despite the energetic and honest efforts of Secretary Stimson to end this particular Manchurian problem, it ended in failure. The first test of the Paris Pact had shown the definite weakness of that agreement —the absence of any machinery to force a settlement of international disputes. Moreover, the external interference, especially by the United States, helped to cause Russia to insist, even by force, upon regaining her former rights in North Manchuria and obtaining additional privileges.

THE MENACE OF JAPAN

Scarcely had this American failure in the Far East been shown than another problem arose which indicated still more clearly the weakness of both the Paris Pact and the League of Nations.

Beneath the surface, the relations between the United States and

Japan had not been satisfactory for many years. Japan blamed the United States for its inability to secure all of the Twenty-One Demands from China in 1915, for the retreat from Shantung after the war, and for the inferior naval position in the Washington Treaty. Nor did the breaking of the Gentlemen's Agreement in the Johnson-Lodge Immigration Act of 1924 help the situation. On the other hand, Japanese intention of dominating the Far East was clearly shown in 1923 when Baron Ishii asserted on the occasion of the abrogation of the Lansing-Ishii agreement: "Japan's special interests in China continue to live in all their vigor." He insisted that they did not result from "benefits conferred upon Japan by the United States," but from "realities deriving from nature and geography."

Although maintaining a façade of parliamentary institutions, Japan was not by any means a democracy. The government was dominated by aristocratic old families, by the higher ranks in the army and navy, and by the individuals who controlled the country's highly concentrated industrial and commercial activities—particularly the Mitsui and the Mitsubishi families. All of these dominant groups were ambitious to extend Japanese power and influence, although they differed considerably on methods. The moderates, particularly to be found among Japanese big businessmen, thought in terms of economic penetration. By a "friendship policy" toward China, a subtle mixture of diplomatic pressure oiled by judicious bribery, they hoped to win an increasing share in the trade and investment opportunities of that undeveloped country, while they avoided serious trouble with the Western powers through a reasonable degree of collaboration with the League of Nations and the various international conferences. The moderates maintained an uneasy ascendancy through most of the twenties, but they were increasingly threatened by the militarist factions who were impatient with these tactics. The extremists were ambitious to extend Japanese political control; they wished to dominate the more valuable parts of China and to expel the hated Occidentals from the western Pacific area. China's progress toward unification and modernization late in the twenties was not at all to their liking.[1]

[1] In 1931 Chinese authorities made public the so-called Tanaka and Honjo Memorials, which they asserted to be ultrasecret Japanese documents representing the real intentions of the Japanese government. Their authenticity is questionable, but they have considerable interest, nevertheless, in view of subsequent developments. The first, allegedly drafted for the emperor by Premier Baron Tanaka in 1927, urged the construction of strategic railroads throughout Mongolia and Manchuria to tap the valuable resources of these areas and give Japan economic control. This in turn would prepare the ground for political domination of these regions and would be a steppingstone for the eventual conquest of all China. The Memorial of General Honjo, head of the

The moderates' position was greatly weakened by events after 1929. The great depression accentuated Japanese economic problems, already serious because seventy million people were endeavoring to make a living in a small and essentially poor country. The extremists regarded this as final proof of the need for Japanese expansion. Their discontent was increased by the refusal of Britain and the United States to grant Japan naval parity at the London Conference of 1930. The temptation to embark upon a program of aggressiveness was great because of the obvious demoralization of the Occident, where monetary chaos, governmental deficits, debt and armament controversies, and general loss of nerve made it unlikely that the Western powers could take any decisive step. As for the United States and its Open-Door policy, Japanese realists believed that it had been largely based on bluff since its first pronouncement.

The showdown came in Manchuria—long a Far Eastern trouble spot. Since the war with Russia, Japan had had extensive treaty rights in the southern part of that province—particularly in the South Manchuria Railroad zone. A quiet struggle for power had been for some time in progress between the Japanese who wanted to extend their influence and the Chinese who wished to interpret Japanese rights very narrowly. The incident which gave the Japanese army its excuse for drastic action was the alleged blowing up of a section of track along the main line of the South Manchuria Railroad, just a few miles from the important center of Mukden on the evening of September 18, 1931. Immediate blame was placed upon the Chinese, despite the latter's denial. Japanese troops guarding the line under the provisions of the Treaty of Peking of 1905 quickly attacked the small Chinese force in the vicinity, and just as promptly the Japanese army in Manchuria seized Mukden and several other strategic points. Although the Japanese authorities asserted that the military forces were acting in self-defense, it appeared to many observers that this was but the beginning of a well-laid plan to conquer Manchuria.

Three days later China, unable to cope with the situation, appealed both to the League and to the United States to try to effect a settlement. Secretary Stimson immediately announced that he was following the problem closely to ascertain whether the Mukden incident contravened the Paris Pact and the Nine-Power Treaty. At the same time

Japanese army in Manchuria, also allegedly prepared in 1927, included proposals for the conquest of Australia, the Philippines, and the East Indies, as well as China, and went on to plan for Japanese domination over Africa and most of Europe. Japan and the United States would then divide the world and, if the United States should prove hostile, Japan would be strong enough to crush this rival as well.

he notified Sir Eric Drummond, the League's Secretary General, that the United States would frankly cooperate with the League in its efforts to settle the strife. Stimson gave little credence to the statement of the Japanese ambassador that the attacks had been made without the knowledge of the Tokyo government.

For the next few days Stimson took no further action, hoping that the two Far Eastern nations might be able to reach a satisfactory settlement, but on September 25 he addressed similar notes to both parties in which he urged them not to extend the conflict. Neither the League nor the American request for a peaceful solution worked, for although both Asiatic parties asserted they were moving toward that objective, fighting broke out anew in early October. Consequently, on October 5, Stimson decided that the United States should conduct an independent investigation to uphold both the Pact and the Treaty, while at the same time cooperating with the League "to reinforce what the League does." With the latter purpose in mind, Stimson secured the consent of President Hoover to have the American consul at Geneva, Prentiss Gilbert, sit in on the meetings of the League Council concerning the enforcement of the Paris Pact. This promise to cooperate with the League and the participation of an American in open League meetings was a far cry from the American attitude of the previous decade, but three quarters of the American press supported the policy.

Despite the Sino-Japanese charges and countercharges as to responsibility for the Manchurian trouble, the United States came to the conclusion on October 8 that Japan was the aggressor. On that date Japanese planes bombed the unfortified city of Chinchow, thereby bringing death to a number of civilians. Almost at once Secretary Stimson sent a sharp note to the Japanese Foreign Office:

The Secretary of State cannot understand how the bombing of Chinchow can be minimized. . . . Chinchow is more than 50 miles from the Japanese railway zone and it is situated in territory where the Chinese have an entire right to maintain troops. . . . Bombing of an unfortified and unwarned town is one of the most extreme of military actions, deprecated even in time of war . . .

No attention was paid to this note, nor did Japan heed the League warning that she was breaking the Paris Pact. Moreover, it was her negative vote that prevented the League Council from approving a resolution calling for the retirement of Japanese troops from the Manchurian region outside of the railway zone before November 15 and for the prompt beginning of direct peace negotiations between Japan and China.

Prentiss Gilbert could not vote upon the attempted League action, but that did not mean that the United States was not interested in the proposition. True, Stimson did not believe it wise to set a date for the final retirement of Japan, but he did think that there must be an amicable settlement of the Manchurian controversy because Japan's actions had "destroyed the administrative integrity of China" in that region in defiance of the Nine-Power Treaty. Japan would have to withdraw her troops as an indication that she was not using force to attain her ends. The American Secretary insisted that the problem of respective treaty rights in Manchuria could be settled only after Japan had given up her armed actions.

Since Gilbert's attendance at the League sessions appeared not to be accomplishing much, there was substituted what was referred to as independent cooperation, in line with the initial policy of the United States. Ambassador Dawes was instructed to be in Paris during the Council sessions for consultation with the Council. And on December 10, 1931, the League decided on still another method of attacking the problem. It set up a commission, headed by Lord Lytton of Great Britain, to make an on-the-scene study of the Sino-Japanese conflict and report to the Council on its findings.[1]

[1] The other countries represented were Italy, France, Germany, and the United States. The American member was General Frank R. McCoy.

Is He In or Out? (By Fitzpatrick in the *St. Louis Post-Dispatch*.)

On the same day that the Lytton Commission was set up, President Hoover delivered his annual message to Congress. In it he asserted that the United States was committed to the maintenance of China's territorial integrity. This could best be done through full cooperation with the League, rather than through independent action, for "unity of effort to maintain peace" would thereby be achieved. Yet he insisted that such cooperation would not lead to American membership in the League because "in all the negotiations the Department of State has maintained complete freedom of judgment and action as to participation in any measures which might finally be determined upon."

The threat of League action, even in cooperation with the United States, did not deter Japan from her objective. By early January, 1932, all of South Manchuria was in her hands. The United States refused to recognize this conquest, however, and on January 7 Secretary Stimson notified the powers concerned with the Nine-Power Treaty that his country

can not admit the legality of any situation *de facto* nor does it intend to recognize any treaty or agreement entered into . . . which may impair the treaty rights of the United States or its citizens in China, including those which relate to the sovereignty, the independence, or the territorial and administrative integrity of the Republic of China, or to the international policy relative to China, commonly known as the open-door treaty; and that it does not intend to recognize any situation . . . brought about by means contrary . . . to . . . the pact of Paris. . . .

This became known as the "Stimson Doctrine," despite the fact that the policy of nonrecognition did not originate with Hoover's Secretary of State. Yet Stimson in a sense made it international in scope by basing it in part upon the Paris Pact which so many of the nations had signed.

At home the doctrine was received with mixed feelings. Some believed it was worthless because there was no real force to back it up; it was more of a statement of policy than a big stick. Another faction considered it might lead to trouble for the United States. To others it was the natural consequence to the Paris Pact; it was a means through which an aggressor might be actually deterred from waging war. And still another element regarded the doctrine as a basic part of international attitude toward Far Eastern problems.

Stimson believed that that announcement would be well received by the European powers. He was in for a rude shock, however, when a spokesman for the British government expressed the opinion that Japan's promises to respect the Open Door would be carried out. As a result of this British position, the Stimson Doctrine was definitely weakened because Japan realized that her opposition was divided. Moreover, she concluded that the United States, torn by partisan strife and hard hit by the depression, was in no position to force her to back down. While it was true that most Americans thought that China was being mistreated, this opinion did not carry beyond the extension of expressions of sympathy. The American people were more interested in ending the depression than in what happened in Manchuria. Nor was the State Department ready to make an issue of the Stimson Doctrine. Indeed, the more vigorous notes to Japan were not published until some time after they were sent and the press was cautioned not to play up the troubles in the Far East.

Encouraged by the lack of cooperation among the Western powers, Japan broadened her aggression. In late January, 1932, she attacked Shanghai and in the ensuing bombing thousands of civilians lost their lives. Only then did American public opinion really express itself against Japanese actions. Newspaper after newspaper started to refer to the incident in scathing terms. Stimson likened the feeling to that expressed in 1914 when Germany invaded Belgium. Even Britain was stirred because Japan was striking closer to the British spheres of influence.

When Stimson requested the British Foreign Secretary to collaborate in a stern and forceful note to Japan, stressing this time simply the breaking of the Nine-Power Treaty, Sir John Simon's reply was noncommittal. This may have been because Britain still had faith in the League and the Lytton Commission, and thus did not wish to join in any other peace movement, particularly when the proposer was not a member of the League and had never been willing to undertake any responsibility for the actual enforcement of international obligations. Or it may have been because of the British desire to appease Japan, and thereby save Hong Kong and the British interests generally in Central China.

Realizing that unilateral action by the United States would not bring results, Secretary Stimson, with the full support and collaboration of President Hoover and Senator Borah, who was chairman of the Foreign Relations Committee, decided to express the American position in an open letter to Borah. This letter would be universally published, would probably be read by the officials of the governments concerned, and, Stimson hoped, might stir up public opinion in many parts of the world in support of the American position. And being a letter to an American rather than an official note to Japan, resulting failure would not be so injurious to American prestige.

On February 23, 1932, this long letter to Borah was released. After tracing the history of Far Eastern relations from the Open Door through the attack on Shanghai, Stimson stressed the importance of upholding the Nine-Power Treaty and the Paris Pact. Then he continued:

That is the view of this Government. We see no reason for abandoning the enlightened principles which are embodied in these treaties. We believe that this situation would have been avoided had these covenants been faithfully observed, and no evidence has come to us to indicate that a due compliance with them would have interfered with the adequate protection of the legitimate rights in China of the signatories of those treaties and their nations. . . . If a similar decision should be reached and a similar position taken by the other governments of the world, a caveat will be placed upon such action which . . . will effectively bar the legality hereafter of any title or right sought to be obtained by pressure or treaty violation . . .

The American press in general loudly praised the policy expressed in this letter, and on March 11, 1932, the League Assembly approved of a resolution that was similar to the Stimson Doctrine without a dissenting vote. Many believe that the Stimson letter played a part in influencing Japan to effect a compromise with China under which Japanese troops withdrew from Shanghai at the end of May, 1932.

Yet meantime Japan was still in control of Manchuria. True, she attempted to forestall criticism by establishing a government there in February, which declared itself independent of China. Early in March, this "independent" state adopted the name of "Manchukuo" and selected Henry Pu-yi, deposed emperor of China, as regent. But the other powers, including the United States, refused to be duped by these events. They knew that Pu-yi was nothing more than a puppet of Japan and that Japan had been responsible for the "independence" movement. Consequently, recognition was not granted to Manchukuo, in line with the Stimson Doctrine.

The next six months witnessed efforts by Japan to defend her actions and continued refusals of the other powers to change their positions. Finally on September 15, 1932, Japan made a more definite break by recognizing the new state and concluding an alliance with it. Then on October 1 the long-awaited Lytton Report was published. After condemning Japan for its actions in defiance of existing commitments, the Report refused to accept Manchukuo as a sovereign state. Manchuria should be returned to China, but certain rights of Russia and Japan should be recognized. The League Assembly approved of these findings, and Secretary Stimson asserted he was in substantial agreement. Japan, however, refused to follow the wishes of the League and maintained her dominant control over Manchukuo; the League did not attempt to use force to drive her out.

During the whole controversy, the United States consistently upheld the Paris Pact and the Nine-Power Treaty. Throughout she was ready to cooperate with the League or with other powers generally. When collaboration was not forthcoming, the United States was ready to play a lone hand in supporting the Stimson Doctrine of nonrecognition. Whether the American public would have supported the administration if force had been attempted is problematical; in all probability it would not. The whole affair showed that the Kellogg-Briand Pact was powerless and that the League as a medium of peace was not much better.

Throughout the Hoover regime, the United States showed a greater degree of international cooperation than previously. The support of the London Naval Conference, the granting of respite on debts, the efforts to settle the Far Eastern problems were all indications of that. Nevertheless, the United States refused to consider actual membership in the League and even failed to act upon the World Court proposal. In her relations to the Latin-American republics and to her own insular possessions, the foundations for an important change in American policy had been laid.

19

The New Deal Begins

Politics during the thirties were destined to revolve in a strikingly different orbit than the politics of the twenties. Old issues that had seemed dead during the complacent days of prosperity suddenly came to life again, while a multitude of new demands made themselves imperatively felt. Out of this conflict of forces came the New Deal—a simple name to describe a complex thing—composed of desperate emergency measures, fundamental reforms, practical politics, and idealistic experiments. So heated was the partisanship evoked by the New Deal that most men either praised it as wholly good or damned it as entirely bad; balanced judgments were rare. Fully as controversial as the measures themselves was their sponsor, the only man in American history to be elected four times to the presidency.

THE EMERGENCE OF FRANKLIN ROOSEVELT

Franklin Delano Roosevelt was born January 30, 1882, at Hyde Park, New York. He was descended from the same seventeenth-century Dutch ancestor, Nicholas Roosevelt, from whom Theodore Roosevelt also traced descent. James Roosevelt, his father, was a wealthy landowner who had had a successful business career as well. His mother, Sara Delano, belonged to a still wealthier family and one equally aristocratic. Young Franklin received the education of a rich man's son. Instructed by private tutors until the age of fourteen, he then attended the exclusive Groton School and received his collegiate training at Harvard, where he gave a short preview of his future career by utilizing his post as editor of the *Crimson* to launch an energetic and successful crusade for better fire protection for the college dormitories. He subsequently studied law at Columbia University Law School and, after being admitted to the bar, accepted employment with a Wall Street legal firm.

Yet his chosen profession had small appeal for him. He spent much of his time at the family home at Hyde Park and, when an opportunity arose for him to enter local politics, he took it eagerly. The assignment was not a promising one—to run as Democratic candidate for the State Senate in a district where no Democrat was supposed to have a chance for election—but the twenty-eight-year-old candidate threw himself wholeheartedly into the contest. He hired a bright red automobile—certain to attract attention in 1910 when automobiles of any color were uncommon—and visited every part of the district, making three times as many speeches as his opponent. As a result partly of his campaigning and partly of the political trend of 1910 which was strongly anti-Taft and anti-Republican, Roosevelt secured election to his first public office. Soon after he took his seat at Albany an opportunity arose for him to earn a reputation for progressivism. The Tammany boss, Charles E. Murphy, was trying to compel the legislature to elect a candidate known as "Blue-Eyed Billy" Sheehan to the United States Senate. Young Roosevelt led a Democratic insurgent revolt against the boss's orders and was able to force Murphy to accept a compromise candidate. The episode received newspaper publicity and gave Roosevelt a prominence most unusual for a freshman legislator. He was reelected to the State Senate in 1912.

The following year he received his first introduction to the Washington official scene. Because he was an asset to his party in a day when the name Roosevelt possessed political magic and also because he had been an energetic campaigner for Wilson, the young politician was named to the responsible post of Assistant Secretary of the Navy—a position once held by Theodore Roosevelt. Unusual opportunities now came his way, particularly when the country became involved in war with Germany. He performed his duties in competent fashion, he made important friends, and received an invaluable education in national politics.

In 1920 at the age of thirty-eight he was nominated for the vice-presidency. It was an honor which many shrewd politicians would have declined since the Democrats were confronted with certain defeat, but Roosevelt accepted it as an opportunity. He made a long campaign tour during which thousands of people came to know him as a tall and strikingly handsome young man with a fascinating smile and an attractive voice. Despite the humiliating defeat of the party, many predicted a brilliant future for this candidate.

The next year, however, Roosevelt was stricken with infantile paralysis. For months he was a helpless victim of this cruel disease and it was generally assumed that his political career was ended. Yet the disaster was not without its compensation. Although his legs were never again strong enough to permit him to walk without support, his struggle with invalidism both demonstrated and deepened the extraordinary courage which came to be his most valuable asset in days of crisis. He himself explained it this way: "Once I spent two years lying in bed, trying to move my big toe. That was the hardest job I ever had to do. After that, anything else seems easy."

Rest and exercise at Warm Springs, Georgia, restored Roosevelt to good health and in 1928 at the urging of the Democratic presidential candidate, Al Smith, he consented to run for governor of New York. Securing election in the year of a Republican landslide, when Smith himself failed to carry the Empire State, Roosevelt returned quickly to a central place on the political stage. When he was reelected in 1930 by a margin even greater than those previously won by the popular Smith, Governor Roosevelt became at once the leading possibility for the next Democratic nomination for the presidency. His administration at Albany was characterized by caution rather than boldness, but he did win favor with both Democratic and Republican progressives by securing enactment of a program of unemployment relief and by championing the cause of public control of the hydroelectrical power which might be generated in connection with the building of a St. Lawrence seaway.

Long before the Democratic convention of 1932 an astute campaign to secure the nomination for the New York governor was in progress. James A. Farley was traveling the country, making friends and lining up delegates; Roosevelt's secretary and shrewd political adviser, Louis McHenry Howe, was coaching his protégé on practical politics, and a group of college professors—presently to be known as the "Brain Trust"—was assembling for Roosevelt the data on government and economics which he was eager to have. The Governor himself was the movement's best asset. His voice proved unusually adapted to transmission by radio broadcast and millions of Americans became familiar with it during the months of preconvention campaigning. In a speech of April 7, 1932, he put his finger upon what many felt was the fundamental fallacy of the Hoover policies when he called for plans "that build from the bottom up and not from the top down, that put their faith once more in the forgotten man at the bottom of the economic pyramid." Even more did he identify himself with the mood of the hour when he declared on May 22, 1932, in a speech at Oglethorpe University:

The country needs and, unless I mistake its temper, the country demands bold, persistent experimentation. It is common sense to take a method and try it. If it fails, admit it frankly and try another. But above all, try something. The millions who are in want will not stand by silently forever while the things to satisfy their needs are within easy reach.

THE ELECTION OF 1932

On June 14, 1932, the Republican National Convention opened its session at Chicago. There was no question of President Hoover's renomination—he was still the titular head and, in the face of probable defeat, no one seriously challenged him. The party platform was largely devoted to praise of the measures which Hoover had sponsored in dealing with the economic crisis. Not only was the Hawley-Smoot Tariff upheld, but a pledge to extend the protectionist principle was incorporated. The policies of the Federal Farm Board were defended and the party went on record in support of "any plan which will help to balance production against demand, and thereby raise agricultural prices, provided it is economically sound and administratively workable without burdensome bureaucracy." A sharp fight developed over the prohibition issue. The majority report opposed a submission to the people of a proposal limited to the issue of retention or repeal of the Eighteenth Amendment, but favored a vague formula under which the voters were to pass upon a proposed amendment "which, while retaining in the Federal Government power to preserve the gains already made in dealing with the evils inherent in the liquor traffic, shall allow States to deal with the problem as their citizens may determine, but subject always to the power of the Federal Government to protect those States where prohibition may exist and safeguard our citizens everywhere from the return of the saloon and attendant abuses." Opposing this, a minority report advocated that Congress immediately propose an amendment to the Constitution repealing the Eighteenth Amendment and returning the liquor problem to the states. After a bitter fight the majority report—the so-called wet-dry plank—was carried by a vote of 690 to 460. Hoover was renominated for the presidency on the first ballot with only a light and scattered opposition. The renomination of Vice-President Curtis, however, precipitated a real contest. While he did win on the first ballot, he received only 634 votes as compared with 513 cast for other candidates.

The Democratic Convention also met in Chicago. The party platform proved to be in refreshing contrast to most such documents. It was comparatively brief and the commitments were clear—embarrassingly clear in the case of a few of them which later failed to be carried out. The document called for the repeal of the Eighteenth Amendment, the reduction of government expenses by 25 per cent, an annually balanced budget, an enlarged program of public works and unemployment relief, the enactment of state unemployment and old-age pension laws, regulation of the sale of securities and banking reform, a modification of the tariff through reciprocal trade agreements, aid for the farmer through control of crop surpluses, and the independence of the Philippines.

Roosevelt's political managers had secured the support of more than half the delegates, but this did not assure his nomination since the two-thirds rule was still in effect and there were a number of other candidates in the running. The most formidable of these was Alfred E. Smith, eager for vindication after his defeat of 1928 and strongly supported by a faction of wealthy and powerful conservatives, headed by the party chairman, John J. Raskob. A third figure with strong backing was Speaker of the House John Nance Garner of Texas. The anti-Roosevelt forces hoped to block the nomination of the New York governor and secure the prize for some compromise candidate. Their strategy depended on keeping in the contest not only Smith and Garner, but as many favorite sons as possible. But after Roosevelt's vote had climbed from 666 to 682 on the first three ballots, Speaker Garner decided to withdraw so as to prevent any such disastrous deadlock as that of the 1924 convention from developing. Two powerful delegations, those of California and Texas, now swung to the support of Roosevelt. Senator William Gibbs McAdoo of California enjoyed his revenge against Smith, who had blocked his nomination in 1924, by announcing the shift of the California delegation's vote from Garner to Roosevelt; this was the break which set the Roosevelt band wagon into triumphant progress. On the fourth ballot the New York governor secured the coveted prize with 945 votes to 190½ cast for Smith and 13 scattered among other candidates. Garner's reward came at once; he was unanimously nominated for the vice-presidency on the first ballot.

The Democratic presidential candidate demonstrated his impatience with meaningless tradition by traveling to Chicago by plane to accept his nomination at once instead of waiting for the customary notification ceremony. He brought the tired delegates to a high state of enthusiasm with an aggressive speech which concluded with these words:

I pledge you, I pledge myself, to a new deal for the American people. Let us all here assembled constitute ourselves prophets of a new order of competence and of courage. . . . Give me your help, not to win votes alone, but to win in this crusade to restore America to its own people.

By this bold gesture Roosevelt captured the attention of the electorate and he never lost it during the long campaign. The Chicago meeting had left some bitterness, particularly among the Smith faction, but Farley, now national chairman, succeeded in bringing about at least a surface harmony before the contest was over. Roosevelt ignored the advice of many of the older leaders that he should confine himself to a front-porch campaign. Instead he visited every section of the country, including even the South which no Democratic presidential candidate had troubled to canvass since the Civil War. Roosevelt's speeches made the most of the weaknesses in the Republican record, while offering the outlines of an alternative policy without any very precise statement of details. They were progressive enough on the issues of farm relief and public utilities to win the support of Republicans like Senators Norris, Hiram Johnson, and Bronson Cutting of New Mexico, as well as the Progressive La Follette. But at the same time the candidate's promise to balance the budget and his cautiousness on the tariff issue held in line the conservatives of his own party. Throughout the campaign he demonstrated a mastery of the difficult art of maintaining the backing of widely divergent elements. What Roosevelt said, however, was probably less important than what he did. Letting millions of people see and hear him was worth many votes. Not only did they fall under the magic of his famous smile, but they could see for themselves that he was in vigorous good health. Thus were scotched rumors that he was a helpless invalid.

Late in the campaign President Hoover became conscious of the precarious position of the Republicans. He abandoned his own front-porch tactics and made an extensive campaign tour, climaxing his efforts with a strongly worded speech in Madison Square Garden, New York. Were the Democratic tariff proposals to be put into effect, he asserted, the grass would grow in streets of a hundred cities. The Democratic promise to put the unemployed to work he characterized as "cruel" because it was "absolutely impossible of realization." He defined the issue of the campaign as whether or not the "American system" was to be maintained.

Election day gave convincing evidence of the revolution in American public opinion since 1928. Hoover, who four years before had carried forty states, now gained but six: Connecticut, Delaware, Maine, New Hampshire, Pennsylvania, and Vermont. The electoral vote was: Roosevelt, 472, and Hoover, 59; the popular vote: Roosevelt, 22,821,857, and Hoover, 15,761,841; the minor party figures showed Norman Thomas (Socialist) with 884,781, and William Foster (Communist).

with 102,991. The Congressional election results were equally decisive. The Democrats secured 59 seats in the Senate to 36 for the Republicans and 1 for the Farmer-Laborites; in the House the division was 313 Democrats, 117 Republicans, and 5 independents. Political observers were wont to assert that these results were not so much a Democratic victory as they were a Republican defeat. So dissatisfied were the majority of voters with existing conditions that they cast their ballots for Roosevelt in order to turn the Republicans out. Actually the Democratic promises were so general that they did not afford much that was tangible; but the voters were sure that a change could not be for the worse and might conceivably be for the better.

THE LAME DUCKS

During the twenties Senator Norris had conducted a long crusade for a Constitutional amendment which would provide for the inauguration of the President in January after his election rather than in March and which would eliminate lame-duck sessions of the old Congress. Despite the obvious merits of the proposal and the fact that the Senate passed it five times between 1923 and 1931, it failed to secure the approval of the House, due largely to the hostility of Speaker Nicholas Longworth and the Republican Old Guard. After Longworth's death and the election of Speaker Garner, however, the Twentieth Amendment to the Constitution passed both chambers and was submitted to the states in March, 1932. Less than a year later, more than three quarters of the states having ratified it, the so-called Lame Duck Amendment was declared in effect on February 6, 1933.[1]

[1] The text of the Twentieth Amendment is as follows:
Section 1. The terms of the President and Vice-President shall end at noon on the 20th day of January, and the terms of Senators and Representatives at noon on the 3rd day of January, of the years in which such terms would have ended if this article had not been ratified; and the terms of their successors shall then begin.
Section 2. The Congress shall assemble at least once in every year, and such meeting shall begin at noon on the 3rd day of January, unless they shall by law appoint a different day.
Section 3. If, at the time fixed for the beginning of the term of the President, the President elect shall have died, the Vice-President elect shall become President. If a President shall not have been chosen before the time fixed for the beginning of his term, or if the President elect shall have failed to qualify, then the Vice-President elect shall act as President until a President shall have qualified; and the Congress may by law provide for the case wherein neither a President elect nor a Vice-President elect shall have qualified, declaring who shall then act as President, or the manner in which one who is to act shall be selected, and such person shall act accordingly until a President or Vice-President shall have qualified.
Section 4. The Congress may by law provide for the case of the death of any of the persons from whom the House of Representatives may choose a President whenever

Unfortunately the reform came too late to prevent the most glaring illustration in the country's history of the evils of the old system. For four months after a decisive vote of no confidence had been registered against the Hoover administration it continued in office, and for three of those months a Lame Duck Congress was in session. It is little wonder that the resulting confusion and uncertainty precipitated the nation into the most critical period of the whole depression.

Congress and the President could not agree on measures for balancing the budget nor on banking reform. A new Bankruptcy Act was passed, but in a form which disappointed Hoover. Against the latter's strong objections, a House resolution was enacted requiring publicity for loans made by the Reconstruction Finance Corporation. Hoover asserted that the practice led to bank runs and lack of confidence in institutions which had had to avail themselves of RFC assistance. Among the few acts of a positive character taken by the old Congress was the approval of the Twenty-first Amendment to the Constitution. This provided for the repeal of the Eighteenth Amendment, but prohibited the transportation or importation of intoxicating liquors into any state in violation of the laws thereof. The amendment was unique among such proposals in stipulating that its ratification must be secured through special conventions in the several states.

Within a week after the election Hoover began to feel the embarrassment of his position. A world disarmament conference was intermittently in progress, a world economic conference was in prospect, and the question of war debts was pressing for settlement. On November 22, 1932, the President and Secretary of the Treasury Ogden Mills conferred on these problems with the President-elect and his adviser, Professor Raymond Moley of Columbia University. The meeting was not very successful, nor were the numerous letters and telegrams which Hoover and Roosevelt exchanged. Hoover felt that he could not initiate policies in these matters without a pledge from the President-elect that the policies would not be repudiated after March 4; but Roosevelt asserted in a letter to Hoover: "I think you will realize that it would be unwise for me to accept an apparent joint responsibility with you when, as a matter of constitutional fact, I would be wholly lacking in any attendant authority." Both men were right; the difficulty lay not with them, but with the as yet unreformed Constitutional provision

the right of choice shall have devolved upon them, and for the case of the death of any of the persons from whom the Senate may choose a Vice-President whenever the right of choice shall have devolved upon them.

that required so long an interregnum. This did not mean, however, that no cooperation at all between the outgoing and incoming administrations was achieved. On the contrary, there was agreement on many points and Hoover received assurances that there would not be any major reorientation of American foreign policy.

BANKING CHAOS

But problems of foreign relations were as nothing compared with the crucial issues of domestic policy that arose during the last month of Hoover's term. Depositors more and more lost confidence in banks and withdrew their savings; many who trusted the banks did not trust the incoming administration and the result was the same—they hoarded their money. The situation threatened disaster for the whole country. The Federal reserve banks were under great strain; they were being compelled to put constantly larger amounts of currency into circulation while their gold stocks were being seriously depleted. Gold was not only being hidden away by domestic hoarders, but was being exported in large volume.

The danger was great that sound institutions would be pulled under along with unsound ones. State governments struggling with the situation resorted to temporary bank holidays—periods during which all transactions between the banks and the public were halted while the situation eased. During 1932 there were several such local bank holidays in the Middle West; the banks of Nevada had to be closed for six weeks on one occasion. But these incidents did not begin to alarm the general public until February, 1933. On the fourth of that month the governor of Louisiana had to proclaim a week-end bank holiday for the city of New Orleans; on the fourteenth the governor of Michigan announced an eight-day state-wide banking holiday in order to save the banks of Detroit from disaster. Many of that city's financial institutions failed to reopen, and those that did could operate only under rigid restrictions. The Michigan crisis had a serious effect on the situation in all the other states.

To President Hoover the crisis reflected nothing but the country's alarm over what the new administration might do. On February 17, 1933, he wrote to the President-elect requesting that the latter should assure the nation "that there will be no tampering or inflation of the currency; that the budget will be unquestionably balanced, even if further taxation is necessary; that the Government credit will be maintained by refusal to exhaust it in the issue of securities." The demand was an astonishing one and indeed its implication was fully realized by

President Hoover at the time, for he wrote to Senator Reed of Pennsylvania: "I realize that if these declarations be made by the President-elect, he will have ratified the whole major program of the Republican Administration; that is, it means the abandonment of 90 per cent of the so-called new deal." Roosevelt refused to allow his hands to be thus tied by his predecessor. He did, however, choose this occasion to announce that the two most important cabinet posts in the new administration would be held by men who could by no stretch of the imagination be portrayed as radicals: Senator Cordell Hull of Tennessee was to be his Secretary of State and William H. Woodin of New York, president of the American Car and Foundry Company, his Secretary of the Treasury. Many days before the inauguration of his chief, Woodin and a group of Democratic experts were in earnest conference with Secretary Mills and other Treasury officials over the banking crisis.

Meantime the situation went from bad to worse. On February 25 a bank holiday was declared in Maryland and restrictions on withdrawals were soon instituted in Indiana, Arkansas, and Ohio. Seventeen other states took similar action during the first three days of March. The night before Inauguration Day the officials of the outgoing administration and the new were agreed that the banking holiday must be made general and together they exercised pressure on Governor Lehman of New York and the executives of other states to proclaim temporary holidays. By noon of March 4 when Roosevelt took the oath of office scarcely a bank in the country was engaged in normal operations.

THE NEW PRESIDENT

Throughout the morning of March 4 the news of the crisis spread through the nation and the groups who crowded around radios at noon to listen to the new President's inaugural address were bewildered and somber. What they heard was tonic not only in its phraseology, but in the calm and courageous manner of its delivery. "This great Nation," declared Roosevelt, "will endure as it has endured, will revive and will prosper. So, first of all, let me assert my firm belief that the only thing we have to fear is fear itself—nameless, unreasoning, unjustified terror which paralyzes needed efforts to convert retreat into advance." He announced that Congress would meet at once in special session and stated his confidence that he could secure the passage of necessary measures. If Congress should fail to act, however, he would ask that body "for the one remaining instrument to meet the crisis—broad Executive power to wage a war against the emergency, as great as the power that would be given to me if we were in fact invaded by a foreign foe." International relations, he asserted, were "in point of time and necessity secondary to the establishment of a sound national economy." But he indicated the main line of foreign policy which he hoped to pursue: "In the field of world policy I would dedicate this Nation to the policy of the good neighbor—the neighbor who resolutely respects himself and, because he does so, respects the rights of others—the neighbor who respects his obligations and respects the sanctity of his agreements in and with a world of neighbors."

Besides Hull and Woodin, the new cabinet included James A. Farley as Postmaster General, George H. Dern of Utah as Secretary of War, Senator Claude A. Swanson of Virginia as Secretary of the Navy, and Daniel C. Roper of South Carolina as Secretary of Commerce. The distinction of being the first woman ever selected for a cabinet post was bestowed upon Frances Perkins of New York who became Secretary of Labor. Senator Thomas J. Walsh of Montana, famous as the investigator of the Teapot Dome scandal, was scheduled to be Attorney General, but died suddenly before Inauguration Day. The post went instead to Homer S. Cummings of Connecticut. The cabinet was completed with the appointment of two converted Republicans, Henry A. Wallace of Iowa and Harold L. Ickes of Illinois to the positions of Secretary of Agriculture and Secretary of the Interior respectively.[1] More influential in shaping the policies of the new administration than many of these cabinet members, however, were certain individuals placed in subordinate posts. Prominent among these were Raymond Moley, who was made Assistant Secretary of State, Lewis A. Douglas, the Director of the Budget, Rexford G. Tugwell, Assistant Secretary of Agriculture, and Adolph A. Berle, Jr., who accepted a post in the Reconstruction Finance Corporation. The new President showed a lively interest in the ideas presented by college professors and young lawyers—many of the latter being recommended to him by Professor Felix Frankfurter of Harvard Law School. Roosevelt's "Brain Trust" soon gained a horrendous reputation among businessmen and old-line politicians for dangerous radicalism, but in reality Moley, who was the

[1] Secretary of State Hull was succeeded by Edward M. Stettinius, Jr., of New York in 1944; Secretary of the Treasury Woodin by Henry Morgenthau, Jr., of New York in 1934; Secretary of War Dern by Harry H. Woodring of Kansas in 1936 and Henry L. Stimson of New York in 1940; Secretary of the Navy Swanson by Charles Edison of New Jersey in 1940, Frank Knox of Illinois in 1940, and James Forrestal of New York in 1944; Postmaster General Farley by Frank C. Walker of Pennsylvania in 1940; Attorney General Cummings by Frank Murphy of Michigan in 1939, Robert H. Jackson of New York in 1940, and Francis Biddle of Pennsylvania in 1941; Secretary of Agriculture Wallace by Claude R. Wickard of Indiana in 1940; Secretary of Commerce Roper by Harry Hopkins of Iowa in 1939, Jesse Jones of Texas in 1940, and by Henry Wallace in 1945.

most powerful of Roosevelt's advisers in 1933, was very conservative on most issues and the others were usually less radical than they were painted.

REOPENING THE BANKS

The action which Roosevelt had promised began at once. On the day after his inauguration the President called the new Congress into special session. Pending that event he issued a sweeping executive proclamation ordering a national bank holiday during which all banking transactions must be suspended except those which might be permitted by the Secretary of the Treasury. Authority for this drastic step was found in the Trading-with-the-Enemy Act of 1917, a piece of World War I legislation which was still on the books. By the time that Congress convened on March 9 an Emergency Banking Bill had been drafted; the measure was passed almost unanimously by the two Houses and received the President's signature the same day. It con-

Even Washing Behind the Ears Isn't Going to Be Enough This Time. (By Carlisle in the *New York Herald Tribune*.)

firmed all of the measures which had been taken and gave the President further emergency powers to control foreign exchange, gold and currency movements, and banking in general. The Comptroller of the Currency was empowered to appoint a conservator, when necessary, to conserve the assets of closed national banks without liquidation. National banks were authorized to issue and sell preferred stock to the RFC so that they might obtain funds without creating claims superior to those of their depositors. The pressing need for currency was met by permitting the banks to borrow on all sound assets from the Federal reserve banks and then allowing these assets to be used as the basis for the issuance of Federal reserve bank notes, which did not require the 40 per cent gold backing of Federal reserve notes.

Throughout the week the Treasury Department worked day and night on the banking problem. With the cooperation of the Federal reserve banks the financial condition of hundreds of institutions all over the country was reviewed to discover as speedily as possible which might be permitted to reopen and which must remain closed while their affairs were set in order. It was decided that on Monday, March 13, the sound banks located in the twelve Federal reserve bank cities should be permitted to open, to be followed the next day by those situated in some 250 cities where there were recognized clearinghouse associations; those elsewhere in the country would be licensed on succeeding days as rapidly as their condition could be determined.

The measures which had been decided upon represented a bipartisan effort. The teamwork had begun well before Inauguration Day and it continued for many days thereafter, the outgoing Treasury officials working side by side with the new staff. But when all the safeguards of a technical character which could be devised had been provided for, there still remained a psychological obstacle of the most serious nature to be surmounted. When the banks reopened, would the public have confidence in them? Or would bank runs and hoarding again be the order of the day? It was at this point that the new President made his own most important contribution. On Sunday evening, March 12, he delivered the first of his so-called fireside chats—an informal radio talk addressed directly to the common man. Simply and clearly he explained the measures which had been taken and promised his listeners that they might trust the institutions which would begin operations again during the next few days. "I can assure you," he said, "that it is safer to keep your money in a reopened bank than under the mattress."

The reopening proved successful. Within three days about 76 per cent of the member banks of the Federal Reserve System were doing business again. Nonmember state banks had to be licensed by the state banking authorities and the process sometimes took longer, but 72 per cent of them had reopened by April 12. More than four thousand banks failed to secure licenses during these early weeks; many of these reorganized and opened later, sometimes with no loss to their depositors, sometimes with a partial loss. Many hundreds were so hopelessly insolvent that they had to be liquidated, but even here the loss to depositors was rarely 100 per cent. As gratifying as the successful reopening of so large a proportion of the banks was the renewed confidence showed by the public. Hoarding ceased and paper currency flowed back to the banks, gold also was returned, and bank deposits had by the middle of April increased over $1,000,000,000.

First aid had been successfully rendered to the banking system, but as yet the abuses which had led to the crisis remained uncorrected. It was a problem to which the administration returned at a later date.

The executive orders under which the banks had been closed and then reopened contained several important restrictions. No gold, gold bullion, or gold certificates might be paid out by the banks without the authorization of the Secretary of the Treasury, nor could gold in any form be exported without a Treasury license. All transactions in foreign exchange were prohibited except such as might be undertaken for legitimate and normal business requirements. The purpose of these regulations was not only to conserve the gold stock of the country, but to permit the dollar to depreciate in its relationship to foreign currencies so as to raise the domestic price level and stimulate exports. For the first time since 1879 the currency of the United States could not be redeemed in gold.

THE HUNDRED DAYS

The special session of the Seventy-third Congress which opened on March 9, 1933, adjourned on June 16, exactly 104 days after Roosevelt's inauguration. Never before in American history had so much important legislation been passed in so short a time nor had so many new policies been instituted as during these so-called Hundred Days. The unusual record was possible because the prestige of the new President was great, and not only did Congress have a secure Democratic majority, but Republicans and Democrats alike were so sobered by the emergency as to accept a large amount of executive leadership. Moreover, public opinion throughout the nation favored a maximum of action and a minimum of debate. Most of the bill drafting was done by presidential advisers rather than in Congressional committees.

Two days after the enactment of the Emergency Banking Law, the Economy Act was passed. The President was given wide powers to cut the salaries of Federal employees by as much as 15 per cent and to reduce as well the pensions and allowances of war veterans. Roosevelt made prompt use of his authority and his courage in braving the wrath of the politically powerful groups affected did much to restore business confidence. The action was well timed to strengthen the administration's attack on the banking crisis.

But inconsistent though it seemed to many, Federal emergency appropriations were increased at the same time that regular expenditures were being reduced. The President was able to secure early Congressional approval for a project which would have appealed to the first Roosevelt in the White House as much as it did to the second. The Civilian Conservation Corps (CCC) was created to give temporary employment to about 300,000 men—250,000 unmarried men between the ages of eighteen and twenty-five, 25,000 veterans of World War I, and 25,000 experienced woodsmen. Most of the young men received but $30 a month, $25 of which was sent to their families. They were taken off the city streets, however, given board and lodging in camps, and put to work on useful projects in the national forests.

The funds which had been made available in 1932 through the Reconstruction Finance Corporation for loans to the states for relief activities were now almost exhausted; Congress made a new appropriation of $500,000,000. A few significant changes were introduced. Money was advanced to the states in the form of grants rather than loans, and a new agency, the Federal Emergency Relief Administration (FERA), was created to carry out the provisions of the law. The actual expenditure of the funds, however, still remained in state and local agencies. To head the FERA the President summoned to Washington Harry L. Hopkins of New York, long engaged in social work, who had directed the New York State Unemployment Relief Administration when Roosevelt was at Albany.

Meantime, advocates of a large public-works program impressed upon the President the benefits that would flow from their proposals. Not only would employment be given to many workers, but a demand for steel, cement, and other materials would be stimulated. The final appropriation, embodied in Title II of the National Industrial Recovery Act (NIRA), was $3,300,000,000—the largest appropriation which had ever been made by any government during peacetime. The Public Works Administration (PWA) was headed by Secretary of the Interior Ickes, an outspoken and honest official, whose deliberation and care in perusing each of the projects submitted for his approval was the despair of many of the other New Dealers.

The unemployed were not the only group who needed immediate help. The problem of unmanageable private debts threatened to crush debtors and creditors alike. The Emergency Farm Mortgage Act authorized the Federal Land Banks to undertake a wholesale refinancing of farm mortgages. Short-term overdue obligations at high rates of interest were replaced with new long-term mortgages at lower rates. In many cases the principal was scaled down as well. The law not only enabled many thousands of farmers to escape foreclosure proceedings, but served equally the interests of the banks and the insurance companies which had held the old defaulted obligations. Similar in purpose was the Home Owners Loan Corporation (HOLC), created by Congress to relieve both the mortgagors and the mortgagees of residential real estate. In the three-year period during which it was authorized to make loans, the HOLC advanced more than $3,000,000,000 to over a million home owners.

The Reconstruction Finance Corporation was not only continued by the Roosevelt administration but was given much broader powers. In addition to loaning money to banks in distress it could now strengthen them by purchasing capital stock, and did so during the next four years to the extent of a billion-dollar investment in six thousand banks. Money was made available for payments to depositors who had funds tied up in closed banks. Direct loans to small businessmen were permitted, while advances to farmers on the security of their crops assumed large volume. Loans from the RFC proved to be the lifeblood for almost every phase of the recovery program.

It will be noted that the measures so far discussed differed from the Hoover depression policies more in the scale upon which they were carried out than in the underlying philosophy. The Roosevelt program, like the Hoover plan, was designed to bolster up the credit structure of the country and prevent wholesale liquidation. Capitalism had been granted a reprieve.

The New Dealers believed, however, that all such measures to save the banks, the corporations, the railroads, the home owners, and the farmers would be futile unless economic activity could be stimulated. The income of millions of farmers and workers must be substantially raised if real recovery were to be attained. This was the purpose of the two most controversial measures passed during the Hundred Days— the Agricultural Adjustment Act of May 12, 1933, and the National Industrial Recovery Act of June 16, 1933. Discussion of these highly significant experiments will be postponed for a later chapter along with certain other early New Deal measures—the establishment of the Tennessee Valley Authority, the Truth-in-Securities Act, and the Glass-Steagall Act.

One further thing the legislators did for their constituents, and this earlier than almost anything else: they gave them beer. The Volstead Act was amended by a law signed by the President on March 22, 1933. The manufacture and sale of beer and wine with an alcoholic content of not greater than 3.2 per cent by weight was now permitted. The step was urged on the ground that the tax revenue which the legalization would bring into the Treasury was sorely needed. Thus was anticipated the final termination of the prohibition experiment which came with the ratification of the Twenty-first Amendment on December 5, 1933.

THE PROGRESS OF RECOVERY

The nation's psychological response to the Hundred Days was striking. Most of the dark pessimism of the winter was overcome and there was a general belief that recovery would now be both complete and speedy. Stock-market prices rose rapidly and industrial production expanded greatly. But this flurry of intense activity was almost entirely speculative. Prices in Wall Street reflected the expectation that corporation profits were going to increase, while manufacturers and merchants, anticipating higher labor and materials costs, were filling their warehouses with products which they hoped to sell at higher prices. Since purchasing power had not yet been created to sustain this higher level of production, business activity began to decline again during the summer and fall of 1933.

Roosevelt sought to reverse this trend by two experiments. The first was an attempt at controlled inflation through the gold purchase plan to be discussed in the next chapter. The second was the Civil Works Administration program advocated and administered by Harry Hopkins. As the end of 1933 approached, it was obvious that although employment figures were much higher than in March, there were several million unemployed who were threatened with serious suffering during the winter. Most of the PWA projects being planned under the conscientious scrutiny of Secretary Ickes were still in the blueprint stage. What was needed in the opinion of the administration was a program in which unemployed but able-bodied men would be put to work at once in their own communities on projects of civic value. Unlike FERA the program was to be administered by Federal appointees.

Hopkins acted with great speed. Given charge of the CWA in November, he had more than four million men at work by the middle of January, 1934. From the beginning the policy was intended as a temporary one and it was terminated in the spring. The CWA experiment cost $933,000,000. Whether it was worth it was a matter of controversy. Purely as a relief measure it unquestionably cost more than the subsistence doles through which most state and local relief had been hitherto provided. But it was contended that the morale of the unemployed was better maintained when they did work and received respectable wages. Most—although by no means all—of the projects, moreover were of real value to the communities.[1] Another purpose which it was hoped that the CWA would serve was that of pump-priming—that is, creating purchasing power which would stimulate industrial activity. Once again it is impossible to say whether the program contributed to this end. Business activity did increase during the first quarter of 1934, but like the earlier revival of 1933 much of the ground gained was lost later in the year.

The Congressional session of 1934 resulted in a rounding out of the policies which had been initiated the preceding year. Important monetary legislation was passed along with several bills increasing the powers of the new Federal credit agencies. Banking and stock-exchange reform was taken a step further. Particularly important was the passage of the Reciprocal Trade Agreements Act since it represented a victory for the Hull internationalist point of view over the type of economic nationalism championed by Raymond Moley.

In November, 1934, the voters had an opportunity to register their opinion on the steps which the administration had taken. That most of them heartily approved is indicated by the fact that the Democratic majority in the Senate increased from 22 to 42 and in the House from 191 to 209.

THE SECOND NEW DEAL

Strengthened by this new mandate, Roosevelt secured from Congress the enactment of a legislative program in 1935 comparable in scope to the measures of 1933. But not for this reason alone have the policies instituted in 1935 been described as a Second New Deal. They represented an important shift in emphasis. The First New Deal had been

[1] Among the hundreds of types of work engaged in, the most important were: painting, plastering, and plumbing in public buildings such as schools, landscaping, installing fire alarms, removing old street-car tracks, building parking spaces, resurfacing of highways, and alleviating flood menaces. Despite a widely held impression only a small proportion of those on CWA rolls raked leaves.

dedicated primarily to recovery, and only incidentally to reform. The emphasis was now reversed. "When a man is convalescing from illness," Roosevelt declared in his first message to the new Congress, "wisdom dictates not only cure of the symptoms, but removal of their cause." The administration had shifted to the left by this time; the honeymoon period of its relations with business was over; its most dependable support was in the future to come from labor. The shift had its visible embodiment in the departure from the Washington scene of such men as Raymond Moley, General Hugh Johnson, and George Peek. Most prominent among the President's advisers now were Harry Hopkins and two able protégés of Professor Frankfurter, Thomas Corcoran and Benjamin Cohen.

It was during the period of the Second New Deal that such important laws as the Social Security Act, the Wagner-Connery Act, and the Public Utilities Holding Company Act were passed and that the Works Progress Administration and the Resettlement Administration were set up. There were many factors contributing to the shaping of a more far-reaching program than that of the First New Deal. The hope that the social objectives of the administration could be largely achieved through NRA codes was disappointed by the failure of the various conflicting interests to reconcile their differences. Before these difficulties could be adjusted, the whole experiment was halted by the Supreme Court's decision in the Schechter poultry case on May 27, 1935. Still dissatisfied with the degree of economic recovery, the administration felt the need of taking more aggressive steps to create purchasing power. There was, moreover, increasing danger that discontented groups would abandon the New Deal and throw their support to such extremist programs as those being agitated with apparently great effect by Huey Long, Dr. Townsend, and Father Coughlin. Labor also was in a more militant mood with John L. Lewis's Committee for Industrial Organization, the CIO in its first form, seeking to unionize the mass-production industries and demanding that the government support the effort.

SPENDING AND THE BUDGET

The problem of unemployment continued to plague the nation. The number of workers in private industry rose slowly from depression lows, but the population was meanwhile increasing and new jobs were not being created as rapidly as new workers were available to fill them. Throughout the eight years, 1933–1940, unemployment figures did not drop much below eight million and they averaged about ten million.

Despite repeated reaffirmations by President Roosevelt of the hope that the budget might soon be brought back into balance, the continuance of unemployment on such a scale made it necessary to provide large emergency appropriations. Following the short-lived CWA experiment, Federal relief expenditures were confined to PWA and FERA channels. But both of these programs had their limitations. Large public-works projects were expensive, they were not always available in the areas of greatest economic need, and they gave employment almost exclusively to construction workers, whereas many of the unemployed were to be found among the white-collar group—clerks, teachers, musicians, actors, artists, and even doctors and nurses. On the other hand, most of the locally administered FERA money went for direct relief— doles which provided only a bare subsistence. Such relief was cheaper in money than any other form of assistance, but it was expensive in other terms. The reliefers were given no real purchasing power which would stimulate the country's economy, while protracted idleness deprived the individuals themselves both of the will to work and whatever skills they might once have possessed. In the words of the President: "To dole out relief in this way is to administer a narcotic, a subtle destroyer of the human spirit. . . . The Federal Government must and shall quit this business of relief."

The policy now adopted was to turn the care of unemployables back to the sole responsibility of the states and local communities, while providing work through Federally directed projects to as many as possible of the able-bodied on the relief rolls. On May 6, 1935, the Works Progress Administration (WPA) was created with Harry Hopkins as Administrator. Hopkins acted with characteristic speed in setting up his organization; by December about 2,667,000 were receiving employment through this new agency. Up to October 1, 1937, the WPA had built 11,000 public buildings and repaired 30,000 others, had laid over 43,000 miles of roads and repaired 146,000 miles, and had constructed thousands of bridges, culverts, sidewalks, athletic fields, playgrounds, swimming pools, dams, levees, and sewers. More than 9,000,000 trees had been planted and over 29,000,000 library books renovated. Women were given work on sewing and canning projects; doctors and nurses operated clinics; musicians were organized in WPA orchestras which gave free concerts; actors, writers, and teachers were given similar opportunities to practice their professions. Those employed in these multifarious activities received wages which were substantially higher than the payments under the FERA had been, but not so high as under either the PWA or CWA projects, on which the general rule

Harry Hopkins and Daughter, Diane, President Roosevelt, Secretary of State Hull, and Secretary of the Treasury Morgenthau. (Acme.)

had been to pay wages similar to those prevailing for that kind of work in private employment. The lower wage rates of WPA were set both as a measure of economy and as an inducement to the workers to secure private employment whenever possible.

A particularly disquieting problem was that of young people in families on relief. The number of these was estimated in 1935 to be about 2,900,000. The natural course for such youngsters was to quit school and look for jobs. But this was deplored both because it aggravated the unemployment problem and because it interrupted the education of the young people, with potentially serious results for themselves and the community. To deal with this situation a National Youth Administration (NYA) was established within the WPA. High-school and college students were given part-time employment on projects helpful to the institutions which they were attending. The amount which could be earned was small, but it was enough in many cases to make it possible for the students to stay in school. The NYA also organized vocational-training classes.

New Deal spending was hotly attacked and as resolutely defended. Critics asserted that much of the work relief was expended for what some cynic named "boondoggling"—made work of no real value. Popular jokes depicted the WPA worker as leaning on his shovel much more than he dug with it. The more serious charges against relief spending were that it jeopardized the solvency of the Federal government and that it was made to serve political purposes. But New Deal supporters, while not claiming that all WPA projects were worthwhile or all WPA workers conscientious, asserted that no responsibility of the government was more important than that of preventing suffering. The great justification of the Hopkins program was that it served this end and at the same time produced in the aggregate an immense amount of useful work. The cost was well within the capacity of the government and was not large when compared with what would be unquestionably expended in a wartime emergency. Politics and graft might sometimes be discovered in local WPA situations, but defenders of the agency pointed out that evidence of such abuses was really not very great considering the magnitude of the program.

The New Deal was expensive. Between March, 1933, and December, 1936, $13,200,000,000 was added to the national debt, whose total rose to $33,900,000,000. This sum was by no means unmanageable. As a matter of fact, through refunding operations which took advantage of lower interest rates, the Treasury was able to reduce the annual carrying charges so that it cost the Federal government less for interest payments in 1936 than it had in 1934. The continuing deficit was, nevertheless, embarrassing to an administration which had come to power on a platform pledging economy. To emphasize the emergency character of the excess spending, the Treasury reports differentiated between ordinary expenditures and such recovery and relief items as agricultural aid, relief, public works, home-owners aid, and the RFC. The point was stressed that the ordinary budget was in balance and that borrowing was necessitated entirely by the relief items. The administration argued that as national income increased, emergency expenditures could be tapered off while revenue would automatically increase until the budget was balanced again.

In his effort to keep the ordinary budget in balance, Roosevelt secured the enactment of new tax levies and resisted pressure to restore the cuts which had been made in 1933 in the salaries of Federal employees and in benefit payments to the veterans. But on the economy issue Congress rebelled. On March 28, 1934, the Independent Offices Appropriations Act—passed over the President's veto—reduced the maximum pay cut for government employees from 15 per cent to 10 per cent from February 1, 1934, to June 30, 1934, and to 5 per cent thereafter. This final 5 per cent cut was ended on July 1, 1935. Meantime, pressure from the veterans' lobby had resulted in restoring their benefit payments.

THE BONUS VICTORIOUS

The most serious issue involving the veterans was the increasing demand for the immediate payment of the bonus. In 1935 Congress passed a measure which would have authorized the issuance of Treasury notes or greenbacks to pay the full maturity value of the certificates. Not only did Roosevelt veto the measure, but he went before Congress in person on May 22, 1935, to state his objections. He pointed out that to pay in 1935 an obligation of $2,200,000,000 not due until 1945 was in its effect the granting of an additional bonus of $1,600,000,000. His principal argument, however, was that the government's obligation during the depression was to all the unemployed and that able-bodied veterans ought not to be entitled to special treatment. In the President's words:

The herculean task of the United States Government today is to take care that its citizens have the necessities of life. We are seeking honestly and honorably to do this, irrespective of class or group. Rightly, we give preferential treatment to those men who were wounded, disabled, or who became ill as a result of war service. Rightly, we give care to those who subsequently have become ill. The others—and they represent the great majority—are today in the prime of life, are today in full bodily vigor. They are American citizens who should be accorded equal privileges and equal rights to enjoy life, liberty, and the pursuit of happiness—no less and no more.

The House voted 322 to 98 to override the veto, but in the Senate the President's action was sustained, although even there 54 Senators favored overriding the veto to the 40 who supported it.

Roosevelt's opposition only delayed the measure's passage. In January, 1936, a new bill, the Adjusted Payment Compensation Bill, passed Congress. In its latest form the project was less objectionable than its 1932 or 1935 version since it eliminated the inflationary provision for paying the bonus in greenbacks and stipulated that the veterans should receive redeemable, nine-year, interest-bearing bonds. Although the President still refused to approve the measure, it was finally enacted into law over his veto by votes of 326 to 61 in the House and 76 to 19 in the Senate. Roosevelt advised all veterans who could to hold their new bonds as an investment rather than cash them, but most of them preferred to have the money at once. Congressional generosity had made the government liable to immediate demands of about $2,400,000-000,[1] and of this total the veterans collected about $1,700,000,000 during the course of the next few months.

THE 1936 BOOM

Whether as a result of the New Deal, as the administration supporters insisted, or in spite of the New Deal, as Republican critics charged, the fact was undeniable that by Election Day, 1936, the country was enjoying a substantial degree of prosperity. National income had been $40,000,000,000 in 1932; it was $60,000,000,000 in 1936. Industrial production by December, 1936, was not only double its 1932 level, but somewhat higher than it had been in the fabulous year 1929. In October, 1936, Roosevelt was able to announce that for the first time in fifty-five years an entire twelve months had passed without a single national bank failure.

Conditions were sufficiently good to assure the triumphant reelection of the President. But the New Deal policies toward business, agriculture, and labor were, despite the election results, matters of the most violent controversy. The next two chapters will be devoted to a detailed analysis of these measures.

[1] This was a larger sum than provided for in the 1935 bill because Congress was forgiving the interest on sums which the veterans had borrowed against their certificates since 1931.

20

Business and the New Deal

NO CONTRAST BETWEEN 1929 AND 1933 IS MORE STRIKING THAN THE changed position which businessmen held in public esteem. In the earlier year the leaders in industry and banking enjoyed great prestige in all but radical eyes. The popular magazines featured success stories; enterprising reporters secured interviews in which the opinions of the business tycoons were solicited on every conceivable subject. By 1933, however, few newspapers were interested in quoting the pronouncements of the fallen heroes; instead, their columns were full of stories of ruined brokers who had committed suicide, industrial leaders who had fled the country in an attempt to avoid criminal prosecution—like the utilities magnate, Samuel Insull, and bankers who had been ousted in disgrace from positions of financial trust—like Charles E. Mitchell of the National City Bank. Such sensational cases were of course exceptional, but, combined with the shock of the depression, they helped to undermine popular confidence in the wisdom and integrity of businessmen as a class. The bankers and industrialists were themselves baffled and discouraged by the financial crisis. For the moment their self-confidence was seriously shaken and they accepted leadership from Washington with much less protest than they would have under ordinary circumstances. Many businessmen were in fact almost effusively grateful for the emergency measures of the Hundred Days whereby the nation's credit structure was salvaged. But this era of good feeling was brief. As the country emerged from the most desperate phase of the depression, the bankers and industrialists were eager to return to a minimum of government control. Other classes in the population, however, still retained their depression-born suspicions of business practices. As the New Deal in response to this turned increasingly to regulation and reform, it aroused the militant hostility of most of the business community.

MONETARY POLICY

Nothing better illustrates the difference in point of view between Hoover and Roosevelt than their attitude toward the country's monetary system. The Republican President had regarded the maintenance of the existing gold standard as perhaps his most important trust; he viewed with horror the suggestion of the slightest deviation from it. Roosevelt refused to adopt this fetish. In his campaign speeches he pledged himself to "sound money," but it was obvious that he was leaving himself free to deviate from conventional orthodoxy if a moderate and controlled inflation seemed advisable. Money was, in the new President's philosophy, a means to an end rather than an end in itself. If one kind of money contributed more to recovery than another, then by that pragmatic test the "soundness" of that money was demonstrated.

If Roosevelt's ideas on money were unorthodox, they were moderate when contrasted with the extreme inflationary demands of many members of his party. Senator Burton K. Wheeler of Montana had revived Bryan's old demand for the free and unlimited coinage of silver at the ratio of sixteen to one. An amendment to the Agricultural Adjustment Act which would have established the Wheeler policy failed of adoption by the Senate by only ten votes on April 17, 1933, and would have passed had the administration not used its influence against it. Other inflationists sought to compel the Treasury to issue several billion dollars in greenbacks. Some form of currency or monetary experimentation was inevitable and Roosevelt met the situation by inducing Congress to grant him wide powers with discretion to choose whatever form of action seemed best. The necessary authorization was contained in the so-called Thomas Amendment or Title III of the Agricultural Adjustment Act of May 12, 1933. Under this the President might (1) issue as much as $3,000,000,000 in greenbacks or legal tender notes to pay maturing Federal obligations or to purchase the outstanding bonds of the United States, (2) reduce the gold content of the dollar by as much as 50 per cent, (3) provide for the unlimited coinage of both gold and silver at a ratio he might fix, (4) accept silver up to the amount of $200,000,000 in debt payments from foreign governments and issue silver certificates upon the bullion so received.

Having obtained a grant of power over the monetary system unprecedented in American history, Roosevelt proceeded cautiously. He shunned both the greenback and free-silver panaceas. Instead, he continued with a line of policy upon which he had embarked during the first week after his inauguration—that of passive devaluation of the dollar. It will be remembered that the Emergency Banking Act had given the President power to control transactions in gold and that the executive order reopening the banks had provided that no gold, gold bullion, or gold certificates might be paid out by the banks without the authorization of the Secretary of the Treasury, nor might gold be exported in any form without a Treasury license. On April 5, 1933, the President ordered all persons owning gold coin, gold certificates, or gold bullion to deliver the same to the Federal reserve banks and receive in exchange an equivalent amount of any other form of coin or currency. On April 19 the Treasury announced that no further licenses for the export of gold would be granted.

These steps had a dual purpose: to reduce the value of the dollar in foreign exchange and to raise the domestic price level. The first of these goals seemed essential to the President because of the abnormal conditions of 1933. England and most of the other countries of the world had abandoned the gold standard. So long as the United States clung to it, the American dollar was expensive in terms of these foreign currencies, thus making it difficult for foreigners to buy American goods. To reduce the foreign exchange value of the dollar, therefore, would encourage American exports. The raising of the domestic price level seemed equally necessary. The downward spiral of prices which had characterized the depression made it more and more difficult for debtors to meet their obligations and discouraged both industrialists from manufacturing for future sale and merchants from buying more than they could quickly sell. The 1933 price level could be fairly described as deflated; the policies undertaken to raise that level were more accurately labeled reflationary than inflationary. In Roosevelt's words:

The Administration has the definite objective of raising commodity prices to such an extent that those who have borrowed money will, on the average, be able to repay that money in the same kind of dollar which they borrowed. We do not seek to let them get such a cheap dollar that they will be able to pay back a great deal less than they borrowed. In other words, we seek to correct a wrong and not to create another wrong in the opposite direction.

Obviously the cheapening of the dollar would result in a windfall to creditors if they could force their debtors to pay in gold rather than in currency. To prevent this, Congress by joint resolution of June 5, 1933, voided any clause requiring payment in gold in any past or future obligation, whether government or private. Congress's power to enact such a provision was upheld by the Supreme Court in the Gold Clause cases of 1935.

The London Economic Conference—discussed more fully in a later chapter—made it necessary for Roosevelt to decide early in July, 1933, whether recovery could best be served by entering a stabilization agreement with the other powers or by continuing his policy of lowering the value of the dollar in foreign exchange and raising the domestic price level. He chose the latter path despite its lethal effect on the Conference.

Until October, 1933, the administration's policy was one of passive devaluation. That is, the dollar was simply divorced from gold with the intention of allowing its value to sink in terms of other currencies. But during the autumn the President, presumably under the influence of Professor George F. Warren of Cornell University, initiated a more aggressive campaign to secure his aims. The RFC began on October 28 the practice of buying gold—at first newly mined domestic gold, but later foreign as well—at a price substantially above the world market. The first purchases were at $31.36 per ounce. The price was gradually raised until on January 16, 1934, it reached $34.45. In view of the fact that an ounce of gold before March 4, 1933, had been worth $20.67, this was equivalent to a devaluation of the dollar by approximately 40 per cent.

This experiment was terminated by the Gold Reserve Act of January 30, 1934. Title to all gold owned by the Federal reserve banks was transferred to the United States Treasury in return for dollar certificates; gold coin was abolished as a component of the American monetary system, but gold in bullion form was to be held in the Treasury as a reserve against the currency; the President was authorized to fix the gold content of the dollar between 50 and 60 per cent of its old weight; $2,000,000,000 of the profit which would accrue to the Treasury through the revaluation of its gold holdings was to be utilized as a stabilization fund to enable the Treasury to maintain the dollar at a reasonable ratio with foreign currencies through operations in the foreign exchange market. By presidential proclamation of January 31, 1934, the weight of the gold dollar was fixed at 15 5/21 grains ninetenths fine. Measured by the old gold dollar (25.8 grains), the new dollar was worth 59.06 cents; gold was priced at $35 an ounce as against the old price of $20.67.

Although the President still retained power to change the weight of the dollar within a designated range, he abstained from any further action. Instead, the policy of the administration was now to hold the dollar steady in the foreign exchange market through the operations of the stabilization fund. When in 1936 a new wave of competitive currency depreciation threatened to develop, the United States joined

Britain and France in an agreement to cooperate in maintaining an equilibrium among their respective currencies.

It is impossible to say that the gold policy either succeeded or failed. Domestic prices rose during 1933 and exports increased, but many other factors than monetary policy were at work. Furthermore, prices did not follow a uniform course. While manufactured goods held their price gains of the spring and early summer, agricultural prices, after a rapid upward spurt, drifted downward again for the balance of the year. Experience with the gold-purchase plan seemed to indicate that the general price level did not respond as directly to a change in the gold value of the dollar as the Warren school of theorists had believed. Too many other factors—among them the volume of credit, the rate of government spending, the supply and demand for goods, the activities of speculators—were at work.

Perhaps the most serious criticism to be made of the gold policy is that it represented a type of economic nationalism all too common in the world of 1933. To be sure, the steps which the United States took in the foreign exchange market were essentially defensive since most of the other nations had already resorted to currency depreciation, but the American policy was, nevertheless, a cause for serious anxiety to other countries. Despite the restrictions on transactions in gold resorted to by governments everywhere, the purchasing program resulted in attracting an abnormally large proportion of the world's gold supply to the United States.

On the other hand, the period of monetary experimentation had at least one healthy result. Most of the dire predictions regarding the results which would follow any deviation from the orthodoxy of the old gold standard proved to be groundless. When Americans learned that life went on as usual even when one could not redeem his currency in gold coin, another of the inhibiting fears which had shackled the country in 1932 was vanquished.

THE SILVER PURCHASE PLAN

The administration's silver policy, although bearing points of resemblance to the gold plan, had this fundamental difference: it was forced upon the President somewhat against his will. Senators and Representatives from the silver-producing states were anxious to remonetize silver in order to rescue the white metal from the disastrously low price which it was bringing at the beginning of 1933. Their position in Congress was strong because they held the balance of power between the inflationists and the anti-inflationists. Their first victory was in securing recognition for silver in the Thomas amendment described above. When the President showed little inclination to use his optional powers, the silverites redoubled their efforts to secure mandatory legislation. They soon forced Roosevelt to make important concessions out of fear that if he failed to do so, some much more drastic step might be forced upon him. At the London Economic Conference the United States joined certain of the other silver-producing countries in agreeing to a silver-purchasing policy. In conformity with this the Treasury began in December, 1933, to buy newly mined American silver at well above its world price.

The silverites won their most important victory in the passage of the Silver Purchase Act of June 19, 1934. Congress fixed the following objective:

It is hereby declared to be the policy of the United States that the proportion of silver to gold in the monetary stocks of the United States should be increased, with the ultimate objective of having and maintaining one-fourth of the monetary value of such stocks in silver.

The Treasury was directed to purchase domestic and foreign silver until either the prescribed proportion of the two metals was reached or the price of silver rose above its monetary value of $1.293 per ounce. Silver certificates were to be issued in proportion to these increasing silver stocks. To prevent speculators from taking advantage of the situation, the President was empowered to nationalize the country's nonindustrial silver stock.

As a result of this legislation, the Treasury was obliged to buy the entire output of the domestic silver mines at an artificially high price and to make extensive purchases of foreign silver as well. This amounted to a very substantial subsidy to the silver producers. The policy made grave difficulties for China, Mexico, and other countries on a silver standard. Among its few satisfactory results was that of creating foreign purchasing power for the benefit of American exporters.

NRA: EXPERIMENT IN INDUSTRIAL SELF-GOVERNMENT

Perhaps the most interesting of Roosevelt's speeches during the 1932 campaign had been that delivered before the Commonwealth Club in San Francisco, California. In it he said:

As I see it, the task of Government in its relation to business is to assist the development of an economic declaration of rights, an economic constitutional order. . . . Happily, the times indicate that to create such an order not only is the proper policy of Government, but it is the only line of safety for our economic structures as well. We know, now, that these economic units cannot exist unless prosperity is uniform, that is, unless purchasing power is well distributed throughout every group in the Nation. . . . That is why some enlightened industries themselves endeavor to limit the freedom of action of each man and business group within the industry in the common interest of all; why business men everywhere are asking a form of organization which will bring the scheme of things into balance, even though it may in some measure qualify the freedom of action of individual units within the business.

In this passage Roosevelt showed his interest in a movement which had been enlisting the support of many industrial and financial leaders. Competition, at least in its most aggressive manifestations, had grown unpopular—particularly during the depression. This led to a demand that the trade associations should be expanded in membership and allowed to organize cooperative measures for stabilizing production, prices, and marketing practices. Since such activities were not permitted under the antitrust laws, it was proposed that the latter should be amended, suspended, or repealed. A concrete proposal based on these principles was put forward by Gerard Swope, president of the General Electric Company, in the autumn of 1931, while a somewhat similar plan was developed under the auspices of the United States Chamber of Commerce. Hoover had been cold to the movement, but Roosevelt had been influenced by such advisers as Bernard Baruch, General Hugh Johnson, and Raymond Moley to give the idea his sympathetic consideration.

Meantime, labor leaders were insisting with increasing emphasis on the need for shortening the standard work week. They asserted that the principal cause of the depression was unemployment brought on by the increased productivity of the individual worker. In order to create the purchasing power to consume the products of the improved machines, hours should be radically shortened and employment spread as widely as possible. To achieve this end Senator Hugo L. Black of Alabama had introduced as early as December, 1932, a bill which would have limited work in factories to thirty hours a week. Although strongly opposed by the Chamber of Commerce, the Black Thirty-Hour Bill, reintroduced during the Hundred Days, passed the Senate in April, 1933. In the House the proposal had the support of Representative William P. Connery of Massachusetts, the Chairman of the Committee on Labor, who suggested adding strengthening amendments. Secretary of Labor Perkins intervened to advise that any bill fixing maximum hours would be dangerous to labor unless it also dealt with minimum wages.

As this Black-Connery-Perkins project took form, the business world became greatly alarmed. Bowing to their opposition, the President disassociated himself from the Thirty-Hour Bill and set his advisers at the task of drafting a measure which would reconcile both the demand of the industrialists for relaxation of the antitrust laws and that of labor for reducing hours.

The result was the National Industrial Recovery Act, which provided for drafting of "codes of fair competition" by industrial groups or associations. These codes were to be submitted to the President or to some representative designated by him, whose duty it was to make sure that the associations were "truly representative," and that the proposed codes were "not designed to promote monopolies, or to eliminate or oppress enterprises." When the President was satisfied with the provisions of a particular code, he gave it his formal approval; then all units in the industry were bound to the code and might be punished for violations, whether or not they had participated in its formulation. If an industry failed to submit a code, the President might impose one after notice and hearing. The President was further authorized to enter into voluntary agreements with industrialists or labor organizations if such agreements would aid in effecting the objectives of the act. Pro-

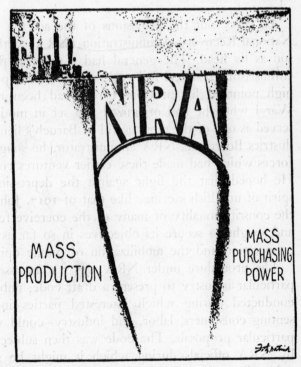

MASS PRODUCTION

MASS PURCHASING POWER

Bridging the Gap. (By Fitzpatrick in the *St. Louis Post-Dispatch*.)

tection to labor was provided by Section 7-A which required that every code and agreement must contain terms guaranteeing to employees the right of collective bargaining by representatives of their own choosing, free from restraint or coercion by employers. The measure was to be in force for two years and, during that period, approved code activities were to be exempt from the antitrust laws.

The bill encountered opposition from some of the old-line progressives like Senator Borah who disliked the relaxation of the antitrust laws, but, with business and labor both supporting it, the measure was passed and became law on June 16, 1933. President Roosevelt displayed his enthusiasm for the experiment in a statement issued the same day:

History probably will record the National Industrial Recovery Act as the most important and far-reaching legislation ever enacted by the American Congress. It represents a supreme effort to stabilize for all time the many factors which make for the prosperity of the Nation, and the preservation of American standards.

Its goal is the assurance of a reasonable profit to industry and living wages for labor with the elimination of the piratical methods and practices which have not only harassed honest business but also contributed to the ills of labor.

To carry out the provisions of the act the President established a National Recovery Administration (NRA) with General Hugh Johnson as its head. The general had a colorful personality, tremendous enthusiasm, great zeal for work, and a flair for pungent expression. The high point of his previous career had been reached during World War I when he had organized and set in motion the draft and then served as one of the most useful of Baruch's lieutenants in the War Industries Board. As NRA administrator, he sought to put at work the forces which had made these earlier ventures conspicuously successful. He hoped that the fight against the depression would call forth a spirit of unselfish sacrifice like that of 1917. Johnson was suspicious of the constitutionality of many of the coercive features of the new law and sought to secure its objectives in so far as possible by voluntary cooperation and the mobilization of public opinion.

The procedure under NRA was for an association representing a particular industry to present a draft code; public hearings were then conducted during which interested parties—including boards representing consumers, labor, and industry—could voice opposition to its particular proposals. The code was then subjected to intensive study by NRA officials during which it might be substantially amended. After all conflicting opinions had been reconciled in so far as possible, the code received the approval of the administrator and the President.

On July 9, 1933, the President announced his approval of the first of the NRA codes, that covering the cotton textile industry. Among other things it provided for a forty-hour work week with a limit of two shifts, minimum wages of $13 a week in the North and $12 in the South, and the abolition of child labor. Roosevelt was particularly elated over the last of these accomplishments, saying of the child-labor clause: "After years of fruitless effort and discussion, this ancient atrocity went out in a day, because this law permits employers to do by agreement that which none of them could do separately and live in competition."

There were more than two hundred codes submitted to NRA during July alone, making it obvious that it would be many months before the whole field of industry could be dealt with. Consequently, some short cut for achieving at once the agency's more important objectives was needed. This was provided by the President's Reemployment Agreement (PRA) of July 27, 1933, to which all employers were invited to subscribe at once. It pledged them to abstain from employing children, to limit hours of labor in stores and banks to forty and in factories to thirty-five, and to pay minimum wages of not less than 30 cents per hour. This document was popularly referred to as the Blanket Code—a misleading term since it was an entirely voluntary agreement entered upon by the individual employer with the President. Its purpose was through spreading work and raising substandard wages to create the purchasing power to sustain the industrial recovery which had developed on a somewhat speculative basis during the summer of 1933. Price raises appeared to be materializing faster than wage increases, and the administration hoped to reverse the process.

Employers who agreed to abide by either the PRA or the provisions of the code of fair competition for their particular industry were entitled to display an official symbol featuring a blue eagle and the words "NRA—We do our part." The dynamic General Johnson now organized a vast Blue Eagle campaign patterned on the Liberty Loan drives of World War I days. Local volunteer committees were organized to solicit the cooperation of businessmen and consumers, innumerable speeches were made, and parades arranged. Within four months, Johnson claimed, 96 per cent of commerce and industry were displaying the Blue Eagle, 2,785,000 workers had been put back on payrolls, and annual purchasing power had been increased by $3,000,000,000.

It had been hoped that the Blue Eagle drive would encourage the drafting of specific codes to substitute for the rather rigid requirements

Grover Whalen, New York NRA Chairman, Presents an NRA Flag to General Johnson, *left.* (Acme.)

of the PRA. Such proved to be the case and eventually 557 basic codes received NRA approval. By February, 1934, the code-making process was virtually completed and all but a very small segment of American industry had been covered. Not only manufacturing, but such economic activities as wholesale trade, retail trade, construction, and the service industries were all operating under NRA organization.

The various codes differed greatly, yet some of their more characteristic features may be listed. They always forbade child labor; maximum hours of work were variously fixed at between thirty-five and forty-eight weekly, with the average about forty; minimum wages were established usually at about 40 cents an hour, with most codes providing for geographical differentials and exceptions for certain classes of employees; the right of collective bargaining was recognized as required by Section 7-A. Most of the codes banned false advertising, commercial bribery, harassing litigation, and the like—practices which were already unlawful but which still prevailed in certain areas. More controversial were the provisions which permitted control of production or limitations on pricing. The cotton textile code limited the number of hours which the plants could operate. Several codes forbade the acquisition of new machinery or the entry of new units into the industry without special authorization. In a few natural-resource industries like lumber and timber, copper, and petroleum, definite production quotas were set. In the lumber, bituminous coal, and petroleum codes, moreover, prices were fixed. This was exceptional, for the provision in most codes was simply that goods must not be sold "below cost"—a formula which in many fields proved difficult of application. More than half the codes prescribed the open-price system and many required a waiting period between filing price changes and putting them in effect. Also common were strict rules regarding the amount of discount which might be allowed for prompt payment of accounts and the condition under which merchandise might be returned. Contrary to the advice of NRA officials, the tendency of the sponsors was to make the codes increasingly elaborate, dealing with trade practices in bewildering detail.

NRA UNDER FIRE

The honeymoon period of NRA was soon over and the experiment became the target of increasingly serious criticism. Section 7–A was resented by many employers. The Ford Motor Company asserted its traditional independence by refusing to associate itself with the automobile code because of the collective-bargaining clause. Other employers gave outward acquiescence to that principle, but sought to encourage the development of company unions, rather than independent ones with national affiliations. While NRA was being criticized by the employers for its prolabor bias, it was under simultaneous attack from the union leaders for not protecting more resolutely the right of the workers to organize.

Small businessmen were divided in their attitude toward the codes. Many industries had been rescued from imminent disaster. According to General Johnson, the bituminous coal code brought 4500 small operators back into production, the lumber code saved 1500 small sawmills, and the retail and wholesale codes by their ban upon loss leaders and other cutthroat competitive weapons saved tens of thousands of small merchants. Despite this, however, the codes were often bitterly resented. The wage and hour requirements were much more burdensome to small employers than to large and the former found little to comfort them in the President's statement that "no business which depends for existence on paying less than living wages to its workers has any right to continue in this country." A more legitimate criticism of NRA was that in the formulation of the codes and in their administration by industry-designated code authorities, big business in the nature of things was usually much better represented than small. Rules modifying trade practices were likely to benefit the units already best established in the field and to add to the difficulties of weak competitors. The filing of information with the code authorities was likewise apt to be prejudicial to the smaller concerns struggling to maintain their position.

Because of the widespread criticism that NRA was operating for the benefit of big business, Roosevelt appointed in the spring of 1934 a National Review Board under the chairmanship of Clarence Darrow, famous as a criminal lawyer and champion of the underdog, to ascertain and report whether any of the codes were "designed to promote monopolies or to eliminate or oppress small enterprises or operate to discriminate against them. . . ." Greatly to the disappointment of the NRA officials, the Darrow Board ignored the very considerable body of evidence showing that the codes had protected small business and concentrated exclusively on assembling evidence that pointed to the contrary tendency. The result was not a judicious appraisal of the actual situation, but a blistering indictment of the whole experiment. Enemies of NRA gave great publicity to the adverse findings of this report, yet laid little stress on its most remarkable conclusion—that oppression of small businessmen was inevitable under capitalism and that the only answer to the problem was socialism.

Meantime, consumers had their own grievances against NRA. Although an advisory board representing their interest was present in the hearings upon each code, its voice was inevitably weak as compared with the spokesmen for organized industry and organized labor. Just how much of the sharp advance in prices that occurred in many areas was fairly attributable to the codes and how much to other factors it is impossible to say; consumer resentment, however, was focused almost exclusively on NRA. The administration realized the seriousness of this resentment and sought to mollify the consumer by various steps. When the experiment was first launched the President appealed to industry not to abuse its opportunity. He said:

I am fully aware that wage increases will eventually raise costs, but I ask that managements give first consideration to the improvement of operating figures by greatly increased sales to be expected from the rising purchasing power of the public. That is good economics and good business. The aim of this whole effort is to restore our rich domestic market by raising its vast consuming capacity. If we now inflate prices as fast and as far as we increase wages, the whole project will be set at naught.

In passing upon the codes, the NRA officials were at first quite tolerant of provisions which tended toward price fixing, but they became increasingly opposed to such devices. Attempts to protect the consumer, however, had the effect of alienating the industrialists to whom the opportunity which NRA offered for escaping from ruinous price wars was the experiment's chief merit.

The decline in NRA's popularity was of the utmost importance. The agency's striking success in securing the initial cooperation of the business world was due to its overwhelming popular support during the first months. Fear of public opinion was likewise the most powerful force in gaining general compliance with code provisions. A threat to deprive a violator of his Blue Eagle usually brought him into line. As criticism of the NRA increased, however, more and more businessmen

Business, an Almost Unwilling Groom. But you see he met her only a few days ago. (By Darling in the *New York Herald Tribune*.)

felt that they could abrogate code provisions with impunity. Since open defiance of the codes threatened the whole experiment, the agency was impelled to order "crackdowns" and to prosecute more and more offenders. But such attempts at coercion angered still further the agency's critics.

General Johnson became a particular victim of attack. His explosive energy and outspokenness, which the country had found exhilarating in 1933, were less and less admired as time went on. The vigorous language with which he defended NRA against attack by those whom he described as "chiselers" and "social Neanderthals" was of course resented by those who felt that he was referring to them. Even within the agency there was an anti-Johnson faction formed by those who believed that NRA should be drastically reorganized. In September, 1934, the President bowed to the storm and accepted the General's resignation. Instead of a single administrator, a National Industrial Recovery Board was now appointed to supervise the agency. In March, 1935, the Board was itself reorganized and Donald Richberg, originally General Counsel of NRA, was named chairman.

Whether the experiment should be continued after the expiration of the original National Industrial Recovery Act in June, 1935, was one of the principal problems confronting Congress in the spring of that year. The President asked that the act be extended for an additional two years, asserting that the fundamental purposes and principles were sound and that to abandon them would "spell the return of industrial and labor chaos." He acknowledged, however, the need for amendments which would include a more definite statement by Congress "in order to clarify the legislative purpose and to guide the execution of the law." The fundamental principles of the antitrust laws should be more adequately applied. Monopolies and private price fixing within industry should not be allowed or condoned. In the administration of the law he recognized the need for simplifying the provisions of the codes as well as for better coordinating the various codes with each other.

Even to this simplified and reformed NRA there was strong opposition in Congress, particularly in the Senate. Some kind of extension of the act, however, would probably have been provided had not a decision of the Supreme Court on May 27, 1935, applied the *coup de grace* to the whole undertaking. In A.L.A. Schechter Poultry Corporation *v.* United States the Court unanimously reversed the decision of the lower courts under which the defendants had been convicted of violating the provisions of the live-poultry code. The Court declared that the National

Industrial Recovery Act was unconstitutional in so far as it delegated legislative power to the President without adequate standards to guide him in its exercise and in so far as it provided for Federal regulation of hours and wages in enterprises like the Schechter concern whose business was entirely intrastate in character. This spelled the end of code enforcement attempts and Congress repealed all compulsory features of the act, but provided for a skeleton NRA to liquidate the agency, collect and analyze statistical and other information bearing upon the great experiment, and explore the possibilities of continuing some of its features through purely voluntary agreements among businessmen. The latter proved impracticable and NRA expired completely in April, 1936.

From the beginning NRA had been handicapped by the incompatibility of its two main objectives—that of stimulating speedy recovery and that of providing for an organization of industry and drafting of codes of fair competition which would be of permanent benefit. The first called for the utmost haste; the second for caution and deliberation. Given the conditions of 1933, it is not surprising that the demands of recovery received priority. The result was that NRA made a considerable success of its short-term objectives—that of speeding production, increasing purchasing power, and establishing a truce on cutthroat competitive methods. But the atmosphere of excitement and haste which contributed to immediate success was prejudicial to the achievement of the agency's long-range objectives. The codes attempted too much and contained many ill-advised provisions. The result was a fatal deterioration of public support and this, even more than the Supreme Court's decision, was evidence of NRA's eventual collapse. Nevertheless the agency's failure was far from complete. Public opinion and subsequent legislation consolidated many of the gains which had been made: the abolition of child labor, the recognition of labor's right to organize, the establishment of certain standards of maximum hours and minimum wages, and the restraint upon ruthless exploitation of the country's natural resources.

SUCCESSORS TO NRA

To several groups the death of NRA threatened the loss of particular gains. Consequently these interests sought by independent legislation to prevent the recurrence of pre-1933 conditions. Labor's protection came in the National Labor Relations Act of 1935 and the Fair Labor Standards Act of 1938, while the bituminous coal industry, the oil industry, and the independent retailers found their substitutes for NRA in both state and Federal laws.

Bituminous coal has been described in an earlier chapter as one of the sick industries of the twenties. NRA had brought some relief, and soon after the Schechter decision Congress sought to continue these benefits through the Guffey-Snyder Bituminous Coal Stabilization Act, the so-called little NRA. A National Bituminous Coal Commission, representative of industry, labor, and the public, promulgated a code for the industry and established minimum prices. Labor was guaranteed the right of collective bargaining and maximum hours and minimum wage agreements by producers of two thirds of the tonnage and representatives of over one half of the mine workers bound the entire industry. Compliance was required through a 15 per cent tax on all coal produced under noncode conditions. The little NRA suffered the same fate as its parent, however, when the Supreme Court, in Carter v. Carter Coal Company, invalidated it in 1936 on the grounds that its labor provisions unconstitutionally delegated legislative powers. The following year a new measure, the Guffey-Vinson Act, by omitting the mandatory labor provisions of the original law, succeeded in putting the stabilization of the bituminous coal industry on a basis which the Supreme Court sustained in Sunshine Anthracite Coal Company v. Adkins (1940).

Although petroleum refining was highly concentrated in some twenty corporations, about one half of the crude oil of the nation came from the wells of small independent producers. During the depression, serious overproduction developed, with ruinous results on prices. The public interest was very definitely involved since chaotic conditions in the industry were resulting in serious waste of an essential natural resource. The situation led the legislatures of the oil-producing states to enact legislation establishing maximum quotas for the individual producers. Two problems subsequently developed: that of correlating the policies of the various states so that one did not profit unduly through the conservation measures undertaken by another, and that of curbing trade in so-called hot oil—oil produced in violation of the state-imposed quotas. Federal assistance seemed to be required; therefore Section 9 of NIRA made special provision for the petroleum industry. But in the so-called Hot Oil case (Panama Refining Company v. Ryan, 1935), that section was declared unconstitutional even before the rest of NIRA. A substitute was provided in the Connally Act of 1935, forbidding interstate commerce in contraband oil produced in excess of state-fixed quotas. Supervision of this measure was delegated by the President to Secretary of the Interior Ickes. Meantime, a mechanism for agreement upon state quotas had been worked out through interstate compacts of the oil-producing commonwealths.

Independent wholesalers and retailers, worried over the increasingly serious competition of the chain stores, also demanded protective legislation after NRA's demise. Exempted from the price-discrimination prohibition of the Clayton Act of 1914 were differentials based upon quantity sales—an obvious advantage to the chains. This was amended by the Robinson-Patman Act of 1936 to forbid such price discriminations unless it could be proved that such discounts for quantity sales were no greater than the actual savings in cost to the seller. Independent druggists and other interested groups, however, demanded still more protection. They secured from the legislatures of most of the states so-called fair-trade acts, which legalized contracts under which manufacturers bound retailers not to sell their products at less than a prescribed minimum retail price. Despite President Roosevelt's opposition, Congress cooperated by passing the Miller-Tydings Act in 1937 which exempted such price maintenance agreements from attack under the Sherman Antitrust Act. A third line of defense set up by the independents was through laws enacted in more than half the states under which chain stores were subjected to special taxes, graduated according to the number of separate stores which each maintained. Representative Wright Patman of Texas waged an aggressive but unsuccessful fight in Congress for a Federal tax on chain stores.

TRUST BUSTING AGAIN

One of the unexpected results of the NRA experiment was to restore to the antitrust laws a portion of their old-time popularity. Throughout the twenties the laws had been under attack as based upon an outmoded and indefensible philosophy. But the eagerness with which many businessmen resorted to devices for price fixing and limiting production under the protection of NRA codes served to educate the consuming public in the merits of the Sherman Act.

Early in his administration President Roosevelt attempted to restore the Federal Trade Commission to the functions for which it was originally intended by removing Chairman Humphrey, the Coolidge appointee whose conservative policies had been so welcome to big business. The Supreme Court rebuked this effort by ruling that members of such quasi-judicial commissions might not be removed by the President except for cause and after public hearings. Humphrey had meanwhile died, however, and this event, coupled with other opportunities to make appointments, permitted Roosevelt to revitalize the agency. The FTC's powers were broadened in 1938 by the Wheeler-Lea Act which made the commission's orders legally binding unless they were appealed to the courts within sixty days.

The most notable efforts to revive the antitrust laws, however, came from the Department of Justice. In 1938 the President appointed Thurman Arnold of the Yale Law School as Assistant Attorney General in charge of the Antitrust Division. Arnold was the country's leading critic of business practices which restrained competition—"bottlenecks of business" as he described them. The division now received much larger appropriations than ever before and began a series of carefully prepared cases. Considerable success was achieved despite the fact that the litigation received much less publicity than the famous antitrust suits of earlier days. Instead of a dissolution order difficult of enforcement, the outcome of Arnold's cases was frequently a "consent decree" —an agreed settlement between the government and the defendants in which the latter undertook to abstain from certain practices which were in restraint of competition. A degree of reform was thus forced upon certain automobile finance corporations in 1939 and upon the "block-booking" practices of the motion-picture industry in 1940. Arnold was sufficiently consistent in his philosophy to attack restrictive policies of the building-trade unions as well as of the contractors.

Meantime, one of the most significant investigations ever made of the workings of American capitalism was undertaken by the Temporary National Economic Committee (TNEC), established by Congress in 1938 upon the President's recommendation. Through public hearings and extensive research, a wealth of material was assembled relating to the degree of concentration of control in the American economic system, as well as the methods and effects of that concentration. The TNEC's reports appeared to prepare the ground for new legislation dealing with such matters as abuse of patent laws, but the onset of war had the inevitable effect of postponing such measures.

NEW DEAL TAX POLICIES

The administration's ambition to retard the growth of big business and the accumulation of excessive private fortunes was reflected in its recommendations for tax revision. The estate-tax and the gift-tax rates were increased in 1934 and 1935, making them for the first time a major source of Federal revenue. The surtax rates on individual incomes were raised to a maximum of 75 per cent on incomes in excess of $5,000,000. The corporation income tax was revised from a flat 13¾ per cent to a graduated rate of from 12 per cent to 15 per cent, while an excess-profits levy reminiscent of World War I days was restored to the tax structure.

These changes, mostly incorporated in the Revenue Act of 1935, were much resented by businessmen. Even more disliked was the tax on undistributed corporation profits, introduced in the Revenue Act of 1936. This step was taken to discourage the accumulation of unnecessarily large corporate surpluses, a form of oversaving which, by reducing dividend payments to stockholders, destroyed purchasing power and reduced the government's revenues from personal income taxes. Spokesmen for business, however, defended these surpluses as a necessary insurance against hard times and as providing the funds for plant expansion.

Conservative Democrats and Republicans mustered enough strength in 1938 to modify somewhat the New Deal tax structure. In the Revenue Act of that year Congress radically reduced the undistributed-profits tax and otherwise lightened the tax burden of the corporations. Roosevelt acknowledged the need for revision to encourage investment, but he criticized the Congressional program as "an infinitely greater tax concession to the man who makes a very great profit than to the man who makes a comparatively small profit. It helps the very few, therefore, at the expense of the many." He allowed the bill to become law,

Bounce. (By Bishop in the *St. Louis Star-Times*.)

but without his signature. The conservatives won another victory the next year when the undistributed-profits tax was entirely repealed.

REGULATION AND REFORM

Some of the most important New Deal legislation dealt with the protection of depositors, investors, and consumers from abuses to which the depression had called attention.

The Glass-Steagall Banking Act of June 16, 1933, strengthened the banking structure with three principal provisions: the Federal reserve banks were given enlarged powers to curb speculative expansion of credit by member banks; commercial banks were prohibited from engaging in investment banking or maintaining security affiliates; and a Federal Deposit Insurance Corporation (FDIC) was established to guarantee depositors against losses to the extent of $2500. The principle of insuring bank deposits was regarded with considerable misgivings in 1933 and the policy was adopted on a temporary basis. The results were so satisfactory, however, that in 1934 the insurance plan was continued for another year and the coverage was increased to $5000. In the Banking Act of 1935, the guarantee was made permanent. Ten years after the original enactment of the plan more than 13,000 banks, holding deposits of $97,000,000,000, were affiliated with the FDIC.

No area of economic life was more in need of regulation and reform than the business of trading in securities. Elementary safeguards to ensure that the investor should have adequate information on new issues had never been set up in the United States, even though England had had such laws since 1844. The shocking abuses which had been permitted to flourish were revealed in the investigations of the Senate Committee on Banking and Currency for which Ferdinand Pecora of New York served as counsel. The committee's hearings, which began in 1932 and continued until 1934, prepared the ground for the banking legislation just described and also for the Securities Act of 1933 and the Securities and Exchange Act of 1934.

The 1933 law, often called the Truth-in-Securities Act, prohibited the public sale in interstate commerce or through the mails of new security issues unless a registration statement had been filed with the Federal Trade Commission. In 1934 this was amended to require registration instead with the new Securities and Exchange Commission (SEC). The statement, a digest of which had to be included in the prospectus given to all persons to whom the securities were offered for sale, had to include information concerning the character and scope of the business, its corporate structure, the purposes for which the new money was to be used, and pertinent facts concerning the prior record of earnings in the case of an established concern or the character of the promoters in the case of a new enterprise. In order that both the commission and prospective investors might have an adequate opportunity to study this data, no public offering of the securities could be made until twenty days after the filing of the registration statement. In case of insufficient information or material falsehood in the statement, the commission was empowered to stop the marketing of the stocks or bonds. Willful violation of the law was punishable by a fine of not more than $5000 or imprisonment for not more than five years, or both. Moreover, persons suffering losses resulting from false registration statements might sue those responsible for the falsehood for civil damages. The new law did not guarantee the investor against loss; it simply ensured that he would have access to a certain minimum of accurate information about the enterprise in which he was being invited to risk his money.

The Securities Act of 1933 applied only to new issues; the problem of regulating trade in the old was dealt with in the Securities and Exchange Act of 1934. This established the SEC, a bipartisan board of five members appointed by the President for five-year terms. The law had three main objectives: (1) to make available to investors information regarding the affairs of corporations whose securities were traded in the securities market; (2) to prevent the diversion into security transactions of a disproportionate amount of the nation's credit resources; and (3) to eliminate manipulation and other abuses in the market. To effect the first, the act required the registration of all securities traded on the national exchanges and filing of up-to-date information on the business of corporations. To effect the second, the Federal Reserve Board was given power to regulate margin requirements, while the SEC was authorized to restrict borrowings by brokers and others doing business upon the exchanges. To effect the third, the SEC was granted broad powers over the stock exchanges of the country as well as over individual brokers whose registration with the commission was required. Protection against manipulation of stocks by insiders to the detriment of small stockholders was provided in the requirement that officers, directors, and those holding 10 per cent or more of the stock of any particular corporation had to file a monthly statement of transactions in the securities of their own company. In similar fashion the commodity exchanges of the nation were regulated under a 1936 law.

The New York Stock Exchange was extremely jealous of its powers of self-government. It regarded the new legislation and the new regulatory body with great suspicion. This was somewhat dissipated through the cautious policy of SEC's first chairman, Joseph P. Kennedy, who had been himself a successful trader. Kennedy permitted the Exchange to undertake its own housecleaning. Sixteen rules, drawn up in conference with the SEC, were voluntarily adopted by the New York body as a means of curbing manipulative practices. The results were not satisfactory and, after Kennedy's retirement, the second chairman, James M. Landis, inaugurated more active policies. The real showdown, however, was delayed until 1937 when William O. Douglas took over the headship of SEC. Douglas insisted that the Exchange should be completely reorganized to take the control out of the hands of men who were dealing in stocks primarily on their own account and place it with those doing business with the general public. This suggestion found a sympathetic response among an insurgent faction within the Exchange itself, but the "Old Guard" at first resisted reform. At just this juncture, however, an incident occurred which revealed all too clearly the abuses which the old regime had permitted. Richard Whitney, a former president of the Exchange, was indicted for grand larceny. In the words of an SEC report: "For at least 3½ years prior to its collapse, Richard Whitney and Company had done business as a member firm while insolvent. Richard Whitney's own misappropriation of customers' securities had commenced as far back as 1926, and, subsequent to 1936, had continued undetected as a regular practice." In the face of these disclosures Old Guard resistance collapsed and the New York Stock Exchange was completely reorganized with William M. Martin, Jr., who had been a leader in the reform movement, as its new president. The new Board of Governors cooperated closely with the SEC, while the latter gladly turned over to the Exchange the principal responsibility for self-policing and self-reform.[1]

Additional responsibilities were entrusted to the SEC by the Public Utility Holding Company Act of 1936. This law required that all public-utility holding companies register with the SEC and file specified information on their corporate organization. The commission was directed to examine each company in order "to determine the extent to which the corporate structure of such holding company system and the companies therein may be simplified, unnecessary complexities therein

[1] Likewise instrumental in bringing reform was the "recession" of 1937, during which stocks fell rapidly. President Roosevelt charged that the decline was brought on by anti-New Dealers in an effort to discredit the administration. He threatened to seek new and broader regulatory measures. To forestall such a step, the Exchange decided to do its own housecleaning.

eliminated, voting power fairly and equitably distributed among the holders of securities thereof, and the properties and business thereof confined to those necessary or appropriate to the operations of an integrated public utility system." As soon as practicable after January 1, 1938, the commission was to require each registered holding company to limit its operation to a single integrated public-utility system, although permission might be granted to control more than one system if such control was necessary to economical management, was exercised over a contiguous geographical area, and did not constitute so large a combination as to impair the advantages of localized management, efficient operation, or effective regulation. Even in the case of integrated systems, however, no holding companies beyond the second degree were to be allowed.[1]

One of the most bitter battles of the thirties was fought over this piece of legislation. To liberals, utility holding-company abuses had been a familiar story since 1928 when the FTC began its important investigation of the industry, and the law of 1936 contained only the minimum safeguards which the situation demanded. But the corporations under attack put up a desperate defense. They protested that the outlawing of nonintegrated companies and companies pyramided beyond the second degree was a "death sentence." Congress was deluged with letters and telegrams of protest from investors, but a Senate investigation, aggressively conducted by Senator Hugo Black of Alabama, revealed that many of the messages had originated with holding-company lobbyists rather than their supposed senders.

The corporations' resistance to the measure did not end with its passage. Most of them challenged the law by refusing to register with the SEC until the validity of this requirement was affirmed by the Supreme Court in the Electric Bond and Share case in 1938. In actually enforcing the "death sentence," the commission proceeded cautiously and sought to promote voluntary reorganization to as large a degree as possible. Less publicized but more immediately effective provisions of the law authorized the SEC to discourage the issuance of unnecessarily risky securities and the assumption of fixed charges beyond the normal earning capacity of the companies. A uniform system of accounts was set up as a protection to the investor and an assistance to state regulatory commissions.

The principle of government regulation already established in various areas was strengthened by the establishment of the Federal Communi-

---

[1] This meant that an operating company might be controlled by a holding company and this first holding company by a second, but further pyramiding was prohibited.

cations Commission (FCC) in 1934 to supervise the telephone, telegraph, and radio industries and by the much-expanded powers given to the Federal Power Commission by the Federal Power Act of 1935. Consumers were given greater protection through the passage of the Food, Drug, and Cosmetic Act of 1938, a considerably stronger law than the pioneer act of 1906.

THE TENNESSEE VALLEY AUTHORITY

During the second month of his administration, the President appealed to Congress to carry out Senator Norris's Muscle Shoals project in a form that surpassed the dreams of that veteran progressive. Roosevelt said:

It is clear that the Muscle Shoals development is but a small part of the potential public usefulness of the entire Tennessee River. Such use, if envisioned in its entirety, transcends mere power development; it enters the wide fields of flood control, soil erosion, afforestation, elimination from agricultural use of marginal lands, and distribution and diversification of industry. In short, this power development of war days leads logically to national planning for a complete river watershed involving many States and the future lives and welfare of millions. It touches and gives life to all forms of human concerns.

I, therefore, suggest to the Congress legislation to create a Tennessee Valley Authority, a corporation clothed with the power of Government but possessed of the flexibility and initiative of a private enterprise. It should be charged with the broadest duty of planning for the proper use, conservation and development of the natural resources of the Tennessee River drainage basin and its adjoining territory for the general social and economic welfare of the Nation.

Congress passed the requested legislation and on May 18, 1933, the Tennessee Valley Authority Act received the President's signature. The law created a public corporation to be administered by three directors appointed by the President. Arthur E. Morgan, president of Antioch College, served as chairman until 1938, when a quarrel between him and his fellow directors led to his removal and the elevation to the chairmanship of David E. Lilienthal of Wisconsin, who had been an influential figure in the TVA since its organization.

The first great activity of the agency was dam building—for the plan contemplated much more than the operation of Wilson Dam over which controversy had raged since World War I. Twenty-one dams eventually came under TVA's control, and of these sixteen were new ones constructed by TVA itself.

Highly controversial was the authority given TVA by Congress to

Senator George Norris at Norris Dam, Part of TVA. (Acme.)

generate and sell electricity. The private power companies would not
greatly have objected to this if the power had been sold wholesale to
them for transmission and distribution. But Congress laid down a very
different policy. TVA was directed to "give preference to states,
counties, municipalities, and co-operative organizations of citizens or

farmers, not organized or doing business for profit, but primarily for the purpose of supplying electricity to its own citizens or members. . . ." Against this effort to promote a public power business in competition to private industry, the utility companies put up a spirited fight in the courts. Although the constitutionality of the provisions permitting TVA to sell surplus electric power was upheld by the Supreme Court in 1936 (Ashwander v. TVA), this did not end the legal battle. A score of issues were raised, sweeping injunctions were issued in the lower courts, and several cases were taken to the Supreme Court. On every major issue TVA was sustained, but the litigation cost millions of dollars and hampered the agency's power activities for years. Eventually, in 1939, Commonwealth and Southern, the holding company whose subsidiaries were most affected, accepted a negotiated settlement. For $78,600,000 the company sold its Tennessee electrical properties to TVA and local public agencies. It was a substantially larger sum than the public power representatives had wanted to pay and Wendell Willkie, president of Commonwealth and Southern, received nation-wide publicity because of his fight in behalf of the investors. Parallel negotiations led to the purchase of other private utility properties in Mississippi and Alabama. After a hard struggle TVA had thus prepared the way to distribute electricity to public agencies without the necessity of wasteful duplication of facilities.

The agency did not deal directly with domestic consumers. Instead it sold its power wholesale to municipalities and cooperative associations. In 1943 it was doing business with eighty-three of the former, including the cities of Knoxville, Nashville, Memphis, and Chattanooga, and forty-five of the latter. It also sold directly to big industrial plants and many new enterprises were attracted to the area, particularly during World War II.

One of the most interesting aspects of the TVA experiment was the pioneering which the agency did with a radically low rate structure. To reduce rates, it was demonstrated, was to encourage the much wider use of electricity. In twelve communities served by TVA from 1934 to 1942 the consumption of electricity in homes increased during these years by 196 per cent as compared with 63 per cent for the nation. Public power advocates contended that the TVA experiment provided a "yardstick" whereby the reasonableness of private-utility rates all over the country could be measured. The spokesmen for the private industry bitterly denied this, saying that the comparison was unfair since TVA and the public agencies with which it dealt did not have to pay taxes and make a profit. This was largely untrue because TVA made annual payments of some $2,000,000 to state and county governments in lieu of taxes, while the municipalities and cooperatives followed similar practices. Both TVA and the public agencies, moreover, claimed to follow conservative accounting methods in calculating operating costs and allowing for depreciation. But, although the conditions under which TVA was doing business were more nearly similar to the private utilities than the latter were willing to admit, it nevertheless remained true that the comparison between TVA rates and private rates was likely to be misleading, and that the fairness of the rates in any particular part of the country had to be judged on the basis of the particular situation.

Whether TVA had provided a fair yardstick or not, private utilities responded to its challenge. An emphasis on rate reduction and increased consumption characterized the entire industry during the thirties. According to TVA Chairman Lilienthal, electric rates dropped only 2 per cent in the seven years before TVA as compared with a decrease of approximately 33 per cent during the seven years after 1933.

Public attention was largely concentrated on TVA's power program because of its challenging and controversial character. Less known were its other activities. The great TVA dams were multipurpose structures. One of their principal objectives was to promote navigation. Great artificial lakes connected by a system of locks provided 650 miles of navigable waterway to stimulate the economic life of the area. The dams also prevented floods. No major river in the world was so fully controlled as the Tennessee. By holding back or releasing the waters impounded behind nine dams on the main stream and twelve on the tributaries, a vast region could be protected against inundation. Moreover, TVA manufactured fertilizer, largely for demonstration purposes, rehabilitated impoverished farmers, educated them in better agricultural methods, and promoted reforestation.

So enthusiastic was the President over the success of TVA that in 1937 he advocated the establishment of similar regional-planning agencies in six other areas of the country: the Atlantic Seaboard, the Great Lakes-Ohio Valley, the Missouri Valley, the Southwest, the Colorado Valley, and the Columbia Valley. Although Congress was not prepared to entertain so bold a proposal, it did provide generous appropriations for the building of large dams in various parts of the nation. Such projects as Bonneville and Grand Coulee on the Columbia, Fort Peck on the Missouri, Big Thompson on the Colorado, and the Central Valley in California, built for various purposes such as navigation, flood control, and irrigation, all contemplated the generation of public power.

Another favorite Roosevelt dream, however, the St. Lawrence Seaway, failed of realization during the thirties because of the opposition of private power interests and the railroads.

Farmers, to whom electricity was a servant even more useful than to city dwellers, had been largely excluded from its benefits under rugged individualism. Private companies had found it profitable to extend service to less than 8 per cent of the nation's farms. Roosevelt sought to remedy the situation in 1936 by setting up the Rural Electrification Administration (REA) and allotting to it $100,000,000 of Emergency Relief Administration funds. The experiment was given a more secure basis the next year when Congress passed the Rural Electrification Act. Farmers were encouraged to form cooperatives which would erect transmission lines and furnish electricity to persons in rural areas not receiving central-station service. Such associations were to be assisted through low-interest loans from the REA. The administration endeavored to avoid controversy by not promoting cooperatives in areas already serviced by private industry and by encouraging farmers' associations to purchase electricity wholesale from the corporations rather than attempting to build their own generating plants. Even so the utility companies did not relish distribution through cooperatives and undertook a rural electrification program of their own. The result of this wholesome competition in good works was gratifying. By 1943 more than eight hundred cooperatives were providing farmers with electricity and their activities combined with those of purely private industry were serving the needs of 2,500,000 farms, some 26 per cent of the nation's total.

PUBLIC HOUSING

Government competition with private enterprise, the ultimate sin in conservative eyes, invaded the real-estate field as well as that of electrical energy.

One of the hardest hit industries of the depression was that of housebuilding. For the New Deal to attempt to stimulate construction was an obvious step in its recovery program. To a large extent, this was done through the encouragement of private business. In 1934 Congress authorized the establishment of a Federal Housing Administration (FHA). This agency was empowered to insure loans made by private lending institutions for both the repair of old dwellings and the construction of new. In the former case only 20 per cent of the loan was insured, but for new construction the guarantee was much more generous. On property valued at less than $6000 fully insured mortgages might be written for as much as 90 per cent of the value and carry a maturity of twenty-five years; on more expensive properties the limit was 80 per cent with a twenty-year maturity. The act originally set 5 per cent as the maximum interest, but this was reduced in 1939 to 4½ per cent.

Although FHA stimulated the building of homes for families in the middle-income brackets, it was no answer to the more desperate needs of the low-income group composing from one third to one half of the entire population. Many of the latter were living under slum conditions in the cities. To build decent homes cheaply enough to be sold or rented to such people was apparently beyond the abilities of private enterprise. There was, moreover, a powerful landlord interest at stake in perpetuating a situation where the poor had to live crowded together in dilapidated old properties. As early as 1933 low-cost housing and slum-clearance programs had been designated as a desirable area for expenditure under the PWA. But results were inadequate until legislation was passed in 1937 establishing the United States Housing Administration (USHA). This body was empowered to make long-term low-interest loans to state or local public-housing agencies for slum clearance and low-rent housing construction which met its standards. The requirement was laid down that tenants must be selected from the lowest income groups "who cannot afford to pay enough to cause private enterprise . . . to build an adequate supply of decent, safe, and sanitary dwellings for their use." As a Federal subsidy for these projects, the USHA was authorized to remit the interest and advance an annual sum equivalent to ½ per cent of the construction loan, provided this grant were necessary to the maintenance of low rents and provided the local agency were also making a contribution. By November, 1939, 296 public-housing projects were in progress under this program. These promised better homes for 650,000 persons, but this was only a fraction of the number needed. The administration appealed to Congress for authorization to expand the project, but the bill to effect this was defeated in the House through the votes of those who were opposed to Federal spending in general and those who were impressed by the loud protests of the real-estate interests.

TRANSPORTATION POLICY

In dealing with the air-transport industry and the merchant marine the New Deal sought certain reforms, yet in the end fell back upon a policy of generous subsidy similar to that of preceding Republican administrations.

In 1933 the government's air-mail contracts fell under vigorous criticism. It was alleged that the Hoover administration had permitted collusive bidding, had favored the big companies, and had made excessive expenditures. Despite the depression, Federal payments to the air lines had mounted from $9,345,000 in 1929 to $19,500,000 in 1933. Early in 1934 Postmaster General Farley canceled the contracts and for some weeks the army flew the mail. The results were unfortunate. A series of severe February storms swept the country and the army pilots and equipment were found inadequate for these abnormal conditions. Ten flyers lost their lives within a month, causing a public outcry which largely diverted attention from the abuses of the old system. The Air Mail Act of 1934 restored contract operations, but under safeguards assuring genuinely competitive bidding. The government made a substantial saving and in 1937 Farley was able to boast that although two and a half times as much air mail was being transported as in 1932, the cost to the government was $7,000,000 less.

But the air lines claimed that the new contracts were not adequate to maintain the industry on a profitable basis and in 1938 Congress established the Civil Aeronautical Authority (CAA) with extensive powers not only to regulate aviation but to adjust air-mail payments to the needs of the different classes of carriers. By 1939 total payments had risen to about $18,000,000, but this figure is hardly comparable to the one of 1933 since the volume of mail had increased very greatly.

The merchant marine subsidy program was even more vulnerable to criticism than that in the field of aviation. Despite annual payments amounting to about $29,000,000, the American merchant marine fleet was rapidly reaching the point of total obsolescence. In this field, also, the Roosevelt administration elected to continue the subsidy policy with what it hoped would be effective reforms. By the Merchant Marine Act of 1936 a new United States Maritime Commission was created. This body was authorized to grant direct subsidies instead of the discredited mail contracts. Payments were to be of two kinds: one to promote construction and the other to assist the private owners in meeting their operating costs. If the subsidy program proved ineffective, the commission was empowered to build ships on its own account, sell or charter them if possible, and operate them itself if necessary. The commission announced a program of sponsoring the building of five hundred new ships in ten years, but with the onset of war this seemed far too modest a goal and a period of feverish construction like that of World War I ensued.

Toward the railroads the New Deal undertook no radically new de-

partures in policy. The Emergency Transportation Act of 1933 authorized the appointment of a Federal Coordinator of Transportation, a
temporary post to which Roosevelt named Joseph B. Eastman of the
ICC. The coordinator's recommendations to the railroads for economies
in operation met resistance from both management and labor, but his
advice to the government on future transportation policy had greater
influence. "Theoretically and logically," Eastman pointed out, "public
ownership and operation meet the known ills of the present situation
better than any other remedy." In view of the practical difficulties of
such a course of action, however, he recommended an extension and improvement of the existing system of Federal regulation of privately
owned and operated carriers. Congress responded by extending the
jurisdiction of the ICC to include motor and water carriers, the first by
the Motor Carrier Act of 1935, the second by the Transportation Act
of 1940.

SOCIALISM AND THE NEW DEAL

A favorite conservative accusation was that the New Deal was
socialistic. Nevertheless a review of the record reveals that this was
mostly name-calling. There was a measure of socialism in the Roosevelt
policies toward electrical power and public housing, but even in these
fields the application of the philosophy was strictly limited. An administration really committed to advancing socialism would certainly have
proceeded very differently, particularly in dealing with the banks, the
railroads, the coal mines, and the merchant marine—strategic areas of
the national economy which were prostrate and dependent on government assistance in 1933. The most characteristic New Deal policies
were those designed to pull private enterprise out of the ditch, refuel it
with loans, and set it back on the road again with some attempt to add
governors to the machinery to prevent it from again smashing up.
Roosevelt conceived his mission to be to save capitalism rather than to
destroy it. Whether that was a virtue or a defect depended on the point
of view. And whether the steps actually taken did in the aggregate
strengthen private enterprise or weaken it was a question on which men
might honestly differ.

21

Agriculture and Labor, 1933–1939

O NE OF THE MOST NOTABLE OF CONTEMPORARY TRENDS HAS BEEN toward the strengthening of economic pressure groups. Business, agri-culture, and labor have resorted increasingly to organization in order to advance their respective interests and have thrown their political weight for or against the major parties according to what each would promise for the group. The Republican disaster of 1932 grew in large part out of the conviction of farmers and workers that the Hoover administra-tion had been less responsive to their needs than to those of business. The New Deal gained power on a pledge to right the balance. To restore the prosperity of agriculture and labor, however, was more than a compelling political obligation of the Roosevelt administration; it co-incided with the conviction held by the President and his advisers that business could not prosper unless the purchasing power of the farmers and the workers was materially increased.

AGRICULTURAL ADJUSTMENT ACT OF 1933

In his campaign speech of September 14, 1932, at Topeka, Kansas, Roosevelt had denounced Hoover for his unwillingness to consider the farm-relief programs advanced by the great farm organizations. He recognized that the agricultural spokesmen seemed to differ somewhat in their demands, but he promised:

It will be my purpose, my friends, to compose the conflicting elements of these various plans, to gather the benefit of long study and consideration of them, to coordinate efforts to the end that agreement may be reached upon the details of a distinct policy, aimed at producing the result to which all these efforts and plans are directed—the restoration of agriculture to economical equality with other industries within the United States. I seek to give to that portion of the crop consumed in the United States a benefit equivalent to a tariff sufficient to give you farmers an adequate price.

On March 8, four days after his inauguration, Roosevelt took steps to carry out this pledge. Through Secretary of Agriculture Wallace an invitation to confer with him was extended to some fifty representative farm leaders, prominent in the Farm Bureau, the Grange, the Farmer's Union, the farm cooperative organizations, and the farm press. The conference agreed on a set of recommendations, which were presented to the President on March 11. The problem of actually drafting a bill to incorporate these principles was—after the fashion of the Hundred Days—entrusted to a group of presidential advisers. Roosevelt transmitted the result of these labors to Congress on March 16. "I tell you frankly," he said, "that it is a new and untrod path, but I tell you with equal frankness that an unprecedented condition calls for the trial of new means to rescue agriculture. If a fair administrative trial of it is made and it does not produce the hoped-for results I shall be the first to acknowledge it and advise you."

The Agricultural Adjustment Act as finally passed and signed on May 10, 1933, showed the influence of Congressional points of view as well as those of the farm leaders and the braintrusters. The President was granted broad inflationary powers and provision was made for the refinancing of farm mortgages through the Farm Credit Administration. But principal interest lay in Title I of the Act which gave the Secretary of Agriculture extraordinary powers to raise the farmers' income. The purpose was to give agricultural commodities a purchasing power with respect to articles farmers bought equivalent to the purchasing power of agricultural commodities in the base period of 1909–1914. To gain this end, two principal methods were provided. In the case of seven basic commodities—wheat, cotton, corn, hogs, rice, tobacco, and milk and its products [1]—the Secretary was authorized to make agreements with individual farmers under which the latter would receive benefit payments for reducing the acreage of their crops or their production of livestock. The revenue for these payments was to be raised through a "processing tax"—an excise levy paid by the manufacturer on the first processing of the basic commodities for the domestic market. The other method provided was to authorize the Secretary of Agriculture to enter into marketing agreements with processors, farmers' associations, and others engaged in the handling of farm products. Thus steps could be taken through voluntary agreements—exempt from the antitrust laws—to establish marketing quotas which would maintain prices by curbing the sale of surpluses—not only of the basic com-

---

[1] The act was amended in 1934 to add sugar, beef and dairy cattle, peanuts, rye, flax, barley, and grain sorghums.

modities eligible for benefit payments but of other agricultural products as well. The Secretary was also granted broad powers to loan money on the security of crops, purchase surplus commodities, and subsidize exports.

THE FIRST AAA

To carry out the provisions of the act Secretary Wallace set up the Agricultural Adjustment Administration (AAA). George N. Peek, one of the authors of the bill and an advocate of farm-relief measures since McNary-Haugen days, was appointed to head the agency. Peek disagreed with Wallace, however, on fundamental issues of policy. The former was an economic nationalist who believed that emphasis should be placed on an aggressive campaign to sell the agricultural surplus abroad. He favored benefit payments but opposed curbs on production unless the surplus was excessive. Secretary Wallace, on the other hand, believed that American farm production must be curbed drastically to make it less dependent on the vagaries of the world market, although he was hopeful that this might be temporary and that through reciprocal trade agreements and tariff concessions foreign markets for American farm products might be restored. Increasing friction between the two men led to Peek's resignation in December, 1933, and the appointment of Chester A. Davis as administrator.

An attempt was made to decentralize the administration of the AAA. By utilizing the county agents of the extension service, contacts were made with individual farmers and local farm organizations so that county production-control associations could be set up. Restriction of acreage was entirely voluntary, but the opportunity to qualify for benefit payments was enough to induce a majority of the growers of staples to cooperate.

The first steps taken under AAA were particularly controversial because they involved large-scale destruction of commodities already growing. This was necessary in the opinion of the administration since the establishment of the agency came too late in the year to prevent the planting of crops and the breeding of livestock that threatened to glut the market. In the case of cotton, for example, 40,000,000 acres were in production in June, 1933—an acreage which seemed excessive under the conditions prevailing in the world market by at least 10,000,000 acres. An emergency program was launched under which the farmers were asked to rent to the Secretary of Agriculture at least one quarter of their acreage at from $6.00 to $20 an acre, according to its productivity. Over one million such contracts were made and cotton plants on about 10,400,000 acres of land were plowed under. For not producing an estimated 4,400,000 bales of cotton, the growers received approximately $113,000,000 in benefit payments. Even more shocking to Eastern conservatives was the purchase and slaughter of thousands of little pigs and pregnant sows to prevent a hog surplus. This massacre of the innocents was given great publicity in the press, although the fact that much of the meat was distributed to the needy through relief agencies received less comment.

The plowing up of crops already planted and the slaughtering of animals already bred, however, were only emergency procedures. The long-range plans of AAA called for limitations upon production in advance. During the next three years the system had an extensive trial. Production of the basic staples was reduced and prices were raised—sometimes with the help of additional measures as in 1933 when cotton loans at above the market price were made available to farmers to induce them to hold some of their harvest off the market, or in 1934 when compulsory marketing quotas were applied to the sale of raw cotton

How Would They Like to Trade Doctors? (By Darling in the *New York Herald Tribune*.)

and tobacco by special legislation. Better prices plus benefit payments increased farm income from $4,500,000,000 in 1932 to $6,900,000,000 in 1935. Even allowing for a substantial rise in prices which the farmer had to pay for things he purchased, this was equivalent to a 35 per cent increase in his real income. The effect of AAA policies upon the production and prices of certain of the basic commodities is indicated in the following chart:

| | Cotton | | Corn | | Wheat | |
	Net Output (mil. bales)	Price ($ per bale)	Net Output (mil. bus.)	Price (¢ per bu.)	Net Output (mil. bus.)	Price (¢ per bu.)
1932	13.0	32.60	587.2	31.9	548.5	38.2
1933	13.05	50.85	437.0	52.2	401.6	74.4
1934	9.64	61.80	170.1	81.5	360.1	84.8
1935	10.64	55.45	409.5	65.5	455.6	83.2

The reduced output and increased prices of these years could not, however, be attributed solely to AAA. Government spending for relief, dollar devaluation, the creation of increased purchasing power through NRA, and natural forces of recovery were all at work and it is impossible to isolate the effect of any one factor. Of great importance, also, was the serious drought of 1934, which reduced production and raised prices more drastically than AAA had planned.

Farmers grumbled about many aspects of the program. Despite efforts made to administer it democratically, the experiment did involve some interference with the American farmer's cherished individualism and —what was perhaps more serious—it established precedents which might lead to more distasteful forms of regimentation in the future. Some farmers were legitimately worried about the ultimate results on exports of a policy of reducing production and raising prices. Not all farmers shared equally in the benefits of the act. Producers of the basic commodities usually gained more than growers of other products, while large farmers gained more than the small. Whatever the misgivings about some features of AAA, however, referendums revealed that the overwhelming majority of farmers desired to have the experiment continued at least until some more desirable alternative could be presented.

Consumers of course were less enthusiastic. They were required to contribute to the rehabilitation of agriculture both in increased prices and in the processing taxes which the manufacturers passed on to them. But spokesmen for agriculture promptly pointed out that for many decades consumers had been paying a similar, if less obvious, subsidy to manufacturers through the operations of the protective tariff. And they also asserted that "the economics of scarcity" had not originated with them, but with industrialists who had sought by fair means and foul to control production in order to maintain prices.

THE SUPREME COURT INTERVENES

On January 6, 1936, in the so-called Hoosac Mills case (United States *v.* Butler), the Supreme Court dealt a crippling blow to the AAA. The issue was the constitutionality of the processing tax; a majority of the Court held that this was invalid since it had been levied, not for the general welfare, but for the purpose of regulating agricultural production. Speaking for himself and five of the other judges, Justice Roberts declared:

The act invades the reserved rights of the states. It is a statutory plan to regulate and control agricultural production, a matter beyond the powers delegated to the federal government. The tax, the appropriation of funds raised, and the direction of their disbursement, are but parts of the plan. They are but means to an unconstitutional end.

Three justices, Stone, Brandeis, and Cardozo, disagreed with this reasoning. Justice Stone asserted that the decision of the majority depended on "a tortured construction of the Constitution" and was "addressed to the mind accustomed to believe that it is the business of courts to sit in judgment on the wisdom of legislative action"; he held "that the power to tax and spend includes the power to relieve a nation-wide economy maladjustment by conditional gifts of money."

Although such AAA activities as surplus removal operations, crop loans, and the establishment and enforcement of marketing agreements were not affected by this decision, the system of contracts under which the government promised benefit payments in return for the farmer's reduction of acreage was completely ruled out. AAA officials and farm-organization representatives, convinced that the results might be disastrous, quickly brought forward an alternative policy.

AGRICULTURAL CONSERVATION

On February 29, 1936, the President gave his approval to the Soil Conservation and Domestic Allotment Act, an amendment and extension of the less ambitious Soil Erosion Act of 1935. The Secretary of Agriculture was authorized to make payments to farmers who employed methods which maintained and restored the fertility of the soil and prevented erosion. Producers could qualify for these payments by decreasing the acreage planted to soil-depleting crops—cotton, tobacco, corn, wheat, and other grains, and increasing the acreage planted to soil-conserving crops—legumes and perennial grasses, or crops like soy beans and cow peas which were valuable as fertilizer when plowed under. Other conservation practices entitling the user to benefits might be the application of fertilizer, the planting of trees, or the terracing and furrowing of pastures on the contour. The AAA was continued under the same name to carry out the provisions of the new law, but some of the procedures which had been rebuked by the Hoosac Mills decision were abandoned. Contracts were not made with the individual farmers and the benefit payments were appropriated out of the general revenues rather than from the proceeds of a special levy like the processing tax.

Agricultural conservation had much to commend it. The folly of many of the agricultural practices of World War I and the postwar period had been dramatically illustrated during the thirties. Parched by hot sun and scanty rainfall, millions of acres of Western land had been ruined. Great dust storms had blown away the thin topsoil, thousands of farms had been abandoned, and hundreds of thousands of farmers had been reduced to the status of migratory agricultural laborers. The conservation program won the cooperation of two thirds of the 6,800,-000 farmers of the country.

But the new law did not prove effective as a curb on the production of agricultural surpluses. The aggregate production of the fifty-three leading crops was larger in 1937 than in any previous year in American history. Large surpluses of cotton, wheat, and other crops began to accumulate and the situation threatened to develop another tragedy like that of 1932—particularly since a general economic recession was in progress.

THE EVER-NORMAL GRANARY

To meet this situation, a new Agricultural Adjustment Act received the approval of Congress and the President, becoming law on February 16, 1938. This measure provided for a variety of procedures, but underlying the whole was the philosophy which Secretary Wallace had been formulating and urging upon the nation. Farm policy, the Secretary argued, should be directed not only to securing for agriculture its fair proportion of the national income, but to guaranteeing to consumers an adequate food supply through years of plenty and scarcity alike. By enabling the farmer to store nonperishable staples, an ever-normal granary would be provided.

The act of 1938 stressed again the importance of conservation. Farmers, cooperating with the Secretary of Agriculture, were eligible for benefit payments. It was now required, however, that the farmer should plant no more acreage in a particular commodity than his allotment under a national quota large enough to meet normal domestic consumption and export requirements for the following marketing year, and to provide also a reserve or carry-over supply of the commodity. If a farmer kept within his acreage allotment and otherwise followed soil-conserving policies, he qualified for benefit payments.

All farmers were eligible for these payments, but producers of cotton, wheat, corn, tobacco, and rice were granted certain additional protection. In the first place, growers of these staples who cooperated with the AAA program, were eligible for price-adjustment or parity payments whenever Congress made appropriations available for this purpose. These payments were intended to provide the growers with a return as nearly equal to parity price as the funds so appropriated would permit.[1]

Another type of assistance was available through the Commodity Credit Corporation which was empowered to make loans on the security of any agricultural product and was specifically directed to do so in the case of cotton, corn, and wheat whenever the crop of these was larger than necessary to meet domestic requirements or when the price declined more than a certain percentage below parity. Farmers cooperating in the AAA program might secure loans ranging from 52 per cent to 75 per cent of parity. These commodity loans not only permitted the storage of grain—often on the farmer's own premises, but had the effect of putting a floor under agricultural prices. Producers of wheat, moreover, were also given an opportunity to secure crop insurance against losses due to unavoidable causes, such as drought, flood, and disease. Premiums were paid in wheat, stored by the Federal Crop Insurance Corporation.[2]

In the case of cotton, wheat, corn, tobacco, and rice, marketing quotas might under certain conditions be imposed. The supply of the particular commodity had to be in excess of normal by a specified amount and two thirds of the growers had to approve the step in a special referendum. Once imposed, however, the marketing quotas applied both to farmers cooperating with the AAA and those who were not. All

[1] Parity was defined as "that price for the commodity which will give to the commodity a purchasing power with respect to articles that farmers buy equivalent to the purchasing power of such commodity in the base period. The base period is August, 1909, to July, 1914, except for tobacco where the base period is August, 1919, to July, 1929."

[2] The crop insurance plan was extended to cotton in 1942.

sales in excess of individual quotas were subjected to heavy penalty. Another method of dealing with the surplus problem was provided by continuing and expanding the operations already initiated by the Federal Surplus Commodities Corporation, which bought up and distributed agricultural surpluses through relief channels or through subsidized exports.

Although the Agricultural Adjustment Act of 1938 returned to a system of paying benefits to farmers who restricted their acreage, the processing tax was avoided. The program was financed by annual Congressional appropriations of $500,000,000 for benefit payments and about $212,000,000 for parity payments.

Agriculture had obviously joined the ranks of the subsidized industries. Many observers regretted the development, but no very feasible alternative was suggested and Republican counterproposals were notoriously vague. And at least it could be said that in return for their annual contribution, the taxpayers were now being assured an ample food supply and certain minimum safeguards for the nation's soil resources.

THE FOOD STAMP PLAN

The greatest paradox in the farm situation was that the agricultural surplus was constituting a major problem of government during a decade in which millions of Americans did not have enough to eat and wear. As far back as the Hoover administration, government agencies had taken the obvious step of making gifts of surplus commodities to relief agencies, and this practice had continued and been expanded under the New Deal. Rational though it seemed to link relief and surplus-removal, many interested parties were dissatisfied. Families on relief had to accept whatever was offered to them whether or not it coincided with their needs; wholesalers and retailers resented the distribution of supplies through noncommercial channels.

At Rochester, New York, in May 1939, a new method of handling the problem was tried out through the cooperation of Federal and local agencies. Families on relief were given an opportunity to buy weekly, on an entirely voluntary basis, a minimum of $1.00 or a maximum of $1.50 worth of orange stamps for each member of the family. For each dollar's worth of stamps purchased, the family was given free 50 cents' worth of blue stamps. The stamps might be used at any grocery store. The orange stamps were acceptable for any food sold in the establishment, but the blue ones could be used only to purchase foods designated as "surplus" by the Secretary of Agriculture. The storekeeper deposited the stamps with his bank, while the latter received payment for them from the government. In this way surplus commodities found their way into the hands of low-income consumers without the necessity of government purchase and distribution. It was of course a subsidy, but it was a subsidy for consumption rather than for restriction of production and hence less distasteful to many citizens.

The trial at Rochester was successful and the Food Stamp Plan was extended over the next two years to some 150 cities before the country's involvement in war removed for the time being any problem of an agricultural surplus. The experiment had great significance, not because the particular plan evolved could be considered final or completely satisfactory, but because it pointed in what seemed to many the right direction—toward helping the farmer by creating new purchasing power within the country.

FARM SECURITY ADMINISTRATION

In 1937 the President's Special Committee on Farm Tenancy issued a report of a most disquieting character. "For the past 55 years," it stated, "the entire period for which we have statistics on land tenure, there has been a continuous and marked decrease in the proportion of operating owners and an accompanying increase in the proportion of tenants. Tenancy has increased from 25 per cent of all farmers in 1880 to 42 per cent in 1935." Yet this growth of tenancy was only part of the problem. Agricultural insecurity was the lot not only of tenants and sharecroppers, but of farm laborers, families on submarginal land, families on holdings of inadequate size, owner-families hopelessly in debt, and farm young people unable to obtain farms. According to another study based upon the agricultural census of 1935, 1,700,000 farm families, representing nearly 8,000,000 men, women, and children, received net incomes of less than $500 per year, including the value of products sold, traded, or used.

To this vast company of the agricultural underprivileged, AAA had little to offer. A program to meet the problem of rural poverty was slow in developing, although efforts toward linking temporary relief payments with steps to rehabilitate farm families in trouble were made in several of the states early in the thirties. As the Federal government became involved in financing relief, it gave increasing attention to the problem. In 1934 a rural rehabilitation division was set up as a branch of the Federal Emergency Relief Administration. The next year the Resettlement Administration was established as an independent agency to carry out a more ambitious program under Federal direction. In

1937 the Resettlement Administration was replaced by the Farm Security Administration (FSA) in the Department of Agriculture.

The FSA fell heir to numerous experimental projects dating back to the early days of the New Deal. About 160 resettlement communities and subsistence homesteads had been laid out in various parts of the country. They followed no uniform pattern. In some cases they were settled with farm families who had been living on submarginal land which the government had purchased and taken out of cultivation; in other cases relief families who had had farming experience were transferred to the country from the cities or from communities dependent on coal mining or logging where operations had ceased because of the depression. In some of the projects the colonists did full-time farming; in others they did part-time farming and worked the rest of the time either in specially established local industries or in some near-by town. In some, operations were carried on cooperatively, in others individually. Three so-called Greenbelt towns, located near Washington, Cincinnati, and Milwaukee, had been developed to demonstrate the practicability of scientific town planning, the wise use of land, and the mass production of housing units and hence were not for farmers at all. Activities of this kind were fascinating social experiments, but they were extremely vulnerable to criticism. They furnished all too much ammunition for those who wanted to depict the New Dealers as impractical utopians or as Communists bent on destroying the American economic system. At the insistence of Congress, the FSA gradually liquidated the homestead projects, giving the settlers the first opportunity to buy.

Other FSA activities, however, aroused less opposition. In case of flood, drought, or complete impoverishment due to erosion the agency made outright grants of money, but this was exceptional. The usual procedure was to loan money to the distressed farmer, contingent upon his accepting guidance in farm and home management which was intended to make him self-supporting. Under the Bankhead-Jones Act of 1937 selected tenants and laborers might be advanced sufficient funds to purchase their farms. Such loans for this purpose averaged $5000 each and were repayable within forty years at 3 per cent interest. Most of the FSA loans, however, were more modest in size and purpose; they were short-term advances for seed, fertilizer, livestock, farming equipment, clothing, necessary medical care, repairs, and similar purposes. In the case of farmers hopelessly in debt, voluntary adjustments with the creditors were sought whereby the debt might be scaled down to manageable terms. Tenants composed 70 per cent of the FSA clientele and the agency sought to improve their status by replacing the short-term leases, under which it had been customary for at least one third of them to move every year, with long-term written leases so drawn as to reward them for improving the property, but to penalize them for willful neglect. Such farmers were encouraged to diversify their farming, to raise pigs, cows, and chickens for food, to grow and can vegetables, and to recognize the importance of sanitation. Through prepayment of annual fees, FSA families were assured adequate medical care. Pressing needs for such things as water in the dry belt, tractors and expensive machinery, and good breeding stock were met by the organization of cooperative associations, which were eligible for FSA loans and advice. In cooperation with the states and local health agencies, camps were built to provide shelter for migrant workers.

Considering the desperate circumstances of its clientele and the fact that its loans were made only to persons who could not secure credit through other channels, FSA was remarkably successful in its financial operations. Up to June 30, 1945, almost 90 per cent of its loans had been repaid when they fell due. This was evidence that a considerable amount of agricultural rehabilitation had actually been accomplished. Vastly more needed to be done, however, and FSA appropriations were always low as compared with those for other purposes—due in part to the suspicion with which the larger farmers viewed these efforts to improve the status of tenants and laborers.

LABOR UNDER NRA

Trade unionism, which had flourished during World War I, lost ground throughout the twenties and then suffered further serious setbacks during the depression. Total membership was estimated at 5,047,-800 in 1920, 3,442,600 in 1929, and only 2,973,000 in 1933.

The situation was radically altered, however, during the first year of the New Deal. Section 7-A of the National Industrial Recovery Act declared:

1) . . . employees shall have the right to organize and bargain collectively through representatives of their own choosing, and shall be free from the interference, restraint, or coercion of employers of labor, or their agents, in the designation of such representatives or in self-organization or in other concerted activities for the purpose of collective bargaining or other mutual aid or protection;

2) . . . no employees and no one seeking employment shall be required as a condition of employment to join any company union or to refrain from joining, organizing, or assisting a labor organization of his own choosing.

Union organizers made skillful use of this declaration of policy. In the coal mines, for example, the news was carried from pit to pit that the United States guaranteed the right to join unions. Often the issue was further simplified. Taking advantage of Roosevelt's phenomenal popularity during the summer of 1933, great banners were prepared carrying the legend: "President Roosevelt wants you to join a union."

The workers' response astonished even the labor leaders themselves. Total union membership at the beginning of 1935 was estimated at 4,200,000, showing an increase of 1,200,000 since 1933. Particularly important was the progress of organization in entirely new fields. During the first four months after the establishment of NRA, the American Federation of Labor chartered 584 directly affiliated federal unions with 300,000 members. Between July, 1933, and July, 1934, 106 federal locals were established in the automobile field where there had been no AFL unions before, while in the rubber-tire industry a similar revolution occurred.

But labor's rejoicing proved to some extent premature. Many employers sought to fulfill the collective-bargaining stipulation of Section 7-A by encouraging company unions. These more than doubled in number between 1933 and 1935, while their coverage of employees rose from 1,263,194 in 1932 to about 2,500,000 at the beginning of 1935. The system was strong in the larger plants generally and in the iron and steel, chemical, and transportation equipment industries in particular. Moreover, despite NRA, the most resolute of antiunion employers succeeded in preventing organization altogether. In April, 1935, replies to a Bureau of Labor Statistics questionnaire from firms hiring nearly two million workers revealed that about 30 per cent of these workers were employed by companies which bargained collectively with trade unions, about 20 per cent in establishments where a company union system prevailed, about 7 per cent where both company and trade unions were dealt with, while more than 43 per cent worked in plants where there was no recognized labor organization at all.

Labor protested against many of the code provisions. They asserted that both in the drafting and the administering of these industry was given too much power. For example, the automobile code contained a so-called merit clause, which read: ". . . employers in this industry may exercise their right to select, retain, or advance employees on the basis of individual merit, without regard to their membership or nonmembership in any organization." Under cover of this provision, it was alleged, active unionists were discharged or otherwise discriminated against. In the hour and wage provisions of the codes, labor usually fared poorly in the unorganized industries. Innumerable disputes arose between AFL unions, unaffiliated independent unions, and company unions over the right to bargain for employees in particular plants. This led in some cases to assigning the rival unions proportional representation in a specially created bargaining agency and in others to dealing separately with majority and minority groups.

Such grievances as these, plus the wages and hour demands to be expected during a period of increased production and rising prices, led to an epidemic of strikes in 1933 and 1934. Since these threatened to retard recovery and injure the NRA experiment, President Roosevelt appointed on August 5, 1933, a National Labor Board, composed of three representatives of industry and three of labor with Senator Wagner of New York as impartial chairman. This body heard complaints, settled strikes, and conducted elections to determine collective-bargaining representatives. The board was a purely executive creation under the general authority of NRA, but so long as the prestige of the latter was high, the panel had a reasonable degree of success in its activities. During 1934, however, when NRA was under severe attack, the board suffered a series of defeats due to the unwillingness of management and labor to accept its jurisdiction and to abide by its decisions. Special labor boards provided under the automobile, textile, steel, and coal codes had similar difficulties. Nor was the situation materially improved when the National Labor Board was replaced with a National Labor Relations Board (NLRB). The latter was a three-man panel appointed by the President under specific Congressional authorization, but it too lacked sanctions to compel obedience to its rulings. Moreover, Section 7-A, which it was attempting to apply, was altogether too general in its phrasing.

THE NATIONAL LABOR RELATIONS ACT

In their disillusionment, unionists dubbed NRA the "National Run Around" and demanded additional protection for their right to organize. A bill for this purpose, introduced by Senator Wagner in 1934 without the President's support, failed. Reintroduced the next year, the measure still found the administration cool, yet it displayed increased strength in the two Houses of Congress. Such was the situation when the Supreme Court's Schechter decision destroyed NRA. Left now without even the safeguards of Section 7-A, labor redoubled its demands for the Wagner Bill. The result was the passage and approval by the President on July 5, 1935, of the Wagner-Connery or National Labor Relations Act.

The law authorized the establishment of a new National Labor Relations Board (NLRB) of three members appointed by the President with the consent of the Senate. The general guarantee of Section 7-A was reenacted in almost identical language, but it was now implemented with a series of specific rules. Five unfair labor practices were listed: employers were forbidden: (1) to interfere with, restrain, or coerce employees in the exercise of the right to bargain collectively, (2) to dominate any labor organization or give financial or other support to it, (3) to discriminate in employing, discharging, or otherwise dealing with employees in order to encourage or discourage membership in any labor organization, (4) to discharge or otherwise discriminate against any employee who filed charges or testified before the NLRB, or (5) to refuse to bargain collectively with the representatives of their employees. The act provided that in any bargaining unit the representatives chosen by the majority of the employees should be the exclusive representatives of all the employees. In case of dispute, the NLRB was authorized to investigate and certify the proper employee representatives. To assist in this decision, the board might take a secret ballot or utilize any other suitable method. The NLRB could issue "cease and desist" orders against employers who violated the act, but these were enforceable only through petition to the Federal courts.

The National Association of Manufacturers and other spokesmen for businessmen protested strenuously against the passage of this legislation. They contended that it was one-sided since it defined unfair conduct on the part of employers without doing so for the unions themselves. Their opposition did not cease when the bill became law. Taking advantage of the contention that the act was unconstitutional, most of the large employers of the country determined to ignore it pending a test of the legal issues. As a result, the law was largely inoperative during the first two years of its existence. In 1937, however, the Supreme Court upheld the validity of the measure in Associated Press v. NLRB, NLRB v. Jones and Laughlin Steel Corporation, and several other cases.

With its authority thoroughly supported by the courts, the NLRB became a very powerful body. By the end of 1939 it had ordered the disestablishment of 340 company unions. The formation of new organizations of this type practically ceased, while the old company unions which survived were completely reorganized to give them more independence. Meantime, general trade-union membership continued to grow until in 1941 about eleven million workers were affiliated with some organization. This growth was not, of course, to be attributed solely to the Wagner-Connery Act and the NLRB, but these served at least as a strong deterrent to such methods as employers had used in the past to counteract the efforts of the organizers. Businessmen continued to complain of the one-sidedness of the act and asserted that the NLRB was prolabor in its policies. These protests induced the House of Representatives to pass a series of amendments to the act in 1940, but the Senate took no action. President Roosevelt undertook to still criticism by appointing Harry A. Millis to head the NLRB in place of J. Warren Madden, who had guided the Board through its first stormy period. The war distracted attention from the issue, but it seemed certain to arise again later.

SOCIAL SECURITY

Another foundation stone of the Second New Deal was the Social Security Act of August, 1935. Behind its passage lay a reversal in prevailing American opinion. Old-age pensions, unemployment insurance, and provisions for sickness and accident benefits under government administration had been commonplace in Europe before World War I. But most Americans had regarded such proposals as intolerable paternalism, and the belief had persisted that saving against old age and misfortune was an individual problem. The depression provided a cruel disillusionment. Thousands of thrifty citizens saw their savings of years swept away by bank failures, while the impossibility for the average individual to guarantee his own security in a complex economic system was demonstrated in many other ways as well. By 1932 there was a widespread demand for government action. The American Federation of Labor passed resolutions asking unemployment insurance with compulsory payments by employers and the state—reversing its earlier hostility to the proposal, while the Democratic National Platform included a plank advocating both unemployment and old-age insurance under state laws.

But building a social security system on exclusively state legislation offered many difficulties. Each state hesitated to burden employers with pay-roll taxes lest factories be moved to other states where no such levies were imposed. Some Federal program to coordinate action on a national basis seemed to be required. To study the problem, President Roosevelt appointed in June, 1934, a Committee on Economic Security with Secretary of Labor Perkins as chairman and a number of advisory groups composed of technical experts. The efforts of these several bodies resulted in a Report on Economic Security which recommended a comprehensive system based upon joint Federal-state action. The

President endorsed the program in a message transmitting the report to Congress on January 17, 1935.

None too early was the administration taking up the problem. Local clubs all over the country were agitating for the Townsend Old Age Revolving Pension Plan, a scheme concocted by Dr. Francis A. Townsend, a retired physician, under which every individual over sixty years of age was to be paid $200 each month to be entirely spent within the next thirty days. Thus at one step, so its sponsors argued, security for the aged would be provided along with perpetual prosperity for the country. Even more extreme programs were being advanced by Senator Huey Long of Louisiana with his Share-the-Wealth plan for guaranteeing to each citizen an income of $5000 and by the radio priest, Father Charles E. Coughlin of Royal Oak, Michigan, with his demands for radical inflation. Beside such reckless proposals as these the recommendations of the administration seemed mild and in fact most of the witnesses appearing at the hearings on the bill were Townsendites demanding the substitution of the $200-a-month plan. The Social Security Act passed Congress by substantial majorities and received the President's signature on August 14, 1935.

The new law dealt with old-age pensions, unemployment insurance, public assistance to the needy aged, the needy blind, and dependent children, and an extension of additional aid for maternal and child welfare services and public health facilities. The only one of these programs exclusively administered by the Federal government was that providing for old-age insurance. All employers and employees except those in certain exempted categories were required to pay a pay-roll tax equivalent to 1 per cent of the salary of each employee. This tax was to be gradually increased until it reached 3 per cent in 1949. These revenues were to be used to build up reserves in the Federal Treasury out of which after January 1, 1942, retired workers were to receive pensions for life of from $10 to $85 monthly, depending upon their average wages and the length of time they had been contributing under the plan.

Provision for unemployment insurance was left to the states, but, in order to encourage the establishment of such plans, a Federal unemployment tax starting at 1 per cent but rising to 2 per cent in 1937 and to 3 per cent in 1938 was levied upon all employers—except those in exempted categories. The employers, however, were to be allowed a credit up to 90 per cent for any contributions made to state unemployment funds. From the 10 per cent which was retained in such cases the Federal government made grants to the states to assist them with administrative expenses. The inducement proved adequate to secure the enactment of unemployment insurance laws in all of the states by July 31, 1937.

In other sections the Social Security Act provided for Federal grants-in-aid up to $15 per month for states which would match this contribution and administer a program of public assistance to old people in need of relief who were not covered by the insurance plan. Similar Federal grants were available to states which adopted plans for aiding the blind and dependent children. Federal aid on a somewhat different basis was extended for certain health and welfare activities and for vocational rehabilitation.

The law was criticized in various quarters. Employers complained of their new tax burdens and bookkeeping problems. Liberals were displeased because agricultural laborers, domestics, and many others had not been brought under the system and because the benefits were small. Economists considered the pay-roll tax as deflationary in effect and unnecessarily heavy since the Federal government with its power to tax was not under the same necessity as private insurance companies to accumulate huge reserves.

Whatever the misgivings about various details, however, social secur-

Bringing the Prodigal Home. (By Bishop in the *St. Louis Star-Times*.)

ity in principle soon won general acceptance. Republican efforts during the campaign of 1936 to turn the workers against the law because of the pay-roll deductions found little response and it became apparent that the popular demand was not for repeal but for liberalization. By various amendments adopted by Congress in 1939 benefits were enlarged and provision was made for protecting the widow and children of the worker in case of his death.

BIRTH OF THE CIO

For years there had been dissension within AFL ranks over the issue of industrial unionism. An aggressive faction had insisted that the mass-production industries like autos, rubber, steel, and electrical equipment would never be adequately organized except by new unions founded along industrial lines. But the established craft unions regarded with great suspicion the creation of any more industrial unions than necessary. When Section 7-A suddenly opened up an opportunity for invading the unorganized industries, the problem was postponed for the time being by chartering federal locals directly responsible to the AFL officers. This soon proved unsatisfactory. The craft unions were anxious to use such locals as recruiting agencies for their organizations and insisted upon a broad construction of their jurisdictional rights. Yet such groups as the auto workers and the rubber workers were just as insistent that they be brought together in single unions for each industry. Many of the old-line leaders, their critics charged, were not only too much interested in protecting vested interests, but too cautious and conservative in temperament to take full advantage of new conditions. This was particularly true in the case of steel, the most important anti-union citadel of the country where the Amalgamated Association of Iron, Steel, and Tin Workers, an old-line craft union which had suffered defeat after defeat during its unhappy history, took no effective steps to organize the plants of the major companies, yet resented all efforts put forth to achieve this end through other channels with the result that company unionism was greatly extended throughout the industry.

Dissension within the AFL reached a crisis at the 1935 convention at Atlantic City. Strongly worded majority and minority reports came from the resolutions committee. Eight committee members emphasized the duty of protecting the jurisdictional rights of all trade unions organized upon craft lines; six opposed this, contending that "in those industries where the work performed by a majority of the workers is of such a nature that it might fall within the jurisdictional claim of more than one craft union, or no established craft union, it is declared that industrial organization is the only form that will be acceptable to the workers or adequately meet their needs." The AFL, the minority report continued, "must recognize the right of these workers to organize into industrial unions and be granted unrestricted charters which guarantee the right to accept into membership all workers employed in the industry." Sharp debate followed, climaxed by a fist fight in which John L. Lewis of the United Mine Workers knocked down William L. Hutcheson of the Carpenter's Union with a right to the chin. But although triumphant in single combat, the burly champion of industrial unionism was short on votes. When the convention was polled, the majority report safeguarding craft unionism was adopted.

On November 9, 1935, just a few weeks after the tumultuous Atlantic City convention, eight heads of AFL international unions met at Washington and formed the Committee for Industrial Organization (CIO) of which Lewis was named chairman. The new group announced that its functions would be "educational and advisory" and professed loyalty to the AFL in its projected campaign to promote organization of the workers in the mass production and unorganized industries of

Picketing. (By Kirby. Reproduced by permission of the *New York World-Telegram.* Copyright, 1937.)

the nation. But President William Green and the AFL executive committee regarded the CIO's activities as rebellion against the majority decisions at Atlantic City and ordered the group to dissolve. When the group not only failed to do this, but induced the Amalgamated Iron, Steel, and Tin Workers to accept its leadership and financial backing in an aggressive move to organize the steel workers, the AFL heads took drastic disciplinary action. In August, 1936, the executive council declared ten unions which had associated with the CIO guilty of dualism, insurrection, and rebellion and ordered their suspension. With the insurgent groups unrepresented, the Tampa convention of the AFL voted to uphold the action of their executive council.

Yet the rebels remained unrepentant. All peace efforts failed and in 1938 the CIO, keeping its initials but changing its name to the Congress of Industrial Organizations, adopted a constitution and accepted its status as a separate federation of American labor unions. This was in many ways an unfortunate development because the AFL and the CIO devoted energies to fighting each other which they might better have reserved for promoting the primary interests of labor. Particularly exasperating to employers and the public were the jurisdictional disputes between the two which frequently led to work stoppages having nothing to do with basic labor-management relations. Despite the split, however, labor was usually able to present a united front during political campaigns or when antiunion legislation was threatened. The very fact of their rivalry, moreover, led to energetic organizing efforts that greatly increased the membership of both federations. John L. Lewis provided the CIO with pugnacious leadership until 1940, when he resigned after a failure to carry the movement with him in support of Willkie in the presidential campaign. He was succeeded by Philip Murray, originally a Mine Workers' official but more recently head of the conspicuously successful Steel Workers Organizing Committee (SWOC). Lewis took his union with him out of the CIO and for the next several years the United Mine Workers, one of the most powerful of American unions, remained independent of both camps.

FIGHTING FOR RECOGNITION

Throughout the years 1936 and 1937 the country was plagued by strikes. This development was almost inevitable since the workers were now resolved to join trade unions and secure contracts, while management was in many areas determined not to put its labor relations on this basis. Despite the prohibitions of the National Labor Relations Act employers sought to combat unionism by using labor spies, discriminating against trade-union members, and promoting rival company unions. Angered by management's defiance of law, the workers resorted more and more to a technique which, as the courts eventually decided, was itself illegal. This was the sit-down strike in which employees, without quitting the plant, simply refused to work. Used successfully in 1933 against the Hormel Packing Company in Austin, Minnesota, the weapon was frequently resorted to during the next few years, particularly around the Detroit area. The philosophy behind this development was well expressed in the auto workers' song:

> When they tie the can to a union man,
>   Sit down! Sit down!
> When they give him the sack they'll take him back,
>   Sit down! Sit down!
> When the speed-up comes, just twiddle your thumbs,
>   Sit down! Sit down!
> When the boss won't talk don't take a walk,
>   Sit down! Sit down!

Another center where sit-down strikes were numerous was Akron, Ohio, the home of the rubber-tire industry. Employers were following an antiunion policy and during 1935 there were frequent work stoppages. Serious trouble developed at the Goodyear plants when the management attempted to reduce costs by increasing hours, reducing wages, and laying off workers. A five-weeks strike began February 17, 1936. One of the longest picket lines in labor history was employed and there was some disorder. But Governor Davey did not consider the trouble sufficient to require the use of state troops, while company efforts to organize vigilantes and back-to-work movements were frustrated by the strikers with the support of the Akron newspapers. On March 22 the strike ended without recognition of the United Rubber Workers or the dissolution of the company union, yet with substantial concessions to the strikers on other issues.

The prestige of the newly organized CIO had been at stake. The Goodyear workers had been largely unorganized when the strike began, but the CIO at once intervened and rendered valuable help. The strike was sufficiently successful to bring the United Rubber Workers thousands of members during the next few months. In 1935 there had been only 3000 union members in the rubber industry; the number jumped to 33,000 in 1936 and to 70,000 in 1937. The United Rubber Workers formally joined the CIO in July, 1936. At the Goodyear plants production was interrupted on 94 out of 275 working days between March 21 and December 31, 1936, while operations at Firestone were stopped for eight weeks in 1937. Serious labor troubles continued until the constitutionality of the National Labor Relations Act was upheld by the Supreme Court in 1937 and the industry abandoned its attempts to promote company unionism and avoid recognition of the United Rubber Workers.

During 1936 the United Automobile Workers, CIO, also made progress despite the opposition of the large companies—an opposition that led the General Motors Corporation to spend $994,855 on private detective services between January 1, 1934, and July 31, 1936. A variety of grievances brought increasingly frequent work stoppages until finally in January and February, 1937, one of the greatest struggles in American industrial history was fought out. Seventeen of the General Motors plants were strikebound and these were so strategically located as to halt production in most of the company's other plants for lack of parts. Two weeks after the strike began 112,800 of the corporation's 150,000 production workers were idle.

The focal point of the conflict was Flint, Michigan, where the sit-down strategy was employed in its boldest form. For six weeks the strikers held key General Motors plants. An attempt by the Flint police to prevent food from being carried to the sit-downers precipitated a three-hour battle in which the police used tear gas and buckshot, while the strikers fought back with sticks, metal pipes, nuts and bolts, soda-pop bottles, coffee mugs, automobile door hinges, and cold water from the plant's hoses. After this episode Governor Frank Murphy ordered 1500 Michigan national guardsmen into the city, but he refused to command them to expel the strikers from the plants and he directed that there should be no further attempt to halt the entry of food. The corporation was successful in securing an order from a Federal circuit court judge directing the strikers to evacuate the plants under penalty of imprisonment for contempt of court and of having a fine of $15,000,000—the estimated value of the plants—assessed against them. But the workers defied the order and the authorities decided against any attempt to carry it out by force.

Governor Murphy was determined to avoid bloodshed at all cost and, ignoring the legal issues involved in the strike, he bent all his efforts toward securing a peaceful settlement. The management at first refused to negotiate until their property was evacuated, but at length after a direct appeal from President Roosevelt it accepted Governor Murphy's mediation. On February 11, 1937, a settlement was announced. The United Automobile Workers was to be recognized for at least six months as the exclusive bargaining agent for the workers in the seven-

Battle Between Police and Sit-down Strikers at Flint, Michigan, During General Motors Strike, 1937. (Acme.)

teen strikebound plants. In all other General Motors plants the union was to be recognized as the agent of its members. All strikers were to be rehired and there was to be no future discrimination against union members. The company and the union were to settle other outstanding grievances through negotiations leading to a signed contract. It was a CIO triumph and after brief trials of strength the other auto plants soon fell in line. Ford attempted to hold out longer than any of the others, but after a ten-day strike in 1941 it too surrendered and signed a contract granting the United Automobile Workers for the first time the closed shop, the checkoff, and the union label.

The legality of the sit-down strike became a matter of heated controversy. The Roosevelt administration avoided any clear-cut pronouncement on the issue and Congress was divided: conservatives like Senator Vandenberg of Michigan and Tydings of Maryland condemned labor's aggressive tactics in strong terms, while liberals like Senators Wagner and Norris contended that management's sit-down against the National Labor Relations Act had given the workers ample justification. They called attention also to the hearings before the LaFollette

Committee on Civil Liberties in which many unsavory details relating to the antiunion tactics of the employers were being revealed. When in 1939 the issue reached the Supreme Court in the case of NLRB *v.* Fansteel Metallurgical Corporation, the sit-down strike was finally pronounced illegal.

Meantime the issue of union recognition was being fought out in the steel industry. The Steel Workers Organizing Committee with Philip Murray at its head and a substantial portion of its expenses advanced by Lewis's United Mine Workers waged an aggressive campaign. One of its most successful stratagems was that of winning over the leaders and rank-and-file of the company unions themselves. So strong was the movement that in March, 1937, the United States Steel Corporation, without risking a strike, recognized the SWOC and permitted the negotiation of contracts with all its subsidiaries.

Several other steel companies followed the lead of the industry's largest unit, but a group of smaller independents elected to resist. The SWOC's struggle with Little Steel, as this group was called, precipitated the bloodiest labor battles of the thirties. At the Republic Steel Company's plants at Chicago ten strikers were killed in a fracas with the police on Memorial Day, 1937; similar incidents led to loss of life in the three Ohio cities of Youngstown, Massillon, and Cleveland. In the end the strikes against Little Steel failed and the defeat was a serious one to CIO. Labor's aggressive tactics had brought it into disfavor with most of the American white-collar class. Tom Girdler, president of Republic Steel, received considerable acclaim for his defiance of the CIO and John L. Lewis was widely denounced. The unpopularity of the CIO was so great in the summer of 1937 that even the President himself seemed to feel its influence. Referring to the bitter struggle between the CIO and Girdler's Republic Steel, he exclaimed: "A plague on both your houses."

A favorite allegation against the CIO was that it was a Communist outfit. This was certainly untrue so far as its high command was concerned. Neither Lewis, nor Murray, nor Sidney Hillman of the Amalgamated Clothing Workers, nor any other CIO leader of comparable prominence had any connection or sympathy with the Communist party. Among local leaders and local unions there was to be sure a certain degree of Communist infiltration, but this arose mostly out of the determination of the movement to use any talent that was offered without scrutinizing too critically its political coloring. The bitterness of the great strikes of 1936 and 1937 was not due to their Communist character, however, but rather to the nature of the issue involved. In almost every case this was not primarily wages and hours but the life or death of the union itself.

In the long run the CIO withstood all attacks and established itself permanently not only in the rubber, auto, and steel industries, but in the electrical, textile, and canning fields as well. Even white-collar workers like newspaper reporters and store clerks organized. As remarkable as the penetration of unionism into new fields was the growth of the older unions, both AFL and CIO. Between 1933 and 1941 the United Mine Workers (CIO) and the Amalgamated Clothing Workers (CIO) both doubled in membership, while the Teamsters Brotherhood (AFL) had a sixfold increase and the Hotel and Restaurant Employees (AFL) jumped over ninefold. Even Little Steel itself abandoned its antiunion policy and signed contracts in 1941 after the NLRB ordered the reinstatement of the workers it had discharged in breaking the union in 1937.

WAGE AND HOUR LEGISLATION

For awhile after the overthrow of NRA, the minimum-wage and maximum-hour provisions of the codes were maintained in many fields by voluntary agreement. But, as old abuses reappeared, labor began to insist on Federal legislation defining fair labor standards. A beginning toward this goal was taken in the Walsh-Healy Government Contracts Act of 1936, which required that all producers who made contracts with the Federal government involving amounts of $10,000 or more must pay not less than the prevailing rate of wages in the locality, must maintain an eight-hour day and a forty-hour week, and must not employ boys under sixteen nor girls under eighteen. Similar requirements were laid down for air lines carrying mail or passengers by the Air Transport Act of 1936.

The proposal for a general wage-hour law met strong opposition. Southern legislators were afraid that one of the principal attractions which had drawn industry to their section would be lost. Northern businessmen felt that their costs might be raised, and farmers feared that higher industrial wages would increase their problems with agricultural labor. A wage-hour bill recommended by the President passed the Senate in 1937, but failed in the House. In 1938, however, the Fair Labor Standards Act was finally passed and received the President's signature on June 25. The law applied to employees engaged in interstate commerce or in producing goods for interstate commerce, but a number of sizable groups were specifically excluded—agricultural laborers, domestic servants, and seamen, for example. The wages of all employees covered by the act were to be not less than 25 cents an hour; this minimum was to be gradually raised until it reached 40 cents an hour in 1945. Similarly maximum hours under the law were fixed at forty-four to be reduced by stages until a forty-hour week was provided in 1940. When the employee worked more than the maximum, he was entitled to time-and-a-half pay for the overtime. The act forbade the employment of children under sixteen years of age in most occupations and their employment under eighteen in occupations found by the Children's Bureau to be specially hazardous. The law contained many exceptions and opportunities for discretion on the part of the Wage and Hour Division of the Department of Labor to which its administration was entrusted.

The immediate result of the act was to raise the wages of about 300,000 persons who were receiving less than the 25-cent minimum and to shorten the working hours of some 1,300,000 workers. As the standards were gradually raised, more and more of the labor force found themselves benefited. Since these standards were in themselves very modest, the operation of the law reveals much about the sweating of labor which preceded its enactment.

Since a generation before the Supreme Court had been unwilling to uphold the power of Congress even to prohibit child labor, there was grave doubt about the constitutionality of the new law. But the Court's decision in the United States v. Darby Lumber Co. (1941) supported the act and gave impressive evidence of the vastly extended powers for which the Court was now able to find Constitutional sanction.

The Fair Labor Standards Act was the culmination of the New Deal's efforts to fulfill its obligations to agriculture and labor. The record was impressive, yet it did not win the universal approval even of the groups it was designed to please. The small farmers accused the administration of sacrificing their interests to those of the large; the large farmers were as certain that the administration had coddled unjustifiably the tenants and agricultural laborers. And the two labor camps each accused the New Deal and the NLRB of favoritism to its rival. In terms of votes, however, the elections of 1938 and 1940 found labor reasonably satisfied and willing to vote Democratic. But the farmers regarded the administration's labor policies with increasing suspicion, and, despite the benefits they themselves had received, they returned more and more to the Republican fold.

22

The New Deal Militant

THE YEARS 1936 TO 1939 WITNESSED A BITTER STRUGGLE BETWEEN THE Roosevelt liberals and their conservative critics. It was a fight that crossed party lines, with many one-time Republicans supporting the President while right-wing Democrats rebelled against his leadership. The first round of the battle, the election of 1936, was won by Roosevelt in decisive fashion, but succeeding rounds were less astutely fought. In the struggle for judicial reform, in the attempted purge of the right-wing Democrats, and in the Congressional election of 1938 the President suffered setbacks. Despite minor victories, however, the conservatives were not able to regain control of the government nor force the reversal of any basic New Deal policy.

THE ELECTION OF 1936

The first determined effort to unseat the Roosevelt faction was through the organization of the Liberty League in August, 1934. The DuPonts and other wealthy industrial and financial leaders provided the movement with ample funds, while conservative Democrats like Alfred E. Smith, ex-Governor Joseph B. Ely of Massachusetts, and Jouett Shouse, formerly chairman of the Democratic Executive Committee, cooperated with it in trying to break the President's hold over his own party. Although the League's activities were unsuccessful in the Congressional election of 1934, it redoubled its efforts the next year. The measures of the Second New Deal, particularly the National Labor Relations Act, were strenuously opposed, while the Supreme Court's anti-New Deal decisions provided support for the contention that the Constitution itself was endangered through the "Roosevelt dictatorship." The climax of the campaign occurred in January, 1936, when Al Smith belabored the administration for an hour to the delight of a banquet hall full of rich Liberty Leaguers in Washington. Nevertheless, the affair had unexpected repercussions. No less than twelve members of the DuPont family had been counted among Smith's audience, and the spectacle of the rich and privileged now making a hero of the Happy Warrior whom most of them had opposed in 1928 appeared to the rest of the country as ridiculous.

As the Liberty League lost ground, wealthy anti-New Dealers turned to other devices. Thousands of dollars were advanced to Governor Eugene Talmadge of Georgia, spokesman for the most narrow and demagogic type of Southern conservatives, to organize a revolt against Roosevelt in his section. It was hoped that by feeding this and other local quarrels within the Democratic party a substantial anti-Roosevelt bloc could be sent to the national convention. But Postmaster General Farley directed an astute preconvention campaign. Wherever insurgency appeared, he tried to get the issue before the Democratic voters, and in all the presidential preference primaries Roosevelt's undiminished popularity with the Democratic rank and file was demonstrated.

The leading contenders for the Republican nomination were ex-President Hoover, Senator Borah, Senator Vandenberg of Michigan, Colonel Frank Knox, formerly a Bull Mooser and now a wealthy Chicago newspaper publisher, and Governor Alfred M. Landon of Kansas. Despite the greater prominence of the other candidates, Governor Landon won the nomination on the first ballot at the Cleveland National Convention early in June. His easy victory was due to the great publicity which he had been receiving from the Hearst papers and from most of the rest of the press as well. He seemed to have many assets for leading the anti-New Deal fight in 1936. Conservatives were impressed by his success in keeping the Kansas state budget balanced during a period in which most units of government were spending much more than they took in, while the liberal wing of the Republican party accepted him more readily than they would have many other candidates because he came from the farm belt and because he had been a Theodore Roosevelt supporter in 1912. His background was that of a small Midwestern businessman, and the Republican leaders believed that this fact would add point to their contention that the New Deal was the enemy of small business. The lack of color in the candidate's personality was obvious, but it was hoped that this might be an asset if the voters were tired of Roosevelt exuberance. Besides the ticket was balanced by the nomination of the aggressive Colonel Knox for the vice-presidency.

Although hopefully undertaken, the Republican campaign of 1936 was ill-starred from the beginning. The party platform and the speeches of the candidates both illustrated the party dilemma. The New Deal had to be denounced as a whole while it was being accepted in most of its significant parts. "America is in peril" were the first words of the platform and Democratic violations of the Constitution, extravagance, bureaucracy, and appeal to class prejudice were cited as evidence. Nevertheless, the Republicans pledged themselves to the effective regulation of public utilities, securities, and other forms of business enterprise, to emergency benefit payments for farmers, to guaranteeing labor's right to organize, and to relief for the unemployed. Such clear-cut issues as the platform raised were largely confined to pledges to balance the budget immediately, to repeal the Reciprocal Trade Agreements Act, and to seek with government assistance to sell the agricultural surplus abroad.

The Democratic convention at Philadelphia was a triumph for Roosevelt. Not only were he and Garner renominated without opposition, but the platform was a thoroughly New Deal document. "We hold this truth to be self-evident," it proclaimed, "that government in a modern civilization has certain inescapable obligations to its citizens, among which are: (1) protection of the family and the home; (2) establishment of a democracy of opportunity for all the people; (3) aid to those overtaken by disaster." And the platform pointed with pride to the administration's achievements under each of these headings, while promising more progress in the future. As another New Deal triumph, selection of party nominees by a simple majority vote was substituted for the two-thirds rule.

Once again Roosevelt appeared before the convention in person to accept the nomination. It was one of the most successful of his political speeches. The delegates were roused to great enthusiasm by the President's condemnation of "economic royalists" and by the stirring conclusion in which he declared:

There is a mysterious cycle in human events. To some generations much is given. Of other generations much is expected. This generation of Americans has a rendezvous with destiny.

In this world of ours in other lands, there are some people, who, in times past, have lived and fought for freedom, and seem to have grown too weary to carry on the fight. . . .

I believe in my heart that only our success can stir their ancient hope. They begin to know that here in America we are waging a great and successful war. It is not alone a war against want and destitution and economic demoralization. It is more than that; it is a war for the survival of democracy. We are fighting to save a great and precious form of government for ourselves and for the world.

I accept the commission you have tendered me. I join with you. I am enlisted for the duration of the war.

For a time during the 1936 campaign great importance was laid on the emergence of a new third party. For many months the old-line politicians had feared that the numerous admirers of Huey Long, Dr. Townsend, and Father Coughlin might join forces in a single broad mass movement, and the formation of the Union Party in June, 1936, was intended to bring about exactly this result. But several factors contributed to making the new party much less formidable than expected. In the first place, Huey Long was dead. His had been one of the most curious careers in American politics. An enormously clever and effective demagogue, he had secured election as governor of Louisiana in 1928. His political machine was corrupt and dictatorial, but he gave better roads and schools to his poor constituents. Elected United States Senator in 1930, he secured wide publicity from the start. His speeches, both in the Senate and over the radio, were rambling and violent, yet they were highly entertaining and never lacked for auditors. His "Share the Wealth" movement with its slogan "Every Man a King" won hundreds of thousands of adherents in 1935, and his ambition to gain the White House had Farley and the Democratic high command seriously worried. They did not believe that Huey could achieve his goal, but they did fear that as a third-party candidate he might win enough votes to throw the election to the Republicans. In September, 1935, however, the Louisiana politician was assassinated in his home state and the Reverend Gerald L. K. Smith, who attempted to assume his mantle, was a much less formidable character. Instead of a colorful figure like Long, the Union party chose as its standard-bearer a rather drab North Dakota legislator, Representative William Lemke, hitherto little known except as an earnest advocate of farm relief and inflation. Father Coughlin was so confident of his own influence with his radio listeners that he promised to retire from broadcasting if Lemke did not poll at least twelve million votes, but the priest's attempts to create enthusiasm for "Liberty Bill" were unavailing. In the end the Union party secured only 900,000 votes. Small though this was as compared with Coughlin's predictions, it was larger than the 190,000 which went to Norman Thomas, the Socialist candidate, and the 80,000 to Browder, the Communist.

The only real contest was between Roosevelt and Landon, and even that proved to be a very unequal one. Despite the fact that a number of prominent Democrats followed Al Smith in "taking a walk"—deserting their party nominee and supporting Landon—the mass of the voters was moving in the opposite direction. Landon's campaigning proved ineffective, while Roosevelt's was adroit and bold. When the votes were counted, Landon found himself defeated more decisively than any previous Republican candidate for the presidency. He had carried only two states and won only eight electoral votes as against Roosevelt's 523. The popular vote was: Roosevelt, 27,476,673, Landon, 16,679,583.

THE SECOND INAUGURAL

Roosevelt took the presidential oath for the second time on January 20, 1937—the first inauguration on the new date provided by the Lame Duck Amendment. The ceremony took place in a heavy rainstorm—an appropriate setting for the first act of what was to be a tempestuous period in national politics. There was little of complacency in the inaugural address. Asking the question: Have we reached "the goal of our vision?" the President replied:

I see a great nation, upon a great continent, blessed with a great wealth of natural resources. . . .

But here is the challenge to our democracy: In this nation I see tens of millions of its citizens—a substantial part of its whole population—who at this very moment are denied the greater part of what the very lowest standards of today call the necessities of life.

I see millions of families trying to live on incomes so meager that the pall of family disaster hangs over them day by day.

I see millions whose daily lives in the city and on farm continue under conditions labeled indecent by a so-called polite society half a century ago.

I see millions denied education, recreation, and the opportunity to better their lot and the lot of their children.

I see millions lacking the means to buy the products of farm and factory and by their poverty denying work and productiveness to many other millions.

I see one-third of a nation ill-housed, ill-clad, ill-nourished.

Obviously the second Roosevelt administration was being dedicated not merely to holding and defending ground already won, but to new offensives under the standard of social justice. The President's conservative opponents, speculating uneasily on where the first blow would be struck, did not have long to wait. On February 5 the Chief Executive dispatched a message to Congress calling for reorganization of the entire Federal judiciary. Even a country which had learned always to expect the unexpected was stunned by the audacity of this maneuver.

THE SUPREME COURT AND THE PROGRESSIVE MOVEMENT

No discussion of the President's proposals and the great debate which they precipitated would be meaningful unless the issue were placed in its historical perspective.

The power exercised by the Supreme Court in declaring Federal and state laws unconstitutional was not explicitly granted in the Constitution, and it is debatable whether the framers of that document intended the Court to perform such a function. When under the strong leadership of John Marshall the Supreme Court actually began to invalidate Federal and state laws, there were numerous protests but the precedents for its doing so were successfully established. The power of the Court to invalidate an act of Congress, however, stood on weaker ground than that of negating an act of a state legislature and the judges acted with particular caution in the former case. During the first seventy years of national history the Supreme Court declared acts of Congress unconstitutional on only two occasions.

Following the Civil War, however, the Court became much bolder in invalidating Federal laws, there being twenty-three such cases between 1860 and 1900 and thirty-five from 1900 to 1930. One at least of the disallowed laws, the income-tax provision of 1894, was the embodiment of a great popular demand and the Court's decision shocked millions of citizens. The Court was accused of using its great power to shield the wealthy against paying their proper share of Federal taxes. Such censure was all the more bitter because of the increasing frequency with which the Federal judiciary was setting aside state legislation which attempted to reform or regulate business. Between .1890 and 1937, 228 state laws were invalidated on the ground that they deprived "persons"—frequently corporations—of property "without due process of law."

By 1900 it was already apparent that the Supreme Court had great usefulness as a conservative stronghold for property interests threatened through either Federal or state legislation. The progressives became increasingly dismayed over the obstacles placed in their path by the judiciary everywhere, and the recall of judges and of judicial decisions became, as we have seen, one of the most important progressive demands before World War I.

Theodore Roosevelt sought to liberalize the judiciary by new appointments. In 1902 he named Oliver Wendell Holmes, Jr., of Massachusetts to the Supreme Court largely because of Holmes's prolabor decisions as a judge in his home state. The Rough Rider was much disappointed when Holmes dissented from the majority decision in the Northern Securities case, but despite the new judge's lack of enthusiasm for the Sherman Act he soon proved a liberal influence of the greatest importance. Again and again during his thirty years as a Supreme Court justice Holmes was destined to thrill progressives with his bold and brilliantly phrased opinions, the most memorable of them being dissents from the decisions of his more conservative colleagues. Roosevelt's two other appointments were much less effective for his purpose.

That Roosevelt named only three men to the Supreme Court in almost eight years in the White House illustrates the good fortune which the conservatives had in maintaining their dominance in that strategic fortress. The conservative Taft had six opportunities to name justices during his four-year term, while the liberal Wilson had only three during the next eight years. On the other hand, the Old Guard Harding made four appointments in less than two and a half years and his Republican successors, Coolidge and Hoover, made one and three appointments respectively. The assumption that progressive Presidents always named progressive judges and conservative Presidents conservative judges is not always valid—as the choice of the reactionary McReynolds by Wilson and the appointments of the liberals, Stone and Cardozo, by Coolidge and Hoover illustrate. Yet in general it proved true that the Chief Executives selected judges who inclined toward their own philosophy of government. The jealousy with which the conservatives regarded their control of the Court was best shown by the extreme bitterness of the fight against the confirmation of Louis D. Brandeis when this progressive lawyer from Massachusetts was named to the bench in 1916. No less than six former presidents of the American Bar Association, including Taft and Root, contended that Brandeis was "not a fit person to be a member of the Supreme Court of the United States." President Wilson stuck by his nominee, however, and secured his confirmation after a hard fight.

Conservative success in keeping control of the Court showed its results in that body's decisions. In 1905 the justices declared invalid an act of the New York legislature limiting the hours which bakery employees could work to sixty a week and ten a day on the grounds that it violated the Fourteenth Amendment by depriving the workers of their liberty of contract (Lochner v. New York). Justice Holmes wrote one of the first of his famous dissents on this occasion, saying:

Some of these laws embody convictions or prejudices which judges are likely to share. Some may not. But a constitution is not intended to embody a particular economic theory, whether of paternalism . . . or of laissez faire. It is made for people of fundamentally different views, and the accident of our finding certain opinions natural and familiar, or novel, and even shocking, ought not to conclude our judgment upon the question whether statutes embodying them conflict with the Constitution of the United States.

On the question of maximum-hour laws the Court gradually gave way. In Muller *v.* Oregon (1908) such a law applying to women laundry workers was upheld on the grounds that women might need this special protection. Finally in 1917 a general ten-hour factory law enacted by Oregon progressives was held valid in a five-to-three decision.

But minimum-wage laws, even to protect women, failed to win acceptance. In the case of Adkins *v.* Children's Hospital (1923) the Supreme Court by a vote of five to three declared unconstitutional an act of Congress establishing minimum wages for women and children in the District of Columbia. The line of reasoning employed by the majority was such as to make it certain that similar state laws would be invalidated and the decision stood as an effective barrier in the way of protecting women workers from sweatshop conditions.

State laws regulating child labor were not interfered with, but two attempts of Congress during the Wilson administration to pass a Federal law on the subject were invalidated by the Court.[1]

Organized labor's grievances against the judiciary have been frequently alluded to, but it should be added that the Supreme Court went to the extent of invalidating Federal and state laws that had been specifically enacted to protect the right of collective bargaining. In 1908 a Federal provision prohibiting yellow-dog contracts in the relations of the railroads with their employees was declared unconstitutional (Adair *v.* United States), while in 1915 a similar state law was invalidated (Coppage *v.* Kansas). The Court even denied the right of a state legislature to limit the power of its own state judges to issue injunctions in labor disputes. This latter decision, handed down in 1921 in the case of Truax *v.* Corrigan, provoked Justice Holmes to say in his dissenting opinion:

There is nothing that I more deprecate than the use of the Fourteenth Amendment beyond the absolute compulsion of its words to prevent the making of social experiments that an important part of the community desires, in the insulated chambers afforded by the several States, even though the experiments may seem futile or even noxious to me and to those whose judgment I most respect.

Even during the twenties when the progressive movement was in eclipse the Federal judiciary was under chronic attack because of its

[1] Hammer *v.* Dagenhart (1918) and Bailey *v.* Drexel Furniture Company (1922).

conservatism. The platform on which LaFollette and Wheeler ran during the third-party venture of 1924 urged a constitutional amendment under which a law declared unconstitutional by the Supreme Court might be reenacted by Congress and exempted from further judicial challenge. Senator Borah was the author of a bill which would have required the concurrence of seven members of the Court to declare an act of Congress unconstitutional. Such proposals were doomed to failure, but in 1930 the progressive bloc was able to prevent the confirmation of the supposedly antilabor John J. Parker as a Supreme Court justice and to put up a strong, though unsuccessful, fight against the confirmation of Chief Justice Hughes.

THE SUPREME COURT AND THE NEW DEAL

Not until 1934 did cases involving the New Deal begin to reach the Supreme Court. Both friend and foe of the Roosevelt measures watched eagerly for an indication of the attitude which the justices would take. Nervous New Dealers found some reassurance in the Court's decisions upholding a Minnesota mortgage-moratorium act and a New York milk-control law (Home Building and Loan Association v. Blaisdell, Nebbia v. New York). Neither case involved a Federal measure, but both involved the powers of government to deal with an economic emergency. Realistic members of the administration noted, however, that these were both five-to-four decisions. It was obvious that four of the justices—McReynolds, Sutherland, Van Devanter, and Butler—would view any new intervention of government into the economic sphere with extreme suspicion. Observers familiar with the record of the judges were not surprised at this; the Court was readily analyzed as containing four ultraconservatives—the justices just named, three liberals—Brandeis, Cardozo, and Stone, and two middle-of-the-roaders —Chief Justice Hughes and Justice Roberts. Therefore the fate of the New Deal was to depend largely on the way in which the last two exercised their balance of power.

The administration received its first serious judicial setback on January 7, 1935, in the "Hot Oil" case (Panama Refining Company v. Ryan) in which all of the Supreme Court judges except Cardozo concurred in holding section 9-A of the National Industrial Recovery Act invalid. The grounds of the decision were important since they hinged largely on the opinion that the section violated the Constitution by delegating legislative power to the Executive—the first instance of an act of Congress being set aside for this reason. Because the delegation of emergency powers to the President had been a prominent feature of the legislation of the Hundred Days, the decision had implications of the most serious kind.

The next important phase of the New Deal to pass under review was the Congressional resolution of June 5, 1933, under which any clause in a public or private contract specifying payment in gold was voided and the obligation was made payable dollar for dollar in any legal tender currency. The windfall to creditors and the utter financial confusion which would have followed the invalidation of this law after the country had been using the devaluated dollar for many months were obvious, yet that disaster was only narrowly averted. By five-to-four decisions on February 18, 1935, the Court upheld the resolution as regards private contracts, but denied the power of Congress to modify the obligations of United States bonds. The plaintiff was not, however, allowed to recover against the government since he had not proved any actual damage.[1]

On May 6, 1935, Justice Roberts sided with the four ultras of the Court in invalidating the Railroad Retirement Act of 1934—a compulsory pension measure for railroad employees which had anticipated the general Social Security Act by a year.[2] The Chief Justice himself was shocked by the implications of the decision and wrote a vigorous dissent:

I am unable to concur in the decision in this case. The gravest aspect of the decision is that it does not rest simply upon a condemnation of particular features of the Railroad Retirement Act, but denies to Congress the power to pass any compulsory pension act for railroad employees. . . . That is a conclusion of such serious and far-reaching importance that it overshadows all other questions raised by the Act. . . . I think that the conclusion thus reached is a departure from sound principles and places an unwarranted limitation upon the commerce clause of the Constitution. . . .

The New Deal's Black Monday in court came on May 27, 1935. By three unanimous decisions the Frazier-Lemke Farm Mortgage Act of 1934 was found invalid, the President's removal of William E. Humphrey from the Federal Trade Commission was declared illegal, and the general code-making procedure under NRA was ruled unconstitutional.[3] It was the last of these decisions which the President found most upsetting. Not only did it destroy an agency for reform from which he hoped much good could still eventuate, but, what was more

[1] The so-called Gold Clauses Cases—Norman v. Ohio Railroad Company, Perry v. United States, etc.

[2] Railroad Retirement Board v. Alton Railroad Company.

[3] Louisville Bank v. Radford, Humphrey's Executor v. United States, A. L. A. Schechter Corporation v. United States.

serious, the Court's opinion seemed to construe the commerce clause more narrowly than any decision for decades. "We have been relegated," Roosevelt told his press conference, "to the horse-and-buggy definition of interstate commerce."

The year 1936 was equally difficult for those who had to argue New Deal cases before the courts. On January 6, the first Agricultural Adjustment Act was declared unconstitutional, with the judges dividing six to three (United States *v.* Butler)—perhaps the most criticized of all the anti-Roosevelt decisions. On February 17 the government won one of its few victories when the power of the TVA to sell surplus electricity generated at Wilson Dam was recognized by all the justices except McReynolds (Ashwander *v.* TVA). But in June the power of the SEC was narrowly circumscribed (Jones *v.* SEC), while a month later the New Deal suffered another major defeat in the invalidation of the first Bituminous Coal Conservation Act (Carter *v.* Carter Coal Company). Five justices concurred in voiding the entire law, despite the opinion of Chief Justice Hughes that only its labor provisions were unconstitutional and that its price-fixing clauses should be upheld. Justices Cardozo, Stone, and Brandeis agreed that the price-fixing provisions were within the power of Congress and asserted that for the purposes of the case in hand it was unnecessary to consider the validity of its other clauses. Hughes again joined the liberal minority in dissenting from the decisions under which the Federal Municipal Bankruptcy Act of 1934 (Ashton *v.* Cameron County District) and the New York Minimum Wage Act (Morehead *v.* Tipaldo) were declared unconstitutional. The latter case emphasized the predicament in which liberals found themselves. While on the one hand the Court was setting aside Federal laws which attempted to provide for minimum labor standards on the ground that they invaded the powers of the states, on the other hand it was denying the power of the state legislatures to pass similar laws on the ground that these violated the Fourteenth Amendment. A legal "no-man's land" had been created where neither Federal nor state governments could act.

The extent of the administration's difficulties is by no means adequately indicated by this account of Supreme Court cases. The lower ranks of the Federal judiciary were also largely staffed with conservatives, and these District and Circuit Court judges were no less eager to hamstring the Roosevelt reforms. Sixteen hundred injunctions restraining officers of the Federal government from carrying out acts of Congress were granted. A variety of legal devices were resorted to by anti-New Deal lawyers to invite judicial intervention. Such agencies as the TVA, SEC, and NLRB found themselves for the time being almost powerless to carry out the functions for which they had been created.

THE JUDICIARY REORGANIZATION BILL

Behind the scenes the administration was considering ways and means of removing these judicial obstacles. Many Roosevelt supporters offered their suggestions and the practicability of each was weighed. This study was in progress throughout the year 1936, but it was carried on very quietly because the President wanted the campaign issue of that year to be the New Deal as a whole rather than any highly controversial new proposal. The avoidance of the judiciary issue during the campaign was not only the course of political expediency, but it was also a practical necessity due to the difficulty encountered by the administration in framing a concrete plan. The most logical remedy appeared to be a constitutional amendment whereby the power of Congress and the state legislature, to deal effectively with twentieth-century economic problems would be affirmed in unequivocal language. But however ideal this proposal was in the abstract, it seemed outside the realm of practical politics. The drafting of an amendment acceptable to two thirds of Congress would have been difficult in the first place; its acceptance by three quarters of the states would have been next to impossible. The fate of the Child Labor Amendment which had been adopted by Congress in 1924 and was still eight states short of the thirty-six necessary for ratification made the administration unwilling to rest the fate of its policies on a similar procedure. Another popular proposal was that of requiring seven, eight, or all of the judges to concur in a decision before the Supreme Court could invalidate a law. Roosevelt and his advisers decided, however, that in all probability any such measure enacted by Congress would itself be declared unconstitutional by the justices. To other suggestions, equally serious objections were raised and, by a process of elimination, the President and Attorney-General Homer Cummings hit at length on the proposal transmitted to Congress in the presidential message of February 5, 1937.

This message on "judicial reorganization" took as its thesis the necessity for legislative action to quiet the complaints of the citizens over "the complexities, the delays, and the expense of litigation in United States courts." The overcrowded dockets proved "the need for additional judges" in all the ranks of the Federal judiciary. "A part of the problem of obtaining a sufficient number of judges to dispose of cases," the President asserted, "is the capacity of the judges themselves. This brings forward the question of aged or infirm judges—a subject of delicacy and yet one which requires frank discussion." He then alluded to the voluntary retirement act of 1869 which permitted judges to retire on a full pension at the age of seventy. Despite this provision, however, many continued on the bench long past this age. In exceptional cases they retained their full mental and physical vigor, but the less fortunate ones were "often unable to perceive their own infirmities." The President's answer to the problem was embodied in the draft bill which accompanied the message. It provided that, when any Federal judge attained the age of seventy and had held a commission as judge for at least ten years and within six months thereafter had not resigned or retired, the President should appoint with the consent of the Senate one additional judge. Not more than fifty judges might be appointed under the act and no judge might be named to the Supreme Court if the appointment would result in more than fifteen members of that body. Similar restrictions were laid down for appointments to the lower courts. The rest of the bill dealt with procedural

Fall In! (By Seibel in *The Richmond Times-Despatch*.)

reforms, most of which were not very controversial in character.

The message of February 5 was less ably composed than most Roosevelt documents. Its best sentence asserted: "A constant and systematic addition of younger blood will vitalize the courts and better equip them to recognize and apply the essential concepts of justice in the light of the needs and the facts of an ever-changing world." But evidence of the existing Court's failure to adapt itself to new problems was not presented. Instead, the principal stress was laid upon the alleged inability of the elderly judges to keep up with their work. In later years Roosevelt himself commented: "I made one major mistake when I first presented the plan. I did not place enough emphasis upon the real mischief—the kind of decisions which, as a studied and continued policy, had been coming down from the Supreme Court."

The blunder was a serious one. Six of the nine justices of the Court were over seventy; the effect of the bill, therefore, would be to give the President six new appointments regardless of whether the elderly incumbents chose to continue to serve or to retire. The proposal was to pack the Court, and the indirection of the presidential message only made the maneuver seem more Machiavellian than it actually was.

A month later in a radio address to the nation, Roosevelt argued for his plan more effectively. He charged the Court itself with violating the spirit of the Constitution by "assuming the power to pass on the wisdom of these Acts of Congress—and to approve or disapprove the public policy written into these laws." To support the accusation he quoted the dissenting opinions of the liberal justices. Facing squarely the criticism that he would be "packing the Court," he denied that he wanted to appoint justices whom he could control on specific cases and continued:

But if by that phrase the charge is made that I would appoint and the Senate would confirm Justices worthy to sit beside present members of the Court who understand those modern conditions; that I will appoint Justices who will not undertake to override the judgment of the Congress on legislative policy; that I will appoint Justices who will act as Justices and not as legislators—if the appointment of such Justices can be called "packing the Courts," then I say that I, and with me the vast majority of the American people, favor doing just that thing—now.

This radio address came too late, however, to overcome the bad impression caused by the deviousness of the first move. Conservatives, of course, denounced the measure in ringing terms both in and out of Congress. They warned the country that Roosevelt, in his reckless bid for power, was attempting to dominate the judiciary and overthrow the

Constitution. It was an issue tailor-made for the anti-New Dealers who had long hoped to alarm the nation and precipitate a popular rebellion against the President. In newspaper editorials, over the radio, and even from the pulpit came fierce denunciation. Congressmen were deluged with letters and telegrams protesting against the presidential proposal.

In so far as these cries of alarm originated in Republican or Liberty League circles, the President could afford to shrug them off. Again and again he had seen similar opposition develop, only to be easily overridden when the votes were counted in the halls of Congress or at the polling places. Even the revolt of conservative Democrats like Senators Carter Glass and Harry F. Byrd of Virginia was not alarming since they had opposed New Deal measures before. What the President had not anticipated, however, was that his proposal would antagonize a dangerously large number of legislators who had hitherto been loyal to his program. Many of these were at heart conservative and, now that the election was past, were anxious to assert their independence of the White House. They were sincerely shocked by the President's proposal and embittered by the fact that he had presented it to Congress without previous consultation. The most unexpected blow of all came when the leadership in the antireorganization-bill fight was assumed by Senator Wheeler of Montana who had always been regarded as a spokesman for the extreme liberals. Wheeler's position was curious. He was bitterly opposed to the Roosevelt plan as a dangerous expansion of the powers of the Executive, but he himself was the sponsor of a more radical measure—a proposed constitutional amendment which would have permitted a two-thirds Congressional vote to overrule any decision of the Court in which an act of Congress was held unconstitutional. Conservative Republicans, having learned the bitter lesson that their prominent participation in a fight against a New Deal proposal was likely to increase rather than decrease its popularity, kept in the background while the Democrats quarreled among themselves.

Public opinion, it soon developed, was sharply divided on the issue. Even the heads of the nation's law schools were of two minds. At the hearings before the Senate Judiciary Committee, the deans of Columbia, Michigan, Fordham, and New York University law schools opposed the reorganization bill; those of Yale, Northwestern, and Notre Dame supported it; so also did former deans of Pennsylvania and Duke. Six New England college presidents condemned the measure, but Professors Edward S. Corwin of Princeton and Charles Grove Haines of the University of California (Los Angeles), two of the country's leading authorities on the Constitution, defended it.

Had the issue come to a vote within the first few weeks after the presidential proposal was presented, it is probable that it would have passed by a narrow margin. Between March and June, however, developments occurred within the Supreme Court itself which profoundly affected the issue.

THE NEW DEAL BECOMES CONSTITUTIONAL

One of the results of the form which the President's reorganization proposal had taken was to give a new solidarity to the institution under attack. Justice Brandeis, who was both the oldest and the most liberal member of the Supreme Court, resented the imputation that the age of the judges prevented the Court from keeping up with its business, while liberal and conservative justices alike opposed the creation of new places on the bench. In answer to an inquiry from Senator Wheeler, Chief Justice Hughes composed a letter in which Justices Van Devanter and Brandeis concurred effectively defending the Court against the charge that it was slow and inefficient.

Hughes's letter gave a mighty lift to the Wheeler faction, but an even greater one was afforded when Justice Roberts deserted the conservative side of the bench and voted with Hughes, Stone, Cardozo, and Brandeis to uphold the constitutionality of a Washington minimum-wage law. This important decision (West Coast Hotel Co. *v.* Parrish) read by the Chief Justice on March 29 overruled the Adkins decision of 1923 and that in the New York Minimum Wage case of 1936. Justice Roberts's change of mind in less than a year was obvious, but Hughes glossed over the reversal by contending that the issue had not been properly presented in 1936 by the attorneys in charge of the New York case.

Additional evidence that the Court could reform itself without outside assistance was offered on April 12 when a series of five-to-four decisions upheld the National Labor Relations Act.[1] Justice McReynolds in his dissenting opinions argued that principles laid down in the Schechter and Carter cases should have been followed, but Hughes and Roberts once again sided with the liberals in asserting that the labor practices involved in these cases threatened to obstruct interstate commerce and that the Federal government therefore had the power to act.

A third major victory for New Deal principles was embodied in a series of decisions upholding the Social Security Act, the taxes levied

[1] NLRB *v.* Jones and Laughlin Steel Corporation, Associated Press *v.* NLRB, etc.

under it, and the state unemployment insurance laws passed in cooperation with the Federal program.[1]

The President and his advisers felt that their attack upon the judiciary
had already brought results. They attributed the new liberalism of Chief
Justice Hughes and Justice Roberts largely to the desire of these two
astute men to save the Court from unwelcome change. Most commenta-
tors have agreed that such a motive was either consciously or uncon-
sciously guiding the judges during their reexamination of the Constitution during the 1937 session. It should be pointed out, however, that
Justice Roberts's shift on the issue of minimum-wage legislation occurred before the presidential message on judicial reorganization was
sent to Congress. Other factors influencing the Court may have been
the conclusive results of the 1936 election and the sit-down strikes,
which gave impressive evidence of the need for legislation in the field
of labor relations. Moreover, the laws of the Second New Deal were
drafted in less haste than those of the First and thus left fewer grounds
for their invalidation.

As a final gesture to demonstrate that the radical Roosevelt proposal
was unnecessary, Justice Van Devanter retired from the bench in June,
thus opening the way for the first change in the personnel of the Court
in five years. The justice's action was facilitated by the knowledge that
under the Supreme Court Retirement Act which had been recently
passed by Congress he could leave the bench without resigning, thereby
enjoying immunity from certain taxes and being assured that his compensation could never be reduced.

DEATH OF THE COURT BILL

Legislators who had been supporting the reorganization bill out of a
sense of loyalty to the party and the President rather than conviction
now advised Roosevelt to abandon his project since it had already
served the purpose of inducing the Court to take a more charitable
view of New Deal legislation. The President refused to accept this
counsel, however, on the grounds that the liberal margin in the Court
was too narrow and uncertain. If a Constitutional "no-man's land" had
been eliminated, it was only to create a "Roberts's land." Even the
retirement of Van Devanter did not reassure the President because he
was committed to appoint to the vacancy Senator Joseph Robinson of
Arkansas, Democratic leader of the Upper House. Robinson had been
a thoroughly loyal New Deal lieutenant as a legislator, but it was feared

[1] Helvering *v.* Davis, Carmichael *v.* Southern Coal Company, etc.

that as a judge he was likely to revert to a more conservative philosophy.

On June 14 the reorganization bill suffered a blow of staggering proportions. Not only did seven Democrats on the Senate Judiciary Committee join with three Republicans in a majority report against the bill (a minority of eight committee members recommended passage), but they appended their names to a scathing condemnation of the project:

We recommend the rejection of this bill as a needless, futile, and utterly dangerous abandonment of constitutional principle. . . .

It is a measure which should be so emphatically rejected that its parallel will never again be presented to the free representatives of the free people of America.

Convinced at length that the bill in its original form could not pass, the President assented to the substitution of a modified plan under which he would be empowered to make two new appointments instead of six. But the opposition was determined to defeat this also. The Senate became involved in an extremely heated debate with tempers on all sides being worn thin. When Senator Robinson, his strength overtaxed by the legislative battle, fell dead in his apartment, the compromise bill received its final blow.

The last chapter was written on July 22 when the Senate, by a vote of seventy to twenty, recommitted the measure to the Judiciary Committee. Eventually a law providing for procedural reforms in the lower courts, but leaving the Supreme Court strictly alone, was quietly enacted into law.

THE NEW DEAL COURT

The defeat of Roosevelt's reorganization plan was a great moral victory for the opponents of the New Deal. Equally important were its implications as a revolt against the President's leadership of the Democratic party. Yet it did not prevent his securing his ultimate end—the liberalization of the Supreme Court. Within the next four years Roosevelt had the opportunity to appoint not six but seven justices. Justice Sutherland followed Van Devanter into retirement within seven months; Cardozo died in 1938; Butler and Brandeis both retired in 1939, to be followed by McReynolds and Hughes in 1941. By the end of the latter year Roberts and Stone were the only pre-Roosevelt appointees still on the bench.

Roosevelt's first appointment in August, 1937, was made before the excitement of the reorganization-bill controversy had died down. The naming of Senator Hugo L. Black of Alabama, one of the most ardent

New Dealers, to the post vacated by Van Devanter was a bitter dose for conservatives to swallow. But the tradition of senatorial courtesy led to Black's confirmation by a vote of sixty-three to sixteen. The new justice quietly took the oath and left for a European vacation before taking up his new duties. At long last the country seemed in a position to forget the court issue when suddenly the whole controversy was reopened by a series of newspaper articles charging Black had joined the Ku Klux Klan in 1926. Those who had disliked the appointment in the first place now put up a vociferous demand for Black's resignation. So great was the outcry that the new justice felt compelled to cut short his vacation and return home. In a statement over the radio he admitted that he had once accepted membership in the Klan, but asserted that this membership had terminated long ago and that he did not hold any of the racial or religious prejudices which characterized that organization.

Black's difficulties did not end with his radio statement. An attempt was made to prevent his assuming his duties through petition to the Supreme Court itself. When this motion was not entertained, the new justice took his place on the bench, but became the victim of a campaign charging him with incompetence. Despite all attacks, however, Black stuck to his post and gradually won a large measure of respect. The irrevelance of the Klan charge was demonstrated by his strongly worded decisions upholding Negro rights. The feeling of conservatives that Black had advanced and unorthodox views was, however, quite true. He had little respect for past decisions of the Court on issues where he thought the trend of its opinions had been wrong. This was illustrated by his criticism of the doctrine that corporations were persons entitled to the protection of the Fourteenth Amendment—an interpretation which the Court had been acting upon since 1886.

No subsequent Roosevelt appointment aroused a comparable outcry. There was some opposition to Felix Frankfurter in 1941 because of the reputation for radicalism which he had received during the Sacco and Vanzetti case, as well as during his behind-the-scenes activities in behalf of the New Deal. On the bench, however, Justice Frankfurter proved to be more conservative than most of the other New Deal appointees. The other new judges were Stanley Reed of Kentucky, who was elevated from the post of Solicitor General, William O. Douglas of Connecticut from the SEC, Frank Murphy of Michigan and Robert H. Jackson of New York, both former Attorneys General, and Senator James F. Byrnes of South Carolina. When in 1942 Roosevelt decided to avail himself of Byrnes's executive abilities in the war administration, he appointed Wiley B. Rutledge of Iowa, a circuit court judge, to fill the vacant place. Much of the criticism of the President's policy toward the judiciary was quieted when he elevated the widely respected Justice Harlan F. Stone of New York to the Chief Justiceship upon the retirement of Hughes in 1941.

As might be expected, the liberal trend in Supreme Court decisions begun in 1937 was not reversed. Such important New Deal laws as the Agricultural Adjustment Act of 1938 and the Fair Labor Standards Act were upheld.[1] The unanimous approval given to the latter in the so-called Darby case of 1941 was one of the administration's greatest judicial victories since it overruled Hammer v. Dagenhart, a barrier to Federal regulation of child labor since 1918.

But unanimity of opinion was no more a characteristic of the Roosevelt court than it had been of its predecessors. Dissenting opinions were frequent and they were often sharply written. None of the justices was conservative in the McReynolds, Van Devanter, Sutherland, and Butler tradition and the groupings of the justices were much more fluid than they had been before 1937. In general, however, Justices Black, Murphy, and Douglas were to be found on the extreme left of the new bench, while Roberts, Hughes, and Stone were on the right, with Frankfurter, Reed, and Jackson holding strategic middle positions.

EXECUTIVE REORGANIZATION

Ever since Theodore Roosevelt's day the need for reorganization of the executive department of the Federal government had been recognized. Every President thereafter had urged that something be done. Limited steps had in fact been taken, but the task was too complex for detailed Congressional legislation. Presidents Taft, Wilson, and Hoover had been in agreement on the principle that effective reform could only be secured through a grant of authority to the President. The little that they had been able to accomplish, however, was no real answer to the problem. The rapid multiplication of government activities, indeed, made the situation increasingly worse.

Consequently, on January 12, 1937, President Roosevelt sent to Congress a special message requesting legislation for the reorganization of the executive branch of the government. The charge made against his Supreme Court plan—that it represented a hastily contrived scheme upon which no sufficient advice had been sought—could not be made against this proposal. On the contrary, the President was transmitting a plan

---

[1] Mulford v. Smith, United States v. Darby.

carefully formulated by a Committee on Administrative Management consisting of three of the country's leading authorities on public administration: Louis Brownlow and Charles E. Merriam of Chicago and Luther Gulick of New York. There were five major recommendations: (1) expansion of the White House staff so that the President might have a group of able assistants to keep him in touch with administrative affairs; (2) strengthening the managerial agencies of the government, particularly those dealing with the budget, with efficiency research, with personnel, and with planning; (3) extension of the merit system "upward, outward, and downward to cover practically all non-policy-determining posts" and reorganization of the civil service system under a single responsible administration; (4) overhauling the hundred independent agencies and commissions and placing them by executive order under one or another of twelve executive departments (the ten existing departments plus two new ones—Social Welfare and Public Works); and (5) reform of the auditing procedures of the government.

Because of preoccupation with the Supreme Court fight, Congress made little progress in dealing with this proposal during the 1937 session. In 1938, however, a reorganization bill passed the Senate. There were several safeguards and departures from the presidential plan: no provision was made for a Department of Public Works, the regulatory commissions like the Interstate Commerce Commission were to be left alone, all executive orders issued under the act were subject to disapproval by Congress within sixty days by joint resolution. It was difficult to see how a grant of power to the President in these terms could undermine republican government, yet such was the accusation hurled at the bill by the anti-New Dealers. The measure was labeled "a dictator bill" and all the propaganda techniques which had been so effective in the Supreme Court fight were once again employed.

The President felt compelled to answer these charges and did so in the form of an open letter on March 29, 1938. He was as much opposed as anybody, he said, to the idea of an American dictatorship for three simple reasons:

A: I have no inclination to be a dictator.

B: I have none of the qualifications which would make me a successful dictator.

C: I have too much historical background and too much knowledge of existing dictatorships to make me desire any form of dictatorship for a democracy like the United States of America.

Despite this disclaimer the House was sufficiently impressed by the clamor of the opposition to kill the measure. Once again a presidential project had been defeated through defection in the Democratic ranks. The principal rebel on this occasion was Representative John O'Connor of New York.

In 1939, however, a modified bill was passed without serious trouble. It provided for six administrative assistants to the President and directed him to formulate plans for abolishing unnecessary government agencies or for grouping or consolidating them to promote economy and efficiency. He was to transmit these reorganization plans to Congress after which they would become effective unless the legislature within sixty days passed concurrent resolutions disapproving them. During 1939 and 1940 Roosevelt submitted five such reorganization plans, none of which Congress disallowed. The powers granted to the President, however, fell short of what he had originally asked by failing to provide for any new executive departments, by exempting from reorganization a number of the independent boards and commissions, by not revamping the auditing system, and by not bringing the civil service system under a single administrator.

THE RECESSION

Meantime, new economic problems had arisen to plague the administration. For a few months of welcome variety in late 1936 and early 1937 the administration was worried by an excess of prosperity. Industrial production was high, the stock market was buoyant, and commodity prices were rising rapidly. It was feared indeed that the country might be entering upon a period of wild speculation like that of the late twenties. The administration shifted rather abruptly to deflationary policies. The WPA rolls were greatly reduced, economy was enjoined upon the government departments, and the balancing of the budget within a year was contemplated. The board of governors of the Federal Reserve System increased the reserve requirements of member banks by 50 per cent as a curb on inflation.

After August, 1937, however, the situation radically altered. Industrial production declined and prices fell. Unemployment once again became a serious problem. This new depression—or recession as the administration preferred to call it—was short-lived. Recovery began in June, 1938, and by December much of the lost ground had been regained. While it lasted, however, the setback was serious and discouraging. Inevitably it struck a damaging blow at the prestige of the Roosevelt administration.

Many economists attributed the recession to natural factors operating quite independently of government policy. Nevertheless, in the supercharged political atmosphere of 1937 the country's new economic troubles became the subject of the wildest accusations. New Dealers asserted that there was a deliberate "strike of capital," that businessmen were recklessly contributing to economic distress in order to force a change of government policy. Anti-New Dealers with similar intemperance blamed the whole situation on the antibusiness attitude of the administration.

Disagreements as to the causes of the recession led to different proposals for its cure. The conservative prescription, which had considerable Congressional support, called for a halt on government spending, tax relief to the corporations, and a recess on social legislation. Without subscribing to this whole program, right-wing New Dealers like Secretary of the Treasury Morgenthau sympathized with it to the extent of advising economy and budget-balancing. On the other hand, more radical advisers urged completely different measures. They attributed the recession to premature reductions in relief expenditures and argued for an enlarged spending program. Marriner S. Eccles of the Federal Reserve Board and Harry Hopkins, the WPA administrator, were spokesmen for this philosophy. The President was evidently reluctant at first to champion the principle because he allowed the recession to continue for over eight months before he appealed to Congress for funds to expand WPA and PWA activities again. But in a message of April 12, 1938, he indicated his acceptance of the tenets of the spending school. The country's economic troubles he attributed to the fact that "production in many important lines of goods outran the ability of the public to purchase them." This led him to assert:

Today's purchasing power—the citizen's income of today—is not sufficient to drive the economic system at higher speed. Responsibility of government requires us at this time to supplement the normal processes and in so supplementing to make sure that the addition is adequate. We must start again on a long steady upward incline in national income. . . .

Let us unanimously recognize that the Federal debt, whether it be twenty-five billions or forty billions, can only be paid if the Nation obtains a vastly increased citizen income. I repeat that if this citizen income can be raised to $80,000,000,000 a year the national government and the overwhelming majority of state and local governments will be "out of the red."

Congress responded to the presidential pleas by authorizing more than $5,000,000,000 worth of emergency expenditures. Hopkins again showed himself a master of the art of putting such a program quickly into operation. Monthly WPA expenditures for wages during the final months of 1938 were double what they had been a year before. The

PWA, administered by Secretary Ickes, also greatly increased its activities, although this was necessarily a somewhat slower process.

Increased government expenditures were paralleled by business recovery, but whether this was cause and effect depended on the point of view. The advocates of compensatory spending asserted that it was and that if the government would not stop at half measures but would double or triple expenditures for public projects, the unemployment problem would be completely solved. This reasoning was, of course, anathema to conservatives who insisted instead that, if the government would put its financial house in order, the resulting wave of confidence would ensure a really sound business recovery. They regarded the advocacy of deficit spending as a long-range policy as evidence that the New Deal was incapable of solving the country's problems. The acrimonious debate between these two points of view was still raging when the onset of war completely changed the economic picture.

ATTEMPTED PURGE

Events since the 1936 election had given additional proof of what had long been evident—the complete lack of agreement among Democrats upon basic principles. Some Democrats were advocates of increased Federal power, others clung to traditional states-rights doctrines; some championed the right of labor to organize, others desired to curb labor unions; some sought through government intervention to broaden greatly the opportunities of the underprivileged, others wished to fortify the position of the dominant economic and social groups.

In 1938 Roosevelt attempted the ambitious task of rectifying this situation. He appealed to the Democratic voters to repudiate the party conservatives and nominate only liberals in the state primaries. In a radio address on June 24 he asserted: "An election cannot give a country a firm sense of direction if it has two or more national parties which merely have different names but are as alike in their principles and aims as peas in the same pod." He indicated that he would play a personal role in the ensuing campaign:

As the head of the Democratic Party, however, charged with the responsibility of carrying out the definitely liberal declarations of principles set forth in the 1936 Democratic platform, I feel that I have every right to speak in those few instances where there may be a clear issue between candidates for a Democratic nomination involving these principles, or involving a clear misuse of my name.

The boldness of the President's effort was best exemplified by his address at Barnesville, Georgia, on August 11, 1938, when he appealed to the Georgia Democrats to repudiate their Senator, Walter F. George, while the latter was sitting on the platform only a few feet away. George, Roosevelt said, was his personal friend, he was a gentleman and a scholar, but on most public questions he and the President did "not speak the same language." With equal directness he subsequently asked for the defeat of Senator Millard Tydings of Maryland and Representative John O'Connor of New York, while requesting the approval of Senator Alben Barkley of Kentucky. These were the only contests in which he intervened directly, but lesser administration figures became involved in a number of other primaries.

This effort to drive the conservative Democrats out of Congress was promptly labeled "a purge" by the opposition press. Had the term been intended simply in its dictionary meaning of "a cleansing," the President would presumably have been glad to accept it as descriptive of what he was attempting. But in 1938 the connotations of the word were far more extensive. Hitler had consolidated his position in Germany by a so-called purge, Stalin had done so in the Soviet Union, and the use of the term in connection with Roosevelt obviously implied that he too was involved in an undemocratic attempt to crush all who opposed him on any issue. Although the President insisted that his objection to certain legislators was on the ground of their general political philosophy, his critics asserted that he was primarily intent on revenging himself on the Democrats who had opposed the Supreme Court Bill. Nor did the President's opponents base their condemnation

The New Deal as Don Quixote. (By Berryman in *The Evening Star*, Washington, D. C.)

merely on the motivation of his conduct; they insisted that whatever the grounds, it was wrong for a Chief Executive to interfere in such local primary contests.

Only in New York and Kentucky was Roosevelt's intervention effective. Representative O'Connor was defeated in the Democratic primary and then defeated again in the November election when he ran as a Republican, while Senator Barkley won his primary contest. But in Georgia and Maryland the proscribed candidates won decisive victories, and such was the result in practically every other instance where conservative Democrats had been marked for retirement. The primaries had as their general result the strengthening rather than the weakening of the anti-New Deal faction.

Roosevelt's attempt to liberalize his party was badly timed. The political tide was running at last in the opposite direction. This had been demonstrated in the Supreme Court and reorganization fights, and it was given further proof by the November elections of 1938. In the Senate the Democrats dropped from 75 seats to 69, while the Republicans were climbing from 17 to 23. In the House the Democrats dropped from 333 to 262 and the Republicans rose from 89 to 169. Even more impressive were the Republican gubernatorial victories in a number of the key states.

THE HATCH ACTS

The revival of the WPA plus the unusual bitterness of the political campaign of 1938 focused attention on the potentialities of the relief administration for bribing or coercing the voters. Despite New Deal denials, charges were rife that such abuses were widespread. The Senate appointed the so-called Sheppard Committee on Campaign Practices to examine these charges; the findings of this Democratic-dominated committee indicated in January, 1939, that in Pennsylvania, Kentucky, and Tennessee the local WPA agents were using the relief organization to promote the New Deal vote. While it is difficult to say how much actual political manipulation of relief there had been, there was enough evidence of irregularities to induce Congress to pass and the President to sign the so-called Hatch Act of August 2, 1939.

Entitled "an act to prevent pernicious political activities," the measure made it unlawful for any person to intimidate, threaten, or coerce any other person for the purpose of influencing his vote in any Federal election. Specifically, it was to be unlawful to deprive or attempt to deprive any person of relief on account of race, creed, color, political activity, support of or opposition to any candidate or any political party in any election. The solicitation of campaign contributions from relief workers was also forbidden. But the act went beyond prohibiting abuses in relief administration to interdict all officers or employees in the executive branch of the Federal government, except policy-making officials, from taking any active part in political management or in political campaigns.

A second Hatch Act was passed in July, 1940, to apply to state officials who received any part of their compensation from Federal funds. It also restricted the amount which any political committee might spend in a single year to $3,000,000 and limited the amount which any single individual or corporation might contribute to $5,000.

RECESS ON REFORM

Roosevelt had crowded proposal upon proposal during his first five years in office because he was convinced that the progressive movement runs in cycles. Unless the reforms on which he had set his heart could be speedily achieved, they might be long delayed due to the changing mood of the public. The soundness of this analysis was proved by the anti-New Deal reaction which set in during his second term. The results of the 1938 elections convinced the President that the time had come to go on the defensive so far as his domestic program was concerned, and during the next years no really new campaigns were begun. Some of the earlier laws, like the Social Security Act, were improved. A few untenable positions like the tax on undistributed corporation profits were surrendered. On the whole, however, the Roosevelt strategy was concentrated on holding the ground already won and resisting such conservative counterattacks as that directed against the National Labor Relations Act.

The President's more conservative mood was intensified by his growing preoccupation with the world situation. Developments in Europe and Asia soon overshadowed every issue of domestic politics.

23

Foreign Policy, 1933–1937

PRESIDENT FRANKLIN D. ROOSEVELT TOOK OFFICE DURING TROUBLESOME times in the diplomatic world. Japan had just successfully defied the League of Nations and the Stimson Doctrine. Benito Mussolini was beginning to formulate plans for an African empire to renew the power that once was Rome's. Adolf Hitler had recently emerged as the most powerful figure in Germany and was bent on wiping out the stain of the Versailles Treaty. International trade was rapidly declining in the face of growing nationalism, and with that decline the war debts and reparations problems were becoming more difficult to solve. Moreover, international economy was disrupted by the currency situation. The seeds of chaos then being sown threatened a harvest of world-wide strife and discord.

THE ATTITUDE OF THE NEW DEAL

The campaign of 1932 indicated that the Democrats were largely concerned with clearing up troubles at home. Little was said in their platform about international affairs, and then only in general terms. The key parts of that platform were:

A sound currency to be preserved at all hazards, and an international monetary conference called, on the invitation of our Government to consider the rehabilitation of silver and related questions.

. . . reciprocal tariff agreements with other Nations and an international economic conference designed to restore international trade and facilitate exchange.

A firm foreign policy, including peace with all the world and the settlement of international disputes by arbitration; no interference in the internal affairs of other Nations; the sanctity of treaties and the maintenance of good faith and of good-will in financial obligations; adherence to the World Court with the pending reservations; the Pact of Paris, abolishing war as an instrument of national policy, to be made effective by provisions for consultation and conference in case of threatened violation of treaties; international agreement for reduction of armaments; and cooperation with Nations of the Western Hemisphere to maintain the spirit of the Monroe Doctrine. We oppose cancellation of due debts owing to the United States by foreign Nations.

Although the leaders responsible for these planks had been trained in the Wilsonian school of internationalism, they failed to include anything about the League of Nations. Even the candidate, who had been a strong Wilsonian in 1920, refused to endanger the party's election chances by reviving the issue of American entry into the League. With the exception of the advocacy of reciprocal trade agreements, the Democratic position on international affairs was strikingly similar to the Hoover theses. As the campaign progressed, however, it became apparent that the New Deal was rejecting an international economic outlook, under which American farmers and manufacturers would have to fix their prices to compete in a world market, in favor of a planned national economy based primarily upon the readjustment of domestic costs and domestic prices.

THE DECLINE OF WORLD TRADE

Regardless of which point of view was correct, President Roosevelt on taking office was faced with numerous complications in the international field. Following the enactment of the Hawley-Smoot Tariff, other countries proceeded to raise their own economic barriers to foreign trade on the assumption that high import duties would provide a safeguard for their domestic products against the sharp fall of world prices, for their gold reserves, and for their labor situation. Even Britain, long considered a champion of free trade, succumbed to this trend in November, 1931, by placing high duties on numerous commodities which she had to import.

The result was that international trade fell off sharply in the years immediately preceding Roosevelt's first inauguration. In 1929, the total value of the exports and imports of 110 countries was slightly more than $68,000,000,000, in 1930 it dropped to $55,000,000,000, in 1931 to less than $40,000,000,000, and in 1932 to $26,000,000,000. A decline of approximately 62 per cent in three years was a cause for worry, if for no other reason than that the payment of war debts was affected; if the debtor nations did not build up their trade, they would not accrue the wherewithal to send their semiannual installments to the United States.

THE LONDON ECONOMIC CONFERENCE

Perhaps the way to solve the numerous interrelated problems was through an international conference. Such a conference had been proposed by the European nations at the time of the Lausanne meeting. The invitation reached the United States just about the time of the Democratic convention and gave the party an opportunity to include a plank advocating American participation. President Hoover was also in agreement with the proposal and in August, 1932, he secured permission to have the United States represented on the Organizing Committee and the Preparatory Committee of Experts which met at Geneva to discuss the matters which would be taken up at the international conference. On the proposed agenda were such problems as world unemployment, the decline of commodity prices, international trade, monetary chaos, and debts and reparations.

During April and May, 1933, Ramsay MacDonald of Britain, Prime Minister Bennett of Canada, Edouard Herriot of France, and representatives of numerous other countries visited President Roosevelt to discuss the impending meeting. In a "fireside chat" of May 7, the President said: "The international conference that lies before us must succeed. The future of the world demands it and we have each of us pledged ourselves to the best joint efforts to this end." Nine days later he sent an appeal to the heads of the fifty-four other nations invited in which he asserted: "The Conference must establish order in place of the present chaos by a stabilization of currencies, by freeing the flow of world trade, and by international action to raise price levels. It must, in short, supplement individual domestic programs for economic recovery, by wise and considered international action." Despite these glowing statements about the need of the conference and the implied promise of American cooperation, the United States had taken steps, even during the Hoover administration, which made the success of the meeting unlikely. The questions of tariffs, war debts, and reparations were ruled off the agenda of the conference. It is difficult to see how international economics could have been improved and stabilized without a discussion of these matters.

The Economic Conference finally opened in London on June 12, 1933. The American delegation, headed by Secretary of State Cordell Hull,[1] was anxious to secure accord, but it was handicapped both by

---

[1] The other members were: Senators Key Pittman of Nevada and James Couzens of Michigan, Representative S. D. McReynolds of Tennessee, James Cox of Ohio, and Ralph Morrison of Texas.

the prohibitions placed upon it and by the changing policy back home. The various delegation leaders started the discussion with hopeful generalities, an indication that not much had been accomplished in the preliminary meetings. Prime Minister MacDonald announced that the question of war debts, although barred from consideration at the meeting, would have to be discussed eventually. While his statement was undoubtedly true, it antagonized the American Congress which had been largely responsible for the prohibition.

The issue of currency stabilization was the first concrete matter taken up. The so-called gold countries—France, Belgium, Italy, Holland, and Switzerland—wanted gold to be the medium for such stabilization. The American delegation refused to agree because the dollar was declining in international exchange; in turn, American prosperity apparently was beginning to return. Were stabilization on a gold standard to be adopted internationally, that hoped-for prosperity might be only an illusion. When the conference threatened to break up, however, the American delegation accepted a compromise: the gold countries should continue the gold standard at existing parities; those which had gone off gold were to return as soon as possible and in the meantime would try to prevent speculation in currency exchange.

As soon as President Roosevelt learned of this compromise, he wired the American delegation on July 3, 1933:

I would regard it as a catastrophe amounting to a world tragedy if the great Conference of Nations, called to bring about a more real and permanent financial stability and a greater prosperity to the masses of all Nations, should, in advance of any serious effort to consider these broader problems, allow itself to be diverted by the proposal of a purely artificial and temporary experiment affecting the monetary exchange of a few Nations only.

Although this repudiation of the compromise was approved in the United States, where prices had already started to fall as a result of fears over currency stabilization, it was vigorously denounced at the London Conference. The American government was charged with bad faith, for it had shown its willingness to agree to stabilization during earlier conferences. President Roosevelt defended his action by placing the blame on the few gold countries which, he asserted, were seeking only temporary expedients; but considering that he himself had said that international development should come before domestic economic policies and then had opposed stabilization, his step was not entirely consistent.

With the July 3 statement the London Conference really came to an end. While it is true that Secretary Hull did try to salvage something from the wreckage, his efforts were useless. The British delegation also attempted to secure some stabilization between the pound sterling and the dollar, but the Americans found their hands tied by the domestic policy of their country. Regardless of who was to blame, the failure of the London Economic Conference was a bitter blow to the betterment of international economic accord. Efforts at cooperation dwindled thereafter and economic nationalism, which had been growing for some time, was given additional impetus. Nor did recriminations help the situation to any degree. From the European point of view, however, the New Deal had started off poorly in international affairs.

THE EUROPEAN NATIONS DEFAULT

Closely associated in the European mind with the restoration of international economic improvement was the matter of war debts. As has been mentioned, the Lausanne Conference provided for practically canceling German reparations if the European debtors of the United States could make a satisfactory arrangement for decreasing their own obligations. The United States was not willing to cancel the war debts, but both President Hoover and President-elect Roosevelt were ready to conduct separate discussions with each debtor nation, even though they disagreed as to the medium for such discussions. By December 15, 1932, the moratorium was over and the semiannual installments were due again. Five nations defaulted; the remainder made their full payments. Britain, in an accompanying note, urged the reopening of the whole debt question as a "contribution . . . to world revival."

The Roosevelt administration consistently refused to support cancellation or a general conference to consider lowering the European obligations. That latter position was indicated clearly when the United States banned the problem from the London Economic Conference agenda.

Three days after that conference opened the next debt payments became due. The European nations were faced with three choices: paying the installment in full; deferring—or from the American point of view defaulting—in hope of reaching a new agreement; or making partial or token payment which would recognize the debt responsibility, but at the same time indicate the need for reduction. The nations which had defaulted the previous December once again failed to make any payment. Finland paid her full obligation. The remaining countries followed the lead of Great Britain in making token payments "as an acknowledgement of the debt pending a final settlement." The British argument was that full payment might interfere with the success of the London Conference, for in the past when such payments were made world prices inevitably went down; the object of the conference was to stabilize them. Thus of the $143,600,000 due the United States, only $11,369,000 was received.

President Roosevelt announced that "inasmuch as the payment made is accompanied by a clear acknowledgment of the debt itself . . . I have no personal hesitation in saying that I do not characterize the resultant situation as a default." He accepted the token amounts and the Treasury Department credited them to the countries concerned. As to the requests for reconsideration, the President said that they were up to Congress and he urged the token payers to send their representations to that body as soon as possible.

Congress, representing the current American opinion, was in no temper to review the war-debt issue. The emphasis placed upon domestic recovery, the "poor sportsmanship"—as Senator Johnson called it—of the London Conference in alluding to war debts, and the fact that European nations could find money to spend on armaments all combined to develop opposition to lowering the obligations to the United States. Consequently, the State Department did not even bother to present the requests of the token payers to the legislature. Thus the European debtors continued either to default entirely or to make partial payments—with the exception of Finland.

THE JOHNSON DEBT DEFAULT ACT

It was in such a mood that Congress overwhelmingly passed the Johnson Debt Default Act in April, 1934. The original bill, sponsored by archisolationist Senator Hiram Johnson of California, had been introduced in 1933 to prohibit any citizen of the United States from buying or selling any securities of a country in arrears or in default of its war debt under penalty of fine or imprisonment. The State Department objected strenuously to the proposal because it would apply to bonds that had already been sold; consequently, many American investors would suffer. Therefore the bill was laid on the table until January, 1934, when it was amended to read that no loans could be made to any nations in default or in arrears, nor could such countries sell any of their securities in the United States. Although there was debate for nearly three months, the passage of the Johnson Bill was never in doubt and it was signed by President Roosevelt on April 13, 1934.

Actually, the Johnson Act did not achieve its objective of compelling the debtor nations to resume their payments. On the contrary, on the next installment date, June 15, 1934, the token payers stopped making even partial payments. Moreover, the Johnson Act checkmated any possible conferences for reducing the obligations. Its passage may have thwarted international economic recovery by preventing the possibility of American loans to foreign nations. Nor did it help the role of the United States in international affairs because Europe regarded it as vindictive. Finally, it was not in line with the asserted Roosevelt policy of trying to promote better relations; the President's signature of the measure was probably motivated by his desire for Congressional support of his domestic recovery program.

THE HULL RECIPROCAL TRADE PROGRAM

While it appeared that the United States thus far had not helped the international economic situation through its position in connection with the London Economic Conference, its stand on war debts, and the passage of the Johnson Act, actually Secretary of State Hull was hard at work on a reciprocal trade program. The Democratic platform had advocated such a program and Candidate Roosevelt had continuously urged it during the course of his campaign. The general thesis was that the existing Hawley-Smoot Tariff was in large part responsible for existing world ills because it tended to suppress international trade. Reciprocal agreements, on the other hand, would not only revive such trade but would build up international prosperity, help to stabilize currencies, and enable the European debtors to pay their obligations. Moreover, they might help to promote American economic recovery by assisting industry and agriculture in finding broader markets.

On March 2, 1934, the President asked Congress for permission "to enter into executive commercial agreements with foreign Nations" and "within carefully guarded limits, to modify existing duties and import restrictions in such a way as will benefit American agriculture and industry." He pointed out that world trade had declined 70 per cent since 1929 and that American exports had fallen off 52 per cent during the same period. "This has meant," he continued, "idle hands, still machines, ships tied to their docks, despairing farm households, and hungry industrial families." The proposal had the unqualified support of Secretary Hull, who indeed may have been the original sponsor of it, having introduced a somewhat similar plan when he was a member of Congress in 1916.

Almost immediately a bill was introduced embodying the President's plan. Attacks from numerous quarters were made. Some who opposed it were fearful lest their own special business interests would suffer; others were against it because they believed that tariff protection was necessary for national prosperity; still another faction considered it un-constitutional because it delegated both taxing and treaty-making power to the executive branch. Despite the fact that the bill encountered more opposition than any other measure thus far in the New Deal, it was passed by substantial majorities—mainly Democratic—in both Houses and signed by the President on June 12, 1934.

Called an Act to amend the Tariff Act of 1930, the measure was popularly known as the "Hull Trade Agreement Act." It provided first of all that the President be authorized to negotiate trade agreements with other nations to obtain new markets for American products. In order to do this, he could raise or lower the Hawley-Smoot rates up to 50 per cent. No decrease in rates would be granted to countries dis-criminating against American goods. A special Executive Committee on Commercial Policy, consisting of several cabinet members and repre-sentatives of the Tariff Commission, was to assist the President, and all interested parties could give their criticisms and suggestions before the agreement became effective. Once arrangements between the United States and another country were completed, the President was to put the agreement into effect by executive proclamation, no action of Con-gress being necessary. The act was to remain in effect for three years.

Secretary Hull, who was really in charge of negotiating the reciprocal agreements, then strove for certain things. First of all he tried to speed up the exchange of commodities produced by one of the parties and needed by the other. Next, he attempted to secure special concessions for American surplus goods. Then, in turn, he granted similar conces-sions in American markets for staples of the other signatory. But he seldom allowed reductions on imports which competed strongly with domestic products.

The first reciprocal agreement was with Cuba, proclaimed in effect on August 24, 1934. By the time the three years were up, fifteen other nations had completed arrangements with the United States for reciprocity, and three agreements were pending.[1] Immediately trade with these nations grew rapidly. For example, during the first year of the operation of the treaty with Belgium, American exports jumped $11,000,000, an increase of 24 per cent; for the first year of the Canadian agreement, the export increase was more than $60,000,000. And whereas American trade with nonsignatories increased 25 per cent, that with signatories grew by 40 per cent. The administration consistently sup-

---

[1] The other fifteen were: Belgium, Brazil, Canada, Colombia, Costa Rica, El Salvador, Finland, France, Guatemala, Haiti, Honduras, Netherlands, Nicaragua, Sweden, and Switzerland.

ported the most-favored-nation principle, and tariff reductions granted under the special agreements with individual nations were automatically extended to all other countries with which the United States had commercial treaties. So the effect of the Hull program was to modify greatly the whole tariff structure.

In 1937 the Trade Agreements Act was extended for another three years, during which time more reciprocal arrangements were effected, principally with Great Britain and most of the remaining nations of Latin America. In addition to helping American business, these treaties influenced other countries to conclude similar agreements with their neighbors. Thus the flow of international trade began again, and thereby better feeling developed among the numerous signatories. Since 1940 Congress has continued to extend the measure.

The United States likewise helped American exporters by establishing the Export-Import Bank early in 1934. This new institution, authorized under a provision of the National Industrial Recovery Act, loaned money to other countries, headed by Cuba, China, and Brazil, so that they could stabilize their currrencies and their exchange, which in turn would make possible more American sales. In addition, many countries received American credit so that they could buy equipment, such as rolling stock, building supplies, and machinery in the United States.

RECOGNITION OF THE SOVIET UNION

Russia was still unrecognized when President Roosevelt took office, but American liberals were eager for a change of policy and American exporters were pressing for restoration of diplomatic relations so that their trade would be safeguarded. The initiative which led to recognition was taken by Maxim Litvinov, head of the Soviet delegation to the London Economic Conference, when he proposed to Secretary Hull that the differences between the two nations might be patched up.

Secretary Hull informed President Roosevelt of the olive-branch suggestion with the result that Litvinov was invited to Washington in November, 1933. Meantime, the way was being paved toward restoration of friendship when the Reconstruction Finance Corporation made a loan to American exporters to facilitate the Russian purchase of American cotton.

After a series of conversations, notes were exchanged between Roosevelt and Litvinov on November 16, 1933. In these notes the Soviet emissary promised that his government would not promote propaganda in any manner in the United States nor allow any organization to develop within Soviet territory which sought the overthrow of the American government. Moreover, Americans in Russia were to be granted freedom of conscience and worship, as well as fair trials if accused of crimes. After diplomatic relations were restored, the Soviet government promised to negotiate on the issue of the debts contracted under preceding Russian regimes. As these statements of Soviet policy were satisfactory to President Roosevelt, he announced American recognition of the Soviet Union the same day.

In general this recognition was well received by the American people, despite the fact that there were some who felt that the Red menace of post-World War I days was still great. There were high hopes of an immediate increase of American exports to Russia. Indeed, one of the reasons for establishing the Export-Import Bank was to speed up commercial relations between the two countries. The failure of the debt negotiations, however, made operative the Johnson Debt Default Act, and no loans could be extended to the Soviet. Without loans, the expected trade boom did not materialize. As time passed, there was also the feeling in American circles that Russia was not living up to her promise concerning propagandist activities. Yet diplomatic recognition of Russia was in line with the Roosevelt inaugural promise to be a good neighbor. And perhaps behind that recognition was the administration desire to secure additional support against Japanese aggression.

THE GOOD NEIGHBOR

The Good Neighbor policy of the New Deal, however, is primarily associated with American relations with Latin America. This was indicated by an address which President Roosevelt made before the governing board of the Pan American Union on April 12, 1933. In it he said:

The essential qualities of a true Pan Americanism must be the same as those which constitute a good neighbor. . . . Friendship among Nations, as among individuals, calls for constructive efforts to muster the forces of humanity in order that an atmosphere of close understanding and cooperation may be cultivated. It involves mutual obligations and responsibilities. . . . In this spirit the people of every Republic on our continent are coming to a deep understanding of the fact that the Monroe Doctrine . . . was and is directed at the maintenance of independence by the peoples of the continent. . . . It is of vital importance to every Nation of this continent that the American Governments, individually, take, without further delay, such action as may be possible to abolish all unnecessary and artificial barriers and restrictions which now hamper the healthy flow of trade between the peoples of the American Republics.

While the emphasis in this speech was placed upon increased trade and commerce, the Roosevelt administration was quick to show that it was also interested in maintaining a policy of nonintervention and in concluding dollar diplomacy. Fulfillment of these aims was aided immeasurably by Secretary of State Cordell Hull, whose informal dealings with Latin-American leaders accomplished more good than straight-laced diplomatic action, and by his assistant, Sumner Welles, whose knowledge of Latin-American problems furnished the basis for many of the Good Neighbor policies.

One of the first opportunities to show that the Good Neighbor was more than a promise was offered during the seventh regular Pan-American Conference held at Montevideo, Uruguay, in December, 1933. Secretary Hull, who headed the American delegation, made no effort to assume a commanding position in open discussions, but used behind-the-scene diplomacy to secure his ends. He was able to secure tacit support for future reciprocity and, in return for American backing for the Argentine Anti-War Pact, he prevailed upon the Latin-American republics to endorse all of the other commitments to outlaw war. The most important action of the Montevideo meeting was approval of Article VIII: "No State has a right to intervene in the internal or external affairs of another." The American backing of this article showed a definite change of heart since the Havana Conference of 1928. And on December 28, 1933, President Roosevelt announced his support of this new position when he said: "The definite policy of the United States [with respect to Latin America] from now on is one opposed to armed intervention." Another step toward peaceful relations was taken when provision was made for permanent bilateral commissions of inquiry and consultation. Moreover, the meeting secured a temporary truce between Bolivia and Paraguay, who had been fighting over the Gran Chaco. A number of cultural and economic questions were also amicably discussed. All in all, the Montevideo Conference ended on a note of great accord; most of the fears and suspicions which Latin Americans had of the United States were erased for the time being.

COMPLETING THE WITHDRAWAL FROM HAITI

Putting the Good Neighbor into more practical effect in regard to Haiti, President Roosevelt finally found the solution which had evaded his predecessor by concluding through the new minister, Norman Armour, an executive agreement with Haitian President Vincent. This arrangement, known as "the Agreement of August 7, 1933," provided for complete Haitian control of the national guard by October 1, 1934, at which time the last of the American marines would be withdrawn.

In collaboration with President Roosevelt, a fiscal representative would be named by Vincent to supervise collection of customs after January 1, 1934.

This financial arrangement was not wholly satisfactory to the Haitians, so, taking advantage of the nonintervention assertion of the Montevideo meeting, President Vincent sought an end to American fiscal control. On the invitation of President Roosevelt, Vincent went to Washington where, in April, 1934, he obtained a promise that new financial and commercial arrangements would be worked out. Three months later, Roosevelt visited Haiti and, after looking over the situation, he ordered the last of the marines to be withdrawn by August 15. At the same time provision was made for the sale by the National City Bank of New York of control of the National Bank of Haiti to the Haitian government and the conclusion of American fiscal control. By the summer of 1935 these financial arrangements were completed and Haiti was once more in full control of all her affairs. American dollar diplomacy in the West Indies was thereby at an end.

Meantime, the United States had helped to ensure Haitian financial competence by signing a reciprocal trade agreement with her in March, 1935. Under its terms, Haiti could send cocoa, rum, and fruit to the United States at considerably less than the Hawley-Smoot rates, while the insular authorities granted similar reductions on American machinery and automotive equipment.

THE ABROGATION OF THE PLATT AMENDMENT

As has been stated, the situation in Cuba was growing tense during the closing days of the Hoover administration. The depression there led to political discontent directed against Dictator Machado. In an effort to end the troubles, President Roosevelt named Sumner Welles as ambassador in the early summer of 1933. Welles tried to solve the difficulties by suggesting that Machado take a leave of absence, but the Cuban executive refused to do so. Thereupon the Cubans took matters into their own hands, staged a general strike on August 4, and forced Machado to flee the country shortly afterward. Then followed months of tumult, with no president or *junta* able to remain in office long. Cries were also raised for the abrogation of the Platt Amendment. While Roosevelt was forced to send a number of warships to Cuban ports to protect American interests, he called upon the ABC powers and Mexico to assist the United States in prevailing upon the Cubans to reestablish orderly government. There was no thought of unilateral action or intervention.

Not until January, 1934, was a semblance of peace restored to the island with the coming into power of Carlos Mendieta, who was recognized by the United States on January 23. Additional help was given in the form of financial credit through the Export-Import Bank loans and a reciprocal trade treaty. That treaty granted Cuba concessions on sugar, rum, fruits, tobacco, and numerous other items, while she in turn allowed reductions on more than four hundred imports from the United States.

The most important token of the Good Neighbor policy, however, was the abrogation of the Platt Amendment. As early as November, 1933, President Roosevelt had urged the abrogation as a means "of showing by deed our intention of playing the part of a good neighbor to the Cuban people." It was not until May 29, 1934, however, that Roosevelt and the Cuban ambassador signed a treaty providing for the erasure of the Platt Amendment from the Cuban constitution and the voiding of the 1903 treaty which incorporated that amendment. Two days later the United States Senate ratified the treaty, with the Cuban Senate giving its consent on June 9. In support of this action President Roosevelt asserted: "By the consummation of this treaty this Government will make it clear that it not only opposes the policy of armed intervention but that it renounces those rights of intervention and interference in Cuba which have been bestowed upon it by treaty." For defensive purposes, however, Cuba allowed the United States to continue the lease of Guantanamo Bay.

SATISFYING PANAMA

In somewhat similar fashion the United States ended its protectorate over Panama. For many years the people of Panama had disliked that provision of the Hay-Bunau-Varilla Treaty of 1903 which gave the United States the right to intervene to preserve order and to ensure independence. They asserted that those rights actually deprived Panama of sovereignty. The situation was complicated still more when the United States in effect went off the gold standard and tried to pay the annual rental for canal rights in 59-cent dollars instead of the promised gold. Moreover, growing unrest in other parts of the world made the Roosevelt administration realize the need of close accord with Panama for the protection of the canal.

Consequently, on March 2, 1936, a treaty was drawn up under which the United States gave up its rights to intervene in Panama for the protection of the waterway, along with its right under eminent domain to secure additional territories near the terminals. On its part, Panama agreed to cooperate with the United States in defending the canal and the adjacent territory. Financially, the United States promised to pay its annual rental in Panama money at the old gold-exchange rate.

The decision of Japan to withdraw from the naval limitations agreements caused considerable worry in the United States Senate. Would the United States be able to defend the canal adequately under the new proposal? Many thought not. Therefore it was not until July, 1939, that this treaty, in somewhat amended form, was ratified by the American Upper House.

THE WAY TOWARD PHILIPPINE INDEPENDENCE

President Roosevelt took up the Philippine promise where Hoover left off. Filipino objections to the Hawes-Cutting Act were remedied in the McDuffie-Tydings Act of March 23, 1934. During the ten-year probationary period the provision for American control of foreign affairs was retained, all military forces in the islands might be called into American service if danger threatened, immigration differences were worked out to mutual satisfaction, and a special commission would consider the tariff situation. The Philippine Congress approved this act on May 1, 1934.

A special constituent assembly of Filipinos then drew up a constitution, which was approved both by President Roosevelt and the Filipino people by the middle of 1935. In the first election under this document, Manuel Quezon was selected as President of the Commonwealth of the Philippines and he assumed his duties on November 15, 1935. Before the probationary period was up, however, the safety of the Philippines was dangerously challenged. The occupation of the archipelago by the Japanese from 1942 to 1945 drove Quezon into exile in the United States where he died. But in the months after V–J Day the United States fulfilled its pledge. On July 4, 1946, the Philippines became an independent republic, with Manuel Roxas serving as president.

THE GATHERING STORM

Thus far the New Deal in its diplomacy had been motivated by the desire to promote world economic recovery, which in turn would help the United States fulfill its domestic program. If the rest of the world did not cooperate, then the United States could always rely upon the support of the other republics of the hemisphere which had been wooed with the Good Neighbor policy.

As the early years of the New Deal passed, however, it became increasingly evident that there was more to world unrest than simply monetary and commercial dislocation. There was a growing aggressiveness—which may have had behind it economic factors to be sure—which threatened the peace of the world. And like Hoover, President Roosevelt wanted peace everywhere. Despite the fact that his wish to complete the domestic program of recovery took his primary attention, the increasing world tension could not be disregarded.

THE GENEVA CONFERENCE

Approximately a month before Roosevelt was inaugurated the Geneva Disarmament Conference reopened its meetings in an effort to find a solution which had escaped the earlier sessions. Germany, which had been seeking equality of treatment, had been placated and had returned to the meetings. Once again, however, there was failure to reach an agreement during the early weeks. Then in March, Prime Minister MacDonald offered a new proposition: the armies of the European nations should be raised through conscription, the size of each determined according to population; none of the armies should be large; heavy guns and military planes should be kept at a minimum; Germany was to be granted proportional equality with her neighbors; and France, worried over growing German strength, was to be pacified through a meeting of signers of the Paris Pact to determine how it could be enforced. Germany did not like this British plan and sought more rights. When the conference refused, she threatened to build up her armaments anyway.

President Roosevelt then tried his hand in reaching a settlement. At the same time that he urged the other fifty-four countries represented at the London Economic Conference to compromise on financial problems (May 16, 1933), he likewise asked the Geneva delegations to "enter into a solemn and definite pact of non-aggression." Six days later, the new chairman of the American delegation, Norman H. Davis, told the Geneva gathering:

We are ready not only to do our part toward the substantial reduction of armaments, but if this is effected by general international agreement we are also prepared to contribute in other ways to the organization of peace. In particular we are willing to consult the other states in case of a threat to peace with a view to avoiding conflict.

This meant that the United States would cooperate with the League of Nations in any action it took to try to avert war. There was an additional promise that the United States would not attempt to restrain collective efforts to bring an aggressor to terms.

While this American position heartened France, it did not result in carrying the British proposal. Germany still refused to admit that she was being fairly treated. Although Hitler professed a desire for accord, the actions of the German delegation indicated the opposite. June found the meeting still deadlocked so an adjournment was called. Just before the conference was to reconvene on October 16, 1933, Germany stated that she would not be represented and, furthermore, she announced her decision to withdraw from the League of Nations. She knew that her plans were opposed by the United States because on October 9 Hull had informed her ambassador that Americans would "wage a steady contest for the disarmament of the heavily armed nations, rather than become parties to a plan for others to proceed to rearm." While the Geneva Conference held some abortive sessions in the spring of 1934, to all intents and purposes its efforts were fruitless after Germany's retirement. The failure of this conference increased Roosevelt's apprehensions about the possibility of new wars.

The Pyromaniac. (By Kirby. Reproduced by permission of the *New York World-Telegram*. Copyright, 1933.)

THE GROWTH OF ISOLATION

American public opinion, primarily concerned with domestic recovery, had been apathetic toward the whole Geneva proceedings. That apathy had been clearly demonstrated in connection with Secretary Hull's request of April 5, 1933, that Congress pass a measure providing that the President might forbid the exportation of arms and munitions of war when such shipments "might promote or encourage the employment of force in a dispute or conflict between nations." The general purpose would be to cooperate with other peace-loving nations in preventing aggressors from obtaining additional military supplies. Hull qualified his request with the assertion that the embargo would be used "to the sole end of maintaining the peace of the world and with a due and prudent regard for our national policies and national interests."

Although the House of Representatives approved a bill incorporating the Secretary's suggestions, the Senate Foreign Relations Committee amended it so that the embargo would have to be applied against all belligerents, aggressor or otherwise. Despite Hull's plea that the amendment did not have President Roosevelt's approval, the Upper House passed the bill in amended form; the House refused to agree and the measure lapsed—for the time being.

The Senate version was a definite indication of a growing spirit of isolation in the United States. The feeling was increasing that the country must not be drawn into another conflict like that of World War I. Norman Davis expressed the views of most Americans when he said on May 29, 1934, that while the United States would cooperate in an international disarmament program, it would not "participate in European political negotiations and settlements and will not make any commitment whatever to use its armed forces for the settlement of any dispute anywhere."

But why had this spirit developed? It is impossible to place one's finger on any single factor for there were a number of contributing elements. To many Americans, World War I had been fought in vain; the world had not been made safe for democracy. There was a growing feeling that wars were engineered by munitions makers so that they might make money. This view was so powerful that *Fortune* magazine made an investigation which it published in its March, 1934, issue. This report appeared to be so damning that President Roosevelt subsequently asked Hugh Johnson and Bernard Baruch to try to find a formula for ending wartime profits. The Senate was not content, setting up its own investigating committee headed by Gerald P. Nye of North Dakota, an extreme isolationist. After three years of much publicized hearings, the Nye Committee revealed its findings in 1937. This report tried to show that American business leaders had not only profited greatly during World War I, but had evaded the payment of taxes on their ill-gotten gains. Moreover, the Army and Navy Departments had been lax to the point of corruption in granting contracts, political connections were important in obtaining contracts, and American bankers were instrumental in bringing the country into war to save their loans to the Allies. Although the report did not prove its points and the conclusions were not warranted by the evidence obtained, many Americans were impressed by the findings and completely converted to isolationism.

Another factor in the trend was the failure of the debtors to repay the money they had borrowed during World War I. And what made it worse, Americans felt that this money was being used to build up national armaments which would lead to future wars. The League of Nations was looked upon simply as an organization to further the interests of its members. The World Court had to be avoided because it was only a tool of the League. If the United States joined the Court, the nation might be involved in European entanglements which might involve it in war. Even though President Roosevelt said on January 16, 1935: "I hope that at an early date the Senate will advise and consent to the adherence by the United States" to the World Court "to make international justice practicable and serviceable," the Upper House did not provide the necessary two-thirds vote because of isolationist opposition.[1]

Among the so-called intelligentsia the isolationist trend was also strong. The nation was flooded with literature stressing the futility of war and playing up the American need of avoiding entanglements with the rest of the world. Charles and Mary Beard developed this thesis in their writings, as did also Harry Elmer Barnes, himself a propagandist against the German menace prior to the entrance of the United States into World War I. It became the vogue in college classrooms to teach that the Treaty of Versailles was a harsh peace, responsible for much of the world troubles during the twenties, and that the Allies were equally guilty with the Germans of starting the conflict. Consequently, the younger generation were imbued with the psychology of isolation; it might almost be said that their slogan became "Peace at any price."

[1] The vote was fifty-two in favor of adherence, thirty-six against.

THE FAILURE OF NAVAL LIMITATION

This isolationist trend was given added impetus by the results of the London Naval Conference of 1935, provision for which had been made at the 1930 meeting. Preliminary to this conference, delegates from the United States, Great Britain, and Japan had gathered at London in June, 1934. Each group had its formula. The Britons urged continuation of the existing ratios, reduction in size of battleships, either abolition of the submarine or reduction in size and number, and an increase in the number of cruisers. The Americans sought a reduction of existing naval armaments; a 20 per cent decrease was suggested. Also, existing ratios must be maintained. On the other hand, the Japanese delegates wanted equality with the other two; they would agree to reduction, but only on their own terms. The *New York Times* quoted Admiral Yamamoto as saying: "Our aim is not merely to bring the navies of Great Britain and the United States down to our level; we should like to reduce our navy too." All efforts at compromise failed, although the British were more ready to yield to Japanese wishes than were the Americans who were determined that there be no change in the relative strength of the navies. On December 29, 1934, therefore, the Japanese government informed the other signatories of the Washington and London Naval Treaties that it would withdraw from the agreements two years later.

Thus the London Naval Conference of 1935, opening in December, began inauspiciously. Japan still insisted on equality and the United States continued to support the existing ratios. The American delegates took the position that granting of equality would be an admission that Japanese actions in the Far East were approved. Thereupon the Japanese envoys left the conference. The remaining delegations, representing France, Italy, Great Britain, and the United States, then tried to salvage something from the wreckage. On March 25, 1936, they agreed to a new London Naval Treaty. The major parts of that agreement were: Britain and the United States were to continue their tonnage parity and were not to engage in any competitive building; the restrictions on the number of ships in each category were removed; and there were so many escalator or escape clauses that the treaty actually did not mean much. Nevertheless the United States Senate ratified the treaty on May 18, 1936, without a dissenting vote. To many Americans the withdrawal of Japan from the naval limitations agreements and the fact that Britain and France were embarking on new naval construction programs meant that the possibility of war was more immediate. Country after country, large and small, was developing its land armaments. The wise thing to do, therefore, was to try to legislate against war.

NEUTRALITY LEGISLATION

Meantime, growing tension had led to actual war. The truce between Bolivia and Paraguay over the Gran Chaco had ended and the two countries resumed fighting. Italy, flaunting the League, had attacked Ethiopia in the early fall of 1935. These wars, especially the Italo-Ethiopian, it was feared, might broaden to embroil the United States. Whereupon the popular demand for American neutrality grew and Congress answered with the Joint Resolution of August 24, 1935, better known as the "Neutrality Act." This measure, the most sweeping neutrality legislation passed thus far in American history, stipulated that when war broke out between two or more foreign nations, or during the progress of such conflict, the President was empowered to proclaim "such fact." Immediately thereafter, an embargo on arms, munitions, and implements of war to any of the belligerents was to become effective, the designation of such commodities to be made by the President. Control and supervision of the manufacture and sale of munitions of war was placed in the hands of a permanent National Munitions Control Board made up of the Secretaries of State, War, Navy, and Commerce, with the Secretary of State in charge of the administration of the whole measure. Also on presidential proclamation, American citizens would travel at their own risk on ships owned by any of the belligerents. The embargo clauses were temporary in nature, terminating on February 29, 1936.

President Roosevelt gave his approval to this resolution a week later "because it was intended as an expression of the fixed desire of the Government and the people of the United States to avoid any action which might involve us in war." He believed that "the purpose is wholly excellent," but he realized that there were some weaknesses in the resolution which ought to be remedied in future legislation.

The resolution expressed the current opinion that the United States had been drawn into World War I because of American traffic in arms. Were that traffic prohibited, there would be less chance of American embroilment in future struggles. Yet had Congress taken the logical step under such a thesis, it should have made the embargo mandatory upon the outbreak of hostilities, whether or not there was a declaration of war, instead of leaving the matter to the discretion of the President. This discretionary right was probably a concession to Roosevelt, who desired a certain amount of flexibility of action in his efforts to promote peace. Definition of what were implements of war might have added weight to the resolution as well.

On October 5, 1935, President Roosevelt proclaimed "that a state of war unhappily exists between Ethiopia and the Kingdom of Italy" and the Neutrality Act provisions were declared in effect. Implements of war were defined and Americans were warned against traveling on ships of the belligerents.

Carrying out this neutrality proclamation ended America's position as the champion of neutral rights on the high seas. Americans who had any dealings with either belligerent were warned that they did so at their own risk; they could not count upon government assistance if, for example, their cargoes were seized. Nor did the act work out as expected. American exporters desirous of profit could and did send to Italy many commodities which were not on the presidential list of implements of war, but which could easily be converted into such. This was not in line with Roosevelt's desire to weaken the aggressor nation—and Italy certainly was that. On the other hand it has been argued that the measure helped Ethiopia because she did not have a merchant marine anyway and never had purchased much from the United States; therefore the embargo did not affect her, although it did Italy.

That the President recognized the weaknesses in the measure was shown in his annual message to Congress on January 3, 1936. He said:

Nations seeking expansion, seeking the rectification of injustices springing from former wars, or seeking outlets for trade . . . fail to demonstrate that patience necessary to attain reasonable and legitimate objectives by peaceful negotiation or by an appeal to the finer instincts of world justice. They have therefore impatiently reverted to the old belief in the law of the sword . . .

Consequently, he urged greater cooperation between the legislature and Executive in promoting more effective neutrality as a means of avoiding war.

The need for speedy Congressional action was shown by the fact that parts of the Neutrality Act of 1935 would terminate at the end of February, 1936. Moreover, the Italo-Ethiopian strife might spread in scope to entangle more countries. Administration leaders in the legislature realized that the well-rounded measure which the President desired might lead to protracted debate between the isolationists and their opponents. Therefore the Neutrality Act of February 29, 1936, was but a stopgap to keep the original legislation alive until a more inclusive measure could be worked out. The original resolution was extended to

May 1, 1937, and several amendments were added to it. No credits or loans could be extended to any belligerent nation; the measure was not to apply to other American republics involved in war with a nation outside the hemisphere; and the discretionary right of the President to proclaim the embargo was changed to a mandatory order to extend it to other countries that might become belligerents.

THE SPANISH CIVIL WAR

This measure of 1936 also had its weakness—it did not concern civil wars. The issue arose in July, 1936, when an internecine struggle broke out in Spain between those who wished to maintain the republican form of government—the so-called Loyalists—and the factions supporting General Francisco Franco and a totalitarian regime. Unfortunately for the cause of peace, Germany and Italy backed the Franco rebels, while Russia began to give aid to the Loyalists despite the fact that twenty-seven nations had established a committee for the purpose of localizing the hostilities and maintaining the principle of nonintervention.

The Spanish Civil War aroused widespread feeling in the United States. The advocates of democracy sympathized with the Loyalists to the extent of establishing innumerable committees to raise funds, clothing, and medical supplies for them. Hundreds if not thousands of adventurous Americans joined the Loyalist army and air force. Many doctors and nurses left for Spain to help the cause. But, on the other hand, there were those who preferred totalitarianism to the dread communism associated with loyalism and countered with similar efforts to assist the Franco forces. Many prominent prelates of the Catholic Church swung their influence to that cause. Despite the fact that the civil war quickly became the testing ground for the strength of two rival ideologies and the struggle threatened to break its theoretically local bonds, the American State Department, voicing the President's wishes, announced on August 6, 1936:

In conformity with its well-established policy of non-interference with internal affairs in another country either in time of peace or in the event of civil strife, this Government will, of course, scrupulously refrain from any interference whatsoever in the unfortunate Spanish situation.

At the same time the Department tried to dissuade American exporters from sending arms to either side on the ground that the spirit of American neutrality would be violated even though there was no specific law to the contrary. In general, the shippers of arms and munitions followed the wishes of the administration, but in December, 1936, a request was made of the government for a license to export planes and war material to the Loyalist government. This request brought the issue to the fore, and early in January, 1937, Congress almost unanimously approved[1] another Joint Resolution, signed by President Roosevelt on January 8, which prohibited the exportation of arms and implements of war to either side in Spain. Thus the civil war was specifically brought under the 1936 neutrality legislation despite loud protests from many Americans, particularly those with Loyalist sympathies. These protests were perhaps justified. The American position was such that regardless of what action the United States took, it would be beneficial to one belligerent or the other. Since Germany and Italy were already helping Franco, the invocation of the neutrality legislation definitely hurt the Loyalists; in fact, it might even be called actual intervention against the Loyalists because it denied them rights customarily enjoyed by *de jure* governments.

When the temporary features of the 1936 acts were about to lapse on May 1, 1937, the international picture had scarcely changed. True, the Italo-Ethiopian War was ended, but only because Italy had overrun all of the enemy territory. The contest in Spain was still being strongly waged and Hitler had defied the Locarno Pact by invading the Rhineland. The situation between Japan and China was such that hostilities might break out at any moment. Consequently, Congress decided to place on the statute books a permanent neutrality measure.

The debate on the new neutrality bill was long and bitter, showing that while the legislators were in agreement on the principle, they were at odds over the means of achieving it. On May 1, 1937, the measure was finally passed and signed by the President. It represented a compromise between those who believed that an embargo must be proclaimed as soon as war broke out between two or more foreign countries and those who felt that the President should have a certain amount of discretion in invoking such an embargo because, as Senator Borah said, "the more discretion within reason the better, for where you are dealing with war conditions it is impossible to foresee what course a nation should pursue." Much of the previous legislation was kept. The President still had the right to proclaim when a state of war existed; when he so proclaimed it would then become unlawful to export arms, munitions, and implements of war to any of the belligerents or to "purchase, sell, or exchange" the securities of such contestants. Nor could any American ships carry arms or implements of war to belligerents or be armed. American citizens were forbidden to travel on

[1] There were no dissenting votes in the Senate; the House vote was 460–1.

ships of a country at war. Finally, under the mandatory provisions, belligerency applied as well to civil wars.

The discretionary powers of the President included the right to prohibit the use of American ports to armed merchant ships and submarines of belligerents or as bases of supply. The chief innovation was the "cash-and-carry" clause: the President could enumerate certain commodities which might not be exported to a warring country "until all right, title, and interest therein shall be transferred to some foreign government"; such goods must not be transported in American ships; in other words, the belligerent must pay for such goods and see that they were then shipped in its own vessels. The National Munitions Control Board was continued, and American republics were exempted from the workings of the measure unless they were "cooperating with a non-American State or States in such war."

Although the Neutrality Act of 1937 contained many more mandatory and discretionary prohibitions than had its predecessors, it actually could provide for what might be called unneutral actions. Undoubtedly the "cash-and-carry" feature benefited the belligerent with money and shipping. It was supposed to be a warning to Germany and Italy that neither would have the advantage of American supplies because they lacked the wherewithal to pay for them. Actually, however, it was not much of a warning. Were either country to go to war, it would certainly be facing a stronger naval power which would prevent it from

Sand. Uncle Sam, ostrichlike, tries not to see the troubles over seas. (By Carlisle in the *New York Herald Tribune*.)

obtaining any American supplies. Therefore, were the act to be invoked under such circumstances, either Germany or Italy would be guaranteed that its enemy would be seriously handicapped in securing American commodities. The measure ran contrary to commitments the United States had with Latin-American countries; there were promises not to sell war material to rebels in those republics, yet the measure stipulated that in case of civil war it must be applied to both the recognized administration and the challengers alike. In similar fashion, there could be no move made to distinguish between the aggressor nation and the one attacked. While international bankers were restricted in their operations, American exporters of goods not on the embargo list were not—provided the belligerent buyer had the cash. As Senator Borah said in criticism of the act on March 1, 1939: "We seek to avoid all risks, all dangers, but we make certain to get all the profits."

The Neutrality Act was immediately proclaimed in effect for the Spanish Civil War by President Roosevelt on May 1, 1937. On the other hand, he did not invoke it after the reopening of hostilities between Japan and China following the incident at Marco Polo Bridge on July 7, 1937, which has been called the beginning of World War II in the Far East. The excuse was that there had been no formal declaration of war and the institution of the Neutrality Act would make more difficult a peaceful and speedy settlement of the strife. The real reason why the measure was not put into practice, however, was because its application would have helped Japan. The administration desired to assist China and could not do so were the Neutrality Act applied to the conflict. Therefore the policy of helping a victim of aggression was placed before the law.

Nevertheless, the publicity attendant upon the contemplated shipment of nineteen planes to China aboard the government-owned *Wichita* in August, 1937, and the American fear that the ship might be sunk by Japan—which would provide the incident that might involve the United States in war, caused President Roosevelt to make the following proclamation on September 14, 1937:

Merchant vessels owned by the Government of the United States will not hereafter, until further notice, be permitted to transport to China or Japan any of the arms, ammunition, or implements of war which were listed in the President's Proclamation of May 1, 1937.

Any other merchant vessels, flying the American flag, which attempt to transport any of the listed articles to China or Japan will, until further notice, do so at their own risk.

The question of applying the Neutrality Act remains in *statu quo*, the Government policy remaining on a 24-hour basis.

As it became increasingly apparent that the Sino-Japanese struggle was more than an incident, President Roosevelt still refused to put the Neutrality Act into effect. He left little doubt in American minds about who was the aggressor—even though he did not mention Japan by name —when he addressed a gathering in Chicago on October 5, 1937. After reviewing "the political situation in the world, which of late has been growing progressively worse," he pointed out that peace-loving nations would suffer unless something were done to prevent "innocent peoples, innocent nations" from "being cruelly sacrificed to a greed for power and supremacy which is devoid of all sense of justice and humane considerations." Then he continued:

If we are to have a world in which we can breathe freely and live in amity without fear—the peace-loving nations must make a concerted effort to uphold laws and principles on which alone peace can rest secure. . . .
When an epidemic of physical disease starts to spread, the community approves and joins in a quarantine of the patients in order to protect the health of the community against the spread of the disease. . . .
America hates war. America hopes for peace. Therefore, America engages in the search for peace.

This so-called quarantine speech proved to be the first formal expression by President Roosevelt against aggressor nations in general and against Japan in particular. It indicated that he was throwing off the cloak of isolation forced upon him by the Neutrality Acts. Yet in so doing he was not seeking war, but joint action of peace-loving nations to secure peace.

THE BUENOS AIRES CONFERENCE
In fact the President had started another movement for the maintenance of peace more than a year before, when, on March 17, 1936, he announced that all of the republics of the hemisphere had agreed to convene at Buenos Aires to discuss the problem of how to meet the existing world chaos. The meeting opened on December 1, 1936, and the importance attached to it may be gleaned from the fact that President Roosevelt went to Argentina to deliver the opening address. He said in part:

This is no conference to form alliances, to divide the spoils of war, to partition countries, to deal with human beings as though they were pawns in the game of chance. Our purpose, under happy auspices, is to assure the continuance of the blessings of peace.

After this stirring opening speech, the conference began its search for greater accord. Secretary Hull, again heading the American delegation, secured unanimous approval for his suggestion that all the previous treaties for peace and arbitration be ratified once again. It was also agreed that when the peace and safety of the Americas were threatened externally or internally, the several republics would meet to find a cooperative solution. Moreover, approval was given to the proposal for a common policy of neutrality in the event of war outside of the hemisphere or between two or more nations within. Likewise all differences among the republics—territorial and financial—must be submitted to arbitration. The accord reached at Buenos Aires indicated that the Monroe Doctrine had in effect become multilateral.

It was partly as a result of this accord that the United States and five Latin-American republics finally found the solution to the Gran Chaco War during the summer of 1938 after the League of Nations failed. Yet the policy of nonintervention and of the Good Neighbor was sorely tried when Mexico expropriated American, British, and Dutch oil properties valued at nearly $500,000,000. The American companies concerned appealed to their government for redress and Secretary Hull sent some vigorous notes to Mexico about seizures without adequate compensation. There was no thought of employing force against Mexico, however, and after several years of jockeying, a joint commission was set up which reached a satisfactory settlement in 1943.

THE "PANAY" INCIDENT

Meantime, American neutrality was given a severe test when Japanese planes bombed and strafed the American gunboat *Panay* and three American merchant craft on the Yangtze River near Nanking on December 12, 1937. No warning was given by the attackers, three Americans were killed, seventy-four were wounded, and the *Panay* and two of the other ships were sunk. Possibly in an effort to prevent witnesses from describing this unprovoked attack, the planes swooped over the boats taking the survivors to shore and machine-gunned them.

Since the *Panay* was plainly marked with two large American flags and was in the Yangtze on the legitimate business of transferring American refugees and supplies from war-torn areas, the Roosevelt administration was naturally distressed. The following day Secretary Hull informed the Japanese ambassador "that the President is deeply shocked and concerned by the news of the indiscriminate bombing of American . . . vessels. . . ." He further sought full Japanese expressions of regret, compensation for the losses, and promises that there would be no recurrence of such attacks.

The Japanese government evidently realized that its forces had gone too far because on December 14 its Foreign Minister sent prompt apology, assured the United States that indemnity would be paid, and that it would "deal appropriately with those responsible for the incident." As evidence of good faith, the Japanese government announced ten days later that the chief of the air force had been removed and that orders had been transmitted to all Japanese forces to use the utmost caution against similar incidents "even at the sacrifice of a strategic advantage in attacking the Chinese troops." Toward the end of April, 1938, Japan made payment of slightly more than $2,200,000 for the deaths, injuries, and property losses sustained in the *Panay* incident.

Although there was a flurry of apprehension in the United States over this affair, which was regarded by some as more serious than the blowing up of the *Maine*, there was no widespread demand for war after the prompt Japanese apology was given. Indeed, the average American did not care too much what was happening in the Far East; he was too concerned with the financial problems at home. If too much were made of the incident, war might result—and he did not want war.

This isolationist, antiwar attitude was further shown by the introduction into the House on December 14, 1937, by Representative Ludlow of Indiana of a proposed amendment to the Constitution. This provided for a national referendum before a declaration of war could be made, except in cases of actual invasion. Early in January, 1938, President Roosevelt used all of the pressure at his command to defeat this Ludlow Amendment. In a letter to Speaker Bankhead he said:

I must frankly state that I consider the proposed amendment would be impracticable in its application and incompatible with our representative form of government. . . . Such an amendment . . . would cripple any President in his conduct of our foreign relations, and it would encourage other nations to believe that they could violate American rights with impunity. I fully realize that the sponsors of this proposal sincerely believe that it would be helpful in keeping the United States out of war. I am convinced that it would have the opposite effect.

Largely as a result of this administration pressure the amendment was defeated, but only by the close vote of 209 to 188. And the American opposition to becoming involved in a Far Eastern war was indicated in a popular poll in which 54 per cent desired to have the United States withdraw entirely from China; only 30 per cent wanted the government to force respect for American rights there.

Thus, as World War II approached, it became increasingly evident that the American people wanted to avoid any entanglements that might embroil them in conflict. In the early years of the Roosevelt regime the President sought to better world accord through international conferences. Both the failure of European nations to agree and the preponderant American interest in domestic recovery prevented the success of these ventures. Roosevelt, in pursuit of the Good Neighbor program, scored greater accomplishments in the Western Hemisphere as the Montevideo and Buenos Aires Conferences showed. The abrogation of the Platt Amendment and the passage of the McDuffie-Tydings Act were other evidences of the Good Neighbor. But because attempts at international cooperation failed, the American people were developing an isolationist—almost peace-at-any-price—attitude as shown by the enactment of the Johnson and Neutrality Acts.

Those Neutrality Acts were based upon a misinterpretation of the causes for American entrance into World War I and consequently upon a belief that no external danger could possibly touch the United States. Moreover, by trying to maintain a policy of extreme isolation, Congress and the people were indirectly admitting that the nation had no outside interests worth defending. Therefore the neutrality legislation amounted to a form of appeasement on the part of the United States. To President Roosevelt, however, the growing use of force by aggressor states so threatened both American and world security that by the end of 1937 he was fully convinced that new cures were needed. And, with the New Deal at home largely complete, he turned his attention more and more to the international scene.

24

Aid to the Democracies

THE MENACE TO THE WORLD'S DEMOCRACIES WAS CLEAR TO THE MORE discerning by the spring of 1938. By that time Adolph Hitler had shown his contempt for treaties by denouncing the Treaty of Versailles and by scrapping the Locarno Pact of 1925. In an effort to promote the German master race and fulfill the theories expressed in *Mein Kampf* he had marched his troops into the Rhineland in March, 1936, and during the Spanish Civil War he had tested the strength of his army, which had grown in defiance of the Versailles Treaty. Moreover, he had persecuted the Jews and other minority groups in Germany. He had arranged an agreement with Italy, known as the Rome-Berlin Axis, which gave him a freer hand in his eventual domination of Austria and in his challenging of France and Great Britain. He was beginning to cast greedy glances toward the territory of neighboring Czechoslovakia. Along with Japan, Germany had resigned from the League of Nations.

The new British Prime Minister, Neville Chamberlain, believed in a policy of appeasement toward this German threat to the peace of Europe, and other Empire statesmen shared his views. Chamberlain argued that German aggressiveness arose out of dissatisfaction with the Treaty of Versailles and the inability to obtain sufficient resources to meet the demands of a growing population. Therefore peace could be preserved by adjusting the complaints. Chamberlain's position had much support in England where many conservatives felt that the real menace to European safety came not from the Nazis of Germany, but from the Communists of the Soviet. The so-called Cliveden set, in their conservative complacency, did not appear to realize that there was much more to the Hitlerian menace than complaints resulting from World War I.

France, convulsed by hard times and political strife, was deteriorating internally and thus was in no position to challenge Germany. The League had failed her and she was compelled to follow Britain's lead in appeasing her natural enemy. Russia was more concerned with the progress of her economic experiments than she was with what was happening in the rest of Europe. Furthermore, she realized that she was the object of distrust.

In the Far East Japan had once more defied the other powers by her attacks on China. Evidently she was attempting to promote the "New Order" there—or the Greater East Asia Co-Prosperity Sphere—under which she would dominate that part of the world, regardless of prior commitments.

APPEASEMENT AT MUNICH

It was in such an atmosphere that the year 1938 opened. President Roosevelt realized the gravity of the situation and, continuing the stand he had taken in his "quarantine" speech of the previous October, he attempted to take the lead in the formulation of American foreign policy instead of acquiescing in the prevalent isolationist point of view. Consequently, in a special message to Congress on January 28, 1938, he said:

We, as a peaceful Nation, cannot and will not abandon active search for an agreement among the nations to limit armaments and end aggression. But it is clear that until such agreement is reached—and I have not given up hope of it—we are compelled to think of our own national safety.

To make that safety possible, he asked appropriations for both 1938 and 1939 to build up army antiaircraft defenses, modernize field equipment, and increase the enlisted reserve, as well as to begin construction on naval ships of all sizes to bring the navy up to treaty strength.

When isolationists in Congress balked at the proposal because they asserted the move might lead the country into war and might result in an entangling agreement for naval cooperation with some other nation, Secretary Hull came to the defense of the plan on February 10. He wrote that the rearmament program was vital for national defense, but was not large enough to enable the United States to enter an aggressive war. Moreover, said the Secretary, it might help the cause of peace by adding greater weight to American influence in world councils. Certainly the United States had no thought of a secret commitment with any other power. The Secretary's appeal, together with the increasing German menace, aided in the passage by Congress of the presidential rearmament proposals in practically their original form.

While laying the groundwork for American defense, however, neither the President nor the Secretary of State relaxed their efforts to prevent a war in Europe. As early as January, 1938, the United States became convinced that Hitler's next move would be to absorb Austria. On the fourteenth Secretary Hull told German Ambassador Dieckhoff that the paramount question facing the world in general and the United States in particular was whether the principles of international law and order should be replaced by the rule of force and aggression. All countries, regardless of their form of government, could consistently cooperate in support of the principle of law and order. This statement was in effect a warning to Germany that the United States would not look with favor upon continued aggression.

The warning was fruitless, for on March 11, 1938, the legions of Hitler moved into Austria in defiance of a three-year-old pledge that the Reich had no desire to acquire its neighbor's territory, and two days later the Fuehrer announced the union of the two countries under his control. The attitude of the United States was quickly shown on March 17 when Hull addressed a meeting of the National Press Club. The United States, he said, might refuse to work with other peace-loving nations for the preservation of law, order, and justice; but to so refuse would mean an abdication of everything that the United States had been working for. Other countries, seeing the American retreat, would attribute it to fear or to unwillingness to protect rightful interests. Consequently, American prestige would be lost, to be followed by danger to American safety; indeed the United States might become "a self-constituted hermit state." Isolation would do no good in the present world. So for the sake of American interests and security, it was essential that the United States maintain its influence in world affairs and work constantly for peace.

Germany paid little attention to the American opposition inasmuch as England and France were doing little or nothing to stem Hitler's actions. In fact, as the summer of 1938 progressed increasingly serious Nazi demands were made for the Sudetenland in Czechoslovakia. A so-called war of nerves—incessant propaganda and sword rattling—initiated the move against this territory which Hitler indicated he must have even though he had to go to war for it. The personal trips which Prime Minister Chamberlain made to Germany to seek a negotiated peace proved abortive.

Believing that the struggle over the Sudetenland might involve Europe in a general war, President Roosevelt sent personal messages to the leaders of Czechoslovakia, Germany, Great Britain, and France on September 26, 1938, in which he said:

The fabric of peace on the continent of Europe, if not throughout the rest of the world, is in immediate danger. The consequences of the rupture are incalculable. Should hostilities break out the lives of millions of men, women and children . . . will most certainly be lost under circumstances of unspeakable horror. The economic system of every country involved is certain to be shattered. The social structure of every country involved may well be completely wrecked.

After pointing out that the United States had no political entanglements, he asserted that the main interest was in settling disputes by peaceful means. The Paris Pact and other treaties bound most nations to preserve the peace. Although he admitted that on the surface the existing problem might seem impossible to solve, "I am persuaded that there is no problem so difficult or so pressing that it cannot be justly solved by the resort to reason rather than by resort to force." Therefore, on behalf of the American people "and for the sake of humanity everywhere" he asked the disputants not to break off their negotiations, but to seek a pacific settlement.

The replies from three of the countries indicated their desire for peace, but Hitler's answer, which traced the inequalities forced on the German people by the Treaty of Versailles, placed the whole burden of responsibility for the present crisis upon Czechoslovakia. In substance, if she wanted peace, she could have it by turning the Sudetenland over to Germany without further ado. If she did not, then Germany would seize it.

Still the Roosevelt administration did not give up hope. Secretary Hull informed American envoys everywhere to use their good services in having the countries wherein they were located send messages to the potential contestants about the need of preserving peace. On the same day, September 27, the President sought the cooperation of Mussolini in settling the problem and sent another appeal to Hitler in which he said:

The question before the world today, Mr. Chancellor, is not the question of errors of judgment or of injustices committed in the past. It is the question of the fate of the world today and tomorrow. . . . Whatever existing differences may be, and whatever their merits may be . . . my appeal was solely that negotiations be continued until a peaceful settlement is found, and that thereby a resort to force be avoided.

American opinion was overwhelmingly for any solution of the controversy which would avoid war. Great was the relief, therefore, at the news that a last-minute conference had been arranged at Munich upon Hitler's invitation. There on September 30, Hitler, Mussolini, Chamberlain, and Daladier of France signed a Four-Power Accord whereby war was averted at the price of giving the Nazis practically a free hand in taking over the Sudetenland. Chamberlain returned to England declaring: "I believe it is peace for our time," and millions of Englishmen, Frenchmen, and Americans hoped that he was right. But this supreme effort to appease Germany soon proved a great mistake. The betrayal of Czechoslovakia destroyed the moral prestige of England and France in the eyes of all the smaller states. The snubbing of Russia aroused her suspicion and resentment, while Germany and Italy had only contempt for the weakness of the Western democracies. American opinion soon reversed itself and condemned the European appeasers. Illogically, however, few Americans saw that the United States shared in the responsibility. Roosevelt no less than Chamberlain had been desperately anxious to preserve peace. Much more important in the underlying situation, moreover, Congress and the country insisted on the futile policy represented by the Neutrality Acts; Hitler could continue his course of aggression in the conviction that the United States would do nothing to help those who resisted him.

The Munich breathing spell was brief. France and England displayed their growing concern with the situation by a great rearmament effort, while as early as October 26, 1938, President Roosevelt declared in a speech before the *New York Herald Tribune* forum:

It is become increasingly clear that peace by fear has no higher or more enduring quality than peace by the sword.
There can be no peace if the reign of law is to be replaced by a recurrent sanctification of sheer force.
There can be no peace if national policy adopts as a deliberate instrument the threat of war.

And the President was deeply shocked shortly afterward by news from Germany of an outbreak of even more violent persecution of the Jews. On November 15 he ordered Ambassador Hugh Wilson to return to the United States—an obvious rebuke to the Nazis. Roosevelt disclosed: "I myself could scarcely believe that such things could occur in a twentieth-century civilization."

THE LIMA CONFERENCE

It was while Europe and Asia were in such turmoil, with the possibility of open war at any moment, that the republics of the Western Hemisphere gathered at Lima, Peru, for their regular Pan-American

Conference. Naturally the chief topics concerned the means by which international law and order could be restored and, were they not successful, how the republics could prevent extrahemisphere dangers from affecting them.

Secretary Hull, once again the chairman of the American delegation, was the most energetic worker at this December meeting and did an exceptionally fine job in promoting President Roosevelt's thesis of November 15 "that national defense has now become a problem of continental defense . . . in cooperation with the other twenty republics and Canada." The result was unanimous approval of the so-called Declaration of American Principles, which reaffirmed the doctrine of nonintervention, proscribed the use of force as an instrument of national or international policy, upheld peaceful settlements of disputes, and avowed that "international cooperation is a necessary condition to the maintenance of the aforementioned principles." Perhaps the foremost action was the approval of the Declaration of Lima. In this all the states affirmed "their continental solidarity and their purpose to collaborate in the maintenance of the principles upon which the said solidarity is based." They agreed "to defend them against all foreign intervention or activity that may threaten them"—an answer to the fifth column menace.[1] Also under that Declaration, "in case the peace, security or territorial integrity of any American Republic is thus threatened by acts of any nature that may impair them, they proclaim their common concern and their determination to make effective their solidarity, co-ordinating their respective sovereign wills by means of the procedure of consultation. . . ." That procedure of consultation was to take the form of meetings of the several foreign ministers when any republic believed that hemisphere safety was endangered. By this means it was hoped that totalitarian threats in both Europe and Asia would not reach American shores and that the pressure of a solid hemisphere bloc might avert another world struggle.

THE OUTBREAK OF WAR

It was well that there was solidarity in the hemisphere because war broke out in Europe before the end of 1939. That President Roosevelt anticipated this was evident from his annual message to Congress on January 4, 1939, when he said:

[1] The "fifth column" was an expression first used during the Spanish Civil War. It refers to subversive agents who go to another country to pave the way, through undermining the confidence of the people and the like, for eventual military invasion.

A war which threatened to envelop the world in flames has been averted, but it has become increasingly clear that world peace is not assured.

All about us rage undeclared wars—military and economic. All about us grow more deadly armaments—military and economic. All about us are threats of new aggression—military and economic.

Then he continued with the assertion that the use of force by enemies of democracy made necessary the employment by peace-loving nations of weapons of defense. So he called upon the legislature for increased appropriations for the army and navy. Moreover he criticized the existing neutrality legislation because it might conceivably result in the United States helping an aggressor nation at the expense of the one attacked. Shortly after this message was delivered, the President sought to build up stock piles of materials that might be needed for American defense.

Such plans and suggestions were obviously the need of the hour. On March 14, 1939, Hitler invaded the remainder of Czechoslovakia, despite his pre-Munich pledge that after he had secured the Sudetenland he had no desire for more territory in Europe. The immediate State Department condemnation of this action as "wanton lawlessness" did not stem the tide. On April 7 Mussolini, desirous of sharing in the spoils, attacked Albania and soon had it under his control. Once again the State Department's verbal opposition to this threat to world peace did no good.

The democratic powers in Europe realized at last the futility of appeasement. Britain and France announced that they would go to the aid of Poland, Rumania, and Greece were they attacked. At the same time they sought agreement with Russia for a bloc to thwart the Rome-Berlin Axis.

To the United States the division of Europe into two camps boded ill for world peace. Consequently President Roosevelt sent notes to Hitler and Mussolini on April 14 in which he traced the growth of aggression during the preceding years. Then he continued with:

I am convinced that the cause of world peace would be greatly advanced if the nations of the world were to obtain a frank statement relating to the present and future policy of Governments.

Because the United States . . . is not involved in the immediate controversies which have arisen in Europe, I trust that you may be willing to make such a statement of policy to me . . . in order that I, acting only with the responsibility and obligation of a friendly intermediary, may communicate such declaration to other nations now apprehensive as to the course which the policy of your Government may take.

The President sought specific assurance that neither would attack or invade the remaining independent countries of Europe and the Middle East, not only for the present, "but also to a future sufficiently long to give every opportunity to work by peaceful means for a more permanent peace." Neither Hitler nor Mussolini saw fit to send a reply to Roosevelt's plea, although the Fuehrer did tell the German people that he had no thought of attacking any more of the Reich's neighbors. Had he not given them definite pledges to that effect?

How much Hitler's promise meant was indicated before the month of April was over. He began to demand of Poland the return to Germany of the city of Danzig, as well as numerous concessions along the Polish Corridor. To make his demands more effective he started to mobilize a large army along the Polish border. The worried British and French governments took this occasion to announce that an attack upon Poland would mean war.

Remonstrating with the German dictator was obviously futile. He understood only the language of force and this language Roosevelt was powerless to use. As a minimum contribution to strengthening the anti-Nazi front, the United States needed to repeal the arms embargo so that England and France could supplement their inadequate war-production facilities with those of America in case of hostilities. But the President's earnest efforts to secure the amendment of the Neutrality Act before Congress adjourned for the summer were unavailing. Not even a White House conference where Roosevelt and Hull presented to the Congressional leaders a candid view of the developing European crisis convinced Senator Borah and his fellow isolationists that war was actually imminent or that the United States had any responsibility in the situation.

Confidence that America would stand aside, therefore, was one of the factors in the situation encouraging Hitler to persist in his reckless course. The war of nerves against Poland continued, while mutual suspicion frustrated efforts to draw the Soviet Union into an anti-Nazi alliance with Britain and France. Instead, the democratic world was stunned when it learned on August 21 that Russia and Germany had concluded a nonaggression pact. Far from being an act of peace, this treaty released Germany from the possibility of a two-front fight in case war materialized and revealed that it would probably be but a matter of days before the march into Poland began.

President Roosevelt once again tried to effect a peaceful settlement by appealing to King Victor Emmanuel of Italy on August 23 with these words:

Were it possible for Your Majesty's Government to formulate proposals for a pacific solution of the present crisis. . . . you are assured of the earnest sympathy of the United States.

The Government of Italy and the United States can today advance those ideals of Christianity which of late seem so often to have been obscured.

The voices of countless millions of human beings ask that they shall not be vainly sacrificed again.

The next day he also sent earnest pleas to both Hitler and President Moszicki of Poland to forego the use of force and to settle their dispute through diplomacy.

The attempts were fruitless, however, because Hitler wanted no peaceful respite. The blame was placed upon Poland because of her unwillingness to give in to all the German demands. On the morning of September 1, 1939, the invasion of Poland started, and two days later France and Britain, living up to their promises, went to her assistance. World War II had begun.

THE IMPACT OF WAR ON THE UNITED STATES

The outbreak of World War II did not come unexpectedly to the people of the United States as had World War I. While it is true that many Americans hoped until the actual invasion of Poland that efforts to maintain peace would be successful, they had been following events in Europe closely in their newspapers and over their radios for several years. Therefore there was not the distinct shock which accompanied the war of 1914.

President Roosevelt was quick to act. After appealing to the participants on September 1 to refrain from bombing civilians, he delivered a fireside chat to the nation two evenings later in which he pointed out that European events of the previous four years had "been based on the use of force and the threat of force." The primary duty of the United States should be to seek "for humanity a final peace" which would end "the continued use of force between nations." Next, he warned the American people to try to "discriminate most carefully between news and rumor." He believed they could do so because they were "the best informed people in all the world at this moment." There must be no talk of sending American troops to Europe for even then he was preparing a proclamation of neutrality. The President did not ask the people to remain neutral in thought, however, because "even a neutral has a right to take account of the facts." He thought that the United States would be able to stay out of the conflict, but he admitted that the war would certainly affect the country in many ways. Yet "as long as it remains within my power to prevent, there will be no blackout of peace in the United States."

On September 5 the President proclaimed the neutrality laws in effect and prohibited the exportation of arms and munitions to the belligerent nations. The following day the Federal Bureau of Investigation was placed in charge of "matters relating to espionage, sabotage, and violations of the neutrality regulations." On the eighth he declared a limited national emergency to safeguard American neutrality and to strengthen national defense. He also made funds available for American citizens who were caught unprepared in Europe.

THE NEUTRALITY ACT OF 1939

Although the President's official position was one of neutrality, it was clear that he favored the cause of the democracies. His numerous utterances were indication that he desired Britain and France to win, and his efforts during the spring and summer of 1939 to secure amendments to the existing neutrality legislation were made so that he could distinguish between aggressor and the attacked. Moreover, he tried during the same period to effect a closer commercial relationship with Britain and France and sought to conclude arrangements for the sale of arms, munitions, and planes to them. In his fireside chat of September 3 his statement that he could not expect Americans to remain neutral in thought was another sign of support for the Allies.

American public opinion (84 per cent according to one poll) undoubtedly desired an Allied victory over Germany, but there was also a strong belief that the United States must stay out of the war. These practically contradictory views made it difficult for the President to put into effect his program for aiding the democracies because the Americans of the isolationist school, under the leadership of Senators Borah and Wheeler, were of the belief that anything but strictest neutrality would involve the nation in hostilities.

Nevertheless, on September 21, 1939, Congress was called into special session for the specific purpose of amending the Neutrality Act. In addressing the legislature, the President said he had been trying to secure the amendment since the beginning of the year because he believed that the existing measure "so alters the historic foreign policy of the United States that it impairs the peaceful relations of the United States with foreign nations." He continued with the assertion, "I regret that Congress passed the Act. I regret equally that I signed that Act." Specifically he wanted changed the embargo provisions which prevented the sale of completed implements of war, but which allowed the selling of uncompleted ones which could be shipped on American vessels. "There in itself . . . lies definite danger to our neutrality and our peace."

Congress could no longer pigeonhole the presidential request, but the debates that followed the introduction of the administration measures were heated in the extreme. Congressmen of the Nye school of thought asserted that the repeal of the arms embargo would mean a repetition of World War I days; American munitions makers would sell to the Allies, make a huge profit, and help involve the nation in war. Still another group in the opposition declared that repeal would be an unneutral step for the United States to take; the war had already begun, and a change in American policy would aid one side to the detriment of the other. And there were those who continued to believe that the Neutrality Act of 1937 was the best means of maintaining American isolation. To them that act concerned American domestic policy only and had nothing to do with international relations. Supporting the administration were those Congressmen who argued that the President was right. The existing legislation was in effect unneutral since it helped the aggressors, who knew that the countries they invaded would not be able to obtain assistance from the United States. Moreover, traditional American rights on the high seas had been given up and the smaller and weaker countries of the world, which had previously looked to the United States for protection, could no longer do so. Some legislators advocated repeal frankly upon the grounds that they believed it was for the best interests of the country to have the Allies win.

Not until November 4, after about six weeks of interventionist-isolationist debate, was the Neutrality Act of 1939 finally approved and signed. The House vote stood 243 to 172, the Senate 55 to 24.[1] The measure kept many of the supposed safeguards of earlier legislation and the cash-and-carry principle was extended to all commodities. The chief changes were: now Congress, as well as the President, could proclaim that a state of war existed; the much discussed embargo on implements of war was dropped; and the President could define danger or combat zones wherein American citizens, ships, and planes could not go.

The President immediately put this new measure into effect with a proclamation of November 4 and accompanied it with the definition of combat areas where American ships could not go. They included all the ports of the belligerents, most of the Bay of Biscay, the English Channel and the waters around the British Isles and the adjacent islands,

[1] A public-opinion poll taken about the time of the passage showed a 56 per cent approval of the measure.

and the Baltic and North Seas. The closing of the last two seas meant that several of the neutral countries such as Belgium, the Netherlands, Denmark, and Sweden could not be reached by American vessels. It was hoped through these proclamations that there would be no incidents to involve the United States in war.

THE PANAMA CONFERENCE

While the Neutrality Bill of 1939 was being debated, steps were taken to safeguard the hemisphere. In line with the decision made at Lima, the several foreign ministers met at Panama in late September to discuss how the Americas could avert the extension of the war from themselves. Unanimous approval was given to the Declaration of Panama on October 2, which stated that "the American republics, as long as they maintain their neutrality, have the undisputed right to conserve free from all hostile acts by any belligerent non-American nation those waters adjacent to the American continents which they consider of primordial interest and direct utility of their relations, whether such hostile act is attempted or carried out by land, sea, or air." The declaration then provided for a safety or neutrality zone roughly 300 miles wide around the Americas wherein no belligerent action should take place. The several republics, jointly or singly, should establish maritime and air patrols to see that the zone was maintained as a neutral area.

Also the foreign ministers initiated an Inter-American Financial and Economic Advisory Committee made up of experts. The purpose was to provide the several republics with advice and information in the fields of commerce and finance, thereby preventing a serious dislocation which might normally follow the outbreak of the European war. Moreover, a Joint Declaration of Continental Solidarity reaffirmed all the cooperative agreements for safety and peace which had been approved at earlier Pan-American conferences. Also the Panama delegates drew up a General Declaration of Neutrality of the American Republics which included the refusal to allow any American territory to be used as bases for belligerent operations or belligerent planes to fly over hemisphere territory, established rules for internment of ships, and set up rules for search.

The United States provided most of the vessels for the patrol of the safety zone and her representatives played prominent roles in the several committees which the Panama Conference established. The warring countries, however, refused to admit the legality of the safety zone and asserted that they would pay no attention to it because their enemies would not. The most notable example of infringement of the zone concerned the German pocket battleship *Graf von Spee* which had been attacking British and French merchantmen in the Atlantic since the opening of the war. Finally in early December, 1939, she was tracked down by three British cruisers and badly damaged in a running fight off the coast of South America. She was forced to seek refuge in Monte-video. The Uruguayan government insisted that she leave after seventy-two hours, but rather than face the British cruisers which were waiting for the kill, she was scuttled by her crew who were subsequently interned. The American republics protested vigorously against the defiance of hemisphere neutrality provisions, and the following April the Neutrality Committee announced that ports of the Americas would be closed to ships of those belligerent nations which refused to recognize the safety zone. The effectiveness of the British blockade, however, prevented many German ships, other than submarines, from reaching American waters after the opening of 1940 so that there were only isolated incidents thereafter.

As in World War I, both contesting groups established blockades which affected neutral shipping and rights. Britain was the first to proclaim a blockade on September 8, 1939, as a means of thwarting submarine attacks. The area included in the blockade was wide and difficult to cover with patrol ships. Germany countered three days later with the announcement that the British Isles were under blockade. In November, 1939, Germany sowed floating magnetic mines in the North Sea and the English Channel in an effort to destroy Allied shipping, only to be answered by an Allied extension of their blockade to cover exports as well as imports. American shipping did not suffer much from these actions because it was prohibited from going into combat areas after the passage of the Neutrality Act of 1939. Furthermore, as the war spread, the proscribed zones were broadened by presidential proclamation to cover most of the Northern countries of Europe (April 10, 1940) following the German invasion of Denmark and Norway, and to include the Mediterranean area and the mouth of the Red Sea (June 11, 1940) after the entrance of Italy into the war. Thus there was not so much note writing as in the first world struggle.

American protests were raised, however, against Britain over the latter's insistence that ships entering blockaded waters must stop at British ports. Once the ships followed this, they were usually detained. Between September, 1939, and May, 1940, a total of 204 vessels were held for an average of five days each by the various belligerents. Britain was the major transgressor, holding 180 of them. The desire for an Allied victory softened the tone of the American objections. Protests were also sent against the searching and censoring of the mails. The foremost incident, much dramatized by the isolationist press in the United States, arose out of the story that mail pouches had been forcibly removed from the Atlantic Clipper when it landed in Bermuda. These objections were as unavailing as they had been in the previous war. Britain knew that the United States would not back up her protests with force and, actually, the United States was not consistent in her objections to searching the mails because she had done the same thing after her entrance into World War I.

There were two prominent incidents involving German infringement of neutral rights. The first occurred on September 3, 1939, when the British *Athenia*, carrying 1400 passengers of whom half were Americans, was torpedoed and sunk without warning off the Hebrides Islands. Thirty Americans were drowned. Germany failed to substantiate her assertions that the *Athenia* carried contraband or was sunk by the British themselves to cause the United States to enter the war. The second incident was the seizing of the American *City of Flint* by a German warship on October 9, 1939, some 1200 miles from New York. A prize crew was put aboard and the ship was taken to Murmansk, then a neutral port. In late October notes of protest were sent both to Germany and Russia. These brought her release to Norwegian authorities. The American point of issue was over the right of Germany to take the *City of Flint* into a neutral port. When the ship was released, the matter was dropped.

THE FALL OF FRANCE

After the initial attacks of World War II and the fall of Poland, both sides settled down during the winter of 1939–1940 [1] along their respective lines along the Western front—the Allies behind the Maginot Line, the Germans protected by their ever stronger Siegfried Line. To some this so-called phony war gave hope of the possibility of a peaceful settlement of differences. However Hitler was still not satisfied by the conquests he had made thus far and on April 9, 1940, he suddenly struck at Denmark, despite a year-old nonaggression pact which he himself had instigated. At this same time and in similar fashion, without the formality of a declaration of war, German troops began their invasion of Norway. Although the Norse, unlike the Danes, attempted to repel the aggressor and secured some help from the British, the fifth-column

[1] The chief fighting of that winter was between Russia and Finland. American sympathies were definitely with Finland, as indicated by the loan made to her in mid-December, 1939.

work which the Germans had organized through the efforts of the traitor, Vidkun Quisling, helped to bring defeat in a few short weeks.

May witnessed even more disastrous blows to the Allied cause as the *blitzkrieg* struck out against Holland, Belgium, Luxembourg, and France. The Maginot Line was outflanked, the British forces were soon separated from their Allies and pinned against the English Channel. Only the extreme heroism of those forces and the skill and bravery of the British people secured their evacuation from Dunkirk. The French were subjected to an overwhelming attack, culminating in their surrender on June 22, 1940. Hitler sought to wipe out the stain of November 11, 1918, by staging the armistice conference in the same railroad car which had been used on that occasion in the same forest of Compiègne. Taking advantage of the French disaster, Mussolini had entered the war on June 10 by attacking from the east.

To Americans the power of the German *blitzkrieg* was astounding. It appeared as though the democracies, now represented solely by the British Empire, could no longer withstand the Axis poundings. Nevertheless, the administration did not give up hope and continued to give moral support. Even more was promised. On the day that Mussolini attacked the French rear, President Roosevelt, after extending the provisions of the Neutrality Act to cover the new belligerent, made a speech to the graduates of the University of Virginia. In it he traced his efforts to dissuade Italy from entering the war and her refusal to consider his proposals. Instead, "the hand that held the dagger has struck it into the back of its neighbor." Because the extension of the war would threaten American rights and institutions, the President announced that the United States "must pursue two obvious and simultaneous courses": the extension of all the material resources of the country to the opponents of force and the promotion of American defense. For the fulfillment of this program there would have to be "full speed ahead."

More and more Americans were standing behind the movements for aid to the democracies and preparedness. To them the fall of France meant that the American and democratic defense frontier was no longer the Maginot Line as President Roosevelt had once intimated. It was now the English Channel and might soon be the Atlantic because the safety of the British Isles was in question after the German air *blitz* of England began in the summer of 1940. None knew whether Britain could hold out against the mounting air attacks and the invasion which was expected at any moment. Were Britain to fall, many Americans believed that the United States would be the next object of German attack. But the United States was not prepared for it; the Atlantic, without the British navy, would no longer be the safeguard which had protected the country for generations. Thus, in addition to striving for preparedness, the United States must go all out in providing aid to Britain so that she might withstand the full power of totalitarian blows.

The first step in giving full aid to Britain had already been taken when the President made his "stab-in-the-back" speech. Using a little-known law of World War I days as the authority, the administration resorted to the "trade-in" method. On June 6 the Navy Department, under orders from President Roosevelt, started delivery of one hundred "overage" scout bombers to the Curtiss-Wright factory at Buffalo, New York, for eventual trade-in for newer models. The turned-in planes were then sent at once to Britain and France. Subsequently the government by this same means sent indirectly to the democracies 100 armed attack planes, 600,000 British Enfield rifles and 800 French 75-millimeter guns of World War I vintage, as well as other stock piles of ammunition, machine guns, and mortars. Although the Federal government did not do the actual selling of these implements of war under the trade-in arrangement, its neutral position might be open to question inasmuch as no effort was made to dispose of similar commodities to the Axis. In similar fashion the United States helped Britain by permitting Canadian fliers to receive training at Florida fields and by allowing her warships to be repaired and refitted in American yards. Moreover, American planes were flown directly across the Canadian border for military use by the neighbor.

THE DESTROYER-BASE DEAL

The supplies which were sold to Britain and the other aids which she obtained were of inestimable assistance to her in her lone defense against the Axis. The help came at a time when she was facing her greatest crisis. But more was deemed necessary to save her from defeat. One way of directly aiding Britain would be to strengthen her navy, and this in turn would diminish the danger of an attack upon America.

Another menace developing from the fall of France and other countries of Europe was that Germany might desire to take over their holdings in the New World, and to do so would bring her right to the American doorstep. The United States had already taken steps at the Havana Conference (see below) to prevent that from happening, but it was essential, so President Roosevelt believed, to secure additional safeguards. Would it not be possible, therefore, to accomplish both objectives at the same time? The President thought so. Consequently, during the summer of 1940 he opened secret negotiations with British Ambassador Lord Lothian for the American lease of British bases in the Western Hemisphere, the "rental" to take the form of fifty overage destroyers which could be recommissioned to help strengthen the British navy. The negotiations were secret because of the expected isolationist opposition in Congress which might hold up completion of the arrangements until too late.

Before the President made the final commitment he sought the opinion of Attorney General Jackson as to the validity of the procedure. Jackson reported on August 27 that there was no doubt of the right of the President to execute an executive agreement, rather than resorting to a treaty. Moreover, he found two old Congressional laws and a decision of the Supreme Court to uphold the presidential right "to dispose of vessels of the Navy and unneeded naval material." Finally, the Attorney General concluded that the transference of the overage destroyers would not run contrary to neutrality laws because they were not built specifically to be turned over to a belligerent nation.

On September 2, 1940, the negotiations were completed. In exchange for the fifty destroyers,[1] which were turned over to Great Britain between September 9 and November 26, the United States secured ninety-nine-year leases for bases in the Bahamas, Jamaica, St. Lucia, Trinidad, Antigua, and British Guiana. In addition, Britain granted the United States similar leases for Newfoundland and Bermuda as "gifts—generously given and gladly received."[2]

The following day the President informed Congress of this deal. He justified his action by saying:

This is not inconsistent in any sense with our status of peace. Still less is it a threat against any nation. It is an epochal and far-reaching act of preparation for continental defense in the face of grave danger. . . .

The value to the Western Hemisphere of these outposts of security is beyond calculation. Their need has long been recognized by our country, and especially by those primarily charged with the duty of charting and organizing our own naval and military defense. They are essential to the protection of the Panama Canal. . . . For these reasons I have taken advantage of the present opportunity to acquire them.

The isolationists in Congress and throughout the country denounced the action as dictatorial, as a violation of American neutrality, as a step in defiance of traditional American policy, and as contrary to interna-

---

[1] The original cost of these destroyers was $75,477,348; the cost of recommissioning them was $20,478,445.

[2] Not until March 27, 1941, were notes exchanged to complete the arrangements.

tional law. But the majority of the American people, after the initial surprise had worn off, praised the action—although perhaps not the method. They showed by this approval that they were ready at last to commit the nation to all-out aid to Britain and to additional defense measures for the hemisphere.

THE HAVANA CONFERENCE

Meantime, an actual move to safeguard the hemisphere was taken at the second meeting of foreign ministers, held at Havana, Cuba, July 21–30, 1940. The immediate reason for this session was the fear of the American republics lest Germany attempt to take over the New World colonies of countries she had occupied. In the independent South American countries, particularly in Chile, Uruguay, and Bolivia, moreover, German fifth-column activities appeared to be increasing in a way suggesting that these areas were included in Nazi plans for world domination. Latin-American trade was badly disorganized by the war and the situation was particularly serious in Brazil and Chile—a situation that made German promises of vast barter deals of raw materials for postwar use particularly seductive. As Secretary Hull, again heading the American delegation, said of this conference: "It is to safeguard the independence, the peace and the well-being of the American republics."

So important were these problems that social and cultural questions were kept at a minimum. The several delegations were in almost complete agreement from the start, despite the German assertions that intra-hemisphere competition and jealousies would result in failure. True, Argentina was at first opposed to the trustee proposal and the United States failed to secure backing for its inter-American cartel plan, but unanimous consent was given to the final resolutions.

The most important of these resolutions was the Act of Havana, which stated that the American republics, jointly or singly, might take over the administration of the threatened territory of non-American nations. A special Inter-American Commission for Territorial Administration was established to afford general supervision of the trusteeships.[1] In addition, a number of decisions reached at Panama were reaffirmed, particularly in connection with the neutrality zone and the

[1] Eventually the United States, Venezuela, and Brazil assumed the trusteeship of Surinam—the former Dutch Guiana, and the United States alone took over Denmark's Greenland. Guadeloupe and Martinique, both French colonies, were not placed under this plan, but the American republics kept watchful eyes on the latter because of the presence of part of the French fleet, which they did not wish to fall into German hands, and because the governor, Admiral Robert, was suspected of being pro-Nazi.

stemming of the fifth-column menace. Further agreements were approved for better financial cooperation among the republics, with the United States helping the cause by announcing, while the conference was in session, a $500,000,000 increase in the lending power of the Export-Import Bank. Finally, the completion of the Pan-American Highway was to be speeded in order to improve the commercial interchange and defense of the hemisphere. At the conclusion of the meeting Secretary Hull said: "The agreements have cleared the decks for effective action whenever such action may become necessary."

THE CAMPAIGN OF 1940

Soon after the fall of France the people of the United States turned their attention temporarily toward the campaign and election of 1940. As in 1916, the world situation played a prominent role in that test of American politics. For the first time in many years diplomatic issues took their place beside matters of domestic concern. Despite the continued efforts of the Democratic administration to keep the country at peace, many Americans believed that it was only a matter of time before the United States again would be at war with Germany. In the domestic picture, the great problem was whether the New Deal had accomplished its objectives; a growing conservative element believed that it had not and that a change to Republicanism would benefit the nation and more speedily return the country to prosperity. Moreover, the conservatives were worried because the third-term precedent was seriously challenged for the first time.

The Republicans, as usual holding their convention first, met in Philadelphia on June 24. The outstanding candidate for the party nomination at the outset was Thomas E. Dewey, the young district attorney of New York City who had gained national fame as a racket buster. His major opponent in the early stages of preconvention jockeying was Senator Robert A. Taft of Ohio, isolationist son of the former President. Another Senator, Arthur H. Vandenberg of Michigan, a semi-isolationist, was a potential dark horse. As the convention approached, however, the tide of popular—rather than political—opinion began to swing in favor of Wendell L. Willkie, a former Democrat. Hoosier born and bred, trained as a lawyer, but experienced as well as a teacher and farmer, Willkie had gained fame as president of Commonwealth and Southern when he had secured for his company the demanded price from the government for subsidiaries taken over by TVA. He was regarded as a liberal conservative who would offer the best fight with the New Deal. His campaign was managed not by politicians but by young novices, of whom the most prominent was Oren Root, a relative of Elihu, through "Willkie-for-President" clubs among the rank and file of Republican voters. This method caught the popular fancy and although Willkie had few delegates openly pledged to him—because his campaign started too late for him to be entered in the primaries—he did have the backing of the convention galleries. On the first ballot Dewey had a commanding lead, but was far short of a majority, with Taft second and Willkie a poor third. From then on, however, Dewey's strength faded, while Taft and Willkie increased their totals. On the sixth ballot, taken early on the morning of June 28, the Willkie band wagon was successful. For the vice-presidency, the Republicans selected Charles L. McNary of Oregon, who was Senate minority leader and active spokesman for the farmers.

The Republican platform denounced the New Deal for its "shifting, contradictory, and overlapping administrations and policies" which had failed "to solve the problem of unemployment and revive opportunity for our youth." The Republicans promised "to re-create opportunity for the youth of America and put our idle millions back to work." The tax system would be revised to stimulate recovery, while private enterprise would be encouraged and "bureaucratic regulations and interference" ended. Social security and similar New Deal reforms would be kept and extended, but in amended form and with abler administration. Waste, discrimination, and politics would be removed from the relief problem by giving most of the task back to the states. A constitutional amendment to limit Presidents to a maximum of two terms was demanded.

In foreign affairs, the Republicans were "firmly opposed to involving this nation in foreign war," but favored "the extension to all peoples fighting for liberty, or whose liberty is threatened, of such aid as shall not be in violation of international law or inconsistent with the requirements of our national defense." That national defense must be promoted for the cause of "Americanism, preparedness and peace."

During the spring of 1940 President Roosevelt remained silent about the possibility of his nomination for a third term, despite the fact that the party leaders had been trying to get him to commit himself during the preceding two years. Nevertheless, his name was entered in numerous state primaries, and in each of them he gained overwhelming victories. Moreover, his political managers saw to it that no other candidates grew strong enough to challenge his leadership. There were a few, however, whose presidential aspirations were obvious: Postmaster Gen-

eral James Farley, who was vigorously against the third term and subsequently broke with the President over it, Security Administrator
Paul V. McNutt, and Vice-President Garner.

When the Democratic convention opened in Chicago in the middle
of July, the President still had not broken his silence. Nevertheless,
his New Deal backers, under the leadership of Harry Hopkins, had a
smooth organization working in a near-by hotel which was in constant communication with the President. Not until Permanent Chairman Alben Barkley concluded his keynote speech was any word received from the President. Then Barkley said he had a special message
for the delegates which the President had worked out the day before.
The gist was that Roosevelt did not seek the nomination and therefore
he released his delegates to vote for any candidate they might choose.
Since he did not specifically say that he would not run if drafted and

Pinning a Tail on the Donkey. (By Seibel in *The Richmond Times-Dispatch*.)

because the convention was "rigged" in his favor, the delegates enthusiastically renominated him the following day on the first ballot. To some political observers this was a clumsy method of the New Deal managers to make it appear that the President did not actually want to run again and therefore the third-term precedent would not react against him; had he not been anxious to run again he could have said so specifically. Moreover, he quickly accepted the nomination by means of a radio message to the assembled delegates in which he said: "My conscience will not let me turn my back upon a call to service." The tense world situation, he asserted, made necessary his wish that his policies must be continued, and that could only be done by keeping the New Deal in office.

Garner was not named again for the vice-presidency. He was now considered too conservative for the New Dealers as he had indicated by opposing some of the legislation Roosevelt desired. Furthermore, earlier in the year the President had said that in order to win and carry on the New Deal program, two liberals would have to be on the Democratic ticket. Consequently, Secretary of Agriculture Henry A. Wallace was substituted at Roosevelt's insistence, but without much enthusiasm on the part of the rank-and-file politicians.

The platform stated that "we will not participate in foreign wars, and we will not send our army, naval or air forces to fight in foreign lands outside of the Americas, except in case of attack." Aid to those fighting aggression was promised, along with preparedness. Promotion of water-power development for the use of all, the enforcement of fair labor standards, defense of "all legitimate business," and the continuance and expansion of the New Deal were likewise promised.

The third-term issue caused numerous Democrats to come out openly in favor of Willkie. Among those who switched were Hugh Johnson, Raymond Moley, and former Budget Director Lewis Douglas. Also going into Willkie's camp were the so-called Jeffersonian Democrats —among them Bainbridge Colby, Alfred Smith, and ex-Governor Joseph Ely of Massachusetts. Those who had opposed Roosevelt's efforts to pack the Supreme Court and to purge the party did not support the President wholeheartedly, and their defection—they did not leave the party—hurt the President. John L. Lewis tried to lead all members of the CIO into the Republican ranks, but he was not successful. The normally Democratic *New York Times* also came out for Willkie. On the other hand, numerous Republican liberals supported the Roosevelt cause because they felt that Willkie's connections with a public-utility company allied him too closely with the Old Guard. Moreover, they thought that the President was better equipped to deal with the world crisis.

Willkie made an extended speaking tour in which he attacked not the basic principles of the New Deal, but the Democratic administration of it. He also found fault with the failure of the New Deal to provide adequate preparedness and urged even more aid to the democracies. He denied that the depression had been conquered by pump-priming and asserted that prosperity resulting from a business revival based upon the manufacture of implements of war was false and temporary. Although the Republican candidate did keep to his conception of the issues, some of his followers did not. They charged that Roosevelt was trying to be a dictator—and they used the destroyer-base deal in an effort to prove that he had made secret commitments with Great Britain that would lead the country into war, that he had agreed to send American troops to foreign lands without Congressional approval, and that he had done little to promote preparedness.

As he had promised in his acceptance speech, President Roosevelt did not campaign at first in the usual sense, but devoted his time to domestic and foreign problems. Yet he did tour the country visiting navy yards, factories, and arsenals, thereby making contact with many voters. When it appeared that Willkie was making rapid political progress, moreover, Roosevelt started to make an active and direct appeal for votes. The reason he gave was that it was necessary for him "to call the attention of the nation to deliberate or unwitting falsifications of fact." In five major speeches Roosevelt stressed the reforms of the New Deal and the need of experience in office. He renewed his promises to try to keep the country out of war.

When the voters went to the polls on election day it was the seriousness of the world situation that swung the day in favor of Roosevelt. The electorate decided that it would be unwise to swap horses. Nevertheless the results were closer than in previous campaigns in which Roosevelt had run. In the popular field he received 27,243,466 votes to Willkie's 22,304,755, while the electoral college gave 449 votes to Roosevelt and 82 to Willkie—who carried ten states. The Democratic popular vote was about half a million below the record-breaking figure of 1936, while Willkie obtained the largest number ever polled by a Republican candidate. The general interest in the election was indicated by the nearly fifty million votes cast. The victorious President maintained his majority in Congress as the Democrats increased their House seats by 6 (for a total of 268 to the Republicans' 162), although there was a slight Democratic drop in the Senate of 3 seats (for a total of 66 to the Republicans' 28).

THE BURKE-WADSWORTH ACT

The election of 1940 was considered by President Roosevelt as a popular mandate to continue his policies of preparedness, hemisphere defense, and all-out aid to the democracies. But even while the campaign was under way he took steps to further his objectives. On August 18, following a meeting with Prime Minister Mackenzie King of Canada in upper New York, Roosevelt announced the establishment of a Permanent Joint Board on Defense to consider "sea, land and air problems" concerning the "defense of the north half of the Western Hemisphere." The first meeting of that board was held at Ottawa on August 26, thereby giving additional proof of solidarity between the two neighbors.

In his acceptance speech of July 19, 1940, the President voiced the need of conscription of man power when he said: "Because of the millions of citizens involved in the conduct of defense, most right-thinking persons are agreed that some form of selection by draft is as necessary and fair today as it was in 1917 and 1918." And while waiting for Congress to enact such a conscription act he secured from the legislature on August 27 authority to call out the National Guard because of "the increasing seriousness of the international situation."

The original conscription measure providing for the first peace-time draft in American history had been introduced into Congress in June, 1940, by Senator Edward Burke, a Democrat from Nebraska, and Representative James Wadsworth, a New York Republican. Called a bill "to provide for the common defense by increasing the personnel of the armed forces of the United States and providing for its training," this measure encountered considerable discussion in the respective committees before it was reported out. Then the debates in both Houses delayed its enactment; the noninterventionists asserted that its passage would surely lead the nation into war; the supporters declared that the army could not wait for voluntary enlistments to build itself up to needed strength. There were also disagreements between the two Houses over the age limits before a compromise was reached on September 14.[1] Two days later the President signed this so-called Burke-Wadsworth Act. Its passage was helped by the support which both Presidential candidates gave it.

[1] The House vote was 232 to 134; in the Senate it was 47 to 25.

The measure provided that all men between the ages of twenty-one and thirty-six—and it was expected that there would be 17,000,000 of them—must register for an eventual year's military service within the limits of the United States. The maximum number to receive such training in a given year was fixed at 900,000. Certain classifications were exempted, but those who served were to be given governmental insurance privileges and were promised that their civilian jobs would be kept open for them. Presidential proclamation fixed October 16 as registration day and President Clarence Dykstra of the University of Wisconsin was named as Selective Service Administrator. The first men so drafted were called for their military training in November.

Meantime, President Roosevelt had made preparedness a bipartisan matter by appointing to his cabinet two Republicans. Henry L. Stimson, who had served in numerous capacities under Republican executives, became the new Secretary of War, while Frank Knox, unsuccessful candidate for the vice-presidency in 1936, took over the administration of the Department of the Navy. Both men filled their respective posts with marked ability and efficiency.

LEND-LEASE

The President still was not satisfied with what had been done to help the defense of the Americas. He knew that on September 27, 1940, Germany, Italy, and Japan had concluded the Tripartite Pact under which they agreed to assist one another in case any power then neutral —meaning the United States—entered the war against one of them. Consequently, in a fireside chat to the nation on December 29, 1940, President Roosevelt described the increasing Axis menace and told of how Hitler had said: "I can beat any other power in the world." Then he reviewed the assistance the United States had given Great Britain and the need to continue and extend that aid because

If Great Britain goes down, the Axis powers will control the continents of Europe, Asia, Africa, Australasia, and the high seas—and they will be in a position to bring enormous military and naval resources against this hemisphere. It is no exaggeration to say that all of us, in all the Americas, would be living at the point of a gun—a gun loaded with explosive bullets, economic as well as military.

The President continued with the assertion that the policy of the nation was "to keep war away from our country and our people." To do this, the country must speed up its production along all lines and see to it that the nations fighting aggression got as many supplies as they needed. "We must become the arsenal of democracy."

This speech set the stage for what the President asked in his annual message to Congress of January 6, 1941. After pointing out that the democracies did not need man power, he asserted that they would soon "need billions of dollars' worth of the weapons of defense." They would soon not be able to pay for those weapons "in ready cash." Despite the "cash-and-carry" provision, it would not be right for the United States to say that they should therefore surrender. Instead, the President asked that the democracies be loaned war materials, not cash, for which "we shall be repaid within a reasonable time following the close of hostilities, in similar materials, or, at our option, in other goods of many kinds, which they can produce and which we need."

Were the United States to extend those material loans, the democracies would win. That victory would make possible a "world founded upon four essential human freedoms"—freedom of speech and expression, freedom of worship, freedom from want, and freedom from fear. This was Roosevelt's first expression of what might be called the victory aims of World War II.

Congress speedily took up the President's request. On January 10, 1941, H.R. 1776 was introduced, a bill "further to promote the defense of the United States." It first of all defined "defense articles" which included weapons, munitions, ships, aircraft, and agricultural and industrial commodities. Then, "notwithstanding the provisions of any other law," the President might authorize the head of any government department or agency "to manufacture in arsenals, factories, and shipyards . . . any defense article for the government of any country whose defense the President deems vital to the defense of the United States." The department or agency might then "sell, transfer title to, exchange, lease, lend, or otherwise dispose of" such articles to that government. These loaned defense commodities must not be convoyed by American naval vessels, and the President must report to Congress at least once every ninety days about lend-lease activities. Moreover, ships of the democracies might he refitted in American ports and information of a defensive nature might be given to such nations.

This so-called lend-lease bill has been called the broadest grant of power ever given to a President, but the administration supporters asserted it was necessary in order to promote speed and efficiency. The noninterventionists immediately condemned the measure. Democratic Senator Clark of Missouri declared it was a method of authorizing the President to declare war; Republican Senator Johnson of California thought that it was "monstrous"; Wheeler of Montana said that he would filibuster against it because it was a "New Deal trip-A foreign policy—plow under every fourth American boy"; La Follette looked on it as "a bold attempt to create a dictatorship to govern our future foreign policy." In special committee hearings they called in "experts" like Charles Lindbergh to testify against the need of such an extreme proposal. A middle group in Congress approved the aid to Britain, but they did believe that the same objective could be accomplished without giving the President so much power. Secretaries Hull, Stimson, and Morgenthau, together with other prominent government officials, gave their unlimited support to the plan, while the President used his influence upon key Congressmen to secure eventual passage of the Lend-Lease Act on March 11.[1] Congress then quickly appropriated $7,000,000,000 to start lend-lease in operation and the President ordered shipments of vital materials to the democracies at once.

The passage of the Lend-Lease Act definitely marked the end of the isolationist policy which the United States had pursued since the close of World War I. It was the logical step to take considering that the na-

[1] The House approved of the bill on February 8 by a vote of 260 to 165 (135 Republicans were on the losing side), the Senate amended and passed it on March 8 by a vote of 60 to 31 (with 17 Republicans and La Follette in the minority), while the House accepted the Senate amendments on March 11 by a vote of 317 to 71. The chief amendment concluded the President's power on June 30, 1943.

Where the War May Be Decided. (By Herblock in the NEA Services, Inc.)

tion had committed itself to the policy that it must aid those opposing aggression. Britain was naturally thankful, and Prime Minister Winston Churchill referred to the act as a "monument of generous, far-seeing statesmanship." Germany tried to play down the effects by saying that American aid would arrive too late to save Britain, but at the same time she called the measure "the most flagrant North American meddling."

The new policy greatly strengthened the antifascist cause. British dollar credits in the United States were practically exhausted and American neutrality legislation stood as a bar to private loans. Already British purchases in the United States were being reduced—a most undesirable development considering the precariousness of the military situation. Lend-lease was based upon the sound premise that the continuance of British and Chinese resistance to aggression was essential to giving America time to strengthen its defenses and the further premise that the most sensible thing to do with the major portion of the implements of war produced in American factories was to place them as expeditiously as possible into the hands of those who would use them against America's potential enemies. Lend-lease had the additional great merit of making the United States government the sole important customer for the arms industry. Instead of a situation wherein representatives of the American armed forces were bidding in competition with the purchasing agents of the other democratic powers, the new policy permitted the United States government to exercise complete power over the allocation of weapons. It could decide which should be kept in the United States and which should be sent abroad.

To be sure, lend-lease marked the end of real neutrality. The nation was openly trying to help one side to the detriment of the other. But the question had become clearly one of American security. To be neutral in a struggle of this character was to acquiesce in the victory of nations whose hostile designs upon the Western Hemisphere were obvious—at least to most observers.

25

Prelude to Pearl Harbor

THE ENACTMENT OF LEND-LEASE AND THE SUBSEQUENT STEADILY IN-creased flow of supplies to the enemies of the Axis brought additional problems. Germany responded with an intensified submarine campaign against Allied ships carrying lend-lease commodities. When the United States undertook to help these reach their destination in safety, inci-dents naturally followed which widened the breach between the two countries. During the period between April and November of 1941 President Roosevelt secured from Congress additional authority to deal with the situation, as well as a thoroughgoing amendment of the Neu-trality Act of 1939, despite the bitter opposition of the isolationists in and out of the legislature.

Strange to say, however, it was not the differences with the European members of the Axis which first brought war to the United States. In-stead, hostilities were precipitated by aggressions of Japan. Although the troubles with Japan were longstanding, the attack upon Pearl Har-bor came as a distinct surprise to most Americans, who had been mainly concerned with the happenings in Europe. The administration had done little to warn the American people of the growing dangers in the Far East. This failure may have been the result of the belief that Japan might be dissuaded from fulfilling her plans, of the fear that the Presi-dent would be accused of warmongering, or of the wish to maintain a united front at home as long as possible—a necessity considering the strength of the isolationist and noninterventionist forces in the United States.

THE ERROR MUST NOT BE REPEATED

As has been shown, there were many Americans who believed that the wisest policy for their country was at all costs to avoid any act which might lead it into war. These so-called isolationists had been largely responsible for the Johnson Debt Default Act of 1934 and the subsequent neutrality legislation. They had hailed the findings of the Nye Committee as proof that World War I had benefited only a few selfish international bankers and munitions makers. They had opposed all efforts to increase the army and the navy, to enact the Selective Service Law, and to pass lend-lease. Such steps, they asserted, would develop a belligerent spirit in the United States and thereby increase the possibility of American participation in foreign war. As in the period from 1914 to 1917, many of these isolationists were honest in their belief that war would be disastrous for the country. Included in this category were many devout Christians, particularly young people.

There were other groups within the isolationist camp, however, who were not so idealistic, but who supported the movement for other and more selfish reasons. Some anti-New Dealers saw in the administration's request for preparedness measures a Roosevelt effort to turn the country's attention from the shortcomings of his domestic policies. Many social reformers regarded the movement toward defense as the beginning of the end for the program of social justice. Up to the time of the German attack on the Soviet Union, American Communists frowned on the possibility of war because they believed it would help to serve only the capitalists. American fascists did not desire either preparedness or war because they wanted victory for the Axis, with the resulting spread of totalitarianism to the United States. Many German-Americans and Italo-Americans opposed the administration because American entrance into the war would spell defeat for their native lands. A few businessmen thought that appeasement of the dictators would bring profitable trade to the country, while Axis agents tried to build up a feeling of security in the United States so that lend-lease would not be afforded the enemies of Germany. Normally these diverse elements would have had little or nothing in common, but now they rallied in mutual support to accomplish their goal—to keep the country out of war. As one writer has said, "Isolationism makes strange bedfellows."

These various groups used numerous means to keep their nonintervention theories alive and before the public. In Congress there were Senators Johnson, Borah, Wheeler, Nye, and La Follette, together with Representatives Hamilton Fish of New York, Clare Hoffman of Michigan, Dewey Short of Missouri, and Stephen Day of Illinois—to mention the most prominent, who were constantly speaking and voting against preparedness bills. From public platforms Charles Lindbergh and others severely condemned the Roosevelt foreign policies. Over the radio Father Charles Coughlin preached in a fascist vein. Books, periodicals, and pamphlets such as Elizabeth Dilling's *Red Network*, Father Coughlin's *Social Justice*, and Gerald Winrod's *The Defender* attempted to spread the isolationist issue.

It was through the agency of special committees, however, that most of the isolationist propaganda was disseminated throughout the United States. Some of these organizations made their appeal chiefly to those of German blood. Under the leadership of Fritz Kuhn, the members of the German-American Bund wore uniforms at their meetings, practiced military drill, and greeted each other with the Nazi salute. Financed in part by the Reich through the German diplomatic corps in the United States, these pro-German committees [1] tried to dissuade Americans from supporting the preparedness measures of the New Deal. They also sang hynms of hate against the British and the Jews.

Many Americans, refusing to join the definitely Nazi organizations, nevertheless did become members of committees which placed their appeal on some different basis. It had been estimated that there were more than seven hundred of these isolationist agencies in the United States at the opening of World War II; most of them were ephemeral, but some were strong and vociferous. One of the most publicized was the American Fellowship Forum, started in the spring of 1939, to promote Nazi ideological warfare, the need for appeasement, and opposition to preparedness. Through *Today's Challenge*, the Forum made its appeal; contributors were Lawrence Dennis, a frank proponent of American fascism, Representative Fish, Senator Lundeen, and George Sylvester Viereck of World War I infamy. Another was William Dudley Pelley's Silver Shirts, which used *The Galilean* to spread the doctrine of a purge of Jews and others whom Pelley asserted were un-American. Verne Marshall, head of the No Foreign Wars Committee, preached in fanatic fashion the need for isolation. He secured the financial backing of William R. Davis, a wealthy oil man, who claimed that he had secured from the Reich a peace plan to which Germany would give its consent, thereby ending hostilities. The State Department, however, never made any mention of the reception of such a plan and the Reich made no comment. After Senator Lee of Oklahoma charged that Davis had a "financial stake in a complete Nazi victory" little more was heard about the supposed peace offer. The Christian Front, which claimed to follow the teachings of Father Coughlin,

[1] Lesser known agencies in America were the League of the Friends of New Germany, the German Legion, the German Edda Kultur League, the Homeland Regional Group, the League of German-American Writers, and the Hindenburg Youth Association.

consisted of a number of platoons claiming a membership of at least 200,000, dedicated to dominating the country even through the use of force.[1] More than twenty isolationist Congressmen, wittingly or not, allowed their franking privileges to be used to send out literature detrimental to preparedness and to the Allied cause.

The America First Committee attempted to gather the membership of these numerous agencies under its wing. Organized in the fall of 1940 by R. Douglas Stuart, Jr., a wealthy student at Yale, it had as its general theme the avoidance of war at any price. The first national chairman was General Robert E. Wood, head of a leading business concern in Chicago. Prominent among the members or those who co-operated were Charles Lindbergh, Laura Ingalls—who had gained fame as an aviatrix, Kathleen Norris, Henry Ford, General Hugh Johnson, and isolationist members of Congress such as Wheeler, Nye, and Rush Holt of West Virginia. This committee sent out hundreds of thousands of pamphlets, millions of letters, innumerable buttons and stickers, and its members made hundreds of speeches against involving the nation in conflict. The most prominent orators were Lindbergh and Wheeler; their speeches indicated that they were in little touch with reality. For example, on April 7, 1941, Lindbergh asserted that Great Britain was a beaten nation; he concluded, therefore, "that we cannot win this war for England, regardless of how much assistance we extend." Six weeks later, he and Wheeler asked for a negotiated peace because, were the United States to enter the war, it would mean the end of democracy on this side of the Atlantic. In September, 1941, the eminent flier declared: "The three most important groups which have been pressing this country toward war are the British, the Jewish and the Roosevelt Administration." He continued with the insistence that those three elements were preparing the path to war under the cloak of defensive preparations, that step by step, without the realization of the American people, they were involving the nation in hostilities, and that they were creating a series of incidents to make it appear that the coming war was being forced on the United States.

It is impossible to say how much influence these isolationist organizations had upon the American mind, nor can the membership be accurately determined. But their efforts were not without effect. The debates in Congress showed that opposition to war was strong, and delaying tactics did hold up preparedness measures. The antiwar spirit

[1] Other prominent committees were: Make Europe Pay War Debts, War Debts Defense, Islands for War Debts, National Committee to Keep America out of Foreign Wars, Christian Mobilizers, American Destiny Party, Save America First, National Workers League, Crusaders for Americanism, and the National Gentile League.

was also active in the colleges as indicated by the thousands of students who signed the Oxford Pledge not to fight under any circumstances and by the flood of petitions sent to Washington urging the administration not to repeat the mistake of 1917. While the majority of those opposed to intervention disclaimed any Nazi influence, their methods sometimes smacked of Hitlerism and there were usually Bundists or members of similar agencies active in the affairs of the committees.

The administration did not conceal its bitterness toward these organizations. For example, on Labor Day of 1941, President Roosevelt asserted that the isolationists were demanding that he "become a modern Benedict Arnold and betray all that I hold dear—my devotion to our freedom—to our churches—to our country." He referred to Lindbergh as an "appeaser and defeatist" in such denunciatory terms that the colonel resigned his commission in the Army Air Force. The President also implied that there was a strong similarity between the writings and speeches of the noninterventionists and the articles which came from the Reich.

Nor was the opposition to the isolationists limited to the administration. A number of Americans established their own committees to counteract the efforts of the America First and other similar agencies. The

Developing a Punch. (By Hungerford in the *Pittsburgh Post-Gazette*.)

most active were the Committee to Defend America by Aiding the Allies and the Fight for Freedom Committee. Pamphlets, speeches, radio talks, and advertisements were used by the internationalists in their fight.

IMPROVING HEMISPHERE DEFENSE

Despite the attacks of the isolationists, the United States continued to take steps which would build up American defense during the spring and summer of 1941. These steps included both giving more assistance to Britain and other countries fighting the Axis and cutting down potential Axis influence in the Western Hemisphere.

For example, just as lend-lease material began to flow from American ports in April, 1941, the United States turned over ten coast-guard cutters to Great Britain to be used primarily in antisubmarine warfare. This action was deemed necessary because of the staggering merchant losses which the British were suffering on the seas and because the Neutrality Act prohibited the United States from convoying American supplies to belligerents.

In the same month Roosevelt and Prime Minister Mackenzie King of Canada issued a joint statement to the effect that "in mobilizing the resources of this continent each country should provide the other with the defense articles which it is best able to produce quickly, and that production should be coordinated to this end." As a result of this agreement, the United States was able to buy hundreds of million dollars worth of strategic material—such as aluminum—from Canada to speed up American defensive preparations, while Canada was provided with essential dollar exchange to balance her unfavorable trade and enable her to buy more American goods.

Likewise in April the United States signed a pact with the Danish Minister in Washington which provided for American defense of Greenland as a Danish colony. The United States secured the right to establish military and naval installations on the island. Not only was this a move to prevent Greenland from falling into German hands as the mother country had and to protect the hemisphere, but it meant as well that the United States might guard British merchantmen as far east as Greenland. In line with this action, Congress approved of Public Law 32, which stipulated

That the United States would not recognize any transfer, and would not acquiesce in any attempt to transfer, any geographic region of this hemisphere from one non-American power to another non-American power; and

That if such transfer or attempt to transfer should appear likely, the

United States shall, in addition to other measures, immediately consult with the other American Republics to determine upon the steps which should be taken to safeguard their common interest.[1]

German protests at these steps were as nothing compared with the cries which were raised against the seizure of her merchant ships in American ports. On March 30, 1941, the United States Coast Guard, under orders of the Treasury Department, had taken over twenty-eight Italian and two German ships lying in American harbors. This was done because the crews of a majority of those ships, acting under orders from their respective governments, had wrecked the machinery and engaged in other acts of sabotage. Consequently, under the Espionage Act of 1917 the United States intervened; the sabotaged ships were a menace to navigation. At the same time thirty-five undamaged Danish ships were brought under American control.[2] German and Italian consular officials immediately sent strenuous objections to Secretary Hull. The German note read:

In the name of my Government I protest most urgently against the aforesaid measures of the United States Government, for which there is no legal basis in international law and which represent in particular a clear violation of the Treaty of Friendship, Commerce and Consular Rights of December 8, 1923, existing between Germany and the United States.

Hull's reply questioned what principle of international law and what clause in the treaty were broken. Then he went on to state that it was a felony under American law for any shipmaster or crew member to injure any vessel within American territorial waters and to threaten thereby navigation.

Then arose the question of what to do with the seized ships. The President found the solution by asking Congress on April 10 to extend his authority to requisition or purchase American vessels to include the recently seized ones. As his reason he gave the need of more shipping to promote American defense, saying

It is obvious that our own ultimate defense will be rendered futile if the growing shortage of shipping facilities is not arrested. It is also obvious that inability to remove accumulating materials from our ports can only result in stoppage of production with attendant unemployment and suspension of production contracts. It is therefore essential, both to our defense plans and to our domestic economy, that we shall not permit the continuance of the immobilization in our harbors of shipping facilities.

[1] The enactment of this resolution was in line with the Havana meeting of 1940 and the separate resolutions of each House of June, 1940.
[2] Following the lead of the United States, nine Latin-American countries also seized the Axis ships within their ports.

On June 6 Congress gave the President the desired authority and on the same day Roosevelt issued a proclamation which empowered the United States Maritime Commission to take over "any foreign merchant vessel which is lying idle in waters within the jurisdiction of the United States . . . and which is necessary to the national defense. . . ." Thus the German, Italian, and Danish ships, together with subsequently seized French ones—including the *Normandie*—were acquired by the United States. Later a number of these were used to carry cargoes to Britain.

Still another blow at the Axis was delivered on June 14 when the President issued an order under the Trading with the Enemy Act of 1917 and subsequent amendments for the freezing of all Axis assets in the United States. By so doing Roosevelt hoped to diminish totalitarian propaganda and sabotage in the country. To serve the same end, another proclamation, this time by the State Department on June 20, ordered the closing of twenty-four German consulates in the United States after July 10 together with the German Library of Information— an important propagandist distributing agency, the German Railway and Tourist Agencies, and the Transocean News Service because they were engaging "in activities wholly outside the scope of their legitimate activities." Subsequently all Italian consulates were also closed.[1]

Nor was the United States finished. Acting under the authority obtained through the declaration of the unlimited national emergency of May 27, 1941, the President issued a "Proclaimed List of Certain Blocked Nationals." This consisted of some eighteen hundred persons and firms in the Western Hemisphere who were "deemed to be acting for the benefit of Germany and Italy"—in other words, they were undermining the American war effort. No American firms were to do business with the black-listed concerns, whose assets held in the United States were to be frozen. This was an unusual action for the United States to take while still a neutral, but it was further proof of the administration's insistence upon keeping Axis influence at a minimum in the hemisphere.

Meantime, the President pushed the defensive zone closer to Europe by ordering the American occupation of Iceland on July 7 because "the United States cannot permit the occupation by Germany of strategic outposts in the Atlantic to be used as air or naval bases for eventual attack against the Western Hemisphere." This pronouncement

---

[1] Germany reciprocated by closing American consulates and American Express offices in the Reich and occupied countries on July 15 because of "grave acts" against Germany. Shortly after Italy followed suit and in addition froze American investments within her territory.

increased the ire of the isolationists who, through the lips of Senator Wheeler, asserted that it would be but a question of time before the nation was involved in war. The Senator also declared that American naval ships had already attacked German submarines, a statement that brought quick denial from Secretary Knox.

But if that were not the case, at least German submarines were attacking American shipping. On May 21, 1941, the *Robin Moor*, clearly marked as an American merchantman, was sunk 700 miles off the coast of Brazil while on her way from Brooklyn to Cape Town. The submarine commander made no effort to help the passengers and crew, who drifted in lifeboats for nearly three weeks before they were rescued. When the news reached the United States on June 9, an immediate protest was sent to the Reich; but the answer certainly was not satisfactory: "Germany will continue to sink every ship with contraband for Britain whatever its name."

Consequently the President sent a special message to Congress on June 20 in which he said:

We must take the sinking of the *Robin Moor* as a warning to the United States not to resist the Nazi movement of world conquest. It is a warning that the United States may use the high seas of the world only with Nazi consent. Were we to yield on this we would inevitably submit to world domination at the hands of the present leaders of the German Reich. We are not yielding and we do not propose to yield.

As definite proof that the United States was not going to yield, the administration condemned the unprovoked German attack upon Russia in June and at the same time announced that lend-lease help would be extended to the Soviet.[1] Moreover, at the request of Chief of Staff George Marshall, the President sent another special message to the legislature in early July asking for the lengthening of military service for the draftees. Their discharge after a year's training, he asserted, would disrupt plans for enlarging the army. The isolationists sought desperately to prevent the enactment of a law to increase the training time to eighteen months; they charged the administration with trying to break a contract made in the Burke-Wadsworth Act and declared that the nation was not in such grave peril as Roosevelt inferred. By August 12, however, the Congress had complied with the President's

[1] This decision also brought vociferous protests from the isolationists. Lindbergh said: "I would a hundred times rather see my country ally herself with England, or even Germany with all her faults, than with the cruelty, the godlessness and the barbarism that exist in Soviet Russia. The only sensible thing for us to do is to build an impregnable defense for America and keep this hemisphere at peace."

request by adding six months to the military service of conscripted men; [1] the extra service was made more palatable through a $10-a-month pay raise after one year.

THE ATLANTIC CHARTER

Despite these preparations, the Axis victories in Europe and Asia, together with continued Allied losses on the high seas, made it essential for more definite planning by the democracies. Therefore President Roosevelt and Prime Minister Churchill, accompanied by their respective civilian and military advisers, met at sea off the coast of Newfoundland August 10–12, 1941. They discussed what aid should be sent the Soviet, what policy should be followed in connection with Japan, and numerous other problems concerning lend-lease and preparedness. The most important and publicized action, however, was the agreement on broad aims and principles for the postwar world. This agreement, known as the "Atlantic Charter," was made public on August 14 and contained the following provisions:

First, their countries seek no aggrandizement, territorial or other;

Second, they desire to see no territorial changes that do not accord with the freely expressed wishes of all the people concerned;

Third, they respect the right of all peoples to choose the form of government under which they will live; and they wish to see sovereign rights and self-government restored to those who have been forcibly deprived of them;

Fourth, they will endeavor, with due respect for their existing obligations, to further the enjoyment by all States, great and small, victor or vanquished, of access, on equal terms, to the trade and to the raw materials of the world which are needed for their economic prosperity;

Fifth, they desire to bring about the fullest collaboration between all nations in the economic field with the object of securing, for all, improved labor standards, economic advancement, and social security;

Sixth, after the final destruction of the Nazi tyranny, they hope to see established a peace which will afford to all nations the means of dwelling within their own boundaries, and which will afford assurance that all men in all the lands may live out their lives in freedom from fear and want;

Seventh, such a peace should enable all men to traverse the high seas and oceans without hindrance;

Eighth, they believe that all of the nations of the world, for realistic as well as spiritual reasons, must come to the abandonment of the use of force. Since no future peace can be maintained if land, sea, or air armaments continue to be employed by nations which threaten, or may threaten, aggression outside of their frontiers, they believe, pending the establishment of a wider and permanent system of general security, that the disarmament of such

[1] The House vote was 203 to 202; the Senate approved by 45 to 30.

nations is essential. They will likewise aid and encourage all other practicable measures which will lighten for peace-loving peoples the crushing burden of armaments.

This Atlantic Charter might be called the Fourteen Points of World War II; true, the Charter was more indefinite than Wilson's statement, but it served about the same purpose—that of establishing a postwar goal for peace and collective security. Moreover, the Charter had greater weight in that it had the approval of heads of two of the strongest nations in the world. It gave oppressed peoples a hope for the future and was the beginning of the United Nations. The very indefiniteness of the Charter provided a latitude lacking in the Fourteen Points.

On the other hand, it more or less committed the United States to cooperate more effectively with the democratic belligerents; it was, perhaps, the natural sequence to lend-lease and other actions of the United States. The Charter was well received in the countries fighting the Axis, in the occupied countries, and in those nations which were sympathetic to the Allied cause. Nevertheless, American isolationists regarded it as bringing the nation closer to war, while the Axis partnership considered it as impossible to fulfill, but at the same time as evidence that the United States was really an ally of Great Britain.

THE SHOOTING WAR

Nor was the Axis slow in retaliating. On September 4 the United States destroyer *Greer*, while carrying mail to Iceland, was attacked by a submarine. Fortunately the *Greer* was not hit by the two torpedoes and she dropped several depth charges in an effort to destroy the U-boat. Immediately the isolationists asserted that the *Greer* had been the attacker or defended the submarine commander on the ground that he might have mistaken the *Greer* for one of the overage destroyers now flying the British flag. The administration, however, did not share these views. President Roosevelt asserted that the attack on the destroyer was deliberate and that the submarine was still being hunted; were it found it would be "eliminated." Then, in a fireside chat to the nation on September 11, the President made known the position he would take when he said:

No act of violence will keep us from maintaining intact two bulwarks of defense: First, our line of supply to the enemies of Hitler, and, second, the freedom of our shipping on the high seas. From now on, if German or Italian vessels of war enter the waters the protection of which is necessary for American defense, they do so at their own peril.

These acts of lawlessness are a manifestation of . . . the Nazi design to abolish the freedom of the seas and to acquire absolute control.

Roosevelt denied it was an act of war to maintain the American patrol to protect shipping. Moreover, he warned that "American naval vessels and American planes will no longer wait until Axis submarines . . . or raiders . . . strike their deadly blow—first." This meant a virtual order to American ships and planes to shoot first.

The isolationists denounced this order as the beginning of a "shooting war." The Reich characterized the President as a dictatorial aggressor who was ready to involve an unwilling nation in war to satisfy his lust for power.

THE REPEAL OF THE NEUTRALITY ACT

Within three weeks after the attack on the *Greer*, the President intimated at a press conference that he would soon ask Congress for permission to arm American merchantmen; this would mean, of course, a partial repeal of the Neutrality Act of 1939. Two days later, on September 25, Senator Kenneth McKellar of Tennessee, who had voted for all the earlier neutrality measures, urged the Upper House to consider the total repeal of the 1939 act because "it has done us no good."

It is impossible to say what chance of success the repeal movement would have had under ordinary circumstances. The isolationists were still very strong in Congress as indicated by the close House vote on extension of military training. Nor was the nation as a whole in favor of the step, even though public-opinion polls showed favor for American convoying of lend-lease material were that the only means of preventing a British defeat. However the cause of repeal was greatly assisted by the actions of Germany herself.

On September 27 the *L. C. White*, an American-owned tanker now under Panama registry,[1] was sunk off the Brazilian bulge well within the limits of the neutrality zone. Secretary Hull immediately characterized the incident as "another act of lawlessness, piracy and attempted frightfulness in connection with the general movement to drive people off the Atlantic Ocean, which is part of the world movement of conquest."

On October 9 the President dealt with the situation in a special message to Congress. In it he said: "Our merchant vessels are sailing the seas on missions connected with the defense of the United States. It is not just that the crews of these vessels should be denied the means of defending their lives and their ships." Consequently he asked for the repeal of the clause prohibiting the arming of American ships, and at the same time intimated that he wished Congress would also remove

[1] Many American ships changed registry to some other neutral hemisphere country in order to avoid the prohibitions of United States neutrality laws.

the "crippling provisions" banning American vessels from combat zones and entering belligerent ports.

Debate on amending the Neutrality Act was cut suddenly short by the news that on October 17 the practically new destroyer *Kearny* had been hit off Iceland with resulting casualties of ten injured and eleven missing. While the *Kearny* did reach port, the incident brought House passage of the bill by an overwhelming vote—259 to 138—within a few hours after the reception of the information.

In the Senate, three Republicans—Austin of Vermont, Bridges of New Hampshire, and Gurney of South Dakota—substituted a measure calling for total repeal of the Neutrality Act because it was "detrimental to the best interests of the United States" which could not exist in a "nazified world." This proposal had the unqualified support of Wendell Willkie, who considered the act in question an "ugly smudge of isolationism." But the Democratic majority preferred to follow the President's wishes by countering with a bill to repeal only three sections of the act: the bans on arming of merchantmen, on entrance into combat zones, and on entering belligerent ports.

Score Board. (By Seibel in the *Richmond Times-Dispatch*.)

The isolationist Senators, led by Wheeler and Nye, rallied their forces on the assumption that repeal would be "the last step before we enter war." A filibuster—like that waged by the willful men of 1917 —was threatened. President Roosevelt added his voice to the active advocates of repeal when he devoted the major share of his Navy Day (October 27) address to the need of freedom of the seas—and he asserted that no ships were safe anywhere.

The crowning factor in the success of the measure, however, was the German sinking of the destroyer *Reuben James* while convoying supplies to Iceland. A majority of the crew of 120 were lost. On November 7, therefore, the Senate approved of the repeal of those three clauses by a vote of 50 to 37, and six days later the House accepted the Senate form by 212 to 194.

The order for arming merchantmen was speedily given, and they were thereafter allowed to go to Allied ports with military supplies. Both these merchantmen and American naval vessels could shoot on sight in order to keep the supply lines open, to maintain freedom of the seas, and strengthen the defense of the hemisphere. The United States was still theoretically neutral, but it was a neutrality in name only. While the isolationists continued to assert that the United States should avoid war, war had already come to America. By November 1 German submarines had taken a toll of eleven American merchant vessels and one destroyer. Two other destroyers and innumerable merchantmen had been attacked but had escaped sinking. To prevent further sinkings, American ships could shoot on sight. Under the circumstances it could be but a matter of time before all-out hostilities developed. Strangely enough, however, they were to break out first on the other side of the world.

MOUNTING JAPANESE AGGRESSION

Following the *Panay* incident, the American people generally turned their backs upon the Far Eastern situation and looked with increasing apprehension at the storm clouds developing over Europe. Nevertheless, in the period from early 1938 until the Pearl Harbor attack, the Roosevelt administration realized that the Japanese menace was mounting rather than diminishing. Because of the isolationist sentiment in the United States, however, that menace was dealt with through words rather than deeds during most of these months.

As 1938 progressed, State Department notes of protest against Japanese encroachments on American rights in China were sent more frequently, as well as criticisms of the Japanese bombings of Chinese civilians. Moreover, the Western powers showed apprehension over the reports that Japan was building a larger navy. On February 5, 1938, Britain, France, and the United States demanded that Japan reveal whether she was constructing any capital ships larger than the 35,000-ton limit placed in the Washington Treaty, but a week later Japan replied that she would not divulge her plans to any outside nation. There was nothing the other nations could do about this rebuff; France and Britain were much too concerned with Hitler's moves, while the United States did not wish to push Japan too strongly because it might mean war.

Nevertheless, the Roosevelt administration tried by other means to show its opposition to Japanese aggressiveness. On July 1, 1938, Secretary Hull informed the manufacturers of airplanes and aircraft parts, as well as exporters of those commodities, that the government was strongly opposed to the selling of such equipment to any nation which used planes to attack and bomb civilian populations. Although there were no teeth in this statement, the manufacturers and exporters in question generally complied with what might be called a moral embargo. In 1939 the State Department similarly frowned upon the exportation of high-octane gasoline and any information as to how to manufacture this aviation fuel. Even before this latter "moral" embargo was placed, the administration persuaded bankers not to extend any financial credit to Japan.

Nor did President Roosevelt proclaim that a state of war existed in the Far East and consequently neither the Neutrality Act of 1937 nor the one of 1939 were put into effect. At first he withheld the proclamation because he hoped that the troubles between Japan and China could be settled quickly in peaceful fashion; as the hostilities expanded, however, he realized that if the neutrality legislation became effective, China, a victim of aggression, with few ships and little money, would be unable to secure American material assistance.

These actions had little effect upon Japanese aggression, except perhaps to make her believe that the United States was definitely unfriendly toward her. Appeasement at Munich encouraged aggression in Asia as well as in Europe and on November 3, 1938, Premier Fumimara Konoye publicly stated for the first time Japan's ambition when he said:

What Japan seeks is the establishment of a new order that will ensure the permanent stability of East Asia. In this lies the ultimate purpose of our present military campaign. This new order has for its foundation a tripartite relationship of mutual aid and co-ordination between Japan, Manchukuo, and China in political, economic, cultural, and other fields.

Then the Premier went on to hope that "other powers will, on their part, correctly appreciate her aims and policy and will adapt their attitude to the new conditions in East Asia."

Unfortunately Konoye's declaration about the New Order for a Greater East Asia Co-Prosperity Sphere neglected to mention that Japan was forcing it upon an unwilling China or what the confines of East Asia would include. The American State Department called attention to some of these omissions. On December 31, 1938, Hull protested strongly that Japanese actions were harming American "rights and interests" in China. Since these interferences were "counter to the provisions of several binding international agreements" to which Japan and the United States were voluntary parties, the United States considered them "unjust and unwarranted." Nor did the United States consider it just for one party to draw up terms for the New Order for regions not under its jurisdiction. Hull then concluded with the assertion that his country would not countenance the abrogation of any of its rights through arbitrary methods. The United States, however, was agreeable to discussing any new proposition which might be satisfactory to all parties concerned.

The Japanese reply to this note was to appoint on January 5, 1939, a more militaristic Premier, Baron Kirchiro Hiranuma, and to extend the sphere of military occupation to include Hainan in February, followed two months later by the seizure of several islands only 700 miles from Singapore. Then in June she began to blockade the British and French concessions in Tientsin. As the war spread, more and more American lives were threatened, more American property destroyed, and more American rights in the Japanese-occupied sections of China interfered with. Since diplomatic efforts failed to right the situation, the United States decided to resort to more drastic steps.

On July 26, 1939, the United States gave Japan the necessary six months' notice for the termination of the 1911 commercial treaty between the two nations. The cancellation of that treaty, with its most-favored-nation clauses, would remove all obstacles to the establishment of an actual embargo against Japan. When the six months' period ended in January, 1940, Japanese-American trade relations were maintained on a day-by-day basis, subject to interruption at any time. But even this threat of ending commercial intercourse did not cause Japan to mend her ways. Although Secretary Hull held many conversations with the Japanese ambassador, sent many notes to the Japanese Foreign Office, and had Ambassador Joseph Grew confer with the Japanese Premier, no satisfactory results were achieved. The military forces of

Japan continued to press their advantage, moving into Hunan Province in September and capturing Nanning two months later. In this progress Japan was aided by the outbreak of the European war which prevented Britain and France from giving much assistance to their nationals in the Far East or from supporting in wholehearted fashion the American protests.

In early June, 1940, Japan took advantage of the collapse of France to move into French Indo-China. Simultaneously she demanded that Britain cease sending arms from Hongkong to the Nationalist forces and close the Burma Road to all military supplies to China. Japan backed up these demands with the implied threat that if Britain did not comply an attack would be made upon Hongkong. Britain, facing the Reich alone now and fearing an invasion, could do nothing except agree to close the road for three months starting July 18. The effect was to cut China almost completely off from the rest of the world.

America showed its disapproval of this development. On July 16 Secretary Hull issued a press release in which he asserted that "this Government has a legitimate interest in the keeping open of arteries of commerce in every part of the world and considers that action . . . would constitute unwarranted interpositions of obstacles to world trade." It was as a result of this American position that Britain reopened the road at the end of the three-month period; the Japanese had probably expected that it would be closed for the duration.

On September 27, 1940, Japan openly asserted its solidarity with the European Axis. The Tripartite Pact, concluded on that date, stated in part:

The Governments of Germany, Italy and Japan consider it the prerequisite of a lasting peace that every nation in the world shall receive the space to which it is entitled. They have, therefore, decided to stand by and co-operate with one another in their efforts in Greater East Asia and the regions of Europe respectively. In so doing it is their prime purpose to establish and maintain a new order of things, calculated to promote the mutual prosperity and welfare of the peoples concerned. . . .

Accordingly, the Governments of Germany, Italy and Japan have agreed as follows:

Article 1. Japan recognizes and respects the leadership of Germany and Italy in the establishment of a new order in Europe.

Article 2. Germany and Italy recognize and respect the leadership of Japan in the establishment of a new order in Greater East Asia.

Article 3. . . . They further undertake to assist one another with all political, economic and military means if one of the three . . . is attacked by a Power at present not involved in the European War or in the Chinese-Japanese conflict.

Although Article 3 was certainly intended as a warning to the United States not to enter either war, President Roosevelt was not swerved from his position by it. In a radio address of October 12, 1940, he proclaimed the need for maintaining democracy in the Western Hemisphere. Then he asserted:

The core of our defense is the faith we have in the institutions we defend. The Americas will not be scared or threatened into the ways the dictators want us to follow.

No combination of dictator countries of Europe and Asia will halt us in the path we see ahead for ourselves and for democracy.

No combination of dictator countries of Europe and Asia will stop the help we are giving to almost the last free people fighting to hold them at bay. . . .

We know now that if we seek to appease them by withholding aid from those who stand in their way, we only hasten the day of their attack on us. . . .

The President's policy, therefore, had several main points. First of all, the United States should not seek war with Japan. Second, it must not back down on its insistence that American rights in the Far East be respected. Third, it must not withhold aid from the defenders of democracy. Fourth, all sorts of pressure, diplomatic and economic, should be used to try to force Japan to cease her aggression. And, finally, the United States was willing to confer with Japan and other nations interested in the Far East for possible satisfactory settlement of the complications.

Additional economic and commercial pressure was already being exerted. On December 15, 1938, the first of a series of loans was made to China. On July 2, 1940, the President signed the Export Control Act which empowered him to stop completely or curtail the export of materials considered vital to the American defense program. Almost immediately Roosevelt announced that, beginning in August, no more export licenses would be granted for shipping aviation gasoline and machine tools to Japan. This was followed in September by a similar ban on scrap iron and steel. These actions were denounced by Ambassador Horinouchi on October 8 as "unfriendly acts" and "discriminatory" measures that might cause "unpredictable results." Hull's answer was sharp and critical. He could not see, he said, how Japan, which had broken so many commitments and had violated so many American rights in China, could object to the validity of the embargoes; "that of all the countries with which I have had to deal during the past eight years the Government of Japan has the least occasion or excuse to accuse this Government of an unfriendly act." And despite Japanese threats, the United States went on to extend the embargo before the spring of 1941 to include arms, ammunition, other implements of war, lead, copper, zinc, aluminum, all petroleum products, and numerous other strategic materials.

TENSION MOUNTS

The opening of 1941 found relations between the United States and Japan more strained. The United States realized still more that the continued Japanese military expansion and occupation of Eastern Asia was a definite menace. Moreover, the Japanese military clique was growing in strength and taking a more active part in the political affairs of the country as well. Members of jingoistic and terrorist societies were assassinating those who advocated peace. The chauvinistic press was attempting to sway the minds of the people in favor of the New Order. If Japan still appeared desirous of maintaining American friendship, that desire was only on the surface.[1]

Japan was not pleased by the American refusal to recognize the New Order nor by the increasing number of commodities which were placed on the American embargo list. Yet there was the feeling that perhaps the United States would not go further than to protest against Japanese aggression. Certainly the isolationists in the American Congress were not willing to antagonize Japan as indicated by the voting down of the presidential request for appropriations to deepen the harbors at Guam and other Pacific islands. That being the case, it is no wonder that the Japanese militarists did not hesitate to proceed with their plans.

It cannot be said that the United States government was not warned of Japanese intentions to strike at her in the near future. On January 15, 1941, Secretary Hull reviewed for the House Foreign Relations Committee the relations with Japan since the Manchurian invasion of 1931. He pointed out that recently an increasing number of statements had been made by Japanese leaders about their plans for the domination of the Far East. The Secretary considered these "a program for the subjugation and ruthless exploitation by one country of nearly half the population of the world." This program should therefore be a "matter of immense significance, importance and concern" to America. Nine days later, Secretary of the Navy Knox became anxious about the situation as shown by his note to War Secretary Stimson:

[1] For example, on October 4, 1940, Foreign Minister Matsuoka is reported to have said: "I fling this challenge to America. If she in her contentment is going to stick blindly and stubbornly to *status quo* in the Pacific, then we will fight America."

If war eventuates with Japan, it is believed easily possible that hostilities would be initiated by a surprise attack upon the Fleet or Naval base at Pearl Harbor. . . . The dangers envisaged in their order of importance and probability are considered to be: (1) air bombing attack; (2) air torpedo plane attack; (3) sabotage; (4) submarine attack; (5) mining; (6) bombardment by gunfire.

This remarkable prediction was followed on January 27 with a report from Ambassador Grew that he had it on reliable authority "that a surprise mass attack on Pearl Harbor was planned by the Japanese military forces, in case of trouble between Japan and the United States; that the attack would involve the use of all the Japanese military facilities."

Despite these warnings, American popular attention was concerned chiefly with events in Europe and the debates then going on in Congress over lend-lease. Trouble in the Far East seemed too remote to affect the United States, and the belief persisted that America would not be drawn into the imbroglio unless she sought war. Indeed, the opinion polls indicated that the primary potential enemy was thought to be Germany, not Japan. It was also felt that, were war to come with Japan, the enemy could be quickly and easily defeated.

Both the United States and Japan asserted they wanted friendly relations restored. The United States took the position largely because of an honest desire to remain at peace. Moreover, America certainly was not prepared either militarily or from the point of view of national unity for hostilities. On the other hand, Japan was still too largely concerned with the conquest of China and Southeastern Asia to provoke war with the United States at the opening of 1941. So she played a diplomatic game in which at least outwardly she indicated a wish for peace.

In line with this policy, a new ambassador, Admiral Kichisaburo Nomura, who had received training at the Naval Academy at Annapolis in his youth, arrived in Washington during February. His primary purpose seems to have been to lull the Americans into a feeling of security about the Far East. And about the same time Premier Konoye said: "The government is not pessimistic concerning future Japanese diplomacy toward the United States." In this statement was the implication that Tokyo would try to promote friendly relations with America.

On March 8 Nomura and Hull began a series of conferences on all outstanding difficulties. The early talks soon indicated Japan had gone so far in her military conquests that she would not be ready to stop or to relinquish her gains. To both Hull and President Roosevelt Japan's course seemed likely to lead to war with the United States, but they hoped to avert hostilities as long as possible. Moreover, the other countries with a stake in the Far East were either too busy with the European struggle or were already occupied by Germany. Although an ABCD (America, Britain, China, and the Dutch) agreement for preserving the status quo in the Pacific was being developed during the spring, that arrangement actually did not mean much. Under the circumstances it seemed best to continue the "peace" talks with Nomura as long as possible.

But, even while these "peace" talks were going on, the United States was pursuing its original policy of trying to stem the Japanese advance by means of economic pressure. With the passage of lend-lease, further credit as well as strategic supplies were extended to China—making a total of more than $100,000,000 since the beginning of 1940. Moreover, lend-lease aid was granted to the Dutch East Indies and Malaya.

FREEZING JAPANESE ASSETS

The diplomacy of 1941 cannot be understood without a realization of the extraordinary importance of Malaya and the Netherlands East Indies. Most of the world's rubber, tin, and quinine came from this area and it had rich supplies of petroleum. Next to the protection of its own territories, the United States held no objective of foreign policy more important than that of keeping this vital area of Southeastern Asia out of hostile hands. Fear that Japan would attack this region had been a leading factor in the appeasement of Japan involved in refraining from a complete embargo—one that would have deprived the Japanese war machine of American gasoline. The threat to Malaya and the East Indies occasioned by Japanese occupation of French Indo-China in 1940 had worried Washington and led to increased diplomatic pressure against the Asiatic aggressor. A crisis over the issue did not arise so long as Japanese forces in French Indo-China were small in numbers and concentrated in the northern part of the country. But in July, 1941, the situation was radically altered. The Vichy government was forced to give its assent to full Japanese control over the country and the Japanese began to strengthen greatly their forces and move them into the south. Such steps could hardly be called defensive; Japan was obviously building up French Indo-China as an offensive base for an attack upon Malaya and the East Indies.

Appeasement had failed and the United States resorted to drastic action. On July 25, 1941, the President announced an executive order freezing all Japanese assets in the United States. The effect of this was to stop all commercial intercourse between the two countries, thus imposing at last a complete embargo. In order to get gasoline and other vital supplies, Japan had now either to attempt to conquer them in Southeastern Asia, involving herself in war with Britain, the Netherlands East Indies government, Australia, and probably the United States, or else she had to induce America to resume trade relations. But the United States, now determined to cease supplying the Japanese war machine, refused to reopen trade unless Japan would abandon its policy of conquest. From such a diplomatic situation the only outcome could be war—unless either Japan or the United States was willing to abandon its position.

Sumner Welles of the State Department clearly stated the American position. He asserted that the occupation of Indo-China was a definite threat to American security because it menaced procurement of raw materials vital to its defense. Moreover, the Japanese advance into Southeastern Asia was in direct defiance of the Tokyo promise to respect the Far Eastern status quo. Welles concluded with: "The Japanese Government is giving clear indication that it is determined to pursue an objective of expansion by force or threat of force." At the same time the United States Navy heads announced that the fleet was practically ready to back up the national policy in the Pacific.

Japan was not prepared for the showdown, however. True she had partially safeguarded her position by signing a nonaggression pact with the Soviet on April 13, thereby ensuring that there would be no attack upon her from the north. But she continued her diplomatic fencing with the United States until her plans were complete. American firms in China were merely taken into "protective custody," with the intimation that this policy would be relaxed if the United States would reciprocate. Japan thus showed she was not desirous of continuing economic reprisals; to do so might cause her relations with America to reach the breaking point. Another example of Japanese appeasement during the summer of 1941 resulted from the so-called Chungking incident. Japanese planes dropped bombs near the American gunboat *Tutuila*, anchored in the Yangtze River, causing slight damage. Without waiting for a protest to come from the State Department, Tokyo sent an apology to Washington and said full reparation would be made.

President Roosevelt refused to be swerved from his embargo policy by the Japanese actions, largely because Japan had not as yet made a definite statement of its position regarding the future of the Far East. At the meeting with Churchill which resulted in the Atlantic Charter, the dangerous Pacific situation was discussed. The Prime Minister favored a stern ultimatum to Tokyo, but Roosevelt felt that it would only serve to force war at once. Instead, he believed he could "baby them along for three months."

THE FAILURE OF THE PEACE TALKS

The Atlantic Charter served to worry Tokyo; it meant possibly the beginning of an actual Anglo-American alliance. Consequently, Nomura, who had not made any satisfactory commitments to Hull, proposed that Roosevelt and Konoye might confer somewhere in the Pacific and thus reach a satisfactory decision. President Roosevelt agreed to such a conference on August 17, but he stipulated that both parties put in writing their Far Eastern policies. Thus a conclusion could be effected more quickly. The proposed meeting never materialized, however, and some observers are of the opinion that it was suggested as a means of seizing the President and holding him as a hostage to force the United States to give in to the Japanese New Order.

If Nomura would not present a conciliatory proposition, Hull was ready to do so. On September 3, he offered the ambassador the points on which a settlement might be reached: (1) both parties should agree to respect the political independence and territorial integrity of all nations; (2) neither party should interfere in the other's affairs; (3) the equality of all countries should be upheld; and (4) the situation in the Pacific could be changed only by peaceful means with the approval of all nations concerned. Although Premier Konoye told Grew that Japan was in full sympathy with these points, Nomura informed Hull that they must not be made retroactive—they could not apply to Manchukuo or the Japanese-occupied parts of China.[1] At the same time the ambassador began to complain that Japan was being encircled by a hostile ring of steel and that she must be allowed additional territory for self-protection.

This diplomatic deadlock clearly threatened war. Further warning came when Konoye was succeeded on October 17 by the militaristic General Hideki Tojo and when reports came from Grew that Japanese leaders were beginning to talk openly about "the final parting of the ways." And probably to lull Americans while the preparations for attacking Pearl Harbor were being completed, on November 5 Tojo sent Saburo Kurusu, a career diplomat, to assist Nomura in the "peace"

---

[1] The Japanese press was urging terms based on the American retirement from the Far East, the ending of all fortification of American islands in the Pacific, and the withdrawal of the American fleet from Pacific waters.

conversations. The terms which Kurusu brought were: (1) the United States must no longer help China; (2) Japan must be allowed a free hand in China; (3) the ring of steel around Japan must be broken; (4) both the New Order and the government of Manchukuo must be recognized and respected by the United States; (5) American freezing orders together with the embargo must be concluded; and (6) a new commercial treaty must replace the one abrogated by the United States.

Although Hull refused to give any consideration to these propositions when they were presented to him on November 17, Nomura and Kurusu repeated the same six points three days later and added demands that the United States must furnish Japan with oil and stop interfering in the relations between Japan and China. If the United States accepted these terms, Japan would not trespass any further into Southeastern Asia and the Pacific. Hull became furious and told the two envoys quite bluntly that nothing could be accomplished as long as Japan maintained her militaristic and aggressive attitude.

The Secretary of State advised the so-called War Cabinet of the United States on November 21 that the Japanese terms were not acceptable, that war was inevitable, and that therefore the American forces in the Pacific should be alerted. Yet he made another effort to maintain peace. On November 26 he informed Nomura and Kurusu of the American propositions, which were approximately the same as the September 4 points, plus the hope that Japan would withdraw from the Axis. The envoys asserted that they would have to secure further word from Tokyo before committing themselves.

While waiting for a reply, the military and naval authorities sent additional warnings to the American forces in the Pacific to be prepared for a possible surprise attack. Moreover, on December 6, President Roosevelt telegraphed Emperor Hirohito, urging him to do his utmost to preserve peace—but received no reply. The following day, the Japanese envoys secured an appointment with Hull for a quarter of two in the afternoon that they might give their answer.

The conference did not begin, however, until 2:20 P.M. Kurusu said the reason for the delay in replying to Hull's proposals of November 26 was because of troubles in decoding Tokyo's answer. That answer proved to be a definite rejection of the American terms. It asserted that the United States was conspiring with Britain and other powers against the New Order and the Japanese efforts to establish peace in the Far East. It implied that the Anglo-American nations were attempting to expand their interests by keeping China and Japan at war. Therefore, concluded the Tokyo note, "in view of the attitude of the American

Government it cannot but consider that it is impossible to reach an agreement through further negotiations."

After carefully reading this answer, Hull, filled with anger, denounced the envoys and their government in no uncertain terms:

I must say that in all my conversations with you during the last nine months I have never uttered one word of untruth. This is borne out absolutely by the record. In all my fifty years of public service I have never seen a document that was more crowded with infamous falsehoods and distortions on a scale so huge that I never imagined until today that any government on this planet was capable of uttering them.

That ended the conference; peace was no longer possible; the two Japanese left in silence.

PEARL HARBOR

War had already come before the envoys presented the Tokyo rejection. At 7:50 A.M. (Hawaiian time—1:20 P.M. E.S.T.) on that fateful December 7, planes from Japanese carriers began dropping bombs on Pearl Harbor. The American military forces commanded by General Walter C. Short and the fleet under Admiral Husband E. Kimmel were caught napping, despite the warnings that had been given about the possibility of a surprise attack.[1] The resulting casualties were great: 2117 navy and marine personnel were killed, 960 were missing and 860 wounded; the army had 226 officers and men killed or mortally wounded and 396 less seriously wounded; there were 80 naval planes destroyed and 70 disabled out of 202; the army lost 97 of its 273 planes;

[1] Several investigations have failed to lay the blame conclusively at anyone's door. The first investigation committee, headed by Justice Roberts, early in 1942 blamed General Short and Admiral Kimmel for failing to take necessary precautions in the face of numerous warnings from Washington. In the summer of 1945 the Army and the Navy made public their special findings. Blame was divided between the two Pacific commanders and the authorities in Washington. The longest investigation, that made by the joint Congressional Investigating Committee and lasting for ten weeks beginning November 15, 1945, resulted in the following majority report: (1) the responsibility for the well-planned and executed attack rested upon Japan; (2) the President and other high government officials in Washington tried their best to avert war with Japan; (3) despite the warning from Washington, the Pacific commanders failed to have their forces sufficiently alerted; and (4) the War Department erred in not making certain that the Hawaiian Department was ready. A minority report of this committee found: (1) that the Washington messages to Hawaii were so indefinite and conflicting that they failed to give the impression of need for wartime alert; (2) President Roosevelt did not effect sufficient cooperation among the several branches in evaluating the information gained through cracking the Japanese code.

Despite the cracking of the code and the knowledge about the "winds" messages, the attack against Hawaii evidently came as a definite surprise to everyone in the United States. While a Japanese attack was expected, testimony indicates that the American authorities believed it would be made in the area of Southeastern Asia.

either sunk or severely damaged were five battleships—the *Arizona,* *Oklahoma, California, Nevada,* and *West Virginia,* along with three destroyers, a mine layer, and a target ship; damaged were three battle-ships, three cruisers, a seaplane tender, and a repair ship.

What made the Japanese duplicity worse was the fact that both Nomura and Kurusu must have known before they entered the last conference with Hull that the attack was already under way. And Kurusu probably left Japan at about the time that the task force set out for its surprise mission. Yet he continued to talk of the possibility of peace for more than two weeks after his arrival in Washington. Of course this was not the first time Japan had so double-crossed her op-ponent; she had done a similar thing in 1904 with Russia.

WAR IS DECLARED

That Sunday evening—it was Monday, December 8 in Tokyo—Am-bassador Grew was notified by the Japanese government "that there has arisen a state of war between Your Excellency's country and Japan beginning today." This was the formal announcement of what had begun twelve hours earlier, and the note went on to assert that the United States was responsible for what had happened.

President Roosevelt was quick to reply. He appeared before the whole Congress, specially convened for the purpose, shortly after mid-day on December 8, to deliver his war message. The President began with the solemn words:

Yesterday, December 7, 1941—a date which will live in infamy—the United States of America was suddenly and deliberately attacked by naval and air forces of the Empire of Japan.

Then he went on to show that peace negotiations were still going on when the Pearl Harbor attack occurred and that the attack must have been planned "many days or even weeks ago." The President also an-nounced that the Japanese had attacked Malaya, Hongkong, Guam, the Philippines, and Wake and Midway Islands.

No matter how long it may take us to overcome this premeditated inva-sion, the American people in their righteous might will win through to absolute victory.

I ask that the Congress declare that since the unprovoked and dastardly attack by Japan on Sunday, December seventh, a state of war has existed between the United States and the Japanese Empire.

Congress acted just as speedily. Within four hours after the presi-dential request, the war declaration was approved, first by the Senate

82 to 0, then by the House 388 to 1.[1] This declaration authorized the President to use all the forces and resources of the United States to "bring the conflict to a successful conclusion." And before the day was over, Britain, true to an earlier promise, also declared war against Japan.

Three days later—December 11—Germany and Italy, in conformance with the Tripartite Agreement and because of numerous American "provocative" acts, declared war against the United States. On the same day, President Roosevelt sent another war message to Congress in which he said:

The long known and long expected has thus taken place. The forces endeavoring to enslave the entire world now are moving toward this hemisphere.

Never before has there been a greater challenge to life, liberty, and civilization.

Delay invites greater danger. Rapid and united effort of all the peoples of the world who are determined to remain free will insure a world victory of the forces of justice and righteousness over the forces of savagery and barbarism.

Both Houses of Congress then passed war declarations against Germany and Italy without a dissenting vote.[2]

Meantime, on the evening of December 9, the President in a fireside chat to the nation gave the general purposes of American participation in the war. He said in part:

The true goal we seek is far above and beyond the ugly field of battle. When we resort to force, as now we must, we are determined that the force shall be directed toward ultimate good as well as against immediate evil. We Americans are not destroyers—we are builders.

We are now in the midst of a war, not for conquest, not for vengeance, but for a world in which this Nation, and all that this Nation represents, will be safe for our children. . . .

And in the dark of this day—and through dark days that may be yet to come—we will know that the vast majority of the members of the human race are on our side. Many of them are fighting with us. All of them are praying for us. For, in representing our cause, we represent theirs as well—our hope and their hope for liberty under God.

[1] Jeanette Rankin of Montana, who also voted against American entrance into World War I, was the sole dissenter.

[2] Bulgaria, Hungary, and Rumania declared war on the United States on December 12. The United States did not retaliate until June 5, 1942. Meantime, a declaration against Thailand was passed on January 25, 1942.

26

Preparing for Total War

THE PEARL HARBOR BLOW CAME AS A STUNNING SHOCK TO THE AMERICAN people. Nevertheless that shock was of immediate value in one respect; it effected a unity that had been lacking for years. The attack upon American soil and the danger of invasion of the United States itself ended the bitter debate that had been raging between the internationalists and the isolationists. Both groups now established common cause, as did also Democrats and Republicans, industrialists and labor. Overnight the American people became united in the conviction that they must help to wipe out the totalitarian threat. This, they now realized, could be done only by girding the United States with full military regalia and making a supreme effort to ensure national survival.

RALLYING ROUND THE FLAG

As concrete proof that partisanship was put aside, outstanding Republicans like Hoover and Landon, together with the minority leaders in Congress, pledged their support to the all-out war effort. Through William Green and Philip Murray, labor was quick to promise full cooperation and, with capital, agreed that industrial disputes, especially in essential fields, must be kept at a minimum. John L. Lewis declared: "When the nation is attacked every American must rally to its support. . . . All other considerations become insignificant."

Isolationists either abruptly changed their position or became strangely silent. Hamilton Fish offered to join the armed forces; Charles Lindbergh said: "We must now turn every effort to building the greatest and most efficient army, navy and air force in the world." While he admitted that he did not believe that force was necessarily the proper method of dealing with the Axis, now that the United States had been attacked, the enemy must be defeated. The carping *Chicago Tribune* suddenly ended its criticism of the administration's foreign

670

policy in favor of "our country, right or wrong." The America First Committee likewise ceased its efforts to obstruct the preparedness movement and most of its leaders resigned from the organization.

This unity made possible a cooperation which led to a mobilization program unparalleled in the history of the world. The army, navy, and air forces were quickly multiplied many times in personnel; industry, on a round-the-clock schedule, began to turn out equipment—planes, guns, tanks, ammunition, uniforms—in numbers and amounts hitherto undreamed of. The government quickly went on a wartime footing and established agencies to deal with every phase of the emergency. Civilians, both men and women, cheerfully prepared to do without many commodities that were needed primarily for the military.

RAISING AN ARMY

Pearl Harbor found the United States still in the preparatory stages as far as the army was concerned. The army personnel numbered nearly 1,600,000 on December 7, 1941, and by far the largest percentage of this total consisted of men who were serving under the Burke-Wadsworth Act and who therefore were not eligible for overseas service. Many of these were unacquainted with either the implements or the strategy of modern warfare. Yet less than four years later, on August 15, 1945, the army had an efficient fighting force of 8,300,000 equipped with the best uniforms and the finest implements in the world. How this was done is a story in itself and only the high lights can be dealt with here.

On the day after Pearl Harbor recruiting offices throughout the country were literally flooded with men and youths seeking to enlist voluntarily. But although volunteers were accepted for some services throughout the war, army officials could not rely upon this unpredictable source. Consequently, the primary dependence for enlarging the army was placed upon conscription. On December 13, 1941, Congress removed the ban on using drafted men for overseas service and a week later the time of such service was extended to the duration and six months. Then in February, 1942, all previously unregistered males within the twenty to forty-four age group were placed within the draft category, and two months later those between the ages of forty-five and sixty-five were ordered to register, not for military service but as potential draftees for work in essential industries. The final amendment of the Burke-Wadsworth Act, announced by presidential proclamation on June 30, 1942, lowered the conscription age for military service to eighteen.

The task of calling up those who had registered was a mighty one. Now under the supervision of General Lewis B. Hershey, the draft was taken care of by 54 state agencies, 515 boards of appeal, and 6443 local boards. The estimated number of workers, most of them volunteers, on these numerous boards was more than 200,000. In general, the local draft agencies tried to prevent undue hardship. The call of married men with children or other dependents was delayed as long as possible. Naturally, however, the system was not uniform because conditions in each draft area varied. Some had a large pool of young, unmarried men with no dependents; in others that pool was small. In the case of the second category, married men were called more quickly. There was also some trouble as the war progressed over interpretations of orders from Hershey headquarters. Although there were some complaints, the draft on the whole worked well.

In similar fashion the navy complement grew. The number of men in the navy at the time of the first Japanese attack was 325,000; at the conclusion of hostilities there were 3,389,000. The marine forces grew from 28,300 to 477,000 during the same period, while the coast guard expanded from 14,000 to 171,000. The growth of naval combat ships showed the same remarkable advance, as the following table indicates: [1]

	1941	1945
Battleships	17	23
Aircraft carriers	7	28
Escort carriers		70
Cruisers	37	72
Destroyers	172	373
Destroyer escorts		365
Submarines	113	240

For ships of all types under the control of the Navy Department, the number increased from 4500 in 1941 to 91,209 at the end of the war. Of the newer types added perhaps the most unusual were those for landing infantry (LCI) and tanks (LCT). The time needed to construct combat craft was materially reduced as the war progressed: battleships could

[1] The chief advocates of a bigger and better navy during the thirties were President Roosevelt and Representative Carl Vinson of Alabama. The first move to build up the navy to Washington Treaty strength came when the President used funds appropriated under the National Industrial Recovery Act for that purpose. Virtually each year from 1934 on Vinson introduced naval construction bills. The most successful was the one of 1938, passed only after long opposition from the isolationists, which provided for the largest building program since the days of World War I. With the outbreak of hostilities in Europe, President Roosevelt secured Congressional approval for a two-ocean navy. This construction was just getting under way at the time of Pearl Harbor.

be built in thirty-two months as compared with the thirty-nine months of pre-Pearl Harbor days; aircraft carriers in sixteen months instead of thirty-two; submarines in seven and a half months rather than in fourteen; and destroyers in five and a half months instead of thirteen. These combat ships were also more heavily armored and carried heavier guns than ever before. Moreover, with the help of more recent devices and inventions, such as radar, they were better prepared offensively and defensively.

Of the specialized branches, the air arms of both army and navy showed the most spectacular improvement. In December, 1941, the number of pilots was pitifully small; by the end of the war the naval, including the marine, branch had nearly 50,000 together with ground crews and other personnel to the number of more than 500,000; for the army, in 1943 alone 65,000 pilots were graduated by the training command, along with 13,783 navigators, 13,998 bombardiers, 81,398 aerial gunners, and approximately 530,000 technicians of various types—indeed, the army air forces totaled approximately 3,000,000 for all categories at their peak. Closely associated with the army air arm were the airborne groups, both parachute and glider battalions, which did such excellent work during the invasions, in the Battle of the Bulge, and in the all-out drive to final victory in Europe. As for the planes, in 1941 the combined army and navy air arms included about 8000, of which a goodly percentage were obsolete. By VJ Day, the navy had close to 40,000 and the army had approximately twice that number. The planes were constantly being improved as far as range, fire power, bomb loads, speed, and fighting ability were concerned. Perhaps the most notable advances were made in jet propulsion and in size—the B–29's with a wing spread of 141 feet and a bomb load capacity of 10 tons. Radar and the bomb sight were of inestimable value too in American air and bombing progress.

To train this vastly increased armed personnel, twelve hundred camps, cantonments, and stations were established throughout the country. An intensive course in military or naval fundamentals lasting from twelve to seventeen weeks was given the new men, after which there was the possibility of attending specialized schools in such fields as gunnery, mechanized warfare, amphibious operations, radar, communications, and officer training. The various branches of the armed services also used many of the colleges and universities of the nation for the training of their men in such specialties as air-force training, engineering, radio and radar, meteorology, and language-and-area. Toward the close of the war the army sent seventeen-year-old pre-inductees to college for training in engineering. Moreover, many college graduates were schooled to assume positions in various phases of military and civilian government in anticipation of the occupation of enemy countries during and after the war.

Beginning June 1, 1942, the pay of the various branches was increased. That of the private and the ordinary seaman was raised from $21 a month to $50, with higher ranks increased in proportion. In the same year the Service Men's Allotment Act was passed to grant $50 a month to wives of those in the armed forces, of which $22 was taken from the pay of the men, plus $12 for the first child and $10 for each other child. In October, 1943, the dependency allotment was increased to $30 for the first child and to $20 for others under the measure establishing the Office of Dependency Benefits (ODB). In anticipation of the discharge of military men, the President signed on June 22, 1944, the measure popularly called the G.I. Bill.[1] First of all, this measure provided a fifty-two week unemployment compensation at $20 a week, together with adjusted compensation for self-employed veterans returning to their old business. Next, the government guaranteed 50 per cent of loans up to $2000 to veterans who were buying homes or setting themselves up in business. A half a billion dollars was appropriated for the construction of hospitals for veterans and to help the United States Employment Service get them jobs. Finally, veterans going to college might secure $500 a year for four years to be used for tuition and books, plus $50 a month ($75 if married) for subsistence.[2]

An unusual feature of the mobilization for World War II was the enlistment of women. The first move was made in May, 1942, when Congress established the Women's Auxiliary Army Corps (WAAC) under the command of Major—later Colonel—Ovieta Hobby; on July 1, 1943, the members of the WAAC were incorporated into the regular army as the Women's Army Corps (WAC). More than 100,000 WACS received training, for which they received the same pay as men for like ratings. They served in such varied capacities as clerks, stenographers, cryptographers, weather observers, link training instructors, laboratory technicians, truck drivers, and small-arms repairers. Although most of the WACS were stationed in the United States, some 15,000 saw service in the various overseas fields of operation. The navy also had its women's

[1] The term "G.I." first referred to anything issued by the government (Government Issue). Gradually it was applied to the enlisted men themselves and is comparable to the doughboy of World War I. Toward the close of World War II the expression became "G.I. Joe."

[2] In December, 1945, the subsistence rates were increased to $65 and $90 respectively.

branch, the WAVES (Women Accepted for Volunteer Emergency Service), organized in July, 1942, under the command of Lieutenant Commander Mildred McAfee. A total of 86,000 women joined up. Until the fall of 1944 they did not serve outside of the United States. Thereafter, some 4000 were on duty in Hawaii, with lesser numbers in Alaska, Puerto Rico, and Bermuda.[1]

Not to be forgotten in the mobilization story were the thousands of doctors, dentists, nurses, medical corpsmen, and pharmacists' mates who performed such invaluable service in taking care of the wounded men.

CIVILIANS AND THE WAR

Despite the long hours of regular work which the war entailed, millions of Americans found time to contribute volunteer services. After the attack on Pearl Harbor the possibility that mainland cities of the United States might be subjected to air raids no longer seemed fantastic. The Office of Civilian Defense (OCD), established several months earlier, suddenly took on vital significance. Five and a half million persons were trained for special duties. Of these, 1,767,000 were neighborhood air-raid wardens, 388,000 were auxiliary firemen, 389,000 were trained to provide emergency medical service, and 350,000 manned aircraft warning stations. Cities provided themselves with air-raid signals, and practice blackouts educated not only the OCD force but the general public in the grim possibilities of modern warfare. Most OCD activities came to seem unrealistic after the Axis powers were thrown on the defensive, but such services as those performed by 77,000 nurses' aides in the dangerously understaffed hospitals were of vital importance.

Other essential work was carried out under the auspices of the Red Cross. Women sewed or knitted as they had during World War I. Much more significant, however, was the blood-donation service. Techniques had been discovered for extracting the plasma from blood and processing it in such a form that it could be sent to battlefields throughout the world. There, mixed with sterile water, the plasma was available to give lifesaving transfusions to wounded servicemen. More to this procedure than to any other single factor could be attributed the remarkable achievement of World War II in cutting down mortality

[1] There was also the United States Marine Corps Women's Reserve under Colonel Ruth Streeter. Organized in February, 1943, about 19,000 enlisted in this branch. After January, 1945, some 5000 were sent to Hawaii. The SPARS, the women's branch of the Coast Guard, started in November, 1942, and numbered 10,000 under command of Captain Dorothy Stratton. The WASPS (Women's Auxiliary Ferrying Service) did not continue throughout the war.

from wounds.[1] Beginning this work in 1941, the Red Cross eventually opened thirty-five blood donor stations in the principal cities, operated more than sixty mobile units, and received prior to VJ Day more than thirteen million blood donations.

Local draft and rationing boards required long hours of volunteer work, while the efforts of thousands of unpaid workers in the centers of the USO (United Service Organization) brightened the off-duty hours of millions of lonely servicemen. Even the housewife in her kitchen helped the war effort as she carefully saved waste fats, tin cans, and waste paper for the salvage drives, while wife, husband, and children all hoed the victory gardens—numbering some twenty million— which were to be found on every vacant lot.

It proved to be easier to contribute war work of a positive nature than to accept cheerfully the numerous disruptions in normal living that the war made necessary. Rationing was a nuisance to all concerned, not only because of the need to stand in line to secure four required ration books, but because of the added time spent in marketing. Even more annoying was the trouble which it took to locate such periodically scarce items as butter, coffee, sugar, meat, cigarettes, women's stockings, and men's underwear. Those scarcities led to the establishment of what were called black markets where unpatriotic—although they would be the last to admit it—citizens could buy scarce commodities without coupons at more than ceiling prices. Such shortages, together with overcrowded transit facilities and crowded housing conditions, were the hardships of the home front over which civilians delighted to grumble, but which did not greatly impress the men in the armed services familiar with conditions in other countries.

MOBILIZATION OF INDUSTRY

It was obvious that the country's greatest advantage over the enemy lay in the gigantic potentialities of its industrial production. Yet the problem of converting factories from peace to war manufacture, of building new plants, and of establishing priorities for the use of raw material and man power, required central planning and direction in a degree unprecedented in democratic America.

The government had the advantage of being able to profit by the experience of World War I and also by several studies of the war mobilization problem which had been made since that time. Despite

[1] General Paul Hawley, chief surgeon of the American forces in the European theater, announced that 96.1 per cent of the 1,375,000 Americans wounded had been saved. He attributed this achievement to the use of plasma, sulfa, penicillin, and the fact that the men were bigger and stronger than the soldiers of World War I.

this, however, many World War I mistakes were repeated, many new ones were made, and it required a long period of trial and error before the final organization was evolved and a competent personnel was recruited. Impatient critics emphasized the President's deficiencies as an administrator; they pointed out that the jurisdictions of the various defense agencies overlapped, that jurisdictional and intra-agency feuds were frequent, and that the Chief Executive was altogether too prone to resolve such difficulties by creating still another coordinating board instead of simplifying and clarifying the lines of authority. All this was true. Yet in a more important sense Roosevelt did a remarkable job. He challenged the nation with seemingly impossible production goals, he assembled a hard-working team, and despite the appearance of muddle the most remarkable record of industrial production in the world's history was achieved.

One reason for the unsatisfactory results obtained by the earlier defense agencies was that they were established before Pearl Harbor while the nation was still at peace and not ready to accept the drastic

Signs of the Times. (By Summers in the *Buffalo Evening News.*)

steps which the imposition of a war economy would have required. Insufficient authority handicapped the activities of the Council of National Defense, established in May, 1940, and the Office of Production Management (OPM) and the Office of Emergency Management (OEM), set up early in 1941. Nor were the first attempts to control prices or to settle labor disputes through the Office of Price Administration and Civilian Supply (OPACS) and the National Defense Mediation Board (NDMB) satisfactory in their results. On May 27, 1941, the President proclaimed a state of "unlimited national emergency," thereby opening the way for the exercise of many of the wartime powers granted Wilson and still on the statute books. Two new agencies created during the summer, however, the Economic Defense Board (EDB) under the direction of Vice-President Wallace and the Supply Priorities and Allocations Board (SPAB) still failed to give the unity and vigor of direction that were required.

Not until President, Congress, and nation were shocked into drastic action by Pearl Harbor did really effective administrative organization evolve. The First War Powers Act, passed by Congress on December 18, 1941, authorized the President to redistribute the tasks of the several boards and agencies in the interests of the most efficient possible prosecution of the war—a counterpart of the Overman Act of World War I. Existing laws were liberalized to facilitate the governments' procurement of essential supplies, while the Trading-with-the-Enemy Act of 1917 was brought up to date to give the President control over all communications and the right to put to use property confiscated from the enemy or enemy aliens.

Under his new authority Roosevelt established the War Production Board (WPB) in January, 1942. Donald Nelson, a Sears Roebuck executive from Chicago, was placed in charge of this new agency, which supplanted both the SPAB and what remained of the OPM. Occupying a post similar to that of Bernard Baruch in 1918, Nelson was answerable only to the President in his efforts to secure adequate supplies and to increase production. The agency was organized into six major divisions: purchases, production, materials, industry operations, labor, and civilian supply, each under a competent director. Following the Baruch precedent, more than two hundred Industry Advisory Committees were established. The antitrust laws were tacitly suspended while the concerns in each industry pooled their patents and divided up the available government contracts. Also sponsored by the WPB were over five thousand labor-management committees formed in individual war plants. Through these channels thousands of practical suggestions for improving techniques and for saving time were received from the workers.

Both to utilize plant equipment and to conserve vital material, all production for civilian use of automobiles, radios, mechanical refrigerators, vacuum cleaners, washing machines, and most electrical appliances was halted during the early months of 1942. Production of hundreds of other metal goods was either stopped entirely or drastically curtailed, while practically all home construction except that approved for defense workers by the National Housing Agency ceased. Many of the nation's smaller industries were hard hit by this transition, but an effort was made to protect their interest through the creation of the Smaller War Plants Corporation (SWPC), which gave out and financed war contracts to small business and assisted them with their engineering problems.

Japanese conquest of 90 per cent of the world's rubber supply during the three months following Pearl Harbor created a crisis of the utmost seriousness. A belated effort at laying in a stock pile of rubber had begun in 1941, but less than a year's supply was accumulated before Malaya and the Netherlands East Indies fell into enemy hands. The sale of new tires except on a strict rationing basis was prohibited on January 5, 1942, and steps were taken to expand synthetic production. Public alarm over the situation was not quieted until the President appointed Bernard Baruch to the chairmanship of a special committee to investigate the problem. On the basis of recommendations made by the Baruch Committee, a program for conserving rubber was instituted which involved gasoline rationing, a 35-mile-per-hour speed limit on the highways, and periodic tire examinations. A vast expansion of synthetic rubber production was called for, to be organized under a special administrator in the WPB. In harmony with this suggestion, Roosevelt appointed William M. Jeffers, an executive of the Union Pacific Railroad, as Rubber Administrator.

Modern war demands global strategy in economic planning as well as in military operations. To preempt vital supplies, to keep them out of the hands of the enemy, to implement foreign policy with rewards and penalties in the form of purchases and sales to particular countries were all important American activities. During the earlier years of the conflict numerous agencies were dealing with such problems, and inevitable clashes of policy resulted. The most publicized of these feuds was that between Vice-President Wallace, the head of the Board of Economic Warfare (BEW), and Secretary of Commerce Jesse Jones, whose Reconstruction Finance Corporation advanced the funds for many of the country's strategic imports. In July, 1943, the President was compelled to intervene by abolishing the BEW and transferring its functions, together with many of those of the RFC subsidiaries, to a new Office of Economic Warfare (OEW) headed by Leo Crowley. This agency in turn was later consolidated with others, including the Office of Lend-Lease Administration, into the Foreign Economic Administration (FEA), which became one of the key agencies for the waging of total war.

Later sections of this chapter will show how the Office of Price Administration struggled to ration scarce items and keep a ceiling on prices and rents, how the National War Labor Board handled disputes over wages, and how the War Food Administration worked to increase agricultural production. One of the great needs was for the effective coordination of these activities. Obviously what was done by OPA affected both industrial production and farm production, while the problems of wage rates and prices were interrelated at every point.

Acting under the Anti-Inflation Act of October 2, 1942, the President established the Office of Economic Stabilization (OES), under the chairmanship of James F. Byrnes of South Carolina, who resigned from the Supreme Court to take over this important post. He was given control over "civilian purchasing power, prices, rents, wages, salaries, profits, rationing, subsidies, and all related matters."

Although the OES did some excellent work in supervising the improvement of production and in holding the line against inflation, there were an increasing number of critics who asserted that Stabilizer Byrnes was loaded down with too much detail, thus impairing the efficiency of OES. These critics demanded the establishment of an agency comparable to Wilson's War Cabinet, which had dealt so effectively with problems of coordination and jurisdictional disputes during World War I. The presidential answer was the organization of the Office of War Mobilization (OWM) on May 28, 1943, which was referred to as "the nearest thing to an orderly planning committee for the home front that has yet been devised." In making the announcement, President Roosevelt said:

We are entering a phase of the war effort when we must streamline our activities, avoid duplication and overlapping, eliminate interdepartmental friction, make decisions with dispatch, and keep both our military machine and our essential civilian economy running in team and at high speed.

The President placed the new agency under the direction of Byrnes, whose powers now became so great that he was popularly referred to as the "Assistant President." Associated with him were Secretary of War Stimson, Secretary of the Navy Knox, the chairman of the Munitions Assignment Board (Harry Hopkins), the chairman of the War Production Board (Donald Nelson), and Byrnes's successor as Economic Stabilizer, Judge Fred M. Vinson of Kentucky. Byrnes and Vinson proved wise choices for their respective posts. They combined integrity and administrative skill with ability to win the confidence of Congress because they had both served for a long time in that branch of the government.

The machinery of economic mobilization often seemed cumbersome. There were terrifying noises emanating from Washington when the gears appeared to clash and angry recriminations were exchanged.[1] As always in wartime, there was much Congressional denunciation of the incompetence of the executive departments. But much more judicious than the work of most such bodies was that performed by the special Senate committee to investigate the national defense program. Intelligently led by Senator Harry S. Truman of Missouri, hitherto inconspicuous as a legislator, the committee performed a useful function in uncovering cases where excess profits had been allowed to contractors or where production schedules had not been met.

Despite occasional evidences of administrative confusion and profiteering, however, the task of economic mobilization was magnificently carried through. In 1940 American war production was insignificant; in 1942 it had jumped to a volume equaling that of Germany, Italy, and Japan combined. But this was only the beginning. In 1943 it was one and one-half times as great as total Axis war production, and in 1944 twice as great. In the words of Donald Nelson:

. . . Between 1941 and the end of 1944 an almost magical transformation of American industry took place. Huge new plants dotted every section of the country. The agricultural South became heavily industrialized. Annual production of steel ingot rose nine million tons. Aluminum production rose from 807 million pounds to 2,179 million. An entirely new, huge, synthetic rubber industry was created. Plane production, in dollar value, was multiplied nearly by ten, tanks by five, naval shipping by more than five, cargo shipping by more than ten. In 1939 our total output of fabricated metal had been 13 billion dollars' worth, and in 1944 it was 70 billions; while in the same period the machine tool industry alone expanded production by more than seven times.[2]

---

[1] Such friction, for example, brought about the resignation of Donald Nelson as WPB head and the appointment of Julius Krug to succeed him.

[2] Jack Goodman, ed., *While You Were Gone: A Report on Wartime Life in the United States* (New York: Simon and Schuster, 1946), p. 224. Copyright, 1946, by Simon and Schuster, Inc.

Stalin himself is reported to have paid tribute to this record at the meeting of the Big Three at Teheran when he proposed a toast to American war production without which the enemy could not have been defeated.

THE PROBLEM OF PRICE CONTROL

Gigantic government expenditures and full employment, during a time when civilian goods were becoming increasingly scarce, threatened to bring about America's greatest inflation since the War for Independence. Yet, although the danger was recognized on all sides, government price fixing was against American tradition and its imposition was long delayed. The impact of war in Europe had already resulted in a sharp rise in the cost of living before the United States became directly involved. Only after six months of discussion, however, did Congress finally give its approval to the Price Control Act on January 30, 1942. This law provided for the establishment of an Office of Price Administration (OPA) and empowered its administrator to fix fair maximum prices on commodities whenever they rose or threatened to rise unduly. Ceiling prices of farm produce, however, could not be set below 110 per cent of parity and any established price had to have the approval of the Secretary of Agriculture. The administrator was also authorized to recommend the stabilization or reduction of rents in defense areas, while his rationing power was extended to cover all commodities sold for personal needs.

The scope of both rationing and price control was gradually expanded over the next several months. Eventually the list of rationed commodities came to include sugar, meat, butter and other fats, canned goods, coffee, shoes, gasoline, and fuel oil. The most ambitious step in the price-control program was the issuance on April 28, 1942, of the General Maximum Price Regulation which imposed wholesale and retail ceiling prices on almost all commodities. The general principle was that prices were not to exceed their highest level during March, 1942. An important omission made necessary by Congress was in the control of most food prices. Not until the original law was amended in October did OPA establish ceilings in this area.

A remarkable feature of OPA was the extent to which its activities were carried out by unpaid volunteers. Teachers were drafted to issue the various ration books, and 5600 local price and rationing boards shouldered the thankless task of passing upon applications for special rations and serving as hearing boards for alleged price violations.

The price control agency became a favorite whipping boy for harassed civilians, both those with things to sell and things to buy. Its first administrator, Leon Henderson, was a vigorous executive and a forceful personality. But his very energy aroused the hostility of Congress and, to save the agency, the President allowed him to resign in December, 1942, and appointed in his place the more diplomatic Prentiss Brown, formerly Senator from Michigan. Although Brown was able to restore peace between OPA and Congress, the agency's less rigorous enforcement policies threatened to defeat the purpose for which it was created. Congress, moreover, put up an insistent demand for personnel with greater practical business experience. In July, 1943, therefore, Roosevelt appointed Chester Bowles, a prominent New York advertising executive who had proved a successful OPA official on the state level, to serve as Brown's deputy. The following October Brown resigned and Bowles was given the post of administrator. The new head proved a good choice. In one of the war administration's most difficult and unpopular posts he achieved a very creditable record.

In the spring of 1943 the need for more drastic price-control policies became evident. The cost of living had advanced almost 8 per cent between May, 1942, and May, 1943. This combined with earlier increases meant a 27 per cent rise in the cost of living since the outbreak of war in 1939. One step to combat the situation was the extension of rent control over the whole nation in October, 1942. Another was the

Advice from the Corner. (By Summers in the *Buffalo Evening News*.)

so-called Hold-the-Line order issued by the President on April 8, 1943. An effort was made to freeze all items affecting the cost of living. Wage and salary increases except in exceptional circumstances were to be prohibited, workers were not to be permitted to change jobs for higher pay, and government agencies regulating common carriers and public utilities were enjoined to disapprove rate increases. Its hands thus strengthened, OPA was successful in restricting the rise of living costs during the next two years to 1.4 per cent. The total increase in the cost of living of less than 29 per cent up to VE Day may be compared with the 63 per cent rise which took place between the outbreak of World War I and the armistice, or the more than 100 per cent increase represented by the prices of 1920.

The validity of the cost of living indexes provided by the Bureau of Labor Statistics was often challenged, particularly by labor spokesmen seeking wage boosts. This was natural because to the average citizen the increase in living costs seemed much greater. In the first place, high wartime taxes, withheld under a new system from wage and salary checks, took a very sizable sum out of each of them. To this should be added the substantial deduction which many workers had authorized for war bonds. There was thus a wide gap between what was earned and what was actually received. Moreover, prices had risen in unequal degree and the consumer was most conscious of those which had gone up sharply. He thought very little, for example, about the fact that rents had risen less than 4 per cent since 1939, but he never forgot that food prices had advanced by 50 per cent. Even more distressing to the consumer was the 40 per cent rise in clothing prices. In actual experience, moreover, the individual usually found that he had to pay more than 40 per cent increase for his clothes due to deterioration of quality and the tendency of items having low ceiling prices to disappear from the market.

Statistics were also deceiving because they failed to take into account the very considerable volume of above-ceiling price transactions; the OPA itself admitted that some 12 per cent of the items in food stores were sold at higher than ceiling prices because of the inadequate funds for enforcement which Congress appropriated for the agency. Yet even though the degree of inflation occurring between 1939 and 1945 was larger than government figures indicated, economic controls had saved billions of dollars for both the government and the consuming public. The OPA served as a brake. It did not entirely stop inflation but it slowed it down until it was no longer dangerous to the war effort.

THE PROBLEM OF TRANSPORTATION

Total mobilization and global war involved enormous strain on the railroads and shipping facilities. World War I precedents were not followed to the extent of bringing the railroads under government operation. Instead, the lines were left under private management, but were closely supervised by the Office of Defense Transportation (ODT) directed by the experienced Joseph B. Eastman. Men, material, and supplies were moved about the country in much greater volume and with less confusion than during World War I—a remarkable achievement since the railroads had less equipment and fewer employees. This was not accomplished without paying a price, however. A number of tragic accidents testified to the seriousness of the tax which the war was levying upon both equipment and personnel.

More vital even than the coordination of the railroads was the efficient use of every precious unit of shipping. In February, 1942, this task was entrusted to the War Shipping Administration (WSA) headed by Vice Admiral Emory S. Land. All the property and powers of the United States Maritime Commission were turned over to the new agency. In addition to the ships thus secured, the WSA acquired title to or secured the use of practically all the nation's privately owned seagoing vessels as well as much of the smaller craft. To this great fleet were added more than four thousand newly constructed ships. Many World War I building records were beaten. The most remarkable exploit perhaps was the construction of a 10,000-ton ship in seventy-eight days, one third of the time required for a similar project during the earlier conflict. This was made possible by radically new techniques, developed particularly in the shipyards belonging to Henry J. Kaiser.

Although shipping was necessarily more highly regimented than was railroad transportation, the actual operation of the merchant marine was through privately owned operating companies—some 130 of which acted as the agents of the WSA. An extensive training program was undertaken to provide more officers and men for the crews. The latter composed some of the war's unsung heroes. Enemy attacks by submarine and plane resulted in approximately six thousand casualties. Several routes like those to the ports of Northern Russia were particularly arduous and dangerous. Despite losses and difficulties of recruitment, however, the merchant marine accomplished its mission of delivering the weapons of war to every theater.

Transocean air travel and transport, still in their infancy when the war began, were enormously expanded. Presidents, prime ministers, and key personnel hopped from continent to continent with surprisingly few mishaps, while air transport for less dramatic missions became routine.

THE FARMERS AND THE WAR

No individual in World War II played as powerful a role as had Herbert Hoover in World War I. The War Food Administration (WFA) of the second conflict, headed by Judge Marvin Jones, was only a pale copy of the famous earlier one. Whereas Hoover had reduced civilian food consumption through a great propaganda campaign, this end was now achieved by an extensive system of OPA-administered rationing. The increased production which Hoover had procured through the incentive of guaranteed high prices was this time secured through a system of subsidies designed in combination with ceiling prices to protect consumers.

Heated debate raged over the merits of the ceiling price-subsidy system. The farmers argued that subsidies placed a burden upon the taxpayer which rightly belonged on the consumer; they demanded that ceilings and subsidies be abandoned and prices be allowed to seek their natural levels. But the administration firmly opposed this policy. Food prices had already risen sufficiently to make the workers restless; a further jump, it was contended, would precipitate a wholesale outbreak of strikes, pay raises, and an upward spiral of inflation. Subsidies admittedly added to the national debt, but they did not increase it nearly so rapidly as would runaway prices during a period when the government was making tremendous purchases. Although Congress twice passed bills which would have killed the subsidy program, both measures were vetoed by the President.

Farmers had other grievances than price controls. Livestock raisers and dairy farmers found feed scarce and expensive. Agricultural machinery was difficult to secure. The armed services and the war industries drew away agricultural man power and labor costs shot up.

Despite all these handicaps, however, the farmers achieved a remarkable production record. Favored during most of the war years with good weather, the largest crops in American agricultural history were harvested. More than 1,000,000,000 bushels of wheat were produced in 1944, while the corn crop exceeded 3,000,000,000 bushels for three years in a row (1942–1944). Meat production kept pace, going over the 20,000,000,000-pound mark annually for the three years 1942–1944, and reaching 25,000,000,000 pounds in the latter year.

Farm income, including government payments, doubled between

1940 and 1943, exceeding $20,000,000,000 in the latter year—a far cry from the 1932 situation when total farm income was less than $5,000,-000,000. Income continued to exceed $20,000,000,000 annually in 1944 and 1945. Of course the increasing cost of things that the farmers had to buy absorbed much of this rise, yet there was a large net gain and there could be little doubt that agriculture was more prosperous than it had been for a generation. One of the healthiest signs was the shrinking agricultural debt. Total farm-mortgage debt which had risen to almost $8,500,000,000 in 1920 and to $9,600,000,000 in 1930, had fallen to $5,270,000,000 by 1945. Farmers were obviously facing the new post-war era in much sounder financial condition than they had the decade of the twenties.

LABOR AND THE WAR

Throughout the thirties the nation had struggled with the problem of unemployment. After Pearl Harbor the situation was transformed. With twelve million men eventually taken into the armed services, where was the labor to be secured to man the nation's industries? The answer was found in the entry into the factories of millions who had never been wage workers—many of them women. The number of persons gainfully employed rose from 45,000,000 in 1940 to more than 60,-000,000 in 1944. A further contribution was provided by millions of hours of overtime work performed in every community.

Less than a week after the United States entered the war a labor-management conference, meeting at the President's call, agreed to refrain from strikes and lockouts affecting essential industry during the war, to settle all labor differences by peaceful means, and to accept the jurisdiction of a war labor board.

Accordingly, on January 12, 1942, Roosevelt established the National War Labor Board (NWLB) composed of twelve members giving equal representation to the public, the workers, and the employers. William H. Davis of New York was designated as chairman. The board acted only on cases where a dispute had failed of settlement through ordinary channels of collective bargaining and the conciliation services of the Department of Labor.

During its first year the new system worked quite effectively. Although almost 3000 strikes occurred, they were quickly settled, and the number of man-days of labor lost was the smallest since 1930. About four hundred of these disputes went to the NWLB; in all but four of these the parties complied with the findings of the board; the cases of noncompliance in essential plants were handled by government seizure and operation. In July, 1942, precedent for the settlement of wage issues all over the country was provided when the board settled a strike in the lesser steel companies' plants by allowing a 15 per cent pay increase to compensate for the rise in the cost of living since January, 1941. This became known as the Little Steel formula and served as a yardstick for wage scales during the balance of the war.

The strike record was not so good in 1943. Workers were distressed by the increased cost of living which, despite OPA, continued until the Hold-the-Line order of May, 1943. Jurisdictional disputes between rival unions increased, as did work stoppages caused by quarrels between management and labor over questions of factory discipline. Many strikes were "wildcatters"—unauthorized by the unions. Employers and employees blamed each other for the situation. The former accused the workers of infringing upon the prerogatives of management; the latter asserted that the employers were trying to discredit unionism with the public by provoking work stoppages through petty acts of tyranny. In all there were 3752 strikes in 1943 involving the loss of 13,500,529 man-days of labor—three times the amount of time lost the previous year.

Most serious of the controversies were those which led to several work stoppages by John L. Lewis's coal miners. The struggle lasted throughout the greater part of the year, during which Lewis defied the NWLB, Fuel Administrator Ickes, and the government generally. Although the administration refused to admit it, Lewis in effect broke the Little Steel formula through obtaining premium pay and additional overtime work.

Congressional concern over the situation led in June, 1943, to the passage of the Smith-Connally War Labor Disputes Act against the opposition of the unions and over the President's veto. Increased powers were granted to the NWLB, a thirty days' notice had to be given before a union might take a strike vote of its membership, explicit sanction was given to presidential seizure of war industries where production was interrupted by labor disputes, and it was made a criminal offense to instigate, direct, or aid strikes in government operated plants or mines. A final provision, particularly resented by labor, prohibited union contributions to political campaign funds. Several states in the South and West passed laws restricting union activities still more stringently.

The strike record of 1944 was somewhat better. While there were more work stoppages—4956—they were for the most part quickly settled and the number of man-days lost fell to 8,721,079.

The most serious strikes inevitably made the newspaper headlines [1] and provoked condemnation of the groups involved. The situation, however, was never actually dangerous, except possibly in connection with the coal strikes. The number of man-days lost was less than 1 per cent of the amount worked. Every time the laborers worked on a legal holiday, as they usually did, the contribution to the war effort was greater than the labor lost through work stoppages for many months. Yet at the same time the percentage of time lost was not always a true yardstick because the stoppages frequently caused tie-ups in other fields which were not indicated in the Department of Labor statistics.

WAR FINANCE

The cost of waging modern warfare has reached figures formerly considered astronomical. By VJ Day World War II had made necessary United States government expenditures of more than $300,000,000,000 —a staggering sum when contrasted with the total American World War I expenditures of some $32,000,000,000.

Despite this huge outlay, the American public raised a larger proportion of war costs out of taxation than ever before. Between Pearl Harbor and VJ Day the United States collected about $123,000,000,000 in revenues, or approximately 40 per cent of its expenditures. This contrasts with 33 per cent during World War I. The record for the fiscal year ending June 30, 1945, was particularly good. Expenditures for that period reached $100,404,000,000, but net receipts were $46,456,000,000, or 46 per cent of outlay.

There was general agreement on the necessity of high wartime taxes. They were essential to preserve the solvency of the government, to prevent the unjustifiable enrichment of those who were profiting from the booming wartime economy, and perhaps most of all to reduce the threat of inflation. The actual rates which should be fixed for the various brackets of income, however, were matters for heated debate. Months of such controversy were the prelude to the enactment in October, 1942, of "the greatest tax bill in history." The tax base was broadened to require payment of income taxes by all persons receiving more than $1200 if married and $500 if single. The normal tax rate was

---

[1] One of the most publicized, although not particularly serious, disputes involved the government seizure of Montgomery Ward and Company, whose head, Sewall Avery, refused to follow the orders of the NWLB. Avery denied that his concern was engaged in war work, but President Roosevelt insisted that the strike affected the morale of the nation. In another case James Petrillo, head of the musicians' union, also defied the government, but was not punished. This resulted in much criticism of the administration's position.

increased from 4 to 6 per cent, but this was an insignificant burden compared with the imposition of surtaxes ranging from 13 per cent on the first $2000 of taxable income to 82 per cent on income exceeding $200,000. Nor was this all; income exceeding $624 in the case of a single person and a somewhat larger figure for one married was subjected to a 5 per cent "Victory tax" withheld by the employer.

These new rates represented a revolution in taxation. The number of people paying income taxes to the Federal government had been only four million in 1939 and seventeen million in 1941, but the direct taxes levied under the 1942 legislation were calculated to reach fifty million persons. Under the 1939 rates a married couple with no children having $3000 gross income had paid little if any income tax; under the 1941 rates such a couple paid about $109; under the 1942 rates the tax was $340.

Corporation taxes were also raised so that the maximum normal and surtax rates on the largest incomes totaled 40 per cent. In addition to this, excess profits were taxed at the rate of 90 per cent, subject, however, to certain postwar rebates to aid reconversion.

These taxes, plus either new or increased excise levies on liquor, beer, telephone service, travel tickets, amusements, and telegraph messages, greatly increased the revenues of the government, but they involved many annoyances and inconveniences to all concerned in tax matters. The income-tax forms had become almost impossibly complicated to fill out, the Treasury Department's problem of enforcement had become unmanageable, and the system of making these huge taxes payable on March 15 after the completion of the year on which the tax was levied threatened to result in wholesale defaults. As a much needed reform, Beardsley H. Ruml, a New York financial expert connected with both the Federal reserve bank and R. H. Macy and Company, became an evangelical proponent of a "pay-as-you-go" plan under which employers would withhold the Federal income tax from wages and salaries as they were paid. In order to put all taxpayers on a current basis, Ruml insisted that the government should forgive the 1942 tax. The latter proposal was unsatisfactory to the Roosevelt administration, but public demand led in June, 1943, to the passage of a Revenue Act which represented a modified version of the Ruml plan. Taxpayers were required to file returns for both 1942 and 1943 income, but 75 per cent of their tax for whichever year was smaller was forgiven. Beginning July 1, 1943, income-tax payments were put on a current basis; wage and salary owners had their taxes deducted and paid to the government at the source; those whose income was in other forms were obliged to estimate their income and make quarterly payments to the Treasury.

Despite these large taxes, net corporate income was at record heights as were also the individual incomes of many citizens. In view of this wartime prosperity, President Roosevelt asked early in 1944 for the imposition of additional taxes to the amount of $10,500,000,000. Wendell Willkie also urged higher taxes to curb inflation and lessen the burden of debt which would be left for the postwar generation. The majority of Congressmen believed, however, that the existing burdens were about as heavy as the country could bear. Although they consented to increase the excise levies and raise the excess profits tax to approximately 95 per cent, the new bill provided for only about $2,200,000,000 additional revenue, and the net result was considerably less because Congress had taken the opportunity to freeze the Social Security levy at 1 per cent instead of permitting it to jump to 2 as provided by earlier law. To show his strong disapproval of the Congressional action, the President took the unusual step of vetoing a revenue measure. Roosevelt's message was so strongly worded that the Democratic leader in the Upper House, Senator Alben Barkley of Kentucky, in an angry speech demanded that the veto be overriden. Barkley's advice was followed in a vote of 299 to 95 in the House and 72 to 14 in the Senate, while the rebellious leader was unanimously re-elected to the post from which he had resigned in protest over the President's message. Roosevelt attempted to smooth the ruffled feathers of the legislators by a telegram to Barkley in which he denied that he had intended to attack the integrity of Congress.

Even after the pay-as-you-go innovation, the income-tax structure was still extremely complicated. Protest against this led to the passage in May, 1944, of the Individual Income Tax Act, sometimes called the Tax Simplification Act. The new law relieved millions of taxpayers whose income was received exclusively from wages or salaries of the necessity of filing returns, it simplified the forms for other taxpayers, and merged the troublesome Victory Tax with the regular levies. The actual tax imposed on each size income remained about the same as before.

When tax burdens had been laid on the country as great as Congress believed could be borne, there still remained a huge deficit which had to be raised by borrowing. The public debt, which stood at $48,961,-000,000 on June 30, 1941, climbed to $258,682,000,000 by June 30, 1945. Every effort was made to borrow as much as possible from individual citizens. This was not essential to raise the money because the banks readily subscribed whatever sums were asked of them. But government borrowing from the banks was highly inflationary since it increased the amount of money in circulation. Bond purchases by individuals, on the other hand, decreased the volume of money available to bid up the price of goods. Thus this method constituted one of the best safeguards against inflation.

Eight great war-bond drives were organized. Thousands of volunteer solicitors conducted house-to-house canvasses. Banks, theaters, and department stores set up booths where bonds could be purchased, while the appeal to do so was repeated many times in the newspapers, in magazines, over the radio, and in the movies. A particularly effective technique was to induce wage earners and salaried workers to authorize their employers to make regular deductions from their pay checks for bond purchases—a method that had the special advantage of selling bonds even when the special drives were not being conducted. In the single month of April, 1945, twenty-five million persons bought $485,-000,000 worth of bonds in this way. The sale of "E" Bonds, the type particularly designed for the small investor, totaled about $40,000,-000,000 between May 1, 1941, and December 31, 1945.

One of the most interesting developments of the war years was the vast accumulation of savings of all types. Despite much easy spending of war earnings, the liquid savings of the American public are estimated to have reached $129,000,000,000 by the spring of 1945. This impulse to save helped to keep down prices during the war and created a backlog of purchasing power for the postwar years, but its unusual volume held at the same time inflationary dangers for the future.

CENSORSHIP AND INFORMATION

By executive order of December 19, 1941, President Roosevelt established the Office of Censorship with power to censor all communications passing between the United States and any foreign country. The task of censoring mail was a huge one, requiring the services of some ten thousand employees who deleted all mention of the movements of troops and ships, details of war production, descriptions of fortifications, air-raid preparations, or weather reports.

Within the country the newspapers and radio agreed to a system of voluntary censorship. Codes of wartime practices were prepared after consultation between government officials and representatives of the publishing and broadcasting industries. Unless it were given out by the appropriate government authorities, the newspapers and radio stations were asked not to reveal information regarding troop and ship movements, attacks by air upon the United States, airplanes' characteristics and activities, fortifications, production, weather, maps and photographs of any of the foregoing, and movements of the President or other high military or diplomatic officials. To act as Director of Censorship, Roosevelt appointed Byron Price, a veteran journalist and Associated Press executive. Price handled his delicate task in competent fashion and violations of the letter or spirit of the code were few.

It will be noted that the newspapers had been asked not to publish news that might involve military security unless it had been cleared with the proper authorities. This made the War and Navy Departments the real arbiters in most cases of what might or might not be released. Their tendency, particularly during the earlier months of American participation in the war, was to err on the side of overcaution with the result that censorship appeared to be sometimes used to shield the reading public from bad news—like the full truth about Pearl Harbor, or from any mention of military blunders—like the incident in which American gunfire shot down American paratroopers in the attack upon Sicily.

On June 13, 1942, partly as the result of pressure from writers and publishers, the Office of War Information (OWI) was established with Elmer Davis, widely respected as an essayist and radio commentator, as Director.[1] The OWI was authorized to utilize the press, radio, motion picture, and other facilities for the purpose of developing an informed and intelligent understanding, both at home and abroad, of the status and progress of the war, and of the war policies and aims of the government. It was given, moreover, extensive powers to coordinate the war informational activities of all Federal departments.

It was hoped that the Davis agency would make accessible larger rations of war news. Strict censorship policies by the War and Navy Departments, however, continued to defeat this end. The greatest success of OWI was achieved in the important field of propaganda. Despite useful work within the United States, OWI's domestic branch was largely liquidated in 1943 when Congress, suspicious that the agency would serve a political purpose during the presidential campaign the next year, cut its appropriations. But the foreign branch, engaged in propaganda in enemy and neutral countries, survived Congressional attacks and conducted an intensive program through all available media. Particularly notable were its short-wave radio activities. It operated 16

[1] An earlier agency, the Office of Facts and Figures (OFF), under the direction of Archibald MacLeish, had not had sufficient power to coordinate the informational material emanating from the various government bureaus.

transmitters and sent out 2700 programs weekly in 24 different languages. It discovered that the most effective propaganda in a news-starved world was straight factual material about war developments, American war production, and plans for postwar reconstruction. Unquestionably the weapon of psychological warfare undermined the enemy's will to resist and was especially effective in hastening the surrender of Italy.

DEALING WITH DISLOYALTY

On the whole, the war brought remarkably little interference with freedom of opinion in the United States. The President and Mrs. Roosevelt, the OPA, the OWI, and the various war administrations were subjected to frequent and violent criticism. Sometimes the attacks were mere partisanship, but on other occasions they represented honest points of difference. Often freedom of speech proved a source of positive democratic strength since it led to the improvement of weak points in the defense organization and the rectification of mistakes.

There was much less of the witch-hunting atmosphere than during World War I. Partly, this reflected the moderation and good judgment of Attorney General Biddle. Partly, it resulted from the circumstance that Communists and Socialists did not follow the extreme antiwar line that they had in 1917. The former, in fact, because of the German attack upon Soviet Russia, became the most outspoken group in the country in urging the subordination of every other end to the winning of the war. The Socialists were not so strongly prowar, but after Pearl Harbor they could hardly condemn the struggle as merely one of capitalist imperialism.

The administration did not attempt to jail radicals merely because they had unpopular economic or social philosophies; but it did proceed against certain individuals and groups whose activities threatened to interfere with the war effort by promoting racial hatred, encouraging evasion of military service, or disseminating enemy propaganda. Newspapers like Father Coughlin's *Social Justice* were barred from the mails, while George Sylvester Viereck, a paid Nazi agent, and various domestic fascists like William Dudley Pelley, George Christians, and Ralph Townsend were arrested, some of them receiving prison sentences under the espionage laws. But the government's most ambitious project—a mass sedition trial of twenty-eight pro-Nazis—miscarried. The death of the presiding judge after many weary weeks of court proceedings, enlivened principally by the antics of the defendants and their lawyers, resulted in a mistrial; the group never again came to trial on the conspiracy charge, although several of them were tried and punished on other grounds. Such individuals, however, were few in number and the country supported the war with greater unanimity than in any previous contest. The enemy made occasional efforts to land agents and saboteurs by submarine, but these were frustrated through the vigilance of the Federal Bureau of Investigation.

The so-called Dies Committee or the Special Committee to Investigate un-American Activities, first authorized by the House of Representatives in 1938, was active throughout the war. Its activities had the support of a majority of Congressmen and it received generous appropriations. Its supporters claimed for it important achievements in exposing subversive movements threatening national security, but the committee was under continual fire from liberals. Its chairman, Representative Martin Dies of Texas, was accused of being much more alive to the dangers of communism than of fascism, of applying the brand of Communist recklessly to every liberal or labor leader whom he disliked, and of specializing in driving the more advanced New Dealers from their government posts. Particularly criticized was Dies's attempt to silence Walter Winchell, the newspaper columnist and radio commentator, who had been vitriolic in his comments on Dies and other Congressmen whom Winchell considered profascist—like Hamilton Fish of New York, John Rankin of Mississippi, and Clare Hoffman of Michigan.

The most serious violation of civil liberties was the treatment of Japanese-Americans. Early in 1942 the army removed all persons of Japanese descent from three West Coast states and lodged them in relocation centers farther inland. This drastic step was justified on the contention that it was necessary to prevent spy activities and sabotage in an essential military zone. But two thirds of the 110,000 evacuees were citizens of the United States. The Supreme Court finally passed upon the legal issues involved in December, 1944, holding that the mass evacuation had been legal under the war powers of the President, but that American citizens against whom no charge had been filed and whose loyalty was not questioned could not be detained after removal from the military zone. Meantime, the War Department repealed its ban against the return of loyal evacuees to the coast, but certain elements of the public in the West bitterly opposed the return of the Japanese-Americans. Over the course of the next eighteen months, no less than fifty-nine acts of violence were committed in attempts to terrorize the returning evacuees. Although the majority of West Coast opinion condemned such tactics, many of the Japanese-Americans decided to find new homes in parts of the country where they would encounter less prejudice. The harsh treatment of this group was probably inevitable considering the shock of the Pearl Harbor attack and the revulsion against all things Japanese which followed. But it is only just to the Japanese-Americans to stress that 17,600 of them served with the United States armed services, that Japanese-American battle units had outstanding records in action, and that no Japanese-American was convicted of either sabotage or espionage on the mainland or in Hawaii during the war.

German and Italian groups were dealt with less rigorously. Citizens were not molested unless accused of specific acts of disloyalty. All enemy aliens over fourteen years of age, however, were required to register and to secure a "certificate of identification." They were barred from the Panama Canal Zone and other vital defense areas and ordered to surrender all firearms, ammunition, cameras, and short-wave radios in their possession. Alien enemies considered dangerous were interned; but only 1228 Germans and 232 Italians were so treated as contrasted with 2151 Japanese. By early 1944, most of the Italians had been released, but the German internees were kept under guard until the end of the war.

POLITICS AS USUAL

Unlike the unwritten British Constitution, the Constitution of the United States did not permit postponement of elections during wartime. To many observers this seemed unfortunate; political campaigns were regarded as intrusions upon the war effort, a dangerous democratic luxury during a compelling national emergency. On the other hand, elections in wartime had much to be said for them. They provided an important popular referendum on the civilian direction of the war. More important, freedom of political debate and honest elections gave impressive evidence of the democratic values which America was fighting to preserve.

The Congressional election of 1942 came at a dark moment of the war. For eleven months after Pearl Harbor the United States had been on the defensive and had suffered the humiliation of losing all her possessions in the western Pacific. On the home front civilians were undergoing the inconveniences of shortages and rationing, of rising prices and increased taxes, and of numerous bottlenecks in industry and transportation. Not yet had the war administrative machinery been properly coordinated nor had the best administrators been discovered through trial and error. Under the circumstances it was not surprising that the mid-term elections showed a strong antiadministration trend. Democratic strength in the House fell from 267 to 222, while the Republicans were rising from 162 to 209. In the Senate the Democrats fell from 66 seats to 57, while the Republicans rose from 28 to 38. Another casualty of the 1942 election was the famous independent, Senator George Norris of Nebraska, whose seat was captured by the conservative Republican, Kenneth S. Wherry.

The results of the election were actually more serious for the President than the statistics indicated. The dwindling Democratic majorities in both Houses gave the balance of power to conservative Southern Democrats, who often allied themselves with the Republicans. This coalition was no less determined than the New Deal Democrats to secure complete victory over the Axis. It accepted also the principle that the United States must support international machinery to maintain peace in the future. But on domestic issues the coalition was rebellious. The attacks upon the OPA and OWI have already been noted, as well as the Smith-Connally Act and the rejection of the administration's tax recommendations in 1944. Contending that they were no longer needed, such relief agencies as the Works Progress Administration, the Civilian Conservation Corps, and the National Youth Administration were liquidated. Only for the last of these agencies did the New Dealers put up a fight, asserting that it should be continued as a training program for the war industries; but the conservatives had their way. One of the most disturbing victories of the anti-New Deal coalition was achieved when they killed the National Resources Planning Board, an agency which had been trying to formulate a well-coordinated program for the postwar period. In the interests of national unity President Roosevelt announced that "Dr. New Deal" had been dismissed and that "Dr. Win-the-War" was now in charge, but this gesture of appeasement resulted principally in distressing the President's liberal supporters without reconciling the conservatives.

The Global War

WORLD WAR II WAS A GLOBAL WAR IN THE TRUEST SENSE OF THE WORD. Rival military forces faced each other in battle on the continents of Europe, Asia, Africa, and North America, as well as upon hundreds of islands in the Pacific. Naval encounters were fought on literally the seven seas. Destruction from the air was dealt every continent except South America. The number of men involved in actual combat reached the highest total in world history, as did also the number of civilians affected. The amount of property destroyed reached nearly astronomical figures. Considering the scope of this global contest, the following account of World War II will be primarily concerned with the major exploits of the American armed forces. Moreover, limitations of space will prevent a detailed study of the strategy of each phase. Instead, it will be the purpose to give a bird's-eye view of the events from the attack upon Pearl Harbor in early December, 1941, through the surrender of Japan in mid-August, 1945.

THE RIVAL FORCES

The major countries involved in this epic struggle were: on the Allied side, the United States, Great Britain, Russia, and China, with considerable help given by the Netherlands East Indies; on the Axis side, Germany, Italy, and Japan, with assistance from Hungary, Finland, Bulgaria, and Rumania. The combined Allied military strength in December, 1941, has been estimated at from 9,700,000 men to 15,700,000; that of the Axis at from 10,660,000 to 13,650,000. The Allied air power is said to have been between 12,100 and 15,300 planes to the Axis's 13,200 to 18,400. For the respective naval ships in operation or under construction, the estimate for the Allies was 1394, and for the Axis, 790.

In the beginning, the Axis had numerous advantages. Both in Europe and in Asia it was fighting along interior lines and nearer the home front; thus the supply lanes were shorter and the deficit in sea transportation facilities was not so sorely felt. Moreover, both Germany and Japan opened their attacks unexpectedly and, while they had been preparing for many years, their foes were largely unprepared. They were both able thereby to overrun large areas from which they obtained supplies which they needed to continue their war efforts. Their ruthless destruction of people and property tended to cower large sections, and the very speed and daring of their original onslaughts swept everything ahead.

The Allies, with their long lines of communication, were at a definite disadvantage. For example, the United States was approximately 3000 miles away from the European arena and more than twice as far as that from the Far Eastern. The problem of logistics had to be solved before the full American weight could be used to help the other Allies. Moreover, the speedy Japanese attacks of December, 1941, and the months immediately following deprived the Allies of numerous essential materials, such as rubber and tin, while the German advance conquered important agricultural, mineral, and oil areas.

What the Axis did not count upon, however, was the Allied will to win. The sneak attack upon Pearl Harbor, which almost destroyed the American Pacific fleet, did not break the American morale. Instead, the United States immediately began to mobilize its fighting and industrial strength to wipe out the stain. And England was able to withstand the terrible air *blitz* following the fall of France and show the stamina of a bulldog, while Russia survived the initial German attack and was starting to show its immense recuperative power. Through excellent cooperation, the United States, Britain, and Russia were gradually able to formulate definite plans for attack and, aided by the increasing supplies of men, money, and equipment which the United States was able to throw into the struggle, the Axis advantages were slowly but surely wiped away. Indeed, fighting along the interior line in the long run proved a disadvantage because the Allies were able to concentrate their full power upon the concentrated areas held by the enemy and because Axis supplies ran short in the long and furious contest.

A BLACK BEGINNING

In the Pacific theater the six months following Pearl Harbor were indeed dark days for the United States and its Allies. The Japanese swept forward quickly, aided by three important circumstances: (1) the American Pacific fleet had been largely put out of action on December 7, 1941; (2) the Allies had been concentrating principally on the European phase of the struggle; and (3) the distance of the Allies from the scene of conflict made it difficult for them to send men and supplies quickly enough to stem the Japanese advance. Consequently, before the end of 1941 the Japanese had taken Thailand, moved into Malaya and seized Hongkong on the Asiatic mainland, had captured Guam, Wake, and the northern Gilbert Islands, and had made several landings in the Philippines. Moreover, during the Malayan campaign, they had dealt another disastrous blow at Allied seapower by sinking two powerful British warships, the *Prince of Wales* and the *Repulse*, with bombs and torpedoes dropped from land-based planes.

January, 1942, witnessed additional Japanese victories. They moved closer to Burma on the west, they pushed deeper into the Philippines where they seized Manila and the important naval base of Cavite, and they began their invasion of the rich and strategic Netherlands East Indies. The Americans and their Allies were beginning to strike back, however, as American troops were arriving in Australia and occupying the Fiji Islands to begin the formation of a ring through which the Japanese could not penetrate. A sharp blow was struck at a Japanese transport fleet in the Strait of Macassar, but without permanently stopping the enemy advance into Borneo.

The following month brought more bad news to the Allies. On February 15 the great naval base at Singapore fell in the face of bold and enterprising Japanese maneuvers that brought them through the vast jungles of Malaya to attack the base from the rear. Furthermore, the Allied hope of holding the remainder of the Dutch East Indies faded when their fleet lost the battle of the Java Sea which lasted from February 27 through March 1. Batavia and Java fell before the middle of March and Japanese landings were made in the Solomons. On the continent of Asia the enemy seized Rangoon, the Burmese capital, thus threatening the vital supply route to China.

The American defense was improving and the counterattacks were starting to take more definite form by this time. The navy, under the command of Admiral Chester W. Nimitz ably assisted by Vice Admiral William F. Halsey, Jr., was beginning to strike back. Task forces with carrier planes had already raided the Marshalls, Gilberts, Wake, and Marcus, as well as numerous Japanese occupied bases in New Guinea. The army, in charge of General Douglas MacArthur, was building up a base in Australia.

Yet the worst news of all was soon to come. Americans had been watching the desperate battles put up in the Philippines by the outnumbered American and Filipino troops.[1] The multipronged Japanese invasions which had opened in December, 1941, could not be stemmed and the enemy control of the seas prevented reinforcements and supplies from reaching the hard-pressed defenders. On Christmas Day MacArthur declared Manila an open city to save the more than 600,000 civilians from attack, but two days later the Japanese disregarded the proclamation by staging a disastrous bombing. On January 2, 1942, the city fell, as well as the near-by naval base of Cavite. The Americans retreated to the Bataan Peninsula where they put up an historic defense in the face of great odds. Although constantly pounded from land and air they held out day after day. Help could not get through to reach the beleaguered men. President Roosevelt, believing that defeat could not be prevented, ordered MacArthur to leave for Australia, which he reached on March 15, and General Jonathan Wainwright assumed command of what remained of the American forces. On April 9 Bataan finally fell, but those who could escaped to the island of Corregidor. Then there started another round-the-clock bombing until the occupants of the Rock, as the Corregidor fortress was called, worn out by sleeplessness, suffering from malaria for which no quinine was available, and weakened by scarcity of food, had to give up on May 6, thereby bringing organized resistance in the Philippines to an end. Many of the more than thirty thousand troops and a similar number of civilians who were captured perished during the infamous "death march" of Bataan. The heroic defense of both Bataan and Corregidor was not in vain, however, because it upset the Japanese timetable and gave the Allies a valuable breathing spell which was used to good advantage in organizing the outer defense ring to check the Japanese advance. But even while the Philippines were being conquered, Lashio, a key point on the Burma Road, fell into Japanese hands, as well as important bases closer to Australia.

There were a few bright spots in the picture for the Allies. On April 15, 1942, General James Doolittle and his band of daring aviators took off from the deck of the *Hornet*—referred to by Roosevelt as Shangri-La—and bombed the city of Tokyo.[2] Three weeks later an American squadron prevented Japan from breaking the line of com-

[1] MacArthur had been in the Philippines since the middle 1930's building up the Filipino armed forces. When the war clouds began to gather, President Roosevelt placed him in command of a joint American-Filipino army. Although MacArthur did an excellent job, the troops were not sufficiently numerous nor well enough equipped to cope for long with the larger Japanese forces.

[2] This raid was more of a morale booster than anything else. Actually it was a bad maneuver from the tactical point of view because it could not establish anything and served only to make the Japanese strengthen their air defenses.

munication to Australia by winning the battle of the Coral Sea.[1] On May 5 British troops landed on Madagascar, which they eventually subdued, to end Japanese expansion in that direction.

On the whole, however, the period up to the beginning of June, 1942, was one of important Japanese victories. The enemy had gained control of Thailand, Malaya, Burma, the Dutch East Indies, the islands of the western Pacific, and was threatening Australia. And in so doing the Japanese had gained not only important strategic advantages, but immensely valuable economic resources—petroleum, rubber, and tin. Despite the darkness of the picture, the Allies seemed confident that they could hold the Japanese advance where it then was and, with growing military, naval, and air strength, could start hitting back. Consequently, the attention of the Allies shifted to the European and African theaters and the effort to crush Hitler and Mussolini.

THE INVASION AND CONQUEST OF AFRICA

At a White House conference between President Roosevelt and Prime Minister Churchill toward the close of December, 1941, it was agreed that the major Anglo-American objective should be the defeat of the European members of the Axis. The first prominent battleground for American troops was in North Africa, where the British and the Italo-German forces had been struggling for supremacy since the summer of 1940. Neither side had gained any permanent advantage as the two rival forces took turns in driving each other along the northern coast.

This African arena was of vast importance to the Allies. Control of it meant the maintenance of British domination of the Mediterranean and the lifeline to India and the Far East. To the United States victory was important because German occupation of the west coast and of Dakar in particular would bring the Axis within 1600 miles of Brazil to threaten the Western Hemisphere. Moreover, an Allied victory would pave the way for an invasion of the European fortress from the south.

The plans for an Allied invasion were only in the formative stage when alarming news arrived on June 21, 1942, that General Erwin Rommel's Afrika Korps had captured the important center of Tobruk and had swept on to a position approximately 50 miles from Alexandria. It seemed as though nothing could save Egypt and the Suez Canal from falling into Axis hands. But the victory-shouting Germans did not

---

[1] In this battle, lasting from May 4 to May 8, the United States lost the carrier *Lexington* and the *Yorktown* was badly hit, but several large Japanese ships were sunk.

count upon the cooperation which followed. General Bernard Montgomery and his British Eighth Army dug in at El Alamein to hold the line while reinforcements were pouring in. Australian troops, American planes and heavier tanks (the General Sherman), and other additional equipment arrived in time, despite the difficult problem of distance.

On October 23, 1942, Montgomery's men opened the counterattack that was to drive the enemy back and virtually destroy the Italian army in Africa, which the Germans made no effort to save. Yet the Montgomery offensive was but one arm of the pincer movement in this final campaign. Roosevelt and Churchill had been conferring in Washington when the gloomy news of the fall of Tobruk reached them. Then and there they started laying plans for an Anglo-American invasion of Africa from the northwest calculated to hem in the Axis troops and force their surrender.

The first step in the invasion plans followed shortly after that conference was over. American agents in Africa began negotiations with several French officers to loosen them from Vichy ties and efforts were also made to deal with the anti-Vichy leaders. In mid-October, 1942, General Mark Clark and a group of Commandos landed secretly on the North African coast to complete arrangements for the actual invasion without French interference.

Finally, on November 8, an armada of British and American ships, consisting of 500 transports convoyed by 350 naval ships of various types, landed some 400,000 men at Casablanca, Oran, and Algiers. Under the command of General Dwight D. (Ike) Eisenhower, the invaders faced some opposition from both Germans and French, but Algiers fell the first day, Oran the second, and Casablanca the third. The surrender of most of the French forces followed speedily, due in large part to the fact that Admiral Jean Darlan, hitherto of the Vichy regime, fell into American hands early in the invasion and agreed to give the "cease fire" order. Despite a good deal of criticism, Eisenhower appointed Darlan as political head of the occupied territories.[1] Dakar gave up before the end of the month, thereby ending the potential menace against the Western Hemisphere.

The primary objective of the invasion, however, was to pinch off the Rommel forces in North Africa. Therefore the Allied troops which had landed at Algiers immediately opened their eastward drive into

[1] Many Frenchmen were angered by the Allied attacks upon the French army and fleet, and especially by the destruction of the *Jean Bart*. On the other hand, the eventual collaboration of the French leaders in Africa with the invaders led the Reich to occupy the remainder of France. The French fleet at Toulon, however, was largely scuttled by patriots to prevent the ships from falling into German hands.

Tunisia with the hope of seizing Bizerte and Tunis, with their important naval and air installations. They were beaten to these goals by the Germans, however, who had overcome the shock of the invasion by this time and were speeding troops by air from Europe to rescue the situation. This German opposition, plus the deep mud, held up the Allied advance for several months. Meantime, Montgomery was rolling along swiftly from the east and finally in January, 1943, forced the Afrika Korps into Tunisia, where the enemy found protection behind the Mareth Line. General Henri Giraud, who had succeeded Darlan after the latter's assassination, gave additional help to the Allied cause when an army of Fighting French pushed northward from Lake Chad to join the British and Americans.

Yet victory was not easy. In February the Germans tried to break out of the Tunisian trap. They struck suddenly at the Americans, forcing them back through Faid Pass, and then won the bloody battle of Kasserine Pass, helped by their heavier tanks. Fortunately there was no complete break-through, but in their counterattack the Germans won back nearly 4000 square miles of territory and drove the Americans back into Algeria. Despite these victories, Rommel was unable to cut off Americans from the British forces in the north.

The American defeat was partially compensated by the fact that the troops had received their first real baptism of fire and, although compelled to retreat, had not broken. Moreover, as the Chief of Staff, General Marshall, said, the leaders realized that a mistake had been made in training too many men for mechanical warfare and not enough for the infantry. Throughout February, 1943, the American army was regrouped and reinforcements and additional equipment arrived. Then toward the close of the month the attack against Rommel opened again. Kasserine Pass was regained after another bitter struggle. The town of Gafsa fell into Allied hands by March 15, while on the east the Mareth Line crumbled to enable the British to seize Sfax and Sousse. The Afrika Korps was forced into the so-called Tunis-Bizerte pocket where it united with the German troops under General Jurgen von Arnim.

Once in this pocket it was but a question of time before the Germans had to surrender. American bombers pounded the steadily diminishing trap and at the same time prevented German transports from carrying away more than a few of the beleaguered men. Allied artillery from land and sea smashed at the defenses, while the infantry infiltrated the enemy lines. Yet the Germans made the most of the hills and other natural fortifications of the region. Not until the end of April were there signs of a break as the combined American, British, and French

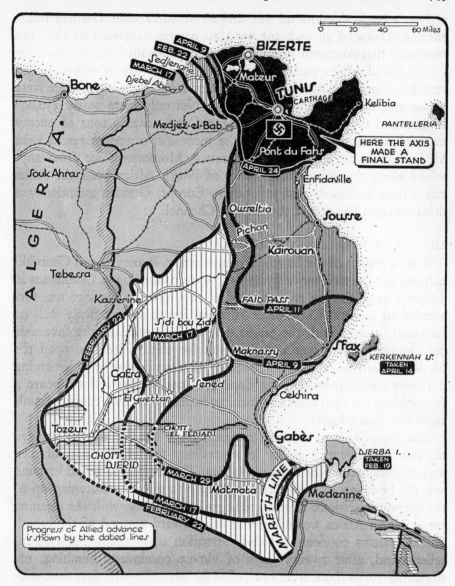

Battle for Tunisia. (From Francis Brown, *The War in Maps*. By permission of Oxford University Press, New York.)

divisions redoubled their efforts. On May 3 the Americans captured Mateur, thus severing connections between Tunis and Bizerte. Finally, four days later, the British First Army stormed into Tunis and the American Second Corps under General Omar Bradley, with the assistance of the French, compelled the surrender of Bizerte. Those victories, gained through full cooperation among the three Allied armies and their respective ground, sea, and air arms, brought German resistance in Africa to an end, for on May 9 what remained of the Axis troops on that continent surrendered unconditionally.

The fall of Africa was the first great Allied victory in which Americans participated. Although the cost in men had been high—there were 70,000 casualties—the results justified it. Not only were nearly 350,000 Italians and Germans killed or captured and 200,000 tons of enemy material seized or destroyed, but the successful campaign rescued the Mediterranean lifeline from Axis control. Moreover, since from anywhere along the thousands of miles of North Africa coast the Allies might open an assault against southern Europe, German attention was diverted from Russia and the English Channel.

THE INVASION OF SICILY AND ITALY

In anticipation of the North African victory, Roosevelt and Churchill mapped out the next move while they were conferring at Casablanca in January, 1943. On the twenty-third of that month a message was forwarded to General Eisenhower "that an attack against Sicily will be launched in 1943 with the target date as the period of the favorable July moon." There was a dual reason for this project: to open the Mediterranean to Allied commerce of all descriptions, thereby saving a 12,000 mile trip around the Cape of Good Hope; and to secure a foothold on the European continent preparatory to the eventual assault upon the Reich itself.

The completion of the plan required time, but Eisenhower showed marked administrative ability in supervising the mobilization of men and supplies needed for the undertaking. The prelude to actual invasion was the bombing of both Sicily and Italy to start the softening-up of the enemy possessions. This move began in mid-May while the cleaning up of North Africa was still going on. Toward the end of the month Allied aviators concentrated their attention upon the island of Pantelleria and, after twenty days of almost continuous bombing, ten thousand troops there were compelled to surrender—the first time such a victory was achieved through air power and without actual invasion. Shortly after, the islands of Lampedusa, Linosa, and Lampione were also conquered to end a menace to Allied shipping in the Mediterranean and to provide steppingstones to Sicily.

It was on July 9, 1943, that the invasion of Sicily began with the landing of American airborne troops, followed quickly by the debarkation of more than 150,000 American, British, Canadian, and French infantry, artillery, and tank groups which had been transported in

2500 vessels of all sizes and descriptions. The two main forces were the British Eighth Army under Montgomery and the American Seventh under General George S. Patton, Jr., which had gained fame in the African campaign. Patton was a fearless and rough-tongued leader who was referred to as Old Blood and Guts; he was, moreover, an expert in tank warfare. In thirty-eight days of vicious fighting, during which Allied cooperation in all branches was again shown, the island was over-run and the enemy forced to surrender. A feature of the victory was the strategy of General Patton in using his tanks to divide the opposition. Total Allied losses were approximately 25,000; that of the Germans and Italians, more than 150,000—or nearly half the number in Sicily at the time of the original attack.

Even while the Sicilian campaign was being fought the Allies were pounding the Italian peninsula from sea and air, directing their bombs and shells toward ports and military installations. Even Rome itself did not escape, for on July 19 more than five hundred American bombers dropped 1000 tons of missiles on railroad yards and airfields within the city.[1] These numerous attacks made Italian leaders realize that their country was the next object of invasion. An appeal to Hitler for more German support was turned down. Indeed the Fuehrer had insisted that the Italian boot as far north as the Po River should be evacuated by the Axis. Mussolini announced that he was forced to give in to Hitler's wish. This was too much for even the Fascist Grand Council to bear, so the members turned against Il Duce by a vote of nineteen to six. Consequently, on the evening of July 25, 1943, King Victor Emmanuel announced Mussolini's resignation and the appointment of Marshal Pietro Badoglio as Prime Minister. Although Badoglio proclaimed that Italy would continue fighting, the Italian populace was now demanding peace.

The continued pounding of Italy by Allied airmen brought increased grumbling from the inhabitants. This fact, plus the realization that the success of the Sicilian campaign would soon result in the invasion of Italy proper, led Badoglio to change his mind. He made secret contact with General Eisenhower for an Italian surrender, which he hoped could be consummated without Hitler's knowledge. Eisenhower had

---

[1] Up to this time every effort had been made to spare attacks on Rome because of its religious importance. Now, however, the Allies realized it had become vital as a military and communications center. When the pleas to have it declared an open city were turned down by the Italians and Germans, the fliers were rigidly briefed so that when they did attack they avoided Vatican City and destroyed practically no religious shrines. The Germans raised the cry of vandalism, ignoring what they themselves had done to churches in Allied countries.

instructions to accept only unconditional surrender, thereby making terms of the greatest advantage to the Allies. While the negotiations were being conducted, General Montgomery and his Eighth Army on September 3 moved across the Strait of Messina with the help of an air covering, secured a comparatively easy beachhead at Reggio Calabria on the toe of the Italian boot, and started northward.

This maneuver speeded the Italian decision to withdraw from the war, and on the same day an armistice was signed, with Eisenhower announcing the unconditional surrender on September 8.[1] Although Allied morale was considerably raised by this act which destroyed one member of the Axis, the material advantage was not great because German forces occupied most of Italy and continued to dispute the Allied invasion. On September 9, a second beachhead was established, this one by Americans and British under General Mark Clark, at Salerno, near Naples. The specific purpose was to seize the important base and port of Naples and to form subsequently a junction with Montgomery's men pushing along Calabria, thereby cutting off the Germans in southern Italy. It was easier said than done, however, because the enemy took full advantage of the natural fortifications and heavily mined roads to slow the Allied advance. Not until September 16 did the American Fifth and the British Eighth link up, and then most of the Germans had succeeded in escaping the trap. The following day a third invasion unit landed at Taranto on the Italian heel. Still the Germans refused to turn and run, so it was October 1 before Naples fell.

The surrender of that base, plus the Allied seizure of Sardinia and Corsica, were bitter blows to the enemy, but the Germans continued to maintain a stiff resistance. They were aided by the very severe winter of 1943–1944 and by the short battle line across the Italian peninsula which enabled them to concentrate their forces. Yet they were prevented from bringing all of their troops south from the Po River line through fear that General Patton, whose whereabouts was unknown, might strike at their rear. The Reich armies retreated slowly until they reached the Gustav Line, whose main stronghold was Cassino; there they held out for many weeks in spite of the sharp attacks of the Allies. During this stalemate General Eisenhower was called back to Britain

[1] Although the document was secret, subsequent events proved that the following must have been among its provisions: that Italy cease hostilities immediately and try to prevent Germany from using Italian equipment, etc., against the Allies; that all Allied prisoners in Italian hands be released at once; that the Italian fleet, merchant marine, and airfields be turned over to the Allies as quickly as possible; and that Corsica and other islands be made available for Allied operations. When Germany refused to evacuate Italy, the latter declared war on the Reich, October 13, 1943, and was recognized as a cobelligerent by the Allies, but was not granted Allied status.

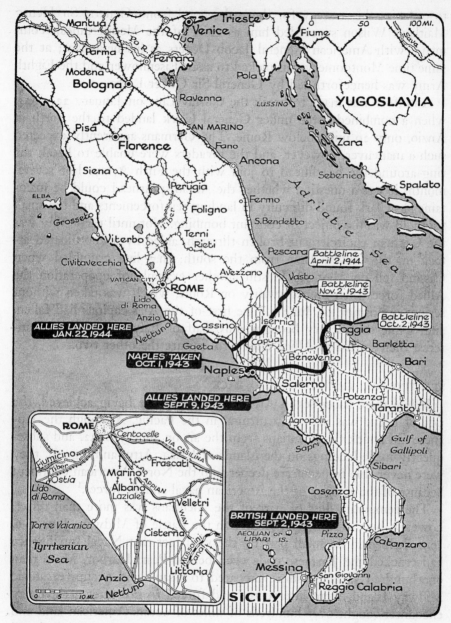

Invasion of Italy. (From Francis Brown, *The War in Maps.* By permission of Oxford University Press, New York.)

to organize the strategy for the real second front. General Sir Henry Maitland Wilson succeeded him as chief of the Mediterranean command, with American General Jacob Devers as his lieutenant; at the same time Montgomery was picked to assist Eisenhower and the Eighth Army was henceforth led by General Sir Oliver Leese.

An effort was made to break the Gustav Line on January 22, 1944, when a combined force under General Clark landed to the north at Anzio, only 20 miles below Rome. The Germans apparently expected such a maneuver, however, and the invaders were unable to break the ring around the beachhead to join with the Fifth Army. For several months it was a question whether the Anzio spearhead could be maintained as Clark found difficulty in landing reinforcements and the small foothold was the object of constant bombing. Not until early May was the German encirclement broken through, aided by a coordinated attack on the Gustav Line from the south; that line crumbled when Cassino fell on May 18. In still another example of cooperation the Allied forces then moved swiftly on Rome, which was taken without serious opposition on June 4. The first of the Axis capitals had fallen, and, while the victory brought only half of Italy under control, interest then shifted to Allied efforts to capture the other two.

STARTING ON THE LONG ROAD BACK

While these successes in Africa and Italy were being achieved, the tide of battle was definitely turning in the Pacific. Although the Japanese did attack the Aleutians from the air on June 3, 1942, and subsequently made landings on the islands of Kiska, Attu, and Agattu, they were never able to penetrate deeper into the North American continent because of the activity of the American naval and air forces.[1]

The temporary loss of part of the Aleutians was more than offset, however, by the American victory in the Battle of Midway, June 3–6, 1942, helped in no small part by the vital fact that Naval Intelligence had cracked the Japanese code even before Pearl Harbor. More than one hundred Japanese ships, prepared to assault and occupy strategic Midway Island, were intercepted and forced to flee after a three-day encounter fought over hundreds of miles of ocean. American land and carrier-based bombers destroyed four Japanese carriers, one cruiser, and 258 planes. The American losses were the carrier *Yorktown*, the de-

[1] In May, 1943, the Americans began their real counterattack by seizing Attu and Agattu after a heavy bombardment. Thus Kiska was by-passed and the Japanese withdrew secretly in August just before the Americans were ready to stage their all-out move to drive the enemy out.

stroyer *Hammann*, and 150 planes. This battle was the most crippling defeat inflicted on the Japanese navy up to that time. Combined with previous losses, particularly in the Coral Sea disaster, Midway left the enemy too weak to match the ever-growing American armada in the Pacific. Consequently, plans to start toward Tokyo could be put into operation and, with the Japanese naval threat ended, more American strength could be released to the European theater.

The first great blow at Japanese conquests was delivered when the marines, under the command of General Alexander A. Vandegrift, opened their assaults upon the islands of Tulagi, Gavutu, and Guadalcanal of the Solomon group. The first two objectives were attained fairly quickly, but on Guadalcanal there was fierce resistance which was not wiped out until February 9, 1943. The struggle almost ended in disaster for the Americans at the very outset as the Japanese fleet made a surprise attack on the night of August 9 to sink three American and one Australian heavy cruisers in the Battle of Savo Island, an encounter which temporarily prevented needed Allied supplies from being landed. The marines were not to be denied, however, and they soon gained control of the island's main airstrip which was renamed "Henderson Field." This was of untold advantage because it enabled the Americans to put their airpower to good use in the subsequent phases of the struggle. In addition to the severe land and air fighting, in which casualties on both sides were high, there were fought four sea battles, culminating in the so-called Battle of Guadalcanal. In these several encounters the enemy lost at least forty-seven important ships, while they in turn sank the carriers *Wasp* and *Hornet*, together with numerous destroyers and cruisers. By eventually winning Guadalcanal, the Americans gained more than simply a small island in the Pacific. They learned valuable lessons in jungle fighting which were to serve in good stead later on; they learned as well the value of naval and air cooperation with invasion forces; they had a steppingstone for future conquests; and they had dealt additional grievous losses to the Japanese navy which could not be replaced.

During this long struggle over Guadalcanal, General MacArthur was striking at the enemy from another direction. The Japanese had gained control of the larger part of New Guinea and were moving uncomfortably close to Port Moresby, a potential jumping-off spot for the invasion of Australia. The Australians checked the advance on September 25 and opened a counterattack with the help of the American air forces which brought in supplies and prevented the enemy from landing reinforcements. American troops then added their strength and by the end of the year the two important bases of Gona and Buna had been recaptured by the Allies. It required another year of desperate fighting before New Guinea was effectively dominated.

Throughout that year of 1943 the American marines, fliers, and fleet were putting into practice the lessons learned at Guadalcanal. The most important encounters were the mopping up of the rest of the Solomons, the conquest of the Gilberts in November after the bloody battles of Makin and Tarawa (November 21–23), and the invasion of New Britain in December. Several naval battles were fought as well—Bismarck Sea (March 2–6), Kula Gulf (July 5–6, 12–13), and Vella Gulf (August 6–7)—in all of which the Japanese losses far exceeded the American.

By the end of 1943 the Americans had their invasion pattern well worked out. The first move was usually a series of reconnaissance flights to obtain pictures of the objectives. This was followed by a heavy air bombardment aimed at wrecking airfields and destroying military supplies and installations. Then the task force [1] would arrive on the scene and set the stage for the actual invasion by attacking the objective from sea and air to prevent the enemy from either escaping or sending in reinforcements and to wreck coastal defenses and sear the beaches. With preparations complete, the invasion forces, usually headed by marines, would be landed from new types of naval craft—such as landing-craft infantry and amphibious tractors, to be joined quickly by tanks. The navy stood off shore and planes flew overhead to shell and bomb ahead of the advancing troops.

It was this pattern of attack that won for the Americans in 1944 the Marshalls, where the initial campaign was directed against Kwajalein on January 31, the Admiralty Islands (February), the Mariannas (the struggle for Saipan lasted from June 15 to July 9), Guam (August-September)—to win back one of the important American islands—and Palau and Halmahera (September), the last Japanese bases in the open Pacific. Moreover, these conquests practically neutralized the prominent naval base at Truk, which was no longer able to obtain supplies as the Japanese communication lines were cut. The Japanese navy was being slowly but surely diminished in size, and what remained of it retired to home bases to prepare for the inevitable Allied attack upon Japan proper.[2] At the same time the Japanese air force was being whittled down, although it put up a strong resistance.

[1] The most famous was Task Force 58 under Admiral Marc Mitscher.
[2] The later conquests were aided by the first Philippine Sea victory (June 19–20) in which four Japanese carriers, three cruisers, three destroyers, one battleship, four tankers and more than four hundred planes were destroyed. In comparison, American losses under Admiral Spruance were negligible.

One of the most heartening incidents of 1944 in the Pacific theater, however, came in October. The attacks on Palau and Halmahera had brought the Americans within several hundred miles of the Philippines. During the remainder of September and in the first weeks of October American fliers were regularly bombing and strafing the archipelago, and the navy was helping to sweep the sea of Japanese naval and merchant craft. Although the natural initial objective appeared to be the island of Mindoro, on October 19 MacArthur struck swiftly at Leyte in the central part of the Philippine chain. Several landings were quickly made and footholds secured; shortly afterward the principal airstrip fell into American hands. The American promise to return had been made good. In a desperate move to isolate the invaders, the Japanese brought up their fleet, only to suffer the greatest defeat in their naval history. In the second Philippine Sea engagement, Admiral Thomas Kinkaid, with his Seventh Fleet, and Admiral William Halsey, with his Third, succeeded in destroying or badly damaging approximately thirty ships of different sizes and classes during a running two-day battle (October 23–24). The announced American losses totaled only a fraction of that number. The Japanese disaster might not have been so great had they not divided their fleet and had not Kinkaid and Halsey shown remarkable initiative and daring.

Mopping up on Leyte proved slow work as typhoons, heavy rains, and resulting mud slowed up the American advance. Moreover, ten thousand Japanese reinforcements were brought to the island by the "Tokyo Express"—a large, speedy transport system. Consequently, it was not until Christmas time that the numerous prongs of the American invaders were able to close in on the enemy and bring its opposition to an end. Meantime, additional landings were made on Samar and Mindoro, while planes from Saipan and from carriers were blasting at Tokyo, Formosa, Okinawa, and Iwo Jima, and the American navy was cutting deeper into the communication lines between Japan and her outlying conquests.

With the opening of 1945 the combined American land, sea, and air arms were poised to complete the destruction of the enemy. On January 5 MacArthur's men landed at Lingayen Gulf on the island of Luzon and immediately started their push toward Manila, only 100 miles away. Aided by the navy, which thwarted the Tokyo Express, and the fliers who destroyed Japanese installations, the land forces captured the Philippine capital on February 5, followed within two weeks by the seizure of Bataan and Corregidor—aided by paratroops. Gradually the other islands of the archipelago were brought under American control and on July 5, 1945, MacArthur proclaimed that the Philippines were liberated and his campaign there was "virtually closed."

Other Allied maneuvers, however, endangered the Japanese homeland more directly than did the fall of the Philippines. For example, in the middle of February the invasion of the Bonins opened. The landing on Iwo Jima (February 19) brought fanatical resistance because the island was only slightly more than 700 miles from Tokyo. It was an essential objective for the Americans because it was a menace to the superfortresses on their way from the Mariannas to attack Japan. The marines gradually overcame the stubborn opposition, captured Mount Suribachi on February 23, and three weeks later (March 17) the complete conquest of the island was announced. The American casualties were high—approximately twenty thousand—definite evidence of the fury of the opposition. Furthermore, suicidal attacks by *kamikaze*[1] fliers damaged or sank many American naval craft.

Still more furious was the struggle for Okinawa in the Ryukyus, about halfway between Iwo and Japan. After a ten-day naval and air bombardment, General Simon Buckner's Tenth Army and some marine divisions made their simultaneous initial beachheads to open a contest that was to last for ten weeks. The Japanese troops were ordered not to surrender because the home government realized that its hope of escaping defeat was "anchored solely on Okinawa." In the face of this resistance, the Americans had to cut the enemy lines into several segments and defeat each before final victory was achieved on June 21. The losses on both sides were stupendous; for example the Japanese dead alone numbered more than one hundred thousand, while the American casualties neared eighty thousand. Moreover, *kamikaze* attacks sank thirty-three American ships and damaged forty-five more; aircraft destruction reached the astounding figure of at least three thousand Japanese planes and one thousand American. In the face of these losses there was a promising note: in spite of indoctrination and orders, nearly eight thousand Japanese surrendered. This was a definite sign that the enemy was starting to crack as the homeland was endangered.

On another Far Eastern front—the China-Burma-India—the tide was also turning. After the Americans under General Joseph Stilwell, along with British, Indian, and Chinese troops, had been driven out of Burma and into India in 1942, conditions were very black. Not only was the

---

[1] *Kamikaze* fliers were fanatical Japanese who flew their planes at terrifying speed directly at an objective, such as a ship, with the hope that in the resulting crash the objective would be destroyed, even though they themselves were killed. The losses from these attacks were great for American airmen, and gunners found it difficult to cope with such attacks.

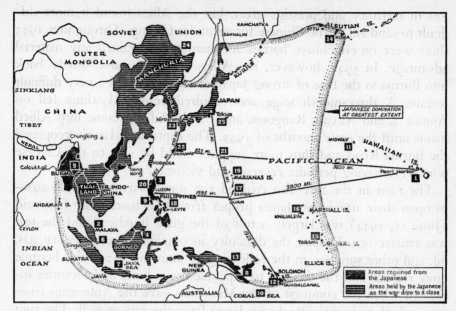

Twenty-Five Highlights in the History of the War with Japan. (Courtesy of the *New York Times*.)

1941   1 *Dec.* *7*—Japanese planes attack Pearl Harbor
  2 *Dec.* *8*—Malay campaign launched by Japanese
  3 *Dec.* *10*—Landings made on Luzon
  4 *Dec.* *22*—Borneo invasion begun

1942   5 *Jan.* *19*—Conquest of Burma begun
  6 *Feb.* *15*—Singapore falls to Japanese
  7 *Feb.* *27*—Allies routed in Battle of Java Sea
  8 *Mar.* *8*—First Japanese landings in New Guinea
  9 *May* *6*—Surrender of Corregidor
  10 *May* *4-8*—Japanese defeated in Battle of Coral Sea
  11 *June* *3-6*—Japanese turned back in Battle of Midway
  12 *Aug.* *7*—American forces land on Guadalcanal

1943   13 *Mar.* *5*—Japanese routed in Battle of Bismarck Sea
  14 *Aug.* *15*—Allied forces retake Kiska
  15 *Nov.* *20-24*—Tarawa and Makin Islands recaptured

1944   16 *Feb.* *1*—First Japanese territory invaded at Kwajalein
  17 *June* *14*—Invasion of Marianas begun
  18 *Oct.* *20-26*—Landings on Leyte, Battle of Leyte Gulf
  19 *Nov.* *24*—First B-29 raids from Marianas bases

1945   20 *Jan.* *9*—American forces land on Luzon
  21 *Feb.* *17*—Landing on Iwo Jima
  22 *April* *1*—Invasion of Okinawa begun
  23 *Aug.* *6*—First atomic bomb dropped on Hiroshima
  24 *Aug.* *9*—Russia invades Manchuria following war declaration
  25 *Aug.* *11*—Tokyo learns Allied answer to surrender offer

loss of territory and prestige great, but the Allies found it more difficult to send aid to the Chinese forces under Chiang. Throughout 1943 there were no conclusive battles and neither side gained any material advantage. In 1944, however, the Allies began to move slowly back into Burma in the face of strong Japanese resistance and a very difficult terrain. A three-month seige was required before Myitkina fell on August 3, and Akyab, Rangoon, and Lashio did not come into Allied hands until the early months of 1945. The capture of Lashio reopened the Burma Road and thus more supplies could be sent to the Chinese who were having periodic reverses and victories.[1]

The turn in the tide also enabled the superfortresses—the B–29's—to open their attacks on Japan proper from CBI bases. The first raid (June 15, 1944) was largely a test of the giant bombers, and the test was satisfactory. Despite the difficulty in obtaining the necessary gas, oil, and other supplies, in the following autumn the B–29 raids became quite regular and the damage to Japanese home bases and factories increased when the conquest of the Mariannas gave the Americans bases from which to launch attacks on Japan from the east as well. The ruin of Japanese industrial cities mounted with each passing month of 1945.[2] With her air force largely depleted, her navy forced under cover, her conquests—with the exception of those in China and Manchuria—almost entirely lost, with her homeland subjected to almost constant bombing, and with morale beginning to crack, Japan faced a dismal future, a future made darker by the fact that on April 5 Russia gave the necessary one-year notice for the cancellation of her neutrality pact with Japan —a prelude to war. Slightly more than a month later the news of the unconditional surrender of Germany reached Tokyo.

PREPARATIONS FOR D DAY

Events leading to that German disaster began with the opening of the long-awaited second front in Europe. Russia had insisted that such an operation be conducted since the entrance of the United States into the war. A second front, she asserted, was the only way to defeat Germany, and the sooner it was opened the better. Churchill urged delay, however, and it was not until Stalin, Roosevelt, and Churchill

[1] Until the reopening of the Burma Road, supplies had to be sent by way of the Ledo Road, largely constructed by American engineers, or by plane over the dangerous "hump" as the Himalayas were called by the fliers.

[2] Between November 24, 1944, and August 1, 1945, 311 bombing missions were conducted by the B–29's. Eighty-two industrial targets were hit in sixty-two cities, 158 square miles of urban industrial regions were burned, and more than eight million persons were rendered homeless. The major targets were Tokyo, Osaka, Nagoya, and Kobe. In addition, the fliers laid mines in forty-four sea areas.

met at Teheran in December, 1943, that agreement was reached. Then Eisenhower received the following message:

You will enter the continent of Europe and, in conjunction with the other Allied Nations, undertake operations aimed at the heart of Germany and the destruction of her armed forces.

The task of getting men, supplies, and transportation facilities ready for this gigantic operation was tremendous. Although the first American troops had arrived in North Ireland in January, 1942, most of them, together with those who landed in the ensuing months, had been used in the African and Italian campaigns. Thus, in the midsummer of 1943 there was only one American division (about 15,000 men) in the British Isles. From that time on, however, the influx was rapid, helped by the fact that the Mediterranean needs were not so great and the Japanese menace was dwindling. Consequently, transportation facilities were concentrated on building up the necessary stock piles for the continental invasion. By the first of June, 1944, the American army personnel in Britain numbered 1,533,000, and supplies were so abundant that within a month after landing each man was fully equipped.

The softening up of Germany through air bombardment had begun in 1942, but not until July, 1943, when Marshal Harris's Royal Air Force swept over Germany at night while General Eaker's American Eighth Air Force took over during the day, did round-the-clock attacks begin. With the passing months the number of raids, planes included in those raids, and the tonnage of missiles dropped increased greatly. For example, on June 6, 1944, the American strength stood at 3000 heavy bombers, and 6500 planes of other types; and in the thirty-three months after August, 1942, the Eighth Air Force rained 1,550,000 tons of bombs on the continent.

The main objectives of these raids were communications centers, munition plants, synthetic-oil factories, submarine pens, dams, and rocket-bomb stations. According to General Marshall, these attacks cut down German fuel supplies 95 per cent, and in the month of May, 1944 alone, some 900 locomotives and 16,000 freight cars were destroyed.

Up until February, 1944, the German *Luftwaffe* put up a desperate resistance. Then, however, in an effort to end the constant bombing, the German fliers were ordered to make an all-out attack against the invaders. During a week of raging battle over the industrial centers of Germany a large share of the German air fleet was destroyed. This fact, plus the dwindling German gasoline and oil reserves, made subsequent

Allied air attacks less dangerous, although the flak sent up from German ground guns still took its toll of Allied planes. Another boon to the softening-up process was the so-called shuttle bombing, in which planes from England continued on to occupied sections of Italy after bombing their objectives, thus making unnecessary a trip back over the targets, where the defense would be more active. A second shuttle run was instituted just before D Day between Italy and Russia, while shortly thereafter a third was begun between England and Russia.

D DAY

In addition to getting men, ships, and supplies ready and softening up the enemy, General Eisenhower and his staff had to consider where and when the beachhead should be established. After considerable study Normandy was selected as the site and June 5, 1944, as the most favorable time from the point of view of tide, wind, and moonlight—an essential for the airborne troops. An unexpected storm, however, caused a sudden change in plans after everything was in readiness and the second front actually opened a day late—on June 6. At 2 A.M. American and British airborne troops were landed to gain control of strategic areas inland from the invasion beaches. An aerial attack started about an hour later, followed at six o'clock by a naval bombardment. Then at six-thirty assault troops, carried in a variety of crafts, went ashore in the face of enemy fire, mines, barbed wire, and underwater entanglements. The American First Army, commanded by General Bradley, eventually secured beachheads in the Carentan-Bayeau area, while the British and Canadians under General Miles Dempsey found their footholds in the Bayeau-Caen region. Despite a determined enemy resistance, reinforcements piled ashore all day, along with tanks and other equipment. Within twenty-four hours the beachheads were secure, and the greatest amphibious operation in history was a success.

Again only cooperation could have achieved the result. The credit belongs equally to the staff of experts who planned the maneuver, the weather experts, those who found the proper place to attack, the navies which carried the men to the Normandy beaches and then stood by to protect them, the air forces which had been steadily pounding the interior and which helped to prevent the Germans from bringing up supplies, the airborne infantry which led the actual invasion, the divers who removed the undersea obstacles, the sappers who destroyed many of the mines, the supply and ordnance branches who helped to make everything ready, and the ordinary soldiers who resolutely carried out their assignments.

United States Troops Storming Normandy Beaches, D Day, 1944. (Brown Bros.)

The movement into the interior might have been speedy had the invaders been able to secure a large port where additional reinforcements of all types could have been landed quickly and easily. But due to stubborn enemy defense of Cherbourg, special docks or breakwaters, of which the most notable was Omaha Beach, had to be floated across the Channel, as substitutes. Although Cherbourg finally fell on June 27, it was so badly damaged by air attack and enemy explosives that it was of little use as a port of debarkation.

On July 5 Eisenhower attributed the slowness of the advance to three factors: the stubborn fighting of the Germany infantrymen; the nature of the countryside; and the bad weather which prevented the Allied air arm from attacking and engaging in reconnaissance work. By the end of July, however, conditions were brighter. An average of 30,000 troops were being landed daily, along with 30,000 tons of supplies. General Bradley was completing the organization of the armies under his command: the American First, headed by General Courtney Hodges, and the Third under General Patton. At the same time General Montgomery was consolidating the Canadian First under General Crerar and the British Second commanded by General Dempsey.

After a heavy bombardment, Bradley's so-called Central Group was finally able to break out of the beachhead before the end of the month by seizing St. Lo, while the Montgomery forces were taking the strongly held Caen. Then General Patton showed the initiative and daring for which he was famous. On August 2 his tank corps stormed through a breach at Avranches into Brittany, and from there he continued on his way toward Paris. Meantime, the Allies were protecting his flank by moving deeper inland; a pincers developed to form the Falaise pocket, in which approximately a hundred thousand of the enemy were captured. The stubborn defense of Panzer units prevented the pocket from closing completely, but the Germans who escaped through the narrow corridor fled from Normandy in confusion.

THE OVERRUNNING OF FRANCE

The harassed Germans then were forced to face another front in France. On August 15 General Alexander Patch's American Seventh Army, made up of Americans and French, effected a landing in the south against unexpectedly weak resistance. Marseilles, Cannes, and Toulon were occupied within two weeks after the beachhead was established, and then Patch moved northward to join up eventually with Patton, who had run roughshod through Chartres, Tours, Troyes, and numerous other cities to flank Paris.

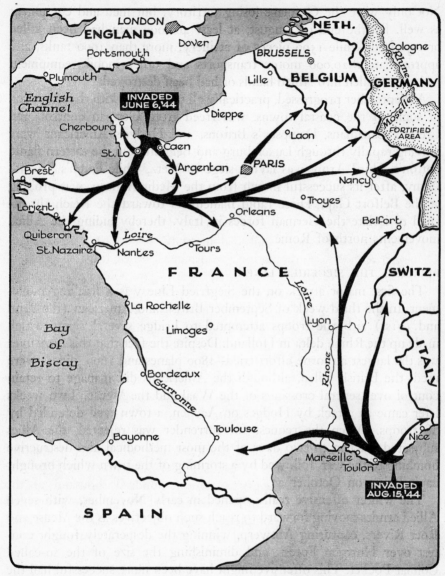

Battle of France. (From Francis Brown, *The War in Maps*. By permission of Oxford University Press, New York.)

While that junction was being effected, Bradley and Montgomery were rushing along the Seine to force the surrender of Paris on August 25, aided by the activities of two underground factions, the French Forces of the Interior (FFI) and the Maquis. Actually the fall of Paris in itself was not important, except to morale, because the Germans were retreating at such a fast rate that the city was soon far behind the lines.

Not only were the Germans losing territory, but men and equipment as well. By the end of August, at least 400,000 men had been killed or captured, while 1500 pieces of artillery, more than 1000 tanks, and approximately 20,000 motor transports and other mobile equipment had either fallen into Allied hands or had been destroyed.

As September progressed, practically all of France, with the exception of some of the coastal towns, was freed from German control, and Crerar's Canadians, Dempsey's Britons, and Hodge's Americans were moving rapidly through Luxemburg and Belgium. On the eastern flank, Patton's Third Army was laying siege to Metz, while Patch's Seventh Army, after its successful march from the Mediterranean, was probing at the Belfort Gap. These rapid maneuvers toward the Reich threatened to isolate the German forces in Italy, thereby aiding the Allied movements north of Rome.

PIERCING THE SIEGFRIED LINE

The first major attack on the Siegfried Line was a flanking movement. In the third week of September British and American (the 82nd and 101st) airborne troops attempted to bridge several rivers which made up the Rhine delta in Holland. Despite the fact that this maneuver was the largest airborne effort tried—2800 planes and 1600 gliders were used—the British failed, although the Americans did manage to retain control over several crossings of the Waal and the Meuse. Two weeks later came an attack by Hodges on Aachen, a town well defended by SS troops. When the request for surrender was rejected, the Allies subjected Aachen to two days of the most methodical and destructive bombing of the war, followed by a storming of the town which brought capitulation on October 21.

The winter offensive really opened in early November, with seven Allied armies moving forward to reach such objectives as the Meuse and Roer Rivers, capturing Antwerp, winning the desperately fought contest over Hurtgen Forest, and diminishing the size of the so-called Colmar Pocket. This offensive might have been more successful had the weather been better and the supply lines been able to keep up with the advancing troops. Moreover, Eisenhower was compelled to weaken some of the front line by putting in "green" divisions in order that the hammer blows might be continued against the main points of attack.

THE BATTLE OF THE BULGE

The Germans under General von Runstedt discovered one of these weak links and, aided by a heavy fog, massed twenty-four divisions along a 75-mile front between Trier and Monschau. On December 16 he suddenly counterattacked and broke through in an effort to reach the coast. For a time it appeared as though this move would be successful. The enemy overran 700 square miles of Belgian and Luxemburg territory and came within 4 miles of the Meuse before the Allies rallied. General Montgomery on the north prevented the bulge from widening in that direction, while Patton, after a forced march, used his Third Army to hold the southern flank. Providentially the 82nd and 101st airborne divisions were at Reims. They were speeded to the front lines to begin pinching the bulge.[1] By Christmas the worst danger was over as a change in the weather brought ideal flying conditions to enable the Allied airmen to cooperate with the ground troops in turning the tide. This Battle of Ardennes, better known as the Battle of the Bulge, proved to be the last important German offensive of the war. Although the enemy inflicted heavy losses in men and equipment, it lost still more. The German reserve strength was ebbing rapidly, the oil supply was dwindling, the communications were more and more disrupted as the Allied bombing grew in intensity, and the Russians were staging a great drive on their front.

THE SURRENDER OF GERMANY

As the year 1945 opened, it became apparent that Germany could not hold out much longer. The middle of January saw most of the

[1] The 101st gained fame by holding Bastogne against overwhelming odds. General McAuliffe refused to surrender the town, replying to the German request with the answer: "Nuts!" Eventually he was relieved by Patton's great dash. The 82nd, less publicized, held open the gap on the west to allow the entrapped divisions of the First Army to escape.

"Just as We Were about to Take a Snooze." (By Carlisle in the *New York Herald Tribune*.)

Ardennes Bulge wiped out, and by the end of the month the Westwall was thoroughly pierced. In February, Holland was largely in Allied hands and the attack on the Saar Basin opened. By early March four Allied armies were on the bank of the Rhine. Germany was losing her industrial regions—a blow just as important as the military defeats. Cologne fell to the First Army on March 6, and the following day the Allies enjoyed a bit of unexpected good luck when the undamaged Ludendorff Bridge across the Rhine at Remagen was captured to enable an easy Allied crossing. The Germans rushed reinforcements to minimize the Allied bridgehead, but in so doing made possible the Allied spanning of the river at other points.

As March progressed the attack upon the center of the Reich proceeded swiftly. City after city in the Ruhr capitulated, the Allied armies were linking up for the final drive and sending out spearheads which made the German confusion greater. Many of the enemy, usually the old men and boys who had been hastily recruited in defense of the Fatherland, surrendered—at the rate of more than twenty-five thousand a day. The Western front was moving ahead as rapidly as were the Russians from the east. The German pocket grew smaller and smaller as, during April, Hanover, Stuttgart, and numerous other key cities surrendered to the Allied *blitzkrieg* which surpassed that of the Germans in the early stages of the war. By the middle of the month the Anglo-American forces were not more than 50 miles from Berlin. A week later Patton's speedy tanks reached Czechoslovakia to cut the Austrian region from contact with the Reich capital, which was already under Russian fire. Another successful cut through the Reich was completed when the Russians and Americans joined at Torgau on the Elbe on April 27.

In Italy, too, the Germans were facing defeat. Although they had stubbornly contested the Allied drive northward from Rome and had held the Gothic Line along the Po for months, they could not stem the coordinated attack which began on April 11, 1945. The Italian people, sensing Allied victory, seized and executed Mussolini on April 29 before he could escape to Switzerland. The German troops could not get out through the Brenner Pass and on May 2 they surrendered unconditionally, along with the divisions in Austria which had been trapped by Patton's lunge.

It was on the same day, May 2, that Berlin, largely gutted by air attack, fires, and fighting, came into Russian hands. The day before, Admiral Karl Doenitz announced the suicide of Adolph Hitler, who

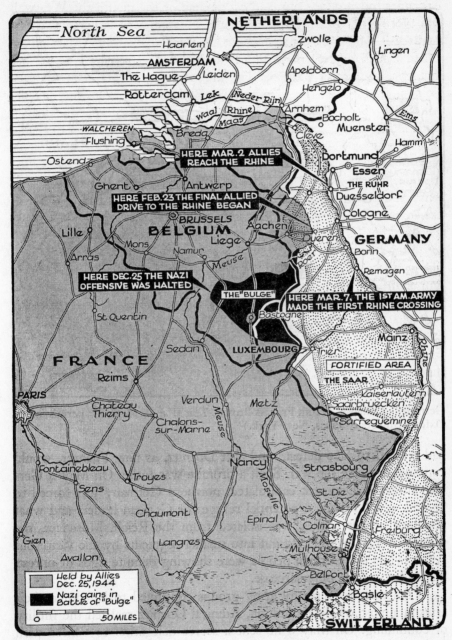

Battle of the Rhine. (From Francis Brown, *The War in Maps*. By permission of Oxford University Press, New York.)

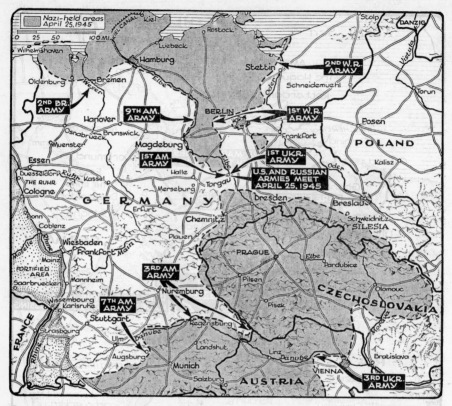

Germany's Collapse. (From Francis Brown, *The War in Maps*. By permission of Oxford University Press, New York.)

had refused to face defeat,[1] and that Doenitz, as new Fuehrer, would continue to wage the war. Such a promise was futile. On May 4 German forces in Denmark capitulated, northern Germany was forced to give in, and Norway, a potential refuge for German leaders and what remained of her armies, was isolated from the Reich. Moreover, the German forces were being cut into smaller segments by the victorious Allies, while the German people were showing definite signs of unrest. Surrender was the only surcease.

As the various Germany army groups continued to lay down their arms in almost wholesale fashion, Admiral Doenitz realized the futility of continuing. On May 6 he sent a secret delegation to confer with General Walter Bedell Smith, Eisenhower's Chief of Staff. The meeting was held at a little red schoolhouse in Reims. The Germans at first re-

---

[1] The circumstances surrounding Hitler's death are still a mystery. What evidence there is indicates that he committed suicide with his recent bride in Berlin. His body has never been identified, however, and many people still doubt his demise.

fused to agree to the unconditional surrender terms which the Allies insisted upon, but with the arrival of German Chief of Staff General Gustav Jodl early on the morning of May 7 (European time), they gave in and signed the Act of Military Surrender, witnessed by General Smith for the Supreme Allied Command and representatives of Russia and France.[1] The following day the formal surrender terms were concluded at Berlin with representatives of the Allied powers present, the terms becoming effective at 12:01 A.M. (European time) of May 9. The most important clause in the surrender document was:

> We . . . agree to unconditional capitulation of all our armed forces on land, sea and air, and also all forces at present under German command, to the high command of the Red Army and at the same time to the Allied Expeditionary Forces.

Although some fighting continued thereafter, particularly in the Breslau area, World War II was at an end as far as Germany was concerned. The news of the surrender was followed by celebrations in all parts of the Allied world. Yet in the United States in particular there was an undercurrent of sadness that President Roosevelt, who had died on April 12, could not witness the triumph for which he had worked so long and hard.

THE END OF THE AXIS: VICTORY OVER JAPAN

On July 26, 1945, the United States, Britain, and China sent a joint note to Japan threatening her with utter destruction unless she would surrender unconditionally. Although her home islands were facing increasingly disastrous and constant air attacks, although she had lost practically all of her conquests, and although she was virtually isolated by Allied naval power, her spokesman, Premier Suzuki, rejected the ultimatum on July 29.

Redoubled Allied attacks by land, sea, and air showed that the promise of destruction was no empty threat. When Japanese resistance continued, the Allies decided to play their ace—a new weapon of revolutionary significance. On August 6 a superfortress dropped an atomic bomb on Hiroshima. The explosive force of this bomb was at least the equivalent of 20,000 tons of TNT and it virtually destroyed the city. Scarcely had Japan recovered sufficiently to realize the implications of

---

[1] After signing the unconditional surrender document, Jodl is reported to have said: "With this signature the German people and armed forces are for better or worse delivered into the victors' hands. In this war, which has lasted more than five years, both have achieved and suffered more than perhaps any other people in the world."

this event than she faced another sharp blow; on August 8 Russia, adhering to the promise made to Britain and America at Yalta the previous February, informed Japan that the next day war would begin between the two countries. Soviet troops swiftly invaded Manchuria and Korea to conclude all possibility that Japanese troops on the Asiatic mainland could hold out. On that same fateful day for Japan (August 9) Nagasaki was destroyed by a second and deadlier atomic bomb, while B–29's ravaged the home islands from tip to tip.

Finally comprehending that the July 26 ultimatum was more than an idle gesture, on August 10 the Japanese government announced its willingness to start surrender negotiations, provided that Emperor Hirohito were allowed to keep his throne. In answer the Allies asserted that the emperor's position could not be guaranteed. He could continue on the throne only until the Allies fully occupied Japan and the unconditional surrender terms were fulfilled. Then there must be a free election under Allied supervision to determine the future leader and type of government. A three-day delay followed, caused in part by the fact that negotiations were conducted through Switzerland and the messages had to be translated. Finally, at 7 P.M. on August 14, President Truman announced to the American people by radio that Japan had accepted the Allied terms. The wild celebration which followed surpassed those of VE Day and Armistice Day, 1918. Five days later a Japanese delegation signed the preliminary surrender document at Manila, with General MacArthur acting for the victors. Then on September 2, aboard the American battleship *Missouri* anchored in Tokyo Bay, the formal surrender occurred.

These terms provided for the surrender of Japanese forces everywhere, with subsequent prompt demobilization and the turning over to the Allies—or the destruction—of all military supplies and equipment. Moreover, the emperor and the government were compelled to agree to obey all orders of the Allied Supreme Command which, under General MacArthur, would supervise the occupation of Japan in joint fashion. Provision was also made for the trial of war criminals, for the establishment of democratic institutions, and for the regulation of Japanese economy.

Although many of the Japanese divisions in outlying regions continued fighting for some time after September 2, to all intents and purposes World War II had ended. Lasting nearly six years, with the United States participating for three years and nine months, it was the greatest, the most widespread, the most destructive, and the most costly war in history. Victory was gained by the Allies in large part through co-

Japanese Envoys Sign Surrender Document on Battleship *Missouri*, Sept. 2, 1945.
(Brown Bros.)

operation, not only among themselves, but among the various branches of their respective services. Naval power played no small part in the Allied triumph for World War II was the greatest naval war in history; in the struggle for control of the Pacific the American navy was of paramount importance. Logistics also played a prominent role; the Allied ability to transport supplies many thousands of miles gradually offset the shorter lines of the Axis, and the members of the respective merchant marines deserve no less credit for ultimate victory than do those in the Allied armies, navies, and air forces.

It has been estimated that more than eighty million men were under arms at one time or another during the course of the war. Of these, fourteen million were killed and millions more wounded. Civilian populaces also suffered greatly from the direct and indirect effects of the struggle. Many communities were wiped out or badly damaged by air assault, V-bombs,[1] shell fire, fires, and infantry attack. Large industrial and agricultural areas were destroyed in both Europe and Asia. The estimated cost of the war in monetary terms reached nearly the trillion dollar mark.

As for the United States, the casualties were much greater than in World War I. The latest Army figures (through January 1, 1946) reveal that 307,554 were killed in action, died of other causes connected with military service, or were declared dead after having been missing a year; 1424 were still listed as missing; and 598,935 were wounded. The Navy report, including the marines and coast guard, listed 66,629 killed and 80,299 wounded. The total casualty list was around the 1,120,000 mark. The naval ship losses totaled 696 craft in all categories, and merchant ships sunk numbered 538. The monetary cost was around $300,000,000,000. Moreover, the United States was compelled to draw on future reserves of iron, tin, rubber, oil, wood, and numerous other commodities which could have been better used for the peacetime needs of present and future generations. Industry was diverted from civilian production and many a youth was retarded in his normal development by military service. Millions of Americans pondered whether victory was worth the cost. Defeat, they realized, would have cost eternally more. But merely to have escaped defeat was not enough. A just and lasting peace would be the only gain sufficiently precious to balance the great sacrifice.

[1] In 1944 and 1945 Germany launched V-1 and the more destructive and powerful V-2 rocket-robot bombs against England. Thousands of lives were lost and many homes destroyed by these missiles.

28

Tribulations of Truman

IN NOVEMBER, 1944, THE FIRST WARTIME PRESIDENTIAL ELECTION IN
the United States since 1864 was held. Despite signs of revived Republican strength, Roosevelt was able to win one more great electoral victory before his sudden death the following April. Reserved for his
successor, however, were the triumphs of VE and VJ Days. Reserved
also were the perplexities of a new postwar period—reminiscent in
many ways of the days of 1919 and 1920. Once again Congress rebelled
against continuance of executive domination, millions of soldiers sought
speedy return to America and to civilian life, businessmen clamored to
be free from the heavy hand of government regulation, labor struggled
to hold its wartime gains, and weary taxpayers urged relief from their
burdens. By no means, however, did history blindly repeat itself; indeed
on some issues—particularly those involving international relations—the
country's leaders displayed a determination to profit by the mistakes of
the earlier period.

THE ELECTION OF 1944

Wendell Willkie made a spirited fight to win a second Republican
nomination to the Presidency in 1944. He had become one of the country's most evangelical advocates of internationalism following a trip
around the world by air in 1942. His experiences in visiting Britain,
Russia, the Near and Middle East, and China made a powerful impression on him; he poured out his convictions in the short but persuasive
book, *One World*, which sold two million copies during the next two
years and headed the best seller list for sixteen consecutive weeks. On
domestic issues also he did some effective writing, impressing many who
had not voted for him in 1940 with the genuineness of his liberalism.
But Willkie's frankness and courage were in the end his undoing. He
staked everything on capturing the Wisconsin primary in April, 1944,

731

hoping to defeat isolationism in a traditional stronghold. He was badly beaten, however, not only by Governor Thomas E. Dewey of New York, but by other Republican aspirants as well. In the face of this setback, Willkie retired from the race despite the strong position he still held in public-opinion polls.

Meantime, Dewey's star rose steadily. His greatest asset was his record as a vote getter in the pivotal state of New York. His election as governor in 1942 was the first such Republican victory since 1920 and offered hope that he might be able to defeat Roosevelt in the latter's home state. The governor's other advantages were his youth, his reputation for efficiency, and the wide fame that he had won through his earlier success in prosecuting racketeers and corrupt politicians. Two other Republican governors, John Bricker of Ohio and Harold Stassen of Minnesota, were prominently mentioned for the nomination, but they were unable to overtake their New York rival.

In June, the National Convention, meeting in Chicago, nominated Governor Dewey on the first ballot and selected Governor Bricker as his running mate. The platform incorporated the so-called Mackinac Declaration agreed to by the party leaders the previous year. It called for "responsible participation by the United States in a postwar organization among sovereign nations to prevent military aggression and to obtain permanent peace with organized justice in the world." The platform further pledged the party not only to prosecute the war to total victory, but to bring home at the earliest possible time after the cessation of hostilities all members of the armed forces who did not have unexpired enlistments and who did not volunteer for further overseas duty. The party devoted itself "to reestablishing liberty at home," to taking the government out of competition with private industry, and to terminating rationing, price fixing, and all other emergency powers after the close of the war. It also went on record as opposing excessive centralization of government, wasteful spending, and arrogant bureaucracy, and as favoring a permanent Fair Employment Practices Commission, a strengthened and broadened social security system, and a constitutional amendment limiting the presidency to two terms.

Roosevelt's renomination for a fourth term by the Democrats was inevitable. Millions of citizens regarded the President's continuance in office as essential to prevent interruption of the war effort and to provide experienced leadership for the postwar period. From the standpoint of party expediency, moreover, it was unlikely that any other Democrat could win the November election. Serious anti-Roosevelt sentiment in the party was confined to Texas and certain other areas of the South where New Deal policies benefiting organized labor, tenant farmers, and Negroes were bitterly resented. Only one man, however, could have prevented the renomination of Roosevelt and that was Roosevelt himself. After he announced his willingness to run again on the eve of the Chicago Convention, the only question was how large the anti-Roosevelt vote would be. The answer was provided by the first ballot when Senator Harry Byrd of Virginia received 89 votes and James A. Farley 1 vote, while the President was rolling up a total of 1066.

The real fight was waged over the second place on the ticket. Vice-President Henry A. Wallace had not been the inconspicuous figure that tradition associated with that office. Instead, he had become a prominent public character through his vigorous championship of the rights of the underprivileged everywhere. In his widely read book, *The Century of the Common Man*, the Vice-President argued that enduring peace depended upon raising the standard of living throughout the world. This type of internationalism was distorted by Wallace's critics to mean that he advocated "a quart of milk for every Hottentot." In the columns of the opposition press he was portrayed as the embodiment of all that was most impractical and visionary in the New Deal. Yet the idealism which had aroused the hostility of conservatives won the enthusiastic support of many liberals. Whether Wallace should be renominated became a hotly debated issue within Democratic ranks.

Such was the opposition to Wallace among the Southern Democrats and the machine politicians of the North that his renomination could have been won only if Roosevelt had vigorously insisted upon it. This the President, striving for party harmony, refrained from doing. In a letter made public shortly before the convention, he testified to his admiration for Wallace and stated that, if he were a delegate, he would vote for Wallace; but he disclaimed any intention of dictating to the convention. The first choice of the party conservatives would have been War Mobilizer James F. Byrnes. But the CIO's hostility to this suggestion made the choice of some compromise candidate essential. The President suggested either Supreme Court Justice William O. Douglas or Senator Harry S. Truman of Missouri. With this help Senator Truman secured the nomination on the second ballot, but not until the incumbent Vice-President had made an impressive showing on the initial roll call. Paradoxically Wallace displayed greater political strength in defeat than he had in victory four years before.

The preamble of the platform read: "The Democratic party stands on its record in peace and in war. To speed victory, establish and maintain peace, and guarantee full employment and provide prosperity—this is its platform. We do not here detail scores of planks. We cite action." This was the keynote of the Democratic campaign. The country was asked to give the President a vote of confidence to continue the international and domestic policies with which he had become identified.

The contest was not lacking in bitterness. The most active workers in the Roosevelt cause were to be found in the Political Action Committee, organized by the CIO and supported by special contributions from union members, since the direct use of union funds was forbidden by the Smith-Connally Act. Astutely led by the veteran unionist, Sidney Hillman, the PAC waged a most energetic campaign. Its great success was based on effective publicity and house-to-house activity by thousands of enthusiastic amateurs working to get out the vote. But these aggressive tactics—so sharply different from the traditional ones of the AFL—were bitterly denounced by the Republicans. The PAC was branded as Communist and its efforts were asserted to be illegal. The fact that Roosevelt had ascertained the attitude of the PAC on Truman before giving the latter his endorsement was twisted to mean that the unionists had captured the Democratic party. "Clear it with Sidney" was the taunt repeatedly thrown against the administration, but the attack upon Hillman boomeranged to a certain extent since many of the foreign-born and Jewish voters felt that the Republicans were playing upon racial prejudice. Another hotly controverted issue was the soldier vote. The New Dealers contended for a simple Federal ballot; the Republicans in alliance with Southern Democrats defeated the proposal and left the matter to the states. Each side accused the other of trying to manipulate the situation for partisan advantage. Governor Dewey toured the country and attacked the administration in a series of vigorous speeches. He asserted that the government was in the hands of "tired old men" and called for a thorough "housecleaning." The President responded with much of his old-time fire, lashing out at his critics in one particularly aggressive speech before the Teamsters' Union in Washington.

The November election provided another Democratic triumph. Roosevelt carried 36 states and secured 432 electoral votes as against Dewey's 12 states and 99 electoral votes. The popular vote was much closer, with Roosevelt receiving 25,603,152 votes, Dewey, 22,006,616 [1] —the smallest margin of victory since 1916. The new Senate contained

---

[1] The minor party vote was insignificant. Thomas, Socialist, received 80,419; Watson, Prohibition, 74,758; Teichert, Socialist-Labor, 45,335.

57 Democrats, 38 Republicans, and 1 independent—the same division of strength as in the old, but the House received a reinforcement in the Democratic ranks—242 of the administration party being elected to 190 Republicans and 2 independents. Isolationism was strongly rebuked by the voters, both in the party primaries and in the November election. Senator Gerald Nye of North Dakota, Senator Bennett Clark of Missouri, Representative Hamilton Fish of New York, and Representative Stephen Day of Illinois all failed of reelection. The new Congress was also without the services of Martin Dies, who had decided—on the professed ground of ill-health—to give up his seat.

DEATH OF A WARRIOR

The fourth term was brief. On January 20, 1945, simple inauguration ceremonies appropriate to wartime were conducted on the White House grounds. "We have learned that we cannot live alone . . ." Roosevelt asserted in his inaugural address, "We have learned to be citizens of the world, members of the human community." Within a few days he embarked for the Crimea where he participated in the important Yalta Conference with Churchill and Stalin. Upon his return he appeared before Congress to explain some of the decisions taken there and to appeal for strong support for the forthcoming San Francisco Conference at which the Charter of the United Nations Organization would be drafted.

Meantime, a sharp controversy over domestic issues had been precipitated by the President's dismissal of the conservative Texan, Jesse Jones, from his post as Secretary of Commerce and the nomination of Henry Wallace to replace him. The whole conservative-liberal battle was reopened and in an aggravated form, because the post of Secretary of Commerce now had connected with it vast powers over the Reconstruction Finance Corporation and other Federal lending agencies. Inheritance of the whole kingdom over which Jesse Jones had reigned would give the ex-Vice-President a magnificent opportunity to push his own program for the achievement of full employment in the postwar economy. A bitter struggle was fought out in Congress,[1] resulting finally in neither side winning a clear decision. By the so-called George Bill the Secretary of Commerce was divested of all power over the Federal lending agencies, but, with his wings thus clipped, Wallace achieved confirmation as Secretary.

---

[1] The bitterness was accentuated by the belief in certain quarters that Jones was being punished for his supposed part in the Texas revolt and because Roosevelt admitted that Wallace was being rewarded for his loyalty in the 1944 campaign.

This, however, was the last important battle of the Rooseveltian period. The strain of war had levied a heavy toll on the President's health. He had spent his energies with characteristic prodigality during the presidential campaign, even driving in an open car through the rain in New York City as if to answer the charge that he was a tired old man. But the exertions of the fall, followed by the hard trip to Yalta, exhausted him and he went to Warm Springs, Georgia, where he had often renewed his strength in the past. There, resting and working in an environment which he loved, he was unexpectedly stricken with a cerebral hemorrhage on April 12, 1945, and died within a few hours. Released after his death was a speech he had been working upon during these last days; its closing words afforded an appropriate valedictory from the fallen war leader to the nation:

The only limit to our realization of tomorrow will be our doubts of today. Let us move forward with strong and active faith.

THE NEW TEAM

The death of Roosevelt brought to the White House a man of very different personality and background. Born on a Missouri farm on May 8, 1884, Harry S. Truman received no more than a high-school education before going to work. After holding minor clerical jobs in Kansas City, he returned to the farm where he continued to make his living until the United States became involved in World War I. Here he achieved his first minor distinction. His long service with the Missouri National Guard enabled him to secure a captaincy in the field artillery and a period of active command in France. He won commendation for his coolness under fire and returned a major. A postwar venture in the haberdashery business failed, but a modest start in politics was achieved in 1924 when he was elected judge of the Jackson County Court, an administrative board. He was defeated for reelection, but later returned to the court as presiding judge. In 1934 the notorious Kansas City boss, Tom Pendergast, engineered Truman's election as United States Senator. His first term at Washington was marked by loyalty to the New Deal but was otherwise undistinguished. After his reelection in 1940, however, Truman began to emerge as one of the most respected members of the Congress—in large part because of the energy and good sense which he displayed as chairman of the special committee to investigate the national defense program.

Like most vice-presidential candidates, Truman had been selected more for the political strength he would give to the party ticket than on the basis of his qualifications for the post of Chief Executive. When he suddenly assumed the highest position in the government, the country had need to appraise his qualities in a new perspective. There were some misgivings. Truman's close connection during his early career with Pendergast was disturbing, as was also his provincial background and limited acquaintance with broad issues. Yet friends pointed out that Truman's integrity had never been challenged, that he was a hard and earnest worker, and that he had a sincere desire to do the right thing. Perhaps his most impressive asset seemed to be his intimate friendships in Congress, which it was hoped would lead to closer cooperation between the executive and legislative branches than had obtained during the later years of the Roosevelt regime.

As has been customary under such circumstances, the new President promised to carry out the policies of his predecessor and requested the cabinet members to remain at their posts. Anti-New Dealers hoped that Truman would hold to this line of conduct only briefly and that as soon as comported with propriety he would move sharply to the right. In this they were doomed to disappointment. No abrupt repudiation of the New Deal ensued; indeed Truman's recommendations for legislation followed closely the program which had developed under Roosevelt. In the personnel of government, however, important changes were soon made. One cabinet change followed another until by the end of the year Secretary of the Navy Forrestal, Secretary of the In-

Truman at the Helm. (By Berryman in *The Evening Star*, Washington, D. C.)

terior Ickes, and Secretary of Commerce Wallace were the only hold-overs.[1] The most trusted advisers of the new President appeared to be Secretary of State Byrnes, Secretary of the Treasury Vinson, and John F. Snyder, a St. Louis banker whom Truman chose to head the important Office of War Mobilization and Reconversion (OWMR), the successor to OWM. Vinson and Snyder achieved additional prestige in June, 1946, when the former became Chief Justice of the United States after the death of Harlan Stone and the latter succeeded to the post of Secretary of the Treasury.

Although this initial shake-up was well received, some of Truman's later appointments encountered sharp criticism. The President was accused of being overgenerous in rewarding his former political associates from Missouri, while it was alleged that several of his other nominations were motivated more by gratitude for partisan services rendered than for merit. Such criticism came to a head in February and March, 1946, when President Truman asked the Senate to confirm the appointment of Edwin M. Pauley, a wealthy oil operator from California, as Under Secretary of the Navy. Pauley had been treasurer of the Democratic National Committee during the 1944 campaign, and opponents of his nomination accused him of attempting to use his influence to stop Federal litigation opposed to the interests of the California oil magnates. The star witness for the opposition was Secretary of the Interior Ickes. When the President supported Pauley and suggested that Ickes had been mistaken in his allegations, the veteran Secretary resigned, warning that another Teapot Dome affair might result were an oil man to be placed in a responsible post in the Navy Department. Convinced at last that Pauley could not be confirmed, Truman withdrew the nomination, whereupon the Senate Naval Affairs Committee affirmed their confidence in the Californian's integrity. The retirement of Ickes under these circumstances was a damaging blow to the administration, but the President retrieved some of his lost ground by appointing to the Interior post Julius A. Krug of Wisconsin, who had won wide respect for his effective work as successor to Donald Nelson on the War Production Board.

The death of Chief Justice Stone in May, 1946, posed a delicate problem for Truman. His first impulse was to elevate one of the other members of the Court to the head of the bench, but this proved im-

---

[1] James F. Byrnes of South Carolina became Secretary of State; Fred M. Vinson of Kentucky, Secretary of the Treasury; Robert P. Patterson of New York, Secretary of War; Tom A. Clark of Texas, Attorney General; Robert E. Hannegan of Missouri, Postmaster General; Clinton P. Anderson of New Mexico, Secretary of Agriculture; and Lewis P. Schwellenbach of Washington, Secretary of Labor.

Secretary of State Byrnes, President Truman, and Secretary of Commerce Wallace. (Acme.)

possible due to sharp personal rivalries among the judges. Although composed entirely of Roosevelt and Truman appointees, the Court was divided into warring factions. Black, Douglas, Murphy, and Rutledge belonged to the extreme liberal faction; Jackson, Frankfurter, and Burton were now counted as conservatives, while Reed occupied a middle position. President Truman sought to restore peace on the bench by appointing the able and genial Fred M. Vinson to the Chief Justiceship. The difficult problem which confronted the new head was illustrated when Justice Jackson took the unprecedented step of issuing a public statement sharply criticizing certain aspects of Justice Black's judicial conduct.

DEMOBILIZATION

The American soldier had fought with determination and courage not because he loved war, but because he hated it. No desire was stronger than to do the disagreeable job as quickly and efficiently as possible so that he might go back home. And waiting for him in almost every American household were lonely and anxious parents, a wife, or a sweetheart hoping impatiently for the war's end. Inevitably the defeat of the enemy first in Europe and then in the Pacific brought an overwhelming demand for as rapid and complete a demobilization as possible.

The first step toward meeting this was taken in May, 1945, just after VE Day. A point system for the discharge of enlisted men was announced under which such factors as length of service, time overseas, decorations and battle stars, and number of children were given a designated weight. For the time being, however, the continuance of the war in the Pacific meant that the proportion of men who could expect to be released was small. The unexpectedly rapid collapse of Japan made it possible to liberalize the system in September. The number of points necessary for discharge was reduced and men were mustered out at the rate of several hundred thousand a month. Under pressure from Congress and the public, the services speeded up demobilization until in the month of December, 1945, 1,112,000 were released from the army and 419,000 from the navy. Since the surrender of Germany there had been five million discharges from the army and one and a half million from the navy.

In January, 1946, however, a change of policy became necessary. The occupation of Germany, Austria, Italy, and Japan, as well as the garrisoning of bases throughout the world required large forces. With new enlistments lagging and draft boards following more lenient postwar policies, new personnel was not being secured in large enough numbers to permit demobilization to continue at so rapid a rate. The army therefore announced that the number of monthly discharges would be sharply curtailed and that men overseas might be required to wait until replacements were available even though they were eligible for release. The order resulted in serious demonstrations by bored and homesick soldiers in places as far removed as Manila, Yokohama, Vienna, and Frankfort. Congress was beset with letters and deputations from

"Bring-Daddy-Back-Home" clubs. The uproar quieted down after General Eisenhower, now Chief of Staff, clarified the army policy in appearances before Congressional committees and in a radio address to the nation. Although unable to promise that the discharge rate of December, 1945, could be continued, he did pledge that all men who had been in the army two years or more would be released by July 1, 1946. The General forbade mass demonstrations of the sort that had been occurring, but ordered officers overseas to listen to the complaints of individual soldiers. After this flare-up, demobilization proceeded with reasonable smoothness. Plans for July 1, 1946, called for an army of 1,550,000 men and a navy of 700,000, as compared with 8,300,000 and 4,054,000 in the two services on VE Day.

A continuance of the policy of discharging soldiers after twenty-four months of service would reduce the army by December, 1946, to half a million less than the 1,500,000 minimum considered necessary for America's immediate postwar commitments. To meet this situation President Truman asked that the draft be continued beyond May 15, 1946, when it was scheduled to expire. On this issue as on that of discharge Congress was sensitive to the outspoken hostility of millions of voters to conscription in peacetime. Not until the last minute did the legislators provide for an extension, and then for only forty-five days or until July 1. The measure exempted eighteen- and nineteen-year-olds as well as fathers.

A few days before this stopgap law expired, Congress finally agreed upon a bill continuing selective service for another year. Men from nineteen through forty-four were eligible for induction, but fathers and veterans who had served any time overseas or six months in the United States were exempted, while eighteen months was made the limit of service for draftees. The size of the army was fixed at 1,550,000 men until July 1, 1947, when it was to be reduced to 1,070,000; the size of the navy, including the marine corps, was fixed at 664,000. Separate legislation provided for pay increases at all ranks, the largest percentage raises being those accorded to privates and apprentice seamen whose monthly stipend was increased from $50 to $75. Enlistments increased with the result that a conscription "holiday" was declared from September, 1946, until the end of the year. The holiday was subsequently extended until March 31, 1947 when selective service was finally terminated.

A proposal widely supported by the nation during the war and recommended by both Presidents Roosevelt and Truman to Congress was for a permanent system of universal military training for all physically fit young men. After VJ Day, however, it became apparent that the proposal would have strong opposition, particularly from educators and clergymen.

RECONVERSION

The soaring national debt as well as the pressing need for civilian goods dictated a rapid reconversion of American industry from war to peace production. Victory in Europe permitted the first cutbacks, but wholesale reconversion did not commence until shortly after the surrender of Japan. Then the Army and the Navy promptly canceled $35,000,000,000 worth of war contracts, while 229 WPB controls were removed. The 150 which were retained dealt with commodities still critically scarce, like tin, rubber, lumber, paper pulp, and textiles. Reconversion Director Snyder announced that the Reconstruction Finance Corporation, in cooperation with commercial banks, was ready to make loans against canceled war contracts, finance plant reconversion or purchase, and make business loans to veterans. Sale of surplus government property was speedily organized. The extent of this operation is suggested by the fact that 252 factories and plants built by the government at a cost of nearly $1,500,000,000 were placed on sale, to say nothing of a tremendous quantity of machine tools, trucks, jeeps, and miscellaneous equipment of all types.

Both the harassed businessman and the individual wage earner welcomed a measure of relief from the wartime tax burden. In November, 1945, Congress passed a new revenue act estimated to reduce taxes by almost $6,000,000,000. All excess-profit levies were eliminated, while corporation income-tax rates were reduced from 6 to 4 per cent. Extending the $500 exemptions for taxpayers and dependents to normal as well as surtaxes released about twelve million individuals from the necessity of paying any income tax. For thirty-six million other individuals the tax burden, though still heavy, was reduced through the scaling down of surtax rates and a 5 per cent over-all reduction.

In October, 1945, Director Snyder had predicted many serious reconversion problems. Unemployment, he feared, would rise until there might be as many as eight million out of work by the next spring. This picture proved unnecessarily gloomy. In April, 1946, Snyder was able to report that unemployment caused by reconversion had apparently passed its peak and was down to about three million. Production of civilian goods had reached the rate of $150,000,000,000 a year—the highest in history, 18 per cent more than on VJ Day and 26 per cent more than in 1939.

For the time being there was an almost insatiable market. Savings of more than $140,000,000,000 were available for the purchase of new homes, new cars, new radios, more clothing, and more food. The principal postwar grievance was that production, though statistically impressive, still fell far short of demand. To purchase an automobile or an electrical appliance it was necessary to wait months after the order was placed, while the returned veteran found it no easy task to locate his new outfit of civilian clothes. Black markets continued to flourish in the scarce fields.

Particularly acute was the housing shortage. Millions found it necessary to purchase real estate at sharply inflated prices in order to secure shelter. New construction languished for many reasons, but particularly because of an acute lumber shortage. To the difficult post of Housing Expediter the President appointed Wilson Wyatt, who had attracted attention by his unusually efficient record as mayor of Louisville, Kentucky. In February, 1946, just five weeks after his appointment, Wyatt proposed a bold plan of attack. He called for the building of 1,200,000 homes in 1946 and 1,500,000 in 1947. He asked for the recruitment and training of a million and a half new workers in the building trades and requested Congress to appropriate $600,000,000 for subsidies to manufacturers of construction materials to keep costs down. The Patman Bill embodying these recommendations became law in April, 1946. Included in its provisions was the guaranty of a government market for as many as two hundred thousand prefabricated houses—an experiment that might have a profound influence on the future of the building industry. Congress also passed an emergency measure appropriating $253,727,000 for temporary homes—trailers and converted military barracks and war housing—to meet the desperate immediate needs of veterans and the families of men still in the services. Many of these homes were eventually located in the neighborhood of colleges and universities to house the veterans who had resumed their education under the GI Bill of Rights.

STRIKES

The greatest reconversion problem proved to be labor unrest—as might have been predicted either from the experience of 1919 and 1920 or by an analysis of the powerful forces being built up during the war years. Labor unions were stronger than ever before. In 1935 there had been less than four million union members; that number had risen to eleven million by 1941 and to fourteen and a half million by 1945. The workers had enjoyed heavy earnings during the war, largely through overtime pay and bonuses. The national average for factory workers increased from $23.19 weekly in 1939 to $47.16 in 1945. With the coming of peace, labor feared that its income would be sharply reduced unless it could force raises in hourly rates that would compensate for the loss of overtime. Such a reduction in take-home pay would be a serious blow at a time when prices were 33 per cent higher than in 1941 according to the Bureau of Labor Statistics. All over the country workers began to demand a raise of 30 per cent—which would give as much pay for forty hours of work as had been received for forty-eight hours during the war. Management pronounced this unreasonable and inflationary. Any such pay raise would throw business into the red unless price increases were made—and these were forbidden by OPA.

A warning of impending trouble came within a month after VJ Day when almost 500,000 workers became involved in local work stoppages. But it was obvious that the real crisis would come when the big unions pressed their demands against the country's major corporations. The Truman administration attempted to head off the storm by inducing industry to make voluntary wage increases and by convening a Labor-Management Conference at Washington during November, 1945, but all efforts to improve the machinery of collective bargaining failed.

On November 21, some 180,000 workers walked out of General Motors plants in twenty different states. The strike was fought out along far different lines than the bloody conflict of 1937. On labor's side there was no attempt to take possession of corporation property; on management's side there was no aggressive strikebreaking. It was a contest of attrition lasting 113 days. Spokesman for the workers was Walter Reuther, UAW vice-president, who employed new and ingenious tactics. The workers' demand for a 30 per cent raise in wages —from $1.12 to $1.46 per hour—was accompanied by an elaborate brief which argued that the corporation could make this concession without increasing prices on its products and still earn almost double the annual profit it had made during the 1935–1939 period. Reuther offered to reduce the wage demand if the corporation could prove that it could not be granted without a rise in prices. The company refused to permit investigation of its accounts and countered with an offer of a 10 per cent raise with a forty-five hour week—to raise the employees' take-home pay to 6 per cent above wartime levels. This exchange provided ample ammunition for a campaign to enlist the support of public opinion for the two sides. Pickets of the UAW stressed the failure of General Motors to open its books, while the company purchased advertising space to denounce Reuther's challenge to private enterprise.

The President intervened through the appointment of a fact-finding commission, but this body's recommendation of a wage increase of 19.5 cents an hour (a little over 17 per cent) was refused by the company. Not until March 13, 1946, was a settlement finally reached on the basis of an 18.5-cent pay raise and liberal vacation allowances. Comparable concessions had already been granted by Ford and Chrysler without strikes.

THE BULGE IN THE LINE

The General Motors strike was only one of the major struggles fought out early in 1946. Two hundred thousand workers employed by General Electric, Westinghouse, and the electrical division of General Motors struck on January 15; 263,000 employees of the meat-packing houses went out the next day; 750,000 steel workers walked out on the twentieth. Other serious contests were those involving the telephone and telegraph maintenance workers, the agricultural machinery employees, the New York City tugboat crews, and the employees of various municipal and private utility companies. By the last week in January approximately 1,650,000 men were on strike and the whole reconversion effort was threatened with paralysis. Congress began to talk in terms of drastic legislative remedies, while the Truman administration hunted feverishly for some magic formula that would dispel the conflict.

Greatest in size and seriousness for the whole economy was the tie-up in steel, which reduced output of that critical material to 89,000 tons a week as compared with the 88,000,000-ton rate achieved during the war. The issue had been defined clearly during the preceding fall when Philip Murray on behalf of the workers demanded a 25-cent-an-hour wage increase to hold pay at its wartime level. Benjamin F. Fairless, president of the United States Steel Corporation and spokesman for the entire industry in the wage negotiations, said that he would not discuss wage adjustments unless the government consented to a $7.00 per ton rise in the price of steel. President Truman sought to avert the strike by announcing that the government would permit a price increase of about $4.00 a ton if the industry would settle its labor controversy. When Murray and Fairless were unable to come to terms, the President then suggested an 18.5-cent-an-hour raise as a reasonable compromise. Murray accepted this recommendation, but Fairless rejected it and the strike became inevitable. Some 800 plants in 250 cities and 25 states were involved. There was little violence; as in the General Motors strike both sides appealed for the support of public opinion.

It was government price policy, however, that was the major factor involved. To what extent should prices be allowed to rise to enable management to pay higher wages and still make the amount of profit to which it thought itself entitled? Chester Bowles, head of OPA, was spokesman for a faction opposed to any major price changes. He contended that adequate wage increases could be made and industry still make a profit due to the repeal of the excess-profits tax and the assured market for a large volume of goods. Price raises would lead the country into a disastrous spiral of inflation. But another group of administration advisers, headed by Reconversion Director Snyder, advocated relaxation on the price line in order to stimulate a large volume of production, which they considered to be the best weapon against inflation. A compromise between these two points of view was embodied in the policy which President Truman announced on February 14. It was assumed that labor was entitled to wage increases to match the 33 per cent rise in the cost of living since January, 1941. If such raises would bring company earnings below their prewar averages, price increases would be permitted, but the wage raises would require the approval of the Wage Stabilization Board if they were to be used as the basis for price relief. As an assurance to the country that the price increases would be kept within strict bounds, the President elevated Bowles to the post of Economic Stabilizer and gave him the right of appeal directly to the White House in case of a conflict of policy with his nominal chief Snyder. Bowles's position at OPA was given to another advocate of rigid price control, Paul A. Porter, chairman of the Federal Communications Commission. Truman described his new policy as "a bulge in the line." He asked for Congressional cooperation in ensuring against any "break-through" by extending OPA for another year after its expiration date of June 30, 1946.

The new formula was first employed to settle the steel strike. The government permitted a $5.00 per ton price raise, whereupon the industry conceded the 18.5-cent pay increase which the President had recommended. The men returned to work on February 18. It was obvious, of course, that the higher price of steel would be reflected in the price of automobiles and thousands of other items made of the product. The new wage pattern was widely copied. The strikes in the electrical industry and elsewhere were settled and wage increases were made by many other companies after peaceful negotiation. The amount granted was usually from 18 to 20 cents an hour. Combined with the 15 per cent which most workers had received during the war under the

Little Steel formula, the total raise since 1941 approximated the 33 per cent increase in living costs during this period.

THE MAY CRISIS

The improved situation of March, 1946, was a false dawn. The Truman administration had still ahead its most difficult labor problems. The first of the new challenges came from that militant veteran, John L. Lewis. Enemies—of whom Lewis had a legion, within the labor movement as well as outside of it—asserted that the miners' chieftain was piqued by the gains which Philip Murray had won for the steelworkers and was eager to capture the center of the stage once again for himself. In January, 1946, Lewis brought his 600,000 mine workers back into the AFL and it was widely predicted that his shrewdness and ruthlessness would eventually result in his gaining leadership of the whole federation. But whatever part personal ambition may have played in motivating his conduct, Lewis was without doubt sincere in his desire to take advantage of a supreme opportunity to win better working conditions for one of the nation's most hazardous occupations.

Negotiations for a new bituminous contract to replace the one which would expire on March 31, 1946, broke down completely. Lewis postponed any discussion of wage rates while he fought to win from the operators stricter safety rules and contributions to a huge health and welfare fund to be administered exclusively by the union. He quoted impressive statistics to support his demands: according to the United States Bureau of Mines, 17,626 persons had been killed and 855,056 injured in mine accidents in 14 years, while insurance rates for miners were 277 per cent above standard. The fund, according to Lewis, would permit modern medical service, standardized hospitalization, and insurance at reasonable premiums. The operators objected, however, to turning over money which they estimated might run as high as $70,000,000 annually to the exclusive control of Lewis.

The deadlock had its inevitable result when 400,000 bituminous miners went out on strike on April 1. During the next six weeks the situation became steadily more serious as the country's stock pile approached the vanishing point. By early May steel output dropped to 57 per cent of capacity; Detroit's auto factories closed down, throwing 350,000 out of work; Chicago and other cities adopted "brown-out" restrictions to conserve electricity; the railroads curtailed their passenger service by 25 per cent; and the Office of Defense Transportation imposed a drastic freight embargo allowing only the most vital commodities to move. At last when a complete industrial shutdown threatened, Lewis relaxed his pressure and sent the miners back to work on May 13 for a twelve-day truce.

By this adroit move Lewis sidestepped an avalanche of public resentment and allowed its impact to be taken by another branch of the labor movement—the Brotherhoods of Locomotive Engineers and Railroad Trainmen, who took the unprecedented step of tying up the nation's railroads on May 23. The dispute which led to this crisis began in July, 1945, when all twenty of the railroad brotherhoods served demands upon the carriers for wage increases averaging $2.50 a day and for changes in the working rules. When no settlement was reached, eighteen of the brotherhoods agreed to an arbitration of the dispute. The trainmen and engineers, however, followed a different course. A strike call for March 11 was issued, but President Truman averted an immediate showdown by appointing a fact-finding board as provided in the Railroad Labor Act of 1926. On April 18 the board recommended a wage increase of $1.28 a day (16 cents an hour) and seven changes in working rules. The two brotherhoods rejected these proposals as unsatisfactory and issued a new strike call.

Are You Sure You Didn't Miss Anything? (By Herblock in *The Washington Post.*)

On May 17 President Truman ordered government seizure of the lines, but he found it no less difficult to arrange a settlement than had the operators. Five days later he suggested a wage increase of 18.5 cents an hour with no change in the working rules for a year. The compromise was accepted and incorporated in a contract between the carriers and all the other brotherhoods, but the trainmen and the engineers continued to demand rule changes.

On May 23 these two dissident brotherhoods went out on strike. The only conveyances they would handle were milk, army hospital, and troop trains. Supervisory personnel ran a few other special trains, but otherwise the tie-up was complete, with neither passengers nor freight able to move except through the overstrained facilities of buses, taxis, trucks, and planes. Improvised relays of mail trucks kept first-class mail moving, but an embargo on all other mail became necessary.

Such a complete paralysis of the nation's economic life was intolerable and the President resorted to vigorous action. On the evening of May 24 he made a radio address, asserting his determination to use every power at his disposal to get the trains moving unless the strike was called off by five o'clock the next afternoon. To back up this threat he called upon the army and secured a promise of cooperation from the eighteen nonstriking brotherhoods. But his greatest weapon was public opinion, now thoroughly aroused. A few minutes before the five o'clock deadline on the twenty-fifth, A. F. Whitney and Alvaney Johnson, the heads of the striking brotherhoods, surrendered. They accepted the presidential recommendations already agreed to by the other brotherhoods and the strike was over.

John L. Lewis, a better strategist than the inept Whitney and Johnson, managed to win a substantial victory. On May 22, near the end of the twelve-day truce, the government took over the mines; a week later Secretary of the Interior Krug and Lewis signed a contract providing for a wage increase of 18.5 cents an hour, increased vacation pay, and much stricter safety rules. The controversial welfare-fund issue was compromised by an agreement that 5 cents on each ton of bituminous coal mined should be assigned to a "welfare and retirement" fund to be administered by a board representing both the operators and the unions, but that a separate medical fund should be managed by the union alone.

CONGRESS AND THE LABOR ISSUE

Inevitably the great strikes strengthened the hands of those who wanted to regulate the unions. The President himself was sufficiently disturbed by the situation to suggest new legislation. In December, 1945, he proposed that the principle of the Railroad Act of 1926 be extended to other important industries: there should be a cooling-off period of thirty days between a breakdown in collective bargaining and the commencement of a strike or lockout; during this period the issues should be presented to a fact-finding commission appointed by the President; the commission's recommendations would not be legally binding, but public opinion would exert strong pressure upon the contestants to accept them. On May 25—the day on which the railroad strike reached its climax—Truman appeared before Congress to ask for temporary legislation of a drastic character: if the workers in any essential industry taken over by the government under its wartime powers ignored the President's appeal to return to work, their union leaders might be subjected to injunction proceedings, recalcitrant union leaders and employers might be subjected to criminal penalties, strikers might be deprived of their seniority rights and drafted into the armed forces; when an industry was being operated by the government during such an emergency, its net profits would go to the Treasury of the United States. So great was the excitement over the railroad tie-up that the House passed a bill embodying these emergency powers by a vote of 306 to 13 within an hour after the presidential message. But the Senate was more cautious. Drafting of strikers was unpleasantly reminiscent of involuntary servitude, while conservatives disapproved of government confiscation of profits. The administration bill was radically amended and sent back to the House, where it was allowed to languish along with the President's earlier request for fact-finding machinery.

Congress finally determined on an independent course of action. Despite loud protests by all branches of organized labor, the legislators finally passed and sent to the President on May 29, 1946, the so-called Case Federal Mediation Bill which provided for a Federal Mediation Board to intercede in labor disputes, a sixty-day cooling-off period between the calling of a strike and its execution, penalties for workers who struck during this period, union liability for damages resulting from strikes, authority for injunctions to bar certain strike activities, and a ban on employer contributions to welfare funds administered solely by unions.

President Truman waited until June 11 before he returned the bill with a long veto message. The measure, he said, struck at symptoms and ignored underlying causes. It would have prevented none of the big strikes of 1946; indeed, like the Smith-Connally Act, it would promote rather than lessen industrial strife. Then the President renewed his request for temporary legislation; permanent measures required more study and a different approach. Industrial peace might best be promoted by providing adequate insurance against unemployment, health and medical services for families of low and moderate incomes at costs they could afford, by raising the legal minimum wage, and by continuing the price control and stabilization law. An attempt to override the veto failed in the House by five votes and, with this impasse, the attempt to write major labor legislation was over for the moment, although Congress and the President did agree in July upon the so-called Hobbs Act, providing penalties up to a $10,000 fine and twenty years' imprisonment for interference by threats of violence or by robbery or extortion with the movement of goods in interstate commerce.

TRUMAN AND CONGRESS

The deadlock between Congress and the President on strike legislation was paralleled on many other issues. Truman's honeymoon was of short duration and before many months he found himself involved in the conflicts with the legislative branch which are so characteristic of the American system of government. His recent graduation from the Senate seemed only to encourage his former colleagues to match their judgments against his without any inhibitions.

I Do My Best to Save Them. (By Herblock in *The Washington Post*.)

The President's difficulties with Congress largely concerned domestic issues. On international affairs he had for the time being remarkable backing. The legislators ratified the United Nations Charter, the Bretton Woods agreement, and renewed the Reciprocal Trade Agreements Act in a form which permitted the President to make concessions as great as 50 per cent on the rates embodied in earlier agreements. Greater opposition was aroused by an Anglo-American pact whereby hard-pressed Britain was to be allowed a $3,750,000,000 credit in return for a liberalization of its empire trade policies, but this too was eventually approved by joint resolution. Congress postponed action, however, on domestic measures which the President urged soon after taking office— measures authorizing governmental planning to ensure full employment, increased unemployment benefits up to $25 a week for twenty-six weeks during reconversion, and the extension of the Selective Service Act.

On September 6, 1945, Truman sent his first fully articulated program —his so-called twenty-one points—to the Capitol. It was a distinctly New Deal document reiterating the earlier requests which Congress had failed to act upon and calling for an increase in the legal minimum wage from 40 to 65 cents an hour, an expanded and liberalized social security plan to include health insurance, a national housing and slum clearance program, long-range planning to develop natural resources and to carry on essential public works, assistance for the farmer and the small businessman, a permanent Fair Employment Practices Act, and government assistance and direction for scientific research. For the transitional period he requested a continuance of his war powers, of price and wage control, as well as of selective service.

The President soon discovered, however, what Roosevelt had had to contend with during his later years. The Democratic majority in the two Houses was deceptive. Conservative Southern Democrats—many of them holding strategic committee posts—were ready to cooperate with Republicans in blocking an extension of the New Deal. Where they lacked votes for a frontal attack, they were successful in amending bills until they bore little resemblance to the administration proposals. The President found it hard to overcome this coalition, even though on some issues he had the support of liberal Republicans. One of Truman's few impressive victories was achieved in December, 1945, when Congress granted him more extensive powers than those granted to Franklin Roosevelt or any other predecessor to reorganize the executive departments. Only the Interstate Commerce Commission, the Federal Trade Commission, the Securities Exchange Commission, and a few other independent boards were exempted. The need for improving the machinery of government was recognized in another form when, on August 2, 1946, the Legislative Reorganization Act became law. This measure raised the salaries of Congressmen to $12,500 and allowed them an additional $2500 for expenses, provided for the establishment of more regular consultation between the executive and legislative branches, and—most important—for simplifying the complex and overlapping Congressional committee system. Robert M. LaFollette, Jr. was the outstanding leader in achieving this overdue reform.

FULL EMPLOYMENT BILL

America's wartime economy fascinated imaginative citizens. The achievement of huge production goals planned in advance, the expansion of productive facilities, and the disappearance of unemployment were immensely impressive. Why could not a peacetime economy be set in motion that would make full use of the nation's enormous productive capacity and afford employment to all who were able and willing to work? Practical men as well as idealists were forced to think along these lines. As a matter of realistic finances, how could a national debt of $270,000,000,000 be carried and a probable peacetime budget of $25,000,000,000 be balanced unless the national income were raised to a figure which would have been considered fantastic in 1939?

Before the war was over, such economists as Alvin Hansen, Seymour E. Harris, and Stuart Chase had written extensively on the theme of full employment. Their postwar prescription stressed such points as the achievement of mass purchasing power, effective competition, low prices, and the stimulation of foreign trade through the judicious extension of credit during the immediate postwar period and greatly enlarged imports as a permanent policy. Although private enterprise must bear the major responsibility for postwar prosperity, these economists emphasized the need of government intervention in the form of a continuance of controls until the danger of runaway inflation was past and, above all, intelligent planning of public works and other forms of governmental investment to take up the slack when private investment fell off and unemployment threatened. These ideas influenced the politicians. During the election of 1944, the Democratic platform, the speeches of President Roosevelt, and the literature of the CIO Political Action Committee all stressed the full-employment theme. The Truman administration accepted this legacy gladly. The President urged the passage of the full-employment bill sponsored by Senators Murray of Montana and Wagner of New York, while the program was popularized by Secretary Wallace's *Sixty Million Jobs* and Economic Stabilizer Bowles's *Tomorrow without Fear*.

Many Americans accepted the aspiration of full employment without subscribing to the idea that a postwar New Deal was necessary to achieve it. Governor Dewey and the Republicans fought their 1944 campaign on the contention that the principal obstacle to the achievement of peacetime prosperity was excessive governmental interference. Give business a free hand and watch it boom, they argued. The Bible of the anti-New Dealers became Friedrich Hayek's *The Road to Serfdom* in which a distinguished Austrian emigré economist asserted that governmental planning and intervention in the economic sphere led inevitably to totalitarian political institutions. The National Association of Manufacturers entered upon a period of great activity after VJ Day and the burden of its message was the necessity of removing wartime controls as speedily as possible in order to attain the goals of full production and maximum employment.

The New Deal formula for postwar planning was incorporated in the Murray-Wagner Full Employment Bill. As originally drafted this was a far-reaching proposal. The obligation of the Federal government to maintain full employment was recognized, provision was made for the appointment of a board of economists who would draw up a national production and employment budget showing how much assistance would be required from governmental spending to maintain full employment, and Congress was to be committed to provide adequate Federal funds to meet these needs.

In its original form the bill was highly unpalatable to conservatives of both parties. The implication that the right to work should be guaranteed and Federal spending to prevent unemployment accepted as a fixed policy raised specters of continued deficit spending, while the production budget spoke in the hateful language of economic planning. On the other hand, conservatives could not afford to put themselves on record as opposed to the measure's basic purpose. Attack therefore took the form of amendments watering down the bill's phraseology.

As finally passed and signed by the President on February 20, 1946, the Maximum Employment Act was a compromise. It set a goal of "maximum" rather than "full" employment; it eliminated the national production budget and substituted an "economic report" to be prepared annually by a board of three economists; instead of committing Congress "to provide Federal expenditure" to maintain full employment, it called upon the Federal government to "coordinate and utilize all its plans, functions, and resources" to this end. Approved by over-whelming majorities (by a vote of 320 to 84 in the House and without a dissenting vote in the Senate), the measure was recognized to mean much or little according to the interpretation placed upon it. Conservatives accepted it as a harmless "New Year's resolution" which left Congress entirely free to implement it or not as it saw fit in the future; liberals hailed it as a landmark, a recognition of a basic new responsibility of government.

PRICE CONTROL

The debate over economic policy assumed a more acute form in the controversy over the continuance of price control. In magazine articles, in radio talks, and in statements before Congressional committees, Chester Bowles, first as head of OPA and then as Economic Stabilizer, hammered at his contention that only price control stood between the country and a repetition of the economic pattern of 1919 and 1920—runaway inflation followed by depression. So long as the demand for goods ran so far in advance of their supply, OPA was necessary. When full production was achieved, controls could be gradually relaxed. Bowles's argument had a great appeal to the nation's consumers as the quantity of mail to Congressmen demanding a continuance of OPA demonstrated. But, as always, consumers' interests were pressed upon the government with less effectiveness than were the interests of special pressure groups. The National Association of Manufacturers engaged in a huge advertising campaign to convince Congress and the public that the best way to combat inflation was to remove price controls. Higher prices, so the argument ran, would stimulate higher production; the law of supply and demand, if allowed to operate, would soon correct unreasonably high prices. Price ceilings, on the contrary, denied to the manufacturer a reasonable profit and deterred production or diverted it to the black market, thereby contributing to inflation. The argument was persuasive, but OPA defenders rejected some of its premises; they denied that businessmen were being required to operate at a loss or that price control did in fact deter production.

Other groups also attacked OPA. Spokesmen for agriculture contended that the high cost of farm labor, of feed, and other things which the farmer had to purchase made price increases imperative. They wanted an end to the subsidy system and a removal of price control on agricultural commodities. If that could not be achieved, they wanted new legal definitions of parity which would compel a substantial increase in price ceilings. Congressmen were particularly impressed by the farm demands because of the extreme shortage of meat, butter, and cooking fats and the growing black market in these extremely important items.

The OPA was due to expire on June 30, 1946, unless Congress gave it a new lease on life. For six months before this date President Truman urged prompt action on the issue in order to end uncertainty and the withholding of goods from the market in hope of higher prices. But the debate in Congress was long and bitter. Legislators willing to continue the agency with all its wartime powers and legislators wanting to kill it completely were both in a minority; the majority favored extension—but with provisions that would limit the agency's authority and force concessions on certain of its policies. Not until three days before the June 30 deadline did Congress finally pass a measure. This bill extended the Price Control Act for another year, but contained a number of what Bowles called booby-trap amendments. The so-called Taft amendment provided that the manufacturer should receive for each article the profit he had made on that item in 1941 and that he might add to the 1941 selling price all increases in cost which had occurred since that time. The Wherry amendment forbade the OPA to require wholesalers or retailers to absorb any part of the manufacturer's markup.

The President was under great pressure from his Congressional leaders to sign this measure, which they insisted was the best that could be secured. But the government officials most concerned with the battle against inflation urged a veto. In order to emphasize his disapproval of the measure as well as to answer critics who asserted that he was trying to perpetuate himself in power, Chester Bowles resigned. The President's final decision caught most of the country by surprise. On June 29 he sent the OPA bill back to Congress with a strong veto message, declaring it was an "impossible" measure which provided "a sure formula for inflation." He condemned particularly the Taft and Wherry amendments.

The result of the Congressional delay and the presidential veto was a three weeks' period during which OPA was without legal powers while the legislators debated their next step. Despite appeals to hold the price line on a voluntary basis, sharp price increases occurred all over the country. Some of these were inevitable since Federal subsidies had been terminated along with price control on June 30. But steak and butter at from $0.80 to $1.00 a pound reflected more a shrewd estimate of what the market would bear than a minimum raise to cover increased cost of production. Consumer resistance brought down some of the unreasonable prices and the restraint of manufacturers who did not want to strengthen the arguments of the price-control advocates held down others. Yet the danger of runaway inflation was enough to induce Congress to pass finally a compromise measure extending the life of OPA until June 30, 1947, and restoring controls over rents and most commodities. The new law required an adjustment of price ceilings to permit the same margin of profits as enjoyed by manufacturers in 1940; meat, poultry, grains, dairy products, and a number of other key commodities were to be exempted from control until August 20; and a three-man "decontrol" board was created with power to lift ceilings at will and to recontrol commodities when necessary. On July 25 the President signed the new bill despite the fact that it was scarcely more workable than the measure he had vetoed earlier. In the twenty-six days during which controls had been inoperative, Bureau of Labor statistics showed that the prices of twenty-eight basic commodities had risen 24.8 per cent as against an increase of only 13.1 per cent in the preceding three years since the "hold-the-line" order of May 17, 1943. State laws in areas like New York, however, had prevented rents from mounting above the 1943 level.

Political Dilemma. (By Berryman in *The Evening Star*, Washington, D. C.)

THE MEAT CRISIS

A worse formula for dealing with the meat situation could scarcely have been devised. For almost two months livestock raisers hurried their product to market, impelled both by high prices and uncertainty as to what the decontrol board would do on August 20. Following the mandate of Congress, the new board studied the problem and decided that since prices had risen unreasonably and meat was in short supply, controls should be restored. Although Secretary of Agriculture Anderson overruled OPA's directive that prices should be reduced to their June 30 level, the moderate increase in ceiling prices permitted was not sufficient to appease the meat industry. With the reimposition of price control, meat practically disappeared from the market to the vast discontent of the consumers. Producers simply held their stock, fattening them up against the day when they might force a relaxation of government policy. The President's first inclination was to stand firm; on September 26 he asserted: "The present level of livestock ceilings . . . is a fair and equitable one and one which should be sufficient to bring forth the maximum production of meat. An increase in prices or the abandoment of price control on meat now would, in the long run, add to rather than solve our difficulties."

But Democratic politicians, already fearful of the political upheaval to be expected in a postwar election, beseeched the President to give the voters meat. On October 14 he complied. In a radio address to the nation he announced not only the immediate termination of meat controls, but a policy of abandoning all price ceilings except those on rents as rapidly as was "compatible with economic security." The step was inevitable. Events had proved the near impossibility of holding down prices in some areas of the national economy while controls were lessened in others. Premature relaxation of rationing after VJ Day, the "bulge-in-the-line" policy, Congressional failure to pass an adequate OPA extension bill before the June 30 deadline, and contradictions in executive policy had all contributed to the situation which confronted the nation in October. Inflation had arrived as all who lived on fixed incomes could testify. How serious would be its results would depend on the level of production which could be achieved. The renewal of the bituminous coal controversy with a new strike in November was not a happy augury. The spiral of inflation seemed inexorable. The rising cost of living led to new wage demands, while wage raises led in their turn to higher prices. Managers, workers, and farmers each laid the blame on the shoulders of the other groups.

REPUBLICAN LANDSLIDE

The meat crisis and the impending coal strike were only two of the handicaps which the Democrats encountered in the political campaign of 1946. Ever since 1938 the Republicans had been demonstrating increased strength; only the war emergency and Roosevelt's great personal hold on the voters had prevented more decisive opposition gains. With the termination of both these influences, a strong swing to the Republicans was predicted on every side. The Democrats were blamed —sometimes with reason, sometimes without—for every postwar annoyance—for shortages of housing and civilian goods, for the unbalanced Federal budget and heavy taxes, for the activities of the Communists, and, above all, for the nation's labor troubles. Various episodes in which the President made ill-considered statements on important matters of policy, only to have to retract them or explain them away, weakened confidence in his competence, while intraparty quarrels steadily diminished the Democrats' chances. To sum up the whole opposition case, some inspired partisan coined the slogan: "Had enough? Vote Republican."

When the votes were counted on November 5, the full extent of the Republican swing was revealed. Democratic strength in the House was cut from 241 to 188, while the Republicans were increasing their representation from 192 to 246. The new Senate contained 51 Republicans and 45 Democrats as compared with 39 Republicans and 56 Democrats in the old. The Republicans now had control of both branches of the legislature for the first time since 1930. Swept to defeat were such ardent New Dealers as Joseph Guffey of Pennsylvania, Abe Murdock of Utah, and James Huffman of Ohio; several others retained their seats only by the narrowest of margins. Candidates endorsed by the PAC usually did not fare well and the Democratic machines in numerous cities broke down. On the other hand, Governor Dewey, the Republican standard-bearer in 1944, gained new prestige by rolling up an extraordinary 680,000 vote majority in the New York gubernatorial contest, while Senator Arthur Vandenberg of Michigan and Senator-elect John Bricker of Ohio, two other possibilities for the 1948 Republican nomination, enjoyed decisive electoral triumphs. Senator Taft of Ohio was not up for reelection, but his presidential stock also enjoyed a rise because of the influential role he was expected to play in the new Congress. Perhaps prematurely the Republicans were counting the next election as already won and were speculating excitedly on which of the party leaders would achieve the White House.

SHOWDOWN ON COAL

The impatience of the electorate with continued labor difficulties was shared by the Truman administration. This was evident from its handling of the coal crisis soon after the election. Nominal control of the bituminous mines had been retained since May, 1946, by the government because of the unwillingness of some of the operators to accept the terms of the settlement negotiated by Secretary Krug with the United Mine Workers. In November Lewis attempted to reopen the contract and, when the government refused, the Mine Workers' head declared the contract terminated, thus giving the signal for a new walkout of the miners on November 21. Lewis's action was in defiance of a temporary injunction which the government had secured from Federal District Court Justice T. Alan Goldsborough. After a stormy trial, Lewis and the UMW were found guilty of contempt of court and on December 4 Goldsborough fined the former $10,000 and the latter $3,500,000.

But while the government wrestled with the union, economic activity throughout the country slowed down alarmingly. Factories closed for lack of coal, blast furnaces were shut down, railroad passenger service was sharply curtailed, a rigid freight embargo was ordered, and communities reverted to the "brown-outs" of wartime. Great was the nation's relief, therefore, when on December 7 Lewis suddenly changed his tactics and ordered the miners to resume work until March 31, 1947, while the legal issues were considered by the Supreme Court.

On March 6 the Supreme Court finally announced its decision. By a seven-to-two vote Judge Goldsborough's verdict that Lewis and the Union were guilty of contempt of court was upheld. By a narrower margin, five to four, the Court ruled that the Norris-La Guardia Act did not apply to labor disputes between the government and its employees. The gargantuan fine against the union, however, was reduced to $700,000, with the proviso that the full $3,500,000 would have to be paid if the union failed to comply with the lower court's restraining order. This meant that Lewis must withdraw his threat to renew the strike on March 31.

Lewis gave notice of his intention to comply with the decision, but on March 25 a grim tragedy intervened. In the worst mine disaster since 1928, more than a hundred miners were killed at Centralia, Illinois. The union chief immediately blamed the Federal government for allowing the mine to be operated after the revelation by an inspector five days before the explosion of fifty-one safety-code violations. Consequently, on March 29 Lewis called upon the miners to halt work for one week as a "period of mourning . . . to honor our war dead." So despite the Supreme Court decision, the miners laid down their tools on March 31 and, under the circumstances, they ran little danger of further punishment. The mines resumed operation only after much wrangling between Lewis and Secretary Krug over the relative degree of responsibility which union and government should bear in seeing that safety provisions were carried out.

REVIVAL OF LAISSEZ FAIRE

President Truman obviously accepted the November, 1946, election returns as evidence that the country had "had enough" of wartime regulation. Four days after the election he issued an executive order dropping all controls on prices and wages, but continuing those on rents, sugar, and rice. Paul Porter retired from his post in OPA on December 4 and that agency began a process of gradual liquidation. Meantime, because the President was unwilling to give him adequate support in his program, Wilson Wyatt resigned as National Housing Expediter. On December 14 Truman swept away the priorities system and removed the $10,000 sales ceiling for new homes, as well as the $80 maximum rental. This represented a virtual abandonment of the administration's effort to compel the construction industry to concentrate on the building of modest homes at prices the veterans could afford to pay. Additional steps in the abandonment of controls were the presidential proclamation of December 31, 1946, announcing the end of hostilities and the executive order of June 11, 1947, terminating sugar rationing. Rent control was continued by Congress until March 1, 1948, but with the provision that landlords and tenants might agree upon leases for as much as 15 per cent higher rent than the previous ceiling.

The country paid heavily for its eagerness to return to laissez faire. In the first ten months that followed the breakdown of price control on June 30, 1946, wholesale prices rose 31 per cent—nearly four times the rise of the preceding thirty-seven months of stringent control. Labor found its 18.5-cent wage increase of 1946 cancelled by the soaring cost of living and pressed new wage demands. The United States Steel Corporation and General Motors agreed to new 15 cent raises in collective bargaining with the unions, thus setting a 1947 wage pattern that was widely followed.

Having abandoned the effort to control inflation by coercive measures, the President attempted persuasion. On April 21, 1947, he declared: "If we are to avoid a recession we must act before it starts. Prices must be brought down. I speak first to those businessmen who have it within their power to reduce their prices." This appeal brought some response. The city of Newburyport, Massachusetts, pioneered in a voluntary experiment in reducing retail prices, while a few of the leading corporations took steps in the same direction. But the tide of inflation was running too strongly to be much affected by piecemeal efforts of this character.

REPUBLICAN ASCENDANCY

In January, 1947, the Eightieth Congress began its sessions. The Republicans, with a majority in both Houses, undertook to put through legislation which would fulfill their campaign pledges to cut expenditures, reduce taxes, and curb labor union abuses.

President Truman's budget for the year ending June 30, 1948, fell under speedy attack. Although it contemplated lower expenditures than had been possible for the six previous years, the total of $37,500,000,000 was still huge by prewar standards. Even the most open-handed of the New Deal budgets had only been for about $9,000,000,000. The House of Representatives resolved to cut the President's recommendations by $6,000,000,000; the Senate more realistically set a goal of $4,500,000,000 reduction. Even this was difficult to approach when Congress began consideration of specific items. Few legislators were rash enough to demand radical cuts in the largest category of expenditure—$11,300,000,000 for national defense. Other items like $7,300,000,000 for the veterans' services and $5,000,000 for interest on the public debt were also practically immune. Even in areas like power development and reclamation where Eastern Republicans like Representative John Taber of New York were eager to apply the axe, Western party members counselled caution.

Despite the probability that the budget cuts would be less extensive than first promised, the Republicans believed that it was feasible to reduce taxes. Postwar prosperity was bringing in a volume of Federal revenues beyond the expectations of the Treasury experts [1] and it seemed possible to repeat the Republican financial formula of the twenties—to balance the budget, reduce the public debt, and still cut taxes. Representative Harold Knutson of Minnesota, chairman of the House Ways and Means Committee, called for a straight 20 per cent reduction in the income tax. This would so obviously benefit large taxpayers more than small, however, that it aroused immediate protest. The eventual bill passed by Congress in June, 1947, provided for only a 10.5 per cent cut

[1] There was every indication that the fiscal year ending June 30, 1947, would result in a surplus for the first time in seventeen years.

on the highest brackets of income, while granting a 30 per cent cut on the lowest. Even in this modified form, with the cuts to become effective on July 1, 1947 instead of at the beginning of that year, the measure was vetoed by the President. He said: "The right kind of tax reduction, at the right time, is an objective to which I am deeply committed. But I have reached the conclusion that this bill represents the wrong kind of tax reduction, at the wrong time." It was the wrong time, he believed, because of the great inflation; it was the wrong kind because it failed to give relief where it was needed most. According to the President, the measure would provide in "take-home" pay an increase of only 1.2 per cent for an average family with $2500 income while granting an increase of 18.6 per cent to families with $50,000 incomes and 62.3 per cent to those with $500,000. The Republican leaders denounced Truman for following Roosevelt's example in vetoing a tax measure, but the attempt to override the action failed in the House by two votes.[1]

THE TAFT-HARTLEY ACT

The President was less successful in his efforts to prevent the passage of drastic legislation regulating the labor unions. The opportunity for which the National Association of Manufacturers and other employer groups had been waiting since the passage of the National Labor Relations Act of 1935 at length arrived. The Republicans were in control of Congress and the unions had lost favor with the public through the postwar strikes. A bill passed in the House under the leadership of Representative Fred A. Hartley, Jr., of New Jersey went too far to win the support of the Senate, which drafted a somewhat more moderate plan. Senator Taft took the most prominent role in the deliberations of the Upper House and also in the conferences where the two branches of the legislature reached a compromise.

As finally sent by Congress to the President on June 9, the Taft-Hartley Labor-Management Relations Act of 1947 amended the Wagner Act in many particulars. Unions might now be sued by employers for breach of contract or for damages suffered through jurisdictional strikes and secondary boycotts. The closed shop in which employers agreed to hire only union members was prohibited; the union shop, wherein employees might be compelled to join a union after they were hired, was permitted—but only under rigid safeguards. A sixty-day cooling-off period was required before a strike or lockout could be called. Unions were required to publish financial statements and were debarred from making contributions and expenditures for political

[1] The vote was 268 to 137.

purposes. They lost their rights under the Wagner Act if any officer were demonstrated to be a Communist. Union dues could not be deducted from the employee's pay check without his individual consent. The government was empowered to secure injunctions against unions postponing for eighty days any strike that would affect the national health or safety. Bureaucratic machinery for dealing with labor was expanded through an enlargement of the National Labor Relations Board from three to five members with a powerful special counsel, the establishment of a new conciliation service outside the Labor Department, and provision for a new Senate-House committee to study labor-management relations.

President Truman vetoed the bill in a long and caustic message. In his opinion:

> The bill taken as a whole would reverse the basic direction of our national labor policy, inject the Government into private economic affairs on an unprecedented scale, and conflict with important principles of our democratic society. Its provisions would cause more strikes, not fewer. It would contribute neither to industrial peace nor to economic stability and progress. It would be a dangerous stride in the direction of a totally managed economy. It contains seeds of discord which would plague this nation for years to come.

But Congress was unimpressed. On the same day as the veto, June 20, the House voted to override by 331 to 83. Senate opponents of the measure delayed the issue briefly with a filibuster, but on June 23 the Upper House repassed the measure by a vote of 68 to 25. The Democrats split, with only twenty-two supporting the President and twenty opposing him.

Even more than the tax bill veto, the conflict between Truman and the Republicans on labor legislation provided clearcut issues on which the election of 1948 would probably be fought.[1] The union leaders called for defeat of those Congressmen who had voted to override the President and at the same time began to lay plans for testing the constitutionality of the new law. On the other hand, the Republicans accused Truman of playing politics and of failing to adhere to his November, 1946, promise that he would cooperate with Congress.

---

[1] The Eightieth Congress also passed and sent to the states for consideration an amendment to the Constitution which would limit the presidency to two terms.

29

Problems of Peace and World Organization

Even more important than the country's domestic troubles were its problems in international relations. The rejection of isolationism after the shock of Pearl Harbor was—for the time being at least—complete. The wartime cooperation of the nations combatting the Axis expanded from the military field into economic and cultural spheres. Meantime there evolved the idea of the United Nations—a new international association to succeed the more or less discredited League of Nations. The United States was now willing to accept important responsibilities in the preservation of peace and willing also to play a leading role in such projects as an international bank, an international stabilization fund, and international agencies for relief and rehabilitation.

But cooperation in wartime proved easier than postwar harmony. So acrimonious were the disputes of the former allies after their great victory that discouraged Americans frequently wondered whether the stable new world society to which they now aspired would ever be built.

BETTER HEMISPHERE ACCORD

Following the Havana Conference of 1940 the hemisphere republics cooperated in closing German-backed schools, in canceling leases of German and Italian airlines, in rounding up suspected spies, in freezing Axis assets, and in seizing Axis ships. Moreover, most of the Latin-American countries signed pacts under which they promised to sell their surplus strategic supplies only to the United States and to countries fighting the totalitarian nations. The importance of these agreements was accentuated after Japan had swept over Malaya and other raw-material regions of the Pacific. Several of the republics also granted the United States permission to establish temporary air bases and naval

765

stations within their territories, thereby helping in the defense of the Panama Canal and of the hemisphere.

On the part of the United States, additional credit was extended to numerous Latin-American republics through the Export-Import Bank and Lend-Lease. These loans were used for stabilizing their currencies, for developing local industries, for improving communication and transportation, and for generally bettering their national defense.

When the news of Pearl Harbor reached the hemisphere, nine Latin American republics [1] quickly aligned themselves with the United States by declaring war on the Axis, while several others severed relations. A conference of the foreign ministers of the hemisphere republics was held at Rio de Janeiro in January, 1942, to decide on a course of common action. The United States hoped for an agreement whereby all the republics would declare war, but the time was not ripe. The strongest step that seemed possible was for them all to sever relations with the Axis, but President Castillo of Argentina at the last moment instructed his foreign minister that he must not go even that far. Consequently, the resolution finally adopted used the following evasive formula:

The American Republics, in accord with the procedures established by their own laws and in conformity with the position and circumstances obtaining in each country in the existing continental conflict, recommend the breaking of their diplomatic relations with Japan, Germany and Italy . . .

With the exception of Argentina and Chile,[2] all of the republics promptly followed this suggestion.

The delegates at Rio also agreed not to resume relations with the totalitarian states separately "in order that their action may have a solidary character." Provision was made as well for integrating the defenses, both military and economic, of the hemisphere.

United States influence played a prominent part in the declarations of war against the Axis by Mexico in 1942 and by Bolivia and Colombia the following year. Finally in February, 1945, the rest, with the exception of Argentina, made their war declarations, possibly as a result of United States pressure. Latin American military effort in the war was small, although Brazil sent some divisions to Italy where they gave a good account of themselves. The major contribution, as in World War I, was in helping to supply the United Nations with necessities;

[1] Costa Rica, Cuba, the Dominican Republic, El Salvador, Guatemala, Haiti, Honduras, Nicaragua, and Panama.

[2] In October, 1942, Sumner Welles of the State Department openly accused Chile of favoring the Axis. This speech brought numerous demonstrations in Chile which caused her to break diplomatic relations with the Axis in January, 1943.

moreover, with Latin American cooperation, the United States had less to worry about the fifth-column menace in the hemisphere and could therefore devote its attention primarily to the war.

FASCISM IN ARGENTINA

Argentina did not cooperate in most of these enterprises. A fierce competitor with the United States in agricultural exports and jealous of the North American nation's leading role in hemisphere affairs, Argentina had become strongly nationalistic. Fearful of too much democracy, many of her wealthy leaders were believers in totalitarian government and sympathized with the Axis from the opening of World War II. This feeling was accentuated when the autocratic Ramon Castillo became acting president in the summer of 1941. Under a state of siege—comparable to an unlimited emergency in the United States, he suppressed many popular liberties and gathered around him aides with fascist views. The United States hoped that conditions would change when in June, 1943, a *coup d'état* brought Pedro Ramirez to the presidency, but the situation became worse instead of better. There was even more democratic suppression and apparently more connivance with the Axis. In the fall of 1943 Secretary Hull engaged upon an energetic diplomatic offensive against the Ramirez regime. Fearing the imposition of economic sanctions by the United States and Great Britain, Ramirez averted the blow by severing relations with Germany on January 26, 1944.

That severance proved unpopular among the Argentine military. Consequently, toward the end of February, the so-called Colonels' Clique overthrew Ramirez and placed Edelmiro Farrell in the presidency; the real power, however, was exercised by Colonel Juan Perón. When it became evident that there would be no change in the Argentine position, the United States, along with many other republics, refused to recognize the new administration. And as the situation worsened, Ambassador Armour was recalled in July, 1944, followed the next month by the announcement that Argentine credit in the United States was to be frozen. Shortly thereafter American ships were barred by the State Department from entering Argentine ports.

THE ACT OF CHAPULTEPEC

In anticipation of the end of hostilities and to prepare for the postwar era, all of the republics except Argentina were represented at a conference in Mexico City during February and March, 1945. In some sixty resolutions, the delegates showed the greatest degree of accord and cooperation that had been developed up to that time. The most important decision reached was the Act of Chapultepec, of which the major parts were:

That every attack of a State against the integrity or the inviolability of the territory or against the sovereignty or political independence of an American State, shall . . . be considered as an act of aggression against the other States which sign this act. . . .

That in case acts of aggression occur, or there may be reasons to believe that an aggression is being prepared by any other State against . . . an American State, the States signatory to this act will consult amongst themselves in order to agree upon the measures it may be advisable to take.

The act referred to aggression not only from without the hemisphere, but from within as well. Thus it is believed that the measure was largely directed against Argentina. The fact that the United States had the only army and navy capable of thwarting aggression meant that the smaller and weaker republics were willing to allow the United States to protect them. And in turn that willingness indicated that the fear of American imperialism had largely ended.

The conference also showed a lively interest in a strong United Nations organization. The delegates agreed that none of the republics should afford asylum to war criminals and that the efforts to wipe out Axis influence should be continued. Moreover, a number of resolutions were adopted dealing with postwar economic, cultural, and social problems. Although Argentina's misdeeds were deplored, the door was left open for her to rejoin the hemisphere family by declaring war against the Axis and approving all the conference resolutions. These steps the Farrell-Perón government took in an effort to escape from its isolated position.

ANGLO-AMERICAN COOPERATION

With the entrance of the United States into the war, the Anglo-American ties, already demonstrated in the destroyer-base deal, Lend-Lease, and the Atlantic Charter, were more fully strengthened. Fulfilling a promise that Churchill had made to President Roosevelt, a British declaration of war against Japan followed quickly after that of the United States. Moreover, the Prime Minister flew to Washington shortly afterward to hold the first of a new series of conferences with President Roosevelt. In these meetings the two leaders, with their diplomatic and military personnel, worked out a close accord which helped greatly in winning the war. One of the most important decisions of the December, 1941, conference was that the major attacks would be first made against the Reich.

At the next meeting of the two men, held at Washington in June, 1942, the plans for the North African invasion were formulated. Following the successful operation of those plans, Roosevelt and Churchill conferred again at Casablanca in January, 1943.[1] There they agreed to redouble military efforts against the European members of the Axis, now thrown on the defensive, by striking at Sicily and Italy and by furnishing additional help to Russia. Nor was the Asiatic member forgotten when similar assistance was promised to China. These efforts were to be continued until the enemy surrendered unconditionally.

Subsequent conferences between the Anglo-American heads were held throughout the war, usually at either Washington or Quebec. At these meetings other matters of importance, such as more help for China, unified command for the Far Eastern theater, and French governmental problems, were discussed, usually with positive results.

BROADENING ALLIED ACCORD

As the war progressed more satisfactorily, the Soviet and China took an increasing interest in such discussions. Thus Stalin attended the Teheran Conference of November, 1943, where the second-front plans

[1] Stalin was invited to attend this Casablanca meeting, but the press of the Russian offensive caused him to refuse.

The Three Fates. (By Seibel in the *Richmond Times-Dispatch*.)

were worked out, while Chiang Kai-shek met with the Anglo-American leaders at Cairo to fashion the means by which Japan could be defeated, punished, and deprived of her ill-gotten gains.[1]

The final wartime meeting of Roosevelt, Stalin, and Churchill was held at Yalta in the Crimea during February, 1945. Plans for the UN Conference at San Francisco were agreed to, as well as certain principles to govern the treatment of Germany after her defeat. The Far Eastern problem was also discussed and important decisions were made, contingent upon Russia's declaration of war upon Japan.

THE UNITED NATIONS

These meetings were largely concerned with military phases of the war. But even while the struggle was under way, the groundwork was laid for an association of nations to supersede the League of Nations as an agency for maintaining peace after hostilities were over. The general consensus of opinion was that the formulation of this organization should be divorced as much as possible from the drawing up of the final peace terms, thereby avoiding one of the mistakes at Versailles.

In a sense the seed was planted at the time of the formulation of the Atlantic Charter. It began to bud when President Roosevelt and Secretary Hull discussed the possibility of keeping all of the opponents of totalitarianism in line until final victory was achieved. On January 1, 1942, the United States, Great Britain, China, and the Soviet signed the United Nations Declaration which stated that the governments:

Being convinced that complete victory over their enemies is essential to defend life, liberty, independence and religious freedom, and to preserve human rights and justice in their own lands as well as in other lands, and that they are now engaged in a common struggle against savage and brutal forces seeking to subjugate the world, DECLARE:

1. Each Government pledges itself to employ its full resources, military or economic, against those members of the Tripartite Pact and its adherents with which such government is at war.

2. Each Government pledges itself to cooperate with the Governments signatory hereto and not to make a separate armistice or peace with the enemies.

The declaration also provided that "other nations which are, or which may be, rendering material assistance and contributions in the struggle for victory over Hitlerism" might adhere to the agreement. The following day, twenty-two other nations ratified the pact. Then between

[1] Because Russia was not at war with Japan, she was not represented at any conference where Far Eastern military problems were considered, nor was China present at meetings on European matters.

June 14, 1942, and January 1, 1945, nine more countries entered the United Nations fold. At the Yalta Conference the Big Three decided that only signatories of this document could be represented at San Francisco, a decision that resulted in eleven more states declaring war against the Axis and signing the declaration.[1]

The first well-organized demand for broadening the United Nations into an agency which might preserve the peace as well as win the war came from four United States Senators: Joseph Ball of Minnesota, Harold Burton of Ohio, Carl Hatch of New Mexico, and Lister Hill of Alabama in what was popularly called the B_2H_2 Resolution of March, 1943. The proposal was regarded as premature by President Roosevelt who believed that for the time being primary attention should be given to achieving military victory. But, although the resolution was tabled through administration pressure, the fact that four prominent Senators, two from each party, had gone on record as favoring a postwar peace organization was impressive evidence of the change in American opinion since the isolationist decade of the thirties.

The failure of the original proposal did not stem the movement. In June, 1943, Representative James Fulbright of Arkansas followed up with a more specific proposition:

Resolved by the House of Representatives [the Senate concurring] that the Congress hereby expresses itself as favoring the creation of appropriate machinery with power adequate to establish and maintain a just and lasting peace among the nations of the world, and as favoring participation by the United Nations therein.

The press of other duties delayed House action on this Fulbright Resolution until September. Then by the overwhelming vote of 360 to 29 the House registered its approval.

Meantime, the growing demand for a world organization was likewise reflected in a resolution introduced in the Senate by Vandenberg of Michigan and White of Maine. Although this particular proposal died in the Foreign Relations Committee, the House support of the Fulbright Resolution compelled the Upper House to take cognizance of the issue. The Senate would not concur, however, in the House action because the members were sticklers for what they believed proper procedure to safeguard Senate prerogatives. Therefore in October, 1943, Senator Tom Connally of Texas, head of the Foreign Relations Committee, proposed a substitute resolution which likewise called for a conclusive Allied victory and American participation in a postwar

[1] Argentina signed after the Yalta deadline, but the American plea brought her an invitation to San Francisco.

organization which must stop aggression; but the entrance of the United States in such an agency must be accomplished only "through its constitutional processes." Those processes, according to a subsequent amendment, meant that "any treaty made to effect the purposes of this resolution . . . shall be made only by and with the advice and consent of the Senate . . ., provided two-thirds of the Senators . . . concur."

THE MOSCOW CONFERENCE

While the Connally Resolution was being debated, a closer accord than had hitherto been achieved was being worked out at Moscow between the Soviet Union and the Western democracies. Secretary Hull, British Foreign Secretary Anthony Eden, and Russian Foreign Commissar Vyacheslav Molotov developed a program for joint action not only in carrying on the war, but in the peace that was to follow. This Moscow Pact, approved in addition by the Chinese ambassador to the Soviet, was important in that it was the first time that representatives of the four nations openly stated the need for a postwar successor to the League of Nations. Article 4 of that Pact read:

That they recognize the necessity of establishing at the earliest practicable date a general international organization, based on the principle of the sovereign equality of all peace-loving states, and open to membership by all such states, large and small, for the maintenance of international peace and security.

The Foreign Secretaries also announced on October 30, 1943, that a democratic regime must be established in Italy as soon as feasible, that Austria must be freed from German control, and that lists of German war criminals should be made and those found guilty after trial punished.

On November 1 President Roosevelt asserted that the United States was bound by the several resolutions drawn up at the Moscow Conference and that he was especially pleased with that part under which the United Nations promised "to consult with one another . . . with a view to joint action on behalf of the community of nations." With this presidential blessing for an international peace organization, the Senate shelved the Connally Resolution in favor of Article 4 of the Moscow Pact—with the amendment that a two-thirds Senatorial vote would be required before the United States could enter such an organization. Then the amended resolution was adopted by the one-sided vote of eighty-five to five. Thus the Upper House, which had been the stumbling block for Wilson's League, now appeared committed to the cause of internationalism.

NEW AREAS OF INTERNATIONAL COOPERATION

The advocates of postwar cooperation realized that more was needed than simply an organization to prevent aggression. There would have to be cooperation as well to promote the Four Freedoms and to help the millions of civilians who had been displaced or whose homes and lands had been ravaged by war. Knowing that these were more than one-nation problems, the United States invited the other forty-three members of the United Nations to the Food Conference, held at Hot Springs, Virginia, in May, 1943. There plans were made for the establishment of the Food and Agricultural Organization (FAO), a fact-finding agency. When called upon, this agency would make national surveys to determine what foods and in what amounts were needed for a good diet in various parts of the world. Then suggestions would be made for achieving the goal.

In order to meet the problem of relief and rehabilitation, the Dutch, the Norwegians, the Poles, the French, and the British were already formulating their plans for securing stock piles of food and materials in anticipation of peace. Yet, by the fall of 1943, it was generally admitted that the project was too great for any one nation or small group of nations. Moreover, countries all over the world, even though immediately unaffected by scars of battle strife, had a stake. Not only was the humanitarian issue involved, but the military and economic as well. For military security, the advancing Allies would need a satisfied population at their rear—and such a population would be found only where there were sufficient food and other essentials. For the revival of world trade it would be necessary to restore all countries as quickly as possible so that they could buy from and sell to the rest.

To meet these needs, the United Nations Relief and Rehabilitation Administration (UNRRA) was organized late in 1943. Funds for the agency were to be contributed by all the member nations on the basis of their relative national incomes. First under the leadership of ex-governor Herbert Lehman of New York and then under Fiorello La Guardia, former mayor of New York City, UNRRA carried on an ambitious program. Over four billion dollars (about 75 per cent contributed by the United States) was expended in the purchase and shipment of food to destitute countries both in Europe and in Asia. Some controversy attended these efforts and it was charged that despite the nonpartisan efforts of UNRRA personnel relief was often used for political purposes in various countries. The United States therefore declined to support the project after December 31, 1946. But despite criticism UNRRA undoubtedly saved millions of unfortunates from starvation during the immediate post-war years.

BRETTON WOODS

Just as the civilians of war-torn nations needed relief, so also was it realized that some of the countries themselves would face economic problems in the postwar era. They would need funds to stabilize their currencies and money to rebuild their factories, their mills, their shipping, and the like. Only by reestablishing as quickly as possible the economic stability of such nations could world trade and business interchange be restored, to prevent again the troublesome days of the 1930's in the international financial field.

The two foremost advocates of postwar economic assistance were the famous British economist, Lord Keynes, and Dr. Harry White of the American Treasury Department. As early as 1942 each had worked out a plan aimed at solving economic strife among nations. Both of them stirred widespread interest. Other experts from at least thirty countries began to consider the relative merits and to offer amendments. By April, 1944, the best parts of both plans were amalgamated and the Keynes-White formula was then used as the basis for discussion by delegates from forty-three other countries invited by the United States to the Bretton Woods Conference of July, 1944.

After considerable debate the conferees reached agreement on two major matters. The first provided for the establishment of the International Monetary Fund amounting to $8,800,000,000. Each country was to contribute according to a schedule determined by ability to pay. The American quota was fixed at $2,750,000,000. A pledge was made by each participant not to change the value of its currency in radical fashion without the approval of the others. It was hoped that this fund would enable each to obtain more easily the currencies of all others and thus be able to buy the others' goods. The second instituted the International Bank for Reconstruction, capitalized at slightly more than $9,000,000,000. Again each participating nation was allocated its subscription based on wealth, and the United States's amount was $3,175,000,000. The bank was authorized to make direct loans to member nations for the purpose of reconstructing industry and agriculture and to underwrite loans advanced by private bankers for similar purposes.

These Bretton Woods Agreements were called the financial side of UN. They were attempts to avert the economic troubles and consequent international differences which might lead to war. After con-

Churchill, Roosevelt, and Stalin at Yalta, 1945. (Acme.)

siderable debate, in which a number of substitute proposals were offered, the United States Senate ratified American participation in July, 1945.[1]

THE SAN FRANCISCO CONFERENCE

All of these conferences helped to set the stage for the most important meeting of all—the United Nations Conference at San Francisco to work out the formula definitely proposed in the Moscow Pact. The immediate forerunner of that conference was a seven-week session beginning in August, 1944, at Dumbarton Oaks (outside of Washington, D. C.). There Undersecretary of State Stettinius, Sir Alexander Cadogan of Britain, and Andrei Gromyko of the Soviet drew up the

[1] Other signs of international cooperation were: the International Labor Organization (ILO) meeting in Philadelphia in April, 1944, which tried to work out plans for promoting the welfare and security of workers throughout the world; the Aviation Conference at Chicago in November, 1944, where the delegates attempted to solve the problem of international airways; and the Rye (New York) meeting of businessmen from fifty-two countries (November, 1944) to consider the postwar problems of private enterprise.

preliminary plans for an association of nations, subsequently concurred in by V. Wellington Koo of China.

These plans were the principal object of consideration at the San Francisco meeting, for which the Yalta Conference had provided. Forty-eight countries were represented—Argentina at the insistence of the United States—when the well-publicized session opened on April 25, 1945. There were no dominating personages [1] to compare with Wilson, Lloyd George, and Clemenceau, but consequently there were fewer clashes of personality than at Versailles and compromise was made easier.

Since the Dumbarton Oaks plan had been a rough outline, there necessarily had to be considerable discussion over some of its parts during the two-month San Francisco session. Of the Big Five, Russia usually proved most obstinate in yielding. Indeed, when it appeared as though there would be a stalemate over the veto issue, Gromyko, who had succeeded Molotov as chief of the Russia delegation, refused to budge from his position. Thereupon President Truman sent Harry Hopkins to Moscow for a conference with Stalin, who soon instructed Gromyko to yield on the disputed point. The major compromises involved the admission of White Russia and the Ukraine as independent members, [2] the admission of Argentina, the exclusion of Spain, the status of Poland, trusteeships, and the voting and veto power of the Big Five. As a result of these compromises the Charter of the United Nations was, on the whole, satisfactory to all the members.

UNITED NATION OBJECTIVES

According to the preamble, the objectives of UN were: "to save succeeding generations from the scourge of war"; "to reaffirm faith in fundamental human rights, in the dignity and worth of the human person, in the equal rights of men and women and of nations large and small"; and "to promote social progress and better standards of life in larger freedom." These might be accomplished by practicing tolerance, by uniting to ensure international peace and security, by preventing the use of armed force "save in the common interest," and by using

[1] The American delegation consisted of: Secretary of State Stettinius, who had succeeded Cordell Hull in November, 1944, Senators Connally and Vandenberg, Representatives Bloom and Eaton, Commander Harold Stassen, formerly governor of Minnesota, and Dean Virginia Gildersleeve of Barnard College.

[2] Provision for allowing Russia three votes and the consideration of a similar number for the United States had been approved by the Big Three at Yalta. So great was the American opposition to the United States increase that the matter was dropped. At San Francisco, however, Russia insisted on her three votes and won out. Thus there became fifty original members of the United Nations.

international efforts to promote the economic and social welfare of all peoples.

The charter members were the forty-eight nations represented at San Francisco, plus White Russia and the Ukraine which were admitted during the session. Provision was also made for including Poland when its governmental difficulties were straightened out. Other states might join by vote of the General Assembly on showing that they were peace-loving and on ratifying the United Nations Charter. Were any member to break any of the provisions, it could be suspended and, for extreme violation, expelled by the Assembly on recommendation by the Security Council.

THE ASSEMBLY AND SECURITY COUNCIL

The General Assembly was made up of delegates—not to exceed five—from each member state, but each state had only one vote. It might discuss "any questions or any matters within the scope of the present Charter or relatings to the powers and functions of any organs provided for in the present Charter, and . . . make recommendations to the Members of the United Nations or to the Security Council or to both on any such questions or matters." The only restriction concerned disputes already being considered by the Security Council. It had the right to initiate studies concerning the strengthening and codification of international law, the promotion of social, cultural, educational, health, and economic problems, and to "recommend measures for the peaceful adjustment of any situation . . . which it deems likely" to cause trouble. On important matters, a two-thirds vote was required.

Much more powerful was the Security Council of eleven members. Five of these—the United States, Britain, China, France, and Russia—held permanent seats. The other positions were filled by vote of the General Assembly for two-year terms, with retiring members not eligible for immediate reelection. Both types of members were entitled to only one vote each. For approval of any action the vote of seven members was needed and, on important issues such as the use of military power, the Big Five must be unanimous in favor. It was here that the disputed veto power came in; were a member of the Big Five considered as a possible disputant or a threat to peace, that member must refrain from voting when the issue of considering the dispute came before the Council; however the offending member could use its veto power to prevent the imposition of economic or military sanctions.

Directly under the jurisdiction of the Security Council was the Military Staff Committee, consisting of the Chiefs of Staff of the Big Five.

This committee could call out whatever armed forces—military, air, and naval—the United Nations agreed to place at the disposal of the organization when the Security Council deemed it necessary.

Another prominent agency of UN was an Economic and Social Council of eighteen members elected for three-year terms by the General Assembly. According to the Charter, this Council

may make or initiate studies and reports with respect to international economic, social, cultural, educational, health, and related matters and make recommendations with respect to any such matters to the General Assembly, to the Members of the United Nations, and to the specialized agencies concerned.

Among the specialized agencies under its supervision were the International Bank, the International Stabilization Fund, the International Labor Organization, the United Nations Educational, Scientific, and Cultural Organization (UNESCO), and the Food and Agricultural Organization.

The Charter likewise provided for a Trusteeship Council to supervise territories already held under mandate, those lands gained from the Axis in World War II, and the regions voluntarily placed in trusteeship by the nations administering them. Council membership consisted of those states acting as trustees, the remaining members of the Security Council, and as many nontrustee nations—elected by the Assembly—as needed to make the number of nontrustees equal the trustees. The Trusteeship Council must make annual reports to the Assembly. The International Court of Justice, to meet at the Hague, was made up of fifteen judges elected by the Assembly. Not more than one judge could be elected from any one country. All members of UN were considered members of the Court. At the first UN meeting, held in London beginning in January, 1946, a special Atomic Energy Commission, consisting of representatives of the nations on the Security Council and a delegate from Canada, was established. Finally, there was a permanent Secretariat to keep the records and assemble the data needed by the organization.

In the effort to maintain peace, the UN was to function in the following manner: when a dispute arose which might endanger international peace, the parties to it were expected to "seek a solution by negotiation, enquiry, mediation, conciliation, arbitration, judicial settlement, resort to regional agencies or arrangements, or other peaceful means of their own choice." If such negotiations appeared to be failing, the issue could be presented to either the General Assembly or the Security Council for investigation and recommendations for settlement. In the event of a breach of the peace, the Security Council was empowered to order economic sanctions against the offenders; if these were insufficient, the Military Staff Committee could be called upon to end the disturbance through armed force.

The small states criticized UN because of the dominating position of the Big Five; yet in answer those five asserted that they would be more responsible for maintaining the peace of the world and thus should exercise more authority than the rest. The use of the veto power by the Big Five was another subject of criticism, for which the Big Five had less defense. Likewise it was asserted that the organization would not work were a member of the Big Five to spurn the machinery and go to war; but it was argued in turn that if such an event happened, the world would be in so much turmoil that no international agency could maintain peace.

Provision was made that the Charter would become effective when the Big Five and a majority of the remaining members ratified the document according to the constitutional processes of each. Nicaragua was the first to act favorably, but the United States was the initial member of the Big Five to give its approval. The Senate, after remarkably little debate, approved of American membership before the end of July, 1945, by the decisive vote of eighty-nine to two.[1] On October 29 the requisite number of states had both ratified and deposited their ratifications with Secretary of State Byrnes. Thereupon he signed the protocol which declared that the Charter was in force. Before the end of the year, both Houses of Congress gave their approval to the United Nations Participation Act, authorizing the President and the American delegates to use those American armed forces assigned to UN without being compelled to secure special Congressional authority on each occasion. Edward R. Stettinius, former Secretary of State, was named as permanent representative to UN.

THE POTSDAM CONFERENCE

The establishment of UN was but one phase of the effort to prevent future conflicts. The feeling was general that Germany must not be allowed to become a strong nation again; too many times since the 1860's had she gone to war in quest of additional power. Although defeated in World War I, she had been able to grow strong again in large

[1] Senators William Langer of North Dakota and Henrik Shipstead of Minnesota, both Republicans, were the only dissenters. Had the absentees voted, the final result would have been 93–3.

part because the Allies had not continued to cooperate in the enforcement of the terms of the Treaty of Versailles. Such a mistake must not be repeated.

Consequently, at the various wartime conferences decisions had been reached for the subjugation of the Reich. In an effort to consolidate these decisions and to establish the machinery for making them effective, President Truman, Prime Minister Churchill (who was replaced during the meeting by Clement Attlee, his successor as a result of a British election), and Marshal Stalin convened at Potsdam, a Berlin suburb, in July, 1945. In the so-called Potsdam Declaration of July 26, the Big Three approved of the complete disarming of Germany for all time. This action was to be strengthened by wiping out the Nazi organization from top to bottom, by the trial of war criminals, by the establishment of democratic local government, and by the institution of a democratic program of education.

To supervise these changes, Germany was divided into four zones of occupation, allotted to the Russians, British, French, and Americans. The American zone was in the south, bordering on Austria and Czechoslovakia. A general Allied Control Council was placed in charge of the whole occupational management.

In order to prevent Germany from returning to the manufacture of war implements or to a war economy, the Big Three agreed to the decentralization of her industry, including the ending of cartels. The Allies were to supervise her exports, imports, and research projects to ensure that agriculture and "peaceful domestic industries" were primarily promoted. Reparations were to be made in goods and industrial equipment, but not in such amounts that Germany would be unable to get along without outside assistance.

The Potsdam meeting was not a peace conference, nor was a formal congress to deal with all the manifold problems of world settlement after the fashion of the Paris Conference of 1919 in immediate prospect. Indeed the procedure laid down was to postpone a general settlement, while clearing the ground through special agreements on specific issues. A Council of Foreign Ministers representative of the five principal Allies was set up to conduct preliminary discussions and to draft the tentative peace treaties for submission to the United Nations. Treaties for Germany and Austria were not to be considered until those with Italy, Finland, Hungary, Bulgaria, and Rumania had been formulated.

Pending final decisions regarding Germany, the Potsdam Declaration laid down a provisional new boundary in the east. East Prussia was

aggressive war. Critics of the trial contended that this was *ex post facto*
procedure—that plotting aggression had been defined as a crime after
the deed had been done. Justice Jackson argued, however, that since
the Kellog-Briand Pact of 1928 and other international agreements had
condemned recourse to war, such activities as those carried on by German political and military leaders were clearly illegal. He asserted that
the precedent of such an international trial, with individuals being held
responsible for conspiring against the peace, offered great hope as a
deterrent against future aggression. The trial lasted more than ten
months and resulted in the conviction of all but three of the defendants.
Eleven were sentenced to death by hanging; eight were given prison
terms. Goering escaped execution by a last-minute suicide; the other
death sentences were carried out on the morning of October 16, 1946.

Lesser criminals were also tried and punished. Thirty-six officials
and guards from the infamous Dachau concentration camp were
brought before an American military tribunal and condemned to death,
while several German civilians who had participated in the murder of
American aviators were tried and executed.

Reconstruction by MacArthur and Company. (By Poinier in *The Detroit
Free Press.*)

OCCUPATION PROBLEMS: JAPAN

The postwar situation in Japan differed from that in Germany in important particulars. In the first place, the surrender negotiations had resulted in an Allied agreement to retain the emperor and govern through him, with the eventual decision as to his position being left to the Japanese people. Secondly, Japan was occupied for the most part with American forces and American officials secured the principal authority in formulating occupation policy.

As Supreme Allied Commander, General Douglas MacArthur exercised enormous powers over the defeated enemy. During the crucial first weeks of the occupation this authority was controlled only by MacArthur's superiors in Washington. The protests of Russia and other Allies resulted in some modification of the situation by the end of 1945. The foreign ministers of the Big-Three powers, meeting in Moscow in December, agreed to the establishment of a Far Eastern Commission composed of the representatives of the United States, the Soviet Union, Britain, China, France, the Netherlands, Canada, Australia, New Zealand, India, and the Philippine Commonwealth. This eleven-man body with its headquarters at Washington was empowered to formulate principles to govern the control of Japan. Another body, the Allied Council, with representatives of the United States, the Soviet Union, China, and the British Commonwealth, was to sit in Tokyo to advise the Supreme Commander on the spot. But the terms of the Moscow agreement were so drawn as to leave the substance of power still very largely in the hands of the American authorities.

MacArthur acted speedily to dissolve the Imperial General Staff and to disarm and demobilize the army. The jingoistic Black Dragon society was liquidated and the Japanese press was freed from Japanese censorship, although subjected to American. Political prisoners were released and civil liberties proclaimed. The secret police, a citadel of Japanese totalitarianism, was abolished. No elaborate system of military government comparable to that in Germany was set up. MacArthur with a relatively small corps of advisers operated through directives to the emperor and the Japanese cabinet.

Although the Japanese people evidenced no desire for a republic, the form of their political institutions was substantially altered by a new constitution, drafted with MacArthur's approval in March, 1946. This defined the emperor's power as derived from "the sovereign will of the people," and required the advice and approval of the cabinet for all acts of the emperor in matters of state. The Diet, elected by universal suffrage, was to appoint the premier and the Supreme Court, as well as to exercise supreme legislative power. The most drastic clauses of the new document renounced war and the use of force and forbade the maintenance of an army, navy, or air force.

In other particulars the treatment of Japan followed the German precedent more closely. Similar provision was made for the collection of reparations through the confiscation of external assets and through the removal of factories and machinery. The arrest and trial of war criminals was likewise stipulated. Vigorous steps along the latter line were carried out. American military tribunals tried Generals Yamashita and Homa and ordered their execution after hearing shocking testimony of Japanese atrocities in the Philippines under the defendants' commands. Numerous lesser criminals were punished, while former Premier Tojo and other major leaders were brought before a special international tribunal like that at Nuremberg.

ONE WORLD OR TWO?

With the defeat of Germany and Japan the imperative need for subordinating all other issues to the winning of the war ended. Suspicions and rivalries among the victorious Allies found open expression and created serious obstacles both to the drafting of peace treaties and the functioning of the new United Nations. The Soviet Union sought to expand its influence and protect itself against possible attack by incorporating the prewar Baltic states and part of Poland within its own boundaries and by supporting Communist or pro-Russian regimes in neighboring states of eastern Europe and the Balkans. The United States protested repeatedly against the undemocratic character of these regimes, their violations of American property rights, and the obstacles placed in the path of fact-seeking American journalists. Such issues reached a crisis in August, 1946, when Yugoslav fighter planes shot down American transports for allegedly flying over Yugoslav territory without permission. A sharp ultimatum from the State Department brought an apology and promise of compensation for the American lives lost in the incident.

Equal concern was expressed over Soviet policy in other parts of the world. The Russians were accused of using their occupation of Germany and Austria to promote the interests of local Communist parties, of seeking to coerce Turkey into surrendering control of the Dardenelles, and of intriguing in the politics of Iran and other Middle Eastern countries. Suspicion extended to the Far East—to the ultimate objectives of Soviet policy in Korea, in Manchuria, and in China. Observers disputed as to whether Russia's conduct was motivated by a new and dangerous brand of imperialism or was essentially defensive and based upon an exaggerated estimate of her security needs.

Particularly disquieting to Americans was the situation which developed in China. Instead of settling down to the problems of economic reconstruction so urgent in their war-tortured land, the Chinese became involved in a renewal of the old civil war between Chiang Kai-shek's Kuomintang government and the Communists. The continuance of this fighting, it was widely felt, would not only be a tragedy for the Chinese, but would threaten serious complications if the United States and the Soviet Union became involved in aiding the two factions. Immediately after General George C. Marshall's retirement as Chief of Staff, he was sent by President Truman as a special envoy to China to attempt to mediate between the warring factions. All through 1946. Marshall struggled with this exasperating problem only to acknowledge failure and return to the United States in December. Although he had succeeded in arranging an armistice and an agreement to broaden the base of the Chinese government to include all major factions the previous January, hostilities had soon been renewed with each side accusing the other of violating the truce. Marshall placed the blame on the extremists in both camps. One of his first decisions after succeeding to the post of Secretary of State in January, 1947, was that the United States should terminate its mediation efforts and withdraw virtually all the 12,000 American army, navy, and marine corps personnel which had been kept in China since V J Day.

The dilemma in China was paralleled in other parts of the world. In the Mediterranean British policy toward Greece, Italy, Spain, Turkey, and the Arab countries reflected in greater or less degree her fear of Russia, and the United States felt it necessary to give the British a generous measure of support. In part, this arose out of America's new interest in the oil resources of the Middle East. The war had made shocking inroads on domestic reserves of petroleum and future security seemed to demand that the rich supplies of the Arab countries should be kept out of the Soviet sphere of control. Only on Palestine where the British found the strongly pro-Zionist attitude of the American government embarrassing did Anglo-American policies to any great extent diverge. But the differences of England and the United States on this issue did not alter the general picture. The inevitable trend of events seemed to be toward the formation of two hostile camps in world politics—one centered around the Soviet Union, the other around Britain and America.

THE ROCKY ROAD TO PEACE

Negotiating peace treaties in this atmosphere was a long and arduous task. All through 1946 the foreign ministers of the victorious powers struggled with the drafting of treaties for Italy, Bulgaria, Rumania, Hungary, and Finland. In accordance with a line of procedure agreed to by the Big-Three foreign ministers at Moscow in December, 1945, draft treaties were worked out by the great powers which had been at war with each particular Axis satellite; these draft treaties were then reviewed by a peace conference where the smaller nations were represented and the defeated nations were allowed to present their cases; the recommendations of the peace conference were then referred back to the Council of Foreign Ministers of Britain, Russia, France, and the United States for final decisions. Each stage in this cumbersome process was marked by bitter acrimony. Three meetings of the foreign ministers broke up without agreement on the provisions of the draft treaties; the fourth succeeded only by postponing some of its most troublesome problems. The twenty-one-nation conference at Paris was equally stormy, with issue after issue resulting in fifteen-to-six votes, reflecting the division between the Western and Eastern blocs. Not until late in the year when the Big Four took up the problem at New York was the spirit of compromise sufficiently in evidence to permit the completion of the treaties.

Among the questions debated throughout the year, three aroused particular controversy: the disposition of the Italian colonial empire; the rival claims of Italy and Yugoslavia to Trieste and Venezia Giulia; and the control of navigation on the Danube. Each issue involved the relations of the Soviet Union and the Western powers. The colonial problem was compromised fairly early in the negotiations by agreement that the colonies should continue under British administration for one year after the treaty became operative and that their final status should be determined by the Big Four or by the UN Assembly if the Big Four were unable to agree. The debate over Trieste provoked the greatest bitterness. Control of this strategic port was regarded as vital by both the Russian and the anti-Russian blocs. Final agreement provided for the establishment of a Free Territory of Trieste and its immediate environs under a governor responsible to the UN Security Council, while most of Venezia Giulia was to be ceded by Italy to Yugoslavia. The United States put up a strong fight for the principle of free navigation of the Danube; the Russians opposed this as a covert form of economic imperialism. In the end the United States succeeded in having the free navigation principle written into the treaties.

The principal personalities involved in these negotiations were Foreign Secretary Ernest Bevin of Great Britain, Foreign Minister Vyacheslav M. Molotov of Russia, Premier-President Georges Bidault of France, and Secretary of State Byrnes. In his long struggle with Molotov, Byrnes counted heavily on the support of Senators Connally and Vandenberg, who accompanied him to all the important conferences. Thus did the Truman administration seek to ensure itself against any repetition of Wilson's unhappy experiences with the Senate.

Bipartisan support for Byrnes, however, did not mean that his activities escaped criticism. In a political speech at New York on September 12, 1946, Secretary of Commerce Wallace condemned those who would base American policy on "getting tough" with Russia and expressed his conviction that the United States had no more business in the political affairs of eastern Europe than Russia had in the west or in the Americas. These and other opinions expressed by Wallace were resented by Byrnes, Connally, and Vandenberg as an intolerable criticism of their efforts at a time when critical negotiations were in progress. Faced with the unhappy alternative of choosing between his Secretary of State and his Secretary of Commerce, President Truman asked for Wallace's resignation—despite the embarrassing fact that the President had previously given the Wallace speech his public approval.[1]

The completion of the satellite treaties cleared the way for consideration of the future of Germany and Austria. The Big Four foreign ministers met for this purpose at Moscow in March, 1947. By this time Secretary of State Byrnes had been compelled to resign for reasons of health and the burden of speaking for the United States fell upon his successor, General Marshall. After forty-six days the conference broke up without agreeing on either a German or an Austrian treaty. Among the controversies that led to this deadlock the reparations issue was most important. So far as Austria was concerned the statesmen found it impossible to agree upon what assets should be assigned to reparations account, while in the far more difficult case of Germany the whole question of how much Germany should pay and the method of payment was opened up. As compensation for the unparalleled damage wrought by the Nazis on Russian soil, the Soviets demanded $10,000,000,000 reparations. Since the Potsdam formula for payment through the seizure of external assets and industrial equipment would not permit so large a

[1] Wallace's successor as Secretary of Commerce was W. Averell Harriman of New York.

bill to be collected, the Russians asked for payment in goods produced by German industry. The American and British delegations opposed this on the grounds that it would place such an intolerable burden on German economy that the population would be unable to pay for essential food imports. Another point of controversy was over the form of government which should be permitted in Germany. Marshall advocated a federal republic with a very weak central government, while the Russians, fearing that this would open the way for attaching the industrially rich western parts of Germany to an anti-Russian bloc in western Europe, insisted upon a centralized government. The Secretary of State bluntly stated his suspicion of this proposal in a subsequent radio address to the American people. He said:

Agreement was made impossible because the Soviet Union insisted upon proposals which would have established in Germany a centralized government, adapted to the seizure of absolute control of a country which would be doomed economically through inadequate area and excessive population and would be mortgaged to turn over a large part of its production as reparations.

Thus mutual suspicion made it impossible for the time being at least to determine the future of Germany. Yet until a German treaty were made, order and security could hardly be restored in Europe.

THE UNITED NATIONS IN OPERATION

Under these stormy international skies the United Nations began to function. To its organization meeting at London in January, 1946, the United States sent a distinguished delegation composed of Secretary Byrnes, former-Secretary Stettinius, Senators Connally and Vandenberg, and Mrs. Eleanor Roosevelt. Russia's suggestion for delay in setting up of the Security Council was overruled, and this important body was formed at once with Australia, Brazil, Egypt, Mexico, the Netherlands, and Poland elected to the nonpermanent seats. Key officers like Trygve Lie of Norway as Secretary General and Paul-Henri Spaak of Belgium as President of the Assembly were elected. The fifteen judges of the International Court of Justice, including the American, G. H. Hackworth, were chosen, as well as the member nations which would compose the Economic and Social Council.

Both at London in January and at New York in March, when the Security Council began the continuous functioning provided for in the Charter, the UN became dangerously involved in the great contest for power between the Soviet Union on one side and Britain and the United States on the other. Russian diplomats condemned the evidences of British imperialism which they saw in Syria, Indonesia, and Greece, while Britain and the United States concentrated their fire on Soviet policy in Iran. This last problem assumed explosive proportions when the Iranian government protested to the Council over the continued occupation of northern Iran by Russian troops in violation of a treaty under which British, American, and Soviet forces were all to be withdrawn by March 2, 1946. Russia objected to consideration of the dispute on the ground that it was a matter for direct settlement between the two parties. When her request for postponement was voted down, Soviet Representative Gromyko walked out of the Security Council and refused to attend subsequent sessions in which the issue was discussed. Undeterred by this gesture of Russian displeasure, Secretary Byrnes strongly upheld the right of Iran and other small nations to be heard before the Council. Tension over the issue subsided when Soviet troops were at length withdrawn and outstanding controversies between Russia and Iran were compromised in an agreement negotiated directly by the two countries. The Security Council also witnessed bitter exchanges on such issues as Spain—where the Soviet Union and Poland took the lead in urging more drastic anti-Franco steps than Britain and the United States were willing to support—and China—where the continued presence of American troops provoked Russian criticism. On eight different occasions between February and September, 1946, Russia resorted to the veto to defeat Security Council proposals on which it found itself in the minority.

THE PROBLEM OF DISARMAMENT

In October, 1946, the UN Assembly began its first regular session at Flushing, New York. At first it seemed that this would simply provide another arena for the struggle between Russia and the West already being fought out in the Council of Foreign Ministers and in the Security Council. Soviet abuse of the veto power was condemned by the small states, while Molotov attacked prominent British and American statesmen with shocking directness. But hope that more constructive results might be achieved was aroused when the other delegations accepted a Soviet proposal that the subject of world disarmament be put on the agenda.

This brought to the fore a situation which had undoubtedly contributed to international distrust since VJ Day. On one side, British and American leaders were uneasy over the large number of Soviet troops still under arms, both in the occupied countries and at home. On the other, the Russians had good reason for concern at the news that the

United States was continuing to manufacture and store atomic bombs and to strengthen its hold on bases in the western Pacific.

American opinion on the subject of the bomb went through a curious transition. The closing events of the war against Japan were so dramatic that atomic warfare became for a time the most popular subject for discussion. One school of thought contended that the United States should guard closely the secret of the bomb in order to gain permanent military security; the other asserted that the nation should at once share its knowledge with its Soviet ally and with the rest of the world. Neither program was realistic, as the scientists who had developed the bomb attempted patiently to explain. But from hysterical excitement over atomic energy the public presently swung over to a minimizing of its significance. This was largely the unfortunate result of "Operation Crossroads," the navy tests conducted in 1946 at Bikini atoll in the mid-Pacific. When all of the target ships failed to dissolve into mid-air, sensation-craving citizens all too readily dismissed the bomb as "just another weapon"—much overadvertised. Many Americans came to a full realization of what an atomic bomb could do to human flesh and blood packed in a great city only through a reading of John Hersey's *Hiroshima*, which first appeared in *The New Yorker* magazine and then reached a much wider public through publication in book form and through readings over the radio.

At first Congress showed itself as unrealistic and ill-informed as the public in its consideration of the problem of controlling the production of atomic energy. Because of the patient and intelligent work of Senator Brien McMahon of Connecticut and the special Senate committee of which he was chairman, however, Congress enacted farsighted legislation in July, 1946, providing for a five-man United States Atomic Energy Commission to control all domestic aspects of nuclear energy. Civilian rather than military personnel was specified and the chairmanship of this powerful body was eventually entrusted by President Truman to David E. Lilienthal, who for thirteen years previously had been associated with the great TVA experiment. The choice was widely applauded when announced, but confirmation by the Senate was not achieved without a sharp fight. Senator McKellar of Tennessee, who had long feuded with Lilienthal because of the latter's insistence that TVA personnel be selected on a business rather than a patronage basis, sought revenge. His charge that Lilienthal was a Communist sympathizer had so little evidence to back it that it was dismissed in most quarters as absurd. But a substantial faction of conservative Republicans headed by Senator Taft joined forces with McKellar. They assailed the appointee as a "New Dealer" and an enemy of private enterprise. They revived the argument that atomic development should be controlled by the army and navy. Since the Republicans now dominated the Senate, this opposition would have been fatal to Lilienthal's chances had not Senator Vandenberg and a group of internationally-minded Republicans given strong support to the President's nominee. He was finally confirmed by a vote of 51 to 30 on April 9, 1947. It was an important victory for two principles: that atomic power should be developed as an asset belonging to all the people rather than to certain privileged monopolies and that United States atomic policy should be determined upon broad international considerations rather than upon narrow nationalism.

The international issue was involved in the Lilienthal fight because of the TVA executive's prominent role in drafting the so-called "Acheson-Lilienthal report" of March, 1946. This served as the basis for the concrete program which Bernard Baruch presented on behalf of the United States at the opening session of the UN Atomic Energy Commission in June, 1946. It was proposed that an international authority be created to exercise managerial control of all atomic-energy activities potentially dangerous to world security, and to control, inspect, and license all other atomic activities. The atomic bomb itself should be outlawed and the international authority should have power to punish violations of the agreement. The United States promised to stop manufacturing bombs, dispose of its stock of bombs, and make available its scientific information, but only after the international authority was set up and in effective operation.

Gromyko, the Russian spokesman, opposed the broad international control advocated by the American government and particularly the careful stipulation in the Baruch plan that no veto of the acts of the new atomic authority should be permitted. The first Russian counterproposal was for a simple renunciation of atomic weapons by all the powers without provision for international controls or inspection. Over the succeeding months these issues were debated over and over again in the Atomic Energy Commission, in the Assembly, and in the Security Council. The Russian position changed somewhat: the need of an international authority and some form of international inspection was soon recognized. But fundamental differences remained. The Soviet government insisted that as a prerequisite to international control, atomic bombs should be prohibited by international treaty and all atomic energy plants should be turned over to international management. The United States refused to take such steps until the system of international control had actually been made effective. The United States wanted the international authority's power of inspection to be broad and exempt from any veto; the Russians wanted to define it more narrowly. Finally and most important, the United States asserted that once a treaty had been agreed to defining the violations which were to be considered international crimes and specifying measures of enforcement, there should be no legal right, by veto or otherwise, whereby a willful violater should be protected from punishment. The Russians wanted to retain enforcement within the framework of the Security Council where each of the Big Five representatives had a veto.

Meanwhile negotiations for general disarmament marked time. By unanimous agreement on December 14, 1946, the UN Assembly had accepted a sweeping resolution calling for the formulation of practical measures for disarmament which should be submitted to a special Assembly session, for the elimination of atomic and other weapons of mass destruction, for international inspection and safeguards against violations of disarmament agreements, for the speedy establishment of an international police force, for balanced withdrawal of troops stationed in ex-enemy countries, and for the progressive reduction of national armed forces. But disagreement developed over the steps which should be taken to implement these pledges. The Soviet government wanted to consider the atomic energy problem as simply one phase of the whole problem of disarmament; the United States insisted that the atomic energy issue must have priority. Whatever the merits of these two lines of procedure, it was obvious that no realistic disarmament could be achieved until Russia and America worked out their differences not only on the problem of the bomb but on numerous other issues as well.

THE TRUMAN DOCTRINE

Growing concern was felt in Britain and the United States as more and more of Europe fell under the control of pro-Russian governments. By the spring of 1947 these included Finland, Poland, Hungary, Czechoslovakia, Yugoslavia, Rumania, and Bulgaria as well as the Russian occupation zones in Germany and Austria. In Italy and France, moreover, there were large and powerful Communist parties.

Greece had an anti-Communist government, but its hold upon the country was insecure. Economic conditions were desperately bad and numerous guerillas were operating, particularly in northern Greece, attempting to overthrow the royalist regime. The rebels included both Communists and non-Communists, but it was widely felt that their victory would mean extension of Russian influence over yet another country and one of critical importance because of its position in the eastern Mediterranean near the strategic Dardanelles and the oil-rich Middle East. Britain under Churchill had undertaken a policy of providing military and economic support to the threatened regime and the succeeding Labor government continued this policy.

But in March, 1947, a crisis developed. England's own economic position was so precarious that her statesmen decided that she must withdraw her help from Greece at the end of the month. This threatened to be a fatal blow for that shaky Balkan regime and the Truman administration decided to take over the responsibility. On March 12 the President appeared before Congress to ask for approval of a $400,000,000 program of economic and military aid not only for Greece, but for Turkey as well in order to strengthen the defenses of this guardian of the Straits. The request had broad implications as the President gravely acknowledged. In what was promptly dubbed the "Truman Doctrine," he said:

I believe that it must be the policy of the United States to support free peoples who are resisting attempted subjugation by armed minorities or by outside pressures.

I believe that we must assist free peoples to work out their own destinies in their own way.

I believe that our help should be primarily through economic and financial aid which is essential to economic stability and orderly political processes.

Not since before Pearl Harbor had there been such widespread controversy over an issue of American foreign policy as the Truman Doctrine provoked. Many Americans supported it strongly as a much needed step toward checking the expansion of Communism and Soviet influence. Others criticized it as a form of economic imperialism, an interference with the domestic affairs of other nations, and the beginning of a dangerous adventure in power politics that might end in war. It was asserted that this attempt to safeguard democracy was being made for governments that were themselves anti-democratic. Henry Wallace, no longer in public office, was the sharpest critic of the new policy. He condemned it in speeches not only in the United States, but in England and on the European continent as well. So great was the schism between the Wallace faction and the administration on this issue that a third party movement in 1948 appeared to be a distinct possibility.

Many who did not go so far as Wallace did in criticism of the Truman Doctrine regretted the fact that the United States had taken unilateral action without at least attempting to utilize the machinery of the United Nations. Truman defended himself on the ground that the UN was not yet equipped to deal with such problems and Warren Austin, the

United States representative on the Security Council, argued that the American action was intended to strengthen, not weaken, the principle of collective security. But, nevertheless, the supporters of the program thought it best to accept the so-called Vandenberg amendment, under which Congress directed the President to withdraw any or all of the aid in case the Security Council found that action by the UN made its continuance unnecessary or undesirable. The United States waived its right of veto on the issue.

Even with the Vandenberg amendment the proposal to expend $400,000,000 on Greek and Turkish aid was hotly debated. But it was finally approved by Congress on May 15, 1947. Much would depend on the administration of the program to determine whether it would result in genuine rehabilitation or merely in bolstering up reactionary groups in their efforts to stave off change. To head the difficult mission to Greece President Truman selected former Governor Dwight Griswold of Nebraska, a Republican of the Stassen or thorough internationalist faction.

THE MARSHALL PLAN

Needless to say, Greece and Turkey were not the only areas urgently needing economic assistance. At the same time that the $400,000,000 aid plan for those two countries was adopted, Congress appropriated $350,000,000 for relief supplies for Italy, Austria, Poland, China, Trieste, and Greece—a step made necessary by the termination of UNRRA. Earlier than this, Great Britain, France, and Italy had successfully applied to American sources for postwar loans. The Soviet Union had also sought a large American credit to finance desperately needed imports, but negotiations for this had made no progress in view of the general tension between the two countries.

By June, 1947, it was clear that the whole question of American financial assistance to Europe and the rest of the world needed review and clarification. How much would the United States need to expend for such purposes? Should its assistance be available to all European countries or only to those which supported it in world politics and shunned Communism? On June 5 in an address at Harvard University Secretary of State Marshall formulated a healthy new approach to the problem. He said:

Our policy is not directed against any country or doctrine, but against hunger, poverty, desperation and chaos. Its purpose should be the revival of a working economy in the world so as to permit the emergence of political and social conditions in which free institutions can exist. Such assistance

I am convinced must not be on a piecemeal basis as various crises develop. . . . The initiative I think must come from Europe. . . . The program should be a joint one, agreed to by a number, if not all, the European nations.

This invitation was accepted by Great Britain and France with alacrity. They promptly initiated steps to formulate a broad program for European rehabilitation and urged the Soviet Union to join them in the enterprise.

The Marshall plan had much to commend it. It was positive in its approach rather than negative as the Truman Doctrine had been. It offered an opportunity for the European nations with American help to join in a great effort to raise themselves out of their desperate economic quagmire. But at least two great pitfalls lay in the path ahead. Would the Soviet Union overcome its suspicion of "capitalist imperialism" sufficiently to cooperate in the enterprise? If not, the fatal division of the world into two hostile camps would continue. Would the United States Congress approve the substantial American expenditures that would be necessary to make the plan work? If not, Europe might agree only to have its agreement nullified by America's return to a form of isolationism.

HEMISPHERE POLITICS

Overcast international skies impelled the United States to strengthen its ties with Latin America. In March, 1947, President Truman made a good-will trip to Mexico City and a few weeks later Mexican President Alemán visited Washington, where he addressed a joint session of Congress. In June the Truman administration formulated a program for coordinating the defense forces of the Western Hemisphere. The President asked Congressional authorization for the United States to train soldiers, sailors, and airmen of other hemisphere nations, to maintain, repair or replace their military equipment, and to transfer American arms and ships to them. The "Arms for the Americas" plan as this was called was criticized as creating an American military bloc contrary to the spirit of the United Nations and as fortifying the position of Latin American dictators by building up the armed force whereby they could perpetuate themselves in power. But supporters of the plan argued that it would strengthen American defenses against the threat of war with Russia and would check the expansion of Communism into the Western Hemisphere.

A desire to achieve inter-American unity led to an important change in the policy of the United States toward Argentina. It will be recalled that the pro-Axis policy of the latter state had resulted in condemnation by Secretary Hull and a period of strained relations. The breach had been partially repaired in 1945 when the Argentine government accepted the Act of Chapultepec, declared war on the Axis, and was admitted to the United Nations. But events during the succeeding months gave the United States reason to doubt the sincerity of this last-minute conversion. The Argentine government continued its undemocratic domestic policies and took no effective steps to prevent Axis exiles from finding a haven on Argentine soil. The United States consequently reverted to a policy of throwing its weight against a continuance of the dominance of the Perón faction. The high point of this campaign was reached in February, 1946, when the American government made clear its hope that Perón would fail in his campaign to win the Argentine presidency in a general election. A "Blue Book" released by the State Department provided damning evidence of the pro-Axis course which Perón and his associates had followed so long as it seemed safe to do so. But despite this record the South American strong man secured a decisive victory at the polls.

There followed a long debate as to the future course which the United States should take. Spruille Braden, first as ambassador to Argentina and then as an Assistant Secretary of State in charge of American republic affairs, advocated a continuance of the anti-Perón policy; George Messersmith, his successor at Buenos Aires, favored an acceptance of Perón and an effort to bring Argentina once again into full participation in inter-American affairs. In June both men resigned their posts, but accompanying events made it evident that the Messersmith policy had at last won out over the Braden. President Truman announced that the United States was now satisfied with Argentina's compliance with the anti-Nazi provisions of the Act of Chapultepec and was ready to include her in discussions for a Western Hemisphere defense pact.

It was obvious that American foreign policy was now being shaped by fear of Communism rather than of fascism. The outlook for permanent peace was not promising. Yet despite the acrimony over specific issues it was possible for optimists to take comfort in the reflection that the Soviet Union and the United States, whose isolationist courses had so weakened the old League, were taking the leading roles in the new United Nations. In this lay the greatest hope that the rocky road to peace might somehow be eventually conquered.

30

Social Trends during Peace and War

It was not easy to believe in the reality of progress during the years when Americans struggled through the Great Depression and the War for Survival—the name which President Roosevelt thought most appropriate for World War II. Many ideals and human values which had seemed secure in 1914 appeared shattered almost beyond revival by 1947. The observer philosophical enough to scan the whole American scene, however, and to think in terms of decades rather than of years, still found many things to reassure him. Despite discouraging setbacks, substantial advance had been made since 1900 in reducing many age-long inequalities. American society was far from perfect, but its prospects were hopeful enough to keep alive and vital the democratic faith.

RISE OF THE NEGRO

In no area was the long view more required than in considering the position of the Negro in American life. Disenfranchisement, discrimination, poverty, and lack of opportunity were still the black man's lot in 1947. Yet there are degrees in misfortune, and the Negro's situation was much less bad in 1947 than in 1900.

Americans have always believed in education as the most valuable key to every problem, and in this area real progress had been made. In 1910 30 per cent of the Negroes had been illiterate; only 8 per cent were thus handicapped in 1940. As late as 1915 there had been only sixty-four Negro high schools in the country; by 1940 the number had risen to 2500. Almost twenty thousand Negroes were graduated from colleges during the decade of the thirties—more than twice the number of the more prosperous twenties.

Mob violence, so terrifying to the Negroes and so degrading to the whites, was diminishing. More than one hundred Negroes had been lynched in each of the first two years of the century, and there were between fifty and one hundred such incidents annually thereafter until 1917. The relatively good record of only thirty-five lynchings of Negroes in that year was not maintained; in 1919 there were seventy-six—but thereafter the annual number dropped until in 1929 it fell to seven. Once again the gain was not permanent and in 1933 there were twenty-four; but there were less than ten for each of nine years beginning in 1936. The 1944 record of 2 Negroes and no whites lynched stood in welcome contrast to the 106 Negroes and 9 whites killed in 1900.

During World War II Americans were rightly shocked over several race riots. Detroit, whose war industries had attracted both Negroes and Southern whites, was the scene of strife in 1942 and again in 1943. Similar if less serious clashes occurred in the Harlem district of New York City and in Los Angeles. Several fatalities took place in the South when trouble arose between Negro soldiers and white police or civilians, while an ugly clash between white and Negro soldiers occurred at Fort Dix, New Jersey. Disquieting as these events were, there was much less violence than in the terrible year 1919 when race riots had taken place in twenty-six American cities. In the worst of these at Chicago, 15 whites and 23 Negroes had been killed, while 178 whites and 342 Negroes had been wounded. More important than the smaller number of riots during World War II—which might be ascribed principally to good fortune—was the evidence of greater concern over the situation and the positive steps taken in scores of American communities to prevent race relations from deteriorating to the point where there was danger of such incidents. More than one hundred local groups were formally organized to deal with the problem. Such diverse institutions as churches, schools, police departments, and labor unions undertook educational projects and other programs intended to reduce misunderstanding between whites and Negroes.

As the Negro came to enjoy somewhat more security against mob violence, however, he became more concerned over the problem of "legal lynching"—the practice in many states of dealing more drastically with blacks hailed before the law than with whites. Nation-wide publicity was attracted to the so-called Scottsboro case in which an Alabama court sentenced to death nine Negroes charged with attacking two white women. The Federal Supreme Court overruled a first conviction in 1932 on the ground that the defendants were not permitted to have adequate counsel and a second conviction in 1935 because the Negroes

Marian Anderson. (Brown Bros.)

had been systematically excluded from the jury lists. Despite the rulings of the Supreme Court, however, the tacit exclusion of Negroes from jury service continued to be the practice in most rural courts of the South.

Negroes with outstanding talent received an increasing degree of recognition. Upon the death of George Washington Carver in 1943, impressive tribute was paid to his achievements as a scientist. Marian Anderson was acknowledged to belong in the company of the greatest singers of her generation, while the extraordinary musical talent of Roland Hayes, Paul Robeson, and Dorothy Maynor was given due praise. An increasing number of Negroes achieved distinction in literature and the arts. Acclaimed by both white and black sports lovers were such outstanding Negro athletes as heavyweight champion Joe Louis, fleet-footed Jesse Owens, the hero of the 1936 Olympic games, and Jackie Robinson, the first Negro in big-league baseball.

Not so promising, however, were the prospects for Negroes of only ordinary ability. In the vital matter of earning a living, the black man found himself seriously handicapped by racial prejudice. The lot of the sharecropper and tenant in the South tended to deteriorate. Negroes left the land and moved to the cities, particularly those of the North. Yet here they encountered the prejudice not only of employers but of workers who frequently admitted only whites to their labor unions. The CIO sought to encourage more liberal policies, but was by no means able to break down the barriers in all local unions. Negroes usually had to accept the menial tasks which no one else wanted. They were the last to be hired in boom days and the first to be let out when business lagged. No group suffered more during the Great Depression.

Some New Deal policies hurt the Negro. This was true of the crop restriction efforts of the early AAA and of some aspects of the NRA which resulted in Negro employees being discharged rather than being given minimum-wage rates. But other policies were of great benefit. Employment under WPA and other forms of relief saved many Negro families from disaster, while PWA and USHA housing projects were of particular value to a group which had hitherto had to dwell almost exclusively in the slums. On the balance, most Negroes found the New Deal good, and thousands of them in the Northern cities changed their political allegiance—temporarily, at least—from the party of Lincoln to that of Franklin Roosevelt.

As the Negro vote became independent, politicians became more acutely conscious of Negro demands. Although filibusters by Southern Senators prevented votes on the Federal antilynching bills which came before Congress in the thirties and the antipoll-tax measures of the forties, these proposals showed impressive strength. The desire to avoid Federal intervention undoubtedly contributed to significant changes of opinion in the South. Lynching fell under almost universal public condemnation. A few states repealed the poll-tax laws which had served to exclude the Negro from the ballot. On this issue, however, Southern opinion was still conservative, and various legal obstacles as well as extralegal forms of coercion prevented all but a few Negroes in the South from exercising their Constitutional right to vote. This continued to be so even after 1944 when the Supreme Court struck down one of the principal white bulwarks by ruling that Negroes might not be excluded from voting in primary elections.

An impressive victory for the race was won when President Roosevelt on June 25, 1941, issued Executive Order 8802. In part this declared:

. . . the policy of the United States [is] to encourage full participation in the national defense program by all citizens of the United States, regardless of race, creed, color, or national origin, in the firm belief that the democratic way of life within the Nation can be defended successfully only with the help and support of all groups within its borders.

Such affirmations of principle had been made before; what made this one something more than mere words was the appointment of a Fair Employment Practices Committee (FEPC) to investigate complaints and to take steps to redress grievances. The FEPC conducted numerous public hearings and focused publicity on employers and unions which practiced discrimination. The effort to open up new areas of employment for the Negroes was well timed since war production supplied an almost unlimited demand for labor of all kinds. Between 1940 and 1944 the number of Negroes employed in manufacturing and processing increased from 500,000 to around 1,200,000; in government service from 60,000 to 200,000. President Truman advocated the continuance of FEPC as a permanent postwar agency, but the proposal was defeated by the filibustering tactics of Senator Bilbo of Mississippi and other Southern legislators.

Despite this setback, the antidiscrimination cause made progress. The world conflict quickened the conscience of many whites; the inconsistency of waging war against the Nazi theory of the Master Race abroad while denying racial equality at home was obvious. Moreover, the injustice of demanding from Negroes the full obligation of citizenship in the way of military service while denying them many of its privileges became clear to more and more Americans. Governor Dewey of New York succeeded in securing an excellent antidiscrimination law from the state legislature in 1945, and similar measures received serious consideration in a score of other states.

The intense interest which the problem of race relations was now receiving found expression in many forms. Lillian Smith's somber novel, *Strange Fruit*, and Richard Wright's poignant autobiography, *Black Boy*, became best sellers, while several plays on the same theme reached the New York stage. On a different level were the important two-volume study entitled *An American Dilemma* by the Swedish scholar, Gunnar Myrdal, and a number of other excellent sociological treatises which appeared during the thirties and forties. Negroes and whites both contributed to the striking growth of the National Association for the Advancement of Colored People, whose membership increased from 100,000 in 1941 to 500,000 in 1945. The tactics of this organization were too aggressive for most Southern whites, but many of them supported the more moderate Commission on Interracial Cooperation. The changing attitude of more advanced Southern opinion was demonstrated by the campaign launched by the Atlanta *Journal* to secure improved economic opportunities for Negroes, better educational facilities, greater emphasis upon health and housing, and the right to vote in general and primary elections.

The Negro problem was far from solved. Indeed, many observers feared that bloody interracial conflict might break out at any time. Yet the country at least had been shaken out of its easygoing complacency on the issue.

CROSSCURRENTS IN THE SOUTH

During the thirties and forties it was apparent that tendencies of divergent direction were at work in the South. There was much evidence of Southern conservatism. Stress has already been laid on the deep distaste for the New Deal that prevailed in many quarters—a distaste that found concrete embodiment not only in opposition to Roosevelt's renomination in 1944, but in a significant growth of the Republican vote in several Southern states. Within Democratic ranks, Senators Glass and Byrd of Virginia, Smith of South Carolina, George of Georgia, and O'Daniel of Texas were outspoken in their condemnation of many of the objectives and methods of the Roosevelt administration. On the other hand, the New Deal secured some of its strongest support from Senators Pepper of Florida, Hill of Alabama, and Barkley of Kentucky.

Most interesting of the younger generation of Southern liberals was Governor Ellis Arnall of Georgia. Although like others of this group he dealt gingerly with the explosive racial issue, he had to his credit the routing of ex-Governor Eugene Talmadge [1]—a notorious Negro-baiter, the adoption of a drastically reformed state constitution, the modernization of the penal system, and the abolition of the poll tax. Arnall's most publicized endeavor was his struggle to force a revision of railroad-rate

[1] The Talmadge faction enjoyed a brief revival of power in 1946. In a close primary vote Eugene Talmadge secured the Democratic nomination and later the election. But he died before inauguration day and the attempt of the Talmadge-dominated legislature to bestow the governorship on his son, Herman, failed when the state supreme court ruled that Melvin E. Thompson, a protégé of Arnall who had been elected lieutenant governor, should succeed to the vacant post. Prior to this decision, from January to March, both men claimed to be the rightful governor—a striking illustration of the conflicting forces in operation not only in Georgia, but in Southern politics elsewhere.

schedules that discriminated against the South. Impatient with the Interstate Commerce Commission, which he considered under the domination of the railroads, Arnall instituted proceedings under the antitrust
laws—the first such case ever brought by a state. According to the
Georgia governor, Northern railroads, instigated by Northern financial
and industrial interests, "conspired to subject all the railroads of the
United States to the authority of a hierarchy of price-fixing rate mecha-
nisms culminating in the Association of American Railroads." Typical of
the differentials cited in the Georgia case was the rate on canned
vegetables. Each hundred pounds of this commodity shipped from
Griffin, Georgia, to Chicago, a distance of 772 miles, was charged 62
cents, while the rate from Baltimore, Maryland, to Chicago, a distance
of 767 miles, was 47 cents. Leaders in Western states watched the
case with great interest, since they had similar grievances against the
railroads. Whatever the Supreme Court decision might be, there was
evidence that the Interstate Commerce Commission had been prodded
into action and that the nation's rate structures would be revised in the
near future.

The controversy over railroad rates dramatized an issue that was
deeply felt in both South and West. Both sections complained of their
"colonial status." That is, they asserted that Eastern capital dominated
the country's economic life and that this control was used to protect
industry in the East and Middle West and to retard the industrialization
of the rest of the nation. Whatever truth there may have been in this
charge, the war resulted in the building of many industrial plants in
less-developed areas. Electrical power from TVA and from the Columbia River dams was employed in the vast expansion of aluminum manufacture. There was great activity in the steel mills of Birmingham,
Alabama, feverish shipbuilding at New Orleans and elsewhere, new
synthetic rubber plants at Baton Rouge, and tin smelters in Texas.
There was danger, however, that some of this gain would be only
temporary, and that not all of these plants would be operated after
the war was over.

Full pay envelopes and high cotton and tobacco prices meant much
to the South because many of the troubles of both white and black
inhabitants arose from poverty. The per capita income of the South
in 1935 was only $240, exactly half that of the rest of the country. In
1938 President Roosevelt said: "It is my conviction that the South
presents right now the nation's No. 1 economic problem—the nation's
problem, not merely the South's. For we have an economic unbalance
in the nation as a whole, due to this very condition of the South." The

statement aroused the resentment of many sensitive Southerners and, as has been shown, New Deal efforts to deal with the situation met with much opposition.

Although they might resent the intervention of outsiders, intelligent leaders south of the Potomac were themselves acutely conscious of their section's major problems. Francis P. Miller of Virginia was instrumental in the foundation in 1935 of the Southern Policy Committee. This body, along with subsidiary organizations in the various states, focused public opinion on the need for attacking the farm-tenancy problem, for improving public education, and for equalizing tax assessments. Another great effort was that of the Citizen's Fact Finding Movement of Georgia, in which groups having a total membership of 250,000 participated. A third such agency was the Southern Governors' Conference, formed in 1937. The most profound individual student and writer on regional problems was Dr. Howard W. Odum of the University of North Carolina.

There was basic agreement on the needs of the section. These included more diversified industry, better balanced agriculture, more stable land tenure, more careful use of the soil, more education, and greatly expanded public health services. To state the problems and to

Driving the Golden Spike. (By Bishop in the *St. Louis Star-Times*.)

solve them were two different things, yet it seemed safe to predict that in a region where the more thoughtful leaders of opinion had clearly defined such objectives much progress in achieving them might be expected over the next generation. Southern optimists emphasized the area's vast undeveloped resources, both natural and human, and insisted that the South should be regarded not as the nation's No. 1 economic problem, but as its No. 1 economic opportunity.

WOMEN AND THE FAMILY

During World War II more than three million women took jobs who would not have done so otherwise. In addition, millions of farm wives did outside chores which had always been considered men's work. A quarter of a million women enlisted in the WACS, the WAVES, or some other service. It was convincing proof of women's ability to perform any task that did not involve extraordinary physical strength. The effect of the war, however, was not to institute a new trend so much as to accelerate one already strongly established. In 1880, two and a half million women had worked; the number had increased to five million by 1920 and to eleven million by 1940.

Typical of the new woman was Eleanor Roosevelt, the President's wife. Impatient with the purely social duties traditionally imposed upon the First Lady, Mrs. Roosevelt carried on an extraordinary number of activities. At various times she accepted employment as a teacher, lecturer, radio commentator, magazine feature writer, and columnist for the daily press. The earnings which came from such labors she devoted very largely to charity. Her unpaid activities were even more extensive. An indefatigable traveler, she visited every part of the country, attending innumerable conferences and seeing with her own eyes conditions among the underprivileged. During the war years she extended the range of her journeys to cover areas where American soldiers were stationed all the way from Britain to Australia. The First Lady's zeal made her a figure scarcely less controversial than her husband. Many Americans asserted that Mrs. Roosevelt's activities should be devoted to the White House, that her restless traveling was both undignified and meddlesome. On the other hand, she had millions of admirers and defenders; to them she was a great person in her own right, giving herself without stint to causes in which she believed.

Women gained distinction in many different lines of endeavor. Within the field of government they achieved administrative posts, seats in the Senate and the House, governorships, and important diplomatic missions. In the field of literature they may be said to have secured equal recognition with men. Of thirty best sellers between 1901 and 1936, sixteen were by women. Few journalists commanded more respect than Dorothy Thompson, Anne O'Hare McCormick, and Freda Kirchwey.

The extent to which women's ambition for a career undermined the stability of the family was a matter of dispute. An increasing number of women, confronted with the choice of marriage or a job, elected to take both. Critics of the practice blamed it in large part for the rising divorce rate and increasing juvenile delinquency, but it was difficult to prove that the woman who worked was necessarily a worse wife and mother than the woman who stayed in the home.

Whatever its perils, marriage was hardly declining in popularity. In 1910, 59 per cent of all women over the age of fifteen were married, while 30 per cent were single; in 1940, 61 per cent were married, while only 26 per cent were single. The proportion of married women to single must have gone up appreciably thereafter since the war years were characterized by an unusually large number of youthful marriages. The depression of the early thirties had caused the marriage rate to drop to 7.87 per thousand population in 1932, but it climbed to 11.9 by 1940, the highest rate since 1920. The rate jumped to 12.6 in 1941 and to 13.1 in 1942, falling off thereafter to 10.9 in 1944. Many war marriages were entered upon in haste and were strained by separation and the tensions of wartime living. There seemed every indication that the divorce rate, which had climbed from 0.73 per thousand population in 1900 to 2.0 in 1940, would leap upward still further during the postwar years.

The decline in the birth rate, which had disturbed some observers during the twenties and early thirties, was at least temporarily arrested. In the depression year of 1933 the rate had fallen to 16.6 per thousand population; better times brought it up to 17.9 in 1940, while the war resulted in its rising to 21.5 in 1943—the highest since 1925. Youth's eagerness to marry and have children during the darkest period of the war seemed to indicate that it had little fear of the future of the nation.

Wartime conditions brought many parental problems. The juvenile-delinquency rate, which had shown a gratifying decline during the thirties, jumped up sharply. In 1944 there were 56 per cent more court cases than in 1939. The increase in the rate of delinquency was greater for girls than for boys, although the actual number of boy delinquents remained larger than the number of girls. Many communities organized special efforts to deal with the problem. Particularly notable in this respect were the Chicago and Detroit Area Project Plans, the Back of the Yard Plan of Saul J. Alinsky in Chicago, and the Sunbury (Pennsylvania) Council for Youth Welfare.

REVIVAL OF RELIGION

The perplexities of modern life, the troubles of the depression, and the long agony of the war caused many Americans to return to the shelter of the church. Books from the warfronts testified to the comfort which religion had provided for men adrift on rafts in the Pacific or flying on dangerous missions. Many servicemen were impressed by the sacrificial spirit and the fine teamwork of Catholic, Protestant, and Jewish chaplains. The mythical exploits of one of these at Pearl Harbor provided the theme for one of the war's popular songs: "Praise the Lord and Pass the Ammunition." Even more striking was the extraordinary popularity of books with a religious theme. Among the best sellers were Lloyd Douglas's *The Robe*, A. J. Cronin's *Keys to the Kingdom*, Franz Werfel's *Song of Bernadette*, and Sholem Asch's *The Apostle*.

Much interest attended the activities of Monsignor Fulton J. Sheen, who brought into the Catholic fold such notable converts as the journalist Heywood Broun, the industrialist Henry Ford II, the ex-Communist Louis Budenz, and the playwright-politician Claire Booth Luce. In addition to such conversions as these which made the headlines, Catholic authorities during the thirties estimated that about forty thousand Americans each year were accepting Catholicism. This gain was offset, however, by a considerable, although unmeasured, loss of Catholics who ceased to practice their faith.

Convincing vitality also marked the Protestant churches. Some of the excessive denominationalism that had marked the nineteenth century disappeared. The union of various Lutheran bodies resulted in the organization of the United Lutheran Church in 1918 and the American Lutheran Church in 1931. A merger of other groups in 1934 brought the establishment of the Evangelical and Reformed Church with nearly a million members. In 1931 the historic Congregational Church joined with the Christian Church, while in 1939 the largest of all these mergers united eight million members in the Methodist Church. Proposed also was a union of the Presbyterian and Episcopal groups. Churches not formally united showed an increasing degree of cooperative enterprise. The Federal Council of Churches served as a medium for much such activity, while other bodies provided for interdenominational planning in the mission field and for focusing the thinking of Christians upon the problem of postwar organization.

Many Protestant clergymen, ashamed of the church's excessive zeal in whipping up wartime passion during World War I, swung over to radical pacifism. Of 19,000 ministers polled in 1931, 62 per cent expressed a conviction that the church should refuse to sanction or support any future war. Such sentiment became particularly characteristic of Christian young people and students. Indeed, the sentiment was so widespread as to contribute materially to the isolationism of the thirties. When war finally came, a sizable group stuck to these convictions and suffered internment in conscientious objectors' camps rather than submit to conscription into the armed service. The great majority, however, saw at stake in the conflict moral issues important enough to override all other considerations. They pinned their hopes for the future upon victory in a just war and the promotion of good will in the postwar world.

The Billy Sunday type of evangelism was no longer in vogue among most of the older Protestant bodies, which preferred to expand their membership by less bombastic means. This conservatism of appeal seemed defeatist to many more emotional Christians. One of the phenomena of the war years was a series of massive Youth-for-Christ rallies conducted in various parts of the country. Another evidence of revolt against religious intellectualism was the remarkable growth of such groups as the Pentecostal and Holiness sects, the Assemblies of God, the Church of the Nazarene, and Jehovah's Witnesses. Entirely different in its appeal was the Oxford Group or Buchmanite movement which stimulated many rich and well-educated people to a new interest in religion.

THE CHALLENGE OF SCIENCE

The atomic bomb dropped on Hiroshima on August 6, 1945, had intellectual repercussions no less impressive than its material results. Intelligent Americans suddenly realized that the advance of science had been so rapid and revolutionary as to require fundamental readjustments in all political and social relationships. Yet the bomb represented the culmination of merely one line of recent research. Less dramatic but scarcely less significant progress had been made by science in the fields of aviation, electronics, chemicals, and medicine.

Even before the war it was obvious that America was becoming aware of science to an increasing degree. The number of industrial research laboratories in the country increased from around four hundred in the early twenties to approximately twenty-four hundred in the late thirties. During the latter decade, $300,000,000 was being expended for such industrial research each year. One center alone, the Mellon Institute for Industrial Research at Pittsburgh, employed 142 investigators and 76 assistants. Giving valuable support and direction to scientific work throughout the country was the National Research Council, organized in 1916.

The general public accepted as a matter of course the assumption that daily life would be more and more transformed by science. Women wore clothing made of synthetic fabrics and used innumerable gadgets made of plastic in the home. Newspapers printed photographs flashed through space, and householders waited impatiently for television to pass from the experimental to the practical stage. Each year saw new knowledge in the field of nutrition and the manufacture and sale of vitamins became big business. Pneumonia and many other diseases lost much of their terror when treated with the new sulfa drugs or the newer-still miracle worker, penicillin.

The necessities of war telescoped into a few years developments that might have been expected over a generation. Not only did the use of blood plasma transform the treatment of the wounded, but it led to an intensified study of the proteins contained in the plasma. From these investigations came the discovery of serum albumin for the treatment of shock, fibrinogen to combat excessive bleeding, and globulins for the treatment of measles and jaundice. Another line of research led to the production of DDT, an insecticide of astounding efficacy whose use during the war cut down malaria during the Pacific island campaigns and checked the spread of typhus in Italy.

No less impressive was progress in electronics and aviation. Radar permitted antiaircraft gun crews to detect the approach of planes in the darkest night 100 miles away, it enabled plane crews to observe the nature of the terrain beneath them through darkness or cloud or fog, and made marine navigation safer. Aeronautical engineering more than doubled the speed of aircraft and made it possible for them to fly at much higher ceilings. Turbine and jet engines that might revolutionize transportation were developed.

The great importance placed by the government on wartime science was evidenced by the establishment of the Office of Scientific Research and Development (OSRD) under the direction of Dr. Vannevar Bush of the Carnegie Institution. There were two main branches of the agency: the National Defense Research Committee (NDRC) with President James B. Conant of Harvard as chairman, and the Committee on Medical Research (CMR) under Dr. A. Newton Richards of the University of Pennsylvania. The war was unquestionably shortened by many months through the activities of these agencies; indeed, had the enemy been allowed to preempt the field of scientific research, United Nations victory might not have been achieved.

The internationalism of science under normal conditions is evidenced by a listing of the key discoveries which laid the theoretical ground-work for the development of the atomic bomb. In 1905, Albert Einstein, a German by birth but residing in Switzerland, opened up a new line of scientific thought with his hypothesis that matter might be converted into energy. Some five years later, Lord Rutherford in England and Professor Nagaoka in Japan theorized that the chemical atom was not a hard massy particle, ultimate and indivisible, but had a nucleus at the center which contained concentrated matter and energy. Rutherford later demonstrated that bombardment with rays of radium could con-vert atoms of one element into atoms of other elements. Dr. Enrico Fermi in Rome showed that such conversion could be effectively ob-tained by using small atomic fragments called neutrons. This line of research culminated in an epochal experiment in 1939 when Dr. Otto Hahn and Miss Lise Meitner of Berlin, working at the Kaiser Wilhelm Institute, bombarded uranium atoms with neutrons and caused them to divide and fly apart with a velocity of 200,000,000 electron-volts. However little this news might mean to the man in the street, it was of world-shaking significance to the world's physicists. Nuclear matter had been transformed into nuclear energy, energy higher than had ever been attained by man before.

The absence of American names in the foregoing should not be interpreted as an indication that the United States was behind the rest of the world in the study of nuclear physics. On the contrary, the in-vention of the cyclotron or atom-smasher by Dr. Ernest O. Lawrence of the University of California won recognition in the Nobel Prize in Physics in 1939, while equally important landmarks were the discov-ery of deuterium or heavy hydrogen by Dr. Harold C. Urey of Colum-bia and that of U–235, a rare form of uranium, by Professor Arthur J. Dempster of the University of Chicago. The onset of war found the country with a company of brilliant scientists already well grounded in the fundamentals of nuclear physics.

It was fortunate that this was so, because the most fantastic secret chapter of the war was the rivalry between the Allies and the Axis in feverish research to apply atomic energy to wartime use. The Ger-mans worked hard on the problem amid interruptions through sabotage by Allied secret agents and carefully planned bombings of the enemy research centers. Ironically, three of the world's greatest scientists, Lise

Cloud Produced by Explosion of Atomic Bomb at Nagasaki, August 9, 1945. (Brown Bros.)

Meitner, Niels Bohr, a Dane, and Enrico Fermi, who might have given the great secret to the enemy, had been forced out of Germany and Italy because of their alleged Jewish ancestry. As it was, the Nazis might have developed the bomb if the war had lasted a year longer. The possibility of using atomic power for military purposes was brought to President Roosevelt's attention late in 1939 and resulted in the appointment of a committee to survey the problem. Two years later it was decided to expand greatly the research program. At Roosevelt's suggestion British and Canadian scientists working on the problem came to the United States and joined forces with the Americans directed by Dr. Bush in the OSRD. Needs of military security led to the transfer of a major part of the program to the War Department in June, 1942, and Major General Leslie R. Groves was placed in charge.

Extraordinary secrecy shrouded the so-called Manhattan Project. Thousands of persons were employed, but the work was so compartmentalized that only a few highly placed men in government and science knew the whole story. Congress cooperated by making almost $2,000,-000,000 available without asking embarrassing questions. Key plants were erected in areas as remote from each other as Tennessee and Washington, while the country's newest and best equipped physics laboratory was built in an isolated district of New Mexico. Dr. J. Robert Oppenheimer of the University of California was in charge of the New Mexico project, and the *émigrés* Bohr and Fermi gave valuable technical assistance. Near there, on June 16, 1945, the first atomic bomb was dropped, causing an explosion felt 200 miles away and seen for over 100 miles. Two months later, atomic-bomb destruction of Hiroshima and Nagasaki hastened Japanese surrender.

This highly publicized event brought problems of the utmost gravity to American statesmen. Should the secret of the bomb be kept or shared with the Soviet Union and other partners at arms? Should the bomb's use be outlawed or should it be entrusted to the United Nations for use in preserving peace? Should the control of atomic power within the country remain under military control or should it be transferred to civilians? What peacetime uses had this new source of energy? Should this energy be exploited under private ownership or should it be socialized? Despite the large amount of discussion which the bomb precipitated, it was doubtful whether Americans generally realized the urgency of the new problems which science had posed.

BOOM IN EDUCATION

Mathematics, chemistry, physics, and foreign languages had other uses than to train nuclear physicists. During the war years hundreds of thousands of young Americans came to a new realization of the utility of higher learning. Many of the most desirable branches of the services were reserved to those who had had high-school training and some work in college. The navy required a college degree for officers. Thousands of promising soldiers and sailors were sent to college for short terms; some of the most able received a complete training in medicine or engineering. This taste of college life, together with the provisions of the G.I. Bill, contributed to the extraordinary situation which prevailed six months after VJ Day when almost every college in the country was filled to overflowing with returned veterans.

Once again the result of war was to accentuate a trend already well established. In 1900 only 11 per cent of American young people between the ages of fourteen and seventeen were to be found enrolled in full-time high schools. The percentage had risen to 73 by 1940. During the same period the number of American colleges had risen from around five hundred to three times that number, while college enrollment had increased eightfold.

Along with the rapidly expanding enrollment of universities went a bewildering growth in their course offerings. An attempt was made to prepare students for more and more special vocations, while the elective system made it possible to secure an A.B. degree for almost any combination of courses which appealed to the fancy of the student. Many authorities became alarmed. In 1930, Abraham Flexner asserted in *Universities, American, English, German* that there was in the United States no university in the real sense of the term—"no institution, no seat of learning devoted to higher teaching and research. Everywhere the pressure of undergraduates and vocational activities hampers the serious objects for which universities exist."

More emphatic still were the judgments passed on the colleges and universities by President Robert Maynard Hutchins of the University of Chicago. The great criminal in the educational field, according to Hutchins, had been President Eliot of Harvard who "applied his genius, skill, and longevity to the task of robbing American youth of their cultural heritage." President Hutchins urged that the liberal arts college be restricted to general education based upon the study of the greatest books of the Western world and the arts of reading, writing, thinking, and speaking, together with mathematics. He called for a reorganization of American education so that the last two years of high school and the first two years of college might be combined in a well-integrated course of studies leading to the A.B. degree at about the age of twenty. Thereafter, the more competent students would be accepted in the university proper, where they would study metaphysics, social science, and natural science.

Hutchins's ideas were hotly debated both at the University of Chicago and in the educational world generally. At his own institution he succeeded in having some, although by no means all, of his principles carried out. A more radical experiment based upon his philosophy was that embarked upon at St. John's College at Annapolis, Maryland, in which all the students were required to read in their entirety a long list of important books ranging from Homer's *Iliad* to Veblen and Young's *Projective Geometry*.

The idea of directing education back to the so-called Great Tradition was rejected in most quarters. In fact, such new colleges as Bennington and Sarah Lawrence, with their emphasis on the cultivation of the fine arts and their highly individualized programs, were experiments in the opposite direction. Most institutions avoided the two extremes. There was much modification of the curriculum with an increasing emphasis on broad survey or general-education courses during the Freshman and Sophomore years and some departure from narrow departmental majors. In general, it appeared that the complexity of contemporary political and social problems had compelled much hard thinking about the objectives of education, and that most institutions

The Camel and the Needle's Eye. (By Messner in the *Rochester Times-Union*.)

were striving to reorganize their programs of study in the light of these studies. Typical of this movement were the curriculum changes recommended in 1945 at Harvard and Yale.

NEWSPAPERS, MAGAZINES, AND RADIO

In the financial organization of the newspaper field, trends already noted continued. Although no new national chains as extensive as the Hearst or the Scripps-Howard developed, and although the Hearst empire had begun to break up, the smaller chains flourished, while consolidation reduced the number of journals published in most cities. Newspapers became increasingly dependent on the Associated Press and the United Press for their news, so much so that the Supreme Court ruled in 1945 that it was a violation of the antitrust laws for the Associated Press to reject arbitrarily an application for membership because of the veto of a rival journal.

The amount of space devoted to syndicated features also continued to increase. The thirties and the forties witnessed a great rise in the popularity and power of the columnists. The widely printed opinions of Walter Lippmann, David Lawrence, Westbrook Pegler, Drew Pearson, and Walter Winchell had an influence far greater than the ideas expressed in the editorials of the individual newspapers. Indeed, the dwindling prestige of the editorial page was frequently commented upon. The point was strikingly illustrated by the election of 1936 when Roosevelt secured 60 per cent of the popular vote despite the fact that he had the support of only 36 per cent of the country's newspapers. Roosevelt's 1940 and 1944 victories reflected the situation even more clearly since on both occasions only about 22 per cent of the papers supported him.

New Dealers complained bitterly of the antiadministration and anti-labor bias of the American press. They accused the journals of coloring or slanting the news and could sometimes offer proof to support their charges. Yet the more scrupulous papers made it a point of honor to keep their news stories free of editorial bias, and this could usually be done because newspaper reporters tended to be much more sympathetic to the New Deal than were their employers. Contrasting strongly with the conservative point of view reflected by most newspapers was the extreme leftist position taken by the New York *PM* and the Chicago *Sun*, both founded during the thirties and sponsored by the millionaire liberal, Marshall Field.

American newspapers of the thirties differed from those of the early years of the century in the much larger coverage given to foreign affairs.

From being poorly informed on such matters the American public had become perhaps the best informed of all peoples. A generation of intelligent reporting of world affairs did much to educate Americans for new responsibilities in the postwar world.

The intense interest of many Americans in the news led to the establishment in 1923 of the magazine *Time*. The enormous success of this weekly venture brought the founding of *Newsweek* and other periodicals devoted to the concise and cleverly written presentation of current events. The same Henry Luce who made a fortune out of *Time* hit upon another winning formula in 1936 when he purchased *Life* and transformed it from a humorous magazine to one featuring interesting pictures so arranged as to tell a story. This also brought a large number of imitators and competitors into the field, the most successful of which was *Look*. The greatest money-maker of all was the *Reader's Digest*, which guided by the intuition of Dewitt Wallace was so perfectly tailored to suit the taste of the average middle-class American that it achieved a monthly circulation of around eight million by the end of World War II. Once again many imitators entered the field, but none secured anything like the popularity of the prototype.

Meantime, the radio became increasingly important as a medium through which history was both made and reflected. Roosevelt's success in winning four elections and achieving innumerable victories for his policies was to be explained in considerable degree to the influence he gained by speaking directly to the people over the radio. Moreover, the American people had a sense of direct participation in the great event when they listened to the ranting speeches of Hitler, the magnificent oratory of Churchill, or the solemn voice of MacArthur presiding over the Japanese surrender ceremony. During the most critical periods of the war, listeners turned to their radios almost hourly for the latest reports from the fronts. Of the total broadcasting time on the NBC Network, only 3.6 per cent was devoted to news in 1939, but by 1944 it was 20.4 per cent.

Radio provided a varied fare. In addition to news, there were opera and symphony broadcasts for music lovers, a galaxy of high-priced comedians and quiz programs for family entertainment, exciting adventure stories for youngsters, and sentimental serials known as "soap operas" for bored housewives. Radio writing became a high-paid profession, and certain individuals like Norman Corwin, who had an unusual feeling for the possibilities of the new medium, gained wide recognition. But radio had its critics. In many quarters it was asserted that broadcasting was excessively commercialized and that the system of chain broadcasting provided too little of an educational or informational character, as well as too little reflecting the needs and interests of the local community.

BOOKS

Literature during the thirties and forties failed in the opinion of some critics to fulfill the promise of the twenties. No more novels from the pen of Theodore Dreiser appeared until *The Bulwark* was published in 1946, after the great realist's death. Nor did Edith Wharton, Willa Cather, or Ellen Glasgow in their later years produce novels which equaled their earlier work. Sinclair Lewis's *It Can't Happen Here,* published in 1935, showed an awareness of the insidious ubiquity of fascism, but neither this nor any of his later novels was as effective as his satires of the twenties.

On the other hand, John Dos Passos gained his greatest success with the trilogy *U.S.A.,* composed of *The 42nd Parallel* (1930), *Nineteen-Nineteen* (1932), and *The Big Money* (1936). Combining such ingenious devices as The Newsreel and The Camera Eye with sketches of figures like Carnegie, Edison, Debs, Bryan, Roosevelt, and Wilson, and case histories of a dozen fictional characters, Dos Passos surveyed American life from 1900 to 1930 in many varied aspects. What he portrayed was not pleasant; his more unscrupulous characters gained material success, while the few who aspired to improve the world were frustrated. Trade unionists, IWW agitators, and Communists were more sympathetically portrayed than were the figures of the bourgeois world. But despite this radical point of view the author showed himself distrustful of doctrinaire Marxism.

Ernest Hemingway also displayed the ambition to outgrow the narrow individualism of his work of the twenties and to deal with some of the basic social problems of his generation. *To Have and To Hold* (1937), dealing with the career of an American gangster, found less favor than his earlier books, but *For Whom the Bell Tolls* provoked great interest. In portraying the Spanish Civil War, Hemingway combined his old-time facility in describing scenes of bloodshed and violent action with a newly displayed talent for telling a love story of unusual tenderness and a new respect for loyalty, idealism, and human decency. Much of the book's success came, no doubt, from its timeliness; it appeared in 1940, a year of catastrophic democratic defeats.

Perhaps the most promising young writer of the thirties was Thomas Wolfe, whose death in 1938 cut short a career of rich promise. Largely autobiographical, Wolfe's novels, *Look Homeward, Angel* (1929),

Of Time and the River (1935), *The Web and the Rock* (1939), and *You Can't Go Home Again* (1940) portrayed his Carolina boyhood, his life at Harvard and Oxford, his teaching at New York University, and his residence in France. They combined graphic realism with passages so lyrical and rhythmic that they have been taken from their context and published as poetry.

The South produced two important novelists, but neither portrayed his section from the traditionally romantic point of view. William Faulkner of Mississippi wrote morbid and sadistic stories like *Sanctuary* (1931), while Erskine Caldwell depicted the degeneracy of the poor white stock in stories all the more shocking because of the broad humor of their treatment. The dramatization of Caldwell's *Tobacco Road* (first published as a novel in 1932) enjoyed a fabulously long run both on Broadway and on tour.

Other sections of the country were subjected to equally severe literary treatment. In *Young Lonigan: A Boyhood in Chicago Streets* (1932) and its sequels, James T. Farrell drew a savage portrait of the city environment in which he himself was brought up. In *Native Son* (1940) Richard Wright showed how relentless were the forces driving a Negro boy into crime in the slums of a Northern city. Particularly influential in attracting the attention of the country to a great social problem was John Steinbeck's *Grapes of Wrath* (1939), in which the consequences of the dust storms of the thirties were powerfully pointed out, together with a revelation of the exploitation of itinerant agricultural workers. Despite the grimness of his theme, Steinbeck conveyed a belief in basic human goodness and confidence that in the long run this good would prevail. Ironic and satirical rather than brutal was the mood in which the sterility of the so-called cultured circles in New England was laid bare by John Marquand in *The Late George Apley* (1937) and *H. M. Pulham, Esquire* (1941). Fiction's most stimulating response to the catastrophic international situation was to be found in the later novels of the veteran Upton Sinclair.

These were the authors most discussed by the serious-minded during the thirties and forties. But larger royalty checks were enjoyed by the writers who ignored these aspects of life and helped their readers forget contemporary problems. Detective stories continued to be the most popular form of escape literature, but readers with more time derived pleasures from the lengthy historical novels which appeared in large numbers. A few of these, like the works of Kenneth Roberts and Walter Edmonds, were of solid merit. Yet the most sensationally successful were novels like *Gone With the Wind* (1936) by Margaret Mitchell and *Forever Amber* (1945) by Katherine Winsor, which appealed to the reader less as vehicles for learning history than for following the escapades of lovely heroines.

AMERICANS LEARN ABOUT ART

During the thirties and forties there was evidence that more Americans than ever before took a serious interest in the fine arts. Training in painting and music gained a more secure place in education. Native talent was no longer ignored, while the public lionized foreign visitors. Probably little of the artistic production of the period had any claim to greatness, but there was interest and activity, and these offered much promise for the future.

To a much greater extent than ever before the Federal government became a patron of the arts. The Great Depression bore down with particular severity upon painters and by 1935 some four thousand of these were in serious straits. To relieve this group the WPA Art Program, under the direction of Holger Cahill, was organized. During the next five years about 52,000 easel paintings were done by government-paid artists and placed on permanent loan in schools, libraries, and hospitals. Even more remarkable was the stimulus given to mural painting. The WPA program resulted in the installation of over 1500 murals in tax-supported public institutions located in every section of the country. The PWA administration also gave extensive employment to mural painters. Artists as firmly established as George Biddle, Reginald Marsh, and Boardman Robinson contributed to the decoration of the new buildings erected in Washington to house the Justice, Post Office, and Interior Departments. Government-sponsored art ranged all the way from the very fine to the worthless. Competent critics found encouragement, however, in the freshness and enthusiasm of much that was produced. Moreover, from the educational point of view, works of art placed in post offices, hospitals, and schools were much more likely to arouse the interest of the general public than pictures purchased by wealthy customers to be hung in their own homes.

Nor was the government the only new patron. *Life* magazine featured reproductions of contemporary painting and commissioned a number of artists to put on canvas their first-hand impressions of battle scenes during World War II. The advertising business—already the chief sponsor of American journalism and radio—became another purchaser of original works of art. Many leading painters accepted the invitation to practice their craft for the glorification of DeBeers Diamonds, Ltd., Dole Pineapple, Capehart Phonograph-Radio, and the

Pepsi-Cola Company. Even labor-union locals commissioned artists to decorate their halls with murals, and many individuals, who a generation before would have considered art effete, now thronged the museums and purchased paintings for their homes.

It is too early to place a definite evaluation on the works of the individual artists. Comparisons are the more difficult because of the extreme variety in style which characterized the period. Some artists were working with a precision of detail that was almost photographic; others painted in a mood so abstract as to bewilder those who inspected their work. Some were traditionalists following canons of taste well formulated in the past; others were audacious innovators. Combining the thorough technical mastery of the academicians with the force and honesty characteristic of the best of the modernists was Eugene Speicher, acclaimed by many as the country's leading portrait painter. John Marin painted a variety of American scenes ranging from rocky Maine and crowded New York to the barren Southwest in a sensitive style bordering upon the abstract. The cultural richness which America derived from immigration was illustrated by the works of Henry Mattson, whose marine paintings reflected the rugged Swedish environment of his boyhood, and Yasuo Kuniyoshi, whose work was marked by the delicacy and subtlety of his native Japan. Another stimulating influence on American art was the infinite variety provided by the country's regional differences. Life in the Midwestern prairie country found reflection in the paintings of Thomas Hart Benton, Grant Wood, and John Steuart Curry; New York City's perennial fascination for the artist was captured by Reginald Marsh and Edward Hopper; the ugliness of many American small towns was satirized by Charles Burchfield; even Alaska was not beyond the trek of the restless artist, as some of the best of Rockwell Kent's work emphasized. Not easy to classify, but much admired, was the adroitly executed and imaginative painting of John Carroll.

Radio broadcasts taught many Americans that opera and symphony concerts were less formidable than they had imagined. The moving-picture industry was somewhat more timid in promoting serious music, but it did offer employment to some of the more shapely prima donnas and made successful pictures upon the careers of Johann Strauss, Frederic Chopin, and George Gershwin. The most effective medium for broadening the popular interest in music, however, was the phonograph. With better methods of recording and reproduction, recorded music achieved a degree of excellence which provoked genuine enthusiasm. Of course, neither radio nor phonograph offered compensations as rich as personal attendance in the music hall. Opportunities to enjoy this latter experience widened during the thirties and were seized by an increasing number of people. Once again government sponsorship through WPA orchestras and free concerts not only kept musicians alive during the depression, but served an educational function as well.

The American-born artist became much less a novelty on the opera and concert stage. Grace Moore, Gladys Swarthout, Lawrence Tibbett, John Charles Thomas, and many others held their own against foreign talent in the operatic field, while Marian Anderson and Albert Spaulding proved prime drawing cards on the concert stage. Top-ranking native conductors were not so common, but Werner Janssen enjoyed a considerable success in this field during the thirties. Nor was the country so entirely dependent on European composers as formerly. Deems Taylor repeated his earlier success with the opera *Peter Ibbetson,* produced by the Metropolitan in 1931. Other notable American operas were *The Emperor Jones* by Louis Gruenberg and *Merry Mount* by Howard Hanson, staged by the Metropolitan in 1933 and 1934 respectively. Another interesting work was the folk-opera *The Devil and Daniel Webster* (1939), with music by Douglas Moore and libretto by the distinguished poet, Stephen Vincent Benét. In the field of symphonic works, John Alden Carpenter's *Sea Drift* (1934) and Daniel Gregory Mason's *A Lincoln Symphony* (1937) combined thoroughly American themes with an orthodox technique. On the other hand, modernistic efforts like the *Third Symphony* by Roy Harris and *Music for the Theatre* by Aaron Copland represented bold pioneering into new idioms. An American by adoption was Ernest Bloch, whose widely acclaimed symphonic works reflected his Jewish cultural heritage, his Swiss native home, and his affection for America. Growing recognition of the significance of the Negro contribution to the American musical heritage was reflected in the interest aroused by the compositions of William Grant Still, while a new appreciation for Anglo-Saxon folk music was stimulated by the researches of John Powell.

It was perhaps this new enthusiasm for art and music that provided the most hopeful symptom for the American future. Such tastes could never, it is true, be the prime driving forces for any large percentage of the population. But they pointed to a broadening of interest. The Great Depression had dramatized the flimsiness of a civilization based excessively on material prosperity. There were hopeful signs that more Americans were perceiving the truth that making a living was not an end in itself but a means, and that really rich living depended upon a breadth of culture.

FACING THE FUTURE

The United States had made enormous progress since 1900. National wealth and income, productive capacity, and the general standard of living had risen to a degree to arouse the envy of less fortunate nations. More Americans than ever before enjoyed the advantages of education; good literature, good music, good art had never been more accessible to the common citizen. American thinking about fundamental problems had undergone a tremendous transition. A nation, which in 1935 had even been unwilling to associate itself with the World Court, was now proposing an international atomic-energy authority which would override every national sovereignty within its sphere.

But complacency was not in order. The problems which the nation faced had grown at an even faster rate than its resources and its knowledge. The formulation of national policies which would "form a more perfect union, establish justice, insure domestic tranquillity, provide for the common defence, promote the general welfare, and secure the blessings of liberty," was now more complex and difficult than ever before. Nor could these benefits of civil society be enjoyed by the United States in isolation. Until justice, liberty, and economic security prevailed in the world at large, their permanence in America could not be assured. This was the great lesson of recent United States history.

Suggestions for Further Reading

GENERAL.   Suggestive and stimulating are the interpretations given to various aspects of recent American history in Charles A. and Mary Beard, *The Rise of American Civilization*, 4 v. (Macmillan, N. Y., 1927–1942). Mark Sullivan, *Our Times: The United States, 1900–1925*, 6 v. (Scribners, N. Y., 1926–1935), is lively reading throughout and particularly valuable for its intimate picture of politics during the Roosevelt, Taft, and Harding administrations. Many of the chapters in Allan Nevins and Louis Hacker, eds., *The United States and Its Place in World Affairs, 1918–1943* (Heath, N. Y., 1943), are excellent, particularly those dealing with economic trends. The game of politics has an interesting description in Wilfred E. Binkley, *American Political Parties: Their Natural History* (Knopf, N. Y., 1943).

FOREIGN RELATIONS.   Thomas A. Bailey, *A Diplomatic History of the American People* (Crofts, N. Y., 1946), is successful in demonstrating the influence of public opinion on American foreign policy. Samuel F. Bemis, *A Diplomatic History of the United States* (Holt, N. Y., 1943), combines thorough scholarship with keen interpretation.

SOCIAL AND CULTURAL.   The two volumes in *The History of American Life* series dealing with this period are Harold U. Faulkner, *The Quest for Social Justice, 1898–1914* (Macmillan, N. Y., 1931), and Preston W. Slosson, *The Great Crusade and After, 1914–1928* (Macmillan, N. Y., 1931). Like other books in this series, these combine sound scholarship, lively subject matter, and an easy style and contain excellent bibliographies. Brief, but stimulating, are the chapters dealing with this period in Thomas Cochran and William Miller, *The Age of Enterprise: A Social History of Industrial America* (Macmillan, N. Y., 1942).

ECONOMICS.   On the nation's economic development the following surveys are outstanding: Harold U. Faulkner, *American Economic History* (Harper, N. Y., 1943), Edward E. Kirkland, *A History of American Economic Life* (Crofts, N. Y., 1939), and Fred A. Shannon, *America's Economic Growth* (Macmillan, N. Y., 1940).

RELIGIOUS TRENDS.   The best survey of religious trends is William W. Sweet, *The Story of Religion in America* (Harper, N. Y., 1939).

INTELLECTUAL HISTORY.   On intellectual history, Merle Curti, *The Growth of American Thought* (Harper, N. Y., 1943), is indispensable. Also excellent are Oscar Cargill, *Intellectual America: Ideas on the March* (Macmillan,

N. Y., 1941), and Ralph H. Gabriel, *The Course of American Democratic Thought* (Ronald, N. Y., 1940). Although penetrating in its comments, Vernon L. Parrington, *Main Currents in American Thought* (Macmillan, N. Y., 1941), is unfortunately incomplete for this period. It must be supplemented with V. F. Calverton, *The Liberation of American Literature* (Scribners, N. Y., 1932), Alfred Kazin, *On Native Grounds: An Interpretation of Modern American Prose Literature* (Reynal and Hitchcock, N. Y., 1942), and Fred L. Pattee, *The New American Literature, 1890–1930* (Century, N. Y., 1930). On science, Bernard Jaffe, *Men of Science in America: the Role of Science in the Growth of Our Country* (Simon and Schuster, N. Y., 1944), is recommended.

EDUCATION.   Important in tracing educational trends are Merle Curti, *The Social Ideas of American Educators* (Scribners, N. Y., 1935), and Adolph E. Meyer, *The Development of Education in the Twentieth Century* (Prentice-Hall, N. Y., 1939). For journalism, see Frank L. Mott, *American Journalism: A History of Newspapers in the United States* (Macmillan, N. Y., 1941).

THE ARTS.   Standard works on the arts are: Samuel Isham and Royal Cortissoz, *History of American Painting* (Macmillan, N. Y., 1936), Lorado Taft, *The History of American Sculpture* (Macmillan, N. Y., 1924), and Thomas Tallmadge, *The Story of Architecture in America* (Norton, N. Y., 1927).

CHAPTER I. THE GOOD OLD DAYS

In addition to the books listed above, the following are recommended:

IMMIGRATION.   The most scholarly general treatment of the subject is Carl Wittke, *We Who Built America; the Saga of the Immigrant* (Prentice-Hall, N. Y., 1940). Louis Adamic, *A Nation of Nations* (Harper, N. Y., 1945), contains some exaggeration, but is stimulating and well written.

BUSINESS AND INDUSTRY.   Well-balanced and authoritative is A. A. Berle, Jr., and Gardiner C. Means, *The Modern Corporation and Private Property* (Commerce Clearing House, N. Y., 1932). Historically important discussions of the trust problem, reflecting the viewpoints of three different decades are: John Moody, *The Truth About Trusts, a Description and Analysis of the American Trust Movement* (Moody, N. Y., 1904), William Z. Ripley, ed., *Trusts, Pools, and Corporations* (Ginn, Boston, 1916), J. W. Jenks and W. E. Clark, *The Trust Problem* (Doubleday Doran, Garden City, 1929), and H. R. Seager and C. A. Gulick, *Trust and Corporation Problems* (Harper, N. Y., 1929). The role of the bankers is explored in George W. Edwards, *The Evolution of Finance Capitalism* (Longmans Green, N. Y., 1938), and in more popular form in Frederick L. Allen, *The Lords of Creation* (Harper, N. Y., 1935). Allan Nevins, *John D. Rockefeller: The Heroic Age of American Enterprise*, 2 v. (Scribners, N. Y., 1940), is scholarly and well balanced.

LABOR.   Excellent standard works are Selig Perlman and Philip Taft, *History of Labor in the United States, 1896–1932* (Macmillan, N. Y., 1935), and Leo Wolman, *Ebb and Flow in Trade Unionism* (Nat'l Bureau of Econ. Research, N. Y., 1936). Indispensable is Samuel Gompers, *Seventy Years of Life and Labor: an Autobiography*, 2 v. (Dutton, N. Y., 1925). Outstanding monographs are Paul H. Douglas, *Real Wages in the United States: 1896–1926* (Houghton Mifflin, Boston, 1930) and Paul F. Brissenden, *The I. W. W.; a Study of American Syndicalism* (Columbia Univ., N. Y., 1919).

RELIGION AND THE REFORM MOVEMENT.   The following studies are important: Charles H. Hopkins, *The Rise of the Social Gospel in American Protestantism, 1865–1914* (Yale Univ., New Haven, 1940), Peter Odegard, *Pressure Politics, the Story of the Anti-Saloon League* (Columbia Univ., N. Y., 1928).

CHAPTER 2.   THE PROGRESSIVE MOVEMENT

GENERAL.   Although written in a spirit of disillusionment, John Chamberlain, *Farewell to Reform: The Rise, Life and Decay of the Progressive Mind in America* (Day, N. Y., 1933), is valuable for its emphasis on progressivism as a broad cultural movement. Matthew Josephson, *The President Makers . . . 1896–1919* (Harcourt Brace, N. Y., 1940), is provocative and well written. The best description of the muckrakers is in Louis Filler, *Crusaders for American Liberalism* (Harcourt Brace, N. Y., 1939). Also good is Cornelius C. Regier, *The Era of the Muckrakers* (Univ. of North Carolina, Chapel Hill, 1932). An older work, still useful, is Fred E. Haynes, *Social Politics in the United States* (Houghton Mifflin, Boston, 1924).

BIOGRAPHICAL MATERIAL.   The personalities of this period are unusually interesting. Several of them have left fascinating estimates of their own achievements. Theodore Roosevelt, *An Autobiography* (Scribners, N. Y., 1924), Robert M. LaFollette, *Autobiography* (LaFollette Co., Madison, Wis., 1913), and William Jennings Bryan, *Memoirs* (Winston, Phila., 1925), derive their importance from the prominence of their authors. Better written and more reflective are the memoirs of the lesser figures like *American Chronicle, the Autobiography of Ray Stannard Baker* (Scribners, N. Y., 1945), Frederic C. Howe, *The Confessions of a Reformer* (Scribners, N. Y., 1925), Tom L. Johnson, *My Story* (Huebsch, N. Y., 1911), *The Autobiography of Lincoln Steffens* (Harcourt Brace, N. Y., 1931), Oswald Garrison Villard, *Fighting Years* (Harcourt Brace, N. Y., 1939), Brand Whitlock, *Forty Years of It* (Appleton, N. Y., 1925), Allan Nevins, ed., *Letters and Journal of Brand Whitlock*, 2 v. (Appleton-Century, N. Y., 1936), *The Autobiography of William Allen White* (Macmillan, N. Y., 1946).

Among the better biographies are: Henry F. Pringle, *Theodore Roosevelt, a Biography* (Harcourt Brace, N. Y., 1931), Claude Bowers, *Beveridge and the Progressive Era* (Houghton Mifflin, Boston, 1932), Herbert Alonzo Croly, *Marcus Alonzo Hanna: His Life and Work* (Macmillan, N. Y., 1912), Nathaniel W. Stephenson, *Nelson W. Aldrich, a Leader in*

American Politics (Scribners, N. Y., 1930), Joseph Dorfman, *Thorstein Veblen and His America* (Viking, N. Y., 1935), Alphonso T. Mason, *Brandeis; a Free Man's Life* (Viking, N. Y., 1946).

CONSERVATION.   Gifford Pinchot, *The Fight for Conservation* (Doubleday Page, N. Y., 1910), is the work of an active participant. Standard accounts are in Benjamin H. Hibbard, *A History of the Public Land Policies* (Macmillan, N. Y., 1924), and Charles R. Van Hise, *The Conservation of Natural Resources in the United States* (Macmillan, N. Y., 1926).

CHAPTER 3. THE BATTLE OF THE PROGRESSIVES

Most of the titles recommended for Chapter 2 are still useful for the Taft period. These should be supplemented with two outstanding recent studies: Kenneth W. Hechler, *Insurgency: Personalities and Policies of the Taft Era* (Columbia Univ., N. Y., 1940), and George E. Mowry, *Theodore Roosevelt and the Progressive Movement* (Univ. of Wisconsin, Madison, Wis., 1946). The best biography of Taft is Henry F. Pringle, *The Life and Times of William Howard Taft*, 2 v. (Farrar and Rinehart, N. Y., 1939).

One of the best ways of understanding the ideals of the progressives is through a reading of such contemporary documents as Louis D. Brandeis, *Other People's Money* (National Home Library, Washington, 1933), Louis D. Brandeis, *The Curse of Bigness* (Viking, N. Y., 1934), Herbert Croly, *The Promise of American Life* (Macmillan, N. Y., 1909); Walter E. Weyl, *The New Democracy* (Macmillan, N. Y., 1912), Charles McCarthy, *The Wisconsin Idea* (Macmillan, N. Y., 1912).

CHAPTER 4. THE AMERICAN EMPIRE

GENERAL.   The diplomatic histories by Bailey and Bemis cited above may be supplemented with A. L. P. Dennis, *Adventures in American Diplomacy, 1896–1906* (Dutton, N. Y., 1928), which combines an account of some of the principal episodes of the period with a publication of the text of interesting documents. Tyler Dennett, *John Hay: From Poetry to Politics* (Dodd Mead, N. Y., 1933), is an excellent biography of a key figure. The best study of the rise of imperialism is Julius W. Pratt, *Expansionists of 1898* (Johns Hopkins, Baltimore, 1936). An entertaining account of the role of newspapers in bringing on the Spanish-American War is Walter Millis, *The Martial Spirit* (Riverside, Cambridge, 1931). W. D. Puleston, *Mahan: The Life and Work of Captain Alfred Thayer Mahan* (Yale Univ., New Haven, 1939), traces the career of a figure having great influence, while hitherto neglected areas of history are illuminated by Harold and Margaret Sprout, *The Rise of American Naval Power, 1776–1919* (Princeton Univ., Princeton, 1939).

CUBA AND THE DEPENDENCIES.   A good over-all view is contained in William H. Haas, ed., *The American Empire: a Study of the Outlying Territories of the United States* (Univ. of Chicago, Chicago, 1940). Critical discussions of relations with particular areas are Leland H. Jenks, *Our Cuban Colony, a Study in Sugar* (Vanguard, N. Y., 1928), Russell H. Fitzgibbon, *Cuba and the United States, 1900–1935* (Banta, Wis., 1940), Moorfield Story and Marcial Lichauco, *The Conquest of the Philippines by the United States, 1898–1925* (Putnam, N. Y., 1926), Joseph Hayden, *The Philippines, a Study in National Development* (Macmillan, N. Y., 1942).

THE FAR EAST.   The best study of this period is A. Whitney Griswold, *The Far Eastern Policy of the United States* (Harcourt Brace, N. Y., 1938). For essential backgrounds see Tyler Dennett, *Americans in Eastern Asia* (Macmillan, N. Y., 1922). For a general survey, Foster R. Dulles, *Forty Years of American-Japanese Relations* (Appleton-Century, N. Y., 1937), is valuable. Outstanding studies of special phases are Tyler Dennett, *Roosevelt and the Russo-Japanese War* (Doubleday Doran, Garden City, 1925), Thomas A. Bailey, *Theodore Roosevelt and the Japanese-American Crises* (Stanford Univ., Calif., 1934), Eleanor Tupper and George McReynolds, *Japan in American Public Opinion* (Macmillan, N. Y., 1937).

CHAPTER 5. SEARCH FOR SECURITY AND PEACE

GENERAL.   The general works recommended for Chapter 4 are still useful. Also two excellent biographies of leading diplomatists: Philip C. Jessup, *Elihu Root*, 2 v. (Dodd Mead, N. Y., 1938), and Allan Nevins, *Henry White: Thirty Years of American Diplomacy* (Harper, N. Y., 1930).

RELATIONS WITH LATIN AMERICA.   The best interpretative study is Samuel F. Bemis, *The Latin American Policy of the United States, an Historical Interpretation* (Harcourt Brace, N. Y., 1943). Older but still useful is William S. Robertson, *Hispanic American Relations with the United States* (Oxford, N. Y., 1923). On the fundamental policy underlying American action, the indispensable authority is Dexter Perkins, *The Monroe Doctrine, 1867–1907* (Johns Hopkins, Baltimore, 1927); more general is the same author's *Hands Off: A History of the Monroe Doctrine* (Little Brown, Boston, 1941). Howard C. Hill, *Roosevelt and the Caribbean* (Univ. of Chicago, Chicago, 1927), Wilfrid H. Calcott, *The Caribbean Policy of the United States, 1890–1920* (Johns Hopkins, Baltimore, 1942), and Chester Jones, *The Caribbean since 1900* (Prentice-Hall, N. Y., 1936) are able monographs.

An outstanding study of canal diplomacy is Dwight C. Miner, *The Fight for the Panama Route* (Columbia Univ., N. Y., 1940). An historically important indictment of American policy is Sumner Welles, *Naboth's Vineyard: the Dominican Republic, 1844–1924*, 2 v. (Payson and Clark, N. Y., 1928).

ANGLO-AMERICAN RELATIONS.   Lionel M. Gelber, *The Rise of Anglo-American Friendship: a Study in World Politics, 1896–1906* (Oxford, N. Y., 1938), is scholarly but narrowly diplomatic in treatment. Of more general interest is Forrest Davis, *The Atlantic System: The Story of Anglo-American Control of the Seas* (Reynal and Hitchcock, N. Y., 1941).

CHAPTER 6. THE NEW FREEDOM

GENERAL.   The best study of the period is Frederick Paxson, *American Democracy and the World War*, 2 v. (Houghton Mifflin, Boston, 1936–1939). Wilson's own speeches and letters are the indispensable sources upon his ideals and his political methods. For these, consult Ray S. Baker and William E. Dodd, eds., *The Public Papers of Woodrow Wilson*, 6 v. (Harper, N. Y., 1925–1926), and Ray S. Baker, *Woodrow Wilson, Life and Letters*, 8 v. (Doubleday Doran, Garden City, 1927–1938). Of the numerous single-volume studies of Wilson, the most useful are William E. Dodd, *Woodrow Wilson and His Work* (P. Smith, N. Y., 1932), and James Kerney, *The Political Education of Woodrow Wilson* (Century, N. Y., 1926).

MEMOIRS.   Wilson's secretary provides an intimate portrait in Joseph Tumulty, *Woodrow Wilson as I Knew Him* (Doubleday Page, Garden City, 1925). His son-in-law and Secretary of the Treasury deals with the period in William G. McAdoo, *Crowded Years* (Houghton Mifflin, Boston, 1931). Important memoranda on cabinet discussions are provided by the Secretary of Agriculture, David Houston, *Eight Years with Wilson's Cabinet* (Doubleday Page, Garden City, 1926). Personalities and politics are engagingly discussed in the memoirs of Wilson's Secretary of the Navy, Josephus Daniels, *The Wilson Era: Years of Peace* (Univ. of North Carolina, Chapel Hill, 1944).

REFORM LEGISLATION.   Two key figures in the creation of the Federal Reserve System discuss its origin in Carter Glass, *An Adventure in Constructive Finance* (Doubleday Doran, Garden City, 1927), and H. P. Willis, *The Federal Reserve: A Study of the Banking System of the United States* (Doubleday Page, Garden City, 1915). The functioning of the system is elucidated in Edwin W. Kemmerer, *The ABC of the Federal Reserve System . . .* (Princeton Univ., Princeton, 1938). An outstanding monograph is Thomas C. Blaisdell, Jr., *The Federal Trade Commission: an Experiment in the Control of Business* (Columbia Univ., N. Y., 1932).

FOREIGN AFFAIRS.   Wilson's basic attitudes and principles are thoroughly discussed in Harley Notter, *The Origins of the Foreign Policy of Woodrow Wilson* (Johns Hopkins, Baltimore, 1937). Bryan's role is sympathetically related in Merle Curti, *Bryan and World Peace* (Smith College, Northampton, Mass., 1931). For American policy in key areas, see J. Fred Rippy, *The United States and Mexico* (Knopf, N. Y., 1926), and Ludwell L. Montague, *Haiti and the United States, 1900–1935* (Duke Univ., Durham, N. C., 1940).

CHAPTER 7. DIFFICULT NEUTRALITY

GENERAL.   For an understanding of how World War I issues presented themselves to the Wilson administration, the most useful works are Baker, *Wilson, Life and Letters*, cited above, Charles Seymour, *American Diplomacy During the World War* (Johns Hopkins, Baltimore, 1935), and the same author's *American Neutrality, 1914–1917* (Yale Univ., New Haven, 1935). The pioneer revisionist work on American policy was C. Hartley

Grattan, *Why We Fought* (Vanguard, N. Y., 1929). A highly readable account, but with overemphasis on the role of newspapers and propaganda, is Walter Millis, *Road to War: America, 1914–1917* (Houghton Mifflin, Boston, 1935). Critical of Wilson's policies is Alice M. Morrissey, *The American Defense of Neutral Rights, 1914–1917* (Harvard Univ., Cambridge, 1939). Most complete and scholarly of all these studies is Charles C. Tansill, *America Goes to War* (Little Brown, Boston, 1938).

PROPAGANDA.   An important study is Horace C. Peterson, *Propaganda for War, the Campaign against American Neutrality, 1914–1917* (Univ. of Oklahoma, Norman, 1937). Interesting, but to be used with great caution because of its author's record as a German propagandist in two wars is George S. Viereck, *Spreading Germs of Hate* (Liveright, N. Y., 1930).

MEMOIRS.   The influence upon policy of key United States officials may be traced in Charles Seymour, ed., *The Intimate Papers of Colonel House*, 4 v. (Houghton Mifflin, Boston, 1926–1928), Burton J. Hendrick, ed., *The Life and Letters of Walter Hines Page*, 3 v. (Houghton Mifflin, Boston, 1924–1925), James W. Gerard, *My Four Years in Germany* (Doran, N. Y., 1920), Robert Lansing, *War Memoirs* (Bobbs Merrill, N. Y., 1935). The activities of the British Embassy may be followed in Stephen Gwynn, ed., *The Letters and Friendships of Sir Cecil Spring-Rice*, 2 v. (Little Brown, Boston, 1929), while the problems of the German ambassador are discussed in Count J. H. von Bernstorff, *My Three Years in America* (Scribners, N. Y., 1920), and in *Memoirs of Count Bernstorff* (Random House, N. Y., 1936).

CHAPTER 8. FROM PEACE TO WAR

In addition to the works recommended for Chapter 7, the reasons for American entry into World War I are given intelligent analysis by Wilson's Secretary of War and by one of the country's foremost diplomatic historians in Newton D. Baker, *Why We Went to War* (Harper, N. Y., 1936), and Dexter Perkins, *America and Two Wars* (Little Brown, Boston, 1944).

CHAPTER 9. WAR FOR DEMOCRACY

GENERAL.   Of works cited above, Slosson, *The Great Crusade and After*, and volume 2 of Paxson, *American Democracy and the World War*, are of particular value for this period. John S. Bassett, *Our War with Germany: A History* (Knopf, N. Y., 1919), and John B. McMaster, *The United States in the World War*, 2 v. (Appleton, N. Y., 1918–1920), are the work of well-established historians, but are too nearly contemporary with the event to be definitive. For the policies of Wilson's Secretaries of War and Navy, see Frederick Palmer, *Newton D. Baker: America at War*, 2 v. (Dodd Mead, N. Y., 1931), and Josephus Daniels, *The Wilson Era: Years of War and After, 1917–1923* (Univ. of North Carolina, Chapel Hill, 1946).

ECONOMIC MOBILIZATION.   The report of the War Industries Board is included in Bernard M. Baruch, *American Industry in the War . . .* (Prentice-Hall, N. Y., 1941). Extensive but uncritical is Benedict Crowell and Robert F. Wilson, *How America Went to War*, 6 v. (Yale Univ., New Haven,

1921). Less detailed is Grosvenor B. Clarkson, *Industrial America in the World War* (Houghton Mifflin, Boston, 1923). Two wartime railroad administrators tell their stories in McAdoo, *Crowded Years*, and Walker D. Hines, *War History of the American Railroads* (Yale Univ., New Haven, 1928).

MOBILIZATION OF THOUGHT.   George Creel's own account is in his *How We Advertised America* (Harper, N. Y., 1920). More objective are Harold D. Lasswell, *Propaganda Technique in the World War* (Whittlesey House, N. Y., 1927), and James R. Mock and Cedric Larson, *Words That Won the War: Story of the Committee on Public Information* (Princeton Univ., Princeton, 1940).

THE WAR FRONTS.   Most authoritative account of the A. E. F. is John F. Pershing, *My Experiences in the World War*, 2 v. (Stokes, N. Y., 1931). Also good is James G. Harbord, *The American Army in France, 1917–1919* (Little Brown, Boston, 1936). For the war at sea, Thomas G. Frothingham, *The Naval History of the World War*, 3 v. (Harvard Univ., Cambridge, 1925–1926), is recommended. On intervention in Russia, see William S. Graves, *America's Siberian Adventure, 1918–1920* (P. Smith, N. Y., 1941).

CHAPTER 10. THE MAKING OF THE PEACE

GENERAL.   An excellent study is Harry R. Rudin, *Armistice 1918* (Yale Univ., New Haven, 1944). Basic documents for tracing the peace negotiations are in H. W. V. Temperley, *A History of the Peace Conference of Paris*, 6 v. (Hodder and Stoughton, London, 1920–1924), and Ray Stannard Baker, *Woodrow Wilson and the World Settlement*, 3 v. (Doubleday Doran, Garden City, 1922). An interpretive study favorable to Wilson is Paul Birdsall, *Versailles Twenty Years After* (Reynal and Hitchcock, N. Y., 1941). Many contrary judgments are in Thomas A. Bailey, *Woodrow Wilson and the Lost Peace* (Macmillan, N. Y., 1944).

MEMOIRS AND LETTERS.   Highly critical of Wilson is Robert Lansing, *The Peace Negotiations: A Personal Narrative* (Houghton Mifflin, Boston, 1921). Less controversial are the accounts given by the other members of the American delegation: Seymour, *Intimate Papers of Colonel House*, Nevins, *Henry White*, Frederick Palmer, *Bliss, Peacemaker: The Life and Letters of General Tasker Howard Bliss* (Dodd Mead, N. Y., 1934). Behind-the-scenes information of some importance is to be found in Stephen Bonsal, *Unfinished Business* (Doubleday Doran, Garden City, 1944), and his *Suitors and Suppliants* (Prentice-Hall, N. Y., 1946). Other informative works by Americans attached to the peace commission are David H. Miller, *The Drafting of the Covenant*, 2 v. (Putnam, N. Y., 1938), Bernard M. Baruch, *The Making of the Reparations and Economic Sections of the Treaty* (Harper, N. Y., 1920), James T. Shotwell, *At the Paris Peace Conference* (Macmillan, N. Y., 1937). One of the liveliest portraits of the conference is the memoir of an English diplomat, Harold Nicolson, *Peacemaking, 1919* (Harcourt Brace, N. Y., 1939).

CHAPTER II. WILSON REPUDIATED

THE TREATY FIGHT.   The most extensive account, highly sympathetic to Wilson, is Denna Frank Fleming, *The United States and the League of Nations, 1918–1920* (Putnam, N. Y., 1932). More critical is Thomas A. Bailey, *Woodrow Wilson and the Great Betrayal* (Macmillan, N. Y., 1945). The conduct of the Senate is analyzed in W. Stull Holt, *Treaties Defeated by the Senate: A Study of the Struggle between President and Senate over the Conduct of Foreign Relations* (Johns Hopkins, Baltimore, 1933), and Kenneth Colegrove, *The American Senate and World Peace* (Vanguard, N. Y., 1943). Wilson's most dangerous antagonist defends his course of action in Henry Cabot Lodge, *The Senate and the League of Nations* (Scribners, N. Y., 1925). But for an unfavorable estimate of Lodge, see Karl Schriftgiesser, *The Gentleman from Massachusetts: Henry Cabot Lodge* (Little Brown, Boston, 1944). On the tragic failure of Wilson and the pro-League Republicans to make a workable alliance, consult Ruhl J. Bartlett, *The League to Enforce Peace* (Univ. of North Carolina, Chapel Hill, 1944).

POSTWAR DOMESTIC ISSUES.   The best study of this period is James R. Mock and Evangeline Thurber, *Report on Demobilization* (Univ. of Oklahoma, Norman, 1944). The excesses associated with the Red scare are discussed in Zechariah Chafee, Jr., *Free Speech in the United States* (Harvard Univ., Cambridge, 1941). The disintegration of the radical labor movement is described in John S. Gambs, *The Decline of the I. W. W.* (Columbia Univ., N. Y., 1932). On the most critical industrial dispute of the period, see William Z. Foster, *The Great Steel Strike and Its Lessons* (Huebsch, N. Y., 1920); Commission of Inquiry, The Interchurch World Movement, *Report on the Steel Strike of 1919* (Harcourt Brace, N. Y., 1920); Marshall Olds, *Analysis of the Interchurch World Movement Report on the Steel Strike* (Putnam, N. Y., 1923).

CHAPTER 12. THE HARDING REGIME

GENERAL.   Very useful are James C. Malin, *The United States After the World War* (Ginn, Boston, 1930), and Louis M. Hacker, *American Problems of Today: A History of the United States Since the World War* (Crofts, N. Y., 1938). Indispensable for this period is volume 6 of Sullivan, *Our Times*. Entertaining and shrewd is Samuel Hopkins Adams, *Incredible Era: the Life and Times of Warren Gamaliel Harding* (Houghton Mifflin, Boston, 1939). Scholarly biographies of Hughes, Hoover, and Mellon are much needed; a popular discussion of the last-named is Harvey O'Connor, *Mellon's Millions, the Biography of a Fortune* (Day, N. Y., 1933).

SPECIFIC ISSUES.   On the election of 1920, see James M. Cox, *Journey Through My Years* (Simon and Schuster, N. Y., 1946). Immigration legislation is discussed in Wittke, *We Who Built America*, George M. Stephenson, *A History of American Immigration, 1820–1924* (Ginn, Boston, 1926), Roy L. Garis, *Immigration Restriction: A Study of the Opposition to and Regulation of Immigration into the United States* (Macmillan, N. Y., 1927). On the bonus, see Marcus Duffield, *King Legion* (Cape and Smith, N. Y., 1931). Facts revealed in the investigation of the oil-reserve scandals are in M. E. Savage, *The Story of Teapot Dome* (New Republic, N. Y., 1924).

CHAPTER 13. KEEPING COOL WITH COOLIDGE

GENERAL.   Calvin Coolidge, *Autobiography* (Cosmopolitan Book Co., N. Y., 1929) is of very limited usefulness, but Claude M. Fuess, *Calvin Coolidge, the Man from Vermont* (Little Brown, Boston, 1940), and William Allen White, *A Puritan in Babylon* (Macmillan, N. Y., 1938), are excellent.

THE PROGRESSIVE OPPOSITION.   On the most significant liberal of the twenties, see George W. Norris, *Fighting Liberal* (Macmillan, N. Y., 1945), Alfred Lief, *Democracy's Norris: The Biography of a Lonely Crusade* (Stackpole, N. Y., 1939), R. L. Neuberger and S. B. Kahn, *Integrity: the Life of George W. Norris* (Vanguard, N. Y., 1937).

POLITICAL ISSUES.   The best introduction to the farm problem is Wilson Gee, *The Social Economics of Agriculture* (Macmillan, N. Y., 1942). See also John D. Black, *Agricultural Reform in the United States* (McGraw-Hill, N. Y., 1929), and E. Seligman, *The Economics of Farm Relief; a Survey of the Agricultural Problem* (Columbia Univ., N. Y., 1929). For various aspects of the power controversy, Stephen Raushenbush, *The Power Fight* (New Republic, N. Y., 1932), and Ernest Gruening, *The Public Pays: a Study of Power Propaganda* (Vanguard, N. Y., 1931) are recommended.

CHAPTER 14. FOREIGN AFFAIRS, 1921–1929

GENERAL.   The diplomatic histories by Bemis and Bailey, cited in the first section of the reading suggestions, are still very useful and may be supplemented with the interpretive study, Frank H. Simonds, *American Foreign Policy in the Post-War Years* (Johns Hopkins, Baltimore, 1935).

INTERNATIONAL COOPERATION.   Competent discussions are Denna F. Fleming, *The United States and World Organization, 1920–1933* (Columbia Univ., N. Y., 1938), and Russell M. Cooper, *American Consultation in World Affairs* (Macmillan, N. Y., 1934). The amazing irresponsibility of the Senate is emphasized by Denna F. Fleming, *The United States and the World Court* (Doubleday Doran, Garden City, 1945). A more creditable record is that discussed in Benjamin H. Williams, *The United States and Disarmament* (McGraw-Hill, N. Y., 1931). Also important for an understanding of the disarmament issue are Raymond L. Buell, *The Washington Conference* (Appleton, N. Y., 1922), and Harold and Margaret Sprout, *Toward a New Order of Sea Power; American Naval Policy and the World Scene, 1918–1922* (Princeton Univ., Princeton, 1940). On the Pact of Paris, the most valuable authorities are James T. Shotwell, *War as an Instrument of National Policy and Its Renunciation in the Pact of Paris* (Harcourt Brace, N. Y., 1929) and David Bryn-Jones, *Frank B. Kellogg, a Biography* (Putnam, N. Y.,

1937). Two outstanding economists discuss the debts issue in Harold G. Moulton and Leo Pasvolsky, *War Debts and World Prosperity* (Century, N. Y., 1932).

SPECIAL AREAS.   For a discussion of the nonrecognition of the Soviet government, see Frederick L. Schuman, *American Policy toward Russia since 1917* (International Publishers, N. Y., 1928), and Foster Rhea Dulles, *The Road to Teheran: The Story of Russia and America, 1781–1943* (Princeton Univ., Princeton, 1944). The leader of the Philippine independence movement tells his story in Manuel Luis Quezon, *The Good Fight* (Appleton-Century, N. Y., 1946). On relations with Latin America, Graham H. Stuart, *Latin America and the United States* (Appleton-Century, N. Y., 1938), is useful. Essential to an understanding of the Nicaraguan affair are Isaac J. Cox, *Nicaragua and the United States* (World Peace Foundation, Boston, 1927), and Henry L. Stimson, *American Policy in Nicaragua* (Scribners, N. Y., 1927). On the easing of the crisis in Mexican-American relations see the excellent biography, Harold Nicolson, *Dwight Morrow* (Harcourt Brace, N. Y., 1935).

CHAPTER 15. REACTIONARIES AND REBELS

GENERAL.   Slosson, *Great Crusade and After*, Sullivan, *Our Times*, v. 6, Beard, *Rise of American Civilization*, v. 2 and 3, are excellent on the period of the twenties. A treasury of stimulating data and comment is provided by President's Research Committee, *Recent Social Trends in the United States*, 2 v. (McGraw-Hill, N. Y., 1933). Highly entertaining is Frederick L. Allen, *Only Yesterday* (Harper, N. Y., 1931). A harsher judgment of the period is Henry M. Robinson, *Fantastic Interim: a Hindsight History of American Manners, Morals, and Mistakes between Versailles and Pearl Harbor* (Harcourt Brace, N. Y., 1943). Robert S. and Helen M. Lynd, *Middletown: A Study in Contemporary American Culture* (Harcourt Brace, N. Y., 1929), is a well-known sociological study of Muncie, Indiana, during the twenties. An interesting comparison is with Angie Debo, *Prairie City: the Story of an American Community* (Knopf, N. Y., 1944). A good contemporary picture is André Siegfried, *America Comes of Age, a French Analysis* (Harcourt Brace, N. Y., 1927). Severely critical judgments are contained in Harold E. Stearns, ed., *Civilization in the United States: An Inquiry by Thirty Americans* (Harcourt Brace, N. Y., 1922).

SPECIAL PHASES.   The problems of organized labor are discussed in Perlman and Taft, *Labor Movements*, and in L. L. Lorwin and J. A. Flexner, *The American Federation of Labor* (Brookings Institution, Washington, 1933). Important on issues involving civil liberties are Chafee, *Free Speech in the United States*, and Arthur Garfield Hayes, *Let Freedom Ring* (Boni and Liveright, N. Y., 1928); see also Felix Frankfurter, *The Case of Sacco and Vanzetti* (Little Brown, Boston, 1927). Outstanding contemporary studies were John M. Mecklin, *The Ku Klux Klan: a Study of the American Mind* (Harcourt Brace, N. Y., 1924), Herman Feldman, *Prohibition, Its Economic and Industrial Aspects* (Appleton, N. Y., 1927), Charles Merz, *The Dry*

Decade (Doubleday Doran, Garden City, 1931). On architecture see W. A. Starett, *Skyscrapers and the Men Who Build Them* (Scribners, N. Y., 1928), and Frank Lloyd Wright, *An Autobiography* (Longmans Green, N. Y., 1932). On literature and the arts, see titles listed in the first section of the reading suggestions; also Joseph Beach, *American Fiction, 1920–1940* (Macmillan, N. Y., 1941).

CHAPTER 16. PROSPERITY

GENERAL.   The economic histories by Shannon, Faulkner, and Kirkland, recommended above, contain good discussions of this period. A contemporary study of great importance is *Recent Economic Changes in the United States*, 2 v. (McGraw-Hill, N. Y., 1929). A useful summary of this is Edward E. Hunt, *An Audit of America* . . . (McGraw-Hill, N. Y., 1930). Brief but highly suggestive is Stuart Chase, *The Road We Are Traveling, 1914–1942: Guide Lines to America's Future* (Twentieth Century Fund, N. Y., 1942). A Marxian interpretation is Lewis Corey, *The Decline of American Capitalism* (Covici Friede, N. Y., 1934). Important monographs by economists are Simon Kuznets, *National Income and Capital Formation, 1919–1935: A Preliminary Report* (National Bureau of Economic Research, N. Y., 1937), and Spurgeon Bell, *Productivity, Wages, and National Income* (Brookings Institution, Washington, 1940).

SPECIAL INDUSTRIES.   J. G. Glover and W. B. Cornell, eds., *The Development of American Industries: Their Economic Significance* (Prentice-Hall, N. Y., 1932), and H. T. Warshaw, ed., *Representative Industries in the United States* (Holt, N. Y., 1928), have chapters on each major industry written by spokesmen for the industry; they contain much valuable information as well as a generous measure of special pleading. Ralph C. Epstein, *The Automobile Industry: Its Economic and Commercial Development* (A. W. Shaw Co., Chicago, 1928), contains valuable statistical material, while David L. Cohn, *Combustion on Wheels: An Informal History of the Automobile Age* (Houghton Mifflin, Boston, 1944), is a popular account. Henry Ford, *My Life and Work* (Garden City Publishing Co., Garden City, 1922) reveals Ford's economic philosophy. A well-written account of the origins of aviation is in Fred C. Kelly, *The Wright Brothers* (Harcourt Brace, N. Y., 1943), while a critical and informative study of the whole industry is Elsbeth E. Freudenthal, *The Aviation Business: From Kitty Hawk to Wall Street* (Vanguard, N. Y., 1940). The perplexities arising out of the merchant marine problem are illuminated by Paul M. Zeis, *American Shipping Policy* (Princeton Univ., Princeton, 1938). On the movies, see Maurice Bardèche and Robert Brasillach, *History of the Motion Pictures* (Norton, N. Y., 1938), Margaret F. Thorp, *America at the Movies* (Yale Univ., New Haven, 1939), Lewis Jacobs, *The Rise of the American Film; a Critical History* (Harcourt Brace, N. Y., 1939); on radio, see A. N. Goldsmith and Austin C. Lescarboura, *This Thing Called Broadcasting* (Holt, N. Y., 1930), Paul Schubert, *The Electric Word: the Rise of the Radio* (Macmillan, N. Y., 1928). On the railroads, see Sidney L. Miller, *Inland Transportation: Principles and Policies* (McGraw-Hill, N. Y., 1933).

ISSUES OF PUBLIC POLICY. Thoughtful studies are William Z. Ripley, *Main Street and Wall Street* (Little Brown, Boston, 1927), W. E. Mosher and F. G. Crawford, *Public Utility Regulation* (Harper, N. Y., 1933), Twentieth Century Fund, *The Power Industry and the Public Interest* (Twentieth Century Fund, N. Y., 1944), Corporation Survey Commission, *Big Business: Its Growth and Its Place* (Twentieth Century Fund, N. Y., 1937), and Thurman W. Arnold, *The Folklore of Capitalism* (Yale Univ., New Haven, 1937).

CHAPTER 17. HOOVER AND THE DEPRESSION

GENERAL. Hoover's record is sturdily defended in William S. Myers and Walter Newton, *The Hoover Administration: a Documented Narrative* (Scribners, N. Y., 1936). Hoover's own writings reveal both his assets and limitations as statesman; see William S. Myers, ed., *The State Papers and Other Public Writings of Herbert Hoover*, 2 v. (Scribners, N. Y., 1934), and Ray Lyman Wilbur and Arthur M. Hyde, eds., *The Hoover Policies* (Scribners, N. Y., 1937). Theodore Joslin, *Hoover Off the Record* (Doubleday Doran, Garden City, 1935) is a memoir by his secretary.

THE DEPRESSION. Vivid descriptions of the economic collapse are in Allen, *Only Yesterday*, and its sequel, F. L. Allen, *Since Yesterday* (Harper, N. Y., 1940), the Beards, *America in Midpassage* (vol. 3 of *The Rise of American Civilization*), and Gilbert Seldes, *The Years of the Locust* (*America 1929–1932*) (Little Brown, Boston, 1933). A historically important interpretation is that of the Harvard economist, Alvin Hansen, *Fiscal Policy and Business Cycles* (Norton, N. Y., 1941). Problems of government policy are discussed in Josephine C. Brown, *Public Relief, 1929–1939* (Holt, N. Y., 1940). See also the economic histories by Shannon, Faulkner, and Kirkland.

CHAPTER 18. HOOVER'S QUEST FOR WORLD STABILITY

GENERAL. Laudatory of Hoover is William S. Myers, *The Foreign Policies of Herbert Hoover* (Scribners, N. Y., 1940). A more balanced account is to be found in the diplomatic histories by Bailey and Bemis. Valuable contemporary interpretation together with much documentary material is in U. S. State Department, *Press Releases* (after 1939 called *The Department of State Bulletin*), Council on Foreign Relations, *Survey of American Foreign Relations, 1928–1931*, 4 v. (Yale Univ., New Haven, 1928–1931), Foreign Policy Association, *Foreign Policy Reports* (N. Y., 1925 to date).

SPECIAL PHASES. On the London Naval Conference, much valuable information is to be found in Charles G. Dawes, *Journal as Ambassador to Great Britain* (Macmillan, N. Y., 1939). The official record is to be found in State Department Conference Series No. 6, *Proceedings of the London Naval Conference and Supplementary Documents* (Gov't Printing Off., Washington, 1931). An important reorientation of American policy may be traced in Bemis, *Latin American Policy of the United States*. The best discussions of the Far Eastern problem are T. A. Bisson, *American Policy in the Far East, 1931–1940* (Institute of Pacific Relations, N. Y., 1940), and Griswold,

Far Eastern Policy of the United States. Hoover's Secretary of State has provided an important memoir in Henry L. Stimson, *The Far Eastern Crisis; Recollections and Observations* (Council on Foreign Relations, N. Y., 1936).

CHAPTER 19. THE NEW DEAL BEGINS

GENERAL.   Indispensable not only for documentary material but for Roosevelt's subsequent comments on events is Samuel I. Rosenman, comp., *The Public Papers and Addresses of Franklin D. Roosevelt*, 9 v. (Random House and Macmillan, N. Y., 1938–1940). Particularly stimulating on this period is Beard, *America in Midpassage*, and the later Charles A. Beard and George H. E. Smith, *The Old Deal and the New* (Macmillan, N. Y., 1940). Another leading historian provides a generally sympathetic account in Arthur M. Schlesinger, *The New Deal in Action, 1933–1938* (Macmillan, N. Y., 1939). The most detailed discussion is Basil Rauch, *The History of the New Deal* (Creative Age, N. Y., 1944). An interesting foreign appraisal is Editors of the London *Economist*, *The New Deal: An Analysis and Appraisal* (Knopf, N. Y., 1937). J. George Frederick, *The New Deal: A People's Capitalism* (Business Bourse, N. Y., 1944), is Democratic campaign literature, but contains some chapters of interest contributed by pro-Roosevelt businessmen. Still valuable are the accounts of the Washington journalist, Ernest K. Lindley, *The Roosevelt Revolution, First Phase* (Viking, N. Y., 1933), and *Halfway with Roosevelt* (Viking, N. Y., 1937). Definitive biographies of Roosevelt are not yet available, but interesting contemporary appraisals are in Gerald Johnson, *Roosevelt, Dictator or Democrat* (Harper, N. Y., 1941), Compton Mackenzie, *Mr. Roosevelt* (Dutton, N. Y., 1944), Noel F. Busch, *What Manner of Man* (Harper, N. Y., 1944).

MEMOIRS.   Of the rapidly growing mass of this type of material, the most valuable item so far is New Deal Secretary of Labor Frances Perkins, *The Roosevelt I Knew* (Viking, N. Y., 1946). A biased but highly informative account of the early New Deal is Raymond Moley, *After Seven Years* (Harper, N. Y., 1939). Harold L. Ickes, *The Autobiography of a Curmudgeon* (Reynal and Hitchcock, N. Y., 1943), is full and frank only for the years before its author became Secretary of the Interior; a second volume on the post-1933 period is much to be desired. Part of the story is in Harold L. Ickes, *Back to Work: The Story of PWA* (Macmillan, N. Y., 1935). Important on politics, particularly the 1932 and 1936 campaigns, are James A. Farley, *Behind the Ballots: The Personal History of a Politician* (Harcourt Brace, N. Y., 1938), and Charles Michelson, *The Ghost Talks* (Putnam, N. Y., 1944). The reaction to the New Deal of two unusually capable journalists are in Marquis W. Childs, *I Write from Washington* (Harper, N. Y., 1942), and Raymond Clapper, *Watching the World* (McGraw-Hill, N. Y., 1944).

SPECIAL PHASES.   Scholarly studies are Roy V. Peel and Thomas C. Donnelly, *The 1932 Campaign, an Analysis* (Farrar and Rinehart, N. Y., 1935), and Donald S. Howard, *The WPA and Federal Relief Policy* (Russell Sage, N. Y., 1938).

CHAPTER 20. BUSINESS AND THE NEW DEAL

GENERAL.   Most of the works cited for Chapter 19 are equally useful for this. The best discussion of the activities of the various New Deal agencies is in Merle Fainsod and Lincoln Gordon, *Government and the American Economy* (Norton, N. Y., 1941). A severely critical contemporary judgment is Ralph Robey, *Roosevelt versus Recovery* (Harper, N. Y., 1934). Valuable factual findings are in Twentieth Century Fund, *Debts and Recovery: A Study of Changes in the Internal Debt Structure from 1929 to 1937 and a Program for the Future* (Twentieth Century Fund, N. Y., 1938).

NRA.   Indispensable for understanding the point of view of NRA's most important administrator is Hugh S. Johnson, *The Blue Eagle from Egg to Earth* (Doubleday Doran, Garden City, 1935). Johnson's successor adds his comment in Donald R. Richberg, *The Rainbow* (Doubleday Doran, Garden City, 1936). A contemporary appraisal by competent economists is Leverett S. Lyon, *et al., The National Recovery Administration* (Brookings Institution, Washington, 1935). An important post-mortem is President's Committee of Industrial Analysis, *The National Recovery Administration* (Washington, 1935).

TVA AND THE UTILITIES ISSUE.   The broad objectives and administrative philosophy of TVA are lucidly set forth by its principal director, David E. Lilienthal, *TVA: Democracy on the March* (Harper, N. Y., 1944). Interesting illustrative material is available in R. L. Duffus, *The Valley and Its People, a Portrait of T. V. A.* (Knopf, N. Y., 1944). An outstanding scholarly study is C. Herman Pritchett, *The Tennessee Valley Authority, a Study in Public Administration* (Univ. of North Carolina, Chapel Hill, 1943). An English estimate is Julian Huxley, *TVA, Adventure in Planning* (Architectural Press, Cheam, Surrey, 1944). On the explosive general issue of utilities' policy see Bernhard Ostrolenk, *Electricity: For Use or For Profit* (Harper, N. Y., 1936), and M. L. Ramsay, *Pyramids of Power: The Story of Roosevelt, Insull and the Utility Wars* (Bobbs-Merrill, Indianapolis, 1937).

HOUSING.   Reasons for Federal intervention in this field are discussed in Michael W. Straus and Talbot Wegg, *Housing Comes of Age* (Oxford, N. Y., 1938), and Nathan Straus, *The Seven Myths of Housing* (Knopf, N. Y., 1944).

FISCAL AND MONETARY POLICY.   Important scholarly discussions are G. Griffith Johnson, *The Treasury and Monetary Policy, 1933–1938* (Harvard Univ., Cambridge, 1939), Sherwood M. Fine, *Public Spending and Postwar Economic Policy* (Columbia Univ., N. Y., 1944), Henry H. Villard, *Deficit Spending and the National Income* (Farrar and Rinehart, N. Y., 1941), Gerard Colm and Fritz Lehmann, *Economic Consequences of Recent American Tax Policy* (New School for Social Research, N. Y., 1938), Sidney Ratner, *American Taxation: Its History as a Social Force in Democracy* (Norton, N. Y., 1942), Harold M. Groves, *Production, Jobs and Taxes . . .* (McGraw-Hill, N. Y., 1944).

CHAPTER 21. AGRICULTURE AND LABOR

AGRICULTURE.   A wealth of interesting material is to be found in the *Yearbooks* of the Department of Agriculture. The philosophy of the New Deal Secretary of Agriculture is in Henry A. Wallace, *New Frontiers* (Reynal and Hitchcock, N. Y., 1934). Severely critical on many phases are Joseph S. Davis, *On Agricultural Policy, 1926–1938* (Food Research Institute, Stanford Univ., 1939) and Edwin G. Nourse, *Government in Relation to Agriculture* (Brookings Institution, Washington, 1940). The politics underlying farm relief is discussed in Wesley McCune, *The Farm Bloc* (Doubleday Doran, Garden City, 1943). The need for conservation is emphasized in Stuart Chase, *Rich Land, Poor Land: A Study in the Natural Resources of America* (McGraw-Hill, N. Y., 1936). On the problems of the rural underprivileged, see Carey McWilliams, *Ill Fares the Land: Migrants and Migratory Labor in the United States* (Little Brown, Boston, 1942) and Department of Agriculture, *Toward Farm Security* (Govt. Printing Off., Washington, 1941). On all phases, Gee, *Social Economics of Agriculture* (cited for Chapter 13) is excellent.

LABOR.   A general discussion is Herbert Harris, *American Labor* (Yale Univ., New Haven, 1939). On legislation, see John B. Andrews, *Labor Laws in Action* (Harper, N. Y., 1938) and Joseph Rosenfarb, *The National Labor Policy and How It Works* (Harper, N. Y., 1940). Important studies are the three by Robert R. R. Brooks, *When Labor Organizes* (Yale Univ., New Haven, 1938), *Unions of Their Own Choosing* (Yale Univ., New Haven, 1939), and *As Steel Goes . . . : Unionism in a Basic Industry* (Yale Univ., New Haven, 1940). Black aspects are emphasized in Harold Seidman, *Labor Czars: a History of Labor Racketeering* (Liveright, N. Y., 1938). On the rise of the CIO, see J. Raymond Walsh, *C. I. O., Industrial Unionism in America* (Norton, N. Y., 1937), Edward Levinson, *Labor on the March* (Harper, N. Y., 1938), Herbert Harris, *Labor's Civil War* (Knopf, N. Y., 1940). On the most controversial figure in the labor movement, see James A. Wechsler, *Labor Baron, a Portrait of John L. Lewis* (Morrow, N. Y., 1944).

CHAPTER 22. NEW DEAL MILITANT

GENERAL.   See titles listed under Chapter 19.

SUPREME COURT CRISIS.   For essential background, Carl B. Swisher, *American Constitutional Development* (Houghton Mifflin, Boston, 1943) and Benjamin F. Wright, *The Growth of American Constitutional Law* (Houghton Mifflin, Boston, 1942) are the best. An appreciative study of the most famous jurist of the modern period is Francis Biddle, *Mr. Justice Holmes* (Scribners, N. Y., 1942). A leading authority on the Supreme Court criticizes its conduct in Edward S. Corwin, *The Twilight of the Supreme Court: a History of Our Constitutional Theory* (Yale Univ., New Haven, 1934), and *Court over Constitution; a Study in Judicial Review as an Instrument of Popular Government* (Princeton Univ., Princeton, 1938). An irreverent portrait of the court is Drew Pearson and Robert Allen, *The Nine Old Men*

(Doubleday Doran, Garden City, 1936). The best account of the court controversy from the New Deal point of view is Robert H. Jackson, *The Struggle for Judicial Supremacy: A Study of a Crisis in American Power Politics* (Knopf, N. Y., 1941). Detailed and well-informed, although unsympathetic to Roosevelt, is the account of the fight over the Judicial Reorganization Bill in Joseph Alsop and Turner Catledge, *The 168 Days* (Doubleday Doran, Garden City, 1938). The sequel of the controversy is dealt with in Edwin S. Corwin, *Constitutional Revolution, Ltd.* (Pomona College, Claremont, Calif., 1941).

OTHER ISSUES.   The neurotic fringe in American politics is studied in Alfred M. and Elizabeth B. Lee, eds., *The Fine Art of Propaganda: A Study of Father Coughlin's Speeches* (Harcourt Brace, N. Y., 1939). The so-called spending theory is expounded in Alvin H. Hansen, *Full Recovery or Stagnation* (Norton, N. Y., 1938) and Stuart Chase, *Idle Money Idle Men* (Harcourt Brace, N. Y., 1940).

CHAPTER 23. FOREIGN POLICY, 1933–1937

GENERAL.   For competent accounts, see Bailey and Bemis in their diplomatic histories. The official defense of American policy is State Department, *Peace and War: United States Foreign Policy, 1931–1941* (Govt. Printing Off., Washington, 1943). For contemporary items see State Department, *Press Releases*, Foreign Policy Association *Bulletins* and *Reports*, and W. H. Shepardson, *et al.*, eds., *The United States in World Affairs, 1933, 1934-35, 1936, 1937* (Council on Foreign Relations, N. Y., 1934-1938). Pronouncements of presidential policy are to be found in *Public Papers and Addresses of Franklin D. Roosevelt;* also in Wilfred Funk, ed., *Roosevelt's Foreign Policy, 1933-1941* (Funk, N. Y., 1942). On Roosevelt's Secretary of State, see Harold B. Hinton, *Cordell Hull, a Biography* (Doubleday Doran, Garden City, 1942). A critical review of New Deal foreign policy is Charles A. Beard, *American Foreign Policy in the Making, 1932-1940: A Study in Responsibilities* (Yale Univ., New Haven, 1946).

SPECIAL PHASES.   Contemporary academic support for isolationism was provided by Charles A. Beard, *The Open Door at Home: a Trial Philosophy of National Interest* (Macmillan, N. Y., 1934), and Edwin Borchard and William P. Lage, *Neutrality for the United States* (Yale Univ., New Haven, 1937). Important memoirs throwing light on the problems of American diplomacy in three critical areas are Joseph E. Davies, *Mission to Moscow* (Simon and Schuster, N. Y., 1941), William E. Dodd, Jr., and Martha Dodd, *Ambassador Dodd's Diary, 1933-1938* (Harcourt Brace, N. Y., 1941), and Joseph C. Grew, *Ten Years in Japan* (Simon and Schuster, N. Y., 1944). Further information on relations with Russia is in Meno Lovenstein, *American Opinion of Soviet Russia* (Washington, 1941). On the Philippines, see *Joint Preparatory Committee on Philippine Affairs: Report of May 20, 1938*, 3 v. (Govt. Printing Off., Washington, 1938), and Kirk L. Grayson, *Philippine Independence: Motives, Problems and Prospects* (Farrar and Rinehart, N. Y., 1936). On Latin America, see Bemis, *Latin American Policy of the United States*, and Stuart, *Latin America and the United States*.

CHAPTER 24. AID TO THE DEMOCRACIES

GENERAL.   The titles recommended for Chapter 23 may be supplemented
with S. S. Jones and D. P. Myers, eds., *Documents on American Foreign
Relations*, v. 1–6 (World Peace Foundation, Boston, 1939–   ), and Shepardson, *The United States in World Affairs, 1938, 1939, 1940*. Two exceptionally well-informed journalists provide their account in Joseph Alsop and
Robert Kintner, *American White Paper; the Story of American Diplomacy
and the Second World War* (Simon and Schuster, N. Y., 1940). American
policy during the first years of the war is ably discussed by Sumner Welles,
The Time for Decision (Harper, N. Y., 1944).

SPECIAL PHASES.   Much valuable information is contained in the account
of the Lend-Lease administrator, Edward R. Stettinius, Jr., *Lend-Lease,
Weapon for Victory* (Macmillan, N. Y., 1944). The controversy between
the interventionists and the isolationists may be traced in Charles A. Beard,
A Foreign Policy for America (Knopf, N. Y., 1940), Allen W. Dulles and
H. F. Armstrong, *Can America Stay Neutral?* (Harper, N. Y., 1939), Ray-
mond L. Buell, *Isolated America* (Knopf, N. Y., 1940), Charles G. Fenwick,
American Neutrality, Trial and Failure (New York Univ., N. Y., 1940),
Walter Johnson, *The Battle Against Isolation* (Univ. of Chicago, Chicago,
1944), and Harold Lavine and James Wechsler, *War Propaganda and the
United States* (Yale Univ., New Haven, 1940).

Magazines such as *Time, Newsweek*, and *Events*, and the current newspapers are essential to supplement this and the succeeding chapters.

CHAPTER 25. PRELUDE TO PEARL HARBOR

GENERAL.   Of works previously cited, those particularly useful for this
period are State Department, *Peace and War* and *Bulletin;* Shepardson, *The
United States in World Affairs;* Jones and Myers, *Documents on American
Foreign Relations;* Nevins and Hacker, *The United States and Its Place in
World Affairs;* Griswold, *Far Eastern Policy of the United States;* and Grew,
Ten Years in Japan. Written with an apparent access to much inside infor-
mation is Forrest Davis and Ernest K. Lindley, *How War Came, an Ameri-
can White Paper: From the Fall of France to Pearl Harbor* (Simon and
Schuster, N. Y., 1942).

THE FAR EAST.   Essential background for understanding the issues of diplomacy between the United States and Japan is provided in C. A. Buss, *War
and Diplomacy in Eastern Asia* (Macmillan, N. Y., 1941), W. C. Johnstone,
The United States and Japan's New Order (Oxford, N. Y., 1941), Harold
S. Quigley, *Far Eastern War, 1937–1941* (World Peace Foundation, Boston,
1942).

CHAPTER 26. PREPARING FOR TOTAL WAR

Nevins and Hacker, *The United States and Its Place in World Affairs*
has excellent chapters on the wartime economy. The most important authority for industrial mobilization is the memoir of the WPB chief, Donald

Nelson, *Arsenal of Democracy: The Story of American Production* (Harcourt Brace, N. Y., 1946). Jack Goodman, ed., *While You Were Gone: A Report on Wartime Life in the United States* (Simon and Schuster, N. Y., 1946), is uneven in quality, but has good chapters. Mercedes Rosebery, *This Day's Madness: A Story of the American People Against the Background of the War Effort* (Macmillan, N. Y., 1944) is chaotic and impressionistic in treatment, but captures something of the spirit of the times. Highly valuable contemporary accounts are provided in Selden Menefee, *Assignment: U. S. A.* (Reynal and Hitchcock, N. Y., 1943), and John Dos Passos, *State of the Nation* (Houghton Mifflin, Boston, 1944). On wartime economic problems, see Seymour E. Harris, *Economics of America at War* (Norton, N. Y., 1943), and the same author's *Price and Related Controls in the United States* (McGraw-Hill, N. Y., 1945). On the war's most serious infringements of civil liberties, see Carey McWilliams, *Prejudice; Japanese-Americans Symbol of Racial Intolerance* (Little Brown, Boston, 1944).

CHAPTER 27. THE GLOBAL WAR

GENERAL.   Trained historians were employed during and after the war by the War and Navy Departments to collect material and prepare a comprehensive account of the great conflict. The Army series alone will contain some 115 volumes. Obviously no definitive history may be expected before this preliminary task is substantially accomplished. Separate from the major project are a number of brief studies already published by the Army historians under the general title *American Forces in Action;* the most important title is *Omaha Beachhead*, a vivid account of the invasion of Normandy; other studies are *Papuan Campaign, To Bizerte with the II Corps, Salerno, Volturno, The Winter Line, Merrill's Marauders, The Admiralties, Guam,* and *Makin.* Useful summaries based upon the early published sources are Roger W. Shugg and H. A. DeWeerd, *World War II: A Concise History* (Infantry Journal, Washington, 1946), Walter P. Hall, *Iron Out of Calvary: An Interpretive History of the Second World War* (Appleton-Century, N. Y., 1946), Francis T. Miller, *History of World War II* (Winston, Philadelphia, 1946). Waverly Root, *The Secret History of the War*, 3 v. (Scribners, N. Y., 1945–46), is a misnomer in so far as the title suggests that the author had access to confidential information, but it contains some useful detail along with provocative comment.

REPORTS AND MEMOIRS.   The clearest as well as the most authoritative brief account of the climactic phase of the war is *General Marshall's Report: The Winning of the War in Europe and the Pacific . . .* (Simon and Schuster, N. Y., 1945). See also H. A. DeWeerd, ed., *Selected Speeches and Statements of General of the Army George C. Marshall . . .* (Infantry Journal, Washington, 1945). On the European campaign from D Day to the surrender of Germany, an essential source is Dwight D. Eisenhower, *Report by the Supreme Commander to the Combined Chiefs of Staff on the Operations in Europe of the Allied Expeditionary Force 6 June 1944 to 8 May 1945* (Govt. Printing Off., Washington, 1946). Much more detailed is Harry C. Butcher, *My Three Years with Eisenhower* (Simon and Schuster, N. Y.,

844 SUGGESTIONS FOR FURTHER READING

1946). One of the most controversial memoirs, critical of Eisenhower and the British, is Ralph Ingersoll, *Top Secret* (Harcourt Brace, N. Y., 1946). Light on naval campaigns in the Pacific is shed by Ellis M. Zacharias, *Secret Mission: The Story of an Intelligence Officer* (Putnam, N. Y., 1946), Walter Karig and Wellbourne Kelley, *Battle Report: Pearl Harbor to Coral Sea* (Farrar and Rinehart, N. Y., 1944), Ernest J. King, *U. S. Navy at War, 1941–1945, Official Reports to the Secretary of the Navy* (U. S. Navy Dept., Washington, 1946.) The accomplishments of the army and navy air arms are told in part in Lewis H. Brereton, *The Brereton Diaries* (Morrow, N. Y., 1946), and A. R. Buchanan, ed., *The Navy's War: A Mission Completed* (Harper, N. Y., 1946). The Japanese side, to be read with caution, is told in Masuo Kato, *The Lost War* (Knopf, N. Y., 1946). Good accounts of the little-publicized Burma and China fronts are in Jack Belden, *Retreat with Stilwell* (Knopf, N. Y., 1943), and Theodore H. White and Annalee Jacoby, *Thunder Out of China* (Sloan Associates, N. Y., 1946). Unforgettable pictures of ordinary army life on the various fronts are in Ernie Pyle, *Here Is Your War* (Holt, N. Y., 1943), and the same author's *Brave Men* (Holt, N. Y., 1944). Of the many memoirs by journalists, Drew Middleton, *Our Share of Night* (Viking, N. Y., 1946), and Eric Sevareid, *Not So Wild a Dream* (Knopf, N. Y., 1946), are recommended.

Much vivid war reporting is to be found in contemporary newspapers and periodicals. Some of the best was to be found in unexpected places—in publications as different from each other as *The New Yorker*, the *Saturday Evening Post*, and *PM*, for example.

CHAPTER 28. TRIBULATIONS OF TRUMAN

The following books are mentioned in the chapter as having influence on the political developments of the period or on public opinion toward basic American problems: Wendell Willkie, *One World* (Simon and Schuster, N. Y., 1943), Henry A. Wallace, *The Century of the Common Man* (Reynal and Hitchcock, N. Y., 1943), Chester Bowles, *Tomorrow Without Fear* (Simon and Schuster, N. Y., 1946), Henry A. Wallace, *Sixty Million Jobs* (Simon and Schuster, N. Y., 1945), Friedrich A. Hayek, *The Road to Serfdom* (Univ. of Chicago, Chicago, 1944). The last months of the Roosevelt administration and the first of Truman are discussed in Jonathan Daniels, *Frontier on the Potomac* (Macmillan, N. Y., 1946). Only the contemporary press and magazines, however, provide adequate supplementary reading for this recent period.

CHAPTER 29. PROBLEMS OF PEACE AND WORLD ORGANIZATION

INTERNATIONAL ORGANIZATION.   The revival of internationalism in the United States led to the publication of many books and periodical articles. Such influential works as Welles, *Time for Decision*, Willkie, *One World*, Wallace, *Century of the Common Man*, have already been cited. Widely read also were Clarence K. Streit, *Union Now: The Proposal for Interdemocracy Federal Union* (Harper, N. Y., 1940), the same author's *Union Now With Britain* (Harper, N. Y., 1941), Herbert Hoover and Hugh Gibson, *The Problems of a Lasting Peace* (Doubleday Doran, Garden City, 1942), Walter Lippmann, *U. S. Foreign Policy: Shield of the Republic* (Little Brown, Boston, 1943), Emery Reeves, *The Anatomy of Peace* (Harper, N. Y., 1945). Elliott Roosevelt, *As He Saw It* (Duell, Sloan, and Pearce, N. Y., 1946), is a memoir by F. D. R.'s son dealing principally with the late President's conferences with Churchill and Stalin; it contains interesting material but should be used with caution because of the anti-Churchill bias of its author. The genesis of the United Nations Organization is well traced in Vera Micheles Dean, *The Four Cornerstones of Peace* (Whittlesey House, N. Y., 1946).

OCCUPATION PROBLEMS.   On the occupation of Germany, see Julian Bach, Jr., *America's Germany: An Account of the Occupation* (Random House, N. Y., 1946), Saul K. Padover, *Experiment in Germany: The Story of an American Intelligence Officer* (Duell, Sloan, and Pearce, N. Y., 1946), James P. Warburg, *Germany—Nation or No-Man's Land* (Headline Series No. 60, Foreign Policy Association, N. Y., 1946). The chief American prosecutor at the Nuremberg trial makes his accusations in Robert H. Jackson, *The Case Against the Nazi War Criminals* (Knopf, N. Y., 1946). On Japan, see Richard Hart, *Eclipse of the Rising Sun* (Headline Series No. 56, Foreign Policy Association, N. Y., 1946). Recent American policy in the Philippines is criticized in Hernando Abaya, *Betrayal in the Philippines* (A. A. Wyn, N. Y., 1946). An equally serious criticism of American policy in China is in White and Jacoby, *Thunder Out of China.*

POSTWAR FRICTIONS.   Relations of the United States with the other victorious powers are discussed in William T. R. Fox, *The Super-Powers, the United States, Britain, and the Soviet Union* (Harcourt Brace, N. Y., 1944), David Dallin, *The Big Three: the United States, Britain, and Russia* (Yale Univ., New Haven, 1945), Vera M. Dean, *Russia—Menace or Promise* (Headline Series No. 58, Foreign Policy Association, N. Y., 1946). The full seriousness of atomic warfare is to be grasped through John Hersey, *Hiroshima* (Knopf, N. Y., 1946), and Bernard Brodie, ed., *The Absolute Weapon: Atomic Power and World Order* (Harcourt Brace, N. Y., 1946). An important criticism of the Truman administration's foreign policy is Sumner Welles, *Where Are We Heading?* (Harper, N. Y., 1946).

CHAPTER 30. SOCIAL TRENDS DURING PEACE AND WAR

GENERAL.   "Recent Social Trends," *American Journal of Sociology*, XLVII (May, 1942), 803–980, does for the thirties what the more extensive work of the same name did for the twenties. A brilliantly written survey is Frederick L. Allen, *Since Yesterday* (Harper, N. Y., 1940). Harold E. Stearns, ed., *America Now: An Inquiry into Civilization in the United States: By Thirty-Six Americans* (Literary Guild, N. Y., 1938), gives a more optimistic picture than the similar survey under Stearns' editorship of 1922 (cited for Chapter 15). Much interesting information is to be found in U. S. Office of War Information, *American Handbook* (Public Affairs Press, Washington, 1945). Robert and Helen Lynd, *Middletown in Transition:*

A Study in Cultural Conflicts (Harcourt Brace, N. Y., 1937), provides an important sequel to the Lynds' earlier study. A thoughtful commentary is Simeon Strunsky, *The Living Tradition: Change and America* (Doubleday Doran, Garden City, 1939).

THE NEGRO.   The most complete and objective study is the work of a Swedish sociologist, Gunnar Myrdal, *An American Dilemma: The Negro Problem and Modern Democracy*, 2 v. (Harper, N. Y., 1944). Outstanding discussions by American scholars are Horace R. Cayton and George S. Mitchell, *Black Workers and the New Unions* (Univ. of North Carolina, Chapel Hill, 1939), Rayford W. Logan, ed., *What the Negro Wants* (Univ. of North Carolina, Chapel Hill, 1944), Robert C. Weaver, *Negro Labor: A National Problem* (Harcourt Brace, N. Y., 1946), *Minority Peoples in a Nation at War*, vol. 223 of *Annals of American Academy of Political and Social Science* (Sept. 1942). Dynamic forces in the present situation are explained in Edwin R. Embree, *Brown America: The Story of a New Race* (Viking, N. Y., 1931), and Roi Ottley, *'New World A-Coming': Inside Black America* (Houghton Mifflin, Boston, 1943).

SOUTH AND WEST.   Southern liberals survey the needs and possibilities of their section in Jonathan Daniels, *A Southerner Discovers the South* (Macmillan, N. Y., 1938), Virginius Dabney, *Below the Potomac: A Book About the New South* (Appleton-Century, N. Y., 1942), Ellis G. Arnall, *The Shore Dimly Seen* (Lippincott, N. Y., 1946). The revolt against colonialism is discussed in A. G. Mezerik, *The Revolt of the South and West* (Duell, Sloan, and Pearce, N. Y., 1946).

EDUCATION AND THE FAMILY.   General discussions are in R. Freeman Butts, *The College Charts Its Course: Historical Conceptions and Current Proposals* (McGraw-Hill, N. Y., 1939), and Robert L. Kelly, *The American Colleges and the Social Order* (Macmillan, N. Y., 1940). For important opposing points of view, see Robert M. Hutchins, *The Higher Learning in America* (Yale Univ., New Haven, 1936), and Harry D. Gideonse, *The Higher Learning in a Democracy: A Reply to President Hutchins' Critique of the American University* (Farrar and Rinehart, N. Y., 1937). One of the best examinations of the problem is *General Education in a Free Society: Report of the Harvard Committee* (Harvard Univ., Cambridge, 1945). On the changing status of women, see Ernest R. Groves, *The American Woman: The Feminine Side of a Masculine Civilization* (Emerson Books, Inc., N. Y., 1944).

JOURNALISM.   For critical discussions of various aspects, consult Oswald G. Villard, *The Disappearing Daily: Chapters in American Newspaper Evolution* (Knopf, N. Y., 1944), Harold L. Ickes, *America's House of Lords: An Inquiry into the Freedom of the Press* (Harcourt Brace, N. Y., 1939), Charles Fisher, *The Columnists* (Howell Soskin, N. Y., 1944).

LITERATURE AND THE ARTS.   The titles listed in the first section of this bibliography may be supplemented with Henry S. Canby, *Seven Years' Harvest: Notes on Contemporary Literature* (Farrar and Rinehart, N. Y., 1936),

Halford E. Luccock, *American Mirror: Social, Ethical, and Religious Aspects of American Literature, 1930–1940* (Macmillan, N. Y., 1940), David Ewen, *Music Comes to America* (Crowell, N. Y., 1942), John T. Howard, *Our Contemporary Composers: American Music in the Twentieth Century* (Crowell, N. Y., 1941), Homer Saint-Gaudens, *The American Artist and His Times* (Dodd Mead, N. Y., 1941).

Index

Adams, Franklin P., 20
Adams, Samuel Hopkins, 30, 379
Adamson Act (1916), 134, 186
Addams, Jane, 182
Ade, George, 20
Agreed Memorandum (1905), 98
Agricultural Adjustment Act (AAA) (1933), 491, 501, 532–537; (1938), 538–540
Agricultural Marketing Act (1929), 436–438
Agriculture (1900–1914), 4–5; under Wilson, 132–133; in W. W. I, 215–217; in 1920's, 287–291, 327–334; under Hoover, 436–438; under FDR, 532–543; in W. W. II, 686–687; post W. W. II, 755–758
Aguinaldo, Emilio, 88–89
Air Force, United States, W. W. I, 219; W. W. II, 673, 698, 701, 704, 707, 710–717, 727–728
Alaska, 63; boundary controversy, 117
Albert, Heinrich F., 157, 158
Aldrich, Nelson W., 48, 51, 57–58, 127
Aldrich-Vreeland Act (1908), 51
Aleutian Islands, 710
Algeciras Conference (1906), 120–122
Alien Property Custodian, 223; scandal, 298, 405–406
Amalgamated Clothing Workers, 13, 365, 557
America First Committee, 646–647, 671
American Embargo Conference, 182
American Federation of Labor, 3, 10, 55–56, 271–274, 311, 360–365, 433, 544, 550–557, 747
American Fellowship Forum, 646
American Legion, 276, 302–303
American Tobacco Co., 5, 42, 61, 416
Anderson, Clinton P., 758
Anderson, Marian, 800, 822
Anti-Saloon League, 17, 263
Anzio, 710
Arabic Pledge, 174
Arbitration, first Venezuela, 109; second Venezuela, 110; Hague Conferences, 116; Pious Fund, 116–117; Alaska, 117; Hay

treaties, 118; Root treaties, 120; Taft-Knox treaties, 120; Bryan treaties, 137–138
Architecture, 23, 388, 406
Argentina, 119, 596, 766–768, 796–797
Argonne, 232
Arizona, 4, 36, 63
Armed Neutrality, W. W. I, 200–201; W. W. II, 653–656
Armistice, W. W. I, 233–234, 237–239
Army, United States, W. W. I, 185–186, 210–213, 228–233; demobilization, 264–267; W. W. II, 638–639, 671–675; operations, 698–730; demobilization, 740–742
Arnall, Ellis, 803–804
Arnold, Thurman, 518
Art, 22–23, 388–389, 820–822
Asiatic Exclusion League, 3
Atlantic Charter, 652–653
Atom Bomb, 727–728, 791–793, 811–813
Atomic Energy Commission, 778, 792
Austin, Warren, 655, 794–795
Australia, W. W. II, 711–712
Automobiles, 9–10, 394–398
Aviation, W. W. I, 219; in 1920's, 409–411, 530, 557; W. W. II, 685–686; see Air Force, United States

Badoglio, Pietro, 707
Baer, George F., 43–44
Baker, George F., 7, 19
Baker, Newton D., 32, 210–212
Baker, Ray Stannard, 30
Balfour, Arthur J., 207, 341
Ball, Joseph, 771
Ballinger, Richard, 58–61
Banking Act (1935), 520
Banking holiday, 485, 487–489
Banks, 6–8, 51; Federal Reserve, 126–131; under Hoover, 434–443; under FDR, 484–489, 520
Barkley, Alben, 583–584, 691
Barnard, George Gray, 23
Baruch, Bernard M., 214, 218–220, 265, 506, 679, 792
Bataan, 701, 713

849

Beach, Rex, 21
Beard, Charles A., 31, 387, 603
Belgium, atrocities, 155; food, 215–216;
  W. W. II, 722–723
Bellamy, Edward, 27–28
Bellows, George, 23
Benét, Stephen V., 383, 822
Benton, Thomas H., 389, 821
Beresford, Lord Charles, 95
Berger, Victor, 28, 278–279
Berle, Adolf A., 486
Berlin, Irving, 24
Bernstorff, Count Johann von, 152, 157,
  169, 174, 178, 188, 193, 195, 197, 199, 205
Bethmann-Hollweg, Chancellor, 155, 170,
  172, 174, 195
Beveridge, Albert, 63, 66, 75, 384
Bevin, Ernest, 788
Bidault, Georges, 788
Biddle, Francis, 694, 782
Bidlack Treaty (1846), 103–104, 107
Big Business, see Industry, Trusts
Bikini, 791
Billings, Warren K., 367
Birth control, 381–382
Black, Hugo, 506, 523, 576–578, 740
Black market, 677, 743
Black Tom explosion, 158
Blacklist, W. W. I, 188–189; W. W. II, 650
Bliss, Tasker H., 241
Blockade, W. W. I, 162–166; W. W. II,
  627–628
Boas, Franz, 18
Bolsheviks, 235, 244–245, 275–278
Bonds, W. W. I, 222, 237, 429; W. W. II,
  692
Bonus, W. W. I, 266; in 1920's, 302–306;
  under Hoover, 446–448; under FDR,
  498–499
Bonus Army, 447
Bootlegging, 373–376, 427
Borah, William E., 249, 256, 258, 281, 318,
  338–339, 349, 423, 438, 443, 451, 473–474,
  508
Boston police strike, 272–274
Boulder dam, 326–327
Bowles, Chester, 683, 746, 754–756
Boxer rebellion, 96–97
Boy-Ed, Karl, 157–158
Bradley, Omar, 705, 718, 720
Brain trust, 486–487
Brandegee, Frank B., 248, 282
Brandeis, Louis D., 60, 66, 76, 124, 128, 565,
  574, 576
Bretton Woods agreement (1944), 774
Briand, Aristide, 341, 349–350
Bricker, John, 732, 759
Brookhart, Smith, 315
Broun, Heywood, 367

Brown, Prentiss, 683
Bryan, William Jennings, 46, 74–75, 95, 123–
  124, 142, 249; presidential candidate, 27,
  39–40, 54–56; treaty of Paris, 82–83; Fed-
  eral Reserve system, 128–129; "cooling-
  off" treaties, 137–138; and W. W. I, 150–
  173, 183; Scopes trial, 370–373
Bryan-Chamorro Treaty (1916), 141–142
Bryce, James Viscount, 31, 196; report, 155
Buck Stove and Range case, 55
Budget and Accounting Act (1921), 291–
  293
Bulge, battle of, 722–723
Bull Moose, 75–77
Bullitt, William C., 245
Bunau-Varilla, Philippe, 106–107
Bureau of Corporations, 42, 46
Burke Wadsworth Act (1940), 638–639,
  651–652, 671–672
Burleson, Albert S., 124, 223–225, 275
Burma, 659, 700–701, 714–716
Burnham, Daniel, 23
Burton, Harold, 771
Bush, Vannevar, 810
Butler, Nicholas Murray, 349
Butler, William M., 281, 308, 315
Byrd, Harry, 733
Byrd, Richard E., 410
Byrnes, James F., 577, 680–681, 733, 738,
  779, 788

Cabell, James B., 383
Cairo Conference (1943), 770
Caldwell, Erskine, 819
Calles, Plutarco, 352–353, 461
Canada, 10, 593; reciprocity with, 63–65;
  Alaska boundary, 117; W. W. II, 638, 648
Cannon, Joseph G., 51, 65–66
Cantigny, 230
Capone, Al, 376–377
Capper, Arthur, 287, 330
Cardozo, Benjamin, 444, 565
Caribbean, 79; diplomacy (1900–1912),
  109–113; (1913–1921), 139–147; in 1920's,
  351–355; under Hoover, 459–463; under
  FDR, 596–599, 612
Carnegie, Andrew, 115, 181
Carranza, Venustiano, 143–147
Caruso, Enrico, 404
Carver, George W., 800
Casablanca Conference (1943), 769
Case Federal Mediation Bill (1946), 750–
  751
Cather, Willa, 22, 383, 818
Catt, Carrie Chapman, 182
Censorship, W. W. I, 167, 225–226; W. W.
  II, 692–694
Centralia, Washington, 276

Chamberlain, Neville, 615–619
Chaplin, Charlie, 402
Chapultepec, Act of (1945), 767–768, 797
Chase, Gilbert F., 23
Chase, Stuart, 753
Chateau-Thierry, 230
Chautauqua, 20
Chemical industry, 405–406
Cherbourg, 720
Chiang Kai-shek, 465–466, 716, 786
Chicago, University of, 814
Child labor, 28, 63, 134, 509–511, 557–558, 566, 570
China, Open-Door, 95–97; dollar diplomacy, 101–102, 136; W. W. I, 252; in 1920's, 340–344; under Hoover, 465–471; under FDR, 610–611, 612–613; W. W. II, 714–716, 770, 785–786
Christian Front, 646
Christy, Howard Chandler, 23, 226
Chrysler Corporation, 396
Churchill, Winston, American novelist, 21, 30
Churchill, Winston, British statesman, 652, 702–703, 716–717, 735, 768–770, 780
City Manager, 32
Civil liberties, W. W. I, 222–225; in 1920's, 365–367; W. W. II, 694–696
Civil service reform, 37, 38, 51
Civil Works Administration (CWA), 492–493
Civilian Conservation Corps (CCC), 490
Civilian Defense, Office of (OCD), 675
Clark, Champ, 65, 75, 124, 194, 210
Clark, Mark, 708, 710
Clark Memorandum, 357, 458
Clayton Antitrust Act (1914), 131–132
Clayton-Bulwer Treaty (1850), 104, 105
Clemenceau, Georges, 243–252
Cleveland, Grover, 46, 80, 109
Coal mining, 43–45, 274, 362–363, 407, 516
Cohen, Benjamin, 494
Colby, Bainbridge, 348
Colleges, 19, 386–387, 813–816
Colombia, 103, 106–108, 138, 355
Commerce, 10; during W. W. I, 159–161; in 1920's, 416–418; in 1930's, 587–590
Commerce and Labor, Department of, 42, 46, 63; Commerce Dept, 317–319
Commission Government, 32
Committee on Public Information, 225–227
Committee to Defend America by Aiding the Allies, 648
Commodity Credit Corporation (CCC), 539
Communications, 9, 267, 523–524
Communism, 275–278, 311, 362–363, 365, 481
Company unions, 364–365, 544–546
Compiègne, 233, 238, 629

Congress of Industrial Organizations (CIO), 550–557, 734
Connally, Tom, 771, 789
Conservation, under TR, 49–50; under Taft, 58–61; in 1920's, 295–298; under FDR, 524–527, 537–540
Contraband, controversy in W. W. I, 162–164
Coolidge, Calvin, 430, 465; police strike, 272–274; election of 1920, 281–283; becomes President, 294–295; and scandals, 297–299; and immigration, 301–302; and bonus, 305–306; election of 1924, 307–312; second administration, 313–334; foreign affairs, 338–339, 344–359; refuses third term, 422–425
Coral Sea, 702
Corregidor, 701, 713
Cortelyou, George B., 46
Coughlin, Charles, 494, 548, 562, 645–646, 694
Cox, James M., 283–286
Crane, Stephen, 22
Creel, George, 225–227
Crime, 376–378
Croly, Herbert, 76
Cromwell, William N., 106
Crowder, Enoch H., 210, 355
Crowley, Leo T., 680
Cuba, 81–86, 141; under Hoover, 462–463; under FDR, 593, 597–598
Cummings, Homer S., 486, 570
Cummins, Albert B., 35, 315
Cunningham claims, 59–60
Currency, under Hoover, 445; under FDR, 501–505, 588–590; see also Banks, Federal Reserve System, Gold
Curtis, Charles, 282, 423
Curtis, Edwin U., 272–274
Cushing, 171
Czechoslovakia, 616–619, 621
Czolgosz, Leon, 40

D Day, 716–720
Damrosch, Walter, 389
Danbury Hatters' case, 55
Daniels, Josephus, 124, 296
Darlan, Jean, 703–704
Darrow, Clarence, 370–373, 512
Daugherty, Harry M., 281, 287, 298, 317, 412
Davis, Chester A., 534
Davis, Elmer, 693
Davis, John W., 310–312
Davis, Norman H., 600, 602
Davis, William H., 687
Dawes, Charles G., 292, 308, 423, 428, 442–443, 452, 471
Dawes Plan, 347, 456
Dayton, Tennessee, 370–373

Debs, Eugene V., 28, 36, 40, 77, 224, 284, 286
Debts, foreign, W. W. I, 208, 345–347, 455–458, 483, 588–592; national, in 1930's, 319–324; under FDR, 497; W. W. II, 691–692, 753
Defense Transportation, Office of (ODT), 685, 747
DeForest, Lee, 404
DeLeon, Daniel, 27
Demobilization, W. W. I, 264–267; W. W. II, 740–742
Dempsey, Jack, 391–392
Denby, Edwin, 287; and oil, 296–298
Denman, William, 214–215
Depression, of 1907, 50–51; of 1919, 265; of 1921, 267, 393; of 1929, 428–448; of 1937, 580–582
Destroyer-Base deal, 630–632
DeValera, Eamon, 257–258
Devers, Jacob, 710
Dewey, George, 82
Dewey, John, 19
Dewey, Thomas E., 633; election of 1944, 731–735; election of 1946, 759
Díaz, Porfirio, 116, 142
Dies, Martin, 695, 735
Direct primary, 35, 70, 801
Disarmament, during 1920's, 339–345; under Hoover, 451–455; under FDR, 604–605; post W. W. II, 790–793
Divorce, 380–381, 807
Doenitz, Karl, 724–726
Doheny, Edwin L., 296–298
Dollar diplomacy, in China, 101–102, 136; in Latin America, 112–114, 136–137
Dolliver, Jonathan P., 60
Dominican Republic, intervention in, 111–113; and Wilson, 141, 355
Doolittle, James, 701
DosPassos, John, 367, 382, 818
Douglas, William O., 522, 733
Draft, see Selective Service
Drago Doctrine, 119
Dreiser, Theodore, 22, 383, 818
Dumba, Constantin, 157, 158, 173
Dumbarton Oaks (1944), 775–776
Dunne, Finley Peter ("Mr. Dooley"), 20
Durant, William C., 396
Duryea, Charles, 394

Easter Rebellion, 168–169
Eastman, Joseph B., 531, 685
Economic Stabilization, Office of (OES), 680–681
Economy Act (1933), 490
Edison, Thomas A., 402
Education (1900–1920), 19–20; in Cuba, 86; in Philippines, 92; in 1920's, 386–387; of Negro, 798; post W. W. II, 813–816

Eighteenth Amendment (1919), 263, 373–376, 424–425; repeal of, 483, 492
Einstein, Albert, 18, 811
Eisenhower, Dwight D., 703, 706–708, 718–727, 741
Elections, (1900), 36–40; (1904), 45–46; (1908), 53–56; (1910), 60; (1912), 70–77; (1916), 190–194; (1918), 240–241; (1920), 280–286; (1924), 307–312; (1926), 315–316; (1928), 422–426; (1932), 476–482; (1934), 493; (1936), 559–563; (1938), 582–584; (1940), 633–638; (1944), 731–735; (1946), 759
Electricity, 398–402, 524–528
Eliot, T. S., 383
Elk Hills, 295–298
Elkins Act (1903), 48
Ely, Joseph B., 559
Ely, Richard T., 30
Emergency Banking Act (1933), 487–488, 502
Emergency Fleet Corporation, 186, 214–215
Emergency Quota Act (1921), 299–300
Esch-Cummins Act (1920), 267–269, 413
Ethiopia, 605–607
Evangelism, 14–15
Evans, Hiram W., 368–370
Executive Reorganization, 578–580, 752–753
Expediting Act (1903), 43
Export-Import Bank, 594–595, 598, 633, 766

Faid Pass, 704
Fair Employment Practices Committee (FEPC), 752, 802
Fair Labor Standards Act (1938), 514, 557–558
Fairbanks, Charles W., 45, 191
Fairless, Benjamin, 745
Falaba, 171
Fall, Albert B., 286; scandal, 295–298
Family relations, 376–382, 806–808
Far East, 95–102; in 1920's, 339–344; under Hoover, 465–469; under FDR, 610–613, 656–668
Farley, James A., 478, 486, 530, 560, 635, 733
Farm Bloc, 287–291, 320–321, 330–334, 436–438
Farm Credit Administration, 533
Farm Security Administration, 541–543
Farmer-Labor Party, 284, 286, 311
Farmers Alliances, 26
Farrell, James T., 819
Faulkner, William, 819
Federal Bureau of Investigation (FBI), 695
Federal Council of Churches, 14, 16, 381
Federal Deposit Insurance Corporation (FDIC), 520
Federal Emergency Relief Administration (FERA), 490, 541

Federal Farm Board (1916), 436–438
Federal Farm Loan Act (1916), 133
Federal Housing Administration (FHA), 528–529
Federal Land Banks, 133, 331, 443
Federal Power Act (1920), 325, 400; (1935), 524
Federal Power Commission, 325, 400
Federal Reserve Act (1913), 126–131
Federal Reserve System, 51, 126–131, 162; and 1929, 430–431, 442–443, 456, 484, 488
Federal Trade Commission (FTC), 131–132, 316–319, 400–402, 517–518, 523
Fight for Freedom Committee, 648
Finance capitalism, 6–8, 399–400
Fish, Hamilton, 644, 646, 670, 735
Fisher, Irving, 376
Fitzgerald, F. Scott, 379, 382–383
Five-Power Naval Treaty (1922), 341–342
Flagg, James Montgomery, 23, 226
Flaming Youth, 378–380
Florida, land boom, 420
Flynn, William J., 158
Foch, Ferdinand, 229–233, 237–238
Food Administration, W. W. I, 215–217; W. W. II, 686–687
Food and Agricultural Organization (FAO), 773, 778
Food Stamp Plan, 540–541
Foraker Act (1900), 89
Forbes, Charles R., 298, 305
Forbes Commission, 459–460
Ford, Henry, 13, 182, 324–326, 394–396, 511
Fordney-McCumber Tariff (1922), 289–291, 330, 345
Forrestal, James, 737
Foster, William Z., 271, 362, 481
Four Freedoms, 640
Four-minute men, 222, 226
Four-Power Pact (1922), 342–343
Fourteen Points, 235–238, 250–252
France, 95, 97, 111, 118, 349–350; Algeciras conference, 120–122; relations with U. S. (1914–1917), 149–205; in W. W. I, 207–208, 228–233; and naval limitation, 340–345, 452–455; debts, 346; in W. W. II, 628–630, 703–704, 716–722
Franco, Francisco, 607–608
Frankfurter, Felix, 221, 366, 486, 577–578
Frazier-Lemke Act (1934), 568
French, Daniel Chester, 23
French Indo-China, 659, 663
Freud, Sigmund, 380
Friars Land, 91–92
Frost, Robert, 22, 383
Fuel Administration, W. W. I, 217–218
Fulbright, James, 771
Full employment, 753–755
Fuller, Alvin T., 366

Fuller, Melville, 95
Fundamentalism, 370–373
Funston, Frederick, 89

G I Bill, 674, 743, 814
Galveston, Texas, 32
Gardner, Augustus P., 183
Garfield, Harry A., 217–218
Garfield, James R., 56, 67
Garner, John N., 480, 561, 635–636
Gary, Elbert H., 271
General Motors Corporation, 395–396, 554–555, 744–745, 761
Geneva Conference (1927), 344–345, 451; (1933), 600–601
Gentlemen's Agreement (1907), 99
George, Henry, 28–29, 32
George, Walter, 583
Gerard, James, 151
German-American Bund, 645
Germany, 10, 97; and Samoa, 83; second Venezuela, 109–111; Moroccan affair, 120–122; relations with U. S. (1914–1917), 149–205; W. W. I, 227–233; peace with, 335–336; reparations, 347–348; Geneva Conference, 600–601; Spanish Civil War, 607–608; pre W. W. II, 615–642; W. W. II, 643–656; war against U. S., 669; campaigns, 702–710, 716–727; post W. W. II, 779–783
Gershwin, George, 389, 821
Gibson, Charles Dana, 23, 226
Gilbert, Cass, 23
Gilbert, Prentiss, 470–471
Gilbert Islands, invasion of, 712
Girdler, Tom, 556
Glasgow, Ellen, 383, 818
Glass, Carter, 126–131
Glass-Owen Act (1913), 126–131
Glass-Steagall Act (1932), 443, 520
Glavis, Louis R., 58–60
Goering, Hermann, 782–783
Goethals, George W., 108, 215
Gold, 501–504, 588–590
Gold Reserve Act (1934), 503
Gold Standard Act (1900), 39
Goldsborough, T. Allen, 760
Gomez, José, 86
Gompers, Samuel, 10–12, 54–56, 132, 214, 220, 274, 361–362
Good Neighbor policy, 115, 355–357, 458–463, 595–599
Gore-McLemore Resolutions, 176–177, 185
Gorgas, William C., 108
Grange, 25–26, 64
Gray, George, 44, 46
Great Britain, 10, 95–96, 118–121; Samoan Treaty with, 83; Hay Pauncefote, 104–105; first Venezuela, 109; second Vene-

zuela, 109–111; Alaska boundary, 117; Panama tolls, 139; policy toward Mexico, 142–144; relation with U. S. (1914–1917), 149–205; W. W. I mission, 207–208; and naval disarmament, 339–345, 451–455, 604–605; debts, 346; and Far East, 472–475; pre W. W. II, 615–642; W. W. II, 643–656, 698–730, 768–772; post W. W. II, 751, 780–796

Greece, 793–795

Green, William, 362, 365, 440, 552, 670

Greenland, 648

Greer, 653

Grew, Joseph C., 658, 662, 665

Grey, Sir Edward, 164, 166, 167, 175–176, 178, 188, 234

Griffith, David W., 402

Griswold, Dwight, 795

Gromyko, Andrei, 776, 792

Groves, Leslie R., 813

Grundy, Joseph, 316, 439

Guadalcanal, battle of, 711

Guam, 82, 661, 668, 712

Guffey-Snyder Act (1935), 516

Guffey-Vinson Act (1937), 516

Gulflight, 171

Hague Conference (1899), 114–116; (1907), 115, 118–119

Hague Court, 110, 116–118, 120

Haiti, dollar diplomacy, 114; under Wilson, 140–141; under Hoover, 459–460; under FDR, 596–597

Halsey, William F., 700

Handy, W. C., 24

Hanihara, Masanao, 301, 341

Hanna, Marcus A., 25, 37–40, 44–45

Hansen, Alvin H., 435–436, 753

Hansen, Ole, 271, 275

Harding, Warren G., 272; election of 1920, 280–286; tariff legislation, 287–291; budget, 291–292; death of, 293–294; scandals, 295–297; and immigration, 299–300; and bonus, 303–305; tax policy, 320–321; foreign affairs, 335–346

Harlan, John M., 61, 94

Harriman, Edward H., 41–42

Harris, Seymour E., 753

Harrison, Francis B., 134–136, 358

Harvey, George, 72–74, 256, 282

Hatch, Carl, 771

Hatch Acts (1939–1940), 584–585

Hawaiian Islands, 83, 342, 667–668

Hawes-Cutting Act (1933), 464–465

Hawley-Smoot Tariff (1930), 438–440, 445, 587

Hay, John, 81, 96–97, 104–107, 112, 118

Hay-Bunau-Varilla Treaty (1903), 107, 598

Hay-Herran Treaty (1903), 106

Hay-Pauncefote Treaty, first (1900), 104; second (1901), 105, 139

Hayek, Friedrich, 754

Hayes, Arthur Garfield, 367, 371

Hays, Will H., 240, 403

Hearst, William Randolph, 21, 46

Hemingway, Ernest, 382, 818

Henderson, Leon, 683

Hendrick, Burton J., 30

Hepburn Act (1906), 48, 62

Hepburn Canal Bill (1901), 105–106

Herbert, Victor, 24

Herrick, Myron, 151, 153

Hersey, John, 791

Hershey, Lewis B., 672

Hill, James J., 41–42

Hill, Lister, 771

Hillman, Sidney, 365, 734

Hindenburg, Paul von, 198

Hippisley, Alfred, 96

Hirohito, Emperor, 666, 728

Hiroshima, 727, 791, 809

Hitchcock, Gilbert, 249, 260

Hitler, Adolf, 601, 615–619, 707, 724, 782

Hoar, George, 82, 93

Hobbs Act (1946), 751

Hobson, Richmond P., 17

Hodges, Courtney, 720, 722

Holding companies, *see* Trusts

Holmes, Oliver W., Jr., 564–566

Home Owners Loan Corporation (HOLC), 491

Homer, Winslow, 23

Honduras, 113

Hoover, Herbert, 281, 285, 302; W. W. I, 215–217; Secretary of Commerce, 286, 314, 317; election of 1928, 422–427; cabinet, 428; stock crash, 428–432; depression, 432–436; farm policy, 436–438; tariff policy, 438–440; relief policies, 440–448; foreign policy of, 449–475; and election of 1932, 479–482; and bank crisis, 484–485; and world trade, 588

Hopkins, Harry L., 492–493, 494, 495–497, 581, 635, 681, 776

House, Edward M., 74, 123, 128, 262; W. W. I diplomacy, 150–205, 235; peace conference, 240–242

House-Grey Memorandum, 175–176, 187

Housing, under Hoover, 443; under FDR, 528–529; post W. W. II, 743, 761; Negro, 801

Howells, William Dean, 21

Huerta, Victoriano, 142–146

Hughes, Charles Evans, 249, 285, 356; as governor, 35; election of 1916, 190–194; on civil liberties, 279; as Secretary of

State, 286, 335–344; as Chief Justice, 443–444, 567–569, 574–575, 578

Hull, Cordell, 485, 588–589, 592–594, 596, 602, 616–617, 620, 649, 654, 658–669, 767

Humphrey, William E., 316, 318, 517–518, 568

Hurley, Edward N., 215

Hutchins, Robert M., 814–815

Iceland, 650–651

Ickes, Harold L., 486, 490, 516, 582, 738

Immigration, 2; opposition to Japanese, 3, 98–100; literacy test, 134; Emergency Act, 299–300; Johnson Act, 300–302; National Origins Act, 302; under Hoover, 441

Imperialism, 78–80

Income Tax, 37, 62, 125–126; W. W. I, 221–222; in 1920's, 319–324; New Deal, 518–520; W. W. II, 689–691; post W. W. II, 762, 763

Industrial unionism, 362, 550–552

Industrial Workers of the World (IWW), 12, 224, 276, 363, 365

Industry (1900–1914), 5–8; W. W. I, 213–220; post W. W. I, 266–267; in 1920's, 393–421; under Hoover, 432–436; under New Deal, 505–520, 580; W. W. II, 677–682; post W. W. II, 742–743, 804

Inflation, post W. W. I, 266, 270; in 1920's, 419–420; in W. W. II, 682–684; post W. W. II, 743

Initiative, 26, 28

Injunctions in labor disputes, 13, 54–56, 274, 361, 760; Clayton Act, 131–132; Norris-La Guardia Act, 446; Taft-Hartley Act, 763–764

Inland Waterways, 10, 411

Insular cases, 92–95

Insull, Samuel, 400, 500

Inter-American Conferences, Panama (1939), 626; Havana (1940), 632–633, 765; Rio (1942), 766; Mexico (1945), 767–768; see also Pan-American Conferences

Interchurch World Movement, 272

International Ladies' Garment Workers, 13

Interstate Commerce Commission (ICC), 37, 39, 47–49, 62, 268–269, 316, 413, 531, 804

Investments, foreign, in 1920's, 416–418

Iran, 790

Ireland, 168, 257, 260

Irish, during W. W. I, 157, 168, 257–258

Irwin, Will, 20

Isolationism, 602–614, 643–648, 661

Italy, 243, 251, 340–345, 452; second Venezuela affair, 109–111; W. W. I debt, 347;

Ethiopian war, 605–607; war on U. S., 669; W. W. II campaigns in, 707–710, 724; post W. W. II, 787–788

Iwo Jima, 713–714

Jackson, Robert H., 577, 631, 740, 782–783

James, Henry, 21

Japan, 4, 95, 102; U. S. policy toward (1900–1912), 97–101; in W. W. I, 200–201, 251–252; naval limitation, 339–345, 452–455, 604–605; under Hoover, 467–475; under FDR, 610–613; in W. W. II, 656–659; Pearl Harbor attack, 667–668; campaigns, 699–702, 710–716; surrender of, 727–728; post W. W. II, 784–785

Japanese-Americans, 3, 695–696

Jardine, William M., 314, 332

Jazz, 24, 389

Jeffers, William M., 679

Joffre, Joseph J. C., 207–208

Johnson, Alvaney, 749

Johnson, Hiram, 35, 63, 193–194, 256, 258, 281–282, 591–592

Johnson, Hugh S., 210, 331, 494, 506, 508–514

Johnson, Tom L., 32

Johnson Act (1924), 300–302; (1934), 591–592, 644

Jolson, Al, 403

Jones, Jesse, 679, 735

Jones, Samuel M., 31–32

Jones Act (1916), 134–136; (1917), 136

Journalism, see Newspapers

Judiciary Reorganization Bill (1937), 570–576

Kaiser, Henry J., 685

Kasserine Pass, 704

Kearny, 655

Keating-Owen Act (1916), 134

Kellogg, Frank B., 337, 339, 349–350, 352, 355–356, 465

Kellogg-Briand Pact, 349–350, 466, 783

Kelly Act (1925), 409–410

Kennedy, Joseph P., 522

Kent, Rockwell, 389, 821

Kimmel, Husband, 667

Knox, Frank, 69, 443, 560, 639, 661, 681

Knox, Philander, 42, 57, 101, 113–114, 120, 256

Knox Resolution (1920–1921), 261, 335–336

Konoye, Premier, 662, 665

Koo, V. Wellington, 341

Korea, 97–98

Krug, Julius A., 681, 738, 749, 760–761

Ku Klux Klan, 367–370, 402, 577

Kurusu, Saburo, 665–667

Labor, 10–13, 43–45, 54–56; Department of, 124; under Wilson, 133–134; in W. W. I, 220–221; after W. W. I, 269–274; in 1920's, 360–365; and Norris-La Guardia Act, 445; under FDR, 515–516, 543–558; and the courts, 565–566, 568–569, 574–575, 578; in W. W. II, 687–689; post W. W. II, 743–751, 753–755, 760–761, 763–764

LaFollette, Robert M., 48, 296; governor of Wisconsin, 33–35; insurgency under Taft, 58, 62–69; anti-war, 201, 203, 206, 221; election of 1924, 310–311

LaFollette, Robert M., Jr., 315, 555–556, 753

LaFollette Seamen's Act (1916), 133

LaGuardia, Fiorello, 445–446, 773

Lame Duck Amendment (1933), 482–483, 563

Lamont, Thomas W., 432

Landis, James M., 522

Landis, Kenesaw M., 224

Landon, Alfred M., 560–563, 670

Lane, Franklin K., 124; plan, 265–266

Lansing, Robert, 262; W. W. I diplomacy, 150–205; peace mission, 241, 245

Lansing-Ishii Agreement (1917), 344, 468

Latin America, relations with (1900–1912), 103–116; (1913–1920), 136–147; (1920–1929), 350–357, 458–463; under FDR, 595–599, 611–612; during W. W. II, 765–768; post W. W. II, 796–797

Laurier, Sir Wilfred, 65

Laval, Pierre, 456

Lawrence, Ernest O., 811

Lawson, Thomas W., 30

League of Nations, 187–188, 234–237; drafting of, 245–250; fight over, 254–262; and election of 1920, 283–286; in 1920's, 336–339, 350; under Hoover, 449–450, 469–475

League to Enforce Peace, 187–188, 234, 240, 256, 261

Legge, Alexander, 436

Legislative Reorganization Act (1946), 753

Lehman, Herbert, 773

Lemke, William, 562

Lend-lease, 639–642, 663, 766

Lever Act (1917), 216–217, 263, 274

Lewis, John L., 440, 670; strike of 1919, 274; in 1920's, 362–363; CIO, 551–552, 556, 636; W. W. II, 688; post W. W. II, 747–749, 760–761

Lewis, Sinclair, 382, 818

Leyte, campaign for, 713

Liberty League, 559–560

Lie, Trygve, 789

Life, 817, 820

Lilienthal, David E., 524–527, 791–792

Lindbergh, Charles A., 353, 358, 389, 409–410, 644–647, 670

Lindsay, Vachel, 22, 383

Lindsey, Ben B., 379

Lippmann, Walter, 238

Literature (1900–1914), 21–22; in 1920's, 382–386; (1930–1947), 818–820

Little Steel formula, 688

Little Steel strike, 556

Litvinov, Maxim, 594–595

Lloyd, Henry D., 29

Lloyd George, David, 196, 236, 238; peace conference, 243–252, 257

Lodge, Henry Cabot, 117, 282; imperialism, 79; Lodge Corollary, 101; anti-League, 239, 241, 243, 248–250, 254–262; anti-World Court, 338; Washington Conference, 341

Lodge Corollary, 101

Loeb, Jacques, 18

London, Declaration of (1909), 119, 163–166

London, Jack, 22

London Economic Conference (1933), 588–590

London Naval Conference (1930), 452–455; (1935), 604

Long, Huey P., 494, 548, 562

Louis, Joe, 800

Lowden, Frank O., 281–282, 423

Lowell, A. Lawrence, 234, 249

Lowell, Amy, 22

Ludendorff, Erich von, 198, 229, 231

Ludlow Amendment (1937), 613

Lusitania, 166, 172–174

Lusk Committee, 278

Lynching, 798–799

Lytton Commission, 471–472, 474–475

MacArthur, Arthur, 89–90

MacArthur, Douglas, 447, 700–701, 711–712, 713–714, 728, 784–785

MacDonald, Ramsay, 452, 588–589

McAdoo, William G., 124, 162, 218, 220–222, 267, 283–284, 309, 480

McClure, Samuel S., 29

McClure's Magazine, 30

McCormick, Vance, 218

McDuffie-Tydings Act (1934), 599

Machado, Gerardo, 462–463, 597

McKellar, Kenneth, 654, 791–792

Mackenzie King, W. L., 648

McKinley, William, 1, 24, 37–41, 81, 105; policy toward Philippines, 88–90; Far Eastern policy, 95–97

McMahon, Brien, 791

McNary, Charles L., 331–334, 423, 634

McNary-Haugen Bills, 331–334, 423

McNary-Watres Act (1930), 410–411

McReynolds, James C., 565, 567–569, 574–575, 576–578
Madero, Francisco, 142
Magazines, muckraking, 29–30; in 1920's, 385–386; (1930–1947), 817
Magdalena Bay, 100–101
Magoon, Charles E., 86
Mahan, Alfred T., 79–80
Maine, sinking of, 81
Malaya, 663
Manchuria, 97, 101–102, 466–475
Manifest Destiny, 79–80, 85
Manila Bay, battle of, 82
Mann-Elkins Act (1910), 62
Manufacturing, *see* Industry
Marin, John, 389, 821
Marine Corps, United States, 672, 711–714, 730
Maritime Commission, 650
Marne, battle of, 230–231
Marquand, John, 819
Marquis, Don, 20
Marshall, George C., 651, 704, 717, 786, 788, 795–796
Marshall, Thomas R., 75, 191
Marshall Islands, invasion of, 712
Marshall Plan, 795–796
Martine, James, 73, 192
Masters, Edgar Lee, 22
Max, Prince of Baden, 234, 237
Maximum Employment Act (1946), 754–755
Meat crisis, 758
Meat Inspection Act (1906), 47
Medicine, 18, 84; in 1920's, 387; in W. W. II, 675–676, 810
Mellon, Andrew W., 256, 286, 428, 430, 432; fiscal policies, 319–324
Mencken, Henry L., 384
Merchant Marine, in W. W. I, 159, 186; Act of 1920, 269–270; in the 1920's, 408–409; Act of 1936, 530; in W. W. II, 685
Methodist Church, 14, 16, 808
Metropolitan Opera Company, 24
Mexico, Pious Fund controversy, 116–117; Wilson and, 142–147; in W. W. I, 200–201; oil question, 351–353; under Hoover, 461–462; under FDR, 612
Michelson, A. A., 18
Midway Island, battle of, 710–711
Millay, Edna St. Vincent, 367, 383, 389
Miller, Thomas W., 298
Millikan, Robert A., 387
Mitchell, Charles E., 432, 500
Mitchell, John, 43–44
Mitchell, Margaret, 819
Mitchell, William ("Billy"), 409
Modernism, 14, 370–373
Moley, Raymond, 483, 486, 493, 494, 506

Molotov, Vyacheslav, 772, 788
Money trust, 7–8
Monopoly, *see* Trusts
Monroe Doctrine, 116, 349; Roosevelt Corollary, 111, 115; Lodge Corollary, 101; Olney Corollary, 109; second Venezuela, 110; League of Nations and, 250, 259; Clark Memorandum, 357, 458; under FDR, 595–598
Montgomery, Bernard L., 703, 707–708, 710, 720–721, 723
Mooney, Thomas J., 367
Moratorium, 455–456
Morgan, J. P., the elder, 6–7, 41–42, 44, 50, 101; the younger, 6, 161–162, 400; and Company, private bankers, 6
Morgan, Thomas H., 18
Morgenthau, Henry, Jr., 581
Morocco, crisis of (1905–1906), 120–122
Morrow, Dwight, 353, 458
Moscow Conference (1943), 772
Motion pictures, 402–404
Muckrakers, 29–31
Munich Conference (1938), 616–619
Municipal reform, 31–32
Munitions industry, 160–162, 203–204
Murphy, Frank, 554
Murray, Philip, 552, 556, 670, 745, 747
Muscle Shoals, 324–326, 444–445; *see also* Tennessee Valley Authority
Music, 24, 389, 800, 821–822
Mussolini, Benito, 707, 724
Myers, Gustavus, 30
Myrdal, Gunnar, 802

National Association for the Advancement of Colored People, 803
National Association of Manufacturers, 12, 546, 755, 763
National Broadcasting Company, 405
National City Bank, 7, 400, 429
National Defense, Council of, in W. W. I, 213–220; in W. W. II, 678
National Defense Act (1916), 185–186, 324
National Industrial Recovery Act (NIRA), (1933), 490, 491, 505–517, 543–545
National Labor Relations Act (1935), 515, 545–547, 552, 554; amended, 763–764
National Labor Relations Board (NLRB), 545, 763–764
National Monetary Commission, 51, 127
National Origins Act (1929), 302
National Progressive Republican League, 66
National Recovery Administration (NRA), 505–517
National Tuberculosis Association, 18
National Youth Administration (NYA), 496

Navy, United States, fleet around world, 100; W. W. I, 186, 207, 227–228; oil scandals, 295–298; disarmament, 339–345, 451–455, 604–605; Pearl Harbor attack, 667–668; W. W. II, 672–673, 699–703, 710–716, 718–720, 726–729
Negroes, 2, 51, 798–803
Nelson, Donald M., 678, 681
Netherlands East Indies, 663, 700, 702
Neutrality Act (1935), 605–606; (1936), 606–607; (1937), 608–610; (1939), 624–626; amended (1941), 654–656
New Freedom, 76
New Granada, canal treaty with, 103–104, 107–108
New Nationalism, 68
New Panama Canal Company, 104–106
New York Daily News, 385
New York World, 20
Newfoundland, 120
Newlands Act (1902), 49; (1913), 186
Newspapers, 20; in 1920's, 385; (1930–1947), 816–817
Nicaragua, proposed canal, 105–106; financial protectorate, 113–114; Bryan-Chamorro treaty, 141–142; in 1920's, 350–354; under Hoover, 460–461
Nimitz, Chester, 700
Nine-Power Treaty (1922), 343, 468–475
Nineteenth Amendment (1920), 147, 264
Nomura, Kichisaburo, 662, 665–667
Normandy, invasion of, 718–720
Norris, Frank, 22
Norris, George W., 425; insurgency under Taft, 65–66; and W. W. I, 201, 203; insurgency under Coolidge, 314–316, 318; Muscle Shoals, 324–326, 399, 524; insurgency under Hoover, 443–445; defeated, 697
Norris-LaGuardia Anti-Injunction Act (1932), 446, 760
North Africa, campaign for, 702–706
Northern Securities Company, 41–42
Nuremburg trials, 782–783
Nye, Gerald P., 603, 644–646, 656, 735

O'Banion, Dion, 376–377
Obregón, Alvaro, 351–352
O'Connor, John J., 580, 583–584
Odum, Howard W., 805
Oil industry, 8, 295–298, 397, 516–517, 786
O'Keefe, Georgia, 389
Okinawa, battle of, 713–714
O'Leary, Jeremiah, 192–194
Olney, Richard, 104, 109
O'Neill, Eugene, 384
Open-Door policy, 95–97, 100–102, 466–475
Oppenheimer, J. Robert, 813

Orlando, Vittorio, 246, 251
Owens, Jesse, 801

Pact of Paris, 349–350, 466, 783
Page, Walter Hines, 151, 153
Palma, Tomas Estrada, 84–86
Palmer, A. Mitchell, 274, 275, 277–278, 283
Pan American Union, 114–116
Pan-American Conferences, Washington (1889), 114; Mexico City (1901), 114; Rio (1906), 115; Buenos Aires (1910), 115; Santiago (1923), 356; Havana (1928), 596; Montevideo (1933), 596; Buenos Aires (1936), 611–612; Lima (1938), 619–620; see also Inter-American Conferences
Pan-Americanism (1889–1912), 114–116, 138; under Hoover, 458–463; under FDR, 595–599, 611–612
Panama, Republic of, U. S. recognizes independence of, 107; treaty with U. S., 598–599
Panama Canal, 10, 355, 598–599; acquisition of, 103–108; tolls issue, 138–139
Panay incident, 612–613, 656
Panic (1907), 50–52; (1929), 428–432
Papen, Franz von, 157–158
Parcel post, 9, 62
Paris Peace Conference (1919), 241–253
Parker, Alton B., 46, 74
Parker, John J., 444
Parker, Sir Gilbert, 156
Parrington, Vernon L., 387
Passaic, New Jersey, strike, 363
Patch, Alexander, 720–722
Patman, Wright, 447, 517
Patton, George S., 707–708, 720–727, 781
Pauley, Edwin M., 738
Payne-Aldrich Tariff (1909), 57–58, 62, 64
Peace, organizations, 181–193; 1916 moves, 194–198; aims, W. W. I, 234–237; see also Disarmament, Kellogg-Briand Pact, Isolationism
Pearl Harbor, attacked by Japanese, 667–681
Peek, George N., 331, 494, 534
Pelley, William D., 646, 694
Penrose, Boies, 36, 282
Perkins, Frances, 486, 547
Péron, Juan, 767–768, 797
Pershing, John J., in Mexico, 146–147; in W. W. I, 208–209, 213, 228–233, 237
Philippine Commission, first, 88; second, 88–90
Philippine Islands, 93, 95, 98; annexation of, 1, 82; independence, 39; U. S. government in, 88–92; under Wilson, 134–136; in 1920's, 358–359; under Hoover, 463–465; under FDR, 599; in W. W. II, 700–701, 713–714

Phonograph, 24
Pickford, Mary, 402
Pinchot, Gifford, 50, 58–60, 67, 374
Platt, Thomas C., 36, 38–39
Platt Amendment (1901), 84; abrogated, 597–598
Plattsburg camp, 183–184
Plumb, Glenn E., 267
Poetry (1900–1914), 22; in 1920's, 383
Poland, 236, 621–623
Political Action Committee of CIO (PAC), 734, 753
Populist movement, 26–27
Porter, Gene Stratton, 21
Porter, Paul A., 746, 761
Portsmouth, Treaty of (1905), 98
Postal savings, 62
Potsdam Conference (1945), 779–781
Preparedness, during W. W. I, 180–187; during W. W. II, 616–617, 638
Price, Byron, 693
Price Administration, Office of (OPA), 682–684, 686, 688, 746, 755–758, 761
Proctor, William C., 281
Progressive movement, 25–52; under Hoover, 445; and the Supreme Court, 564–567
Progressive party, in 1912, 70–77; in 1916, 190–191; in 1924–1926, 310–316
Prohibition, 16–17; in W. W. I, 216, 263; Eighteenth Amendment, 263; in 1920's, 373–376, 424–425, 427, 479–480; repeal of, 483, 492
Propaganda, and W. W. I, 156–157, 204, 225–227; and W. W. II, 693–694
Protestantism, 14, 381, 808–809
Public utilities, see Electricity, Muscle Shoals, Tennessee Valley Authority, Transportation
Public Utility Holding Company Act (1936), 522–523
Public works, under Hoover, 441–443, 446; under FDR, 490–493, 495–497, 581–582
Public Works Administration (PWA), 490–491, 581–582
Puerto Rico, 82, 86–88, 110, 136, 357–358, 463
Pujo Committee, 127–128
Pulitzer, Joseph, 21
Pure Food and Drugs Act (1906), 47, 524
Purge, the, 582–584

Quay, Matthew S., 36, 38
Quezon, Manuel, 599

Race Riots, 799
Racketeering, 377
Radio, 404–405, 817–818
Railroad Labor Act (1926), 412, 748, 750

Railroad Labor Board, 269, 412
Railroads, extent of, 9; regulation of, 37, 48–49; under Taft, 62; Adamson Act, 134; in W. W. I, 218; Transportation Act of 1920, 267–269; in the 1920's, 411–414; in W. W. II, 685; post W. W. II, 747–749, 804
Railway Brotherhoods, 12, 267, 360, 748–749
Rankin, Jeannette, 203, 669
Raskob, John J., 426, 480
Rationing, 677
Reader's Digest, 817
Real estate, boom of 1920's, 420; after W. W. II, 743
Recall, 35, 63, 70, 75–76
Reciprocal Trade Agreements Act (1934), 493, 592–594, 751
Reciprocity, under Taft, 63–65; under FDR, 493, 592–594; under Truman, 751
Reconstruction Finance Corporation (RFC), 412, 442–443, 448, 483, 490, 491, 735
Red Cross, 437, 675–676
Red scare, 275–278
Reed, Walter, 84
Relief, under Hoover, 441; under FDR, 490, 492–497
Religion, 14–17, 370–373, 808–809
Remagen, bridge captured, 724
Rent control, 682–683, 761
Reparations question, after W. W. I, 238, 347–348, 455–458; after W. W. II, 780, 788–789
Resettlement Administration, 542
Reuben James, sunk, 656
Reuther, Walter, 744
Revenue Acts, W. W. I, 221–222; 1919–1928, 319–324; under FDR, 518–520; W. W. II, 689–692; post W. W. II, 742, 762–763
Richberg, Donald, 514
Riley, James Whitcomb, 22
Rinehart, Mary Roberts, 384
Ritchie, Albert J., 424
Roberts, Owen J., 296, 444, 537, 567–569, 574–575, 578
Robeson, Paul, 800
Robin Moor, sunk, 651
Robinson, Edwin Arlington, 22, 383
Robinson, Jackie, 801
Robinson, Joseph T., 424, 575–576
Rockefeller, John D., 8, 19, 432
Rockhill, W. W., 96
Roman Catholic Church, 14, 381–382, 607, 808
Rome, captured by Allies, 710
Rommel, Erwin, 702–703
Roosevelt, Eleanor, 789, 806

Roosevelt, Franklin Delano, 35, 457; and Haiti, 141; election of 1920, 284; election of 1932, 476–482; bank crisis, 484–489; Hundred Days, 489–492; second New Deal, 493–494; fiscal policy, 494–499; monetary policy, 501–505; NRA, 505–517; trust regulation, 517–518; tax policy, 518–520; regulatory legislation, 522–524; TVA, 524–528; housing, 528–529; transportation, 529–530; agriculture, 532–543; labor, 543–558; election of 1936, 559–563; and Supreme Court, 564–578; reorganization bills, 578–580; recession, 580–582; attempted purge, 582–584; foreign policy (1933–1937), 586–614; (1937–1941), 615–669; election of 1940, 633–638; W. W. II: home front, 670–697; war fronts, 698–730; election of 1944, 731–735; death, 735–736; foreign policy (1941–1945), 765–775; policy toward Negroes, 801–802

Roosevelt, Theodore, 1, 25, 29, 35, 81, 564–565; election of 1900, 38–39; becomes President, 40; trust-busting, 40–43; labor policies, 43–45; election of 1904, 45–46; reforms, 46–48; conservation, 49–50; panic of 1907, 50–52; quarrel with Taft, 67–71; election of 1912, 75–77; advocates expansion, 79–80; policy toward Cuba, 85–86; policy toward Japan, 97–100; Panama Canal policy, 103–108; Caribbean diplomacy, 109–113; and Pan-Americanism, 115–116; arbitration efforts, 116–120; Algeciras Conference, 120–122; and W. W. I, 154–155, 172–173, 183–184, 211; election of 1916, 190–194; and League of Nations, 239, 240, 242; death of, 280

Roosevelt, Theodore, Jr., 302–303, 463

Roosevelt Corollary, 111, 115, 357

Root, Elihu, 240, 341; Secretary of State, 53, 100, 115, 117, 119–120; Secretary of War, 84; convention of 1912, 71; and League of Nations, 249, 285; and World Court, 337, 450

Root-Takahira Agreement (1908), 100

Round Robin, 249

Rubber, 679

Rule of Reason, 61–62

Ruml, Beardsley, 690

Rural Electrification Administration (REA), 528

Russell, Charles E., 30

Russia, 95–96, 102, 235, 244–245; Russo-Japanese War, 97–98; revolution (1917), 202; recognition question, 348, 594–595; and Far East, 466–467; W. W. II, 706, 723–728, 769–771; and UN, 775–777, 780–796

Ruth, George H. ("Babe"), 390–391

Ryder, Albert P., 23

Sabotage, in World War I, 157–159, 222–223; World War II, 649

Sacco-Vanzetti case, 365–367

Saint-Gaudens, Augustus, 23

Saipan, capture of, 712

Samoa, 83

San Francisco, school issue (1906), 99

San Francisco Conference (1945), 775–779

Sandburg, Carl, 22, 383, 384

Sandino, Augusto, 354, 460–461

Sanger, Margaret, 381

Santiago, battle of, 82

Sargent, John Singer, 22–23

Schechter case, 514–515, 568

Science, 17–18, 387, 809–813

Scopes, John Thomas, 370–373

Scottsboro case, 799–800

Sculpture, 23

Seattle, general strike in, 271

Securities Act (1933), 520–522

Securities and Exchange Act (1934), 520–522

Sedition, in W. W. I, 157–159, 222–225; W. W. II, 694–696

Sedition Act (1918), 222–225

Selective Service Act, W. W. I, 210–213; W. W. II, 638–639, 651–652, 671–672, 740–742

Seventeenth Amendment (1913), 35, 62

Shantung, 251–252, 340, 343

Sheen, Fulton J., 808

Sheppard, Morris, 17

Sherman Antitrust Act (1890), enacted, 37; labor and, 13, 55–56; prosecutions, 37, 41–43, 55; under Wilson, 131–132; under Coolidge, 317–319; under FDR, 505–518

Sherman, James S., 53, 71

Shipbuilding, see Merchant Marine

Short, Walter, 667

Sicily, conquered by Allies, 706–707

Silver Purchase Act (1934), 504–505

Simmons, William J., 367–368

Sims, William S., 207, 227–228

Sinclair, Harry F., 296–298

Sinclair, Upton, 47, 819

Single tax, 29

Six-Power Loan, 101–102

Sixteenth Amendment (1913), 62, 125

Sloan, John, 23

Smith, Alfred E., governor of New York, 278; convention of 1924, 309–310; candidate for President (1928), 424–426, 478; and election of 1932, 480; opposes New Deal, 559–560, 563

Smith, Frank L., 316

Smith, Gerald L. K., 562

Smith, J. Allen, 31

Smith, James, 73

Smith-Connally Act (1943), 688

Snyder, John, 738, 742, 746
Social Christianity, 16
Social Security Act (1935), 547–550, 691
Socialism, 27–28, 223–224, 276, 284, 286, 311, 481, 531
Socialist party, 28, 284, 286, 311, 481; in W. W. I, 223, 224
Socialist-Labor party, 27, 276
Soil Conservation Act (1936), 537–538
South, the, 5, 803–806
Soviet Union, see Russia
Spaak, Paul-Henri, 789
Spanish Civil War, 607–610
Spanish-American War, 81–83, 103
Speicher, Eugene, 821
Spooner Amendment (1901), on Philippine Government, 90; (1902), for canal, 106
Sports, 389–392
Spring-Rice, Cecil, 164
Stalin, Josef, 682, 716–717, 735, 769–770, 780
Standard Oil Company, 5, 8, 29, 42, 61–62, 415
Steel Workers Organizing Committee (SWOC), 552, 556
Steffens, Lincoln, 29, 31, 66
Steinbeck, John, 819
Stephenson, David C., 369
Stettinius, Edward R., Jr., 775–776, 779
Stillman, James, 7
Stilwell, Joseph, 714
Stimson, Henry L., 68, 285; mission to Nicaragua, 354; in Philippines, 359; Secretary of State, 428, 452, 460–461, 465–475; Secretary of War, 639, 681
Stimson doctrine, 472–475
Stock market, 1929 crash, 428–432, 520–522; regulation of, 520–522
Stone, Harlan F., 314, 537, 565, 567–569, 578, 738
Street cars, 9
Strikes (1900–1917), 10–13, 43–45, 186–187; (1917–1921), 270–274; (1921–1933), 362–363, 412, 440–441; under FDR, 545, 552–556; W. W. II, 687–688; post W. W. II, 743–751, 760–761
Submarine warfare, during World War I, 169–174, 176–179, 227–228; during W. W. II, 651–656
Sullivan, Louis D., 23, 388
Sunday, William A. ("Billy"), 14–15
Supreme Court, and the Progressive Movement, 564–567; under FDR, 567–578; cases: U. S. v. E. C. Knight Co., 37; Northern Securities, 41–42; Danbury Hatters, 55; Bucks Stove, 55; Insular, 94; U. S. Steel, 132; Hammer v. Dagenhart, 134, 566; Bailey v. Drexel Furniture Co., 134, 566; prohibition, 263; trade association, 317; Duplex, 361; American Steel

Foundries v. Tri-City Trades Council, 361; Truax v. Corrigan, 361, 566; O'Fallon, 413; gold clause, 502, 568; Schechter, 514–515, 568; Carter v. Carter Coal, 516; Sunshine Anthracite Coal Co. v. Adkins, 516; hot oil, 516, 567; Electric Bond and Share, 523; Ashwander v. TVA, 526, 569; Hoosac Mills, 537, 569; NLRB, 546, 556, 574; U. S. v. Darby Lumber Co., 558, 578; Lochner v. N. Y., 565; Muller v. Oregon, 566; Adkins v. Children's Hospital, 566; Adair v. U. S., 566; Coppage v. Kansas, 566; Jones v. SEC, 569; New York Minimum Wage, 569; Railroad Retirement v. Alton Railroad Co., 568; West Coast Hotel Co. v. Parrish, 574; Mine Workers', 760; white primary, 801
Sussex pledge, 177–179, 187, 195, 198–200
Swope, Gerard, 506

Tabloids, 385
Taft, Lorado, 23
Taft, Robert A., 633, 756, 759, 763–764, 791
Taft, William Howard, 17, 86, 220, 240, 565; in the Philippines, 89–92; elected President, 53–56; approves Payne-Aldrich Tariff, 57–58; Ballinger affair, 58–60; reforms, 61–63; reciprocity, 63–65; opposed by insurgents, 65–67; quarrel with Roosevelt, 67–71; election of 1912, 70–77; governor of the Philippines, 89–92; dollar diplomacy: in China, 101–102; in Latin America, 112–114; arbitration efforts, 120; Panama Tolls issue, 138–139; and League of Nations, 234, 249, 256, 260–261
Taft-Hartley Act (1947), 763–764
Talmadge, Eugene, 560, 803
Tampico incident, 144–146
Tarawa, battle of, 712
Tarbell, Ida M., 29
Tariff, Payne-Aldrich, 57–58, 125; reciprocity with Canada, 63–65; concessions to Cuba, 85–86; Underwood, 125–126; Emergency Tariff of 1921, 287–289; Fordney-McCumber Act, 289–291, 316–317; Hawley-Smoot Act, 438–440, 445; under FDR, 592–594
Tarkington, Booth, 21
Taxation, under Wilson, 125–126; W. W. I, 221–222; in 1920's, 319–324; under FDR, 518–520; W. W. II, 689–692; post W. W. II, 762–763
Taylor, Deems, 389, 822
Teapot Dome scandal, 295–298
Teheran Conference (1943), 769
Teller Amendment (1898), 83
Temporary National Economic Committee (TNEC), 518
Tennessee, Scopes trial, 370–373

Tennessee Coal and Iron Company, 50–51, 69

Tennessee Valley Authority (TVA), 524–527

Textile industry, 407, 509, 511

Thayer, Webster, 366

Thomas, Norman, 363, 481

Thompson, Dorothy, 807

Time magazine, 817

Togo, Hideki, 665, 785

Townsend, Dr. Francis, 494, 548, 562

Trade associations, 317–318, 416

Trading-with-the-Enemy Act (1917), 218, 223, 487, 650

Transportation, 9–10; W. W. I, 218; Transportation Act of 1920, 267–269, 413; during the 1920's, 411–414; under FDR, 529–531; W. W. II, 685–686; post W. W. II, 747–749, 804

Treaties, Paris (1898), 82–83; Portsmouth (1905), 98; Hay-Pauncefote, first (1900), 104; second (1901), 105; Hay-Herran (1903), 106; Hay-Bunau-Varilla (1904), 107; Hay arbitration (1904), 118; Root arbitration (1908), 120; Taft-Knox arbitration (1911), 120; Canadian reciprocity (1911), 63–64; Bryan "cooling-off" (1913), 137–138; Colombian (1914), 138; Bryan-Chamorro (1916), 142; Versailles (1919), 241–253, 254–262; with Germany (1921), 336; Five-Power Naval (1922), 342; Four-Power (1922), 342; Nine-Power (1922), 343; with Colombia (1921), 355; Kellogg-Briand (1928), 349–350; London Naval (1930), 452–454; with Cuba (1934), 598; with Panama (1936), 598–599; London Naval (1936), 604; United Nations (1945), 776–779; Axis satellites (1946), 787–788

Trieste, 787

Tripartite Pact, 659

Trudeau, Edward L., 18

Truman, Harry S., 681, 728, 802; election of 1944, 733–734; becomes President, 736–740; domestic policy, 740–764; foreign policy, 775–797

Truman Doctrine (1947), 793–795

Trusts, growth of, 6–9; opposition to, 9, 68–69, 74, 76; prosecution of, 40–43; under Wilson, 131–132; under Coolidge, 317–319; in 1920's, 414–416; under FDR, 505–520

Tugwell, Rexford G., 486

Tunisia, 704–706

Tunney, Gene, 391–392

Turkey, 794–795

Turner, George Kibbe, 30

Twentieth Amendment (1933), 482–483

Twenty-First Amendment (1933), 492

Tydings, Millard, 583

Underwood, Oscar W., 124–126, 341

Underwood Tariff (1913), 125–126

United Automobile Workers (UAW), 554–555

United Mine Workers (UMW), 43–45, 274, 361–363, 557, 747–749, 760–761

United Nations (UN), 770–779, 788–795

United Nations Educational, Scientific and Cultural Organization (UNESCO), 778

United Nations Relief and Rehabilitation Administration (UNRRA), 773–774

United Service Organization (USO), 676

United States Employment Service (USES), 221, 265

United States Housing Authority (USHA), 529

United States Shipping Board, 186, 214–215, 269–270, 408

United States Steel Corporation, 5, 6, 50–51, 68–69; organized, 6; labor relations of, 12; antitrust suit, 68, 132; strike of 1919, 271–272; in 1920's, 415; post W. W. II, 745–747, 761

U'Ren, William S., 35

Urey, Harold C., 811

Valentino, Rudolph, 389, 403

Vandenberg, Arthur H., 633, 759, 771, 789, 792, 795

VanDevanter, Willis, 567–569, 574–577

Vare, William S., 316

Veblen, Thorstein, 30

Venezuela, boundary controversy, 109; blockaded by European powers, 109–111

Vera Cruz, Mexico, occupied by U. S. forces, 145–146

Versailles, Treaty of, 241–253, 603; defeat of, 254–262

Veterans' Bureau, 298, 305–306

Veterans' legislation, 266, 302–306, 446–448, 498–499, 674, 743

Viereck, George Sylvester, 156, 694

Villa, Francisco (Pancho), 146–147

Vinson, Fred M., 681, 738–739

Virgin Islands, purchased by U. S., 140

Viviani, René, 207, 341

Volstead Act (1919), 263, 373–376, 492

Wage Stabilization Board, 746

Wagner, Robert F., 446, 545, 753

Wagner Act, *see* National Labor Relations Act

Wainwright, Jonathan, 701

Walker Commission, 105–106

Wallace, Henry A., 486, 794; Secretary of Agriculture, 532–541; Vice President, 636; W. W. II, 678–679; election of 1944, 733; Secretary of Commerce, 735, 738, 754, 788

Walsh, Frank P., 220, 257, 367

Walsh, Thomas J., 296, 424, 486
Walsh-Healy Contracts Act (1936), 557
War debt question, 345–347, 455–458, 483, 588–592
War Food Administration (WFA), 686–687
War Industries Board, 218–220, 265
War Information, Office of (OWI), 693–694
War Labor Board, W. W. I, 220–221; W. W. II, 687–689
War Mobilization, Office of (OWM), 681–682, 738
War Production Board (WPB), 678–679
War Shipping Administration (WSA), 685
War Trade Board, 218
Warren, Charles B., 314–315
Warren, George F., 503–504
Washington Conference (1921–1922), 339–344, 451
Watson, John B., 387
Weaver, James, 26–27
Webb-Kenyon Act (1913), 17
Welfare capitalism, 13, 364–365
Welles, Sumner, 596, 597, 664
Wheeler, Burton K., 311, 501, 567, 573–576, 647, 651, 656
Wherry, Kenneth, 697, 756
White, Henry, 121, 241–243
Whiteman, Paul, 389
Whitlock, Brand, 31, 151
Whitney, A. F., 749
Whitney, Richard, 522
Wickersham, George B., 57, 61
Wickersham Commission, 427
Wiggin, Kate Douglas, 21
Wiley, Harvey W., 47
Willard, Daniel, 214, 365
William II, Emperor of Germany, 110, 196, 198; Algeciras Conference, 120–122; abdication, 239
Willkie, Wendell L., 526, 633–638, 691, 731–732
Wilson, Woodrow, 35, 280, 283–284, 291–292, 319–320; early career, 71–74; elected President, 74–77; opposes dollar diplomacy, 102, 136–137; Panama tolls, 108, 139; cabinet, 123–124; tariff reform, 125–126, 287–289; Federal Reserve, 126–130; trust policy, 131–132; agriculture and labor, 132–134; and dependencies, 134–136; "cooling-off" treaties, 137–138; Latin American policies, 138–147; problems of neutrality, 149–205; election of 1916, 190–194; war message, 202–203; peacemaking,

234–253; League controversy, 254–262; postwar domestic problems, 262–279
Winsor, Katherine, 820
Wireless telegraphy, 8
Wisconsin, progressive movement in, 33–35
Wolfe, Thomas, 818–819
Women, 35, 147, 264; in 1920's, 380; in W. W. II, 674–675; (1930–1947), 806–808
Women Accepted for Volunteer Emergency Service (WAVES), 675
Women's Army Corps (WAC), 674
Women's Christian Temperance Union, 17
Women's suffrage, 35, 47, 264
Wood, Grant, 821
Wood, Leonard, in Cuba, 83–84; in W. W. I, 183, 211, 213; in Philippines, 136, 358–359; election of 1920, 281–282
Woodin, William H., 485
Woods, Arthur, 441
Works Progress Administration (WPA), 495–497, 580–582, 584–585, 820, 822
World Court, 247, 336–339; under Hoover, 450–451; under FDR, 603
World War I, U. S. neutrality, 149–205; U. S. enters, 201–206; conscription, 210–213; economic mobilization, 213–220; labor, 220–221; finance, 221–222; sedition, 222–225; propaganda, 225–227; campaigns, 227–233; armistice, 233; casualties, 233; peace negotiations, 234–253; demobilization, 264–266
World War II, origins of, 599–623; outbreak of, 623; aid to Allies, 623–667; Pearl Harbor attack, 667–668; U. S. enters, 668–669; home front, 670–697; war fronts, 698–730; casualties, 729–730; demobilization, 740–742; occupation of Germany and Japan, 781–785; peace negotiations, 787–789
Wright, Frank Lloyd, 23, 388
Wright, Harold Bell, 21
Wright, Richard, 802, 819
Wright brothers, 409
Wyatt, Wilson, 743, 761

Yalta Conference (1945), 735, 770–771, 776
Yap, island of, 340, 343
Yellow-dog contract, 361, 446
Yellow journalism, 80–81
Young Plan (1929), 348, 456
Youth problem, 378–380, 807–808
Yugoslavia, 785, 787–788

Zimmermann note, 200–201